JUSTICE BRENNAN

JUSTICE
BRENNAN

· LIBERAL CHAMPION ·

SETH STERN AND
STEPHEN WERMIEL

HOUGHTON MIFFLIN HARCOURT
BOSTON NEW YORK
2010

Library of Congress Cataloging-in-Publication Data
Stern, Seth (Seth Rose), date.
Justice Brennan : liberal champion / Seth Stern and Stephen Wermiel.
p. cm.
Includes index.
ISBN 978-0-547-14925-7
1. Brennan, William J. (William Joseph), 1906–1997.
2. Judges — United States — Biography.
I. Wermiel, Stephen.   II. Title.
KF8745.B68S74 2010
374.73'2634 — dc22
[B]   2010019036

Book design by Victoria Hartman

Printed in the United States of America

DOC 10 9 8 7 6 5 4 3 2 1

To Claire

SETH STERN

To Justice Brennan, Abner Mikva, and Seth Stern,
who made this book possible

To my wife, Rhonda Schwartz, and my daughter, Anne Wermiel,
who never stopped encouraging the effort

STEPHEN WERMIEL

Contents

List of Illustrations

Justice Brennan and Chief Justice Earl Warren and family. Time & Life Pictures/Getty Images

The Warren Court. Harris & Ewing/Courtesy of the Collection of the Supreme Court of the United States

Lunch group at the Milton Kronheim liquor warehouse, late 1960s. Courtesy of the Collection of the Supreme Court of the United States

FOLLOWING PAGE 450

Justice Brennan receives the Laetare Medal, 1969. Catholic News Service

Justice Brennan and Marjorie at a Nantucket cottage, 1975. Photograph by R. Rhodes

Justice Brennan and Marjorie on a Nantucket sand dune. Courtesy of the Brennan family

The Wharf Rat Club, Nantucket. Photograph by Anne Wermiel

The Burger Court meets President Ronald Reagan. The White House/Courtesy of the Collection of the Supreme Court of the United States

Justices Marshall and Brennan at a courthouse dedication, 1985. Ray Lustig photograph © 1985 The Washington Post

Justices Brennan and Blackmun on their way to justices' conference, 1983–84. Courtesy of Jeffrey B. Kindler

Justice Brennan and his second wife, Mary Fowler. Courtesy of the Collection of the Supreme Court of the United States

Brennan speaks at Loyola Law School graduation, 1986. © Bettmann/Corbis

Justice Brennan, in retirement, with his successor, Justice David Souter, 1996. Lois A. Long/Courtesy of the Collection of the Supreme Court of the United States

Herblock cartoon, 1990. © The Herb Block Foundation

William J. Brennan lying in state in the Supreme Court's Great Hall, 1997. Time & Life Pictures/Getty Images

Prologue: Last Surprise

WILLIAM J. BRENNAN JR. left his chambers as usual on the morning of June 27, 1990, when summoned by a buzzer to join his eight colleagues on the United States Supreme Court.

His first-floor chambers had remained largely unchanged since Brennan first arrived at the Court as a little-known New Jersey state judge thirty-four years earlier. Brennan had continued to work at the same desk, and the same wooden mantel clock still rested on the shelf above the fireplace. He preferred the old lamps to the fluorescent lighting other justices had installed. The only distinctive decorating touch in Brennan's chambers was the kelly green carpet covering the floor.

Stepping into the hallway, Brennan might have looked at the figures emerging from the neighboring chambers and thought for just a moment of his former allies Hugo Black, William Douglas, and Earl Warren, with whom he had transformed American constitutional law a quarter century earlier. All three had died long ago.

Brennan's closest remaining allies, Harry Blackmun and Thurgood Marshall, the nation's first African American justice, had, like him, grown old on the Court. Never a tall man, Brennan, now eighty-four, had shrunk as a result of age and illness. He shuffled when he walked the hallway toward the courtroom, and when he locked arms along the way with Blackmun or Marshall, the gesture was as much about steadying his gait as making an intimate connection.

He joined his colleagues in a small room behind the ornate courtroom, where they donned their robes and shook hands as per tradition before walking through the two-story-high curtains into the Court Chamber. As he had done for the last fifteen years, Brennan took the seat to the immediate right of the chief justice, at center, the spot reserved for the longest-serving associate justice.

The Court followed its custom of announcing decisions in reverse order of the author's seniority. The first to speak that day was the second-most-junior justice, Antonin Scalia, fifty-four, who had often sparred with Brennan since joining the Court four years earlier as its most conservative and youngest member. Scalia delivered an opinion severely restricting the ability of environmental and other citizen groups to challenge government action in federal court.

Justice Sandra Day O'Connor, President Reagan's first addition to the Court and the first female U.S. Supreme Court justice in history, followed with four decisions. Justice Byron White, who was the second-most-senior justice after Brennan and who had drifted to the right since President John F. Kennedy appointed him, then followed, with one. The six decisions announced by the members of the Court's conservative wing were a fitting finish to a term in which they had seemed to dominate.

Finally, Chief Justice William H. Rehnquist came to the last opinion of the day — and of the Court's term — and announced that Brennan would deliver it. Brennan leaned forward and pulled himself up in his high leather chair to make sure he could be seen above the raised mahogany bench. He spoke in a strong voice, although one slowed by age and more gravelly than usual due to a lingering cold. Brennan stated that the Court was upholding the constitutionality of two affirmative action programs in which the Federal Communications Commission gave preference to minority-owned companies to operate television and radio stations.

The import of the moment was lost on the crowd of tourists who packed the courtroom, but the handful of lawyers and reporters present were surprised by this unexpected outcome. Support for affirmative action had eroded on the Supreme Court in recent years. A year earlier Brennan had dissented when a majority had severely limited the ability of state and local governments to assist minority-owned businesses. And yet in the FCC case, the Court, by a 5–4 margin, upheld — and even expanded — the legally acceptable justifications for such programs. Once again, Brennan had somehow managed to defy expectations and build a majority.

What no one — including Brennan — knew that day was that this opinion would be the last of the more than 1,350 opinions he delivered as a Supreme Court justice. Less than a month later, Brennan abruptly announced his retirement after suffering a stroke. His opinion in *Metro Broadcasting v. FCC* proved to be the final surprise in a tenure full of surprises, a tenure that spanned five decades.

Little in his career as a corporate labor lawyer and New Jersey state judge suggested that William Brennan would emerge as perhaps the most influential justice of the entire twentieth century. No one could have predicted that Brennan would become the most forceful and effective liberal ever to serve on the Court. In fact, few if any of the eight men who served as president during his tenure could claim to have had such a wide-ranging and lasting impact. Brennan interpreted the Constitution expansively to broaden rights as well as create new ones for minorities, women, the poor, and the press. His decisions helped open the doors of the country's courthouses to citizens seeking redress from their government and ensured that their votes would count equally on Election Day. Behind the scenes, he quietly helped craft a constitutional right to privacy, including access to abortion, and bolstered the rights of criminal defendants. In the process, he came to embody an assertive vision for the courts in which judges aggressively tackled the nation's most complicated and divisive social problems.

Few outside the Court had any idea during the 1960s of the extraordinary influence that Brennan exerted working alongside Chief Justice Warren. And no one could have predicted the success he continued to enjoy under Warren's two Republican-appointed successors, Warren Burger and Rehnquist, largely holding the line against a conservative retrenchment.

Although Brennan's decision in the *Metro Broadcasting* case was subsequently overruled, affirmative action, like much of Brennan's legacy, survives two decades after his retirement and more than a decade after his death. The Court — and all of American politics — is still roiled by the forty-year-long conservative backlash that his decisions about school prayer, the death penalty, and affirmative action helped fuel. And while he remains a hero to two generations of progressive lawyers, including Presidents Bill Clinton and Barack Obama, he is also still the very symbol of judicial activism decried by conservatives. Each time a vacancy opens on the Supreme Court, conservatives vow never to repeat the mistake they say President Eisenhower made in nominating Brennan more than a half century ago.

· PART I: 1906–1956 ·

· 1 ·

BILL'S SON

NEWARK, NEW JERSEY, seemed cloaked in mourning on May 16, 1930. The sudden death two days earlier of City Commissioner William Joseph Brennan Sr. had eclipsed even the economic disaster enveloping the city in the early months of the Great Depression.

Thirty-eight years had passed since Bill Brennan arrived by steamship in the United States at the age of twenty, just another poor, anonymous Irish immigrant. An estimated forty thousand citizens — equivalent to 9 percent of the city's entire population — lined up through the night for a chance to enter the rotunda of City Hall, where his body lay in state. Standing vigil nearby was an honor guard of labor, police, and firemen Bill had led as head of the stationary firemen's union and during four terms as city commissioner. The next morning, six police horsemen and a marching band led off the parade of two thousand political, business, and union leaders accompanying the hearse. Three New Jersey National Guard airplanes dipped low overhead, dropping flowers on the mile-long funeral cortege. Throngs of somber onlookers lining Broad Street lifted their hats as the hearse passed by on its way to St. Patrick's Cathedral.

Seated in a carriage behind the hearse was William J. Brennan Jr. The younger Brennan, twenty-four, had rushed home by propeller plane from Massachusetts, where he was finishing his second year at Harvard Law

School, when it had become clear that his father would not survive a sudden bout of pneumonia. But he had arrived too late to say goodbye to the man who, for decades to come, would dominate his view of the world and the course of his career.

In life, Bill, who stood nearly six feet tall, had overshadowed his still boyish-looking namesake, five feet eight, in every way. Brennan's classmates at Barringer High School teased in their yearbook that the commissioner's son got by thanks to "Dad's reputation" and predicted his ambition was "to follow dad." Brennan had dutifully taken his father's advice and enrolled at the University of Pennsylvania's Wharton School and then Harvard Law, an Ivy League pedigree that far outshone the six grades of school Bill had completed. Brennan, soon to begin his first summer job as a lawyer, probably could not have imagined as he looked out on the massive funeral procession the extent to which he would exceed his father's professional achievements as well. Bill, however, had always expected nothing less from his oldest son.

WILLIAM J. BRENNAN SR. had bloomed late, his first quarter century in Ireland and America filled with far more failures than successes. Born on December 26, 1872, in Roscommon, a poor rural county on the border between central and western Ireland, about fifty miles north of Galway, Bill was the oldest of six children of Patrick Brennan, an illiterate tenant farmer from the tiny village of Cloonshanville, and Elizabeth Kelley, of Leggatinty, an equally small nearby town. Patrick Brennan had "married into" the Kelley farm, moving there and eventually taking over the tenancy. Bill's grandparents likely made do with a couple of cows, sheep and pigs, and some hens, just enough for them to survive the Irish potato famine that devastated Ireland a quarter century before his birth. Bill's parents, born just after the famine, stuck it out in Ireland even as millions of others fled.

Life for Bill, as for his ancestors before him, did not extend much beyond the nearest town of Frenchpark, where farmers gathered on Friday market days to sell animals and produce and to exchange gossip. Bill, who attended primary school intermittently when he was not helping his father on the farm, decided he wanted out. At the age of sixteen he traveled to England to work as an apprentice in an uncle's pottery business at Longton, Staffordshire, near Newcastle. Bill lasted only three years in the position before concluding that neither England nor his uncle's business was for him. In 1892 he set out for the United States. Family lore has it that he landed first in Boston, although Bill ultimately chose Trenton, New Jersey, as his destination.

Trenton, capital of the nation's pottery industry, was a natural choice, given his apprenticeship in the trade. But Bill's timing could not have been worse. The Panic of 1893 soon plunged the nation into a deep depression. Trouble in the pottery industry had started even earlier. Orders dried up, and factories — including the Maddock plant where Bill worked — shut down. With little education and no skills other than in pottery, Bill next followed the path traveled by earlier waves of Irish immigrants in New Jersey: manual labor. He found a job as a laborer on a gravel train on the Philadelphia and Reading Railroad and quickly worked his way up to brakeman on the Lehigh Valley Railroad, although he soon lost that job too, during a strike in 1893. The victim of economic depression, free trade, and a broken strike in just his first months in America, Bill's loyalties would forever lay with the workingman.

LEAVING TRENTON IN the summer of 1894, Bill headed to Newark, a brawny industrial boomtown fifty miles to the north. Although the city was overshadowed by New York, its more cosmopolitan neighbor just a few miles to the east, Newark's civic boosters exaggerated only slightly when they claimed its factories built every product sold in the United States. Downtown, smokestacks dominated the skyline above factories producing everything from beer and chemicals to patent leather and hoisting engines. Webs of telegraph wire and trolley cables ran above its cobblestone streets.

Newark seemed a place of limitless possibilities to immigrants like Bill, who boosted the city's population by a third, to 246,070, during the 1890s. With its population and industry growing rapidly together, however, Newark was also a place of considerable squalor. Nowhere did opportunity and poverty entwine more than in the industrial section of town along the Passaic River known as Down Neck, or the Ironbound, a reference to the railroad lines surrounding the neighborhood. Succeeding waves of new arrivals crowded into dilapidated houses adjacent to the neighborhood's many factories.

By the time Bill arrived in Newark, the children of the Irish immigrants who had first come to the city in large numbers during the famine era had begun to ascend toward middle-class respectability. Bill had to start at the bottom, right alongside the new immigrants from southern and eastern Europe. He laid tracks for the B. M. Shanley Company, then converting streetcars from horse to electric power, and shoveled coal at a licorice factory, a job that made him detest the taste or even the smell of licorice thereafter.

Then, around the dawn of the new century, Bill finally found steady employment at the forty-acre riverfront P. Ballantine & Sons brewery. As a stationary fireman, Bill worked inside the brewery's power plant, where enormous coal-fed boilers belched out the steam powering all the chutes and slides, fermenting vats, and mashers from which poured barrel after barrel of lager. Watching the boiler pressure gauges and repairing them when they broke put Bill in the middle of the boiler-room hierarchy, above the coal shovelers yet below the operating engineers who supervised the power plant. Coal dust filled the air. Temperatures rose well above 100 degrees in the summer. Still, Bill surely preferred the smell of beer to licorice. He enjoyed the camaraderie among the mostly Irish stationary firemen and may have had one of his coworkers to thank for introducing him to his wife.

Family accounts differ about how Bill, handsome, with wavy dark-red hair, met his slim dark-haired wife, Bridget Agnes McDermott. One version of the story suggests that Bill boarded at the same house on Plane Street in Newark as Agnes, as she preferred to be called. In the alternative account, Bill accepted an invitation to have dinner one night at the home of a colleague, and Agnes, the host's niece, joined them at the dinner table. Either way, Bill would have known that they came from the same part of Ireland as soon as he heard Agnes's flat midlands brogue. They soon learned they shared an even closer connection. Agnes, born in 1878, had grown up in Castlerea, a town less than ten miles from his hometown. Given their narrowly circumscribed lives, they almost certainly would never have met back in Roscommon.

Although her father was an illiterate tenant farmer like Bill's, Agnes had finished more years of school than Bill, later telling her children that she scored so high on a national entrance exam, the state offered to pay her way through high school. When her mother refused, based on the notion that girls did not need so much education, Agnes resolved to save up enough money working menial jobs to immigrate to the United States, which she did around 1894, moving in with her aunt in Newark around the same time Bill arrived in the city. Their children knew little about their courtship beyond the fact that Bill and Agnes were married at St. John's Catholic Church in Newark on June 17, 1903. Eight months later Agnes gave birth to their first child, a daughter they named Katherine.

Around the time that Bill became a father, he started on a well-trod path to Irish immigrant success in early-twentieth-century America: up through union ranks and into politics. A member of Local 55 of the International Brotherhood of Stationary Firemen, Bill initially sought a leadership role in the organization because he thought it was poorly run. Members paid their dues to a saloonkeeper who kept no account of their money and doled out jobs as he saw fit. Bill successfully ran for office, becoming the local's business agent. As a union officer he displayed the qualities that later made him a popular politician: honesty, transparency, and a gregarious personality.

ON APRIL 25, 1906, attention in Newark, as in the rest of the country, was focused on San Francisco, where a devastating earthquake had struck exactly one week earlier. Agnes Brennan's thoughts were closer to home that day. Inside the Brennans' wood-frame house at 357 New Street, an unpaved road just beyond downtown, past the Morris Canal and right behind the Daly Hat Company, she went into labor with her second child. Agnes later remembered that someone flagged down the family doctor, named Haggerty, who was on his way to a wedding at nearby St. Joseph's Church and showed up at the house wearing striped pants and a cutaway morning coat. At 1 P.M. Agnes gave birth to her first son, whom they named after Bill.

As if making up for lost time, Agnes, who was twenty-six when her first child was born, spent more than half of her first sixteen years of marriage pregnant. She gave birth to eight children in all and also suffered two miscarriages. The two following William Jr. were also boys: Charlie, born in 1907, and Tom, born in 1910. Then came two more girls, Betty and Peggy, by the time young William was nine. The Brennans moved frequently, outgrowing their modest lodgings. The future Supreme Court justice spent his infancy in three different rentals around the edge of Branch Brook Park, a multiethnic section of Newark that was a step up from Down Neck. The first house he would remember was at 212½ Parker Street, in a predominantly Italian neighborhood just across Bloomfield Avenue from Newark's most affluent section, Forest Hill.

Despite his union position, the elder Brennan found it difficult to support his ever-growing household, and his long hours proved exhausting. After briefly considering the more lucrative job of operating engineer, Bill ultimately decided to stay in the stationary firemen's union, where he rose to become national vice president and leader of both the Essex County and state labor federations. He began traveling around the country on union business, finding time on one such trip in 1911 to write Agnes a playful postcard from Milwaukee. "Well kitten, I hope yourself + kidlets are well. Will be home Tues. P.M. if allowed, Your Hubby." That same year, Bill sat behind union president Timothy Healey as he testified on a foreign trade bill before the U.S. Senate Finance Committee.

Living on the edge of affluence, William Jr. was nevertheless acutely aware of inequality and class differences. As a youngster he was put to work carrying orders for a butcher and recalled being struck by the gap separating the working-class families on his side of Bloomfield Avenue and the upper-class residents of Forest Hill, who lived in stately Victorian and colonial mansions.

At the age of five, Willie Brennan, as he was then known, went off to school at the Sacred Heart Roman Catholic School. Bill and Agnes sent him to parochial school either out of devotion to their faith or mere convenience, given that Sacred Heart was located on Parker Street, just a couple of blocks from their home. Brennan distinguished himself from an early age as a bookworm, much to his parents' satisfaction. They hoped all of their children would obtain the schooling they never had, which they viewed as the key to advancing beyond their station in life. As the oldest son, Brennan carried the heaviest burden of expectations, although with his high grades he generally had no trouble pleasing his father.

Bill dominated the household and brooked no dissent from his children. Brennan and his siblings knew to quiet down as soon as their father walked in the door each night. Inspiring respect, Bill resorted to physical punishment only sparingly. Brennan most vividly remembered the instances where he expected to get punished and did not, such as the time he and his younger brothers hit a baseball through a neighbor's window and the neighbor complained bitterly to Bill. "Boy [my father] did tell us off about watching out for people's property," Brennan remembered. "But that was the end of it." Brennan feared his father most when Bill drank. Although he could enjoy a beer or two with friends without incident, Bill was inclined to drink alone at home when something upset him at work. "He'd get himself potted, and when that would happen, he was not a very pleasant person to have around," Brennan recalled. "We'd just stay out of his way." Those nights of his father's drunken belligerence, seared in his memory, were a troubled foundation for Brennan. Never a problem drinker himself, alcoholism would follow him in his family life.

THE ELDER BRENNAN stood in several inches of slush at the corner of Belmont and Springfield on the night of April 8, 1916, in a downpour of rain mixing with snow. The dreary weather perfectly reflected the dark mood of Bill and his fellow labor organizers as they set out to demonstrate on behalf of striking trolley-car conductors and motormen. Two weeks had passed since a small number of trolley workers had walked off the job, seeking higher pay and a nine-hour day. The Public Service Corporation still refused to recognize the strike. Newark's police department sided with the powerful company, which also controlled the city's gas and electric utilities. Police officers broke up demonstrations and deployed en masse to prevent picketing outside the car barns where trolleys were housed. Union men retaliated by sabotaging at least one trolley car and throwing stones at those operated by nonunion men.

The Newark police had finally granted the union permission to march, but smothered the parade with squads of mounted police. Almost every last police captain, lieutenant, sergeant, and patrolman in the entire department lined both sides of the parade route. Bill, as secretary of the strike committee, would have harbored no illusions at this point about the strike's prospects. Weeks after the march, Newark began a massive celebration of the city's 250th birthday, but Bill was feeling more anger than civic pride that spring as he was elected president of the Essex County Trades Council. He had learned a bitter lesson about how government power could be turned against the workingman.

The trolley workers' strike had failed, but Newark politicians recognized organized labor's growing political strength. In early 1917, seeking a labor representative on the board overseeing the police department, Mayor Thomas Raymond offered the post to Bill, who was viewed as a palatable choice to both the unions and the city's business elite. Bill accepted the offer, although his tenure on the police board was brief. Newark overwhelm-ingly voted in October of that year to replace its mayor and city council with a five-member city commission vested with both executive and legis-lative power. A month later, Bill ran as the labor candidate in a crowded field of eighty-six candidates under the slogan "Civic representation for working people." On election night, the 15,736 votes the elder Brennan re-ceived was the third highest of any candidate, thus assuring him one of the five seats on the commission.

Under the new government structure, each commissioner oversaw a separate part of the city government. Bill chose to run the city's fire and police departments as director of public safety. He was as strict a lawman as he was a father. He pledged to vigorously enforce closing times for sa-loons, dance halls, and cabarets, and docked an officer thirty days' pay for public drunkenness. Yet he also exhibited the same capacity for tolerance he showed with his children, once forgiving a patrolman who stopped him for a driving infraction and then in his zeal insisted on taking Bill to the police station.

Although there was the potential for corruption in the departments he oversaw, Bill himself, by all accounts, stayed honest. But he was not above enjoying the perks of the job, including the use of a city-owned cabin be-side Newark's Pequannock Watershed, which some neighbors criticized as an unnecessary extravagance. He had a chauffeur-driven car at a time when few in the middle class could afford to buy their own automobiles. The job also afforded Bill frequent opportunities to travel. He headed off to annual union and police-chief conventions from Montreal to New Or-leans, and took at least one vacation each winter in Bermuda, Cuba, or Mi-ami, Florida. Conscious of his appeal to the common man, Bill took pains to portray these trips as low-cost affairs. Newspaper stories typically de-scribed the tropical getaways as an opportunity for the commissioner, who suffered frequent bouts of pleurisy, to recuperate from the health problems that plagued him.

Bill is not easily defined according to the labels traditionally affixed to Irish Catholic politicians of the time. He was a loyal Democrat, yet avoided close association with the city's party apparatus. Unlike the stereotypical Irish machine boss of the era, he showed little interest in accumulating power or siphoning off a fortune. Bill's campaign slogan during subsequent reelection campaigns, "A square deal for all, special privileges to none," evoked Teddy Roosevelt's progressive presidential agenda. Once in office, Bill did exhibit liberal tendencies. He warned that police officers who struck defenseless suspects deserved to be dismissed from the force. And he earned the respect of the local chapter of the civil rights group the Urban League by appointing three additional black patrol officers at a time when there was only one African American on the force.

Bill was a progressive in the mold of the Catholic theologian John A. Ryan, a forceful advocate for social justice who would come to be dubbed the New Deal's priest. Ryan's 1906 book, *A Living Wage*, argued that workers deserved an income that allowed for a comfortable living, a workday of reasonable length, and insurance that protected them against accidents, illness, and unemployment. Although there is no evidence that Bill read any of Ryan's books, he echoed Ryan's rhetoric when he explained to reporters why he endorsed a pay increase for police and firemen: "This was only a living wage, and I think the men were entitled to it."

Bill's liberalism did not extend, though, to his attitudes toward civil liberties. He pledged full cooperation with efforts to suppress the sale of magazines and other publications deemed morally objectionable. His tenure as commissioner coincided with a national crackdown on foreign radicals and suspected Communists, a movement he joined without qualms. He declared that any police officer who did nothing in the face of an insult to the American flag did not deserve to wear the uniform. His union sympathies did not extend to allowing radical labor agitator William Z. Foster to speak in Newark in 1924, and he forbade a protest on behalf of the Italian American anarchists Nicola Sacco and Bartolomeo Vanzetti, who were executed in 1927.

Bill's most notable crackdown on free speech came in 1926, when he prohibited the showing of *The Naked Truth*, a silent film in which a father instructs his son about the dangers of venereal disease. The board of censors appointed by Bill had barred Newark's Capitol Theatre from exhibiting the film, concluding that it was not suitable for commercial distribution and could be appropriately shown only free of charge as a public health service, at a YMCA, school building, or church. Bill, who declined an invitation to view the film, threatened to revoke the theater's license and to arrest anyone involved in its exhibition. The decision won praise from

Newark's Episcopal bishop, but a state judge issued an injunction barring the commissioner from interfering, on the grounds that he lacked any authority to engage in such censorship.

NOT LONG AFTER joining the police board, Bill had relocated the family to Vailsburg, a suburban neighborhood on Newark's far western edge. Just a few years earlier most residents of downtown Newark considered Vailsburg a place apart, as a destination for leisurely daytrips to the Electric Park amusement park or Velodrome outdoor bicycle track. Vailsburg had recently proved an appealing residential area for upwardly mobile immigrants relocating from the Ironbound. Many of the newcomers were city workers like Bill and the police and firemen he oversaw, who were required to live within the city's borders. The Brennan family moved into a triple-decker house on Alexander Street, their most significant step yet out of the urban ghetto.

The move to Vailsburg coincided with the end of the younger Brennan's parochial school education. He began attending a public school just up the block from his family's house on Alexander Street. Bill had no intention of circumscribing his children's education to satisfy his church. William Jr. and five of his seven siblings later attended public high school. Only Tom and Betty, viewed as the wild ones, were sent to parochial high schools.

Like so many other immigrants, Brennan's parents had complicated feelings about their ethnic identities. Bill subscribed to the *Irish World* newspaper, joined Irish fraternal organizations such as the Friendly Sons of Saint Patrick and the Ancient Order of Hibernians, and treated Saint Patrick's Day as an important holiday. But while he enjoyed putting his feet up on his desk in his City Hall basement office and regaling visitors with tales of growing up in Ireland, Bill divulged little about his childhood to his own family. Agnes was even more ambivalent about her roots. She insisted that her children attend Sunday Mass but told at least one son she did not believe in the Church doctrine of papal infallibility. Agnes bought every one of the Irish tenor John McCormack's Victor Red Seal records, featuring songs such as "My Wild Irish Rose" and "When Irish Eyes Are Smiling," on the day they went on sale. But she did not want to be known as Bridget, a name closely associated in nineteenth-century America with Irish domestic workers. She was so self-conscious about her Irish brogue that she rarely spoke in front of strangers. And if Bill slipped into Gaelic when talking with friends in their house, she would cut them off by snapping, "You are Americans now!"

Both Bill and Agnes wanted to retain some links to their Irish roots, but not at the expense of their children identifying fully as American. Brennan internalized his parents' desire to live in both worlds. On the one hand, he insisted later, his identity was inseparable from "the kind of family I was born into and the kind of society," which he described as "blue collar, Roman Catholic, [and] Irish." At the same time, he remembered attending Mass as "an agony we went through every Sunday whether you liked it or not." Having left parochial school at a young age, Brennan retained a relatively unsophisticated understanding of Church doctrine. While he continued to attend Sunday school, he had happier memories of playing pool in the church's recreation room for teenagers.

Barringer High School, which Brennan attended beginning in 1920, was a prestigious public school and a magnet for the children of Irish, Italian, and Jewish immigrant parents like Brennan's with big ambitions for their first-generation American offspring. Brennan excelled academically, joined the science and Spanish clubs, wrote for the school newspaper, the *Acropolis,* and, in the first hint of an interest in law, chaired the Constitution Day committee. For much of high school, Brennan was accompanied at Barringer by Charlie, the brother to whom he was closest. They had always shared a bedroom growing up as well as a common sense of mischief, throwing pillows at their sister Betty to get her out of bed in the morning. During Brennan's high school years, the family relocated a couple of blocks to their second home in Vailsburg, a single-family house on North Munn Avenue. Brennan and Charlie went to work together each morning at a dairy farm across the street. Brennan pulled rank as older brother, forcing Charlie to work the earlier shift milking the cows at Martens Dairy while he delivered the bottles later, on his way to school. The family's finances had improved considerably after Bill became a city commissioner. But Brennan continued working after school and on weekends, delivering newspapers, making change for passengers boarding trolley cars downtown, and gassing up cars at a neighborhood filling station. Brennan kept whatever he earned for spending money, allowing him to splurge on his wardrobe. He had developed a taste as a teenager for nice suits and well-shined shoes.

On Sunday nights, Brennan and Charlie invited friends over for dinner.

The house on North Munn was crowded enough even without the additional guests, particularly after the arrival of Brennan's paternal grandmother, who emigrated from Ireland, and the birth of his two youngest siblings: Helen in 1917 and Frank in 1919. Meals at the Brennan household were boisterous affairs where siblings vied to talk about everything from international politics to local high school basketball scores. The girlfriend of one of Brennan's brothers later remembered reading the newspaper from end to end in order to keep up with the conversation. Adding to the lively atmosphere might be Bill's two brothers who lived in New York: Patrick, a firefighter with bright red hair, and Tom, a chauffeur. Still, Agnes never complained. She cooked ham, potato salad, and sheet cake for twenty or more people. After dinner, they rolled up the rug and danced.

BRENNAN WAS FIFTEEN years old when his father ran for reelection in 1921, old enough to participate fully in a political campaign for the first time. He witnessed all the theatrics then typical of Newark's city-commissioner campaigns. There were torch-lit parades and raucous rallies at the Newark armory, where the walls shook from the sounds of marching bands and thousands of cheering attendees. Along the way, Brennan also observed his father's ample political skills — the way Bill remembered names and faces and could fit in so comfortably at a firehouse or corner tavern. Bill's up-by-his-bootstraps rise appealed to voters, and every September beginning in 1921, Bill shored up his image as a man of the people by hosting picnics for thousands of city residents, featuring free soda, hot dogs, and ice cream and lollipops, plus merry-go-rounds and toboggan slides. A savvy student of Newark's changing demographics, Bill realized he could not just rely on his kinsfolk at a time when Italians and Russian immigrants outnumbered Newark's Irish residents. He bought ads in the city's Jewish newspapers and touted his Jewish appointments. In subsequent elections, he also reached out to Newark's small black population.

But Brennan, who spent his adolescence as the son of one of Newark's most famous and closely scrutinized figures, also observed an uglier side of politics. Bill's popularity and political skill could not protect him from harsh attacks by critics unhappy with the less than fervent way he enforced Prohibition. Bill, who had never lived outside the urban "wet" Northeast, had misjudged the support Prohibition enjoyed, particularly in the Midwest and South. In January 1918, even as the first states started ratifying the

Eighteenth Amendment outlawing the manufacture, sale, and transportation of "intoxicating liquors," Bill assured a gathering of liquor wholesalers in Newark that American soldiers fighting in Europe would not tolerate such restrictions on their liberty when they returned home. A year later, just two months after World War I ended, the thirty-sixth and final state needed to ratify the amendment did so. The amendment and the Volstead Act, which spelled out penalties for its violation, went into effect in January 1920.

There is a certain irony that the elder Brennan, a former brewery worker, wound up with the thankless task of helping U.S. Treasury agents enforce Prohibition. Bill had no intention of forsaking alcohol himself. He could no longer enjoy a beer or two at his favorite tavern around the corner from his house, but he continued to drink alcohol in the privacy of his own home, where, unfortunately for his family, he was more apt to become belligerent when drunk. It would not be until 1927 that Bill publicly confessed at an Elks Club lunch that he would finally give up alcohol, but only on his doctor's orders.

Bill had much to lose politically by cracking down on illegal alcohol consumption. Prohibition proved unpopular among Newark's working-class immigrants, the owners of hundreds of saloons where they drank, as well as with the city's vital brewing industry. Production had ceased at the Feigenspan Brewery, but its rooftop sign reading "P.O.N." — an abbreviation for "Pride of Newark" — still lit up every night like a beacon for Prohibition's repeal. Prohibition spawned new forms of lawlessness throughout the country, and particularly in Newark, which earned a reputation as a bootleg capital. Speakeasies sprung up around the city, and speedboats raced out to freighters loaded with bootleg whiskey lingering just off the coast, beyond the three-mile territorial limit.

Bill had little enthusiasm for Prohibition, but there is no evidence that he was among the countless New Jersey police officers and politicians who took bribes from bootleggers like Newark gangster Abner "Longie" Zwillman. However, this was one issue where Bill could find no middle ground that might satisfy everybody. Protestant church groups and the local chapter of the Anti-Saloon League came down hard on Bill for lax enforcement, insinuating that he was a drunk. In February 1922 members of a coalition of church groups heckled Bill and other city officials at a City Hall meeting and demanded that he resign. Brennan read about the attacks on his father's character and took them to heart. At sixteen, he turned away from politics. "I saw what it did to my father, and I wanted no part of it," Brennan recalled. "What a filthy business the whole thing was."

AT THE TIME Brennan applied to college in 1923, most American Catholic students attended church-affiliated colleges. He could have walked to Seton Hall, located two miles from the family's house up South Orange Avenue in neighboring South Orange, New Jersey. But Agnes and Bill had their sights set elsewhere for the first member of either of their families to attend college. Both wanted Brennan to head to the Ivy League.

Agnes thought Bill should go to Princeton, the top school in New Jersey and training ground for the state's Protestant elite. Princeton accepted Brennan, and his high school yearbook even listed it as his destination. But Bill had other ideas. On the eve of the stock market boom that came to define the Roaring Twenties, the loyal union man envisioned his son's future squarely on the side of Wall Street. Knowing little about such matters, Bill relied on the advice of James W. Costello, his close friend and Newark's chief city engineer. Costello had graduated from the University of Pennsylvania, and convinced Bill that that was where his son should go. Bill encouraged Brennan to apply to Penn's Wharton School of Finance and Commerce, as it was known at the time. Having deferred to his father's wishes throughout his childhood, it did not seem to occur to Brennan that he might have a say in the matter.

It was the fulfillment of Bill's ambitions, if not necessarily his own, when Brennan arrived at the University of Pennsylvania in the fall of 1924 as a freshman in the College of Arts and Sciences. (As a sophomore, Brennan transferred to Wharton, where he was soon joined by his younger brother Charlie.) Only ninety miles separated Vailsburg from the Penn campus in Philadelphia, but the distance must have seemed much greater as Brennan moved into one of the Tudor Gothic–style dormitory houses designed to evoke the campuses of England's Oxford and Cambridge. Yet this grandson of an illiterate Irish tenant farmer had little trouble fitting in at the university founded in 1749 by Benjamin Franklin. Brennan spent less time at the Newman Center, where Catholic students congregated, than at the Delta Tau Delta fraternity he joined, where members with names like Brennan and O'Hara remained a distinct minority. He lived in the Delta Tau Delta house for three years, Charlie joining as well. The Brennan brothers blended easily among the three dozen fraternity brothers who posed for a yearbook picture, looking like underaged bankers in their three-piece suits, striped ties, and neatly folded breast-pocket handkerchiefs. Much to his father's delight, Brennan's grade cards were filled with "distinguished" and "good" — the two highest levels.

Each summer, Brennan returned to Newark, where he was employed inspecting a city contractor's street-paving work. He could thank his father's friend James Costello, the city engineer, for the job. It paid well — forty dollars a month, in Brennan's memory, which allowed him to indulge in his preferred high-priced "collegiate" style of dress. He bought $75 custom-made suits and a $105 overcoat he particularly cherished.

Brennan probably wore one of his fancy handmade suits in December 1926 when he attended one of the big events of Newark's Christmas social season: a cotillion at the East Orange Women's Club. Brennan at the time was a boyishly handsome twenty-year-old, with a thin face and hair neatly combed and smoothed with pomade. His most notable feature was his bright green eyes. Brennan noticed a slim blue-eyed brunette he had never seen before and got up the nerve to approach her. Nineteen-year-old Marjorie Leonard had come to the cotillion with another young man as her date, but added Brennan to her dance card. Brennan was slighter in build and shorter than the lifeguard types who typically pursued her, but Marjorie thought Brennan was handsome, intelligent, and a good dancer. They also shared common Irish Catholic roots and grew up only a couple of miles apart, although Marjorie's childhood had been markedly different from Brennan's.

Marjorie's American-born parents came from Belfast, a small town in western New York State best known as where the Irish boxer John L. Sullivan had his training camp. Her father, Hugh Leonard, became a protégé of Sullivan and his trainer, and began wrestling professionally at age sixteen. By the time Marjorie was born, Hugh had become a famous coach at the elite New York Athletic Club and author of an illustrated handbook on wrestling. But when Marjorie was seven years old, Hugh was killed at his summer training quarters in Belfast, struck by lightning when he ran outside during a storm to take a flag down. Her mother, Rose O'Boyle, died when Marjorie was a teenager, leaving Marjorie an orphan under the care of her three older sisters. After graduating from Orange High School, she went straight to work in a clerical job at the New York Insurance Company and lived in an apartment in Orange with Irene, the sister roughly fifteen years her senior who had become her surrogate mother.

Brennan, the Ivy League fraternity brother, was instantly smitten with this vivacious, independent, and strong-willed young woman. He soon began writing Marjorie almost every day. She visited Philadelphia when his fraternity hosted formal parties. Eventually, Brennan brought Marjorie home to meet his family. Having had a different experience of family life growing up, Marjorie seemed uncomfortable at the Brennans' animated dinner table. But she could certainly hold her own with Brennan. During their courtship, Brennan gave Marjorie a fraternity pin, an expensive symbol of commitment. In the middle of an argument they had on a Newark trolley car, she threw it out the window. They looked at each other, equally in shock at what she had done, and got off the trolley at the next stop to search for the pin, which was nowhere to be found.

There was little question about what Brennan would do after graduating college, at least in his father's mind. Long after he had become a successful attorney, Brennan remembered his father encouraging him to pursue a legal career as early as high school. In fact, Bill had envisioned a business career for his oldest son when he encouraged Brennan to apply to Wharton. But, as with Brennan's college choice, Bill's thinking about Brennan's career was heavily influenced by a friend's advice. Jerome Congleton, Newark's city counsel and then mayor, suggested that, as a graduate of a top law school, Brennan could easily find work as an attorney on Wall Street. Brennan finished college in the spring of 1928 at a time when stocks soared to unimaginable new heights every day, and the entire country seemed caught up in a speculative fever. Once again, Brennan's own preferences about his future seemed immaterial.

Brennan, most likely with Bill's considerable input, chose as his destination Harvard Law School, the oldest continually operated law school in the country and, by the time he applied, also the nation's preeminent one. Gaining admission to Harvard Law was not quite as singular an achievement in Brennan's day as it became later. Applicants needed to present little more than a diploma from a reputable college and a deposit toward the $400 annual tuition. The tough part, as these newcomers learned, was the culling that occurred following exams at the end of the first year. Roughly a third of students who arrived under this open admissions policy received letters the summer after they took their first exams telling them not to come back.

Five weeks before graduating college, Brennan engaged in the first rebellious act of his life. He and Marjorie decided to elope. They traveled to Maryland, which had no waiting period for a marriage license and required only a church ceremony. William Mackessy, the priest they approached at a Catholic church in Baltimore, seemed suspicious. "Why aren't you getting married at home?" Brennan recalled Mackessy asking. Brennan, then twenty-two, and Marjorie, twenty-one, did not want to tell the priest that they feared Bill would disapprove of the marriage. Brennan suspected his father would say they should wait until after he graduated law school and could afford to support a wife.

But after a year and a half of dating, neither of them looked forward to being apart for three more years without any formal commitment. Marjorie was the more devout Catholic, having turned to her faith for solace during her traumatic childhood. But she was not about to let the priest interfere with their plans. So when Mackessy wavered, they threatened to head to one of the private chapels in Elkton, a small town in the northeastern corner of Maryland, at the time considered the elopement capital of the East Coast. The priest finally relented and married them, after rounding up as witnesses a couple of women praying at the church. Brennan's first rebellious act was an incomplete one, however. At the age of twenty-two, he still could not openly defy his father, and opted to keep the marriage a secret. Brennan graduated college on June 20, 1928, his family having no idea that he was a married man.

MARJORIE STAYED BEHIND in New Jersey when Brennan headed to Cambridge, Massachusetts, in September 1928 to begin his first semester at Harvard Law School. He was as unaccustomed as the rest of his roughly seven hundred classmates to the unique style of instruction they encountered in the school's amphitheater-shaped classrooms. A half century earlier, Dean Christopher Columbus Langdell had abandoned textbooks and lectures in favor of having students read legal opinions collected in casebooks and answer questions in a Socratic dialogue, using close questioning to tease out the facts of the case and relevant rules of law. This case method helped burnish Harvard Law School's reputation and made it a model for legal education throughout the country. The curriculum had changed little in the intervening years. First-year students were divided into four sections, and enrolled in civil procedure, contracts, criminal law, property, and torts. For Brennan and his classmates the system had one advantage: with a class size of 168 students, no one could get called on too frequently.

Brennan found lodging at a nearby boardinghouse in Harvard Square along with a group of other students. As at Penn, he had no trouble fitting in among his classmates. He became close friends with his fellow boardinghouse residents, including fellow New Jersey native Bill Lord, a graduate of Dartmouth College whose father was president of the Scribner publishing house. But not even his closest law school friends knew Brennan was married. They knew Marjorie only as the girlfriend to whom he wrote long letters while the rest of them went out on dates. During her occasional visits, Marjorie stayed at a Boston hotel for the sake of appearances.

For Brennan and his law school friends, studying took up much of their time. The pressure was intense, perhaps explaining why Brennan smoked cigarettes heavily during his Harvard years. His work paid off. In his second year, Brennan scored high enough to qualify for one of the three organizations reserved for top students. The *Harvard Law Review*, a prestigious student-run journal, invited the highest-scoring dozen or so students; the Board of Student Advisers took the second-best group; and the third batch qualified for the Legal Aid Bureau, which Brennan was invited to join when he returned in the fall of his third year.

Founded in 1913, the student-run Legal Aid Bureau helped Cambridge's poor with landlord-tenant disputes, domestic relations, and personal-injury cases. Brennan was exposed for the first time to real-world legal problems and the plight of the poor. He later credited the Legal Aid Bureau with opening his eyes to law's "compassionate aspects — helping confused and worried little people over problems of rent and family and small inheritances — problems of little or no significance in the large, but which can assume terrifying proportions for the people concerned." Membership in the Legal Aid Bureau put Brennan a notch or two below the top of his class, although the hands-on nature of the work probably suited him better than the more academic-minded *Law Review* anyway. Brennan never showed much interest in theoretical debates or the schools of legal thought developing at the time. He was not anti-intellectual, but he largely considered his education at Wharton and Harvard Law School a means to an end rather than an intellectual exercise to be enjoyed for its own sake. He later recalled his college auction-bridge games in much more vivid detail than any books or authors he read in college or law school.

It was his father who had always had the most influence on Brennan. He had learned to sympathize with the underdog as he watched his father's struggle as a labor leader at a time when, Brennan recalled, society "wanted no part of organized unions." He had soaked up his father's concerns about government power being employed against individuals, as it was during the 1916 trolley workers' strike, and he also saw how government could be a force for good during the thirteen years his father served as a city commissioner. But unlike his father, Brennan's liberalism extended beyond economic matters to issues of civil liberties. And that enlarging upon his father's views may well have begun at Harvard Law School, in a course taught by Professor Zechariah Chafee.

Shaken by the government-sanctioned repression of speech during World War I, Chafee responded by writing *Free Speech*. Published in 1920, the book became a must-read for lawyers grappling with how to strike the proper balance between liberty and the sorts of restraints imposed on speech during emergencies such as wartime. Brennan recalled that it was in Chafee's class on equity during his second year in law school that he first thought seriously about what sort of protections the First Amendment afforded. (Brennan did not enroll in constitutional law, an elective class taught by the renowned scholar Thomas Reed Powell, although he recalled sometimes sitting in on the lectures.) In one class, Chafee spoke excitedly about an unusual free speech case he had come across. Brennan did not realize until the end of the discussion that Chafee was praising the New Jersey state court decision overturning his father's prohibition of the film *The Naked Truth*. Brennan recounted the story to Bill during his next visit home. His father was not amused.

THE DEPRESSION CAUGHT Bill—like most Americans—completely by surprise. He had campaigned for a fourth term on the city commission with the slogan "Continued Prosperity" in the spring of 1929. Everything began changing after the stock market crashed that October, although the devastation was relatively slow to reach Newark. It was not until early 1930 that employment and wages began to decline steadily. Bill's government job meant that the Brennan family did not have much to worry about in the first winter of the Great Depression. They were more concerned about Agnes, who underwent surgery to repair an intestinal blockage in January 1930.

Bill, now fifty-eight, his red hair long since gone gray, continued to struggle with health issues as well. He had been plagued with kidney stones for at least a year, and after the latest attack in May, Bill's doctor had suggested a few days of quiet recuperation. Bill retreated to his city-owned cabin at the Pequannock Watershed for a week, but wound up catching a cold. When a fever he developed worsened, his doctor retrieved him from the cabin, and Bill was admitted to the hospital on May 12.

The next day, the *Newark Star Eagle* reported that the commissioner was in "very serious condition" with pneumonia in both lungs. His doctor predicted Bill would "pull through," but overnight his condition worsened, and he lapsed into a coma early on the morning of May 14. After receiving a call in Cambridge from his family, the younger Brennan frantically tried to find a way back to Newark. His law school friend Bill Lord drove him to the train station, but too late for the departure. He then missed the next available flight out of Boston, and by the time he finally arrived home by plane, it was too late. Bill had died at Newark's Presbyterian Hospital at 10:23 A.M., surrounded by family, including his seventy-seven-year-old mother, Elizabeth, as well as his wife and two of his oldest children, Katherine and Charlie. That night, Bill's body was returned to the Brennans' Munn Avenue home, where he remained overnight. Fourteen years after Bill had marched through the streets of Newark surrounded by hostile mounted policemen, officers escorted Bill's casket through the streets to City Hall, where he lay in state. On May 16, as the funeral Mass began, flights at Newark's airport and traffic downtown halted to observe a moment of silence in his honor.

The outpouring of affection and grief reflected Bill's extraordinary popularity and reputation for honesty. He died at his peak politically, perhaps fortunate not to live long enough to see the city government he helped lead become the target of public anger. Voters were to cast out all but one of his fellow city commissioners in the next election in 1933 amid accusations that several had bought parcels of land later sold to the city at inflated prices. Nor did he live long enough to see his greatest ambition realized:

three of his sons accumulated a total of five Ivy League degrees, and two of his daughters attended college too.

A month after Bill's death, the family suffered another loss when Bill's mother, Elizabeth, died. Bill had left Elizabeth $2,000; the remainder of his estate went to Agnes, who could use whatever financial help she could find. Four of Brennan's siblings still lived at home at the time. Betty and Peggy were in high school, and Helen and Frank were still in grade school. Charlie was still in college at the University of Pennsylvania, and Brennan had a year remaining in law school. The City of Newark offered some assistance, and Brennan's older sister, Katherine, who was working at Prudential, chipped in too.

Prior to his death Bill had used his connections to land his oldest son a summer clerkship at one of Newark's leading law firms. Despite high grades at a top law school, Brennan was not the type of candidate the firm of Pitney, Hardin & Skinner usually selected. John O. H. Pitney and John R. Hardin, two Princeton graduates born in 1860, had founded the firm in 1902. Pitney's brother, Mahlon, was a justice on the U.S. Supreme Court, and two of his sons had helped build the law practice into the firm of choice for New Jersey's top corporations and banks. Like its founders, every Pitney Hardin partner had graduated from Princeton. And none were Catholic. But Bill's colleague on the city commission, Mayor Congleton, had intervened on Brennan's behalf at the firm, nicknamed "Pluck'em, Hook'um & Skin'um" in reference to its aggressive representation of corporate clients.

Congleton's request came as a surprise, according to one of the firm's partners, Waldron Ward. The partners did not necessarily agree with Bill's politics, but Ward recalled they regarded him "as a rugged, honest and able man." Left unstated was the potential future benefit of doing the mayor a favor. Brennan was offered a summer position. He later remembered little about the summer except that it went well enough that eventually he received an offer to join the firm upon graduation.

BRENNAN FACED THE challenge of financing his final year of law school without his father's help when he returned to Cambridge in the fall of 1930. He obtained a scholarship from the school and got a job waiting tables at a boardinghouse, although his standard of living remained high enough that he soon felt free to quit the job. Most people did not have that luxury in Newark, where employment at major manufacturers had fallen 25 percent and residents who could not afford to heat their homes filled wheelbarrows and any available conveyance with cords of wood given away at a city firehouse. Brennan, by contrast, could still afford to see plays and lectures in Boston or dine at his favorite restaurant downtown, Durgin Park, with his law school friends.

Every Monday and Tuesday, Brennan headed to Langdell Hall at 11 A.M. for a course called Public Utilities. The name was a bit of a misnomer, since the instructor felt free to lecture about whatever he pleased, with tangents into politics, economics, philosophy, and history. Five hours of class elapsed before the professor even turned to the first case, examining how the Interstate Commerce Commission regulated railroads. Then he lingered on that one case for a month and four days, dissecting it in such depth that students nicknamed the class "The Case of the Month Club." Felix Frankfurter was trying to show the two hundred assembled students how law was shaped by outside forces rather than something to be studied in isolation.

This forty-eight-year-old professor's biography was as unique on the Harvard faculty as the course he taught. In 1894, at age twelve, he had immigrated to the United States from Austria with his parents and five siblings, settling among other Jewish newcomers on Manhattan's Lower East Side. Despite being a latecomer to English-language instruction, he managed to graduate from City College by the age of nineteen and then to enroll at Harvard Law School, where he was first in his class all three years. His success explains why Frankfurter developed what he admitted was a "quasi-religious" attachment to Harvard Law, which to him embodied the American ideal of meritocracy. Frankfurter did not feel the same way about the New York law firms that would not consider him for a job because he was Jewish. He returned to Harvard Law School as a professor in 1914 and remained active in liberal politics. Frankfurter emerged during the 1920s as a leading crusader on behalf of civil liberties. He was denounced as a radical for his vigorous defense of Sacco and Vanzetti, the Italian American anarchists for whom Brennan's father refused to allow even a protest meeting in Newark.

Brennan, like so many of Frankfurter's students, found both the charismatic professor and his class fascinating. But he was not in the elite circle of top students Frankfurter took under his wing in this era, ranging from Brennan's classmate and future Harvard Law professor Paul Freund, to Dean Acheson, the future secretary of state, to Alger Hiss, later accused of being a Soviet spy. Frankfurter invited these favored few to enroll in his more intimate seminars and to join him for Sunday-afternoon teas at his Brattle Street home near campus. In his domineering way, Frankfurter remained absorbed in his disciples' lives long after they graduated. Brennan, at the time, was unworthy of Frankfurter's attention and forgotten as soon as he graduated in June 1931.

CLOSE TO GRADUATION, Brennan finally came clean about his secret marriage. He'd had no trouble telling his law school friends; the difficulty was in explaining things to his mother. Brennan had dug himself into a deep hole by hiding the marriage for so long. So instead of admitting the truth, he schemed to cover it up by arranging a second wedding ceremony.

Brennan informed his mother that he intended to wed Marjorie, neglecting to mention that they were already married. The trouble started when Brennan went to St. Joseph's Church to pick up a copy of his baptismal certificate while his mother waited outside. "What do you want this for?" asked the skeptical priest, a longtime friend of his father's. Brennan feigned innocence in explaining his intention to wed. "What'd you do with the wife you married in 1928?" the priest replied.

Unbeknownst to Brennan, Father Mackessy, the Baltimore priest who had performed his and Marjorie's wedding, had sent a copy of the marriage certificate to the churches where Brennan and Marjorie had been baptized. Caught in his lie, Brennan left the church and sheepishly admitted the truth to his mother. "That day was a long, long day," Brennan recalled. The priest at Marjorie's church proved more understanding and offered to go ahead with the ceremony. Agnes would not hear of it. "No more skulking around!" she ordered. His mother had taken up the mantle of family monarch after Bill's death, and Brennan had no intention of arguing with her. So instead of a second ceremony, a wedding announcement noting the "secret marriage" ran in the *Newark Evening News* on June 20, 1931. That morning, Brennan and Marjorie set out for a honeymoon in Canada with a stop in Belfast, New York, where Marjorie's parents had grown up.

· 2 ·

LAWYER

Brennan and Marjorie returned from their belated honey-moon in the summer of 1931 and finally moved in together as husband and wife. Rather than settling near Brennan's family in Newark, they found an apartment in neighboring Orange. It was within Marjorie's comfort zone — on the same stretch of Central Avenue where she had grown up and lived with her older sister Irene after her parents died. Marjorie had remained in Orange during the three years she and Brennan lived apart, even as his social and intellectual exposure had grown considerably at Harvard.

Brennan commuted downtown each morning to his new job at Pitney Hardin, on the twenty-first floor of the National Newark and Essex Bank building. Brennan's modest title of clerk and even more meager wages of $75 a month did not quite match the law firm's majestic setting, in a skyscraper that dominated Newark's otherwise unremarkable skyline. Under New Jersey's antiquated rules, new lawyers had to complete a yearlong apprenticeship before they could qualify to take the bar exam and earn the title of attorney. Passing a second test three years later elevated them to the rank of counselor. Brennan's summer clerkship counted toward the total, so he had nine months remaining in his apprenticeship when he started at Pitney Hardin.

As an apprentice lawyer Brennan's responsibilities included serving notices on behalf of the National Newark and Essex Bank to makers of overdue promissory notes. Hiring cabs would have quickly eaten up their wages, so Brennan and Donald Kipp, a law school classmate who had also gone to work for Pitney Hardin, traveled the city by trolley car. Brennan arrived home late most nights, tired, hungry, and dispirited after attending an evening bar-exam course. "It's a dog's life," he wrote a law school friend in May 1932, one month after taking the exam, which, he confided, "wasn't half as nerve-wracking as this endless wait" for the results.

Brennan felt pressed to make ends meet even after he passed the bar exam and the firm bumped up his salary to $165 per month. Along with his other employed siblings, he was helping to support his mother and younger brothers and sisters. Marjorie kept working, too, though she switched from New York Life Insurance Company in Manhattan to a job as a proofreader at the *Orange Daily Courier* newspaper. She did her best to stretch their combined wages, feeding them on $5 a week. They bought an unfinished bed, dresser, and vanity for their apartment and finished the furniture themselves; they also saved money by eating at least one dinner every weekend at the Brennan house in Vailsburg.

Still, Brennan's modest lifestyle would have been the envy of most Newark residents as the Depression continued to worsen. A 1931 survey of Newark families receiving government assistance found most were subsisting on $5 to $15 a week and could afford only a diet of bread, potatoes, and weak soup. Hundreds of men showed up on the first night that winter when Newark converted an old elementary school into housing for transients. Many attorneys struggled, too, supplementing their meager earnings from legal work with second jobs driving taxicabs or working for the postal service.

Brennan earned extra money by taking criminal-defense assignments from a city judge, Daniel J. Brennan (no relation). As with the civil cases he'd encountered in his work with the Harvard Legal Aid Bureau, these criminal cases exposed Brennan to a very different kind of caseload and clientele than his work on behalf of corporate clients at Pitney Hardin. Brennan later enjoyed recounting the story of when he went to trial for the first time, in early 1933, representing a client, William Logan, accused of striking with his car and killing a deaf and mute pedestrian. Brennan had learned during law school the importance of employing character witnesses to testify on a defendant's behalf. He recruited an Irish-born retired policeman who lived near the defendant. But Brennan failed to appreciate the importance of preparing a witness in advance, and put him on the stand without any practice.

"Do you know the reputation of the defendant in his neighborhood for truth and veracity?" Brennan asked the retired police officer.

"I do and he's a fine automobile driver," the puzzled witness replied tentatively.

Brennan asked the same question two more times, and the man answered the same way, in an increasingly irritated tone. Finally the trial judge intervened and said, "Officer, look at me, does the defendant usually tell the truth, do you know?"

"Oh yes, Your Honor," the witness said. "I never knew him to tell a lie."

"Well," said the judge, "that's what Mr. Brennan wanted to know but you see he's a Harvard graduate and he doesn't speak English."

BRENNAN FOUND HIMSELF heavily courted in the spring of 1933 by the Good Government League, a local group dissatisfied with many of the sitting commissioners in the run-up to Newark's first city-commission election since his father's death. But running for office held little appeal to the young attorney. At twenty-seven, Brennan knew it was his famous name rather than his modest qualifications that made him an attractive candidate. He saw no benefit to giving up the security of his job at a prestigious law firm, particularly with Marjorie about to give birth to their first child. He recently had finally felt secure enough financially to rent a house on Highland Avenue in Newark and to buy some new furniture. Marjorie planned to stop working once the baby was born. And his mother pleaded with Brennan not to run for office. She had hated watching Bill attacked in the press and did not want to see her son subjected to the same treatment.

Brennan turned down the offer and instead campaigned on behalf of one of the commissioners the Good Government League sought to depose: his father's friend Jerome Congleton, who had helped him get his job at Pitney Hardin. Brennan felt a tremendous debt of loyalty for the help Congleton provided his family after Bill died. Brennan volunteered to work nights at Congleton's headquarters and delivered his first political speech there three weeks before the election. The crowd greeted Brennan's maiden oration with an ovation. Either impressed by the speech or desperate to capitalize on the family name, Congleton enlisted Brennan as one of his chief campaign surrogates. Brennan delivered fifteen or twenty more speeches on Congleton's behalf throughout the city. But, as he quipped to a newspaper reporter a few months later, "I guess it didn't do Mr. Congleton much good." Congleton was one of the four city commissioners thrown out of office in the election on May 9, 1933.

Even so, Newark newspapers began speculating about Brennan's political future. In an effusive editorial titled "Another William J. Brennan!" the *Ledger* praised the young lawyer as "the worthy son of a worthy sire, who, we believe, is destined to play a big role in Newark's official life."

Ten days before Election Day, Marjorie had given birth to a son, whom they named William J. Brennan III. Newark's two leading newspapers announced the birth in stories in which the baby's late grandfather garnered more ink than the father. Pursuing a career in law rather than politics must have appealed to Brennan as a way to carve out his own identity. He abandoned any thought of running for office after the 1933 election and never again campaigned on behalf of another candidate. As he told the *Newark Evening News* a few years later, "I don't want any part of politics. I'm too busy trying to be a lawyer — and I'm far happier in the practice of law." For the first time in his life, Brennan had made a decision about his career without his father's input.

Although Brennan swore off his father's vocation, he had inherited his gregarious personality. He easily made friends, remembered names and faces, and fit in no matter the setting, just as he had in college and law school. Pitney Hardin was perhaps the most aristocratic circle in which he found himself yet, as typified by Shelton Pitney, the partner with whom he worked most closely at the firm. Pitney, born in 1893, was the son of the late U.S. Supreme Court justice Mahlon Pitney and a nephew of the firm's founder. He joined Pitney Hardin as a partner after graduating Princeton and Harvard Law School, being wounded in World War I, and working two years at the white-shoe New York law firm that later became known as Cravath, Swaine & Moore.

In his rare nonworking hours, Pitney enjoyed cruises on his gaff-rigged schooner, the *Gray Goose,* where he required guests to place drink orders with the onboard steward and then jump into the ocean while he sang

"When the Sun Comes over the Yardarm." If Brennan joined Pitney on one of these cruises, he would have gamely played along, just as he good-naturedly endured his colleagues' taunts when the Princeton football team played the University of Pennsylvania. (Brennan even made a tidy profit of $50 one year wagering all the Princeton alumni that his alma mater would win.) He did not raise any objections, either, to the fact that the only Satur-day the lawyers at his firm were sure to get off was when Princeton played Harvard or Yale at home each fall. Brennan hid any frustration or resent-ment at the firm's genteel snobbery behind an amiable mask. The same geniality also effectively disarmed attorneys Brennan later faced in court and hid the extent of his considerable ambition.

Brennan was much too politic to say or do anything that might alienate any of his law firm colleagues. That is why his memory of openly exulting in Franklin D. Roosevelt's landslide 1932 victory over Republican incum-bent Herbert Hoover — a reaction he recalled as leaving a senior partner aghast — seems so out of character. The firm's conservative senior attor-neys did not look kindly on the way Roosevelt dramatically inserted the federal government into the nation's economy in the early months of his administration, rewriting banking laws and enacting new relief and agri-cultural programs. Brennan, who was as loyal a Democrat as his father, was undoubtedly pleased about Roosevelt's interventionist economic poli-cies. And given how famous his father was in Newark, Brennan's col-leagues probably assumed he shared Bill's Democratic loyalties. Brennan recalled speaking favorably about the president's New Deal agenda. But more credible is the account of Brennan's contemporaries at the law firm who described him as circumspect in his political views. It's fair to con-clude that at work he dealt with his political beliefs in the same way he did his marriage to Marjorie while at law school: something best kept to himself.

JOHN ALLEGAERT FELT a bit shortchanged in 1934 when he first laid eyes on his new attorney. Allegaert needed all the help he could get deal-ing with workers trying to organize a union at the United Color & Pig-ment factory in Newark, where he served as general manager. Pitney Har-din had sent Brennan, who at twenty-eight still looked young for his age. (Although he had taken up smoking a pipe as his father had, the practice only made him look like a young man pretending to be an adult.) Allegaert assumed that the firm simply viewed him as too minor a client to merit a seasoned lawyer. In fact, and not for the first time, one of Pitney Hardin's senior partners had purposely assigned the matter to Brennan because of his late father's union ties.

Brennan's first labor assignment had come shortly after he arrived at the law firm. A bloody battle had broken out in 1931 at the construction site of a three-mile elevated highway over the Meadowlands swamp and the Hackensack and Passaic rivers. The Pulaski Skyway, as it later came to be known, was designed to ease the drive from Newark and Jersey City to the Holland Tunnel and New York City beyond. The contractor, the McClintock-Marshall Company, sparked the "War of the Meadows" by employing nonunion labor on the project. The violence got so bad that workers were transported by tugboat from New York and even slept on barges so they did not need to leave the worksite. Union ironworkers pelted the boats with stones and steel bolts and beat any scabs caught outside the construction site's perimeter. After a particularly nasty skirmish, Brennan was tasked with bailing out some of the McClintock-Marshall workers from one of the Newark police precincts once overseen by his father. The assignment quickly went awry. A police detective at the precinct mistook Brennan for a criminal who had recently escaped the city jail, and it took quite some time for him to convince the officer otherwise.

Despite that inauspicious start, Brennan's was the first name that came to mind when United Color & Pigment's labor dispute reached Pitney Hardin. The company was accused of refusing to rehire workers involved in an organizing drive at its factory. Such labor confrontations were becoming increasingly frequent as the 1930s progressed. A newly rejuvenated labor movement organized workers in an array of trades and industries, tripling union membership to 9 million during the course of the decade. A major piece of New Deal legislation — the National Industrial Recovery Act (NIRA) — played a part in encouraging this rising worker militancy. The law, which allowed industries to form trade associations to set production quotas and fix prices, included a provision guaranteeing the right of employees to organize and bargain collectively. United Color was sued under that provision — section 7(a) — for wrongfully discharging three-dozen workers for their involvement in a strike for higher wages. No one at Pitney Hardin knew much about the new law or thought the claim had much merit.

As with so much else about Brennan's education and early career, he fell into what would become his legal specialty but approached the task handed to him skillfully and energetically. Brennan quickly impressed his new client. He went to Allegaert's office and questioned him at length, rather than requesting that all relevant documents be delivered to the firm. The National Labor Relations Board initially ruled against United Color, directing the company in April 1935 to reinstate fifteen of the fired workers. Potentially more significant was the accompanying order stripping the company of its Blue Eagle, the symbol companies displayed to show compliance with the NIRA. Loss of the Blue Eagle was theoretically a damaging punishment when applied to employers who sold labeled goods or relied on government contracts. But the initial enthusiasm for the Blue Eagle, once displayed everywhere from factory walls and windshields to the thighs of Atlantic City beauty queens, had faded by late 1934. Few consumers seemed interested in participating in boycotts. Companies found it easy to get a favorable court injunction blocking the loss of the Blue Eagle, a strategy pursued by Brennan. He succeeded in obtaining an injunction two weeks later from the District of Columbia Supreme Court. The matter soon became moot when the U.S. Supreme Court ruled the entire NIRA unconstitutional a month later.

Brennan's work in the case earned him a reputation as the firm's resident expert on labor matters. That expertise became all the more valuable after the enactment of the National Labor Relations Act in July 1935. That law, which protected workers' rights to organize and bargain collectively, helped elevate labor law as a distinct field. It also empowered a newly reconstituted National Labor Relations Board to investigate charges of unfair labor practices and to oversee elections in which workers could decide whether they wanted union representation. Companies throughout the country trying to understand the new law's requirements as they resisted union-organizing drives called on Brennan for advice, particularly after the Supreme Court finally upheld the law's constitutionality in April 1937. That year proved to be one of intense and often violent labor conflicts around the country. Brennan traveled frequently to often out-of-the-way destinations on behalf of clients such as the United States Leather Company, which resisted organizing drives at several of its tanneries in rural western Pennsylvania. Brennan's colleague Donald Kipp believed that what Brennan learned about the union movement from his father made him a more effective negotiator. "The labor leaders trusted him," Kipp recalled in 1956. "They knew he was not going to axe them."

The irony of a son of one of Newark's most famous union leaders representing the side of business in labor disputes did not escape notice in the city's newspapers. "So far he has pitted his legal skill against counsel for a great many labor unions, but to date has not had occasion to oppose anyone representing his father's old union," noted one 1939 profile. Newark lawyers and those who later wrote about Brennan often assumed, as one suggested, that "Bill 'Unity and Unionism' Sr. must have twirled in his grave." While the elder Brennan may well have been surprised to learn of his son's focus on labor law, he had always envisioned a future for him working on behalf of corporate America.

As with his political views, Brennan kept to himself any inner conflict he may have felt about representing management. "That was one of the best-kept secrets Bill ever had," said Thomas Morrissey, who joined the firm in 1940 as a new clerk fresh out of Fordham Law School. In what became his characteristic way of interacting with colleagues, Brennan was always sociable but, as Morrissey recalled, "he never told you anything about himself." The closest Brennan ever came to sharing any union sympathies was when he told Morrissey he never let a loaf of bread come into his house that lacked a union label.

More revealing was the obvious pride Brennan took in his relationships with the union lawyers he faced. "I never lost a friend on that side," Brennan later insisted. Indeed, union lawyers who squared off against Brennan were more likely to remember his courteous manner than his aggressive defense of corporate clients. This strong desire to be liked by everyone held true throughout his life, but it seemed especially evident in the context of labor negotiations.

Brennan's caseload continued to grow as the 1930s progressed, thanks largely to his labor work, but he still worried about the future. Brennan shared his concerns with Donald Kipp when he invited his colleague to join him at a World Series game between the New York Giants and the New York Yankees in October 1937. (The tickets were a gift from a client.) Kipp felt equally insecure about his ability to attract new clients and the amount of work he could expect down the road. The two were to laugh about their fears nearly three months later, when the firm invited them both to become partners as of January 1, 1938.

Being tapped as the firm's eleventh partner brought a significant boost in Brennan's salary. He felt secure enough to buy a spacious $15,000 three-story home one town over from Newark in the more prosperous suburb of South Orange, on the western slope of South Mountain. He could now afford a live-in maid, as well as a laundress who came to the house once a week. With the birth of a second baby boy, Hugh, in 1936, the family now numbered four. His new social set included his former client, John Allegaert, who sponsored Brennan's membership at the Orange Lawn Tennis Club. Brennan also began playing golf at the Rock Spring Club in West Orange. He had decisively crossed over the class boundary his father had remained within.

For Marjorie, the new prosperity and upper-middle-class social circle was a considerable change from her earlier life. Unlike Brennan, she had never mingled with people so educationally and socially advantaged. She also needed to adjust to going from the workforce to full-time housewife. She never went back to work after Bill Jr. was born, concentrating instead on raising their children. Marjorie came to enjoy this new life afforded by Brennan's law-firm partnership. She had time to pursue hobbies such as bridge and golf. She still lived close enough to her sisters to see them regularly, and was able to attend her old church, Our Lady of Good Counsel. She made new friends and enjoyed joining a rotation of couples that took turns hosting each other on Friday nights.

The Friday-night dinners were the exception to the rule: Brennan's work schedule left little time for socializing or spending time with his family. He usually worked six days a week, and could often be found one or two nights a week inside his twenty-first-floor office as late as 10 P.M. or even 1 A.M. He rarely made it home on the train in time to eat dinner with his family. And even on the nights when he did, Brennan pulled out a card table in the living room after dinner and worked until bedtime. One of his son Bill's earliest memories was accompanying Brennan to his office on Saturdays and drawing in a coloring book while his father worked. Brennan made a conscious decision to be more lenient with his children than his father had been. "He was the policy maker," recalled Hugh. "[Marjorie] was the enforcer." Brennan was the more likely of the two to excuse the boys' mischief-making. One time, Bill was throwing snowballs at passing cars and accidentally hit one driver in the head. As the incensed driver chased Bill into a patch of woods near their house, Brennan intervened, eliciting from the man the fact that he was out on parole. Brennan convinced him to calm down and leave the scene before his parole officer got involved.

The strain of keeping up his intense work schedule began to wear on Brennan toward the end of the 1930s. On the advice of a fellow lawyer, he decided to take the summer off, renting a cottage for the family at Buck Hill Falls, Pennsylvania, a resort community eighty miles west of South Orange. Marjorie, who loved swimming and tennis and proved a better golfer than her husband, benefited as much as Brennan from the time away. This extended summer vacation became an annual tradition, first at Buck Hill Falls and then on Cape Cod, since Marjorie preferred the beach. Marjorie and the children spent much of the summer away, with Brennan joining them when he could. The annual breaks helped keep Brennan on a more even keel, but in the midst of an ever-grueling pace.

NOT ALL OF Brennan's legal practice involved labor disputes; he was also involved in trusts and estate work and handled complicated tax matters for corporate clients. Brennan, along with senior partner Shelton Pitney, spent a good deal of time after 1938 representing corporations facing large tax assessments on their intangible assets from New Jersey municipalities desperate for more revenue. One of those clients was Duke Power, a major provider of electricity in the Carolinas. And when Doris Duke, the twenty-nine-year-old heiress to the Duke family power and tobacco fortune, was charged with a separate $14 million tax assessment by Hillsborough Township, home to the opulent twenty-seven-hundred-acre family estate, Duke Farms, Brennan joined Shelton Pitney on that case too.

Brennan had never encountered a client quite like the blond, six-foot-one-inch Duke. The only child of James Buchanan Duke, she had inherited $50 million at the age of twelve upon his death, earning her the designation "the richest girl in the world." The gilded isolation of her childhood only increased the public's fascination. Duke grew up to be a spoiled dilettante who looked visibly bored touring West Virginia's impoverished coal country with First Lady Eleanor Roosevelt or visiting the obscure Methodist college in North Carolina that her father's donations had transformed into Duke University. She seemed happiest in Hawaii, where she enjoyed surfing and built Shangri La, the first million-dollar home on Oahu.

Not surprisingly, Duke proved to be a difficult client. Nervous about her upcoming deposition in the case, she summoned Brennan one night at the last minute to Duke Farms. Her abrupt request forced Brennan to leave Marjorie home alone to host a cocktail party for dozens of guests. Brennan had to leave Marjorie and their sons behind again on Sunday, December 7, 1941, to prepare for Duke's deposition. He was meeting at the home of Duke's personal attorney, William Robertson Perkins, in Montclair, New Jersey, that afternoon when Perkins's wife interrupted with news that Japan had attacked the U.S. Naval Base at Pearl Harbor, not far from Duke's Hawaii estate. (Duke, who was not at the meeting, responded to news of the attack by asking friends in Hawaii whether her swimming pool had been damaged.)

On January 20, 1942, Brennan stood in a Somerville, New Jersey, courtroom questioning Duke, who had been well coached for her appearance. She seemed to have listened to Brennan's advice, at least concerning appearances. Duke was dressed demurely, in a wine-colored wool suit and black scarf and with only a crystal bar pin and single ring for jewelry. But when she opened her mouth, she did not do much to help Brennan establish that Hawaii rather than New Jersey was her primary residence. Under questioning by Harry Walberg, the lawyer representing Hillsborough Township, Duke could not explain why she failed to fill out the nonresident space on her application for a New Jersey driver's license.

"Are you in the habit of signing papers without reading them?" Walberg asked.

"Yes, I'm afraid so," Duke replied.

It was an exchange that reporters enjoyed recounting in their stories about the trial.

BY THE TIME Duke appeared in court, Brennan's legal work seemed increasingly trivial to him. His youngest brother, Frank, then a twenty-one-year-old recent graduate of Princeton, had already enlisted in the Army. His brother Charlie could have used his poor eyesight as a way to avoid getting drafted at the age of thirty-four. But Charlie soon left his job as an accountant at United Color & Pigment, a job Brennan might well have helped his younger brother land, and enlisted too. As the Duke case dragged on that winter, Brennan joined his mother, sister, and Charlie on a visit to Frank, who was training outside Boston to be a radar man in the U.S. Army Air Forces. The family posed for pictures in which both Frank and Charlie appear in their military uniforms. Brennan, the shortest and oldest of the three brothers at thirty-six, looks out of place in his civilian overcoat, fedora, sweater, and tie.

Brennan finally got his chance to join his younger brothers in the military on July 3, 1942. He was called out of a conference to take a phone call from Major General Levin H. Campbell Jr., chief of the U.S. Army Ordnance Department. Campbell asked Brennan to come to Washington the following day to talk about joining his staff. It meant forfeiting a holiday weekend with Marjorie and the boys, who had already headed off to Cape Cod. Eager to serve, Brennan did not hesitate. "He was so happy, you'd think he'd just inherited $20 million," recalled Brennan's United Color client John Allegaert, who spoke with Brennan the day the call came. In Washington, Brennan immediately accepted Campbell's offer to join the Ordnance Department as an adviser on labor relations at the rank of major. He took a leave of absence from his law firm on July 29, 1942, the same day he entered active-duty military service. He had to relocate his family to Washington, D.C., and took a significant cut in salary. The potential conflicts of interest his work presented meant that Pitney Hardin could not supplement his income as it did for other attorneys who entered government service during the war.

Brennan joined the Army in the midst of the largest and most rapid military expansion in American history. The Army grew from 1.5 million personnel in the summer of 1942 to 5.4 million by the end of the year. President Roosevelt had called for a tripling of airplane production in 1942 to 60,000 — and then a doubling of that, to 125,000, in 1943. After just 309 tanks were produced in 1940, the president demanded 45,000 in 1942. The war mobilization finally pulled the country out of the Depression. But it also placed enormous strain on the nation's factories and workers, at a time when many were being enlisted or drafted into the military themselves. Continued labor unrest further complicated the rapid mobilization. The sense of common national purpose did not entirely eliminate labor-management tensions. There were three thousand labor strikes during 1942 — including fifty-one that affected war production in a single two-week period before Brennan joined the Army.

The Army needed specialists such as Brennan who could prevent work stoppages or end them quickly once they began. Brennan was tasked with maintaining the peace at dozens of ammunition plants built and owned by the government but managed by private companies, including Quaker Oats and Proctor & Gamble. Brennan's work impressed Undersecretary of War Robert P. Patterson, a fellow Irishman and Harvard Law School graduate. President Roosevelt had enlisted the Republican federal judge before the war started to lead the peacetime industrial mobilization and Army procurement. Patterson, like Shelton Pitney, quickly identified Brennan as an able and amiable subordinate.

In 1943 Brennan and his family relocated yet again, this time to Los Angeles, after Patterson assigned him to lead a team tasked with eliminating manpower shortages plaguing aircraft factories in Southern California. Brennan took a creative approach to the problem, one modeled on a similar program employed at Boeing's factories in Seattle. He pushed to transfer workers from nonessential occupations such as gas attendants and waiters. To reduce absenteeism and turnover, particularly among the growing percentage of female workers, he made building new childcare facilities a priority, and lengthened shopping hours at grocery stores.

Brennan also spoke frequently to civic groups about the impact manpower shortages had on military production, and he tried to prepare West Coast residents for even greater sacrifice as the war effort shifted from Europe to Asia. In January 1944 Brennan helped organize a giant military pageant at the Los Angeles Memorial Coliseum themed "Get on the job and stay on the job." More than two hundred thousand people attended the exhibition, which featured an air show, fifteen hundred soldiers, movie stars like Gary Cooper and Bob Hope, and a giant stage designed by Hollywood crews to look like a Japanese stronghold in the Pacific.

Brennan performed so well in California that Patterson employed him as a personal troubleshooter after he returned to Washington in July 1944. At thirty-eight, Brennan was promoted to full colonel and given an impressive new title: Chief of the Labor Branch of the Industrial Personnel Division. Helping ensure the continued production of vital war materials such as cotton duck and rubber tires was unquestionably important work. But at some level Brennan felt guilty that he operated from the safety of Washington and Los Angeles while his two brothers served on the frontlines. Frank, then a bombardier flying dangerous missions over Europe, had left behind his new wife, Betty, whom he married in February 1944 while stationed in Laredo, Texas. Charlie, a sergeant with the Army's 77th Infantry Division, left behind a fiancée, Pat Purcell, in Newark. Charlie had already earned a Silver Star — the Army's third-highest honor — and a promotion for carrying wounded soldiers to safety on the battlefield on Guam.

Shortly before Christmas in 1944, there was alarming news: Frank had been shot down during a bombing mission over Germany and was missing in action. Just days after he had been promoted to the rank of captain, Frank's B-24 bomber had come under attack by German fighter planes. Frank parachuted to safety through the nose wheel of the crippled bomber. Three other members of the crew survived, while five died. As Christmas approached, the family knew only that Frank was missing. Many more weeks passed before the family finally learned he had been captured and taken to a German prison camp.

Charlie had heard nothing about Frank's disappearance when he wrote Brennan and Marjorie from Leyte, an island in the Philippines, on New Year's Eve. Charlie avoided any mention of the latest fighting; instead he filled the letter with mundane details about the rainy weather, sporadic mail delivery, and the thrill of special holiday meals. He mentioned how much he was looking forward to receiving Christmas packages and then concluded, "Give my best to Bill and Hughie and a Happy New Year to all." By the time the letter reached Brennan in Washington it was February 1945. Just a few days later, the Army notified the family that Charlie had been killed in action on Leyte at the age of thirty-seven. He was among the last American soldiers who died there in the final weeks of mop-up operations before his division packed up and headed to the next island target, Okinawa.

The loss devastated Brennan. He had always been closest to Charlie, who had followed him from the bedroom they shared growing up to Barringer High School, Wharton, and his fraternity, Delta Tau Delta. Now Charlie was dead, and Brennan's youngest brother was a prisoner of war. What is more, their sister's husband lay critically wounded at Walter Reed Hospital in Washington, D.C., with injuries sustained in battle. In characteristic fashion when dealing with something that upset him, Brennan rarely talked about his brother's death beyond passing references to his family about Charlie's bravery. But half a century later, that last letter from Leyte remained close at hand in the upper-right drawer of his desk in his Supreme Court chambers, where he kept his most cherished possessions.

After Charlie's death, Brennan pressed for an assignment closer to the frontlines. He lined up a position in Manila as chief of personnel for U.S. Army Forces in the Western Pacific, charged with the planned invasion of the Japanese mainland. But his labor work within the United States kept getting in the way. There was a railroad strike to sort out and then a heavy-truck shortage threatening to slow the Army's advance through France. Then he was tapped to appear before Congress to explain why the Army opposed the idea of granting special furloughs to soldiers with skills sought by civilian industries. Brennan laid out the Army's view that such a program, in bypassing soldiers who had served longer and accumulated more combat duty than prospective furlough candidates, was unfair and would hurt morale. He would be called on to testify before a congressional committee a second time, in July 1946, regarding two brothers accused of enlisting a congressman to intervene on their behalf to lift a limit on the number of workers authorized for their ammunition plant.

By the time he testified before Congress the first time, in July 1945, on the issue of special furloughs, the war in Europe had ended and the Soviet army had liberated the German prison camp in which his brother Frank had been held. It fell to Brennan to inform Frank about Charlie's death when Frank's troopship arrived home. A month later, in August, Japan unconditionally surrendered after the U.S. atomic bombings of Hiroshima and Nagasaki. Brennan was released from active duty on September 11, 1945, having served three years, three months, and sixteen days. He received the Legion of Merit and a letter of commendation from Undersecretary of War Patterson, who called him "a tower of strength in working for the Army on manpower problems." But in his mind Brennan's contributions to the war effort would never measure up to those of his two younger brothers.

BRENNAN, UNDOUBTEDLY AWARE at the time of his growing value to Pitney Hardin, probably feigned surprise when his partners voted to add his name to the law firm soon after he returned to Newark in the fall of 1945. One Newark newspaper noted the symbolism of an Irish Catholic being added to the names spelled out in gold on the front door of "Newark's most aristocratic law firm." Brennan's achievement was a source of pride to other Irish Catholics at the firm, now known as Pitney, Hardin, Ward & Brennan. One telephone operator crowed about his achievement as if it were her own. But Brennan did not want to dwell on his status as a pioneer. He simply told the newspaper that his firm had "been very nice" to him. "This is a great place to be," a smiling Brennan said as he patted his desktop.

Rather than make a fuss about breaking barriers, Brennan preferred to open doors quietly for others. Joseph Nolan was a night student at Rutgers Law School when he first met Brennan, then serving on the firm's hiring committee. Nolan was understandably pessimistic about getting a job at the firm, which had never hired a night student before. During their conversation, Brennan asked Nolan what his father did. When Nolan replied he was a fireman in Newark, Brennan stated, "You deserve the job." Nolan soon received an offer. In 1947, after graduating from Harvard Law School, Brennan's youngest brother Frank joined the firm as well.

The firm's name change did indeed reflect Brennan's growing value to Pitney Hardin. His wartime work had only boosted his national reputation as a labor lawyer, and he attracted a long list of top corporate clients. His specialty became all the more important in the months after the war ended, as years of pent-up tensions burst to the surface in an unprecedented strike wave. Organized labor emerged from the war stronger than ever, with 14.5 million members representing 35 percent of the workforce, an all-time high. Right from the start, 1946 proved to be the most strike-torn year in all of American history, as workers sought to reverse wage cuts that followed the war's end. It was a singularly chaotic moment in New Jersey, as in the rest of the country. The front page of the *Newark Evening News* featured a daily scorecard in January 1946 tallying up the 1.5 million workers on strike or threatening to strike in the steel, electrical, auto, oil, and meatpacking industries. These walkouts were more than a distant abstraction to average Americans, many of whom lost their long-distance phone service and could find no meat in their neighborhood markets. The federal government considered seizing steel mills and meatpacking plants, and the New Jersey legislature mulled taking over utilities threatened by strikes.

Western Electric called in Brennan when seventeen thousand of its workers went on strike at twenty plants in New Jersey and New York on January 3, 1946. These workers, who manufactured telephone equipment, wires, and cables for the Bell Telephone System, demanded a 30 percent wage increase. The strike turned violent the next day at the largest of those factories, in Kearny, New Jersey. Picketers used the wooden handles on their placards as clubs to beat back managers trying to enter the plant.

Twelve days after the strike began, Brennan went to court on Western Electric's behalf in an attempt to limit the number of picketers who could block access to the Kearny plant's gates. Seeking such an injunction was a standard legal maneuver, although Brennan pursued an unusually aggressive course. He invoked a little-used state law that allowed the chancery judge to issue an injunction without notifying the union in advance. Brennan came to court prepared with twenty-one affidavits from company managers denied access to the plant, movie reels of the picketing, and a copy of a newspaper front page containing pictures of the January 4 scuffle outside the plant gates. The evidence proved compelling enough for Chancery Judge James F. Fielder in Jersey City to issue a temporary injunction without hearing from the union, limiting the union to five or ten picketers per gate.

Just as Fielder made the injunction permanent in February, as Brennan had requested, workers flagrantly began ignoring it. Even as Brennan stood in the judge's chambers to sign the permanent order, hundreds of picketers surrounded the gates in open defiance. The union claimed the workers were acting on their own. Brennan then sought a contempt order, to no avail. In a letter to the Kearny city council and county agencies, Western Electric complained that the situation was "approaching anarchy" and pleaded for indication of whether anyone intended to enforce the injunction. Such open defiance of a judge's order had become routine that winter in strikes in northern New Jersey. Strikers at a Westinghouse plant in Bloomfield that January dispersed only when a posse deputized by the local sheriff approached the picket line brandishing clubs.

The Western Electric strike finally ended in March, but not because of the injunction Brennan obtained or the contempt action he pursued. Rather, the threat of a national telephone strike prompted the two sides to reach an agreement. Brennan continued to pursue the contempt action even after the strike ended. He insisted he had no choice, having been designated a special prosecutor in the matter by the Chancery Court.

The strike taught Brennan a valuable lesson about the limits of judicial power. All his meticulous preparations and the court's favorable rulings meant nothing absent a way to enforce the judgment. The incident also left Brennan uneasy about unions' excessive power and their willingness to disobey the law so flagrantly. Two weeks after the strike ended, he addressed the issue in a speech to the Essex County Bar Association. He first made clear that, except in industries of "vital public importance" such as utilities, he believed strikes "are not too great a penalty for industrial freedom." But then he warned labor leaders that unless they agreed to some "correctives which will do no more than assure an equal balance and wipe out known abuses of labor's power, the forces which in fact will destroy free labor will win the day and labor, not management, will be the greatest loser."

Brennan soon publicly endorsed legislation aimed at rolling back some of the powers granted unions by the National Labor Relations Act. In a September 1946 speech before the Newark Rotary Club, Brennan said the time had arrived "when we must have some remedial legislation which recognizes the changes in the last ten years in labor's influence in our national life." He described organized labor as "a powerful giant enjoying its strength inclined to play bully and giving evidence to dictate its own terms without regard to the common good." Brennan sounded rather conservative in this, his first public talk about a national political issue. After the enactment of the Taft-Hartley Act in June 1947, which put new restrictions on unions' ability to strike, Brennan defended the measure in public debates with union leaders. But Brennan also defended labor against charges of Communist infiltration or sympathies. "In this great conflict between two philosophies we can take great comfort that American trade unions are unalterably the bitter enemies of the Russian virus."

All the new labor work kept Brennan busier than ever. His colleagues marveled at his capacity for hard work and the ease with which he seemed able to meet his numerous obligations. In truth, the pace took a toll on him both physically and psychologically. Brennan felt uneasy about how little time he could spend with his two sons, who were now approaching adolescence. He provided a stable home but was hardly a constant presence, particularly on weeknights. He did his best to carve out time for his sons on the weekend, taking them to Dodgers and Yankees games or to watch the semipro baseball team that played in South Orange. When Hugh said he wanted to play a night baseball game, Brennan set up lamps in every upstairs window to illuminate the backyard. Summers, particularly, allowed the family to spend time together on Cape Cod. Still, his sons noticed his absence. "If Father ever said, 'I will put together a little league team and I will be the coach,' I would have fallen over in a dead faint," recalled Bill, who turned thirteen in 1946. A terrible reminder to Brennan about the costs of continuing at such a pace came suddenly in January 1946. Shelton Pitney died of a heart attack at his home in Morristown, New Jersey, two months shy of his fifty-third birthday.

BRENNAN MANAGED TO find the time for one extracurricular activity: agitating for an overhaul of New Jersey's archaic court system. "Jersey justice" had long ago become an epithet for the state's unwieldy labyrinth of courts with overlapping jurisdiction ruled by judges seemingly answerable to no one. The system was notorious for long delays before cases reached trial, and even longer intervals before judges actually announced decisions. The state's highest court was the sixteen-member Court of Errors and Appeals, which included ten judges and six laymen. Brennan derisively remembered it as "a little larger than a jury, a little smaller than a mob." Making matters worse was the veto power the state's political bosses — particularly Jersey City's ironfisted Frank Hague — exercised on judicial appointments. The presence of loyal judges on the bench helped protect Hague against charges of election fraud.

Brennan first became concerned about the quality of judicial appointments in the early 1930s. He joined a group of young Essex County attorneys who unsuccessfully pressed the governor to submit the names of potential nominees to the state bar association for review in advance. Brennan was particularly outraged when Hague convinced New Jersey's governor to appoint his unqualified thirty-four-year-old son to the state's highest court in 1939. Governor Harry Moore candidly admitted, "I know this appointment will make his dad happy."

One lawyer in particular had made overhauling the courts his cause. Born in Newark in 1888, Arthur T. Vanderbilt had started his own successful Newark law firm and became dean of New York University Law School and president of the American Bar Association. Vanderbilt had also taken an early interest in political reform, enlisting as his allies a group of younger lawyers, many of whom had worked at his law firm during the 1930s. One of those lawyers, Nathan Jacobs, had a background much like Brennan's. Born a year before Brennan in Bayonne, New Jersey, Jacobs had graduated from the University of Pennsylvania three years before Brennan and then went to Harvard Law School. He earned the prestigious Sears Prize as the top-ranked member of his class in 1927, served two years on law review, and came back to earn an S.J.D. degree the same year Brennan graduated. But like Felix Frankfurter, the professor with whom he was close at Harvard, as a Jew Jacobs had had difficulty finding work at any elite law firms. He wound up working at Vanderbilt's firm for six years before cofounding a firm himself. He also taught at what later became Rutgers Law School while serving intermittently in state government and volunteering in Vanderbilt's court-reform effort. Brennan did not know Jacobs during law school but came to respect him greatly through their interactions after the war. He readily accepted Jacobs's invitation to join the editorial board of the *New Jersey Law Journal*, a weekly legal newspaper pushing for reform.

Court reform appealed to Brennan for the same reason his father had first run for office in his union: he wanted to improve an institution he cared about. He shared his father's distaste for corruption and political machines. The fact that connections mattered more than competence in picking judges galled Brennan. Arthur Vanderbilt's efforts finally paid off in June 1947 when Governor Alfred E. Driscoll convened a state constitutional convention. On July 2, 1947, Brennan testified before the convention's judiciary committee, chaired by Nathan Jacobs. It was a bit of staged theater, since Jacobs in all likelihood had helped write the *New Jersey Law Journal* editorial, "A Modern Court Structure for New Jersey," that Brennan read aloud. In August, the convention approved judicial articles creating a new unified and centrally administered state court system overseen by the chief justice of a seven-member state Supreme Court. The multiplicity of lower courts was replaced by a two-part Superior Court with an Appellate Division and trial court in each county. Voters approved the changes in November 1947, and a month later Governor Driscoll named Vanderbilt as his choice for chief justice.

As the new court system was scheduled to go into effect in September 1948, Driscoll enlisted Jacobs to help recruit new judges. Jacobs approached Brennan, along with other members of the *New Jersey Law Journal* editorial board, about becoming lower-court judges. Brennan was understandably reluctant at first. He was being asked to give up his $80,000-a-year job as a named partner at one of the state's premier law firms to become a trial judge for a quarter of the salary. He was well respected within his specialty and Newark's business community, having already been asked to serve as a director of the American Insurance Company. Brennan worked the lunchtime crowd at the Downtown Club, shaking hands like a celebrity. He was assured a secure future at the firm and could expect offers to join many more corporate boards.

Still, the idea of becoming a judge appealed to Brennan. He had long ago grown averse to elected politics, but public service remained an attractive option. He had inherited his father's reformist impulses and liked the idea of helping to build a new court system from scratch. He had grown tired of the long hours at the law firm and, as he put it to the *Boston Globe* in 1956, "I began to believe that I wouldn't be with my family long if I didn't quit the pace." It was not an idle concern. He was forty-two at the time, only a decade younger than Shelton Pitney had been when he died. Neither his father nor his paternal grandfather had lived to sixty. Brennan's mother loved the idea of her oldest son becoming a judge, quite a contrast to the horror she expressed fifteen years earlier at the prospect of him following his father into politics.

Brennan did not immediately accept. The potential financial sacrifice weighed heavily on him. He had put aside savings to help pay for the cost of school for Bill and Hugh. But his three years of military service had set him back some. And just a few months earlier, Brennan and Marjorie had been surprised to learn she was pregnant again. The news had come as a particular shock to Marjorie, who had recently confided to a friend with a baby that she did not envy her. Brennan sat down with his family around the dinner table to talk about the potential impact of his moving in a new direction. "It's going to cost us something," he said.

Brennan later credited Jacobs with finally convincing him to accept the offer: "We saw one another every day, virtually. We were very close friends and it was he who persuaded me that I really ought to get in and help now that I had done so much already to get the new judicial article." Brennan's colleagues at Pitney Hardin were stunned when he informed them of his decision. Kipp remembered that they were walking back from lunch at the annual meeting of the New Jersey Bar Association that November of 1948 when Brennan told him the news. Kipp was happy for Brennan but worried about what his loss would mean to the firm. Those impressed by the news included Brennan's brother Frank, who soon concluded that law firm life was not for him, either. Before settling down to life on a judge's salary, Brennan had a last hurrah of sorts, buying Marjorie a Lincoln Continental convertible.

Governor Driscoll announced Brennan's appointment on January 4,

1949. The news elicited hearty approval from the local press. "The Senate should be eager to confirm this excellent choice," declared a *Star Ledger* editorial. For the first time, Newark's newspapers wrote about Brennan without mentioning his father. In the eyes of his hometown press at least, Brennan had finally become his own man.

ASCENDING THE BENCH

S WORN IN AS a New Jersey Superior Court judge by Chief Justice
Vanderbilt on January 27, 1949, Brennan was almost immediately
thrown into one of the most bitterly contested elections in New Jersey history. He served just north of Newark in Passaic County until mid-
February, when Vanderbilt appointed him to be the top trial-court judge
in Hudson County. Located across the Hudson River from Manhattan,
Hudson County was the state's second-most-populous county and headquarters for Frank Hague's notorious political machine.

Hague had stepped down as mayor of Jersey City in 1947 after thirty
years in the position, anointing his nephew and private secretary, Frank
Hague Eggers, as his heir apparent. Such blatant nepotism did not sit well
with some of Hague's lieutenants, including John V. Kenny, whose saloonkeeper father had loaned Hague $75 to launch his first political campaign a
half century earlier. Kenny organized an insurgent slate of city-commission
candidates to challenge Eggers and the Hague machine. The election,
scheduled for May 10, 1949, would be the greatest test yet of Hague's continued influence as Democratic Party boss.

The tide had clearly begun to turn against Hague since he had stepped
down as mayor. At one campaign rally, tomatoes and boos rained down
from Kenny supporters. That sort of open defiance was once unthinkable

in Jersey City, where Hague could claim, with no hint of irony, "I am the law." This election, voting machines had replaced paper ballots, and state officials were watching registration lists closely: Hague could no longer make ballots cast for his opponents easily disappear or count on votes from residents who had long since died or moved out of the city. Nor could he rely on loyal judges to protect him now that William Brennan Jr. presided in the county's trial courts and his old foe Vanderbilt served as chief justice.

Brennan detested the way Hague had manipulated the legal system, but ruled in his favor, nonetheless, when a dispute related to the election reached him in April 1949. At issue was the order in which candidates' names would appear on the ballot. When Jersey City's deputy clerk reached into a wood drum holding the candidates' names, the card with the Eggers ticket was the first one he pulled out. The selection meant that the Hague-Eggers slate would top the ballot, an outcome that led to the Kenny slate of candidates challenging the drawing in what reporters dubbed the case of "the magic ballot box."

Although Brennan issued one of his first written opinions as a judge in favor of the Hague ticket, he decided against Hague in another election case. One day before the election, Hague's lawyers came before Brennan challenging the validity of poll books that had been transported in a truck allegedly bearing a Kenny campaign banner. Brennan ruled that it would be impractical to conduct a comparison of the poll books with the original election-board records so close to the election. He also ordered the release of three men on the truck who had been taken into custody.

On Election Day, Hague's thirty-two-year reign as Jersey City's boss came to an end when Kenny and his fellow insurgents defeated the entire slate of incumbents. Kenny's lawyers returned to Brennan's Jersey City courtroom the next day seeking an order barring the outgoing administration from destroying or altering official records in their final days in office. Hague's men had been spotted burning everything they could get their hands on in the City Hall incinerator.

BRENNAN'S TRIAL COURT docket rarely measured up to the drama of the Jersey City election or the complexity of his caseload at Pitney Hardin. His typical written opinions involved municipal zoning decisions, contract disputes, and in one instance a lawsuit involving a garbage-removal contract. He had no difficulty transitioning from his previous orientation as a corporate labor lawyer, ruling two times in the summer of 1949 in favor of unions. Brennan rejected a labor injunction sought against striking long-shoremen and upheld a wage increase awarded to a union by an arbitrator. But he still had much to learn about some of the more mundane aspects of judging.

As the judiciary's chief administrator in the county, Brennan's off-the-bench responsibilities included assigning cases to the other judges. Vanderbilt had a mission in mind when he appointed Brennan to Hudson County: a sweeping overhaul of the state's courts and an end to the long delays before cases went to trial. To accomplish that goal, Vanderbilt had stripped trial judges of much of the autonomy they previously enjoyed. He required trial judges to file weekly reports detailing how many hours they spent on the bench, the number of cases and motions they considered, and their pending caseload. Judges accustomed to a large measure of independence resented the strict new oversight. Vanderbilt felt no sympathy. "If any of the judges can't or won't do the job we should excise them from this work in favor of those who can and will," he wrote Brennan.

Many judges and lawyers particularly disliked Vanderbilt's crowning innovation: pretrial conferences. First introduced two decades earlier in Detroit, pretrial conferences were designed to force the parties to discuss the facts, narrow the legal questions, and allow the judge to nudge them toward settlement. If the two sides did not settle, the judge then issued an order to help guide the trial. Vanderbilt had championed pretrial conferences as a means to improve court efficiency ever since he served as American Bar Association president in 1938. Vanderbilt knew that many New Jersey judges silently rebelled or paid mere lip service to the idea, and he deployed the assignment judges to overcome that resistance.

Resistance was particularly fierce in Hudson County, where a clubby band of Hague loyalists still occupied the bench. The success of Vanderbilt's entire reform program hinged on Hudson and Essex counties, which accounted for a combined 40 percent of the state's litigation. Brennan supported Vanderbilt's drive for greater efficiency, approaching the task from the perspective of a Wharton graduate. Believing, as he wrote in 1957, that the "intelligent application" of principles of business management would "cure most of the problems of organization, procedure and management which are plaguing the courts of our land," Brennan conceived of his role as assignment judge as equivalent to the responsibilities a large corporation might entrust to a vice president or branch manager.

Veteran judges under Brennan's supervision did not take kindly at first to receiving orders from the forty-three-year-old novice. His youthful appearance surprised even judges of his own generation. Haydn Proctor, who became a Hudson County trial judge at the same time as Brennan, had expected some grizzled old veteran when he heard that the new presiding judge had been a colonel during the war. Proctor was thus taken aback on first seeing the young-looking judge, who walked in holding a Hershey bar. (Brennan was known to eat chocolate in the late morning for an energy boost.)

Brennan won over judges and lawyers by employing the same skills that had helped him disarm potentially hostile union lawyers. Mark Sullivan, a Hudson County judge who reported to Brennan at the time, found him, "a charmer in his own way. He was firm and tough but he had the ability to bring people around to his way of thinking." Brennan's success at reducing delays and speeding up the docket helped explain why Vanderbilt could boast that the state's trial judges disposed of 98 percent more cases in 1949 than in the previous year. At least on occasion, Brennan became overzealous in the pursuit of greater efficiency. After a Union City lawyer complained that the presiding judge had pressed too hard to settle a case, Brennan professed to Vanderbilt, "I must learn that no provocation justifies harsh treatments."

Vanderbilt had no qualms. In August 1949 he handed Brennan the sensitive task of presiding at an attorney disciplinary hearing. Andrew O. Wittreich was a Jersey City lawyer accused of using thousands of dollars belonging to a seventy-two-year-old client, who was partially paralyzed and illiterate, for personal use, buying, among other things, a new Cadillac sedan. This was one of the first such proceedings since the state Supreme Court had been granted greater control over attorney discipline, and Vanderbilt wanted to show the public he was serious about cracking down on misconduct.

After the three-day hearing concluded, Brennan sent Vanderbilt a handwritten letter that reveals the close relationship they had already established. "Dear Chief," it began, "I'm troubled about several features + need your help." Brennan worried he had done a poor job of explaining his role to Wittreich's attorney, incurred too many expenses conducting the

hearing, and mishandled local newspaper reporters, who had mischaracterized the proceeding in the press. Vanderbilt responded the next day
from his Maine vacation home with a lengthy, reassuring letter. "The only
thing about that Wittrich [sic] matter that disturbs me is that you were delayed a week in getting on your well deserved vacation," he wrote.

Brennan later looked back fondly on his time as a trial judge. He enjoyed having absolute authority over his own courtroom and being able to
decide most matters instantly. But the assignment did not last long. After
only eighteen months in the trial court, Brennan was promoted in August
1950 to be one of six judges serving on the Superior Court's Appellate Division. Jersey City newspaper columnist Jon Byrne lamented Brennan's departure, praising the same traits that would later distinguish him on the
U.S. Supreme Court: "He made friends as he went along and was as genial
to the men in overalls who do the manual work necessary to keep the court
house going as he was with the top flight advocates . . . those of us who
knew him from close association believe he is an ideal American judge."

BRENNAN EXPRESSED SOME hesitance as he prepared to assume his
new post as an appellate judge. "I'm prone to some wild fears and misgivings about everything new I do but you always bring me down to earth,"
he wrote to Vanderbilt. It was an uncharacteristic display of self-doubt for
the judge, and though it might have been aimed as much at flattering Vanderbilt, Brennan had some legitimate grounds for concern. Stripped of his
administrative responsibilities, his sole focus would now be on judging.
And whereas as a trial judge he had considered cases individually, Brennan would now work on them collectively, with two other members of the
Appellate Division. Achieving consensus was a top priority, given the pre-
mium Vanderbilt put on unanimity on New Jersey's new appellate courts.
There was a practical reason for avoiding dissents on the Appellate Division whenever possible: a unanimous three-judge ruling gave the New Jersey Supreme Court discretion over whether to hear a subsequent appeal,
but a dissent triggered an automatic right of appeal for the losing party.

The new role entitled Brennan to a small staff, and in assembling his
team he reached back to his roots at Pitney Hardin, hiring Shelton Pitney's
former secretary, Alice Connell, and Pitney's son James as his first clerk.

Brennan soon developed a warm working relationship with his two Superior Court colleagues. John B. McGeehan, fifty, worked as a Bayonne

deputy revenue commissioner and state legislative counsel before being appointed to the Court of Errors and Appeals in 1945. Wilfred Jayne, sixty-two, was a former Ocean County prosecutor who resigned his state senate seat to become a circuit court judge in 1933. He had been appointed to the new Superior Court in 1948 and elevated to the Appellate Division earlier in 1950.

The men had no difficulty deciding and assigning cases among themselves after oral argument. Jayne, distinguished by a bristling mustache, often helped lighten the mood with his keen sense of humor — a welcome relief from what was largely a bland Appellate Division docket dominated by tort, zoning, workers' compensation, public-employee discharges, contract, and family law cases. They heard few cases asserting federal constitutional violations, because the U.S. Supreme Court had not yet applied most provisions of the Bill of Rights to the states. (As written, the Bill of Rights functioned only as a limitation on the power of the federal government, but the Supreme Court, from the 1920s to the 1960s, gradually made most of its provisions apply to the states as well.)

In the rare instances where a case involved constitutional claims, Brennan did not necessarily show much sympathy for the parties alleging a violation of their rights. He wrote an opinion in 1951 ruling that announcing a verdict when the criminal defendant was absent from the courtroom did not violate the defendant's rights. Brennan similarly ruled against a mother who refused to permit a blood test determining paternity to be administered either to herself or to her child. "The citizen holds his citizenship subject to the duty to furnish to the courts, from time to time and within reasonable limits, such assistance as the courts may demand of him in their effort to ascertain truth in controversies before them," Brennan wrote. Brennan's Appellate Division opinions were workmanlike in tone and language. He showed no particular preference for parties in any type of case, including ones involving labor law. He directed his rare bursts of harsh language at lawyers or judges for mishandling cases.

While serving in the Appellate Division, Brennan continued his court-reform work, but without his former administrative responsibilities, his schedule lightened considerably. He enjoyed the camaraderie of fellow judges who maintained their chambers in the Newark Hall of Records, including Nathan Jacobs, a frequent lunch partner. He worked from home every other Wednesday and cared for his baby daughter, Nancy, born in

February 1949, shortly after Brennan's appointment to the state Superior Court. The arrangement gave Marjorie the chance to attend a matinee. Having adjusted to the unexpected pregnancy, Marjorie was now happy to be raising her first daughter. But the premature death of her sister Irene, who had raised her after her parents died, came as a blow. For Marjorie, the death of her sister, which roughly corresponded with Nancy's birth, made her feel as if she had been orphaned all over again.

THE FINAL STEP in Brennan's swift rise up the ranks of New Jersey's judiciary owes much to the reluctance of a fellow Irish American. Edward J. O'Mara, a Democratic state senator from Jersey City, had first turned down Governor Alfred Driscoll when he offered him a seat on the newly created New Jersey Supreme Court in 1948. At the time, O'Mara cited the obligation of supporting a large family and the recent reorganization of his law firm. Nevertheless, when Justice Henry Ackerson Jr. retired in January 1952, Driscoll looked again to O'Mara as his first choice. Driscoll was a Republican, but needed to appoint a Democrat to maintain the customary bipartisan makeup of the state's high court. At the same time, Brennan's name surfaced in the local press as a contender. Brennan's selection was endorsed by Vanderbilt, who in turn had been urged to support Brennan for the vacancy by, among others, his former partner at Pitney Hardin, Waldron Ward. Ward had written to Vanderbilt to tout Brennan as "the ideal selection." But O'Mara enjoyed one significant advantage over Brennan: he was from Hudson County. Essex County, where Brennan lived, was already overrepresented on the court, particularly since Driscoll had announced plans on February 5, 1952, to nominate Nathan Jacobs to another vacancy on the court.

Driscoll offered the seat to O'Mara over dinner the same night he announced Jacobs's appointment. O'Mara asked for a day to think about the offer and then turned the governor down a second time. Driscoll disclosed O'Mara's decision to reporters at his weekly Thursday press conference in Trenton on February 7. A few minutes later, after an aide slipped a note to the governor confirming Brennan's acceptance, Driscoll announced his new selection, praising Brennan's "rich experience as a practicing lawyer" and the "high quality" of his work as a judge.

Noting Brennan would be the fourth justice from Essex County, the *Newark Evening News* editorial writer observed, "It may be said that this gives one county preponderant representation. But obviously Mr. Driscoll has proceeded on the sound belief that good men are where you find them." In fact, adding a fourth justice from Essex County so concerned Driscoll that, prior to offering the job, he asked Brennan to relocate. Brennan agreed to leave the county where he and Marjorie had spent the greater part of their lives, seeing it as a relatively small price to pay for what had become his ultimate ambition. "I had no intention of being anywhere except on the New Jersey Supreme Court the rest of my life," Brennan recalled later.

Brennan and Jacobs were sworn in together on Monday, March 24, 1952, in Trenton, inside the State House Annex building where the Supreme Court was headquartered. The crowd of fifty onlookers in the court conference room included their friends, family, and Senator O'Mara. The two newcomers immediately took their seats on opposite ends of the bench as they heard arguments in five cases that day. Their positions on the bench and identical educations explain why some labeled them the "Harvard ends," a moniker not always meant as a compliment.

Jacobs and Brennan stood out on the court for more than their identical Ivy League pedigrees. Jacobs, forty-seven, and Brennan, who joined the court just shy of his forty-sixth birthday, were considerably younger than the other five state Supreme Court justices, who were all in their sixties. Except for Vanderbilt, their colleagues could all boast considerably more experience as judges. Harry Heher first joined the Court of Errors and Appeals in 1932, just a year after Brennan graduated from law school. Albert Burling, a former Republican state senator and circuit judge, joined the Supreme Court in 1947. Dayton Oliphant was a former Mercer County prosecutor first appointed to the circuit court in 1927. William Wachenfeld served as a prosecutor in Essex County before his appointment to the bench in 1946.

Brennan was the only true newcomer: Jacobs had sat with all four justices during his tenure on the Court of Errors and Appeals in the late 1940s. The biggest challenge for Jacobs was working alongside Vanderbilt: "My aversion to domination has intensified with the passage of the years and I suspect that the chief's passion for domination has kept pace," he wrote in a June 1952 journal entry. Vanderbilt may have harbored his own misgivings about Jacobs, who, he believed, had not sufficiently sought his advice during the 1947 state constitutional convention.

Brennan had an opportunity to watch Jacobs and Vanderbilt navigate their new relationship when the three of them traveled by train from Newark to Trenton twice a week. The justices gathered to hear arguments on Mondays and to discuss cases on Thursdays. The rest of the week, Brennan worked out of the same chambers he had occupied as an Appellate Division judge, on the third floor of the Newark Hall of Records. Jacobs maintained his chambers there too. Brennan soon discovered one important difference between the Appellate Division and the Supreme Court. Spread out all over the state, Brennan and his colleagues relied almost entirely on written memoranda and letters as the means to communicate with one another.

Brennan offered few insights about his views or judicial style in the ten opinions he wrote in the three months before the court recessed for the summer, on July 1. The cases were standard fare for the court, including a divorce decree contested by estate administrators and a dispute over court jurisdiction in a personal-injury case involving another state's laws. He showed signs of passion in his writing only in the case of a Bridgeton attorney suspended from practicing law for six months after he was sentenced for assaulting the editor of a weekly newspaper. Brennan, in a separate concurring opinion, explained in great detail why he believed the attorney, who wielded a rubber hose and a riding crop in the attack, should have his law license suspended: "Discipline must be imposed not primarily to punish him but to give assurance to the public that the profession is deserving of its trust and confidence and will demand that all lawyers meticulously adhere to the high standards imposed by the profession upon itself."

WHEN THE TERM ended, Brennan fulfilled his promise to Governor Driscoll to relocate from Essex County. He and Marjorie chose Rumson, a seaside town forty-five miles to the southeast in Monmouth County. Rumson was located at the end of a peninsula, surrounded on two sides by the Shrewsbury and Navesink rivers, and on the third by a narrow inlet leading to a barrier-beach island on the Atlantic Ocean. Rumson's proximity to the ocean explains why so many large summer estates were built there in the nineteenth century; by the 1950s only some of those properties had been subdivided into smaller parcels.

The Republican-dominated town, suffused with a genteel upper-crust culture, was perhaps a surprising choice for Brennan and Marjorie. Catholics remained a rarity at Rumson's trio of exclusive clubs: the Rumson Country Club, the Sea Bright Beach Club, and the Sea Bright Lawn Tennis & Cricket Club. The latter, one of the oldest tennis clubs in the country, boasted of importing from England the original sod for its grass courts. The lure for Marjorie was the easy beach access; it was just a quick drive over a small bridge to the shore. Then they found what she came to consider her dream home: a seven-room former carriage house on what were once the grounds of an adjacent estate.

The house at the corner of Conover Lane and Rumson Road was full of charming remnants of its former life. Enormous storefront-size plate glass windows in the living and dining rooms were installed where carriages once departed through double doors. A beam jutting out above a small door on the second story had been used to lift bales into the hayloft. The small symmetrical windows and wooden support columns remained in what were once the stables. Brennan sold their South Orange house for $25,000, which covered the purchase price for the new home. But the Rumson house required extensive renovations costing an additional $18,000 — equivalent to three-quarters of his new annual salary. Marjorie supervised the renovations and redecorating herself. They hired contractors to modernize the kitchen and redo the upstairs bedrooms, which were once servants' quarters. The former barn stalls became a three-car garage. They also did extensive carpentry, plumbing, and landscaping work and painted the house. In the interim, the family moved into an apartment above a neighbor's garage on Conover Lane.

Having lived for most of her life on the densely populated edge of Newark, Marjorie felt as if she had moved to a resort town. She no longer yearned for summer trips to Cape Cod, now that she had such convenient access to swimming, sailing, tennis, golf — and even iceboating during the winter. "Everything is right next door," she explained to a newspaper reporter a few years later. Nancy, then three years old, also loved the new house, despite allergies to the lingering horsehair. She enjoyed playing in the acre-plus yard and the small burial plot between their house and Rumson Road. By the end of the summer, Nancy had the house to herself. Bill went back to college at Colgate, where he was starting his sophomore year that fall of 1952. Hugh enrolled at the Lawrenceville School, a private boarding school near Princeton.

Moving to Rumson required that Brennan relocate to new chambers as well. He settled into a modest two-room suite carved out of state office space in nearby Red Bank. His chambers were located on the second floor at 12 Broad Street, a narrow five-story building on Red Bank's main commercial strip just a couple of blocks from where sailboats docked on the Navesink River. The outer room of his chambers contained just enough workspace for his law clerk, James Pitney, and his secretary, Alice Connell, who both accompanied him in the move. Pitney was later succeeded as law clerk by the son of Waldron Ward, the other Pitney Hardin partner who had done so much to advance Brennan's career.

Brennan preferred an early start to the day, as his third clerk, David Harrison, later discovered, much to his chagrin, at the start of his clerkship in the summer of 1954. Brennan glowered at Harrison when he arrived at nine thirty on his first day, an uncharacteristic display of pique from an otherwise genial boss. Brennan asked his clerks to write memos summarizing cases prior to oral arguments. But he preferred to write his own opinions in longhand on legal pads while seated at a long wooden table in his chambers, his law books spread out around him. Brennan always kept his door open so that his clerk could have access to the modest collection of law books he had inherited from his predecessor. More detailed legal research required a trip to Newark or Trenton. Brennan found his work life in Red Bank somewhat isolating on the three days a week he did not travel to Trenton. He no longer had fellow judges, like Jacobs, as lunch partners, and begged off dining with local attorneys to avoid the appearance of impropriety. Most days, he ate in his chambers with only his secretary and clerk for company.

BRENNAN'S FIRST FULL term was drawing to a close in May 1953 when the New Jersey Supreme Court took up what became the most significant case of his tenure there. John Henry Tune was accused of murdering a Newark man and leaving the body in the basement of the victim's home. Tune signed a fourteen-page confession based on his statements to police during an interrogation at Newark police headquarters. His defense lawyers subsequently tried to obtain a copy of Tune's statements to police, as well as statements made by witnesses in the case. The trial court directed prosecutors to provide Tune's lawyers with copies of his statements, but not those of witnesses. But Vanderbilt, in a majority opinion for the Supreme Court, held that the defense lawyers should not be granted access to either the witnesses' or Tune's statements.

Brennan excoriated the majority in a passionate dissent. "It shocks my sense of justice," he wrote, "that in these circumstances counsel for an accused facing a possible death sentence should be denied inspection of his confession which, were this a civil case, could not be denied." He complained that "the majority view sets aside the presumption of innocence and is blind to the superlatively important public interest in the acquittal of the innocent. To shackle counsel so that they cannot effectively seek out the truth and afford the accused the representation which is not his privilege but his absolute right seriously imperils our bedrock presumption of innocence." To Vanderbilt's argument that greater use of discovery in criminal cases would lead to increased perjury, Brennan responded: "That old hobgoblin perjury, invariably raised with every suggested change in procedure to make easier the discovery of the truth, is again disinterred from the grave where I had thought it was forever buried under the overwhelming weight of the complete rebuttal supplied by our experience in civil causes where liberal discovery has been allowed."

Brennan's dissent in *State v. Tune* is notable in several respects. First, it stands out as a rare example of sparkling prose in Brennan's tenure as a state judge, which was marked largely by tepid writing. Brennan also displayed a willingness to disagree vigorously with Vanderbilt's legal reasoning, despite their close relationship off the bench. By 1953, Brennan had become Vanderbilt's unofficial deputy, the genial face who complemented the chief justice's role as ruthless enforcer. Brennan coauthored the manual on pretrial procedures given to trial judges and lawyers throughout the state and became chairman of the Supreme Court's committee on pretrial conferences and calendar control. "Brennan was the workhorse," recalled Ed McConnell, whom Vanderbilt appointed administrative director of New Jersey's courts in 1953.

Interestingly, and most importantly, although the clerks who worked alongside Brennan most closely at the time later recalled him exhibiting no particular ideological bent, Brennan's dissent in the case would later become a key piece of evidence cited by writers looking for early hints of the liberalism he later displayed on the U.S. Supreme Court. Brennan had certainly not developed anything resembling a coherent judicial philosophy, particularly regarding rights guaranteed under the U.S. Constitution. Brennan did display some other hints of his future jurisprudence, particularly in cases involving civil liberties. He joined an opinion by Vanderbilt holding that distributing King James Bibles in public schools violated provisions of both the United States and New Jersey constitutions prohibiting state establishment of religion. He ruled that Newark's public safety director had imposed an improper prior restraint on speech by denying an operating license to a theater because it had previously operated burlesque shows. The case had obvious parallels to his father's failed attempt to block the showing of the film *The Naked Truth*, and Brennan cited that 1926 court decision in his opinion.

As in *State v. Tune*, Brennan emphasized the importance of protecting the rights of criminal defendants in other cases, though he did not always rule in their favor. He adopted a broad view of the privilege against self-incrimination, which he called "precious to free men as a restraint against high-handed and arrogant inquisitorial practices." Still, he held that witnesses who invoked the right against self-incrimination in a public corruption case could be compelled to answer questions before a grand jury. In a civil lawsuit for damages against a police officer who shot a fleeing suspect, Brennan wrote, "The law values human life too highly to allow an officer to proceed to the extremity of shooting an escaping offender who in fact has committed only a misdemeanor or lesser offense, even though he cannot be taken otherwise." So too did Brennan offer a ringing endorsement of the prohibition on double jeopardy: "The plea of double jeopardy must be honored, though a regrettable defeat of justice may result. Such misadventures are the price of individual protection against arbitrary power."

BRENNAN — AND PARTICULARLY Marjorie — continued to enjoy life in Rumson. As in each earlier phase of his life, Brennan had little trouble blending into the town and its most exclusive institutions. The Brennans joined both the Rumson Country Club, which was only a block away from their home, and the Sea Bright Beach Club. They also joined the new Catholic Church of the Nativity at the border of the neighboring town of Fair Haven. Brennan was a featured speaker at breakfasts for the local Holy Name Society, a Catholic men's group. Marjorie volunteered for the local Community Appeal, eventually becoming its treasurer. Brennan, too, got involved in local civic organizations. He was elected to the board of governors of Monmouth Memorial Hospital, situated near his chambers in Red Bank, and served as a trustee of the Monmouth County Organization for Social Service. He delivered speeches to local groups including the legal aid society and the Rotary Club, and at dinners honoring local judges and prosecutors. He found an escape from his lunch-hour isolation by joining a group of local businessmen, "the Root Beer and Checkers Club," who met across the street from his chambers at a restaurant called the Olde Union House, and participated in their annual golf outings, dinners, and cocktail parties.

Brennan achieved something resembling a balanced work and home life for the first time in his career, despite the twice-weekly 120-mile round-trips to Trenton. He was able to spend more time with his daughter Nancy than he had with his sons when they were her age. Still, much of the parenting burden continued to fall on Marjorie, particularly when it came to disciplining their two teenage sons. Marjorie was the one who stayed up waiting for Bill or Hugh, home on summer vacation or school breaks, to return from late nights out with friends. Hugh remembered Marjorie regularly cooking him early-morning breakfasts and then staying up to talk to him while he ate. Both Bill and Hugh seemed more focused on fun than on their studies. But Brennan, mindful of his own father's domineering presence in his life, was unwilling to confront either of his sons.

Bill had not distinguished himself academically at Colgate, which made it difficult for him to follow his father's path into a legal career. He was rejected by Harvard Law School in the spring of 1955, prompting Dean Erwin Griswold to write Brennan an apologetic letter. "If the matter had been really close, I was prepared to do some special urging with the Admissions Committee," Griswold wrote the judge in May 1955. "However, your son's record at Colgate was rather low." When he wrote Griswold back, Brennan blamed himself for not doing "a better job of seeing to it that he performed up to his capacity to do better." Bill returned to Colgate in the fall of 1955 for an extra semester to make up for missing credits. By that time, he was engaged to Roxey Louise Atwood, a senior at Skidmore College. They planned a June 1956 wedding.

Hugh had also enrolled at Colgate in the fall of 1954, when Bill was a junior there, after being rejected by his first choice, Princeton. He joined a fraternity and by his own admission "was a dreadful kid." Drunk one night, Hugh and his roommate stole the mayor's car as a joke and got caught when they parked behind a local bar. The infraction was serious enough to merit expulsion, but Brennan drove up to the campus to intervene on his son's behalf. Hugh, suspended for a week, drove home with his father, a fifteen-hour roundtrip for Brennan. Such missteps were typical among the children of their parents' friends in Rumson, Hugh later recalled. "A lot of them ended up taking forever to get out of college, getting into trouble with alcohol," he said.

Their parents' social life was no less bibulous. Brennan and Marjorie had found a new set of five or six couples in Rumson with whom they socialized regularly over barbecues, winter buffets, and cocktails. Brennan earned a reputation for making the best martinis. At one point, Brennan, Marjorie, and their friends hired an Arthur Murray instructor to teach them some new dance steps. Brennan and Marjorie, who had first met at a dance, were both good dancers and had enjoyed stepping out. But everyone got so drunk that not much was learned at these weekly sessions. The instructor put her foot down on the last night and insisted on teaching everyone the samba. To the outside world, Marjorie seemed content with the life she and her husband had created in Rumson. But the physical distance from her hometown had not eased the pain caused by the death of her sister Irene, which recalled the earlier trauma of her parents' deaths. Though Brennan may not have realized it at the time, Marjorie's social drinking was an early sign of his wife's growing dependence on alcohol.

The family finances presented Brennan with a more immediate concern. Brennan and Marjorie had never adjusted their lifestyle to his lower income as a judge. Shortly after being named to the Superior Court, Brennan had allowed Bill to transfer from a South Orange public high school to the private Newark Academy for his last two years of secondary school. Then came tuition at Colgate, a private college. Hugh had also attended Newark Academy before transferring to another private school, Lawrenceville. Brennan had only become more overextended since moving to Rumson, despite a modest boost in his salary. There was the continued expense of renovating their home, and membership in the country and beach clubs. And on top of his two sons' college expenses, Brennan was also paying for Nancy to attend Rumson Country Day School. Brennan shielded his children from the family's financial problems and began borrowing heavily.

A GREEN CARNATION graced every lapel and a potted shamrock decorated every table when Brennan stood up to deliver the keynote address to the Charitable Irish Society of Boston at a Saint Patrick's Day dinner on March 17, 1954. Brennan played to the audience of one thousand society members gathered inside Boston's Sheraton Plaza Hotel, beginning his speech with a hearty embrace of his audience's common Irish heritage. "This is the day every year when the whole nation seems to go on a genealogical binge to find a strain of Irish somewhere in the family lineage," Brennan noted. "We who need go back no further than our parents' Roscommon cottages witness the avid search, smugly we must confess, and yet with an inner if unexpressed pride that all America should in that way show its recognition of how completely American are the Americans of Irish ancestry."

Brennan continued in a similar vein of ethnic pride for most of his speech before pivoting, toward the end, to a discussion of the threat posed by Communism. The topic was seemingly inescapable in the midst of the Cold War between the United States and its former wartime ally, the Soviet Union, and Brennan sounded much like Ambassador Henry Cabot Lodge Jr., also a speaker at the dinner, when he warned, "Organized atheistic society is making a determined drive for supremacy by conquest as well as infiltration." But then Brennan's speech took an unexpected turn. He warned the audience against sacrificing "all of the guarantees of justice and fair play and simple human dignity which have made our land what it is" in the name of fighting the Communist threat. Brennan added, "The enemy deludes himself if he thinks he detects in some practices in the contemporary scene reminiscent of the Salem witch hunts, any signs that our courage has failed us and that fear has palsied our hard won concept of justice and fair play."

There was no mistaking the target of Brennan's veiled criticism: Senator Joseph McCarthy, a fellow Irish Catholic. It had been only four years since the obscure first-term Wisconsin Republican had vaulted to national prominence with a February 1950 speech in Wheeling, West Virginia, warning of Communist infiltration within the State Department. The Red

Scare had gripped the country long before McCarthy's Wheeling speech. World War II had barely ended in 1945 when the House Un-American Activities Committee began grilling a parade of witnesses about their alleged Communist ties. Those who declined to answer questions were cited for contempt and even jailed. Loyalty oaths became a prerequisite for employment for everyone from teachers and dockworkers to Hollywood screenwriters. Refusing to sign these oaths could mean consignment to career-ending blacklists.

But McCarthy's explosive accusations—combined in that summer of 1950 with the outbreak of the Korean War and the arrest of Julius and Ethel Rosenberg on charges of passing secrets about the atomic bomb to the Soviet Union—added additional fuel to the anti-Communist hysteria. The fact that the numbers McCarthy offered of suspected Communist infiltrators kept changing and that his claims were based largely on innuendo mattered little to his many admirers. His fellow Republican senators viewed him as useful even if dishonest, particularly after he was credited with helping them win several seats in the fall 1950 midterm elections. When Republicans took control of the Senate in 1953, he was rewarded with a subcommittee chairmanship, allowing him to launch his own investigations.

McCarthy had passed his peak by the time Brennan delivered his Saint Patrick's Day speech. FBI director J. Edgar Hoover, who had supplied McCarthy with investigators, had cut him off in July 1953. Dwight D. Eisenhower, the World War II general turned Republican president, grew tired of his antics, particularly after McCarthy set his sights on the U.S. Army. On March 9, 1954, Edward R. Murrow, then perhaps the nation's most prominent television journalist, dedicated an episode of his popular CBS television news program, *See It Now,* to a devastating portrayal of McCarthy as a bully. But at the time Brennan spoke nine days later, the nation had not yet witnessed McCarthy's televised downfall as he faced off against the Army regarding his investigation of alleged subversion at Fort Monmouth, New Jersey. The climax of the thirty-six days of televised hearings came on June 9, 1954, when Joseph Welch, special counsel for the Army, asked McCarthy, "Have you no sense of decency sir, at long last?"

So, taking a swipe at McCarthy—even a veiled one like Brennan's— remained a risky proposition in March 1954, particularly before a crowd

of Irish Catholics. McCarthy, the country's most famous Catholic politician since 1928 presidential nominee Al Smith, remained a popular figure
among their coreligionists. He had been heartily embraced by both the
Church hierarchy and working-class Catholics who shared his distaste for
Communism. They viewed identifying with his crusade as a way for them
to prove themselves loyal Americans. One day before Brennan delivered
his speech, McCarthy was praised at a Saint Patrick's Day gathering in a
Chicago church for "driving the snakes out of America."

McCarthy was generally less popular among more successful Irish
Catholics like Brennan. His leading critics included Eugene McCarthy, a
Minnesota Democrat, who was then a member of Congress and later a
senator and candidate for president, and Chicago's auxiliary bishop, Bernard Sheil, who condemned McCarthy in April 1954 by saying that anti-
Communism was not "a game to be played so publicity made politicians
can build fame for themselves." But Catholic support for McCarthy remained so high that when the Senate voted to censure him in December 1954, Massachusetts's junior senator, John F. Kennedy, then recovering
from back surgery, skipped the vote out of fear of alienating voters back
home. Kennedy's brother, Robert, served as a counsel for McCarthy's subcommittee.

Brennan had been privately uneasy about the investigative methods
that came to be known as McCarthyism. He disliked the use of secret sessions where he believed "hapless and helpless" victims had their good
names ruined. Brennan decided to speak out publicly when McCarthy ze-
roed in on targets close to Brennan's home — and his heart. Brennan was
outraged by McCarthy's investigation of the Army Signal Corps at Fort
Monmouth, which was just four miles from his home in Rumson. Brennan
was also angered by McCarthy's demands that the Army court-martial
Major Irving Peress, a dentist stationed in New Jersey who refused to answer the senator's questions. Like President Eisenhower, Brennan, the former colonel whose brother was killed in action while serving in the Army,
identified much more closely with the targets than the inquisitor. "The
thing was right on our doorsteps," Brennan recalled later. "What the hell, I
had nothing to lose." But in fact Brennan could not afford to be quite that
cavalier: he faced reappointment after his seven-year term on the state Supreme Court expired, and only then would he be granted tenure. Never-

theless, Brennan indirectly criticized McCarthy in two additional speeches he delivered in subsequent months to New Jersey audiences.

BRENNAN SPOKE MORE often about court reform than about McCarthyism in his increasingly frequent public addresses. He had become Vanderbilt's public relations man, trumpeting New Jersey's court reforms to audiences throughout the state and beyond. Brennan led more than fifty county judges on a two-day tour of state prisons in April 1954. The judges talked with inmates, visited cells and infirmaries, and received a favorable write-up in the *New York Times*. Brennan spoke to the North Carolina Bar Association about pretrial procedures in 1954 and led demonstrations at the American Bar Association convention in Philadelphia and at Suffolk University in Boston in 1955. A savvy protégé, Brennan always made sure to give plenty of credit to Vanderbilt. "I acquired my interest in the subject under his tutelage," the judge told the North Carolina Bar Association.

While Brennan credited the chief justice publicly, privately he had come to share Jacobs's assessment of Vanderbilt as a martinet. Vanderbilt assigned the opinion of the court in every case, regardless of whether he was in the majority or minority. He discouraged dissent and was not pleased when a majority disagreed with his conclusions. Vanderbilt was equally assertive about the role he thought his court should play in state policymaking, and showed little deference to legislators or administrative agencies.

Vanderbilt's autocratic management style as chief justice helps explain why his relationship with Brennan never grew from a business partnership into a true friendship. The two men rarely socialized beyond formal events such as a Friendly Sons of Saint Patrick celebration they both attended in West Orange in 1953. Nevertheless, it was clear to many in New Jersey's legal establishment that Vanderbilt was grooming Brennan to succeed him as chief justice when he reached the mandatory retirement age of seventy in 1958. While Brennan recalled that Vanderbilt never mentioned the idea explicitly, the older man dropped hints suggesting that he believed only Brennan really shared his convictions about how to administer a judicial system.

On Tuesday, May 22, 1956, Brennan delivered his standard court-efficiency speech in the most prominent setting yet: the U.S. Department of Justice's headquarters in Washington, D.C. He was among eighty judges, bar association presidents, and prominent lawyers gathered in the Justice

Department's Great Hall for a conference on court congestion and delay in litigation organized by Attorney General Herbert Brownell. No one attending the conference could doubt how important Brownell considered the issue. "This is the most vital problem confronting the bench and bar of our country today," the attorney general had told attendees the previous day.

Brennan skipped the opening day of the two-day conference, arriving in Washington late Monday night in time for the second session, which focused on state courts. Asked to moderate a panel on the progress of court reform in several states, including New Jersey, Brennan opened the Tuesday-morning panel with a twelve-page speech in which he described how New Jersey's courts had managed to "lick the problem of calendar congestion and keep it licked." In offering his standard recitation of New Jersey's court-reform efforts since 1948, describing pretrial conferences in great detail, Brennan, still a relatively unknown state supreme court justice, caught the attention of the conference's organizers, especially Brownell and William P. Rogers, the deputy attorney general, who presided over much of the conference.

A substantial body of myth subsequently developed about Brennan's speech and what role it played in landing him a spot on the U.S. Supreme Court. One story holds that Brennan was not even supposed to be at the conference; writers later claimed he was a last-minute substitution for an ailing Justice Vanderbilt. Brennan, the story goes, read and received undue credit for the notes of the speech that Vanderbilt was supposed to deliver. If not for the substitution, Brennan might not have wound up a Supreme Court justice.

The myth of the "accidental justice" makes for a good story, but there is substantial evidence contradicting that version of events. Brennan's office files contained an advance copy of the address, marked "For Release at 10:00 A.M. EDT, Tuesday, May 22, 1956," as did the file containing the results of the FBI's background investigation at the time of his subsequent nomination to the U.S. Supreme Court. Both copies match the printed transcript of Brennan's speech at the conference except for an ad-libbed introduction. He had given plenty of similar addresses about court reform, including several beyond New Jersey's borders in 1954 and 1955, and would continue to do so after joining the U.S. Supreme Court. Further, Robert Seaver, who as assistant deputy attorney general did much of the staff work for the conference, later recalled that Vanderbilt had never been on the schedule. And during Brennan's panel, Frederick W. Brune of the Maryland Supreme Court, noted, "It is very regrettable that [Vanderbilt] cannot be here today because, I believe, his court is in session, but I'm very glad they could spare Justice Brennan."

Brennan made a particularly good impression on Deputy Attorney General Rogers, whom he had previously met during the war. Rogers invited Brennan and a select group of other participants to attend a lunch in the attorney general's private dining room with other senior Justice Department officials. Rogers was struck by Brennan's knowledge and attitude about court backlogs. "Unlike other judges, he didn't spend all the lunchtime trying to give excuses as to why the courts were running behind," Rogers recalled a few months later. "He was the one really concerned about court administration." Brennan later recalled corresponding with Rogers through the summer of 1956 about serving on a follow-up committee, an assignment for which Brennan had little enthusiasm.

· PART II: 1956–1962 ·

· 4 ·

IKE'S MISTAKE

B RENNAN COULD NOT hide his irritation when the phone rang on the evening of Friday, September 28, 1956, and he picked up the receiver to find Attorney General Herbert Brownell on the line asking him to come to Washington for a meeting the next morning.

"Uh-oh, here it is," Brennan thought as he waited for Brownell's request. He had been trying to avoid being roped in to serve on a follow-up committee for the Justice Department conference he had attended in May. "Herb," he told the attorney general, "I'm terribly busy."

That very day, Brennan had moved into his new three-room judicial chambers, built to his specifications in a small commercial office building in Red Bank, on the Navesink River. At the moment Brownell called, around 5:30 P.M., Brennan and his new clerk, Clyde Szuch, a recent Harvard Law School graduate from New Jersey, were busy stacking volumes of the state Supreme Court's decisions on the empty shelves that ran the full length of the walls. Brennan was preoccupied with a case the court had taken up upon reconvening after Labor Day about whether to disbar a prominent New Jersey attorney and former judge accused of stealing from an elderly client's estate. The last thing he needed, Brennan thought, was a last-minute trip to Washington.

But Brownell persisted, reminding Brennan that he couldn't say no to an invitation from President Eisenhower. "He wants to see you at nine o'clock tomorrow morning at the White House," Brownell said.

Brennan immediately headed home to Rumson, so rushed to pack his things that Marjorie had to borrow a suitcase from a neighbor when they could not locate their own. Then he traveled the fifty miles to Newark's Penn Station, where he boarded an overnight train to the capital, most likely the Midnight Keystone scheduled to arrive in Washington at 8 A.M.

It all happened so quickly that Brennan would later say he hadn't had much time to think about why the president himself wanted to meet with him first thing on a Saturday morning about serving on a Justice Department committee. And when he blearily got off the train at Washington's Union Station, he did not think much either about why the attorney general himself was waiting at the gate to greet him.

"Come on," Brownell said, "We're going out to my house for breakfast."

"My god in heaven," Brennan thought, "they're really operating on me."

Seated inside Brownell's chauffeured car on the way to his house near American University, the attorney general turned to Brennan and asked, "You know why the president wants to see you, don't you?"

"Herb, I know, but you know how I feel about this thing," Brennan said, still trying to fend off the committee assignment.

"Why you don't know at all, you damn fool," Brownell said with a chuckle. "He wants to talk to you about filling the vacancy of Sherman Minton." Brennan later suggested it was only then that he realized that Eisenhower was considering him for a seat on the United States Supreme Court.

EXACTLY THREE WEEKS had passed between Sherman Minton's letter to the president announcing that he intended to leave the Supreme Court effective October 15 and Brennan's summons to Washington. Minton, an Indiana native, had been appointed to the Court in 1949 by his friend and former colleague in the U.S. Senate, President Harry Truman. Now, seven years later, Minton cited health problems that made continuing his "exacting duties" too difficult. Minton had privately confessed in a December 1955 letter to Truman that his mental and physical health were "slipping fast." But he waited another ten months to retire until he had completed fifteen full years as a federal judge and become eligible for a full pension.

The White House quickly released a letter expressing Eisenhower's "appreciation" for Minton's service and wishing him "contentment and good health" in retirement. The president, or at least his staff, masked his annoyance that the wire services got the news before he did. More irritating was the fact that, just weeks earlier, Minton had endorsed Eisenhower's Democratic rival, Illinois senator Adlai Stevenson, in the upcoming presidential election by saying that the president was "terribly handicapped physically."

Eisenhower probably did not relish the prospect of filling another Supreme Court vacancy. With two Supreme Court nominations under his belt, the novelty of the process had worn off. His first nominee, Chief Justice Earl Warren, had caused plenty of trouble for Eisenhower with the 1954 *Brown v. Board of Education* school-desegregation opinion that had so alienated southern voters. Warren had marshaled a unanimous Court to declare that the Constitution would not permit separate but equal education, threatening the South's entire edifice of segregated life. Eisenhower had privately confided that he believed the decision had set back progress in the region by at least fifteen years and damaged his relationship with southerners. Eisenhower's second nominee to the Court, John Marshall Harlan, had proved far less problematic than Warren. But the president did not need any new potential problems now, in the middle of a reelection rematch against Stevenson that was proving more difficult than expected.

In less than two months, Eisenhower and Vice President Richard Nixon would beat Stevenson and his running mate, Senator Estes Kefauver of Tennessee, by more than 10 million votes, a better margin than during the first Eisenhower-Stevenson matchup in 1952. Eisenhower's victory was helped by two foreign-policy crises that would erupt in the weeks ahead: the joint attack on Egypt by France, Great Britain, and Israel over control of the Suez Canal, and the Soviet invasion of Hungary. But at the time of Minton's resignation in early September, Eisenhower's reelection prospects remained uncertain.

Eisenhower's biggest problem, as Minton had pointed out, was his health. The sixty-six-year-old president had suffered a heart attack in 1955 and spent almost the entire month of June 1956 hospitalized as he recovered from emergency surgery for an intestinal blockage. An August Gallup Poll found that 28 percent of voters thought that Eisenhower's health should be an issue, and 30 percent expected he would have another heart attack during the next four years. Eisenhower's image was not helped by the fact that a young, vigorous senator from Massachusetts named John F. Kennedy was campaigning on Stevenson's behalf throughout the key battleground states of the Northeast. Eisenhower's aides later denied strenuously that election-year politics played any role in selecting Minton's successor. But the election was clearly on Eisenhower's mind as he carried out his duties as president that fall. He worried that intervening in a potential war between Egypt and Israel might cost him the votes of Jews in the Northeast, who would not take kindly to a commander in chief taking sides against the fledgling eight-year-old Jewish state.

On the morning of Minton's announcement, Eisenhower had a good sense of what his third Supreme Court pick should look like. Unhappy with what he viewed as Truman's patronage selections, Eisenhower wanted a nominee with experience on lower courts, whether at the federal or particularly the state level. The Conference of Chief Justices of State Courts had pressed Eisenhower to consider the latter, since no state judge had been appointed to the Court in twenty-seven years. Eisenhower was clear that his nominee should be relatively young and healthy. And he wanted, if at all possible, the nominee to be Catholic.

That last criterion had been on his mind ever since a visit more than two years earlier by Francis Cardinal Spellman, the archbishop of the Catholic Archdiocese of New York. The sixty-seven-year-old, round-faced archbishop presented a cherubic and humble image in public that obscured his status as the most powerful Catholic in America. Spellman quietly made deals and traded favors with such aplomb that it was as if he operated out of Tammany Hall rather than St. Patrick's Cathedral. His ability to cultivate influential people — from popes to presidents — had propelled his rise from obscure Massachusetts priest. Spellman first met Eisenhower during World War II while serving as the Church's top chaplain for the U.S. Armed Forces. Spellman made sure to visit both soldiers at the front and the top generals at headquarters, including Eisenhower, who commanded the Supreme Headquarters Allied Expeditionary Force in Europe. They shared a common personal conservatism and distrust of Communists. The friendship carried over when Eisenhower became president. Spellman was one of the few clergymen invited to one of Eisenhower's occasional small stag dinners, mingling in June 1953 with the president and a dozen guests, including former president Herbert Hoover and General Douglas MacArthur. Spellman was entirely comfortable in the White House, having first become a frequent guest as adviser to President Roosevelt. He was the first priest ever to say Mass there in 1936.

So it was not particularly unusual that Spellman requested a meeting with Eisenhower in the summer of 1954 without mentioning any topic. His conduit was Bernard Shanley, the president's fifty-three-year-old New Jersey–born appointment secretary and unofficial liaison to the Church. It was not until Spellman sat down with the president and Shanley in the White House on the afternoon of July 23, 1954, that the archbishop explained his purpose. He asked the president to consider nominating a Catholic to fill the next vacancy that opened up on the Supreme Court. No Catholic had served on the Court since Justice Frank Murphy, appointed by Roosevelt, died in 1949, ending fifty-five years of consecutive service by a Catholic.

Spellman argued that Eisenhower should appoint a Catholic not just for the sake of maintaining a "Catholic seat." Instead, he emphasized the many issues involving the Catholic Church facing the Court, such as the legality of using public funds to pay for school lunches in parochial schools. Spellman had no use for any strict separation of church and state and had pressed for years for more public aid for New York's parochial schools. Left unsaid was that Spellman sought a conservative Catholic who agreed with his views rather than one like Frank Murphy, who had been an unabashed liberal. When Spellman had finished making his case, Eisenhower seemed convinced. He turned to Shanley and said, "Bernie, I want you to let me know when there is an opening—remind me of what the Cardinal has just said."

Spellman was not the only voice urging Eisenhower to appoint a Catholic to the Court. When Chief Justice Fred Vinson died in 1953, the Catholic magazine *Commonweal* noted, "The president is under no obligation to appoint a Catholic to any position, but in recognition of the fact that Catholics constitute about one-fifth of the total population, it had been deemed equitable, and perhaps politically expedient to allocate a certain number of top appointive positions to members of the Roman Catholic Church." Earl Warren's surrogates quickly lined up Catholic support for his own 1953 bid to succeed Vinson in order to head off calls by prominent Catholics to tap one of their own.

Shanley reminded Eisenhower of Spellman's suggestion when Justice Robert Jackson died suddenly of a heart attack in October 1954. Spellman returned to the White House to make his case to the president four months after his summer visit, during a November 16, 1954, one-on-one meeting while he was in Washington for a meeting of Catholic bishops. Spellman showed the president a resolution the Catholic bishops wanted to vote on during their meeting, urging the president to nominate a Catholic to fill Jackson's seat. The politically savvy prelate told the president he wanted to make sure Eisenhower was informed privately instead of facing a potentially embarrassing public vote by the bishops. Eisenhower found Spellman persuasive enough that he wrote in his diary that night that the bishops' draft resolution "does show the acute sensitiveness of particular groups in the United States in this matter of what they consider to be proper and equitable representation on all important governmental bodies, especially the Supreme Court." Eisenhower nonetheless opted to pick a Presbyterian, John Marshall Harlan, to fill Jackson's seat on the Supreme Court at Attorney General Brownell's urging.

But Eisenhower passed along the Catholic bishops' proposal to Brownell. And when the president met with his attorney general two weeks later, Brownell told Eisenhower he thought the next Supreme Court seat should go to a Catholic unless it was the seat currently held by Felix Frankfurter, the Court's only Jewish member. In March 1955 Eisenhower asked Brownell to draw up a list "of some fine prominent Catholics to nominate to the bench." The idea was still on Eisenhower's mind when he got word of Minton's intended retirement. Appointing a Catholic justice had become an even more attractive idea by the fall of 1956. Both political parties viewed the Catholic vote as vital, fed in part by the machinations of Senator Kennedy earlier in the year as he sought to make himself a more attractive vice presidential candidate. A paper stealthily prepared by a top Kennedy aide but attributed to the Connecticut state Democratic Party chairman argued that a Catholic vice presidential nominee could help retake the northeastern Catholics who had voted for Eisenhower in 1952. Stevenson did not pick Kennedy as his vice presidential nominee, but the paper was widely quoted by the press, feeding the perception of the Catholic vote's importance.

The morning in early September he learned of Minton's intention to retire, Eisenhower called Brownell, his point person for selecting Supreme Court nominees. He told his attorney general to "start thinking again about a very good Catholic, even a conservative Democrat." Brownell's orders were to find an "outstanding man, with court experience, regardless of his political affiliation." Eisenhower repeated the message that evening when he spoke on the telephone to Leonard Hall, the former Connecticut congressman who chaired the Republican National Committee. He told Hall that Minton's retirement made room for a Catholic. Eisenhower said he wanted a conservative Democrat, particularly one who had been on the bench for some time.

Asked at a September 11 press conference about whom he might pick, Eisenhower said, "I have no name in mind." But he mentioned three criteria for any nominee: "the recognition of the American Bar Association," "unimpeachable character and accomplishment," and "reasonable age," meaning someone who was not "very close to retirement age." As is often the case with such nominations, press speculation was widely off the mark. The *New York Times* listed Thomas E. Dewey, the New York governor and former presidential candidate, John Foster Dulles, and Brownell himself as potential successors. Others mentioned William Henry Hastie, an African American judge on the U.S. Court of Appeals for the Third Circuit who had previously served as dean of Howard University's law school and as governor of the U.S. Virgin Islands.

ARMED WITH THE president's criteria, Brownell set out to find a Court nominee who fit the bill. Eisenhower himself had much else on his mind, even besides the upcoming election. At the September 11 press conference, the Supreme Court vacancy was fifth on his agenda after the Suez crisis, Red China, nuclear tests, and the latest charges of Communist subversion by Senator Joseph McCarthy — although ahead of segregation and statehood for Alaska and Hawaii.

Now fifty-two, Brownell, a former New York State assemblyman turned Republican Party strategist, had helped lead the push urging Eisenhower to run for president. On election night, before results had even come in, Eisenhower asked Brownell to be his chief of staff. Brownell said he would prefer to continue practicing law. "How about being Attorney General?" Eisenhower asked. Brownell was one of two close aides Eisenhower entrusted with the sensitive task of filling the rest of his cabinet in the weeks leading up to his inauguration. And the president similarly delegated the job of picking his Supreme Court nominees almost entirely to Brownell. It was Brownell who secretly flew out to McClellan Air Force Base in September 1953, trying to convince California governor Earl Warren to take the job of solicitor general he had already been offered. Eisenhower had promised to name Warren to the Supreme Court eventually. But he never intended to give Warren the job of chief justice, which had suddenly become vacant with Fred Vinson's death. Warren, fresh from a hunting trip, insisted that Eisenhower live up to his pledge and nominate him as chief justice. Warren ultimately prevailed after some savvy behind-the-scenes lobbying. It was also Brownell who picked Harlan to be Eisenhower's second Supreme Court nominee, in 1955. Brownell met Harlan, the grandson and namesake of the nineteenth-century Supreme Court justice, during their days together at a New York law firm in the 1920s. Brownell had previously engineered Harlan's appointment to the U.S. Court of Appeals for the Second Circuit as a steppingstone to the nation's highest court.

Brownell came to view picking Supreme Court nominees as almost routine work after the experience with Warren and Harlan. But as he sat down with his forty-two-year-old deputy attorney general William Rogers and laid out the president's narrow criteria for Minton's successor, Brownell understood the nomination as posing a particular challenge. Only a handful of judges in the entire country satisfied all of Eisenhower's criteria: Democratic, Catholic, and younger than sixty-two. There were only two federal judges who qualified, and one of them had never served as an appellate judge. At the state level, Brennan, at fifty, was the only Catholic appellate judge under the age of sixty. Rogers later recalled that it was he who first broached the possibility of nominating Brennan, referencing the judge's impressive performance at the Justice Department conference in May. With so few other candidates, Brennan quickly became an appealing option. Brownell asked Rogers to handle the initial round of vetting. Rogers quietly began reaching out to people in New Jersey who knew Brennan and researching his legal opinions.

Brownell remained involved, too, calling Arthur Vanderbilt at his home in New Jersey. Brownell knew that Eisenhower, who had previously considered Vanderbilt as a potential Supreme Court nominee, particularly valued the New Jersey chief justice's opinion. When the president hosted members of the Supreme Court for dinner in November 1953, Vanderbilt was the only state supreme court justice invited to attend. For ten minutes, Brownell quizzed Vanderbilt about Brennan. Three or four minutes later, he called again with more questions. And then later that same hour,

Brownell called a third time. Brownell later said he had read all thousand pages of Brennan's four hundred New Jersey Supreme Court opinions, an unthinkable level of involvement by an attorney general today.

Compared to later Supreme Court nominations, though, the Eisenhower administration considered Brennan's nomination in a rather cursory fashion. There were not dozens of lawyers in both the Justice Department and what later became the White House Counsel's office carefully scrutinizing every last detail in the nominee's past. Brennan's nomination was handled almost entirely by Brownell and Rogers and a couple of top aides. Brownell and Rogers, in turn, relied largely on the assurances of those who liked and respected Brennan in New Jersey. And positive feedback is exactly what Brownell and Rogers wanted to hear. Eisenhower's rigid criteria left the two with little flexibility. Brennan fulfilled the specific purposes for which he was chosen: he was a Democrat, a Catholic, and a state court judge; he was comparatively young for a Supreme Court nominee; and he remained committed to reform efforts to reduce delays and backlogs in the nation's courts.

It is easy to point to several opinions Brennan wrote on the New Jersey Supreme Court that might have given a conservative Republican pause. Nevertheless, Brownell concluded that Brennan's opinions were "well reasoned and well written." Plus, there was no question about Brennan's character. Neither Brownell nor Rogers harbored any reservations about the New Jersey judge. Both were moderate Republicans, with ties to Dewey, the New York governor and leader of the middle-of-the-road Republican faction during the late 1940s, rather than Robert Taft, who led the competing conservative isolationist Republican bloc. Brownell, who had chaired the Republican National Committee for four years, surely appreciated the value of picking a nominee who might curry favor with Catholic voters in the Northeast — including Brennan's home state.

Brownell and Rogers appeared to have devoted more energy to ensuring that Brennan was a faithful Catholic than that he was a reliable vote for the Court's conservative bloc. Rogers contacted Archbishop Spellman, and he asked Bernard Shanley, the White House's unofficial Catholic liaison, to speak with Brennan's parish priest. Shanley had known Brennan and his father since childhood, and he and Brennan had crossed paths regularly when both practiced law in New Jersey. But contrary to press accounts after the nomination, neither Shanley nor the administration's other high-ranking official from New Jersey, Labor Secretary James Mitchell, who knew Brennan from the war, played any role in his selection. Shanley acknowledged that the request to call Brennan's priest "was the first inkling I had" of Brennan's possible nomination. Shanley did as he was asked and reported back that Father Donald Hickey thought very highly of Brennan, who had earned Hickey's gratitude by speaking at the church's Holy Communion breakfasts and to its Catholic youth group.

Satisfied that Brennan was both a faithful Catholic and good judge, Brownell was eager to read the Federal Bureau of Investigation's background check — so eager in fact that he had the report delivered to his house at 9:35 P.M. on September 25. The FBI's powerful director, J. Edgar Hoover, had begun conducting background checks on Supreme Court nominations only three years earlier, when Eisenhower selected Warren to be chief justice. On this occasion, Hoover's agents did not have much time for a thorough search. The five-page double-spaced report was delivered to Brownell's home only one day after Hoover had sent out a memo ordering field offices to conduct the investigation. The report concluded, "Our files reflect no derogatory information concerning him." It noted, "Justice Brennan is considered very strict on legal matters in his court, although extremely efficient and fair minded. In lay circles, he is considered an ardent Catholic." With all the vetting complete, Brownell concluded that Brennan "was like manna from Heaven." His was the only name the satisfied attorney general recommended to Eisenhower

On September 28, Brownell, Eisenhower, and Sherman Adams, who functioned as the president's chief of staff, met in the Oval Office for a half hour at 3 P.M. Two hours later, Brownell called Brennan and asked him to come down to Washington the next day.

BRENNAN'S ACCOUNT OF being completely dumbfounded upon learning he was Eisenhower's pick for the Supreme Court made for good newspaper copy, but strains credulity. He was much too shrewd not to realize the purpose of his sudden summons to Washington. In fact, Brennan soon admitted that the possibility of being selected for the Court had crossed his mind after Brownell called to invite him to the White House. "But it seemed so fantastic I dismissed the idea at once," he told *Life* magazine. Prior to his nomination, Brennan assumed the only promotion he could expect was to chief justice of the New Jersey Supreme Court when Arthur Vanderbilt retired.

By the time Brownell ushered him to his car outside Union Station, Brennan almost certainly understood the reason he had been called to Washington. But Brennan always wanted to be seen as a regular guy rather than an ambitious climber, so he may well have played dumb for the benefit of Brownell and reporters. And given the nature of the offer, the shock he expressed upon actually hearing the news from Brownell might well have been genuine.

After breakfast at Brownell's house, the two headed to the White House. Adams met them at a side door and escorted Brennan to the Oval Office. Adams and Brownell made some initial introductions, and then left Brennan alone with the president.

Brennan admired Eisenhower and had earlier hoped he would be the Democratic nominee for president. Eisenhower expressed regret about Vanderbilt's health problems and said he had hoped to appoint him to the Court. Brennan was impressed and flattered by how much the president seemed to know about his work in New Jersey. They talked about Brennan's army service during the war, which, Brennan said, "apparently didn't hurt me at all in Eisenhower's eyes." What never came up, Brennan recalled, was his views on any legal topics. After twenty minutes, Eisenhower was satisfied he had found the right man. But he told Brennan he planned to wait until Monday to announce the nomination in order to have time to inform New Jersey's two senators over the weekend. Eisenhower told Brennan he could tell his wife and children as long as word did not get out.

After leaving the Oval Office, Brownell suggested to Brennan that they head back to the Justice Department, where Brennan could call his family. Brennan reached Marjorie with the news on a telephone from Brownell's private office. Their son, Bill, was also in the house that morning. Bill had postponed plans to attend law school in favor of the Marine Corps, and he was home for a visit from officer training at Quantico, Virginia. Bill had gotten in so late and Brennan had left in such a hurry that Bill did not even know his father had gone to Washington until coming downstairs that morning. When the call came, Bill recalled, "My father — not an inarticulate man — could barely get the words out." Next, Brennan called his mother. He told her to sit down before he delivered the news. All she managed to say over and over again was, "God bless you, my son." Brennan had barely finished with his calls when Brownell came rushing in to say that the president wanted them to return to the White House at once.

"Oh Jesus! He's going to take it back," Brennan recalled thinking.

The president actually had decided to go ahead with the announcement immediately. That morning, William Rogers had gotten back an initial positive review from Bernard Segal, the chairman of the American Bar Association committee charged with vetting judicial nominees. Segal had been a classmate of Brennan's at the University of Pennsylvania. When Brennan and Brownell returned to the White House, Eisenhower told his nominee that he did not see any reason to wait until Monday. They posed for pictures, shaking hands and smiling. Eisenhower did not mention the campaign considerations for pushing up the announcement. Waiting until Monday would have disrupted Eisenhower's plan to leave Sunday night on an overnight train to Cleveland for a Monday speech before flying to Lexington, Kentucky, for a nationwide radio address that night. Plus, moving up the announcement of a justice from New Jersey might steal some of the thunder away from Stevenson, who was scheduled to begin a well-publicized tour of the Catholic-rich Northeast on that Tuesday with a sixty-mile barnstorm through Brennan's home state.

The announcement came so suddenly that James C. Hagerty, the president's press secretary, had few details to offer reporters about the nominee. Only later did Hagerty have time to embellish, telling the *Boston Globe*, "I never saw a man say 'yes' so fast when the President asked him if he'd take the job." The half dozen or so reporters gathered in the press room that Saturday morning knew nothing about the judge sitting smiling before them as Hagerty made the announcement that Eisenhower would make a recess appointment of Brennan to the Court. The decision meant that Brennan would temporarily become a justice when the Court began its new session in just a few days, rather than waiting for the Senate to confirm him. (Roughly equivalent to a school year, the Court's term begins each year on the first Monday in October and usually wraps up by the end of June.) It had been ninety-one years since a president had used the recess-appointment power to pick a member of the Supreme Court when President Eisenhower employed it to select Warren in 1953.

Brennan had no prepared statement and little experience handling the

Washington press corps, but he proved deft at this impromptu news conference. Asked about his political affiliations, the judge, speaking in a soft voice, explained he had been a lifelong Democrat but had never taken an active role in politics. He told reporters he had not voted in the 1952 presidential election because he had not lived in Rumson long enough to establish residence there. Asked for whom he planned to vote in the presidential election just weeks away, Brennan asked reporters to forgive him for not answering the question. He dismissed both his party and religious affiliation. "I really don't understand the political significance of either term," he said.

With the announcement official, Brownell and Rogers drove Brennan to his future place of employment, the Supreme Court, for his first visit there as a nominee. The U.S. Supreme Court had not had a home of its own until this neoclassical marble temple of justice opened in 1935. The justices had previously worked out of their homes and convened right across the street at the Capitol, in the Old Senate Chamber. At the time, Justice Harlan Fiske Stone looked at the new building's accoutrements, which included fluted Corinthian columns, marble candelabras, and two six-ton bronze doors above which the inscription EQUAL JUSTICE UNDER LAW was carved into the frieze, and declared it "almost bombastically pretentious." It left a better impression on Brennan. "This building just awes people, and I was not excused," he recalled later.

There to greet Brennan was the sixty-five-year-old Chief Justice of the United States, Earl Warren. Brennan shook hands for the first time with the broad-chested chief justice, who at six feet one had a resumé as daunting as his physical presence. Brennan had been in high school when Warren first won election as a crime- and corruption-fighting district attorney in northern California's Alameda County. He would hold office in the state for the next twenty-seven years, rising to attorney general and then governor for an unprecedented three terms. In 1948, a year before Brennan took the bench for the first time as a New Jersey trial judge, Warren was tapped as Republican presidential nominee Tom Dewey's running mate. He ran unsuccessfully for the Republican presidential nomination in 1952 and then moved to Washington the following year as chief justice. The closest Brennan had ever come to meeting Warren before was a November 1948 election-night house party in South Orange, where the Republican hosts hung life-size banners of Dewey and Warren on the living room wall.

Brennan, alone among the Republican guests, quietly rejoiced as radio broadcasts gave the first hints of Truman's come-from-behind upset victory that night. Brennan did not mention having rooted against his new boss as Warren showed him around his chambers.

There was no time for Brennan to get a look around the Court or to meet his seven other new colleagues. Warren had made lunch reservations at the University Club, right up Sixteenth Street from the White House. Warren had quickly made himself at home at this clubby eating and athletic outpost for the capital's establishment. He took his clerks there for leisurely lunches on many Saturday afternoons, where he could relax over a couple of scotches and, in later years, watch college football games on television. On this Saturday afternoon, Warren and his guests exchanged pleasantries and small talk about Arthur Vanderbilt, whom Warren said he admired greatly. There was no hint that these two new colleagues would soon form one of the most enduring friendships and important alliances in the history of the Supreme Court. Brennan could not linger too long over lunch, having promised Marjorie he would be home in time for a dinner party she had previously scheduled that night for a few friends and neighbors. He rushed back to Union Station in time to make the afternoon train, the Congressional, back to Newark.

It was not until Brennan walked into Union Station and saw a picture of himself shaking Eisenhower's hand on the front page of the afternoon *Washington Star* that he realized he had forgotten to call Marjorie to let her know that the president had decided to announce his appointment that day. He did not reach her until the train stopped at a station well past Baltimore. So Marjorie was wholly unprepared for the frenzy that descended on their house after Eisenhower's announcement that afternoon. Reporters interrupted her dinner preparations by constantly ringing the doorbell. Well-wishers — including one of Brennan's new colleagues, Justice Harold Burton — kept the phone ringing nonstop. Photographers camped out on the lawn. For Marjorie, it was the first hint of just how different life would be, married to a Supreme Court justice.

Brennan, too, got his first taste of his new life as he got off the train at 7:30 P.M. in Newark's Penn Station, which he had left anonymously just the night before. Brennan and all the other disembarking passengers were startled by the horde of photographers jostling for pictures of him. One of his children had accidentally tipped off the press about his travel plans. His sons, Bill, twenty-three, and Hugh, twenty, were there, too, waiting to drive Brennan back to Rumson in their 1956 Chevy Coupe for the end of the dinner party turned celebration. In getting ready for the party, Marjorie had barely had time to prepare the baked ham and desert melons, completely overcooked the broccoli, and dried up the hollandaise sauce. Not that the meal dampened the mood of the three couples, who remembered only the excitement of the night. Amid all the activity, Brennan had forgot to tell his law clerk, Clyde Szuch, about his appointment. Szuch heard the news that night as he drove home with his wife from a Rutgers football game.

OPENING ALMOST ANY newspaper in the United States on his first full morning as a Supreme Court nominee or the days that followed, Brennan would have discovered mostly glowing coverage, although he would not necessarily have recognized the man being described.

The Associated Press portrayed his as an Irish rags-to-riches tale in a profile titled "Justice Brennan, Son of Irish Immigrants, Came Up the Hard Way to Highest Tribunal." (Brennan would do his best to knock down the myths of a hard-knocks childhood. "I'm no Horatio Alger," he told *Life* magazine that month.) Other reporters described him as an everyman who carried his own bag and was handy in the kitchen with a skillet or pot. The *New York Times* began a pattern that was to continue for the rest of his tenure, in which reporters laced their profiles with stereotyped portrayals of the happy leprechaun. The *Times*' "Man in the News" column described Brennan as "a jaunty judge" in its headline and quoted one unidentified colleague from his time in the War Department who said he was the "friendly Irish type." *Time* magazine later that week headlined its brief profile of Brennan "The Ninth Justice: A Happy Irishman"; in it he was described as "an affable, storytelling Irishman."

As is often the case, guessing where Brennan might fit on the Court proved a tricky business. The *Washington Post* called him a "moderate liberal" and editorialized that his appointment "is a fine example of the great tradition of a qualified and independent judiciary in operation." After noting his "comparative obscurity," the *New York Times* predicted that "he will take his seat, two weeks hence, amid general goodwill, and when the Senate meets again will be confirmed, we imagine, without controversy." Most news outlets suggested Brennan would be a middle-of-the-road justice. One administration official who had known Justice Brennan many years—quite possibly Shanley—conceded to *U.S. News & World Report* that he was "a man with lots of progressive ideas" but added that his views "are very close to President Eisenhower's on many issues."

Those who had observed Brennan more closely provided the most accurate predictions. Immediately after the nomination, New Jersey governor Robert Meyner told the *Trenton Evening Times* that Brennan "will not be as middle of the road as some Republicans seem to think." And J. L. Bernstein of the *Reporter,* a publication of the Passaic County Bar Association, did not have much trouble figuring out where Brennan might find allies on the Court. "Prediction in print is a preoccupation of the foolhardy," Bernstein wrote. "But we have a notion that Justice Brennan, son of a former labor leader, will become a valuable assistant to Chief Justice Earl Warren, son of a former railroad mechanic."

Letters that began arriving at the White House later that week from average Americans suggested that Eisenhower had succeeded in winning the appreciation of at least some Catholic voters in the Northeast. Michael Bowler of the Bronx, who noted he emigrated from Ireland with his wife thirty years earlier, wrote Eisenhower expressing gratitude "for bestowing on Judge Brennan, the son of Irish immigrants, the high honor of judge of the United States Supreme Court." Eisenhower did attract more Catholic voters on Election Day, although it is hard to tell what role Brennan's selection played. He carried New Jersey and other Catholic strongholds such as Rhode Island and New York in both 1952 and 1956. One Catholic vote that Eisenhower did not manage to attract was Brennan himself. Brennan would not vote in 1956 or any election that followed, based on the belief that judges should remain studiously nonpartisan. Three decades later, Brennan would still refuse to say for whom he would have voted had he cast his ballot in 1956.

Judging by Eisenhower's mail, the selection alienated more voters than it pleased.

Congratulatory notes were far outnumbered by the dozens of letters from citizens condemning Eisenhower for picking a Catholic. "Being a Roman Catholic, he is NOT a free agent but an emissary of the Pope—it is the Pope on the Supreme Court bench, not Mr. Brennan," wrote Paula Jackson of Chicago. Even more wrote to complain that Eisenhower had betrayed his own party by picking a Democrat. "Just about ten minutes ago

I heard an announcement on the radio and was so angry I almost exploded," wrote Alice Gothard of Glendale, California, in a letter to Sherman Adams. "He doesn't seem to know that there are good Republicans that he can appoint to offices."

Ironically, Archbishop Spellman, who did more than anyone to make Brennan's nomination possible, was no more satisfied than the people penning the anti-Catholic letters. Spellman was reportedly the first person Shanley called after the nomination was announced, eager to report Eisenhower had selected a Catholic, as the archbishop had advocated for years. The conversation did not go well. Spellman thought that Brennan was neither conservative enough nor likely to be easily swayed by the Catholic hierarchy. During their phone conversation, Shanley tried to explain that he had not had anything to do with Brennan's appointment, which Spellman did not believe. Brennan, too, never believed Shanley's claims that he had played no role in the nomination. Two decades later, during a ceremony where Brennan's portrait was presented to the New Jersey Supreme Court, Brennan approached Shanley and asked him when he would finally admit that he had played a role in the appointment. Once again, Shanley denied it.

PERHAPS SPELLMAN MIGHT have been slightly mollified had he known that Brennan started his first full day as a Supreme Court nominee that Sunday in church. He and Marjorie attended the 9 A.M. Mass at the Church of the Nativity in Fair Haven on September 30. Even in church, Brennan could not escape the spectacle surrounding his selection. Brennan was almost embarrassed by how much a fuss their parish priest, Donald Hickey, made.

The Brennans returned home for a full day of interviews and pictures. Everyone in Brennan's family lent a hand. Hugh and his new wife made coffee for all the neighbors who came by to offer their congratulations. Seven-year-old Nancy at first declined to have her picture taken on the grounds "my nose is scratched" but ultimately relented. Bill, still home from Quantico, joined in the portraits too. Some photographers had the family pose in the yard. Others chose the living room. In most of the photographs, either as a result of accident or design, it is not evident that Brennan's daughter-in-law was five months pregnant with his first grandchild.

The judge portrayed by the press as a jolly leprechaun had managed to obscure his deep concerns about his finances and family. In the course of a year, Hugh had dropped out of college at Colgate and then suddenly married and was expecting a baby. It got worse: Hugh's wife was Roxey Atwood, who had been engaged to his older brother, Bill, the previous year. By the time of Roxey and Bill's anticipated June 1956 wedding, Roxey was instead pregnant with Hugh's child. No reporters made note of this Brennan family secret in their nomination stories, although the local paper later mistakenly referred to Roxey as "Mrs. William J. Brennan 3d."

In addition to worrying how Hugh would afford to support a family, Brennan's financial concerns had deepened. His bills and bank loans had piled up at an alarming rate in recent months. In July 1956, Brennan borrowed $4,082.99 from a friend, Frank W. Ritchie, to help pay off some of his mounting debts. Switching from New Jersey to the nation's highest court would bring nearly a 50 percent pay raise, to $35,000. Nevertheless, the potential cost of moving to Washington and simultaneously maintaining his house in Rumson made Brennan all the more pressed. He would borrow an additional $11,000 in two installments in the coming weeks from the same friend.

ON MONDAY, BRENNAN returned to the New Jersey Supreme Court in Trenton for his last week of work there. Vanderbilt opened the session by expressing "gratification" at Brennan's appointment. "Washington's gain will be our loss," he said from the bench. The pupil had leapfrogged over the mentor. While one Warren biographer later claimed Vanderbilt was surprised and perhaps envious upon hearing news of Brennan's nomination, the overwhelming evidence suggests Vanderbilt had been consulted in advance about the decision.

It is possible that Vanderbilt indulged in the idea that he could have gotten the nod if he, rather than Brennan, had delivered that May speech at the Justice Department. Brownell later recalled a conversation with Vanderbilt's son, who told him his father was unhappy with the appointment. But it seems highly unlikely that Vanderbilt could have been truly embittered that Eisenhower had chosen Brennan over him. The president had made clear that age and good health were important criteria for his Supreme Court nominee. Vanderbilt, at sixty-eight, was well above the sixty-two-year-old threshold and had in addition suffered a stroke nine years earlier.

If in fact Vanderbilt was unhappy about Brennan's nomination, he hid it well both publicly and privately. George Williams, who was with Vanderbilt when Brownell called to inquire about Brennan, recalled that his answers were filled with the highest regard and praise for Brennan. Similarly, Bernard Segal, who conducted the American Bar Association inquiry, reported to Rogers that Vanderbilt "could not have been more enthusiastic." After the nomination was announced, Vanderbilt told reporters Brennan was a "wonderful appointment." Vanderbilt wrote letters to numerous friends and associates in October 1956, all of which supported Brennan.

On the day after Brennan sat on the New Jersey court for the last time, on October 4, Vanderbilt wrote Brennan a single-spaced page-and-a-half-long letter thanking him for his "truly magnificent" service and help on their campaign for judicial efficiency. He added that if Brennan ever felt frustrated by the Supreme Court, he could always return to New Jersey and lead the court he was now leaving. "I think it is no secret that I had hoped that you would be the next Chief Justice of New Jersey," Vanderbilt wrote.

Ill health would force Vanderbilt to miss Brennan's swearing-in ceremony two weeks later. But the two would continue to correspond even after Brennan joined the Supreme Court. In February, Vanderbilt recommended a candidate for the job of administrative director of the Supreme Court. Brennan assured him in a February 1957 note that "your personal recommendation is certain to carry great weight." In May 1957, when the New Jersey State Bar Association awarded Brennan its highest gold medal award, Brennan expressed his thanks for the honor of "receiving it from the hand of one whom all acclaim among the great judges, my former chief and, I am proud to say, always my warm friend, Arthur T. Vanderbilt." Less than a month later, Vanderbilt died of a heart attack at a train station near his home on the way to work at his Newark chambers.

But that was all in the future as Brennan left the New Jersey Supreme Court chambers with the riverfront view he had barely had a chance to enjoy, with a fedora in one hand and his judicial robes draped over the other arm, a tableau neatly captured by *Life* magazine. He had first worn one of these robes as a trial judge in Hudson County and through every promotion since. At home in Rumson, a reminder of his new job already awaited him: two large packages in plain wrapper containing a few of the cases the Supreme Court would take up when its new term began in just a few days.

AS BRENNAN PREPARED to move to Washington, his new colleagues wrote to congratulate him — and also discreetly tried to size him up. Most if not all of the justices viewed Brennan as an entirely unknown quantity. Three admitted to the *Washington Star* shortly after Brennan's nomination that they had never heard of him. Justice William O. Douglas asked one of his clerks, William Cohen, to read all of Brennan's New Jersey Supreme Court opinions. Douglas had certainly been more widely known when he joined the Court in 1939, having earned a reputation as a legal wunderkind professor at Yale Law School and chairman of the Securities and Exchange Commission at the age of thirty-nine. Douglas carefully cultivated his public image, adding dramatic — and often exaggerated — flourishes concerning his overcoming childhood polio and serving in the military during World War I. Douglas's clerk dutifully did as asked and read all of Brennan's opinions, but reported back he could not draw any conclusions about the new justice.

Felix Frankfurter, the seventy-four-year-old justice prone to intrigue, took a more active role in ferreting out intelligence about his new colleague and former student. Frankfurter did not remember Brennan, who had not been among the favorites he invited to join his Harvard Law seminars and Sunday teas or later funneled to New Deal agencies after his friend, Franklin D. Roosevelt, became president in 1933. Frankfurter had turned down Roosevelt's offer to serve as solicitor general, claiming he could be of more use as an outside adviser. He did not say no a second time in January 1939 when Roosevelt offered him the seat on the Supreme Court vacated the previous year by Benjamin Cardozo. Once on the Court, Frankfurter continued to tap Harvard Law's top students as his clerks. On October 4, Frankfurter wrote one of those favored former students, Nathan Jacobs. He asked Jacobs to kindly tell him what he knew "about my brother-designate." Frankfurter, who seemed to love gossip and cutting digs almost as much as the law, admitted to knowing little more about Brennan than "his law school qualities" and "his frequent or rather, his uninhibited dissent from your martinet" chief justice Arthur Vanderbilt. He closed his letter by noting he would have preferred it if Jacobs had received the nomination instead.

Frankfurter could not have been put at ease when he got a report from another one of his former students, Brennan's classmate Paul Freund, who now taught at the school himself. "I am chagrined to have to say that I don't remember him," Freund wrote. Freund reported Brennan's grades, which were unlikely to impress. Frankfurter had ranked first through all three years at Harvard Law School and expected any fellow alumnus tapped for the Court to have a similarly impressive academic record. Freund also noted that Brennan had not taken Constitutional Law. "Possibly he gave himself the pleasure of listening in," Freund wrote. Freund was almost apologetic to Frankfurter for being quoted in the Harvard Law School student newspaper as saying Brennan would make a "great justice." Freund wrote, "I can only hope that my spurious prediction will turn out to be one of those self-fulfilling prophecies." Harvard's student journalists echoed the law school faculty's misgivings about Brennan. A columnist for the *Harvard Crimson* sniffed, "With this commendable but undistinguished background, it is understandable why there were eyebrows raised when the news of Brennan's elevation to the nation's highest tribunal appeared."

His former students' reports and his own suspicions of how the nomination came about left Frankfurter unable to offer more than a tepid prediction to an old confidant: "I confidently expect him to be a congenial colleague and a hard-working, conscientious judge." But when writing Brennan for the first time, Frankfurter was the picture of gracious warmth. "I look forward with high and happy expectations for the time that remains to me in our joint labors of our common, august enterprise, and for the many years beyond that for you," Frankfurter said in his handwritten welcome note. Brennan wrote back as the humble pupil. "I cannot hope that you would remember one so inconspicuous in your classroom back in 1930–1931 but my recollections of your good self are most vivid — and your imprint has been permanent."

BACK IN RUMSON, Marjorie did her best to both prepare for the move and fill the role of poised spouse for the nonstop flow of reporters parading through their home. Just as Brennan was portrayed as the stereotypical "Happy Irishman," Marjorie was characterized as the perfect 1950s homemaker. A typical photograph depicted her smiling as she poured coffee into two cups held by Nancy. "Mrs. Brennan Up in Clouds," declared the headline of an article in the *Newark Evening News,* which described how Marjorie "cooks and does most of the housework in their seven-room home." She was quick to downplay her role in her husband's career. "Sometimes he tells me about a case and asks me what I think," she said. "But whatever I say, it's always the opposite of his opinion." She displayed her most recent needlepoint for reporters and boasted about being able to sew and watch television at the same time.

In her most revealing moment, Marjorie admitted to one reporter that she felt "a little scared" about the move. She confessed she would "be sorry to give up" their Rumson home and hoped to come back to New Jersey during the summers. Marjorie did not reveal the full extent of her ambivalence. She felt genuinely happy for her husband and what he had achieved but was uneasy about what it meant for her. Only a few years earlier, she had been uprooted from the part of northern New Jersey where she had lived almost her entire life and resettled in Rumson. She had come to love the house that she had carefully renovated, the surrounding seaside community, and the many friends she had made. Now she had to give that all up to move again. She had lived in Washington briefly during the war but her husband's lifetime appointment to the Supreme Court meant living there permanently. Given the Brennans' precarious finances, maintaining their home in New Jersey was not an option for the long term.

Life magazine used the spacious yard of their Rumson home as the setting for a photo shoot, resulting in a multipage article that curiously omits Marjorie entirely. *Life*'s photo spread shows Brennan pushing Nancy on the backyard swing, hugging her after she climbs over the backyard fence, and "consoling" her as she says goodbye to her "hitherto inseparable playmate Rusty Young." It is as if Marjorie does not exist — a feeling she would come to have often in Washington.

ON WEDNESDAY, OCTOBER 10, Brennan entered the Supreme Court on his way to meet his new colleagues for the first time. All had impressive credentials and lengthy tenures on the Court. Harold Burton, sixty-eight, had served as mayor of Cleveland and a U.S. senator before joining the Court in 1945. Tom Clark, a fifty-seven-year-old Texan with a penchant for bow ties, had served as Truman's attorney general before being named a justice in 1949. Stanley Reed, seventy-one, came to the Court in 1938 after a stint as Roosevelt's solicitor general, one of four justices who had been there at least fifteen years. Two still nursed thwarted presidential ambitions. Brennan would be the youngest justice by seven years — and the first born in the twentieth century. So he was understandably more than a little intimidated at the prospect of meeting his fellow justices individually — not to mention all eight at once. Chief Justice Warren had asked them all to gather in their private third-floor lounge for the occasion.

Brennan admitted later he was most in awe of Hugo L. Black, the senior associate justice who had served a decade as U.S. senator before being named to the Court in 1937. Brennan knew the seventy-year-old populist politician born in Alabama's hill country had gone from a onetime member of the Ku Klux Klan to a southern outcast when he signed onto the *Brown* decision. If Brennan had known about Black's unpretentious style, it might have left him less nervous about this meeting. Black still preferred the title "Judge" — which he earned serving on the Birmingham police court — over "Mr. Justice." He had insisted on driving his own green 1948 Plymouth while the rest of the justices traveled in limousines for their annual White House visit three years earlier.

Brennan and the chief justice walked in the door of the dimly lit lounge. Warren quickly flipped on the light switch, revealing Brennan's new colleagues in a less than august pose, sitting around a table eating sandwiches while watching television. Warren introduced Brennan to each of the justices, who took turns shaking his hand. Almost immediately after this formality, one of the justices said, "Put out the lights." Brennan or Warren quickly obliged. The brethren were intent on watching the seventh and final game of the World Series between the Brooklyn Dodgers and the New York Yankees live on television that day. In the justices' defense, Game 5 two days earlier had proven to be one of the most dramatic moments in baseball history. The Yankees' Don Larsen pitched the first — and only — perfect game during a World Series. Now tied 3 to 3, this game would determine which of these New York rivals would win the Series.

Still, it was not quite as warm a welcome as Brennan might have envisioned. Eventually John Harlan stepped forward and invited Brennan to join him downstairs in his chambers. Brennan followed the tall, dignified lawyer, who wore London-tailored three-piece suits and the gold watch chain of his namesake grandfather, who was also a Supreme Court justice.

Harlan had built a successful law practice representing major corporations and members of the du Pont family before his friend, Attorney General Brownell, engineered his appointment to the U.S. Court of Appeals for the Second Circuit and then to the Supreme Court. Harlan alone among Brennan's new colleagues came to the high court as a judge. Unlike Brennan, Harlan's ascent to the bench had not hurt him financially: he still maintained a country home in Westport, Connecticut, and his own box at the National Symphony.

When they arrived in his chambers, Harlan asked, "Do you smoke?"

"Yes," Brennan replied tentatively.

"Oh, thank God," Harlan said. "I've been dying, dying around here — nobody smokes."

The Yankees won the game that afternoon 9–0 to take the World Series title. The next night, the justices, without any baseball game to distract them, gathered at the White House for their annual preterm visit with the president. The previous year's meeting had been canceled due to Eisenhower's heart attack. The meeting this year, which included Justice Minton, whom Brennan would replace in five days, lasted an hour. When Eisenhower and the justices gathered for a picture, Brennan stood in the second row behind the president.

Brennan, Marjorie, and Nancy had arrived in Washington a day or two before his visit to the Court and checked into the Brighton Hotel on California Street. The family's first task was finding a more permanent place to live, though Brennan had no intention of giving up his home back in Rumson quite yet. Since his had been a recess appointment, Brennan felt he could not risk selling it and buying a new home in Washington. He worried less about Senate confirmation than the pending presidential election. "If Eisenhower had lost, well, sure I'd have been out," Brennan recalled thinking. He certainly was not counting on Stevenson reappointing him.

They found a furnished apartment to lease for a year from a U.S. Navy captain who had been transferred to San Diego on short notice. The apartment, on Cathedral Avenue not far from American University, was beautifully appointed by the officer's wife, an interior decorator, and was being offered for only $400 month. The owners had combined two adjoining apartments into one by tearing down a wall. Because it was fully furnished, Marjorie would need to bring only a set of china, leaving the rest of their belongings behind in their Rumson home, where Hugh and his wife,

Roxey, moved in. The low rent was welcome news for the Brennans, who could now temporarily maintain two homes. Equally good news was the sound of a school bell ringing as Marjorie toured the apartment for the first time. She followed it to the nearby Annunciation Catholic School and enrolled Nancy as of October 17 — one day after her father was to be sworn in as the ninetieth justice to serve on the United States Supreme Court.

· 5 ·

JOINING THE COURT

J UST PAST NOON on October 16, 1956, Brennan stood at the front of the Supreme Court's marble-covered courtroom, raised his right hand, and repeated the seventy-nine-word judicial oath that officially made him a justice — at least temporarily. Yet no one treated Brennan this day as anything less than a full member of the Court. His new colleagues had all gathered in their oak-paneled conference room just minutes before the public ceremony, to watch Chief Justice Warren administer the constitutional oath in private, as dictated by Court tradition.

Inside the courtroom, the Court's marshal, bedecked in his formal morning clothes bellowed the traditional declaration proclaiming the Court in session. "Oyez! Oyez! Oyez! All persons having business before the Honorable, the Supreme Court of the United States are admonished to draw near and give their attention, for the Court is now sitting. God save the United States and this honorable Court!" The justices then walked in groups of three through the heavy red-velvet draperies and into the courtroom, with its imposing forty-one-foot-high ceiling and interior Ionic columns. Brennan, dressed in the black judicial robe he wore when he first became a judge in 1949, stopped at the clerk's desk on the right side of the elevated mahogany bench until the judicial oath had been administered.

The justices and audience — including several of Brennan's siblings and nine of his nieces and nephews, twenty-six family members in all — stood as the marshal escorted Brennan to the seat reserved for the Court's most junior justice, on the far left side of the bench. Then, without further fanfare, Brennan took his place and heard his first full oral argument as a justice of the United States Supreme Court. It was an appeal by Alfred E. Butler, a Detroit bookseller convicted of violating Michigan's law banning the sale of obscene books. Though Brennan did not realize it at the time, obscenity would be an issue on which he soon would lead — and which would dog him — for years to come. At the end of the oral argument, Brennan and his family lunched in the East Conference Room, which was decorated with flowers sent by his former colleagues on the New Jersey Supreme Court. Brennan flashed a toothy grin as he posed for a row of photographers crouching to take his picture. Newsreel footage shows Marjorie putting a black robe on Brennan's shoulders. His mother, sister, and children, including Bill dressed in his Marine uniform, look on smilingly. After lunch, Brennan returned to the bench for a second argument while his family joined Bernard Shanley on a tour of the White House.

The festivities resumed that night when Brennan and Marjorie accepted an invitation to attend a party at Justice Douglas's house. Brennan did not realize until he arrived bearing champagne that it was Douglas's fifty-eighth birthday, thus establishing a tradition that would continue for nearly two decades of the two jointly celebrating the occasions. Even more significant for Brennan's life in Washington was another guest he met that night. David Bazelon, a forty-seven-year-old judge on the U.S. Court of Appeals for the D.C. Circuit, was just one of the many judges, congressmen, and journalists Douglas had befriended since his days in the New Deal–era Securities and Exchange Commission. Bazelon was the ninth child of Russian Jewish immigrant parents and the first in his family to attend college, paying his way through the University of Illinois and Northwestern University Law School in part by working as a movie usher. He had been made a partner in a Chicago law firm at age thirty-two and, after a stint in the Justice Department, was appointed by Truman in 1949 to the D.C. Circuit.

Brennan had first heard Bazelon's name two years earlier while attending a conference on prison administration. A speaker mentioned a groundbreaking opinion Bazelon had recently authored that redefined insanity in criminal cases. Bazelon ruled that a defendant could not be held responsible for a criminal act if it was the product of mental disease or defect. Brennan went home from the conference, read the ruling, and came away impressed by the opinion and its author. On this night, Brennan and Bazelon began talking about opinions they had each written about defendants' access to evidence in criminal cases. Looking back many years later, Brennan would recall meeting the man he would come to consider his closest friend in Washington, calling the friendship love at first sight. But for his part, Bazelon did not know what to make of this new justice after their lengthy talk that night at Douglas's house. Driving home from the party, Bazelon told his wife, Mickey, that he thought Brennan "had a good bit of the 'blarney' in him."

BRENNAN RETURNED TO the Court the next day for his first full workday as a justice. He heard oral arguments in three cases, which among them would produce his first opinion for the Court, his first dissent — and the most controversial opinion of the term.

Brennan said little during the arguments, establishing a pattern of listening more than speaking that would hold throughout his tenure. The days had long passed since an advocate could argue a case before the Supreme Court for hours. The Court at the time Brennan joined limited lawyers to one hour — and would eventually cut that in half. But Brennan still thought lawyers talked too long. Much to his disappointment, he soon concluded that litigators before the Supreme Court did not do a much better job presenting their cases in their allotted hour than those back in New Jersey.

Unrealistic expectations aside, Brennan's years as a New Jersey judge helped ensure him an easier transition to the Court than some of his colleagues had experienced. Unlike Warren, Brennan had already worked alongside other judges as equals and exercised discretion about which cases to take up. And unlike many former governors, cabinet members, and congressmen who had been elevated to the Court, he found the atmosphere of the institution familiar. Justice Harold Burton, a former senator, compared exchanging a big staff and constant callers for the quiet halls of the Supreme Court as like going "direct from a circus to a monastery."

Brennan, in contrast, was the rare new justice of that era whose staff actually increased when he arrived at the Court. He was entitled to hire two clerks rather than the one he'd had in New Jersey. He brought with him

Clyde Szuch, his New Jersey clerk, and hired Richard Rhodes, who had been slated to clerk for Minton that term. Brennan planned to import another familiar face, Alice Connell, as his secretary. But after Connell suffered a heart attack, Brennan hired Mary Fowler, a forty-year-old member of the Court's secretarial pool, to fill in.

Nevertheless, Brennan's adjustment to the Court was not without difficulties. His previous state court experience, focused largely on more mundane legal issues such as property, contract, and zoning, did not necessarily prepare him to address the kinds of constitutional questions taken up by the Supreme Court. Brennan confessed a few years later to experiencing "considerable astonishment" when he moved from Trenton to Washington and discovered the differences between the two courts. "The work of each has a character, a difficulty, and a complexity of its own, and none of these has its exact counterpart in the other." Brennan took some comfort in cataloging the fears of his distinguished predecessors who had previously made the same leap, noting that Justice Benjamin Cardozo had been unsure whether "perhaps the larger opportunity was where I have been." Even the great Oliver Wendell Holmes, Brennan noted, had called switching from the Massachusetts high court to the Supreme Court "an adventure into the unknown." Brennan successfully hid any misgivings from his clerks, who observed no signs of self-doubt in their boss. It was a theme picked up by the press. "He is never plagued by that crippler of personal enterprise known as self-doubt," the *Saturday Evening Post* reported in 1957.

Brennan might actually have had a little too much confidence about what his new job required. He overcommitted himself with outside and often out-of-town speaking engagements that became increasingly onerous as his first term progressed. He traveled to Connecticut to address a meeting of the state bar association for his first speaking engagement as a justice exactly one week after he joined the Court. Bad weather had forced him to postpone a year earlier, and he gave little thought to canceling now despite his promotion. Brennan delivered his standard stump speech on court efficiency. He gave four more speeches during his second month on the job and a total of seventeen addresses by the end of the term. Brennan provided his audiences no revealing insights about his adjustment to the high court, although he did admit feeling a little overwhelmed by the volume of invitations from universities, lawyer groups, clubs, friends, politicians, and foreign embassies. Not wanting to disappoint people, Brennan found it difficult to say no. In meeting his outside commitments, he relied on his clerks to write about two-thirds of the first drafts of his opinions, after first discussing with them what he wanted to say. He devoted more time to crafting specific language in important cases.

Brennan's first writing assignment was unimportant by design. Supreme Court tradition dictates that the first opinion a new justice writes be uncontroversial, in an effort to ensure the other justices sign on to it unanimously. Even though he disliked tax law, Brennan's first opinion involved a case addressing a highly technical business tax question. Black, Douglas, and Warren were all inclined to vote the other way but changed their minds after reading it. Black explained in a letter to Brennan that he thought "a discussion the other way would better reflect the meaning of the statutory language invoked." In the spirit of accommodating his new colleague, he continued, "Your opinion however is clear and to the point and if Congress wishes it can easily amend the law." But Brennan could not convince one justice — Harlan — to see things his way. After spending the previous night "sweating out" the case, Harlan wrote Brennan to say he still had "grave doubts about the correctness of the Government's position." As a result, he informed Brennan, "I am sorry that I am unable to sign up at once with your 'first,' for I think you have handled the Government's case as strongly and well as it can be put." The case came down 8–1 with Harlan alone in dissent.

FELIX FRANKFURTER COULD not have been more pleased with his former pupil and new colleague. Even before arriving in Washington, Brennan had sought out Frankfurter's advice about how to pick his clerks. Nothing could have flattered Frankfurter more. As a Harvard Law School professor, Frankfurter had supplied clerks for Justices Brandeis, Cardozo, and Holmes. Frankfurter explained to Brennan that he had continued that tradition by relying on Harvard Law professor Henry Hart to select his clerks. Frankfurter could conceive of no other source. "If you want to get good groceries in Washington you go to Magruders," he once explained. "If you wanted to get a lot of first class lawyers, you went to the Harvard Law School." Brennan accepted that logic, enlisting the assistance of his former classmate, Harvard Law professor Paul Freund. Pleased to hear about the arrangement from Freund, Frankfurter immediately dashed off a note to Brennan on October 25 promising that "he will, I am wholly confident, give you great satisfaction."

Creating a conduit for Brennan's clerks from Harvard Law School was just part of Frankfurter's typically assiduous courtship of new colleagues. When Brennan invited him to attend his swearing-in day luncheon, Frankfurter wrote back, "It will give me great pleasure to do so and particularly to meet your mother!" Frankfurter did focus his attention on Brennan's mother at that lunch, helping her to her seat and making sure she was comfortable. "Frankfurter took over," Brennan's brother Frank later recalled. Frankfurter had long ago earned a reputation for wooing every new justice with great vigor. He smothered them with flattering notes and copies of articles, books, and opinions he had written. He lavished attention on clerks, whom he viewed as his entrée into the other justices' chambers, focusing particularly on those who had attended Harvard Law School. Frankfurter invited them to a special black-tie dinner each year at his Georgetown home, where he would hand them cocktails without first asking what they liked to drink. It was all part of Frankfurter's never-ending campaign to win over potential allies or acolytes who would vote with him rather than with Black, his main antagonist on the Court.

A growing philosophical divide had separated Black and Frankfurter since the early 1940s. Frankfurter believed firmly that judges should act with restraint and largely defer to the elected branches rather than strike down laws. Judicial restraint was something he had preached as a professor at a time when a conservative Supreme Court was overturning the progressive economic regulations enacted by Congress that he favored. He continued to advocate restraint as a justice, following in a tradition of his close friends and predecessors on the Court, Oliver Wendell Holmes Jr. and Louis Brandeis.

Black and Douglas had been equally frustrated with the conservative Court's knocking down of economic regulations, but were most concerned that the Court was abdicating its responsibility to protect civil liberties in the name of judicial restraint. For more than a decade, Black, along with Douglas, fought to push the Court to apply the protections of the Bill of Rights to the states. Black interpreted the due process clause of the Fourteenth Amendment, ratified after the Civil War, as requiring that the first eight amendments to the Constitution be applied against the states. Frankfurter, in contrast, believed that the Fourteenth Amendment required only incremental application of the Bill of Rights to the states, leading to less sweeping, less rigorous imposition of standards of procedural fairness on state criminal procedures.

Frankfurter had an unfortunate habit of personalizing disagreements on the Court in a melodramatic fashion. He viewed Black and Douglas — and any new justices who might agree with them — as members of an enemy camp. During most of the 1940s, Black and Douglas could rely on two allies — Frank Murphy and Wiley Rutledge — as they pressed to apply the Bill of Rights to the states and took liberal positions in civil liberties cases. But the bloc shrank when Murphy and Rutledge died unexpectedly within two months of each other in 1949. Their more conservative successors, Minton and Clark, shifted the Court's balance toward Frankfurter's camp.

The balance began to shift back again toward the liberal bloc with the arrival of Warren as chief justice. By the time Brennan joined the Court, Frankfurter was lumping Warren in with Black and Douglas as justices who made decisions on the basis of "their prejudices and their respective pasts and self-conscious desires to join Thomas Paine and T. Jefferson in the Valhalla of 'liberty.'" Black and Frankfurter viewed Brennan, their new and seemingly uncommitted justice, as up for grabs, with good reason. While Brennan had exhibited liberal leanings in some of his opinions in New Jersey, he arrived at the U.S. Supreme Court not yet the vigorous advocate of judicial power he was to become. As a state judge, he had taken as a given that only a few of the protections of the Bill of Rights had been applied as limits on the states and had not yet formulated a firm position on the issue.

More personal reasons contributed to Frankfurter's determination to win over Brennan. The arrival of a former student reminded the seventy-three-year-old Frankfurter that his own time on the Court was running out. "On more than one occasion you have tried to instill in me appropriate respect for the fact that the years creep up on us," Frankfurter wrote that October to eighty-four-year-old Learned Hand, his longtime friend and a famed judge on the U.S. Court of Appeals for the Second Circuit. "You don't have to do it any longer, considering that I face the stark fact of having a former student of mine on the bench with me." Frankfurter got carried away with visions of his former student carrying on his legacy, an impulse Brennan understood. It was the first time two justices who'd been teacher and student served together, Brennan later noted, "And Felix really carried that to great lengths just to make it true."

Frankfurter by late October had already hatched his next plot: a small, intimate dinner for Brennan at his Georgetown home. He hoped his high-powered friends would impress his new colleague—and perhaps teach Brennan something in the process. Frankfurter lined up an impressive roster of guests for the November 17 dinner, including former secretary of state Dean Acheson and his fellow Covington & Burling litigator, the veteran Supreme Court advocate John Lord O'Brian, as well as Monte Lemann, a prominent Harvard Law alumnus and New Orleans attorney.

This was heady stuff for the new arrival from Rumson. But it did not take long for Brennan to figure out what Frankfurter and his allies were up to over dinner and the brandy that followed in Frankfurter's Dumbarton Avenue home. Acheson recounted his experience clerking for Brandeis when he had carelessly cited two cases in a footnote without double-checking them. Brandeis had scolded Acheson for failing to make sure those cases supported the intended point. Acheson told Brennan he was grateful he had not been fired. Brennan understood that Frankfurter was not so subtly trying to send a message via Acheson about the importance of being meticulous. "Felix wanted me to understand that," Brennan later remembered.

Realizing he still had much to learn about how the Court operated, Brennan initially did not mind when Frankfurter reverted to his favorite role of professor. Frankfurter convinced him that it would be a bad idea to cut out federal district and circuit courts from hearing prisoners' petitions for habeas corpus, a mechanism by which courts inquire into the legality of a prisoner's detention. State prisoners used such petitions in federal court to challenge their confinement after they had exhausted their state appeals. As a former state judge, Brennan had needed Frankfurter's convincing that it was correct to allow state courts' findings in these matters to be reviewed by a lower federal court prior to the U.S. Supreme Court. Frankfurter led Brennan to see that bypassing the lower federal courts would overburden the Supreme Court.

Some of Brennan's early votes offered Frankfurter signs of hope that he had found a malleable new ally. The first dissent Brennan joined was written by Frankfurter, and it put Brennan at odds with Douglas, Warren, and

Black. He also joined Frankfurter's concurring opinion in a case that struck down the confessions of an uneducated black man from Alabama who was facing a possible death sentence for burglary with intent to rape. That sort of federal court intervention into state criminal proceedings, Frankfurter argued, was justified only where police or prosecutors offended notions of "fundamental fairness." And the first dissent Brennan wrote also had the two justices on the same side in a case addressing the manner in which a federal trial judge handled two antitrust cases. After he read the result, Frankfurter wrote Brennan one of his typically flattering notes of praise. "I am glad to be joined in this, for it is an effective refutation of the Court's conclusion."

The elder justice kept up the flattery in person, too. With his chambers right next door to Brennan's, Frankfurter would pop in unannounced a couple of times a week. He would stop first in the outer office where Brennan's two clerks worked, schmoozing with them briefly before advancing into the anteroom, where he would chat with Brennan's secretary. Finally, Frankfurter would make his way into Brennan's chambers, once occupied by Brandeis. Frankfurter might begin by innocently asking Brennan what he thought about a certain approach in a case. If Frankfurter disagreed with Brennan's answer, "he'd go into quite a lecture." Frankfurter's advice extended to work habits too. "I'm serious, very serious, but I hope not intrusive Bill in being concerned that you should feel tired by working into the night," Frankfurter wrote him. Brennan took all the attention Frankfurter lavished on him in stride — at least at first.

FRANKFURTER WAS NOT the only justice courting Brennan that fall. He was also being wooed by Chief Justice Warren, albeit with a lighter touch. When Brennan circulated his first opinion, Warren sent him a handwritten congratulatory note that read, "We are all very happy in our association with you and I am sure I voice the feeling of our brethren when I express the hope that this opinion is the first of hundreds to be written by you for the strengthening of our institutions and for the welfare of our people."

Brennan and Marjorie joined the other justices and their wives on a trip to Philadelphia organized by Warren to watch the annual Army-Navy football game. Warren had started the tradition two years earlier, reserving a private car for his guests on a Pennsylvania Railroad train. They ate breakfast and enjoyed morning drinks on the train, attended the game, and then ate dinner together in their own car on the way home that same night. This year, Army and Navy tied 7–7, perhaps a fitting score given Brennan's divided loyalties. The former Army colonel's son would soon graduate from Marine Corps officer training at Quantico, where Brennan was scheduled to be the graduation-ceremony speaker in February 1957.

This was just the first of many football games that Warren and Brennan would enjoy together in the years to come. Warren had started attending Washington Redskins games when he moved to Washington in 1953, and often invited Brennan to join him. Warren's wife, Nina, packed them lunch to eat in the stands. Later, they would move up to the owner's box as guests of Edward Bennett Williams, the Washington power lawyer and part-owner of the Redskins. It certainly was not the quality of the games that drew them to Griffith Stadium and then in 1961 to the new D.C. Stadium (which would later become RFK Stadium). Nor was it a chance to talk about the Court's work. Unlike Frankfurter, who never passed up a chance to expound on his views about law, Warren preferred talking about politics or family rather than cases while watching the game. Brennan became an avid Redskins fan, getting so worked up about one game he watched at home he nearly kicked the television.

Their common interest in football alone did not explain the friendship blossoming between the towering politician of Scandinavian descent and the diminutive Irish judge. Looking back, Brennan could not cite any particular reasons why "we just got along . . . from the very beginning." Brennan, not one for self-reflection, did not mention their similar personalities. But in his written tribute honoring Warren after his death in 1974, Brennan could have been describing himself. Warren was "naturally gregarious and open, with a warm and engaging smile. It was impossible to dislike him. He liked people and people liked him. He was instinctively courteous and sensitive to the feelings of others." In contrast to Frankfurter, both were physically warm and unpretentious. Beneath their gregarious exteriors, however, Brennan and Warren shared a common reserved nature that left them unwilling to share their inner selves with any but the closest of confidants.

Both men also had a history of forming similar relationships in previous jobs. In each phase of his career — in the Army, at the Pitney law firm, and as a judge — Brennan had advanced thanks to close mutually beneficial relationships with older confidants. Most recently, by enlisting Brennan as his court-reform evangelist, Vanderbilt had raised the younger judge's profile both inside New Jersey and beyond, and ultimately made his appointment to the Supreme Court possible. Yet interestingly, Brennan would later angrily reject the idea that Shelton Pitney, Robert Patterson, or Arthur Vanderbilt had ever served as his mentor.

Warren's professional relationships revealed a pattern as well, one dating back to California, of attachments to considerably younger men who dedicated themselves to his interests. Just as Warren had come to rely on such aides to implement policies he laid out abstractly, he came to see that Brennan could play a similar role for him on the Court.

Brennan was not the first justice Warren turned to as an ally on the Court. The chief justice upon his arrival in 1953 had almost immediately developed a close working relationship with Hugo Black. Like Warren, Black was an avuncular former politician who joined the Court after a lengthy career in elected office. Warren asked Black, then the senior associate justice, to preside at the justices' weekly conference until he got his bearings. They traded political and courtroom war stories over steaks and within a couple of years, Warren met with Black before or after conference to strategize about whom to assign cases when they were both in the majority. (The chief justice has the power to assign opinions when in the majority; the senior associate justice in the majority does so when the chief justice dissents.)

But by the time Brennan arrived on the Court, Warren was increasingly aware of the philosophical differences separating him and his older mentor and friend. Warren, the natural pragmatist, was uneasy with Black's absolutism, particularly regarding the First Amendment, which Black interpreted to bar any government limitations on free speech. By contrast, Warren sensed none of the same sort of rigidity in Brennan. "I suppose we just gravitated together," Brennan recalled. It was not just that he and Brennan seemed to approach so many issues the same way. Warren, an astute observer of talent and his own weaknesses, saw that Brennan could theorize about the law in a way he could not.

As chief justice, Warren could employ a powerful tool only he possessed to assign cases to Brennan whenever he was in the majority. Warren's regard for Brennan resulted in some unusually choice assignments for a freshman justice in his first months. The first was an important antitrust case involving E. I. du Pont de Nemours and Company (familiarly known as DuPont), the massive chemical conglomerate, which the Court took up in November.

On November 16, 1956, a buzzer in each justice's chambers rang shortly before 10 A.M. summoning them to gather at their weekly conference, a meeting bound by tradition and secrecy. After shaking hands with each of their colleagues, they sat down at the conference table in the center of the oak-paneled room, with its portrait of Chief Justice John Marshall hanging over the marble fireplace. Brennan, as the most junior justice, answered the door if any of their messengers knocked to deliver notes. No one except the nine justices could enter the room, not secretaries, law clerks, or messengers. The justices on this day took up the Justice Department's seven-year-old antitrust lawsuit against DuPont. At issue was DuPont's 23 percent stake in General Motors, one of its biggest customers, and whether the Clayton Antitrust Act applied to "vertical trusts" in which a company gains control of a potential customer or supplier. A federal district court in Chicago had conducted a seven-month-long trial, and after concluding that the Justice Department had failed to establish illegal action by Du-Pont, had dismissed the case. The Justice Department appealed this rejection of the claims to the Supreme Court. Warren, Black, and Douglas had all shown a willingness to rule against DuPont in another antitrust case that had come before the Court a year earlier. On the crucial question of what was the relevant market potentially being monopolized, all three favored a narrow interpretation that would make it more likely DuPont was found to be monopolizing the car-finishing business. Their position had not gotten majority support the previous year.

Warren, Black, and Douglas all made clear on this day that they favored reversing the trial court's decision and ordering the company to divest itself of General Motors stock. Frankfurter, Burton, and Reed came out for DuPont. Harlan, who had represented two members of the du Pont family and two companies with large holdings in its stock during the seven-month-long trial in 1952 and 1953, recused himself from consideration of the case. That left Brennan as the crucial undecided vote when it was finally his turn to speak. Brennan argued that he was not sure the antitrust laws had been violated, but also said he felt that DuPont probably invested in General Motors to guarantee its market share. He seemed inclined to send the case back to the District Court for a remedy short of divestiture. So he was not willing to go as far as the trio of Black, Douglas, and Warren wanted. But since Black made clear he saw no remedy short of divestiture, Warren could not give him the opinion and hope to keep Brennan onboard. Instead, Warren assigned the opinion to Brennan. The assignment made good strategic sense: giving a case to the least decided justice was often the best way to ensure he did not defect.

Brennan returned to his chambers from the justices' weekly conference meetings almost giddy after landing such plum assignments his first term. "He'd be frankly as excited as a kid with a brand-new toy or an ice-cream cone," recalled Szuch. "He just couldn't believe that he was getting all this great stuff." The high-profile freshman assignments got noticed by clerks in other chambers too. The good assignments also fueled long six-day workweeks for Brennan, his clerks, and secretary. They would work on the *du Pont* case, which proved to be a defining moment for him, over the course of the next seven months. The pace proved so intense that when Brennan asked Mary Fowler, his fill-in secretary, to stay permanently that fall, she opted to return to another job she had lined up in the Clerk's Office.

BRENNAN DID NOT stop working as the Court adjourned for Christmas that December and his family returned to Rumson for a ten-day holiday. He simply relocated to his former state Supreme Court chambers in Red Bank, which he had hardly had a chance to occupy. It seemed all the more unlikely that he ever would, now that President Eisenhower had easily won reelection to a second term. Brennan's nomination had attracted few signs of opposition in the Senate in advance of a confirmation hearing expected after the new Congress convened in January.

Brennan celebrated Christmas in New Jersey, confident about his prospects for confirmation. An even better Christmas gift was that his son, Hugh, had gotten a job at a company in Long Branch and enrolled in night classes at Monmouth College. For Christmas, Hugh and his wife, Roxey, gave Brennan a portrait Roxey had painted of Nancy, which he proudly hung in his chambers at the Court. By springtime, after Hugh had earned a promotion, Brennan would write to one of Roxey's relatives, "When I think back of [sic] our worries of last summer about how he would manage to feed his family I marvel now that we gave it a thought."

The return to New Jersey proved bittersweet for Marjorie. It reminded her how much she missed their life in Rumson. There was no place in their rented apartment in an anonymous Washington high-rise for the tulips she carefully tended back in Rumson. So she crated all the bulbs in special soil and planted them around Justice Harlan's home in Georgetown. Hardly any of the wives of Supreme Court justices found the role easy. They needed to pick activities outside the home carefully, lest they get involved in an organization or cause that might come before the Court. That explains in part why most preferred, in the words of one Supreme Court wife, to "find self-fulfillment in home and a private life." That was not a problem for Marjorie, who harbored no professional ambitions and remained focused on raising Nancy. But she did mostly give up the kind of community-service work she had enjoyed in Rumson.

Marjorie found it particularly difficult to navigate Washington society's rigid social expectations. Some of the more formal protocols had eased. No one still expected the justices' wives to receive hundreds of visitors on designated Mondays, providing both a dance venue and full tea — a tradition that had died during the Great Depression. Yet society ladies still might show up at any time with their calling cards, as Marjorie discovered one day. Marjorie was kneeling in the front yard of the Georgetown home they eventually found, pulling weeds around a magnolia tree, when a well-dressed matron approached the house. Marjorie kept her eyes down and pretended to be the maid rather than greet the guest approaching her front door.

Marjorie compared her standing in Washington to that of a military wife, whose status derived solely from her husband's rank. After attending one too many luncheons where other guests fawned over her, Marjorie observed that she would not have been treated that way if her husband was just some lawyer from Passaic back in New Jersey. Marjorie's close friends knew her as a warm, spunky woman with a whimsical sense of humor and a throaty laugh. But she was shy by nature and not nearly as comfortable around strangers as her husband was. She developed a studied reticence in public, saying little about the Court to anyone, particularly to the press: "They merely want to know what Bill is thinking through me, and I'm not going to tell them." She was more eager to talk about dogs than about the Court or politics when seated at dinner next to famed political columnist Jack Anderson.

In their first months in Washington, the Brennans kept their appearances on the Washington social circuit to a minimum, despite a flood of invitations. Brennan confessed that January that they had accepted only two invitations since his appointment: one to the National Symphony and the other to see *Inherit the Wind,* a play depicting the Scopes evolution trial. The Brennans could not, however, skip an invitation to attend their first state dinner at the White House, given by President Eisenhower in the justices' honor. A picture that ran in the next day's *Washington Post*'s "About Women" page showed Brennan, bedecked in a tuxedo with tails, taking Marjorie's fur shawl. They joined the fifty-seven other guests for dinner in the East Room, where the place settings included gold service plates engraved with the Great Seal of the United States. The men then re-tired to the Blue Room for coffee and liqueurs; the women headed to the Red Room. Her friends sensed how much of a strain it all was on Marjorie. "She was a very lovely person but she wasn't going to conquer Washing-ton," one friend recalled.

But Marjorie kept up the public façade of a content Washington wife. "Both Mrs. Brennan and her husband enjoy living in Washington," *Subur-ban Life* magazine reported. "She likes entertaining their many friends and has worked on so many community and charitable projects that her husband has long since lost track of the number." That rosy version of his wife's experience is what Brennan preferred to remember many years later. "She loved it," said Brennan, who recalled how Marjorie enjoyed attending events at embassies and the White House.

Brennan himself certainly preferred life in Washington over Rumson. He mingled among his intellectual equals and like-minded friends such as David Bazelon, who had quickly included the new justice in his broad social and intellectual circle. Brennan particularly enjoyed the small din-ner thrown in his honor at the Capitol Hill Club by Congressman James Auchincloss of New Jersey that April of 1957, attended by a group of prom-inent lawmakers that included both Speaker of the House Sam Rayburn, a Texas Democrat, and Minority Leader Joseph Martin, a Massachusetts Re-publican. The only drawback on such occasions was dealing with guests who insisted on mixing business with pleasure. Brennan recoiled when Postmaster General Arthur Summerfield cornered him at one party to talk about a case pending before the Court.

Brennan's daughter-in-law was eight months pregnant with his first grandchild when the family convened in Rumson for Christmas. Marjorie returned to New Jersey alone a few weeks later, in January, when Roxey gave birth to an eight-pound baby boy, whom his parents named Hugh Jr. Brennan was enough of a celebrity now that the birth merited a picture in the *Asbury Park Press*. Marjorie and Hugh stood over the hospital bed in which Roxey held the baby in her arms. Marjorie told reporters that her husband "was much too busy to make the trip."

BRENNAN HAD SPENT almost the entire Christmas break working on his second opinion for the Court in a case addressing compensation for injured railroad workers. A Missouri railroad laborer burning weeds alongside tracks had slipped down a ravine and had been injured when an approaching train fanned the flames. The case, which Brennan was assigned essentially at random, had infuriated Frankfurter from the start. He thought the Court had no business getting involved in such an individualized dispute between a railroad and its workers under the Federal Employers Liability Act. Frankfurter wanted the Court to stay out of the matter altogether and voted to deny the petitioner's writ of certiorari, or cert. petition, requesting the Court take up the case. The justices enjoyed broad discretion over what cases they agreed to hear by the time Brennan joined the Court and no formal standards guided their decision in most cases. But by a long-standing "rule of four," the justices would only hear cases where four justices voted to "grant cert."

Black and Warren, the son of a railroad worker himself, vigorously disagreed. They believed the Court should provide relief to these injured workers, even if it meant adjudicating their claims one case at a time. Black, who had sparred with Frankfurter about the issue long before Brennan or Warren arrived, voted to hear every one of the nearly two hundred claims by injured workers that reached the Supreme Court during his tenure. That difference of opinion between Warren and Frankfurter reflected a broader disagreement between them over the role of the Court. Warren believed the job of the Court was to mete out justice. Frankfurter had a very different view, as he explained to Brennan in an April 1957 letter. "I do not conceive that it is my function to decide cases on my notions of justice," Frankfurter wrote. "If it were, I wouldn't be as confident as some others that I knew exactly what justice required in a particular case."

Brennan approached the case from the perspective of a recent state judge. He recalled the first time he encountered the law as a state trial judge in a case where a railroad employee was injured when an urn of coffee boiled over. He dismissed the case after applying the concept of assumption of risk, which holds a plaintiff fully responsible for activities they knew were particularly dangerous. The state appellate courts reversed him, which he later came to view as the correct course of action. "When the state appellate practice does not correct the error, or as sometimes happens, creates it, must not the injured employee perforce turn to the Supreme Court of the United States for vindication of the rights created for him by the Congress?" Brennan said of the case in an April 1959 speech. "There is no other tribunal to which he can go."

In the Missouri case, Brennan wrote an opinion favoring the railroad workers. He interpreted the federal statute as merely requiring workers to prove that the railroad's negligence played some part in causing the injury — rather than being the sole cause, as the state court required. For Brennan, it was just the first of many cases in so many areas of law where he emphasized providing individual civil plaintiffs or criminal defendants maximum access to the courts.

The result, announced from the bench by Brennan on February 25, 1957, absolutely infuriated Frankfurter, who vowed never to participate in another such case again. He wrote a strident thirty-four-page dissent and, for good measure, tacked on two appendices in which he accused his fellow justices of abusing the process by which the justices decide which cases to take up. "This is not the supreme court of review for every case decided 'unjustly' by every court in the country," scolded Frankfurter. This was the first time Brennan was on the receiving end of one of Frankfurter's intemperate piques.

In hindsight, Frankfurter should have been more concerned by Brennan's action in another case announced the same day. Brennan had joined Black, Douglas, and Warren to form a bloc of four dissenters for the first time. The issue in the case — *In re Groban* — was whether a fire marshal could bar the target of an investigation from having an attorney present when answering questions under a subpoena. Brennan initially agreed with Reed's opinion for the Court that the state had no obligation to let an attorney participate. But after thinking it over in the middle of the night, Brennan switched sides at the last minute, convinced by Black that such a ruling would encourage law enforcement to bar attorneys during other kinds of questioning.

The switch helped break the ice between Brennan and Black; Brennan would no longer view his senior colleague as such an intimidating figure. But it also angered Reed, who wrote Brennan a note accusing him of playing "into the hands of those who are careless" with the law. Reed — joined by Frankfurter — still prevailed in the case, which was one of the last he would announce. The seventy-two-year-old justice retired that day after nineteen years on the Court, citing old age. What should have most troubled Frankfurter was that Brennan in *Groban* and two other cases that day had joined what Frankfurter by 1957 had taken to calling the "hard core liberal wing" of the Court, whose "common denominator is a self-willed self-righteous power lust." Up to this point, Brennan had maintained a noticeably centrist voting position and not aligned with any particular bloc. He often had cast his votes with Warren, but was just as likely to join Frankfurter as Douglas. If Brennan started regularly joining with Warren, Douglas, and Black too, it would mean a solid bloc of four liberals, just one shy of a majority.

If Frankfurter picked up on the potential significance of Brennan's votes that day, he gave no hint of it in his voluminous correspondence. Neither did Brennan's actions in *Groban* and the railroad case get much attention in the next day's newspapers on the morning of February 26. Nor was either case on the minds of many senators that day, as the Senate Judiciary Committee finally began Brennan's confirmation hearing after a weeklong delay. Most at issue at the hearing was Brennan's Catholic faith and two of the speeches in which he had taken veiled swipes at Senator Joseph McCarthy long before joining the Court.

Brennan initially attracted few detractors in the Senate. Through the New Year, the only senator to express concern publicly about his nomination was Olin D. Johnston, a South Carolina Democrat on the Senate Judiciary Committee who promised in November to examine Brennan's record "with a fine-tooth comb." A recent civil rights decision prompted the ardent segregationist's sudden interest in Brennan's record. The Supreme Court had summarily affirmed a lower court that knocked down Alabama's state and local laws requiring segregation on buses. Rosa Parks had helped launch an African American boycott of Montgomery's city buses, challenging those laws a year earlier by refusing to give up her seat in the whites-only section. The eleven-word decision by the Supreme Court — issued on the basis of the petition and without oral argument — took the wind out of segregationist efforts to resist the boycott.

After U.S. marshals served notice on city officials of the Supreme Court decision, a twenty-six-year-old minister and leader of the boycott named Martin Luther King Jr. victoriously declared the boycott's conclusion. The modern civil rights protest movement had scored its first big win. Senator Johnston had earlier held up the nomination of a circuit court judge whom he viewed as too sympathetic to civil rights, and now saw a way to take his anger out on the Supreme Court's newest justice too. But another southern Democrat, Senator A. Willis Robertson of Virginia, quickly jumped in and said he "did not anticipate any difficulties" with Brennan's confirmation.

Then, with all looking clear as the Senate returned in January, McCarthy suddenly popped up and announced his opposition to the nominee he labeled "supremely unfit." Although he acknowledged that Brennan appeared to have the votes needed to win confirmation, McCarthy said he would be "derelict" in his duty if he failed to call the Senate's attention to speeches in which Brennan criticized congressional committees exposing Communism. McCarthy accused Brennan of "waging a guerrilla war against committees that pick up individual communists by the scruff of their neck and expose them."

By this time in early 1957, McCarthy's star had dimmed considerably. The days had long passed when McCarthy automatically commanded media attention and elicited the fear of those he targeted with headline-grabbing hearings and often baseless accusations. His public popularity had eroded significantly in the wake of the Army-McCarthy hearings in the spring of 1954. The Senate's censure vote against him that December shredded what little credibility he had left in Congress. "It is safe to assume that McCarthyism, while not dead, has definitely faded away," the *Washington Star* noted in February 1957.

McCarthy's severe drinking required repeated hospitalizations for detoxification. His hands shook from delirium tremens and he suffered from alcohol-induced hallucinations. Many in his own Republican Party viewed McCarthy as little more than an embittered crank and obstructionist by this point. His opposition to Brennan — as well as his plans to testify against the promotion of the Army general with whom he had tangled at the 1954 hearings — came across as cheap score-settling, a badge of honor for Brennan in the eyes of some. "None of the praise heaped upon Justice Brennan when President Eisenhower appointed him to the nation's highest court equals the tribute implied in Senator McCarthy's criticisms of him," an *Asbury Park Press* editorial observed.

Still, Brennan could not entirely dismiss the Republican from Wisconsin, who had ruined careers with equally spurious accusations. So Brennan arrived for his February 26 confirmation hearing in Room 424 of the Senate Office Building girding for a potential confrontation. McCarthy had requested and received permission to join the Senate Judiciary Committee in its questioning of the nominee. Having already appeared before congressional committees twice before, this was not entirely a new experience for Brennan. But he benefited from none of the intense advance preparation afforded later Supreme Court nominees. Nor did Brennan try to ingratiate himself with committee members in advance with courtesy calls on their offices, which he viewed as inappropriate. Brennan even thought it was incorrect to approach his two home state senators, Republicans H. Alexander Smith and Clifford P. Case. They led off the hearing with brief statements of support addressed to the committee, arrayed around a conference table in the cramped hearing room. A crowd of committee staff and reporters stood alongside the walls.

McCarthy, who spoke next as he peered at Brennan through his thick black-framed eyeglasses, took a different view. Sitting just two seats away from Brennan at the conference table, McCarthy said the nominee's record indicated he had "demonstrated an underlying hostility to congressional attempts to expose the Communist conspiracy. I can only conclude that his decisions on the Supreme Court are likely to harm our efforts to fight communism."

McCarthy, in his typical and by now well-worn penchant for the dramatic, declared that he had evidence that Brennan "in his public speeches has referred to congressional investigations of communism, for example, as 'Salem witch hunts,' and 'inquisitions,' and has accused congressional investigating committees of barbarism." Only later did he acknowledge that the evidence came from two speeches Brennan readily provided McCarthy's office. And in his typical display of discourtesy, McCarthy insisted on referring to the witness as "Mr. Brennan" rather than "Mr. Justice Brennan" as did other senators in recognition that he had already been on the Court for four months.

Brennan did not take the redbaiter's bait, opting to placate McCarthy rather than spark a confrontation.

"Do you approve of congressional investigations and exposure of the Communist conspiracy set up?" McCarthy asked.

"Not only do I approve, Senator," Brennan replied. "But personally I cannot think of a more vital function of the Congress than the investigatory function of its committees, and I can't think of a more important or vital objective of any committee investigation than that of rooting out subversives in Government."

But Brennan deflected McCarthy's attempt to get him to agree that Communism "is a conspiracy designed to overthrow the United States Government," citing cases pending before the Court. "Senator, believe me I appreciate that what to one man is the path of duty may to another man be the path of folly, but I simply cannot venture any comment whatever that touches upon any matter pending before the Court."

Brennan backtracked from most of the charges in his speeches and passed up repeated opportunities to criticize McCarthy's methods or broader congressional excesses.

McCarthy asked if Brennan made "any distinction between good investigations of communism and bad investigations." Brennan replied, "There was a general atmosphere that bothered me, and I think a lot of other Americans about this time . . . It was the general notion — not congressional committees — but there was a general feeling of hysteria that I felt was very unfortunate and many things were symptoms of it, not congressional committees."

McCarthy asked if Brennan could cite any instances of epithets being hurled "at the hapless and helpless victims," as he had charged in his speech. Brennan brushed off that language as "artist's license" and replied, "I can't name any specific instances for you, Senator; no."

McCarthy ended his interrogation after less than two hours, making clear that he intended to continue when the committee resumed consideration the next morning. It proved to be an empty threat. McCarthy failed to appear when the hearing resumed. Instead, McCarthy sent a letter to committee chairman James Eastland in which he said, "I am convinced, after yesterday's session, that there is no further doubt about the accuracy of my initial conclusion" about Brennan's fitness. But, McCarthy added, "I am doubtful that further questioning on the subject would serve any useful purpose."

Newspaper reviews panned McCarthy's antics. The *Washington Star* noted, "For a few hours this week the Wisconsin Senator was back in the limelight . . . it soon became evident that Senator McCarthy, the man, has not changed. But somehow, the old 'soft on communism' theme just didn't stick." Brennan, however, came in for some criticism himself from some for reacting so meekly to McCarthy. "At this late date it would have required a minimum of valor for Brennan to affirm his stated convictions or simply to refuse to be drawn into the argument," a *New York Post* editorial lamented. "The tragedy in the Brennan affair is that his capitulation cannot even be defended on the ground of desperate expediency; his confirmation was virtually assured long ago. He was being heckled by a ghost, but he acted as if his adversary were Superman."

Brennan privately defended his low-key approach two months after the hearings to a political science professor by saying he was a sitting justice and had no desire to embarrass the Court by "going to the mat" with McCarthy. In doing so, Brennan successfully employed a confirmation-hearing strategy readily adopted by future nominees and their handlers: win by saying as little as possible. Brennan, who had inherited his father's keen political instincts, understood that this was not the place for a showdown.

Another factor contributed to Brennan's reticence with McCarthy one-on-one. Brennan was an intensely conflict-averse person, as he would prove time and again during the course of his tenure on the Court. His clerk, Szuch recalled, "He'd rather walk out of the room a friend of yours than an enemy of yours." Part of the reason that he enlisted Freund to pick his clerks, Brennan admitted later, was because he could not bear to reject any students he might interview. "If there's a kid sitting across the table from me, I can't tell him no," he said in a 1987 speech. So, while disappointing to McCarthy's critics, Brennan's avoidance of a direct confrontation with the faded redbaiter was certainly within character.

McCarthy's absence left one other obstacle for Brennan before the Judiciary Committee: he would need to confront the question of whether a Catholic could put service to the Court above his faith. The issue was raised by Charles Smith, a representative of the National Liberal League, who made his anti-Catholic bias clear. "We oppose it on the same ground that a Catholic in a predominantly Catholic country would oppose the nomination of a Protestant. This is a predominantly Protestant country. In Catholic nations, we believe, Protestants are not appointed to the highest court." Smith gave voice to lingering unease about Catholics even as a generation of newly prosperous and increasingly assimilated middle-class Catholic veterans was joining the American mainstream. A Catholic priest, Bishop Fulton J. Sheen, hosted one of the nation's top-rated television shows. And yet, no matter how successful or assimilated, Catholics still could not entirely escape doubts about their divided loyalties. Al Smith had to confront such questions when he ran for president in 1928, and so would John F. Kennedy in just three years, on his way to being elected the nation's first Catholic president.

Only seven years had passed since a liberal intellectual, Paul Blanshard, had reached the bestseller list with his book, *American Freedom and Catholic Power,* which portrayed the Catholic hierarchy and Communism as parallel threats to American democracy. A Protestant minister could still take to the pulpit in Manhattan's Riverside Church in 1951 and warn that "Roman Catholicism is engaged in a ceaseless surreptitious pressure to obtain a position of preference in the New World." The fact that five Catholics had preceded Brennan on the Court — including two chief justices — did not inoculate Brennan from the same distrust now.

Tennessee Democrat Estes Kefauver, who had been Stevenson's running mate a few months earlier, objected to the question posed about Brennan's faith, arguing that raising religion to determine a nominee's qualifications could set a dangerous precedent. But Joseph C. O'Mahoney, the Catholic chairman of the Judiciary subcommittee considering Smith's request, opted to ask Brennan the question himself. "You are bound by your religion to follow the pronouncements of the Pope on all matters of faith and morals. There may be some controversies which involve matters of faith and morals and also matters of law and justice. But in matters of law and justice, you are bound by your oath to follow not papal decrees and doctrines, but the laws and precedents of this Nation. If you should be faced with such a mixed issue, would you be able to follow the requirements of your oath or would you be bound by your religious obligations?"

The focus on his faith surprised Brennan. Unlike many Catholics his age, Brennan did not harbor resentment over being excluded from elite institutions because of his faith or bitter memories about Al Smith's experience running for president in 1928. Brennan swallowed his anger about having to address the issue and replied calmly. "I took that oath just as unreservedly as I know you did, and every member and everyone else of our faith in whatever office elected or appointive he may hold," Brennan said. "And I say not that I recognize that there is any obligation superior to that, rather that there isn't any obligation of our faith superior to that. And my answer to the question is categorically that in everything I have ever done, in every office I have held in my life or that I shall ever do in the future, what shall control me is the oath that I took to support the Constitution and laws of the United States and so act upon that cases that come before me for decision that it is that oath and that alone which governs."

Pledging to completely divorce one's religious and legal views remained a prerequisite in this era for a Catholic hoping to gain widespread acceptance in American public life. But this answer designed to reassure non-Catholics also inevitably alienated some Catholics, who believed he had gone too far in accommodating the Church's critics. The Catholic magazine *Commonweal* suggested the "confused and negative discussions" which followed Brennan's testimony could have been prevented had he clarified the "distinctions and assumptions" underlying his statement.

John F. Kennedy sparked similar criticism two years later with a remark published in *Look* magazine: "Whatever one's religion in his private life may be, for the office holder, nothing takes precedence over his oath to uphold the Constitution in all its parts, including the First Amendment and the strict separation of church and state." Brennan naïvely hoped his promise would permanently put to rest any questions about divided loyalties. He would grow increasingly frustrated when the questions continued in subsequent years. Brennan said thirty years later, "Why in God's name I can't get people to understand that, I don't understand."

After a few more questions, the committee adjourned. Brennan's entire confirmation hearing had lasted less than three hours. The committee sent his nomination to the full Senate, which confirmed him on March 19, 1957, three weeks after the hearing had ended. McCarthy uttered the single loud "no" on the Senate floor among the chorus of "ayes." Columnist I. F. Stone accurately predicted, "It looks as if we have just seen the last of low blow Joe." In less than three months, McCarthy would be dead at the age of forty-nine. His death certificate delivered one last fabrication, listing the cause of death as hepatitis rather than cirrhosis of the liver.

Brennan, who was driving back to Washington from New Jersey with Marjorie and Nancy in a car with a broken radio, did not hear about the vote until they returned home that night. The Senate that day also confirmed Charles Whittaker, a fifty-six-year-old federal judge from Missouri, as Justice Reed's successor, the first such simultaneous confirmation in 146 years. According to an obscure statute, when two such commissions bear the same date, the older justice would be registered as more senior. By that measure, Whittaker, who was six years older, would outrank Brennan, who had already been on the Court for nearly five months.

Attorney General Brownell avoided such an outcome by dispatching Brennan's commission by air to Bermuda, where President Eisenhower was meeting with British prime minister Harold MacMillan. Eisenhower signed the commission on March 21, clearing the way for Brennan to take the oath first on March 22 in the presence of his colleagues in the Court's conference room. Whittaker's commission was not dated and issued until March 22 and he took the oath March 25. After five months on the Court, Justice Brennan would no longer have to answer the door for messages during the justices' private conferences and could shift his seat from the far left to the far right on the bench.

BRENNAN HAD BEEN on the Court for only a few months when Warren handed him what was perhaps the term's thorniest problem, one the chief justice found particularly distasteful: obscenity. The thought of his daughters looking at sexually explicit materials made Warren angry. It did not take long for Brennan to notice Warren's puritanism when it came to pornography, a trait in the chief justice that reminded him of his father. "Warren was a terrible prude," Brennan said. "He would not read any of the books or watch the movies."

Until this term, the Supreme Court had managed to avoid ruling on the question of whether the First Amendment's protections extended to obscene materials. And with good reason: unless the Court ruled all obscene materials were constitutionally protected, regulating obscenity would require the inherently difficult task of defining what made a work obscene. Was it enough that a magazine or movie merely treated sex in a disgusting manner? Did it need to arouse lustful thoughts? Or, perhaps, would the material also need to incite improper sexual conduct? No matter what threshold for obscenity the justices established, there was no denying that the impact of sexually explicit material greatly depended on individual tastes, morals, and vulnerabilities.

Despite these uncertainties, several states, starting with Vermont in 1821, had long ago begun enacting obscenity statutes. But obscenity prosecutions became widespread only after the Civil War, thanks largely to the efforts of one man. Anthony Comstock, a former New York dry goods store clerk, became increasingly alarmed by the bawdy books read by his customers and coworkers. The New York Society for the Suppression of Vice led by Comstock from 1893 to 1915 pushed for anti-obscenity laws and prosecutions around the country, most notably under the federal obscenity law named in his honor that prohibited the mailing of obscene publications.

Comstock, who became a U.S. postal inspector, liked to boast about the tons of obscene materials he helped suppress each year. He ensnared in his puritanical net enough works now considered classics by the likes of Balzac, Tolstoy, Joyce, and Dreiser to fill an entire semester of college-level literature. American courts reviewing obscenity prosecutions against authors, their publishers, and booksellers employed a test first adopted in an 1868 British case, *Regina v. Hicklin*. The *Hicklin* rule established a low bar for obscenity. Courts examined whether selected excerpts, rather than the entire work, tended to "deprave and corrupt." By that standard, a brief passage taken out of context could taint an otherwise meritorious literary work. The test also focused on readers deemed most susceptible, such as children and the mentally ill, rather than the public at large.

By the early 1900s, American judges began to rebel against that strict standard, particularly in cases involving works of literary merit. The question of obscenity's constitutional status did not reach the Court until 1948, when lawyers for literary critic Edmund Wilson argued that his First Amendment free speech rights protected his novel *Memoirs of Hecate County* against obscenity charges. Justice Robert Jackson presciently asked the publisher's counsel, "Does your argument mean that we would have to take every obscenity case and decide the constitutional issues on the merits of the literary work? It seems to me that would mean that we would become the High Court of Obscenity." The eight justices tied 4–4, thus leaving the lower court's ruling in place without a definitive ruling on the constitutional question. The lack of clear-cut constitutional protections combined with intermittent state and local prosecutions in the years afterward left some major publishers reluctant to issue works such as Norman Mailer's 1948 novel *The Naked and the Dead* and Vladimir Nabokov's *Lolita*, first published in 1955.

But Comstock's puritanical heirs were fighting a losing battle. Nudity and sex had begun to infiltrate mainstream American culture thoroughly by 1956. Calendars featuring a nude photo of actress Marilyn Monroe posing on a red velvet drape hung in thousands of barbershops and gas stations. The same picture had also appeared in the 1953 inaugural issue of a new magazine called *Playboy. Peyton Place,* a book first published in 1956 that vividly detailed the sex life—including incest and abortion—of a small New England town, quickly shattered sales records for an American novel.

Brennan had encountered his first obscenity case on his maiden day on the bench back in October. At issue in *Butler v. Michigan* was the state's statute that criminalized selling or distributing reading material containing content "tending to the corruption of the morals of youth." Brennan was one of three justices who suggested the case raised constitutional questions. But Frankfurter, writing for a unanimous Court, wrote a narrow opinion that rejected the vague statute as unduly restricting adults' access in order to protect youths. Frankfurter compared it to burning down an entire house "to roast the pig." Frankfurter's narrow approach had won over Brennan. "I confess I originally thought this should have full dress treatment," Brennan wrote him. "It is probably wise, however, to hold that treatment until we are forced to it."

That point came in April when the Court took up an appeal by Samuel Roth, convicted of violating the Comstock Act by mailing obscene books, periodicals, and photographs with titles such as *Wanton by Night* and *Wild Passion.* At trial, Roth's lawyers argued that the law was an unconstitutional restriction on his speech and press freedoms. They urged the Court to allow an infringement on speech only if it would cause a substantive evil. The government argued that the Court had to weigh the value of the speech against the public interest served by the restriction and the form of the restriction imposed.

Roger Fisher, one of the lawyers in the Solicitor General's Office, which argues the government's position before the Supreme Court, coined the term "hard core pornography" to reflect the low value of the speech involved. For added emphasis, Fisher sent a box full of obscene materials seized in the mails over to the Court. Roth had not actually sold any of these books, photos, booklets, and comic books showing people engaged in sexual acts of every kind. Fisher's point was to drive home how vile obscenity could be. The justices passed the box of pornography down the bench during the oral argument, starting at Brennan's end.

The box—and all its contents—wound up in Brennan's chambers when Warren assigned him the case following the April 26 conference. Brennan had joined the five other justices, including Warren, who voted in favor of affirming Roth's conviction. He was never entirely sure why Warren gave him the assignment in the *Roth* case, thus beginning what would become his leading role in obscenity cases for years to come. In fact, Warren did not have many other good options. Black and Douglas voted to overturn the conviction, arguing that the First Amendment prohibited restrictions on any form of expression, including obscenity. Harlan argued that regulating obscenity was the business of the states and believed the federal government should have less leeway. "Everybody knew you couldn't go along with the Black-Douglas approach. But nobody knew what other approach you could take," Brennan said.

Perhaps Warren hoped to further cement their relationship. During his first six months on the Court, Brennan had already proven himself capable of handling a big case in *du Pont*, for which he was still in the process of drafting an opinion. Brennan noted that, unlike most of his colleagues, he had encountered obscenity before on the New Jersey court. That is not to say Brennan was particularly comfortable with obscenity. He confided to clerks that, as a father, he thought certain things should not be legal. The thought that his daughter or even his secretary might see the contents of the box sent over by the Solicitor General's Office horrified him. Szuch hid it under his own desk.

Brennan initially decided to adopt the approach the Court had taken in a 1942 decision upholding the conviction of a New Hampshire man charged under a state law that banned addressing "any offensive, derisive or annoying word to anyone who is lawfully in any street or public place." Walter Chaplinsky was arrested after calling the town marshal "a Goddamned racketeer" and "a damned Fascist." The Supreme Court in that case enunciated a two-tier theory of the First Amendment, under which "well-defined and narrowly limited" categories of speech fall beyond the bounds of constitutional protection. In applying that approach in *Roth*, Brennan said he envisioned formulating a standard outlawing obscenity only on proof that it presented a clear and present danger of some social harm, either to the individual or society generally. Brennan's clerks had written up an opinion taking that approach.

But Brennan changed course after Frankfurter stopped by during one of his regular visits. Frankfurter handed Brennan a memo prepared by one of his own clerks showing that obscenity had not been treated as protected speech in colonial-era statutes. Frankfurter's memo so impressed Brennan that he changed his approach. In his opinion, Brennan noted that the guaranties of freedom of expression in ten of the fourteen states which by 1792 had ratified the Constitution gave no absolute protection for every utterance. Thirteen states provided for the prosecution of libel, and all of those states criminalized either blasphemy or profanity. "In light of this history, it is apparent that the unconditional phrasing of the First Amendment was not intended to protect every utterance," Brennan wrote.

Instead of claiming that obscenity was unprotected speech, Brennan opted to declare that obscenity was not speech at all. That avoided the problem of showing the harmful effect of the materials on society. But that approach still left open the question of what materials qualified as obscene and thus outside the constitutional zone of protection. Brennan's approach provided little clarity. After noting that "sex and obscenity are not synonymous," Brennan wrote, "obscene material is material which deals with sex in a manner appealing to prurient interest." Brennan's clerks were not sure what he meant when he suggested using the term "prurient interest." Brennan told his clerks to check the dictionary. When they reported back finding the definition "to itch," Brennan smiled mischievously and said, "That's precisely right. If you had an itch you had to scratch it and that was prurient interest."

His clerks wrote up a lengthy footnote that cataloged all the definitions of "prurient," including the one in Webster's *New International Dictionary*, which listed "itching" along with "uneasy with desire or longing." In determining what appealed to the prurient interest, Brennan rejected the *Hicklin* test's emphasis on what impact materials had on the most susceptible persons and selected excerpts. Instead, Brennan set forth as the standard "whether, to the average person, applying contemporary community standards, the dominant theme of the material, taken as a whole, appeals to prurient interest." Under that test, Brennan upheld Roth's conviction along with the conviction of the operator of a Los Angeles mail-order business in a companion case involving a California state law.

Brennan had offered, as Warren wanted, at least a temporary solution for the tricky obscenity problem. But the range of opinions offered by his fellow justices augured the trouble ahead. Brennan attracted four of the Court's most conservative members: Frankfurter, Burton, Clark, and Whittaker. Warren concurred only in the result; he thought the opinion went unnecessarily far in loosening the law of obscenity. The chief justice would have focused more narrowly on the defendants' conduct. "They were plainly engaged in the commercial exploitation of the morbid and shameful craving for materials with prurient effect," Warren wrote. Harlan concurred with the majority in the state case but dissented in *Roth*, which he said would "result in a loosening of the tight reins which state and federal courts hold upon the enforcement of obscenity statutes."

Black and Douglas adhered to their absolutist position, rejecting any restrictions on freedom of speech. "I do not think we can approve that standard and be faithful to the command of the First Amendment," Douglas wrote. The press sided with Black and Douglas when the decision was announced in June 1957. Newspaper accounts emphasized that the Court had for the first time ever upheld the right of government officials to ban obscene materials. A *Washington Post* editorial warned of the danger "when legislators and judges conclude that the normal citizen has need of governmental intervention 'to save himself from his own impulses and protect himself from his own ideas.'" In fact, *Roth* soon proved to be the vehicle for easing the nation's obscenity laws.

JUNE 3, 1957, began like any other decision day at the Court. The justices took their seats promptly at noon. Scores of lawyers were introduced, welcomed by the chief justice, and sworn into practice before the Court. As Whittaker read a decision in a minor case, Brennan sat back in his chair and looked fixedly over the heads of spectators toward the frieze on the opposite wall depicting the struggle between good and evil. It was not until

1:30 P.M. that Brennan's turn finally came to announce the first of two major decisions that day which would finally lay bare to the public his leanings as a justice.

The audience perked up noticeably as Brennan identified the first decision he would announce: *United States of America, Appellant v. E. I. du Pont de Nemours and Company et al.* Over the course of the next twenty minutes, Brennan read aloud from his decision for the Court holding that DuPont had violated antitrust laws with its purchase of General Motors stock and returning the case to the District Court to determine an appropriate remedy. "We hold that any acquisition of one corporation of any part of the stock of another corporation, competitor or not, is within the reach of the section whenever the reasonable likelihood appears that the acquisition will result in a restraint or in the creation of a monopoly of any line of commerce."

Harlan looked on from the other end of the bench with dismay. Having represented members of the du Pont family at the seven-month trial, which produced a voluminous 8,283-page transcript, he had as a justice recused himself from the case. Only now did he finally feel free to vent his frustration over the outcome. As Brennan spoke, Harlan wrote Frankfurter a note that read, "Now that my lips are no longer sealed, if there was a more superficial understanding of a really impressive record than Bill's opinion in *du Pont* — I would like to see it. I hardly recognize the case as I listen to him speak."

Frankfurter was so worried that morning about the decision's potential impact on the financial markets, he had suggested to Warren that they hold off announcing it until after the New York Stock Exchange closed for the night. The markets did not tumble after the decision was announced that afternoon, but Wall Street did not like what it heard. "Justice Brennan's opinion introduced new uncertainties into the law and placed virtually every large company under a cloud of suspicion," declared *Fortune,* which called the decision "basically an anti–big business law."

After dispensing with *du Pont,* Brennan announced the opinion of the Court in another case that, much to the justices' surprise, proved even more controversial. Clinton Jencks was president of a New Mexico local union charged in 1953 with falsely filing an affidavit swearing he was not a Communist. His conviction depended largely on the testimony of two paid FBI informers, one of whom had confessed to lying and fabricating information and would begin serving a five-year prison sentence the same month Brennan announced the Court's decision. At issue in Jencks's appeal was whether the trial judge correctly refused to require the government to produce the reports detailing what the informants had said. The Court had taken up the case on Brennan's second day on the bench in October.

The case reminded Brennan of the *State v. Tune* case he had heard back in New Jersey, in which a defendant in a Newark murder trial was denied access to his own confession and witness statements. He viewed *Jencks* through the same prism. For Brennan, the only issue was whether a judge should have access to a witness's prior statements to government agents in order to prove the witness had previously given a different account. While Jencks's lawyers only sought review of the testimony by the judge in the case, both Warren and Brennan went further, arguing that his lawyers should be able to review testimony too. Warren assigned the case to Brennan, who took the lead in discussions of the case at several conferences throughout the term.

Justice Clark, who as Truman's attorney general had initiated prosecutions of the leaders of the Communist Party, had made clear his misgivings about Brennan's approach from the start. The fifty-seven-year-old Texan told his fellow justices at their initial October conference about the case that it would be a "big mistake to open up FBI records on the showing here." He presented a twenty-two-page memo in which he proposed providing FBI reports only where the defense could prove the existence of documents and statements that contradicted testimony in a material way. Clark's anger only grew as his warnings went unheeded. After Brennan announced the decision for the Court from the bench, Clark, sitting next to him, vented his concerns publicly. "Unless the Congress changes the rule announced by the Court today," he warned in his Texas drawl, "those intelligence agencies of our Government engaged in law enforcement may as well close up shop, for the Court has opened their files to the criminal and thus afforded him a Roman holiday for rummaging through confidential information as well as vital national secrets."

Clark had lit a fuse on the still-potent Red Scare powder keg. Brennan and his fellow justices did not appreciate just how explosive such a charge remained. Just as the anti-Communist hysteria Joseph McCarthy stoked predated his rise in 1950, it had now survived his death, a month earlier, in May 1957. The public reaction against Brennan's *Jencks* decision was swift and overwhelmingly negative. Within a day, members of Congress introduced eleven different bills aimed at thwarting it. New Hampshire's attorney general warned that the decision set the nation's war against subversives back twenty-five years. Press coverage was equally alarmist; a typical cartoon in the *Fort Wayne News Sentinel* portrayed the justices digging an escape route for Communist prisoners.

As the term wound down, the *Jencks* and *du Pont* decisions prompted many journalists to rethink their predictions of the previous fall about Brennan's likely middle-of-the-road approach. A new consensus quickly formed among the Washington press corps that Brennan had aligned himself with the Court's liberals. Four days after the *Jencks* decision, the *Wall Street Journal* had this to say: "Liberal leanings show up more and more in Eisenhower's Supreme Court. Warren lines up closely with Black and Douglas on the liberal side. Brennan promises to make it a foursome." *Time* even came up with a nickname for the new bloc: "B.B.D. & W." — a play on the name of a well-known advertising agency. *Life* magazine declared in a July 1 spread on the Warren Court that "as much as any other member, Brennan has made possible the liberal domination of the Warren Court." *Life* scolded Brennan and his fellow justices, declaring, "The Court could have avoided much of this criticism by practicing more 'judicial restraint,' i.e., agreeing whenever possible with the precedents, with Congress and with the lower courts."

Frankfurter, disgusted by what he viewed as the new foursome's willingness to interpret the Constitution according to their whims, started calling them "the framers." His friend, the aging Judge Hand, had a more derisive nickname: the "Jesus Quartet." The direction of the Supreme Court troubled another much younger judge named Warren Burger, who had joined the U.S. Court of Appeals for the D.C. Circuit in April 1956. On July 11, the forty-nine-year-old judge sent a note to his fellow lawyer and childhood friend back in Minnesota, Harry Blackmun. "I have been depressed by the seeming irresponsibility of the Supreme Court," Burger wrote. "They seem to have thrown away all caution [and] restraint . . . and in badly done opinions at that."

The backlash against the *Jencks* decision only seemed to grow as the term drew to a close. The Court further fueled public outrage with four additional subversion decisions released two weeks later. In each of the four cases, the Court ruled against the government's anti-Communist investigations, leading critics to dub the day "Red Monday." Then, to top off the term, Brennan wrote an opinion requiring the United States to turn over to Japan an American serviceman who had killed a Japanese woman while trying to scare her off a U.S. military range in Japan. Having heard a dozen domestic-security cases that term, the justices had sided with the suspected Communists in every one. The Court, many feared, was putting the rights of America's past and current enemies over the nation's security.

Animus toward the Court — particularly in the South — had been building ever since the *Brown* school-desegregation decision three years earlier. In February 1957 the Georgia legislature overwhelmingly passed a resolution calling for Warren's impeachment. But now it was not just southerners denouncing the Court. Segregationists and ardent anti-Communists had discovered a common enemy. In July, Senator William Jenner of Indiana took to the Senate floor complaining, "We've witnessed today the spectacle of a court constantly changing the law, even changing the meaning of the Constitution." But most of the anger that summer — including inside the White House — was directed at the *Jencks* decision. On June 16, radio commentator Fulton Lewis Jr. reported that Attorney General Brownell was in a "Vesuvian eruption" over the case. "His burn — and that of the Justice Department generally — is that the key figure in the ruling was his own appointee, Justice William Brennan Jr., who not only wrote the decision but provided the majority by which a 160-year court practice was overturned, threatening havoc to the FBI."

Brennan had not helped his cause with an opinion that failed to explain fully what portions of FBI reports should be given to defendants, who should make that determination, and when such information could be obtained. By the end of the month, the White House was urging Congress to adopt legislation that would limit the release of full FBI reports. All summer, competing bills made their way through Congress until President Eisenhower signed into law, on September 2, 1957, modest prohibitions on such disclosures.

Brennan was absolutely stunned by the controversy generated by his opinion in what he viewed as a straightforward criminal-procedure case. He could not escape the backlash even in Rumson, where he returned for the summer with his family. Brennan and Marjorie had sold their home shortly after his Senate confirmation and rented for the summer the same apartment above a neighbor's garage on Conover Lane where they had lived briefly when they first moved to Rumson. Hugh and Roxey had remained in New Jersey. Residents stopped Brennan in the local post office to question him about the decision. A one-man protest greeted Brennan and Marjorie when they arrived that July at a Red Bank hotel for a Kiwanis Club ceremony honoring him as the "Outstanding Citizen of 1956." James Bertie, a thirty-three-year-old Korean War veteran, held a sign that read, "Impeach Justice Brennan." Bertie told a local reporter that Brennan's *Jencks* decision was "playing into the hands of the Communists."

Brennan's own mother, Agnes, had second-guessed him for the first — and only — time in his tenure as a judge. "I don't understand, dear," Brennan recalled his mother telling him. "I never had any difficulty being proud of your opinions on the New Jersey Supreme Court. But how could you do this?" Brennan remembered the conversation as taking place over the telephone during one of their weekly Sunday calls; his sisters would recall that it occurred at Agnes's birthday party that summer, at the home of his brother Frank. Either way, this criticism by his mother stung far more than that from any other source. Brennan was always particularly eager to share his achievements with Agnes. One week after joining the Court, Brennan wrote her a letter on his new official letterhead, ending, "How do you like the stationery?"

The furor seemed to rattle the freshman justice. He wrote Frankfurter in August to "confess to considerable concern" for being "the instrument (+ in my first year!) for demeaning the standing of the court." After receiving Brennan's contrite note, Frankfurter wrote back reassuringly, "The past is irremediable; the future of the Court is our keeping," and advised Brennan that "self searching honesty and candor will guide you." But was Brennan genuinely second-guessing his opinion, or merely offering the ritualistic contrition he thought his senior colleague expected? His clerk Richard Rhodes concluded that the experience had actually hardened Brennan. Events soon supported Rhodes's theory. While other justices — particularly Frankfurter — emerged from the summer gun-shy about voting against the government in future subversion cases, Brennan did not. And looking back, Brennan grew only more unrepentant about the case. He blamed the "yellow press" — including the Hearst newspapers and conservative commentators like Fulton Lewis — for suggesting "the Commies had open season on the files of the FBI."

Regardless of what, if anything, Brennan regretted about the decision, he learned a valuable lesson about the delicate political environment in which the Court operated. "Believe me, there's a difference in the climate between Trenton and Washington," he told a college audience a few years later. "The winds of criticism and controversy that swirl around the court in Washington are generally of a higher velocity than those blowing in state capitals — and the temperature is hotter."

· 6 ·

COLD WAR

B RENNAN'S LIFE IN Washington settled into a comfortable routine during his second term on the Court. In October 1957 he
and his family moved out of their apartment and into a home on
Dumbarton Avenue in the increasingly tony neighborhood of Georgetown. The Victorian house, set back on a small hill and shielded by ivy-
covered walls and a white picket fence, stood out even on this short quiet
street, which included some of the oldest and prettiest homes in Georgetown. Brennan could not afford to buy here. Instead, he rented half of
the home from its resident owner, Richard Harkness, a local television
news anchor. His neighbors on this cobblestone and tree-lined stretch of
Dumbarton, dubbed "columnists' row," included two of Washington's most
famous newspaper writers of the time — Joseph Alsop and Drew Pearson
— as well as Felix Frankfurter, who lived almost directly across the street.
Justice Harlan lived just a couple of blocks away, as did the junior senator
from Massachusetts, John F. Kennedy.

Every morning, Brennan woke up without an alarm before 6 A.M., put
on some old clothes and a bulky sweater, went down the two flights of
stairs in front of the house, and set out on his morning walk. His doctor
had diagnosed Brennan with a potential heart problem earlier in the year
and ordered him to shave some weight off his 167-pound frame. As the

doctor suggested, Brennan walked the streets of Georgetown at a brisk pace, usually by himself, stopping only to chat briefly with the newspaper deliveryman. Sometimes his law clerks or those of other justices who lived in the neighborhood would join him. The routine was interrupted one morning when two Washington police officers stopped Brennan, accompanied by his son Bill, who was home on leave from the Marines, as they walked on the grounds of the Georgetown Visitation Preparatory School. Thinking the men were attempting to break into the school, the police only grew more suspicious when the two unshaven figures were unable to produce identification. The officers did not believe Brennan when he identified himself as a Supreme Court justice and his son as a Marine first lieutenant, and decided to take them in for questioning. On the way to the station house, Brennan suggested that they first stop at his house on Dumbarton Avenue so he could provide identification.

When Marjorie answered the door, she quickly sized up the situation. "Lady, these two claim that they belong to you," one of the officers said.

"Never saw them before in my life," Marjorie deadpanned.

"Mommy," Brennan said, using his pet name for her, "this is serious."

"OK," she said. "That's my husband, that's my son."

"What does your husband do?" the worried police officer now asked.

"He's a judge," she responded.

"On what court?" the officer asked.

"The United States Supreme Court," Marjorie replied.

"Oh my God," the officer replied, realizing the magnitude of his error.

Brennan expressed no hard feelings. In fact, he invited the officers in for breakfast. He made them eggs, just as he did most mornings for Marjorie and Nancy before sitting down to read the *New York Times* and *Washington Post*. His early-morning newspaper reading put pressure on his clerks, with whom Brennan regularly engaged in a discussion of the day's headlines on their morning commute to the Court. On this particular morning, playing host to the police officers, Brennan may not have gotten his usual reading done.

Brennan had given up driving himself to work. He wanted Marjorie to have their car during the day, and he had not had much luck with driving since arriving in Washington anyway. In March, a city bus had bashed into the rear of his new car on a rainy morning when Brennan was stopped at a traffic light. Brennan assured the anxious bus driver, "Don't worry about this thing. It happens every time there's a rain and it's nobody's fault at all." The incident would have gone unnoticed if not for the fact that the *St. Louis Post Dispatch*'s Supreme Court reporter was on the bus. He wrote a short article about the accident that was picked up nationally — and didn't hurt Brennan's reputation for geniality. Brennan's clerks worked well as chauffeurs in his second term until the day Daniel O'Hern, a Harvard Law School graduate selected by Professor Freund, forgot to fill up the tank of his 1951 Oldsmobile and they wound up running out of gas not far from the White House on Pennsylvania Avenue.

When Brennan arrived at work on the morning he had breakfasted with the police officers, sitting in his chambers once again at the secretary's desk was Mary Fowler. Brennan's ailing secretary from New Jersey, Alice Connell, had died of a heart attack in July in her small apartment in the Methodist Building, just across the street from the Court. Mary took the job despite her misgivings about the pace. Marjorie, intervening on her husband's behalf, had beseeched her to do it and Frankfurter, whom Fowler had known for years, had convinced her it was the right thing to do. Brennan was most grateful, writing Frankfurter, "I sincerely appreciate your help in getting Mary Fowler to decide to join me. It will be a great thing for me in a relationship which means so much for our work."

IN CONTRAST TO his fixed morning routine, Brennan had not yet hit a stable rhythm on the Court. It was during his second term that he made what he considered the biggest mistake of his entire tenure. He voted to uphold the government's decision to strip the citizenship of a Texas man who had voted in a Mexican election. The case, *Perez v. Brownell,* was one in a pair of so-called denaturalization cases taken up by the Court that term. At issue were two provisions of the Nationality Act of 1940, which made voting in a foreign election or deserting the military grounds for stripping an American's citizenship. In *Trop v. Dulles,* the appellant had been refused a passport on the grounds that he had been convicted of deserting the military during wartime. The Court had first considered the cases the previous term. Brennan initially had sided with Warren, who argued that citizenship was an absolute fundamental right granted by the Fourteenth Amendment that only a citizen himself could renounce. Frankfurter urged the Court to defer to Congress's authority to regulate foreign affairs and war. But the case was held over for the 1957 term, giving Brennan time to rethink his position.

When the justices discussed the case again, Brennan changed his vote to affirm Perez's denaturalization, although he still voted to reverse Trop's. That decision cost Warren his majority in *Perez*. Brennan later credited Frankfurter with changing his mind. Frankfurter stopped by his chambers and talked at length about how foolish Congress was in enacting the statute, but insisted there was nothing in the Constitution prohibiting Congress from "making a damn fool of itself." Rather, Frankfurter argued, the justices should concern themselves only with the statute's constitutionality. Brennan explained his decision in a March 21, 1958, note to Frankfurter by saying Perez's expatriation "is reasonably calculated to effect the ends which Congress seeks to achieve, namely the avoidance of embarrassment to our foreign affairs by the voting of American citizens in foreign elections."

Brennan's explanation in a concurring opinion for why he voted against Perez but not Trop satisfied few readers. One law professor wrote that it reminded him of Mark Twain's line, "The more you explain it, the more I don't understand it." Brennan soon regretted his decision in the case, which he later described as "just dead wrong" — highly unusual for a judge who rarely second-guessed himself. He would repudiate his view in the case when the denaturalization issue came before the Court a few terms later in 1963. "Congress is constitutionally debarred from so employing the drastic, the truly terrifying remedy of expatriation, certainly where no attempt has been made to apply the full panoply of protective safeguards which the Constitution requires as a condition of imposing penal sanctions," Brennan wrote in a concurring opinion in that subsequent case.

If the *Perez* case suggested that Brennan was still feeling his way, another case that term showed him employing some of the successful tactics he would use in coming years to build majorities on the Court. *Speiser v. Randall* involved a California statute that required any veteran who wanted to qualify for a special property-tax exemption to declare that he did not advocate overthrowing the government by force or violence or support a foreign government against the United States in time of hostilities. The Court was badly divided over the case, which Brennan was assigned.

To attract as much support as possible, Brennan opted to take a narrow approach. He avoided the broader constitutional question of whether a state could impose such a test as a condition for obtaining a tax exemption, assuming that it had the power to do so. Instead, Brennan focused on the manner in which California had regulated speech with this provision and wrote an opinion knocking down the law on procedural grounds. Brennan argued that the law improperly put the burden of proof on taxpayers to show they had not engaged in the prohibited forms of advocacy. As a result, Brennan argued, the requirement appeared to penalize people who did nothing more than hold certain opinions and created too great a danger of chilling lawful speech. This sort of focus on the potentially deleterious impact of legislation on legitimate speech would be central to Brennan's First Amendment jurisprudence.

Even this narrow approach did not guarantee Brennan a majority, and he looked to shore up support wherever he could find it. One of Brennan's clerks returned to the justice's chambers after lunch one day and recounted a conversation with Norman Dorsen, a Harlan clerk, who had expressed doubts about Brennan's *Speiser* approach and suggested he would advise his boss not to join the opinion. Not long after, Dorsen received a phone call from Brennan's clerk, who said Brennan wanted to speak with him. Dorsen rushed to Brennan's chambers and was immediately ushered into his office. Brennan got up from his desk and sat beside Dorsen on the couch. "He made me feel as if he had all the time in the world to talk to me about this," Dorsen recalled years later. "Looking back I realize that Brennan was obviously, although graciously, providing me with ammunition and arguments that could be used to induce Harlan to join Brennan's opinion." Harlan did ultimately join Brennan's opinion, but Brennan did not persuade Black and Douglas, who concurred in the result and wanted to address the broader constitutional question. They argued that California did not have the power to penalize beliefs, no matter how abhorrent they might be.

There was little to suggest at the time that Brennan's opinion in *Speiser* would become a building block in the rights revolution that lay ahead. Commentators later pointed to Brennan's use of the Fourteenth Amendment's due process clause in *Speiser* as a novel and significant way of expanding individual rights. Brennan said the Court had to examine not only the underlying constitutional right — free speech, for example — but also whether a state imposed an unfair burden through the procedures by which it regulated. He also raised the notion that a state cannot condition the receipt of public benefits on a requirement that an individual sacrifice a constitutional right; this idea came to be known as a doctrine of unconstitutional conditions. Brennan would use the *Speiser* due process approach in a host of constitutional areas, from free exercise of religion to free speech to the right of defendants to the fairness entitled welfare recipients.

Notwithstanding *Speiser,* the "B.B.D. & W." alliance continued to hold, particularly in criminal procedure and civil liberties cases. Brennan, by 1958, had established himself, in the eyes of one political scientist analyzing his early performance that year, as a fourth justice with "a passionate concern with the rights of persons accused of crimes" who "shows no inclination to subordinate the individual's right to speak freely on public questions to society's right to protect itself from 'dangerous ideas.'" Douglas was impressed enough by Brennan by 1957 to praise his "courage and independence" in a letter to a Yale Law School professor who wrote an article suggesting Brennan would simply mimic Frankfurter. "I would be willing to give odds that he will leave as fine a record on this Court as Holmes, Hughes, Murphy or any of the great," Douglas wrote. Yet without a consistent fifth vote, this foursome usually remained in the minority.

And Brennan stood on the "fringes of the bloc," winding up on the opposite side from Black and/or Douglas in 20 percent of cases. Brennan remained somewhat less willing than Black, Douglas, or Warren to support civil liberties claims and economic underdogs. Even when he voted with the bloc, Brennan was more apt to write his own opinions or join Warren's than to sign on to dissents by Douglas and Black. As in the *Speiser* case, Brennan preferred to base decisions on narrow grounds.

Brennan broke with his allies frequently enough that at the end of the term, *Life* would observe, "Justice Brennan has seemed to lean [toward Frankfurter] of late." So even as Frankfurter derisively referred to them as "the Four" when he scribbled notes on his conference list in March 1958, he had not entirely given up on his former student. "I wish he were less shallow and thereby less cocksure but his honesty cheers me much and gives me considerable hope," Frankfurter wrote Harlan. Frankfurter even joked about their differences of opinion in a January 2, 1958, handwritten note to Brennan. "Even Christmas cheer did not stir in me the thought — or hope — that you would agree with my [opinion], much as it would please me if you did," Frankfurter wrote.

Similarly, Brennan still talked warmly about Frankfurter to his clerks and continued to laugh off the older man's professorial tone during frequent visits. There were still signs of easy rapport and occasional humor in Brennan's correspondence with Frankfurter about cases. And when Brennan rose to speak at Frankfurter's seventy-fifth birthday party in November 1957, he offered a gushing — although perhaps a bit odd — toast for the Court's only Jewish justice.

Brennan told the story of a man in purgatory who wanted to work his way to heaven. Saint Peter gave the man the task of removing a mountain with a shovel. It took him two thousand years to remove the mountain, after which he again stood before Saint Peter. This time Saint Peter directed the man to empty a nearby lake with a teaspoon. It took the man five thousand years to empty the lake, at which time he again presented himself to Saint Peter. This time Saint Peter told the man to go out and find another individual like Felix Frankfurter. The man set out to accomplish this latest task. "He's been gone thirty thousand years," Brennan concluded, "and he hasn't come back yet."

BY THE SPRING of 1958, President Eisenhower was clearly disappointed with the direction of the Court he had so strongly molded with four appointments over five years. "I get more confused every time the Court delivers another opinion," Eisenhower confided in a May 12 letter to William Rogers, who had succeeded Herbert Brownell as attorney general. Reporters and academics seemed to take a certain glee in pointing out the Court's unexpected change of course. Political science professor Daniel Berman wrote, "This capital, which boasts many strange sights, has another paradox to exhibit today: The spectacle of a Republican President unwittingly restoring the liberal balance of a Supreme Court which had been pushed to the Right by his Democratic predecessors."

Eisenhower did not hide his feelings when Justice Harold Burton came to the White House that July with a resignation letter effective October 13. Parkinson's disease had left Burton increasingly frail but he had held out until he became eligible for a full pension. Burton, the only Republican appointed by either Roosevelt or Truman, noted in his diary that Eisenhower "expressed disappointment at the trend of decisions of Chief Justice and Justice Brennan." Eisenhower then turned to Rogers and told him to be more careful in choosing a nominee to replace Burton. What is less certain is whether, when asked if he had made any mistakes as president, Eisen-hower actually uttered the oft-quoted phrase, "Yes: two. And they are both sitting on the Supreme Court." The witty one-liner took on a life of its own among journalists after respected University of Virginia political scientist Henry Abraham included it in his book on Supreme Court appointments, *Justices and Presidents*. Abraham attributed the statement to another book, Elmo Richardson's 1979 biography of Eisenhower. However, Richardson's book explains that the line was part of a conversation between Eisenhower and Republican leader Ralph Cake. A transcript of that conversation shows that Eisenhower did not use those words in reference to Warren and Bren-nan at all. Rogers and Brownell both later insisted that Eisenhower would not have said such a thing, no matter how disappointed he was about some of Warren's and Brennan's decisions. Nor has the Eisenhower Presidential Library ever found the precise statement in the president's papers.

Fred Friendly, the legendary CBS News producer, recalled Eisenhower uttering the line to him and Walter Cronkite, the network's correspondent and future anchor, in May 1961. The two newsmen were sharing lunch with Eisenhower at Gettysburg College, where the retired president maintained an office, before taping an interview. Since the CBS cameras were not yet rolling, the only account of what followed is what Friendly remembered nearly three decades later.

"You know, Mr. President," Friendly said as he made conversation over their turkey sandwiches, "one of the things your administration will be re-membered for is the appointment of Earl Warren."

"I'm surprised to hear you say that," Eisenhower replied. "That was the worst mistake I've ever made."

"Are you saying that's one of the mistakes you made as president?" Friendly asked.

To which Eisenhower put up two fingers and said, "Two. They're both sitting on the Supreme Court: Earl Warren and William Brennan. Bren-nan's just as bad. Those two are very important jobs and I didn't do a very good job with them."

ON THE MORNING of August 25, 1958, President Eisenhower's two al-leged mistakes were sharing a stage in Los Angeles Philharmonic Hall. Brennan looked on from the platform as Chief Justice Warren delivered the opening address at the American Bar Association's annual conference to a standing-room-only crowd. The warm welcome for California's favorite son five years after he had left for Washington contrasted with his experience at the ABA's meeting the previous year in London. Warren had angrily canceled his membership after an ABA committee presented a report criticizing the Court's subversion decisions and endorsed legislation limiting its jurisdiction. This time, there was nothing but applause as Warren warned the crowd of twenty-seven hundred lawyers and their families about the dangers of unjustifiable court delays.

A few hours later, Brennan took up the cause of court efficiency during a lunchtime speech at the Biltmore Bowl, a downtown Los Angeles hotel ballroom that had frequently hosted the Academy Awards ceremony. Warren, who was joined at the head table by FBI director J. Edgar Hoover and Attorney General Rogers, listened as Brennan warned the crowd that the nation's courts needed to adopt modern business procedures to meet the needs of modern society. For one day, it was as if Brennan were back on the stump on behalf of judicial efficiency in New Jersey, with Warren replacing Arthur Vanderbilt.

Brennan and Warren had arrived in California a week earlier, for the opening of the San Francisco Bar Association's meeting on August 18. They mingled in business suits poolside at the Menlo Circus Club among the Bay Area's legal elite, which was about two hundred and fifty miles from where Warren grew up in the dusty town of Bakersfield. Warren still considered California home and usually returned there for at least part of each summer. It was the site of his biggest political triumphs, and also of one episode he did not like to talk about much anymore — his role as state attorney general in helping remove and intern Japanese Americans living on the West Coast during World War II.

Now, Warren was sharing his home state with Brennan, enjoying the most time they had ever spent together outside the Court. They were so friendly by now that Brennan would begin letters to Warren by writing, "My Dear Chief." Except for the Redskins games, though, their friendship rarely extended beyond the Court. Brennan never joined Warren on his hunting or fishing trips, as Justice Clark did. And Brennan always referred to Warren as "Chief" whether they were at the Court, a football game, or traveling together in California. "There has to be a distance between yourself and the Chief Justice," Brennan insisted.

Brennan was no stranger to California, having served there for more than a year during the war. On this return trip, he strung together a vacation with Marjorie and Nancy in between official events. Over the weekend, they had visited Bill, now stationed with the Marines in California. Bill finagled a tour of the aircraft carrier *Yorktown* for his much younger sister, and the family watched the Marine Band raise the flag at El Toro Air Station. Brennan planned to continue his family's California tour later in the week with stops at Stanford University and a conference of the judges of the U.S. Court of Appeals for the Ninth Circuit. But when he arrived in Los Angeles on August 25 for his joint appearance with Warren at Philharmonic Hall, he discovered he would have to cut short this California sojourn. Shortly before taking the stage, Warren had announced that the Court would hold a rare special session later that week to take up the biggest challenge yet to its *Brown v. Board of Education* decision declaring segregated schools unconstitutional. The Court would decide whether the school board in Little Rock, Arkansas, could delay desegregation in the face of local resistance.

Southern defiance had long since dashed blacks' high hopes for rapid progress that followed the Court's *Brown* decision four years earlier. Four states banned public-school desegregation. Politicians throughout the South embraced a pre–Civil War notion of states' rights, arguing that they could interpose the sovereignty of the state between local schools and federal courts. Grassroots Citizens' Councils of America seemed to spring up in every southern town to organize resistance locally. Rioters successfully blocked a federal order desegregating the University of Alabama in February 1956. In March 1956, 101 southern members of Congress signed a "Southern Manifesto," reaffirming their opposition to integration and accusing the Supreme Court of a "clear abuse of judicial power."

The Court itself seemed to put the brakes on rapid school desegregation when it finally announced the remedy in the *Brown* case for school desegregation a year after its initial decision. Instead of intervening with forceful desegregation guidelines, the Court in its *Brown II* decision left it to southern states and localities to proceed to "full compliance" with "all deliberate speed." Neither had Congress nor President Eisenhower shown much enthusiasm for prodding the South. Eisenhower never endorsed the *Brown* decision during his tenure, and as late as July 1957 he publicly stated that he could not imagine a circumstance where he would deploy federal troops to enforce a school-desegregation order.

Two months later, though, Eisenhower reluctantly deployed paratroopers from the Army's 101st Airborne Division to escort nine black teenagers into Little Rock's Central High School. This state capital had become a surprising symbol of southern resistance. Blacks had enrolled in Arkansas' public colleges without incident, and ten school districts had announced plans for gradual desegregation by the end of 1955. Little Rock had a lower percentage of black students than Baltimore, Louisville, or Washington, D.C., which had all desegregated their schools without much trouble. But the process did not go as smoothly in Little Rock, where everyone from the school superintendent to the mayor bungled preparations for desegregation set to begin in September 1957.

Governor Orval Faubus took up the cause of states' rights with newfound fervor in the summer of 1957. One day before the first African American students were set to begin attending Central High School, Faubus announced in a television address that it would "not be possible to restore or maintain order if forcible integration is carried out tomorrow." Faubus surrounded the school with National Guard troops, who kept the black students out until he withdrew the soldiers three weeks later without warning. The nine black teenagers who finally entered the school had little to protect them against the mobs of angry whites outside. When the black students slipped away, the mob turned its fury on out-of-town reporters.

The violence prompted Eisenhower to federalize the National Guard and dispatch Army paratroopers to restore order. The federal troops with their fixed bayonets did not stay long and did little to check the months of harassment and abuse these black students were subjected to inside the school's halls and classrooms. In February 1958 the Little Rock School Board and superintendent petitioned a federal district court to delay desegregation for two and a half years. A district court judge granted the request. The U.S. Court of Appeals for the Eighth Circuit reversed on August 18, 1958, but stayed its order pending Supreme Court review.

As Brennan and his family visited Bill on August 22, the NAACP Legal Defense and Educational Fund (LDF), created in 1940 as the legal arm of the National Association for the Advancement of Colored People, petitioned the Court for an order removing all barriers preventing black students from returning to Central High. After consulting with the three other justices in California and several others by telephone, Warren announced that the Court would hold a special session scheduled for three days later. On Tuesday, Brennan and Warren boarded a plane on their way back to Washington along with Warren's wife and daughter. Nancy and Marjorie, who did not like airplane travel, trailed behind by train. As they sat next to each other on the plane, Brennan recalled turning to Warren and saying, "Well, Chief, do you want me to try to turn something out? I'll be glad to do it." By the time they arrived in Washington, where news photographers waited to snap their pictures inside the terminal, Warren had asked Brennan to prepare a memo as the basis for the Court's consideration of the case.

Brennan was not the only justice Warren sought out for advice as he prepared to take up the Little Rock case, *Cooper v. Aaron*. The chief justice met privately with both Black and Frankfurter the day he returned to Washington to discuss the delicate task ahead. Warren wanted to maintain the unanimity he had almost single-handedly achieved in *Brown* in the face of criticism, still intensifying, of the Court's decision there. Back in Washington, the Senate had voted by a slim majority to set aside Indiana Republican senator William Jenner's bill to limit the Court's jurisdiction, thanks to some last-minute maneuvering by Majority Leader Lyndon B. Johnson. And the Conference of Chief Justices meeting in Pasadena on the eve of the ABA convention had approved a thirty-six-page report condemning the Supreme Court for failing to use "the power of judicial self-restraint" and usurping states' rights.

In Arkansas, Governor Faubus kept up the pressure, convening a special session of the state legislature on August 26 to pass new laws empowering him to fight if the Supreme Court ruled in favor of immediate desegregation. The legislators rushed through bills to allow Faubus to close schools if integration was ordered and to transfer state funds to private, segregated schools. President Eisenhower offered the Court little help, stating at an August 27 press conference that he would like to see "slower movement" toward racial integration in schools. "Faubus's resistance, Eisenhower's posture, all of it created an atmosphere of historic crisis" at the Court, recalled Dennis Lyons, who had begun his clerkship in Justice Brennan's chambers just days earlier.

Such was the uncertain state of affairs as Brennan gathered with his fellow justices for an hourlong conference before taking the bench at noon on August 28. Most of the justices had rushed back to Washington. This included Justice Burton, who, having submitted his letter of resignation to

Eisenhower effective at the start of the new term in October, thought he had already heard his last case. Once the oral argument began, they heard the LDF's chief counsel, Thurgood Marshall, ask that the Court lift the stay granted by the Eighth Circuit. The fifty-year-old African American attorney, dressed in a tan business suit, spoke almost casually and with only an occasional glance at his notebook. It was the easy performance of a veteran who had already argued at least ten cases before the Court.

The grandson of a slave, Marshall had grown up on the edge of the Jim Crow South in middle-class Baltimore, where his father was a railroad car porter and his mother a teacher. Marshall knew he wanted to be a lawyer as a teenager, but did not bother applying to his home-state law school at the University of Maryland, which had not admitted blacks since the 1890s. He opted instead for Howard University, where he grew close to the demanding Harvard Law–educated dean, Charles Hamilton Houston.

As a novice lawyer, Marshall accompanied Houston on trips through the Deep South to tour dilapidated segregated schools, and they soon joined together to fight segregation on behalf of the LDF. Among the earliest targets they successfully desegregated was the University of Maryland's law school. Marshall was named the chief lawyer of the NAACP in 1938 at the age of thirty. There, he successfully challenged, piece by piece, the edifice of segregation. He knocked down teacher pay gaps, all-white primaries, and restrictive covenants, and found time in between to represent blacks accused of crimes in often hostile Deep South towns. Marshall narrowly escaped a Tennessee lynch mob and a firebomb in Montgomery during the bus boycott. The architect of the NAACP's court battle against racial segregation had become one of the most famous blacks in the country after arguing the *Brown* desegregation case before the Supreme Court, earning the nickname "Mr. Civil Rights."

Marshall had been in Little Rock the previous September, petitioning the federal court to go ahead with integration. And now, nearly a year later, he was still arguing the case. On this day, Marshall focused largely on a technical discussion of stays, but urged the Court to get to the underlying merits of postponing integration for two and a half years, which he said was completely "entwined" with the stay problem. He said the Court should not "surrender to obstructionists and mob action," arguing that when banks were robbed, "you don't close the banks — you put the bank robbers in jail." Solicitor General J. Lee Rankin, speaking on behalf of the United States Justice Department, also requested that the Court lift the stay. Richard C. Butler, who argued for delay on behalf of the Little Rock School Board, did himself no favors by citing in his Ozark drawl public opinion polls that showed a majority of the country favored postponing integration in Little Rock. Frankfurter retorted acidly, "I sometimes wonder why we have elections and do not turn it all over to the polls." After a ninety-minute recess, the justices returned to the courtroom at 5:10 P.M. Warren requested further briefs on the underlying question of delaying integration in advance of a second oral argument set for September 11.

When the Court reconvened two weeks later as scheduled, Marshall spoke once again, as did Butler, who argued for a "reasonable delay" in implementing Little Rock's desegregation plan. Brennan asked Butler, "How is this court in a position to allow or sanction or approve a delay sought on the ground that the responsible state officials, rather than be on the side of enforcement of these constitutional rights, have taken actions to frustrate their enforcement?" Butler said the school board was caught in a war between "two sovereignties" and that the conflict was "completely beyond the realm of this school board to solve."

There was little disagreement when the justices met after the three-and-a-half-hour oral argument. The conference quickly agreed with Warren's suggestion that they draft a decision to uphold the Court of Appeals and affirm the duty of state officials to obey the law as previously laid down by the Supreme Court. Frankfurter and Harlan agreed to draft a brief unsigned order on behalf of the full Court to be announced the next day. Brennan would draft the longer opinion of the Court to follow. The groundwork laid between Warren and Brennan on the plane ride back to Washington and in a private meeting the morning before the oral argument had helped him land the assignment. Warren, who had kept for himself the responsibility of building consensus in *Brown*, now delegated to Brennan the task of drafting an opinion that could maintain the unanimity. Brennan returned to his chambers and surprised both of his new clerks with news of his biggest assignment since joining the Court.

BRENNAN WAS SITTING on the porch of his Dumbarton Avenue home in September 1958, working on the Little Rock case, when his neighbor, Richard Harkness, came over to say hello. The two men and their wives had become friends in the year since Brennan moved to Washington. Harkness, a television journalist with the local NBC affiliate, had just returned from a reporting trip in the South that included a swing through Louisiana. Brennan gave no hint of what he was working on but listened closely as Harkness described how much the word "integration" riled up the people he interviewed in the South. Integration, Harkness explained, conjured up southern fears of interracial sex and marriage. The term "desegregation" "didn't bother them as much, didn't go so far," Brennan recalled him explaining. When it came time to write his first draft in the Little Rock case, it was the term "desegregation" that Brennan insisted on using.

Brennan could use all the help he could get to understand better both the South and race relations more generally. He had never lived farther south than Washington, and his only firsthand encounter with racial tensions came during the war, when he was called upon to help resolve a work stoppage caused by conflict between black and white workers at a munitions plant. Brennan had not had much exposure to blacks in his daily life. He had moved away from Newark for college long before the large African American influx began there, as did his mother and six surviving siblings, most of whom now lived in suburban New Jersey. Brennan had moved into Georgetown after rising home values and historic-preservation laws had driven most blacks out.

The few blacks employed at the Court worked in the most menial jobs, including as the justices' messengers, a relic of the era when the justices worked at home and needed to transmit documents among themselves. One quiet comment by Brennan to his clerk Dennis Lyons as the two walked through the Court's Great Hall one evening is revealing. Black maintenance workers were polishing the brass appointments and scrubbing the marble walls. "You know," Brennan said quietly, "I always wonder how these people take it as well as they do."

The one place where Brennan interacted with African Americans as equals was at the small Catholic church he chose to attend just a few blocks up Dumbarton Avenue. Epiphany Church was founded in 1923 as a breakaway parish by 357 African American Catholics fed up with being treated as second-class citizens inside Georgetown's Holy Trinity Church. They wanted their own church where they would not have to wait to receive

Communion until after the white parishioners or be relegated to a segregated gallery. Even as the neighborhood changed, Epiphany's black parishioners clung to this church they had worked so hard to build, where packing crates served as their first altar and their priest slept in the parish hall because they could not afford to rent him a proper home during the Depression. Brennan and his family sat in the pews as the city's first black Catholic pastor, Chester C. Ball, who had started at the church in 1952, led services at Epiphany.

BRENNAN AND HIS clerks spent a week preparing the first draft in the Little Rock case, which was bland by design. Brennan, particularly concerned about losing any of the southern justices, made achieving unanimity his top priority, even if the result was not necessarily stylish writing. Even when he wanted to produce it, writing lively prose did not come naturally to Brennan. He later admitted he sometimes found the process of writing opinions agonizing work. In the years ahead, he would earn a reputation among Supreme Court reporters for his willingness to sacrifice style in order to build consensus. The result, in the word of one journalist, was often "nearly colorless compromises." Brennan's clerks, Peter Fishbein and Dennis Lyons, took turns dictating the eighteen-page opinion to Mary Fowler, who typed it up for distribution to the other justices on September 17, after Warren had a chance to look it over.

No one reading Brennan's first draft would get any sense of the case's import. A pedestrian recitation of the case's development ate up half the opinion. Brennan had hoped to show how the Court had paid careful attention to following its usual procedures. Not until halfway through the opinion did he raise the question presented in the case, which he awkwardly stated as "whether the desegregation process in the Little Rock schools, actually commenced according to an approved plan, may be arrested because the orderly carrying out of the plan has been made difficult by actual and continued threatened mob violence and disorders occurring in a situation of stiffened hostility toward desegregation."

Brennan started from the proposition that *Brown* had held laws requiring racial segregation in public schools to be a denial of the guarantee of equal protection provided by the Fourteenth Amendment. Prior to *Brown*, the Court had read the equal protection clause as requiring equal treatment, not integration. In the infamous case of *Plessy v. Ferguson*, the Court in 1896 found that "separate but equal" streetcars provided sufficient equality. But in *Brown*, the Court said that separate but equal schools still made African American children feel inferior and deprived them of equal opportunity. Starting with *Brown*, the Court began to view decision making based on race with extreme suspicion, unless the purpose was to correct past discrimination.

In *Cooper*, Brennan cited a long list of Court precedents establishing the proposition that "every state legislator and executive and judicial officer is thus solemnly bound not to war against the Constitution" and to "obey its relevant commands as defined by this Court." That placed school authorities "under an immediate duty to formulate a plan promptly . . . to bring about complete desegregation of the public schools 'with all deliberate speed.'" He warned that "delay in any guise to avoid discharge of the constitutional duty to desegregate may not be recognized." The Little Rock School Board was entitled to no delay merely because it had acted in good faith or faced mob violence. "The enforcement of constitutional rights can never yield to such a challenge."

Other justices immediately jumped in with their own ideas. The problem was less what Brennan said but rather how he had presented it. Black suggested playing up the Court's unanimous historical precedents, as he had done repeatedly for other cases in the past. Both Black and Frankfurter also recommended adding a more dramatic ending that might highlight for the public the importance of the issue at stake. Brennan quickly realized after reviewing their feedback that this opinion would be written by committee and that he was more an editor than author. Brennan would later remember the Court's unanimity, rather than the misgivings of some of the other justices, concerning the opinion he had drafted. He never saw the draft dissent Clark wrote out in longhand on two pages of an ABA memo pad. Clark feared Brennan was going too far. "Under our constitution, there is no steerage," Clark wrote. "However, as I understand *Brown*, integration was not to be accomplished through push button action but rather through 'deliberate speed.'" By far the justice most dissatisfied with Brennan's draft was Harlan. Brennan had come to expect opposition from Harlan — who had dissented from his very first opinion — during Harlan's frequent visits to Brennan's chambers.

Such disagreements did not get in the way of the friendship born over a cigarette on the day Brennan had first met his colleagues in October 1956.

Brennan and Harlan had since bonded over rounds of golf and a surprisingly similar taste in jokes. Beneath his stiff patrician exterior, Harlan had a humorous side, and enjoyed teasing Brennan by invoking the language Brennan had quoted from a British judge in his *Roth* obscenity opinion. "So that's a sacred thing?" Harlan would ask Brennan as they considered the latest obscene material to reach the Court.

Here in the Little Rock case, Harlan first shared his concerns with Clark and Frankfurter, showing them an alternative draft he had written before circulating to Brennan on September 23 a shorter substitute for the last five pages of his opinion. Harlan suggested that the opinion note that, while the membership of the Court had changed since the *Brown* decision, all three new members of the Court — including both Harlan and Brennan — supported it. Brennan initially opposed that approach as a "grave mistake." Brennan argued it would lend support to the idea that "the Constitution only has the meaning that can command a majority as that majority may change with shifting membership." He added, "Whatever truth there may be in that idea, I think it would be fatal in this fight to provide ammunition from the mouth of this Court in support of it." But Brennan, ever the keen vote counter, relented in the interest of strong support. So too would he acquiesce when either Harlan or Frankfurter suggested the even more dramatic touch of having all nine justices sign their names to the opinion. Usually, only the author signed, but proponents argued that this was a way to emphasize that the Court spoke with one mind when it came to desegregation.

Brennan was more resistant to Harlan's proposal that they cut out his discussion of *Marbury v. Madison,* the landmark 1803 case in which Chief Justice Marshall had enunciated the principle of judicial review. Brennan equated the Court's interpretation of the Constitution's meaning with the words of the Constitution itself, by suggesting its decisions were "the supreme law of the land." That phrase would become the opinion's most enduring source of controversy, attacked by conservative critics of the Court for decades as evidence of excessive judicial hubris. Brennan rejected Harlan's suggestion that they omit the language, describing it as "a very essential part of what I believe our opinion should contain." He later insisted that expansive definition of judicial review was the only possible way to interpret the Court's decisions.

Black suggested the other significant revision after the justices discussed Brennan's third draft on September 24. Black sketched out in pencil and apparently off the top of his head a new and more dramatic opening for the opinion on three sheets of lined paper. He sharply focused the stakes for the Court and the country. "As this case reaches us it raises questions of the highest importance to the maintenance of our federal system of government," Black began. Brennan, once again avoiding proprietary ownership of his most important opinion yet, incorporated Black's suggestions almost verbatim into a more forceful fourth draft he circulated on September 25. Brennan finally won over Harlan after adopting nearly every change he suggested to this draft.

On September 29, Warren announced the Court's decision from the bench. He began by noting that all nine justices had jointly authored the opinion, a touch of drama that had its intended effect. "It became apparent, at the start of the reading," the *New York Times* observed the next day, "that this was more than an ordinary opinion." Warren looked at each of the justices present in turn as he read the opinion verbatim for forty-five minutes. Brennan was not responsible for the opinion's two most dramatic flourishes, the joint signatures and noting that the newest justices all agreed with *Brown,* but the basic approach and most of the language was his. Yet his central role was completely obscured by the justices' decision to sign the opinion as joint authors, and by the fact that Warren was the one to announce the decision from the bench. Few outside the Court would learn about Brennan's role in the case until two decades later. This would not be the last time that Brennan's central behind-the-scenes efforts in an important case were hidden from public view.

The Court's extraordinary display of unity, however, obscured simmering tensions among the justices. The spark was Frankfurter's announcement three days earlier at conference that he intended to write a concurring opinion in the case. Frankfurter's decision surprised his fellow justices, since he had long advocated maintaining the Court's unanimity in school-desegregation cases. The other justices pleaded with Frankfurter not to write separately, but he could not be persuaded.

Frankfurter believed he had held his tongue long enough, particularly with Brennan. He had been itching to lecture his former student ever since Brennan received the assignment to write the high-profile decision. "After sleeping on it, I have decided to curb my temperamental spontaneity and not talk to Bill Brennan," Frankfurter wrote Harlan the next day. "Cocksureness begets sensitiveness and as his erstwhile teacher, I have to be particularly careful with Bill. He was plainly displeased at the thought of my writing anything before I saw what he will produce, on the assumption that he will take care of all there is to be said. Therefore, I do not think I ought to tell him what I think should be the conception and temper of our opinion."

A frustrated Frankfurter believed that the Court was not doing enough to appeal to moderate southern lawyers. "These are not only men who can be won to desegregation on the merits but they ought to be won and I believe will be won to the transcending issue of the Supreme Court as the authoritative organ of what the Constitution requires," Frankfurter wrote Harlan on September 25. Frankfurter viewed himself as being in a "peculiarly qualified position to address" this audience given his "extensive association . . . with a good many Southern lawyers and law professors" while teaching at Harvard Law School.

Here, Frankfurter displayed the intellectual arrogance that so frequently alienated his colleagues. He naïvely assumed his long-ago associations in New England with a few southern lawyers gave him a full understanding of their home region. Frankfurter wildly overestimated the power of dispassionate reason and the potential influence of southern moderates in a region increasingly closing ranks since the *Brown* decision behind the idea of "massive resistance" to desegregation. He clung to the notion that "vindication of Brown will come not through Court decrees but by winning the minds of the leading influences" in the South. And he knew just who was to blame on the Court for not doing so. "Some of my brethren — particularly the Chief and Bill Brennan — are not only very imperceptive, but cockily so and have a poor limited understanding" of the region, he wrote Harlan. Frankfurter angrily rebuffed the other justices' attempts to get him to drop his concurrence, agreeing only to postpone announcement until after the opinion of the Court was read.

Frankfurter's decision to write separately angered the other justices, particularly Warren and Brennan, who had just spent weeks carefully trying to build unanimity. When Frankfurter circulated his concurrence on October 3, Brennan vented in the margins of the draft with a string of exclamation points and question marks. "Isn't this bound to be confusing to judges faced for the first time with applications against school boards?" Brennan scribbled in the margin. "As an interpretation by [an] author of the basic *Aaron* opinion, won't it be read as allowing them to take hostility into account?"

Brennan and Black threatened to release a competing statement if Frankfurter went forward. Brennan wrote out the text on a piece of scrap paper. "Mr. Justice Black and Mr. Justice Brennan believe that the joint opinion of all the justices handed down on September 29, 1958 adequately explains the views of the Court and they stand by that opinion as delivered. They desire that it be fully understood that the concurring opinion filed this day by Mr. Justice Frankfurter must not be accepted as any dilution or interpretation of the views expressed in the Court's joint opinion."

Harlan defused the standoff by passing around a mock opinion he had drafted, complete with the Court's regular typeface, which called for justices' names to be in full capitalization, and formatting. "I doubt the wisdom of my brother FRANKFURTER filing his separate opinion but since I am unable to find any material difference between that opinion and the Court's opinion — and I am confident on my reading of the former by my Brother FRANKFURTER's express reaffirmation of the latter — I am content to leave his course of action to his own good judgment. I dissent from the action of my other Brethren in filing their separate opinion believing that it is always a mistake to make a mountain of a molehill." Black and Brennan wisely followed Harlan's advice. Frankfurter released his concurring opinion without any public announcement from the bench on October 6. It merited a front-page story in the *New York Times,* which noted that "his words today seemed directed particularly at the moderate forces of the South." But his opinion was quickly forgotten, in contrast to what might have happened if Black and Brennan had released an opinion of their own in retribution.

FRANKFURTER'S PERFORMANCE DURING *Cooper v. Aaron* clearly angered Brennan. But it is wrong to conclude that this case — or any other — can be cited as the definitive turning point or rupture in their relationship. The breakdown happened gradually over the course of several years, and in fact never became as heated — even vicious — as Frankfurter's disagreements with other justices. Brennan, for his part, never publicly exploded at Frankfurter on the bench, as Warren did repeatedly, nor stormed out of the justices' private conference, as Douglas did when Frankfurter began his lengthy lectures. Douglas even threatened to stop going to conference entirely as long as Frankfurter remained on the Court, and took to calling him the "little bastard." Frankfurter, in turn, called Douglas "the most cynical shamelessly amoral character I've ever known." Nor would Brennan ever lunge at Frankfurter, as both Vinson and Black on at least one occasion did during conferences. That was just not Brennan's way, given how much he prided himself on getting along with his colleagues. "If he was unhappy with someone [his instinct] was avoidance rather than direct conflict," recalled Jeffrey Nagin, who clerked for Brennan during the 1959–60 term.

Still, Brennan's relationship with Frankfurter would follow the same trajectory as that of so many justices before him. Frankfurter grew disappointed with Brennan for failing to see things his way and showing continued signs of independence in his votes. Frankfurter had watched so many new justices slip away from his grasp despite his best efforts at persuasion. And now Frankfurter was faced with his former student and imagined heir's increasing alignment with Black, Douglas, and Warren. Frankfurter found himself on the opposite side from Brennan in a pair of high-profile subversion cases during the 1958–59 term. Frankfurter had largely sided with Brennan in favor of the targets of subversion investigations on Red Monday and in *Jencks*. But, more recently, he and Harlan had retreated and voted to uphold the government investigations. Not that Brennan always saw eye-to-eye with the other members of what Frankfurter saw as the enemy camp. He still was not always lining up identically with his allies, particularly in subversion and criminal-procedure cases. The *New York Times* noted that while Warren and Douglas "were consistently with Justice Black in dissent" that term, Brennan was with him only "frequently so." So differences over opinions alone did not explain the chill in relations with Frankfurter.

Brennan, like those before him, grew increasingly alienated by Frankfurter's heavy-handed interpersonal style. Brennan came to view Frankfurter's visits to his chambers and his courtships of his clerks as intrusive. Frankfurter's lectures at conference — which could last nearly as long as one of his fifty-minute classes back at Harvard Law School — became tedious. "We would be inclined to agree with Felix more often in conference if he quoted Holmes less frequently to us," Brennan once said. More and more, the meanness that lay just beneath Frankfurter's warm façade repelled Brennan. "He tried very hard to be a hale fellow well met but it was impossible," Brennan later said. "Some of his excessive intellect would leak out and he'd hurt people."

Brennan and his clerks thought Frankfurter's demeanor darkened after the seventy-six-year-old justice suffered a heart attack in November 1958. He no longer told jokes, and he lost the bounce in his step. Regardless of what, if any, role Frankfurter's illness played, Brennan's relationship with him clearly took a turn for the worse in the 1958–59 term. Frankfurter took to calling Brennan mockingly "the Admiral from Newark" that winter after reading Brennan's opinion in a case involving injured sailors. They exchanged angry memos in a criminal case concerning the issue of double jeopardy. "Brother Frankfurter not too delicately implies that my circulated dissent misrepresented the record. I won't enter into a discussion with him on that score," Brennan wrote his fellow justices. Frankfurter also communicated his displeasure when Brennan decided to take the unusual step of offering a concurring opinion in a case where he was also writing the majority opinion for the Court. "A young fellow like you," Frankfurter lectured Brennan, "will have ample opportunity to say your say when the issues make them relevant."

In April 1959 Brennan jokingly noted Frankfurter's growing disenchantment during a speech to the *Harvard Law Review*'s annual banquet in Cambridge. "I was a student of Professor Frankfurter," said Brennan, who underlined the word "professor" in his prepared text for added emphasis. "And when we disagree on the Court — perhaps you have noticed that this happens not infrequently — he observes that he has no memory of any signs in me of being his prize pupil." A few months later, the pages of the *Harvard Law Review* proved to be a flashpoint in the feuding between Brennan and Frankfurter. Their proxies would exchange heated volleys about a decision Brennan had written in the case of *Irvin v. Dowd*.

Leslie Irvin had been convicted and sentenced to death in December 1955 for a series of six murders around Evansville, Indiana. He escaped from prison a few days later, which complicated his appeal in the eyes of both state and federal courts after his recapture. The state courts said he had forfeited his right to appeal by escaping. Irvin then brought a habeas corpus proceeding in federal court seeking to challenge his detention. But the district court judge said Irvin could not pursue that habeas claim because he had not exhausted all potential state remedies. Brennan initially wrote a broad opinion when the case came up in January 1959. He saw this case as a potential vehicle for broadening criminal defendants' access to appeals in the federal courts. Five justices, including Frankfurter, made clear they would not join that sort of broad opinion. Frankfurter cited his "clear, deeply rooted understanding of the limits of our jurisdiction in re-viewing state convictions." Brennan then set out to write a narrower opin-ion that would win over a fifth vote. He focused particular attention on his newest colleague, Potter Stewart, who at age forty-three had supplanted him as the Court's youngest member at the start of the 1958–59 term.

Attorney General Rogers was confident he had fulfilled Eisenhower's wish to replace Burton with a reliable conservative when he recommended Stewart. This slender-framed, youthful-faced Yale-educated lawyer was born into a wealthy Ohio Republican family; his father had served as both mayor of Cincinnati and a justice on the Ohio Supreme Court. Stewart joined a Cincinnati law firm and then followed his father into local poli-tics. He served as vice mayor and two terms on the city council before Eisenhower tapped him for the U.S. Court of Appeals for the Sixth Circuit in 1954.

Brennan alone among the justices already knew Stewart, having met him at a judicial conference a couple of years earlier. So Stewart turned to Brennan for advice when he received Eisenhower's third recess appoint-ment to the high court. They started talking about life on the Court at Brennan's house over dinner one night shortly before Stewart's confirma-tion hearings, and kept it up well past midnight. Brennan continued his subtle courtship afterward, forwarding to Stewart transcripts of his and Frankfurter's confirmation hearings. Stewart wrote Brennan back the same day to thank him, joking, "They will make good bedside reading." Brennan also sponsored Stewart's membership at the Chevy Chase Country Club, assuring its board of governors that "the Stewarts will make most desirable members."

Brennan had equally high hopes as Eisenhower for Stewart as a mem-ber of the Court. Stewart impressed Brennan with his performance at the confirmation hearing, where his endorsement of the *Brown* desegregation opinion prompted seventeen southern senators to vote against his confir-mation. That decision contributed to Brennan's initial sense that Stewart would think like him in future cases too. But it became quickly apparent that Brennan had misjudged his new colleague. Stewart almost immedi-ately emerged as the key swing vote on a court roughly divided four to four. Stewart showed signs of tilting toward Frankfurter, particularly in subversion cases, although he remained uncommitted in enough cases that both justices and lawyers appearing before the Court courted him rigorously. One litigator joked he should have moved his lectern to Stewart's end of the bench and argued directly in front of him; Stewart replied that the lawyer would have lost, 8–1. Brennan, too, turned on the flattery in a rather transparent way. "Your opinion in the above is not only right but is a model of how opinions should be constructed and written," he wrote Stewart in one case.

In *Irvin v. Dowd,* Brennan set out to convince Stewart to join his bloc of four, a task Brennan knew he had to approach delicately. "You had to work with Potter," Brennan recalled. "He was a real skeptic about any result until he tested it six ways from Sunday by his own methods." Brennan did eventually win over Stewart, by writing a narrow opinion allowing Irvin to pursue his habeas corpus claim in federal court. But Brennan's clerks believed he had sacrificed the opinion's logical clarity in the process. Peter Fishbein thought that while the first draft "was very carefully reasoned and detailed," the second was "not internally consistent." Brennan nonetheless viewed the decision as a victory. Like an effective general, he was proving to be not only a good tactician regarding how to win the current case, but also a keen strategist on how that case fit into the bigger picture. Here, Brennan had built a majority and also taken an incremental step toward his larger goal of expanding state prisoners' ability to file habeas corpus petitions.

Brennan had largely put the case behind him until an article appeared in the *Harvard Law Review* attacking his opinion. The author was Henry Hart, a leading constitutional scholar and federal courts expert at Harvard Law School and a longtime Frankfurter disciple, who had continued to provide Frankfurter with all his clerks. Hart regularly denigrated Black and Douglas — although not Brennan — in his class on federal courts. In this article, Hart managed to channel many of Frankfurter's criticisms of his colleagues. He attacked the railroad injury cases that Frankfurter hated as "a grievous frittering away of the judicial resources of the nation," and criticized the quality of the Court's output.

Hart's main target, though, was Brennan's opinion in *Irvin v. Dowd,* which he condemned for its "studied ambiguity" and as illustrating "concretely what is meant by an inadequately reasoned opinion." He accused the Court of validating critics' claims that it "twists facts and words at its pleasure in order to reach the results it wants to reach." Hart, in a footnote, denied singling out Brennan. "No one of all nine of the Justices succeeded in emerging from it with a position which seems defensible," he charged.

Brennan and his clerks brushed off Hart's complaints as the musings of an out-of-touch academic who failed to understand how a fractured court produced opinions. Brennan had deftly demonstrated his attitude toward academic criticism in a December 1957 letter to Yale Law School professor Fred Rodell, who had written apologetically about a *Yale Law Journal* article critical of Brennan's *Jencks* opinion. "I have always envied the conviction displayed by Law Review editors in their critique on the work of the Court," Brennan wrote. Brennan never had much use for professors and their fancy empirical methods. After listening to one Brown graduate student describe the complicated metrics used by academics to gauge judicial values, he interrupted with a shrug and said, "Why don't you just ask us?"

But Brennan craved academic approval more than he cared to admit. So he certainly did not mind when Thurman Arnold, one of the founders of the prominent Washington law firm Arnold, Fortas & Porter, decided to write a rebuttal. Arnold, who had briefly served as a federal judge, condemned Hart's article as a series of "pompous generalizations dropped on the Court from the heights of Olympus." Arnold wrote: "Theoretically, ambiguity has no place in Supreme Court decisions. But if Professor Hart has ever tried to hold together a majority in favor of an opinion which he had written . . . he would know that compromise in the form of ambiguity may be inevitable." He added in defense of Brennan, without naming him, that "only a man wholly out of touch with reality could expect an opinion writer with such a fragile majority to 'illuminate large areas of the law.'" Arnold and Abe Fortas, another one of the firm's named partners, forwarded a copy of the article to Brennan, who made clear he liked the result. "It's both brilliant and devastating," Brennan wrote Fortas on December 28, 1959. "I thank him for writing it and you both for letting me read it."

By now, Brennan had begun joining Black, Douglas — and particularly Warren — in a reliably cohesive bloc. Brennan sent Warren private notes about cases in advance of their consideration with the tone of a lieutenant reporting to his captain. Even Douglas, who had long ago developed a reputation as a loner, began privately sending Brennan his drafts, marked "for your eyes only." Memos Brennan circulated to all three colleagues at this time suggest he was beginning to emerge as the group's strategist, scouting out opportunities to advance their views and plotting out how a current loss could contribute to future victories. The justices had no control over what cases reached the Court, but they had a great deal of freedom in choosing what cases to take up by granting certiorari. Since it only took four justices' votes to grant cert., their bloc of four could require the Court to take up any case they chose. But it would prove counterproductive to do so if they could not find the fifth justice to vote with them on the merits.

Frankfurter still won more cases than he lost in the 1959–60 term, despite Brennan's firmer alignment with the liberal bloc. But like a spurned suitor, Frankfurter grew increasingly disdainful of Brennan and began sharing it openly with his clerks. "In Frankfurter's mind, Brennan was a great manipulator and great internal politician," said Paul Bender, who clerked for Frankfurter during the 1959–60 term. Frankfurter, who continued to think little of Brennan's intellect, attributed his effectiveness the previous term to his clerk, Lyons, who was rumored to have been one of the highest-ranked students in Harvard Law School's history. Frankfurter left Bender with the impression that he believed "Lyons served Brennan's purpose very effectively and [was] very unprincipled."

Frankfurter's disappointment in his former student was intense by the summer of 1960. Brennan had voted with Black and Douglas about three-quarters of the time, and with Warren in nearly 90 percent of cases the previous term. "This is just a voice out of the past," Warren wrote playfully to Brennan on Beverly Hills Hilton stationery on August 19 after the Court had adjourned for the summer. "I am the fellow who had an office next to the Conference Room but who has for some time past been tramping through the Western states care free and leaving his associates behind to put out the fires that occur in the hot months of July and August." Frankfurter was not feeling quite so carefree as Warren when he joined Brennan and the chief justice at Justice Harlan's house later that month for a dinner honoring Oxford Law professor Arthur Goodhart. The conversation turned to a former student of Goodhart's who was presiding as judge in a prominent British murder trial. Goodhart, dismayed by his former student's performance, exclaimed, "He certainly didn't learn any of that from me." And then Frankfurter spoke up. "When I was a professor, and I was proud of that title as I ever have been of 'justice,' I always thought I was most successful when my students thought for themselves," he said. "But Brennan's carrying it too far."

Yet even as their relationship at the Court deteriorated, the two men's interactions — and particularly those between their families — remained warm back home in Georgetown. Brennan observed a very different and far more sympathetic side of Frankfurter on Dumbarton Avenue. There, he saw not the overbearing Professor Frankfurter but rather a doting husband who nursed his desperately unhappy and incapacitated wife, Marion. She had suffered from psychological problems since the 1920s and been largely confined to her second-story bedroom since the 1940s.

Nancy frequently visited the Frankfurters, who became her surrogate grandparents. She sat talking with Mrs. Frankfurter for hours at a time, played on the mechanical lift that went up and down the stairs, and was assured of an endless supply of cookies. Marjorie encouraged the relationship. One Halloween, she and a friend put stockings over their heads and took Nancy trick-or-treating at Frankfurter's house. Justice Frankfurter opened the door with delight. The Frankfurters, who never had children of their own, embraced Nancy as if she were their granddaughter. Even at the Court, one of Frankfurter's clerks recalled that Nancy was the one person that Frankfurter would drop everything for when she visited. "Dearest Nancy," Frankfurter wrote her. "Don't tell the secrets of the Court, for as time goes on you will discern — not learn! — more and more of them. Your friend, Felix Frankfurter." Unlike at the Court, where he viewed Frankfurter's every move with suspicion, Brennan did not assume Frankfurter had any ulterior motives in treating Nancy so warmly. "He was absolutely insane about children," Brennan said.

Brennan made a concerted effort to spend more time with Nancy than he had with his two sons during their childhoods. He returned home every night to Georgetown with a full briefcase around 5 P.M., ceasing any talk of the Court as soon as he reached the front gate. He got home early enough to tutor Nancy in math and to eat dinner together around 6:30 P.M. Each year, he took her and the two dogs they had adopted since moving to Washington to Epiphany Church for the annual blessing of the animals. He also accompanied Nancy to the National Press Club's annual father-daughter dinner in 1958, where they were pictured sipping soft drinks out of big straws along with an assistant secretary of defense and his daughter. Nancy cut the picture out of the newspaper and saved it for her father.

Brennan and Marjorie also tried to maintain Nancy's connection to New Jersey, returning there in 1959 for a weekend so she could celebrate her tenth birthday with old friends.

The Court community of clerks, justices, and their children offered Nancy an extended family otherwise missing now that they had left New Jersey. Nancy considered the courthouse her playground, where she dribbled balls down the hallway when Brennan worked on Saturdays. Brennan's clerks later taught her how to both play tennis and drive. The other justices supplemented Frankfurter as surrogate uncles. Nancy once sent Warren a birthday card from the whole family, including their pet fish. Warren's daughter, Virginia, acted both as babysitter and older sister. But despite Brennan's best efforts, Nancy, like her two older brothers, later remembered her father's work-life balance as "a knitting of compromised work and compromised family life." Just like her older brother, one of Nancy's most enduring memories of her father growing up was the image of Brennan working at a green card table in the living room after dinner, his papers spread out around him on the floor. Then, around 9 P.M., Brennan would finally put aside his work. He would sit beside Marjorie on their sky-blue sofa, and they would watch television while holding hands until it was time for bed.

BRENNAN LOOKED ON with pride as his older son, Bill, wed Georgianna "Georgie" Franklin, in her parents' home back in South Orange, New Jersey, on September 10, 1960. Bill had straightened out considerably since his wild youth and the five years it took him to graduate from Colgate. Everyone in the family, including his new bride, whom he had known growing up, credited Bill's experience in the Marine Corps with helping him mature. Bill loved his time in the Marines and carried the disciplined, upright bearing of a Leatherneck the rest of his life. He even briefly flirted with making a career out of the military, but instead opted to attend law school like his father.

Bill began at Yale Law School in the fall of 1959. Brennan had talked him out of attending his other top choice, Stanford, on the grounds that it might hurt his job prospects on the East Coast. Brennan did not mention his more selfish concerns about his son permanently planting himself so far away on the West Coast, where Bill had enjoyed living while in the Marines. Brennan could employ the same subtle powers of persuasion both at the Court and at home with equal success. "Papa could be a steam-roller and you'd never know it," Georgie recalled, using the name Brennan's grandchildren called him.

While Bill followed the straight and narrow path to success, Brennan's younger son, Hugh, still gave him cause for concern. Hugh's marriage to Roxey had not lasted much longer than a year, and ended with an annulment. Roxey was already engaged to another young man from Rumson by June 1959. Hugh had trouble holding down a job and developed a serious drinking problem. "He was just an alcoholic," Brennan later bleakly recalled. Rather than remain in New Jersey, Hugh followed his parents and sister to Washington. He was enrolled at George Washington University by the fall of 1959, and Brennan enjoyed the company of his son, who turned twenty-four in March 1960. They played golf together almost every weekend at the Chevy Chase Country Club. But proximity only heightened Brennan's sense of helplessness about Hugh, now seemingly adrift at roughly the same age Brennan had been when he graduated from law school.

· 7 ·

IRISH OR HARVARD

B RENNAN SAT JUST four rows away on the inaugural platform jutting out from the Capitol's East Portico on a bright frozen January
afternoon in 1961 as Chief Justice Warren administered the oath of
office to John F. Kennedy. Only a few months earlier, Brennan had remained skeptical about whether the nation was ready to elect its first Catholic president. He had even made a friendly wager with a priest back in
New Jersey on the eve of the election about whether Kennedy could beat
Vice President Richard Nixon. Brennan once again opted not to vote in
this election, but neither he nor the priest he bet against was disappointed
with the outcome. Now, bundled up in a gray herringbone overcoat and
blue scarf, Brennan watched as the forty-three-year-old Kennedy, who had
abandoned his overcoat and top hat despite the frigid temperature, supplanted him as the highest-ranking Catholic in the U.S. government.

The Irish heritage he shared with the new president had not entitled
Brennan to any special perks at the inauguration. He could not get tickets for all the friends who wanted to attend, one of whom he wrote, "the
Republicans did better by us last time." Nancy took the seat reserved for
Marjorie, who remained in bed at home with an injured back. Seated two
rows in front of Brennan was House Majority Leader John McCormack,
another Massachusetts Irishman who would soon become Speaker of the

House, and one row directly behind him was Mike Mansfield of Montana, who had recently become Senate majority leader, placing Irish Catholics for a brief and unprecedented time in prominent roles atop all three branches of government. In the row in front of Brennan to his immediate right sat the aged poet Robert Frost, who recited "The Gift Outright" as part of the ceremony and gave Kennedy a book of his poems as a present, in which he inscribed, "Be more Irish than Harvard." Conspicuously absent from the ceremony was Archbishop Spellman, who was no happier about Kennedy's victory than he had been about Brennan's nomination. Spellman, afraid to lose his mantle as the nation's most powerful Catholic, had made known he preferred the Republican nominee. Kennedy returned the favor, asking Spellman's rival, Richard Cardinal Cushing, of Boston, to deliver the invocation at the inauguration.

Brennan's only brush with Kennedy this day likely came during the inaugural parade, when the new president greeted members of the Supreme Court. Brennan did not stay long, heading home with Nancy through the snow-covered city to Marjorie and skipping the five inaugural balls that night. He was long since asleep by the time a column of limousines and Secret Service cars pulled up a few houses down Dumbarton Avenue at columnist Joe Alsop's house around 2 A.M. Neighbors hanging out their windows cheered as Kennedy arrived for a nightcap with Alsop and his friends.

Brennan's absence from the late-night celebration on Dumbarton Avenue captured his peripheral position in the Camelot era that followed. He had few ties of note to Kennedy before the election beyond their common heritage, Georgetown addresses, and relative youth in official Washington. That was enough to explain why then-senator Kennedy had suggested Brennan when his younger brother Edward, known as Ted, a student at the University of Virginia's law school, sought to invite a member of the Court to speak at the school. Brennan accepted the invitation to visit Charlottesville and wrote to congratulate Ted a few months later for winning the school's moot court competition in April 1959. But Kennedy and his brothers were much closer to Douglas, who had served with their father at the Securities and Exchange Commission, and eventually to Warren, who may not have been an Irish Catholic but shared a deep dislike of Richard Nixon. It was Warren whom First Lady Jackie Kennedy would ask to deliver a eulogy at Kennedy's funeral less than three years later.

Brennan saw more of Kennedy during his short tenure than he did any other president—they met perhaps a half-dozen times—but that is not saying much. Unlike some of his fellow justices, Brennan never grew particularly close to any of the men who served as president during his time on the Court. The sole intimate moment Brennan shared with Kennedy came at a White House reception shortly after *Look* magazine published a profile of Brennan that reported on his lengthy morning walks. Kennedy poked Brennan in his belly and quipped, "You can't tell me you walk four miles every morning." Brennan's growing influence on the Court remained little known beyond the Court's walls, so Kennedy and his top advisers probably viewed Brennan as a less than central junior player on the Supreme Court. Brennan and Marjorie's class aspirations and glamour quotient were also relatively low for Kennedy's inner circle.

Yet Brennan, perhaps more than anyone else in Washington, understood the difficulty Kennedy faced in balancing his Catholic faith and public duties—and in being both Irish and Harvard. Kennedy grew up more Harvard than Irish, grandson of a congressman, and beneficiary of a fortune amassed by his father that assured a childhood full of mansions and servants. If Brennan's father had crossed over the class line dividing "shanty" from "lace curtain" in the proverbial Irish Catholic social topography, Joseph Kennedy had leaped the fence entirely, providing his family a way of life more common among Boston's Protestant Brahmin elite. In his middle-class Irish Catholic upbringing, Brennan had more in common with Thomas P. "Tip" O'Neill of Cambridge, Massachusetts, who succeeded Kennedy in the House in 1953 when the future president was elected to the Senate. Now beginning his fifth term in Congress, O'Neill was also the son of a local politician with a brother who had attended Harvard Law School. But the closest O'Neill got to the Harvard campus was cutting its lawns at age fourteen. He graduated from Boston College and then got kicked out of its law school. O'Neill, who would go on to be Speaker of the House, was perhaps the only Irish Catholic who would rival Brennan's influence over time in postwar Washington.

Both Brennan and Kennedy had tried their whole lives to retain their identities as Irish Catholics as they advanced through the Protestant establishment. Neither man, however, wanted to be defined solely as Irish Catholic. Educated at Choate and Harvard, Kennedy, like Brennan, mixed largely with non-Catholic students during college. Kennedy shared Bren-

nan's ignorance of Catholic theology. Whether out of obligation to his family or political expediency, he continued attending Sunday Mass nearly
every week as an adult, but avoided marching in Saint Patrick's Day parades or being pictured with priests and nuns. Like his father, Kennedy did
not want to be known as a backslapping Irish politician, a stereotype applied to Brennan ever since he joined the Court.

Before his appointment to the Court, Brennan had gladly and frequently skipped Mass. Brennan's sons remembered him often dropping
them off at Sunday school back in New Jersey on his way to play golf. Since
moving to Washington, however, Brennan joined Marjorie and Nancy
roughly two out of every three Sundays when they walked to Epiphany
Church just up Dumbarton Avenue. Still, Brennan made it a point to attend all sorts of public Church events after joining the Court. He appeared
at a Mass celebrating Pope Pius XII in 1957, and another marking his death
the next year, and was present for the dedication of the National Shrine
in 1959. He judged a student orators' competition at Catholic University
and delivered the commencement address at the Catholic-affiliated Trinity
College in Washington in 1960. He was in the audience at the annual Red
Mass celebrating the legal profession in Washington every January and for
Saint Patrick's Day every March. He joined the John Carroll Society, a
group of professional Catholic men, serving as toastmaster at some of their
events, and befriended the society's founder, Bishop Philip Hannan. Brennan stuck to shrimp salad and clam chowder for lunch at the Court on
Fridays during Lent.

Brennan traveled to Ireland in the summer of 1963, one month after
Kennedy made a similar trip. For Brennan's Irish relatives, his visit was an
even more significant event than the president's, although his photo still
ranked third in importance in their house, behind both Kennedy and Jesus
Christ. Brennan, eager to see his parents' birthplaces in County Roscommon, was disappointed to find his father's home had been razed long ago.
So his Irish relatives made sure to point out a house where his mother
might have been born. "He was happy and accuracy wasn't the order of the
day," recalled his relative Paula Smith. Brennan cemented a lasting bond
with his cousins, Agnes and Harry Crawley of Dublin, with whom he continued to correspond regularly for decades to come.

Brennan took particular comfort in friendships with priests, and he
identified strongly enough with the Church that criticisms by its leaders

would sting, even if they never influenced how he actually voted. The extent to which his Catholic faith influenced his views or judicial philosophy is far more difficult to discern. Brennan's jurisprudence mirrored the lessons he recalled from Sunday school as a child about "taking care of the poor and the weak." His emphasis on "human dignity" as the fundamental value underlying the Constitution echoed the work of John A. Ryan, the Catholic priest and social theorist, just as his father's rhetoric about a "living wage" sounded like Ryan's. But, except for Saint Thomas Aquinas, Brennan never quoted Catholic thinkers. He perhaps best fit the worldview of the liberal Catholic magazine *Commonweal*, summarized by one historian as arguing that members of the faith "must break out of their self-imposed 'ghetto' and involve themselves more actively in the pluralistic society of which they were a part." *Commonweal* Catholics were New Deal liberals who opposed Joseph McCarthy and "espoused an enlightened liberality on matters relating to artistic expression and were regularly chagrined by the moralistic excesses of Catholic 'crusades' against indecency and movies."

Brennan — like John Kennedy — often strived for entrée to institutions that had previously excluded Catholics, from his Newark law firm to his New Jersey shore beach club. He rolled his eyes when people made too big a deal of his Irish roots, and made sure his family knew he disliked eating cabbage. The man who became his best friend in Washington, David Bazelon, was a nonobservant Jew who sprinkled his conversations with Yiddish. Their Georgetown social circle included more Protestants and Jews than Catholics. Brennan also made sure, as his father had, that his children would be comfortable in the non-Catholic world. His son Bill recalled that the only fight he had with his father was over whether he would go to Sunday school, but Brennan and Marjorie did not pressure him later to keep going after his confirmation, when he told them he did not want to attend anymore. Bill drifted away from religion altogether.

Brennan encouraged Nancy to have non-Catholic friends, and she recalled being transferred out of her suburban Washington parochial school, Stone Ridge when, at age eleven, she started talking about becoming a nun. Not surprisingly, Brennan preferred to explain the decision to others in innocuous terms. In his letter informing Stone Ridge's headmaster, Mother Mouton, of the decision, he blamed the strain on Marjorie, with her bad back, of driving Nancy every day. Elsewhere, he said the switch was prompted by an influx of poorly trained teachers from Cuba following the revolution there. All three of his children would marry non-Catholics. Marjorie and Brennan had no problem enlisting a Protestant minister to conduct the wedding ceremony for Bill and Georgie, the granddaughter of a Russian Orthodox bishop, when no Catholic priest was willing to do so. Georgie suspected Catholic priests were afraid to marry the son of such a prominent Catholic to someone who was not a member of the Church. Only one of their three children, Hugh, would remain a practicing Catholic.

There is a certain irony that Brennan and Kennedy, neither of whom considered themselves particularly religious, found it necessary to pledge to compartmentalize their private faith, when it was not likely to guide them anyway. Both worked carefully to avoid even the appearance of undue Church influence while in office. There would be no Masses celebrated inside the Kennedy White House, and few overt displays of Catholicism during his presidency. Brennan similarly avoided any sort of behind-closed-doors events that might give the appearance he was beholden to the Church. When the Papal Nuncio's Office called Brennan's chambers in the late 1950s, inviting him to attend a retreat, Brennan had his clerk return the call and politely decline. All their careful tiptoeing ensured that critics of the Church would have no new ammunition to attack Catholics' alleged divided loyalties. But during the course of Kennedy's brief tenure as president, both men found that the way they divorced their private faith and public life did not always satisfy their own church. And, for both, the intersection of religion and schools proved to be the main source of contention.

Education had long been the central flashpoint in America's debate over church and state. The nineteenth-century surge in Catholic immigration prompted an often tense standoff between the newcomers and America's Protestant majority about what role religion should play in schools—and where Catholic children should be educated. Many Protestants, alarmed by the growing numbers of Catholics flooding American cities, believed public schools infused with a healthy dose of Protestant values were the best way to acculturate the offspring of these newcomers. Readings from the King James Bible and hymn singing joined reading and writing in school curriculums. The presence of Protestant Bible reading and bigoted textbooks sparked confrontations that occasionally turned violent. Many

Catholics responded by enrolling their children in parochial schools run by the Church, which sought public funding. That, in turn, only fed more anti-Catholic sentiment and the public perception that Catholics did not want to join the American mainstream.

For decades the Supreme Court provided no guidance about the propriety of aid for parochial schools. The First Amendment to the Constitution prohibits the federal government from establishing any religion (the establishment clause) or interfering with citizens' ability to exercise their faith freely (the free exercise clause). But until well into the twentieth century, the Supreme Court never applied either of the First Amendment's religion clauses to the states, leaving them more leeway to inject religion into schools. The Supreme Court first took up the issue of public aid for parochial schools in a 1930 case challenging state-financed textbooks in Louisiana. The Court, without reference to the First Amendment, upheld such aid on the grounds that it benefited the child rather than the school or church.

It was not until 1947 that the Supreme Court fully applied the First Amendment's establishment clause against states, in the case of *Everson v. Board of Education*. Justice Black, borrowing a metaphor from Thomas Jefferson, declared the need for a high "wall of separation between church and State" in that case, although he held that New Jersey's law allowing school districts to pay to transport students to parochial schools had not breached that wall. The following year, much to Archbishop Spellman's dismay, the Court held unconstitutional an Illinois law that allowed students "released time" to be instructed in religious subjects inside their public schools. In the years since, the Court had taken an uneven course, upholding New York City's released-time program in which students left public school buildings during the school day for religious instruction, and ducking the question of whether Bibles could be distributed to students in New Jersey public elementary schools.

That was the uncertain state of the law when Kennedy served in Congress during the late 1940s and early 1950s. Congressman Kennedy initially supported aid for parochial schools but changed his position as a senator eyeing a bid for the White House. In 1958 Kennedy introduced a school-aid bill that benefited only public schools. He was the sole presidential hopeful to vote against an amendment to include nonpublic schools. As president, he endorsed an education bill in 1961 that also excluded parochial schools. It was just one of several areas where he broke with the wishes of the Church. By the early 1960s, many bishops were rethinking the wisdom of pushing for public funds for parochial schools. But the Conference of Catholic Bishops, the assembly of the Church hierarchy in the United States, was still dominated by Spellman. He said it was "unthinkable that any American child be denied" this kind of aid because a parent selected a "God-centered education." The Conference voted to oppose Kennedy's education bill, and its maneuvering helped ensure its defeat. Kennedy publicly joked about the loss. "I asked the chief justice whether he thought our new educational bill was constitutional," Kennedy quipped. "He said it was constitutional — it hasn't got a prayer." Privately, he was livid.

Brennan, too, found himself on the opposite side of the Catholic bishops on an issue related to religion and schools. In the spring of 1962 the Supreme Court considered the constitutionality of school prayer for the first time in the case of *Engel v. Vitale*. At issue was a twenty-two-word nondenominational prayer that the New York State Board of Regents, which oversaw public schools in the state, decreed in 1951 should be read aloud by students and teachers at the start of each school day. "Almighty God, we acknowledge our dependence upon Thee, and we beg Thy blessings upon us, our parents, our teachers and our Country." Five parents whose children attended public schools in one Long Island district challenged the law. The New York State courts upheld the government-written prayer as long as students were not compelled to participate over their parents' objections. In 1960 prayer remained commonplace in American schools, whether in the form of Bible reading, school prayer in homeroom, released time for religious instruction, or lunchtime prayer.

The Court had considered no church-state cases from the time Brennan joined the Court until the previous 1960–61 term, when it took up several at once. Brennan had shown himself sympathetic to a strict separation of church and state in these few cases he had heard. The Court had unanimously rejected a Maryland law requiring public officials to affirm a belief in God, but upheld four Sunday-closing laws. In one of the cases, Orthodox Jewish merchants in Philadelphia challenged the law as impinging on their ability to make a living, since they asserted their faith required them to close on Saturday too. Warren, writing for the Court, held that states did have the power to set aside "one day of the week apart from the others as a day of rest, repose, recreation and tranquility." Brennan dissented, arguing such collective goals should not outweigh individual rights.

Brennan had not heard any religion cases involving schools on the U.S. Supreme Court, but had expressed concern about even the voluntary presence of religion in public schools as a justice on the New Jersey Supreme Court. There, in 1954, he faced the same case about distributing Bibles in public schools that the U.S. Supreme Court later dodged. In the course of the New Jersey oral argument, the Board of Education's lawyer claimed the distribution was voluntary, since only children whose parents signed consent slips could receive the Bibles. Brennan disagreed. He described the way Nancy, then age five, would plead with him to buy breakfast cereals she saw advertised on television. He said there was nothing voluntary about him buying those products, and asked the lawyer whether it was fair to describe as voluntary the consent granted by parents when their children came home from school pleading that they be allowed to accept the Bible like other children.

It was immediately apparent on the day the Supreme Court heard oral arguments in the *Engel* school-prayer case in April 1962 that it was of great interest to the Catholic Church. Fears of growing secularism and the declining influence of religious values in public schools prompted many in the Church hierarchy to defend school prayers originally adopted to assimilate their adherents. Brennan, though, readily agreed with the majority of the justices who voted to strike down the mandated school prayer. Only Stewart expressed reservations. Warren assigned the case to Black, who had written many of the Court's previous church-state decisions.

The justices honored Black for completing his twenty-fifth term on the Court on June 25, 1962, before he announced the *Engel* decision. Black declared that the First Amendment's ban on establishment of religion meant that it was not "the business of government to compose official prayers for any group of the American people to recite as part of a religious program carried on by government." Black rejected any suggestion that the Court was expressing hostility to religion, insisting in a footnote that the opinion did not prohibit the "many manifestations in our public life of belief in God," such as singing a national anthem. While the justices did not view the decision as momentous, reporters covering the announcement immediately picked up on its potential significance. "The clear implication of the ruling was that any religious ceremony promoted by the state in public schools would be suspect," Anthony Lewis wrote in the *New York Times.*

The decision generated widespread public outrage, equal to or even more intense than the condemnation generated by the desegregation and Communist-subversion opinions. The justices managed to unite lawmakers and clergy of many persuasions along with most of the public in vociferous opposition. Polls found 85 percent of those surveyed opposed the decision. The case generated the largest volume of mail in the Court's history up to that point. Members of Congress from both parties and every region of the country dropped all other business to denounce the decision and introduce constitutional amendments designed to overrule it. Alabama Democrat George Andrews complained, "They put the Negroes in the schools, and now they've driven God out." Churches of many denominations came out against the decision, including the Episcopal council in Brennan's hometown of Newark.

By far the strongest condemnations came from atop the Catholic Church. Cardinal Cushing of Boston said the decision was fuel for Communist propaganda. Archbishop Spellman called it a "tragic misreading of the prayerfully weighed words of our founding fathers." President Kennedy came to the Court's defense at a June 27 press conference, where it was the subject of the first question posed to him. "I think that it is important for us, if we're going to maintain our constitutional principle, that we support Supreme Court decisions even when we may not agree with them," Kennedy said. That did little to stem criticism against the decision in the Washington Archdiocese, where the official organ, the *Catholic Standard,* accused the Court of committing "one of the most comprehensive brush-offs of American history."

As with the *Jencks* case criticized for aiding Communists, Brennan and his fellow justices were once again caught off-guard by the outrage their decision generated. Black, who usually did not reply to critics, answered some of the letters that came to his chambers. Clark broke with the justices' usual practice of letting opinions speak for themselves, and defended *Engel* publicly at an appearance before the San Francisco Commonwealth Club. He blamed the media for presenting the public with an incomplete version of the Court's decision.

Brennan, too, thought the press coverage was ill-informed, but unlike Clark he did not try to rebut the criticism publicly. "The tradition that judges do not debate decisions or the reasoning on which they rest has roots in history, and I think its discard would be most unfortunate and undesirable," Brennan told *Look* magazine later that year. But he spent much time in the months that followed — including some sleepless nights — thinking about what would happen next time the Court took up a school-prayer case. "I was afraid that I was going to come in for a real lambasting from the Roman Catholic hierarchy," Brennan recalled later. "It's hard now to recapture what the atmosphere was, when the Church was still very domineering and arbitrary."

Brennan did not have long to wait for the next school-prayer case. Eight months later, in February 1963, the Court took up a challenge to laws in Maryland and Pennsylvania that required the reading of Bible passages at the start of each school day. Brennan felt acutely self-conscious about the case, *Abington School District v. Schempp,* far more so than he had a year earlier in the first school-prayer decision. Brennan would later recall that at the time, he felt as if "everybody in the Roman Catholic hierarchy was looking to see what I was going to do." He felt the same sensation of having all eyes upon him at the time when he attended Sunday Mass at Epiphany Church. He alone remained seated as all those around him stood to recite a pledge not to see indecent and immoral motion pictures, which became known as the "pledge of decency." His clerk Robert O'Neil recalled Brennan coming into his chambers one Monday looking pale and tired. When O'Neil asked him what was wrong, Brennan said, "You have no idea what it's like to be the only person in the congregation of a large Catholic church who refuses to stand to recite the pledge of decency. Everybody turns and looks at me. It's a terrible experience."

On the issue of school prayer, at least, Brennan felt he had a venue for explaining himself and the Court's position fully. Brennan believed the authors of the majority opinions in some of the recent cases involving the religion clauses had been sloppy, or at least had not given the attention due a topic of such sensitivity. At his clerks' urging, Brennan began drafting a concurring opinion in the *Schempp* case in which he laid out his views on the First Amendment's establishment clause. He and his clerks worked seven days a week exhaustively researching the issue. Brennan wrote out his opinion in longhand while his clerks added footnotes gleaned from the shelves full of books and articles they found inside the Court's library or borrowed from the Library of Congress and universities. They invoked a diverse set of sources, ranging from court opinions and foreign constitutions to the *American Jewish Yearbook* and Catholic and Episcopal magazines.

The result read less like a court opinion than a historical study, as Brennan traced the history of school prayer back to the English colonies in the seventeenth century and detailed nearly every religion-clause case the Court had ever heard. He took pains to try to prove that the Court had firmly grounded its conclusion in both law and tradition. "The principles which we reaffirm and apply today can hardly be thought novel or radical," Brennan wrote. "They are, in truth, as old as the Republic itself and have always been as integral a part of the First Amendment as the very words of that charter of religious liberty." He rebutted each argument in support of school prayer, such as the idea that prayer might foster better discipline or elevate the spiritual level on which the school day opens. Such goals, he contended, could not be accomplished by violating the limits of the First Amendment. Brennan then offered a list of religious practices and accommodations he believed passed constitutional muster. Those included prayers at the start of legislative sessions, the use of the motto "In God we trust" on currency, and moments of silence.

Brennan showed the seventy-page final product to his fellow justices in May 1963 after two and a half months of effort. He made clear to his colleagues that he wished this to be his statement alone. He would accept no offers to join the opinion. It was the inverse of his confirmation hearing, where he had sought to address the concerns of non-Catholics. Here, Brennan specifically sought to explain to a Catholic audience what justified his breaking with what he viewed as the Church's position. Brennan was not the first Catholic justice to come out on the opposite side of the Church in a sensitive church-state case, but he was the first to try to explain himself in such a public manner. There would be three concurrences in all, their authors' religious affiliations — one Catholic, one Jew, and one Protestant — adding some additional, perhaps unintended, symbolism about American religious pluralism.

Brennan chose his words with great care, often turning to the book of synonyms he kept beside his desk. "I always try to say what I have to say in words that can be understood," he explained to a reporter soon after the decision was announced. "This takes an awful lot of scrubbing." Brennan spoke in his own voice in *Schempp* — he did not have to make any compromises this time for the sake of consensus. He also wrote the majority opinion in another important religion case announced the same day. In *Sherbert v. Verner,* Brennan set forth a rule that would govern the Court's consideration of free-exercise cases for the next quarter century. Under the *Sherbert* test, the government had to prove it had some compelling interest and no alternative means of reaching its goal where it placed a burden on the exercise of religion. In *Sherbert,* the Court ruled that a South Carolina Seventh-day Adventist could not be denied unemployment benefits because of her refusal to work on Saturdays in line with her religious beliefs. The practical effect of *Sherbert* was to require that states accommodate the sincerely held religious beliefs of workers by exempting employees from some requirements for unemployment-compensation eligibility.

But only his *Schempp* concurrence was uniquely Brennan's own. A *Washington Post* reporter called his concurrence in *Schempp* "specific and outspoken," while the *Sherbert* opinion "was much more general and left conspicuous holes." After so much work, the instant criticisms that followed the June 17, 1963, *Schempp* announcement disappointed Brennan. "There were four majority opinions which filled 109 printed pages," he complained later in a speech. "Yet within two hours the critics were in print saying the Court was wrong. It was obvious they could not have read the explanations." Lawmakers dusted off their proposed constitutional amendments authorizing school prayer. Still, Brennan was relieved that the Court's decision in *Schempp,* which had a broader potential impact than the *Engel* case, generated less fury overall. "Indeed, our mail is scant and much of it is approving," Brennan wrote to one law professor who praised his opinion. The decision's real-world impact proved minimal too. Two-thirds of southern schools and half in the Midwest carried on as before and allowed prayer in schools to continue.

JUST OVER SEVEN months later, Marjorie and Nancy joined Brennan at the annual Red Mass at St. Matthew's Cathedral. The grand domed church that served as seat for the bishop of Washington was full as usual for the occasion with prominent Washington lawyers, judges, and members of the cabinet and Congress. Nancy recalled that Marjorie silently fumed as John J. Russell, the bishop of Richmond, criticized the Court's recent school-prayer decisions. "Thank God, our Constitution forbids the State's setting up or favoring any particular form of religion," Russell said. "But that separation of church and state which we all cherish in our country never meant the divorce of government from religion or the separation of law from morality."

Clergy sometimes used the occasion of the Red Mass held in Washington and elsewhere around the country to scold the captive audience of politicians and judges about matters of public policy. In New Orleans, for example, clergy in this era often lectured their audience of lawyers about the need for desegregation. Three Louisiana Catholics — a local political boss, a journalist advocating segregation, and a housewife turned anti-integration agitator — all wound up excommunicated in the early 1960s for defying the Church's position on desegregation. It was not only Catholic officials who could find themselves squirming in a church's pews. In 1967 Lady Bird Johnson remained stone-faced and silently boiled when an Episcopal minister in Williamsburg, Virginia, criticized the war in Vietnam while she and President Johnson sat in the audience.

Marjorie had already sat through a school-prayer lecture by their parish priest at the Brennans' Georgetown church, after which Brennan tried consoling his wife as they walked home. This sort of public chastisement deeply offended Marjorie, who was both protective of her husband and, of the two of them, the more devout spouse. She had taken great comfort in her faith ever since she lost both her parents at a young age. When Marjorie's sister had been sick or her sons in trouble, she performed the novena, a cycle of prayers repeated on nine consecutive days. Brennan joked she had a red telephone to God.

So Marjorie found it hard to hold in her anger after sitting through a second lecture of this kind, inside the home church of the entire archdiocese. Brennan could see Marjorie was furious as they approached the bishop, who stood greeting attendees at the front door of the church after the Mass. Brennan pleaded with his wife under his breath not to make a scene.

"Mommy," he said, using his pet name for her. "It's not that important." Marjorie disagreed. "That's the last straw," she said.

Marjorie kissed the bishop's ring, as expected, before bolting upright and spitting out, "You're not fit for my husband or me to kiss your ring!"

A mortified Brennan, who so strenuously avoided confrontation, quickly greeted the bishop before fleeing down the church's front steps with his family as fast as he could. "My father was so upset," Nancy said.

"He just wanted to get out of there." Brennan had learned how to keep private any anger or disappointment with the Church. For Marjorie, though, there would be no putting the incident behind. She was done going to Mass. "It wasn't safe anymore," Nancy recalled her mother thinking.

The Brennans' growing alienation from their faith coincided with a new spirit of change sweeping through the Catholic Church. The same year Marjorie angrily stormed out of the Red Mass, Catholic parishes began adopting a sweeping series of changes to the liturgy designed to make Mass more welcoming to parishioners. The changes were the result of the Council of Cardinals called earlier by Pope John XXIII, which came to be known as Vatican II. Priests began celebrating Mass in the language of their parishioners rather than in Latin and they now faced them rather than keeping their backs to the pews. Pope John XXIII, during his five-year tenure, also invited dialogue with other faiths and adopted a new, more tolerant stance on religious liberty espoused by the liberal church theologian John Courtney Murray, among others.

Brennan and Marjorie moved away from the Catholic Church just as their son Hugh drew closer to his faith. If his older brother Bill could thank the Marines for helping him mature, the family believed that Hugh found his redemption — both personal and professional — through religion. He had remarried in August 1961 and his new wife, Mary Frances Crown, was a Catholic. Having graduated from George Washington University, Hugh enrolled at Georgetown Law School after the wedding, in the fall of 1961. Although he dropped out of Georgetown, Hugh went on to a successful career in the federal government. Brennan took particular pride in bragging to his friends and family about each of Hugh's promotions and the achievement awards his son earned in succeeding decades. Presidents of both parties later appointed Hugh to the federal Committee for Purchase from People who are Blind or Severely Disabled.

But for Hugh, putting his troubled early years entirely behind him was the price of moving forward. He largely cut off contact with Hugh Jr., the son he'd had with Roxey, except for the occasional letter or gift at Christmas. Hugh had four more children with Mary, none of whom he informed about his earlier marriage or son. Future newspaper and magazine profiles of Brennan would describe Bill's first son as his oldest grandchild. Hugh Jr. had been erased from the family. "It was as if I didn't exist," Hugh Jr.

later recalled. But Brennan kept in touch with Hugh Jr. via letters and gifts, even after Roxey moved to Arizona with him and his younger half sister. Brennan also kept a silent reminder of Hugh's previous life in his chambers. Roxey's painting of Nancy that he received as a Christmas gift in 1956 remained hanging on the wall above the fireplace.

AT LEAST ONE day a week when the Court was not in session, Brennan met at lunchtime with fellow federal judge David Bazelon. Together, they headed in Bazelon's chauffeur-driven car to a gritty industrial section of northeast Washington, stopping at a nondescript warehouse at 2900 V Street. Their unconventional lunch destination was a cafeteria inside a liquor distributorship, a far cry from the wood-paneled dining rooms in the city's elite University or Metropolitan clubs.

It certainly was not the ambiance that attracted some of Washington's most powerful politicians, judges, and lawyers to this small cafeteria where the employees of the liquor warehouse ate. Guests sat in plastic chairs at a wooden table seating ten with a view of the cook and the Coke machine that stood in the corner. The food was not bad, unless you believe the law clerks who occasionally accompanied Brennan and Bazelon, who panned the cafeteria's offerings as bland. Brennan, in contrast, looked forward to the comfort food served up by Annie, the cook: soup and cornbread, an entrée of the day—his favorites were the crabmeat special ordered from Crisfield, a local seafood restaurant, or short ribs—plus a pie or cake she had baked that morning.

The real draw, however, was the host, Milton Kronheim, the owner of the liquor warehouse and one of the most colorful local characters Washington has ever produced. Kronheim, born in 1888 in a crime-infested Washington neighborhood nicknamed Bloodfield, had learned about liquor and politics long ago at the feet of his father, who operated a saloon near the Capitol. Kronheim opened his own wine and liquor shop at age fifteen after dropping out of high school. Prohibition forced him to switch to selling men's clothes and trolling police precincts at night as a bail bondsman, where he earned the appreciation of local politicians he rescued from the drunk tank. Kronheim himself remained a teetotaler his entire life, claiming he did not like the taste of alcohol, although he eagerly returned to the liquor business when Prohibition ended.

Kronheim proved as skillful at collecting powerful friends as he was at selling Southern Comfort. He first started hosting prominent politicians and judges for lunch on Saturdays in the 1920s. In the decades since, a lunch invitation from "Mr. K" at the Mayflower Hotel, where he lived, became something of a status symbol in the city, even after he started hosting his guests inside his warehouse in the early 1950s. He also picked up the tab for aging Truman administration buddies at a separate lunch on Saturdays. Kronheim was not shy about showing off his powerful friends and lunch guests, who included every president since Roosevelt. Framed pictures of them — two thousand in all — covered every inch of the walls of the cafeteria.

Kronheim insisted that he never exploited these friendships, a claim that might have elicited laughs from those in Washington who knew him best, although it is hard to say where Kronheim's true influence ended and his legend began. He was said to have a hand in every local appointment, from Washington police and fire chiefs down to the lieutenants in the firehouse. He landed a judgeship on the city municipal court for his less-than-well-qualified son. He shaped federal legislation that kept sales taxes and spirits taxes so low that customers flocked to Washington to buy his liquor from as far away as New York. Kronheim said simply, "If you had friends and were judicious and didn't assume to have power, you could do things." In 1958 Kronheim pleaded no contest and paid a $2,000 fine on federal charges of conspiring to prevent liquor stores in neighboring Montgomery County from buying directly from distilleries.

By the time Brennan started attending his lunches, Kronheim had largely retired from influence peddling. He focused his energies on his business and philanthropy, quietly giving away large sums to Jewish and civil rights organizations and charities benefitting children. Not that anyone sitting around Kronheim's lunch table gave too much thought to potential conflicts of interest. This was a time before ethics rules limited where congressmen could dine, and when Washington superlawyer Edward Bennett Williams, who regularly argued before the Court, could hand out Redskins tickets to justices over lunch at Kronheim's without raising any eyebrows.

Among those Kronheim counted as close friends was Bazelon, a generation his junior. Kronheim had befriended Bazelon as soon as he moved

Brennan's parents, William J. Brennan Sr. and Bridget Agnes McDermott, sit for their wedding portrait.

Campaign ad for William J. Brennan Sr.'s first reelection as City Commissioner, 1921

William J. Brennan Jr.,
age seventeen

William J. Brennan Sr.,
Newark Commissioner
of Public Safety

Harvard Legal Aid Bureau, 1930–31. Brennan is in the front row at far left.

Marjorie Brennan

Major Brennan, World War II

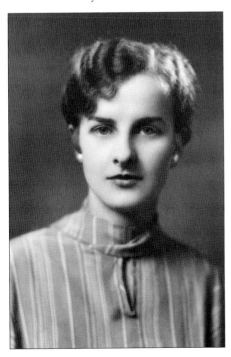

The New Jersey Supreme Court in conference. Chief Justice Arthur Vanderbilt is at head of table; Brennan is to the right of Vanderbilt; Nathan Jacobs is seated beside Brennan.

President Eisenhower greets Brennan in the Oval Office, September 29, 1956, the day Eisenhower announced Brennan's appointment to the U.S. Supreme Court.

Back home in Rumson, New Jersey, September 30, 1956. Brennan is flanked by Marjorie and daughter Nancy; standing are sons Hugh (at left) and William III.

Brennan with Nancy, seven, and Marjorie at the Supreme Court for his swearing-in ceremony, October 16, 1956

Brennan in his judicial robe

Brennan at the Senate Judiciary Committee confirmation hearing, February 1957. Senator Estes Kefauver (D-Tenn.) is at left.

Brennan and Chief Justice Earl Warren, accompanied by Warren's wife and daughter, arrive at Washington National Airport from Los Angeles for the special Court session on the Little Rock school desegregation case, August 1958.

The Warren Court, 1965–1966. Seated, left to right: Tom Clark, Hugo Black, Earl Warren, William O. Douglas, John Harlan. Standing, left to right: Byron White, Brennan, Potter Stewart, Abe Fortas.

Lunch group at the Milton Kronheim liquor warehouse, late 1960s. Seated, left to right: Justice William O. Douglas; 4th Circuit Chief Judge Simon Sobeloff; Kronheim; Chief Justice Earl Warren; Justice Thurgood Marshall. Standing, left to right: Washington lawyer Milton King; D.C. Circuit Chief Judge David Bazelon; former Maryland governor Theodore McKeldin; Washington businessman Stanley Rosensweig; D.C. Circuit Judge Skelly Wright; and Brennan.

to Washington, becoming something of a surrogate father to the young judge, whose own father had died when he was two years old. Bazelon assumed the role of unofficial social director at Kronheim's lunches, helping draw up the guest lists and menu. And so it is not surprising that Bazelon started inviting Brennan along too. What is perhaps more surprising is that here, amid an intimate crowd of powerful men brought together by a Jewish liquor dealer, Brennan would come to feel most at ease in Washington. Kronheim never asked Brennan for any favors, and the only things he gave Brennan besides the subsidized lunches were packages of pecans every Christmas and a birthday telegram each April.

Kronheim understood the appeal of his unassuming cafeteria perfectly. "They can relax out here, loosen up," he said in 1979. "They know they can talk off the record without anything being repeated. I never discuss their business, and they never discuss mine." Brennan, who had enjoyed all-male lunches at the Root Beer and Checkers Club in Red Bank, liked the easy male camaraderie at Kronheim's as much as Bazelon. "They were like a couple of frat boys together," recalled one clerk who served in both of their chambers. Brennan and Bazelon both enjoyed listening to Kronheim hold forth on politics, sports, and local gossip, or hearing the lifelong Washingtonian regale recent transplants to Washington like themselves with tales of the old days.

The two men had grown ever closer in the years since Brennan moved to Washington. They went on morning walks together — as far as their respective courthouses during the week — or through Rock Creek Park on the weekend, although Bazelon did not like getting up quite as early as Brennan. At Bazelon's suggestion, Brennan invested in a real estate project near the new airfield in rural Virginia that would become Dulles Airport. Bazelon had already begun to amass a tremendous fortune, thanks in part to his investments with a Jewish immigrant from Russia named Charlie Schmidoff, who became one of Washington's most successful real estate developers under the name Charles E. Smith. Those investments explain why Bazelon could afford to build a Japanese-style house in Georgetown in 1958 so striking in its architectural detail it would later be featured on the cover of the *Washington Star's* Sunday magazine. Brennan, living on a judge's salary alone, still could not afford to buy a home in Washington.

Many prominent Washingtonians, including Senators Edmund Muskie and Abraham Ribicoff, considered Bazelon among their closest friends. But his bond with Brennan ran deeper due to their experience as judges. "They shared so much intellectually," Bazelon's son, Richard, recalled. Despite the chauffeur-driven car, hand-tailored suits, and Japanese-style designer house, Bazelon, like Brennan, never stopped viewing himself as an outsider or identifying with underdogs. "They were cut out of the same cloth as judges," said Washington lawyer Abe Krash. Bazelon's sympathetic and controversial views about the rights of criminal defendants explain why he would come to be viewed as the prototypical activist liberal judge in the years to come.

BRENNAN CONTINUED TO wrestle with his own judicial philosophy in the early 1960s. His views were still enough of an unknown quantity that the Associated Press could declare in 1962 that "most students of the Court say he has not laid down any general theory to outline his position" akin to Black or Frankfurter. And yet, as early as 1957, Brennan was already talking about his role as a justice in expansive terms and had clearly embraced an active role for the courts as an engine for social change. He did not feel bound simply to interpreting a static set of laws set forth in the Constitution or by prior court precedent. "Courts have a creative job to do when they find that a rule has lost its touch with reality and should be abandoned or reformulated to meet new conditions and new moral values," Brennan said in a 1957 speech at Georgetown University. He invoked the notion of a judge's creative function in a 1959 speech in which he rejected the idea that "THE LAW," as he wrote in his prepared remarks, is "some brooding omnipresence in the sky, wholly unconcerned with the broader, extra legal values pursued by society at large or the individual." Brennan acknowledged that legislators could hand judges and lawyers a solution to some social problems, but that that left judges and lawyers to figure out answers for the rest.

Where no precedent stood in the way, Brennan argued in his 1957 speech at Georgetown, the courts should hammer out new rules respecting those values of the past that "have survived the tests of reason and experience and anticipate what contemporary values will best meet those tests." Adhering to precedent mattered less than accomplishing what he viewed as the primary mission of the justice system: preserving individual freedom "to the fullest extent possible consistent with the public welfare," as Brennan told an audience at Duquesne Law School in Pittsburgh in February 1960. During a lunch with clerks from another chamber during his second term on the Court, Brennan was even blunter about whether he viewed precedent as any obstacle: "Of course I would be bound by decisions of the Court, at least those I've had an opportunity to participate in."

Brennan's most important early speech laying out his judicial philosophy came in February 1961, when he delivered the second annual Madison Lecture at New York University. The Madison Lecture served as something of a bully pulpit for Brennan and the other members of his bloc on the Court. Black had delivered the inaugural lecture the year before, and Warren and Douglas followed Brennan in the two subsequent years. Black had focused in his speech on the applicability of the Bill of Rights to the federal government, reminding the audience that he viewed its protections as preeminent. "There are 'absolutes' in our Bill of Rights," Black said. "They were put there on purpose by men who knew what words meant, and meant their prohibitions to be 'absolutes.'"

Brennan offered a sequel to Black's speech, focusing on the Bill of Rights' applicability to the states. Unlike most of his speeches, which he relied on his clerks to draft, Brennan closeted himself in his chambers working on draft after draft for this one by himself. The result was his most public embrace to date of Black's view that the Fourteenth Amendment incorporated the Bill of Rights' protections as applying to the states. But Brennan, who was often skittish about going as far as Black, rejected his senior colleague's view that the Fourteenth Amendment incorporated all of the amendments en masse. Instead, Brennan cited Justice Cardozo for the idea that the Fourteenth Amendment's due process clause could be used to apply individual rights to the states selectively.

Brennan argued that additional parts of the Bill of Rights—particularly those provisions providing rights to criminal defendants—urgently needed to be applied against the states. As of 1960, few of the protections afforded criminal defendants in the Bill of Rights applied in state courts, where 95 percent of cases wound up. In some parts of the country, police in 1960 could still knock down a door without a warrant or roughly question suspects for hours. Defendants could be tried without a lawyer with no violation of constitutional rights. "Crises at hand and in prospect are creating, and will create, more and more collisions between the citizen and his government," Brennan said. "The need for vigilance to prevent government from whittling away the rights of the individual was never greater."

A watershed moment in the piecemeal incorporation of the Bill of Rights against the states began a month after Brennan delivered the Madison Lecture. In March 1961 the Court took up the case of *Mapp v. Ohio.* Several years earlier, police officers in Cleveland had forcibly entered the home of Dollree Mapp without a warrant as part of an investigation of a recent bombing. The officers did not find the bombing suspect they were looking for, but turned up allegedly obscene materials as they searched among Mapp's photo album, personal papers, and a trunk in her basement. Brennan and his allies thought *Mapp* would be a simple obscenity case, since they did not appear to have the votes to address what they viewed as the underlying injustice of allowing evidence obtained without a warrant to be used against a defendant. Since 1914 the Court had barred the use of such evidence in federal court as a violation of the Fourth Amendment's prohibition on unreasonable searches and seizures. But this so-called exclusionary rule had never been applied to the states on the grounds that the Fourth Amendment did not extend to state criminal cases. Frankfurter took that position in his 1949 opinion for the Court, *Wolf v. Colorado,* and he appeared still to have a majority to reaffirm it now, a dozen years later.

But as the justices left the conference where they discussed the *Mapp* case, Clark turned to Black and Brennan and asked, "Wouldn't this be a good case to apply the exclusionary rule and do what *Wolf* didn't do?" Warren assigned the case to Clark, who wrote a majority opinion declaring that the exclusionary rule would now apply to state prosecutions too. Brennan was elated by the result. "Of course you know I think this is just magnificent and wonderful," he wrote Clark. "I have not joined anything since I came with greater pleasure."

Harlan, who wrote the dissent, saw this for what it was: a major step toward applying the Bill of Rights to the states. "If you don't mind me saying so," the unfailingly polite Harlan wrote Clark, "Your opinion comes perilously close to accepting 'incorporation' for the Fourth A., and will doubtless encourage the 'incorporation' enthusiasts." Frankfurter was far less temperate at the conference where the justices discussed the case. Brennan recounted to his clerks that Frankfurter shook and almost came to tears as he vehemently denounced the decision. The decision was a body blow for Frankfurter's brand of jurisprudence. But worse was to come soon, at Brennan's hand.

BRENNAN WAS PLAYING an ever more important behind-the-scenes role at the Court by 1961. He continued to act as strategist in memos he circulated privately to Black, Douglas, and Warren. Brennan wrote his three allies in March 1961, weighing the merits of voting to grant cert. in a case he viewed as "an ideal opportunity" for applying the *Jencks* rule for defendants' access to evidence to the states. "I suppose there would be a vehement protest against our taking the case and the probabilities are, I guess, that we'd lose out on the merits," Brennan wrote. "The latter probability may be a good reason to pass up this opportunity but I do think we'll wait a long time before we get a question as sharply presented. My inclination is to vote to grant and take a chance. What do you think?"

Around the same time, Warren discreetly regularized Brennan's role as his chief unofficial adviser. Each week, the chief justice entered Brennan's chambers unannounced on Thursday afternoon or Friday morning with his loose-leaf notebook, in which he scribbled notes on the Court's docket. He invariably called Brennan's secretary, Mary Fowler, by the wrong name, "Miss Fuller," before entering Brennan's office and closing the door. Brennan and Warren privately discussed the cases to come before the conference during these meetings, which might last an hour or two.

It was natural, then, that Warren ultimately turned to Brennan to write the opinion, when, in 1961, the Court took up a landmark case about how Tennessee drew up its state legislative districts — a case Warren would later label the most important of his tenure. The case showed Brennan at his best as a tactician and coalition builder, but also highlights his willingness to sacrifice the quality of an opinion's legal reasoning to get the outcome he wanted.

The United States' population had shifted from farm to city over the previous half-century, but the states' legislative maps had not been redrawn accordingly. The result was wildly unequal districts. One state senator represented Los Angeles County, which had a population of more than 6 million people, while another represented three northern California rural counties with a total population of 14,294. These skewed districts allowed rural lawmakers to retain disproportionate power, and they were not about to give it up by redrawing the maps. Tennessee had not redrawn its district maps in nearly fifty years; some of the state's urban districts contained twenty-five times the population of rural ones.

The Court, at Frankfurter's urging, had previously avoided intervening in the apportionment issue, an area he argued should be left to the elected branches of government. "Courts ought not to enter this political thicket," Frankfurter wrote in the controlling 1946 case. He believed the Court was ill-equipped to redress these wrongs and fashion an appropriate remedy. Frankfurter felt no differently now that the Court had the case of *Baker v. Carr* before it fifteen years later. Brennan gave little weight to the idea that the Court should avoid getting involved in "political questions." He thought Frankfurter himself had opened the door to the Court weighing in about legislative districts the year before. Frankfurter had written an opinion rejecting the way Alabama had drawn the boundaries of Tuskegee into a twenty-eight-sided figure designed to exclude 99 percent of the city's African American voters. Frankfurter insisted, however, that the Tuskegee case was a racial-discrimination one rather than a matter of reapportionment.

When the Court first took up *Baker v. Carr,* the Tennessee reapportionment case, in April 1961, everyone — including the lawyers arguing in favor of reapportionment — understood that Potter Stewart would be the key justice in the case. Reminiscent of the lawyer who once joked about moving his lectern directly in front of Stewart, the plaintiffs' lawyers in *Baker v. Carr* directed their arguments at Stewart.

Frankfurter gave a tour de force argument at the April 21 conference, exceeding even his usual flare for melodrama. He spoke for at least ninety minutes, pulling volumes of the Court's cases off the shelves as he darted around the room, gesticulating. Frankfurter warned in a grave voice that the Court would "rue the result" if it got involved in the case. He argued that taking up reapportionment would be an error akin to the disastrous Bay of Pigs invasion in Cuba that had begun the previous week and was just being reported by the press. Brennan disagreed, saying "the purpose of the Fourteenth Amendment was to give equality" and that remedies were not insoluble. The justices went around the table one by one, lining up four to four by the time it was Stewart's time to speak. He remained undecided, and the justices soon agreed to hold over the case for the following term, as Stewart requested.

Frankfurter wasted little time after the October 1961 reargument before resuming his offensive. The next day, October 10, he circulated a sixty-page memorandum laying out why the Court should stay out of reapportionment. "I find it necessary to state in comprehensive detail the problems involved in this case, the disposition of which has such far-reaching implications for the well-being of the Court," he wrote. Brennan countered with an eleven-page chart he told the conference was prepared by his clerk Roy Schotland, which laid out the vast disparities among Tennessee counties. "At the very least, the data show a picture which Tennessee should be required to justify if it is to avoid the conclusion that the 1901 [Apportionment] Act applied to today's facts, is simple caprice."

In between the Frankfurter-Brennan volley of memos, Harlan quietly penned a plea of his own to Stewart and Whittaker. "Unless I am much mistaken, past events in this case plainly indicate that your votes will be determinative of its outcome," Harlan wrote. The justice never known for alarmism warned his two brethren, "The case involves implications whose importance is unmatched by those of any other case coming here in my time." He said, "the independence of the Court, and its aloofness from political vicissitudes, have always been the mainspring of its stability and vitality," and enforced his view that "the only sure way of avoiding this is to keep the gate to the thicket tightly closed."

Harlan's note pleased Frankfurter, who told him, "You have rendered an important service to the Court, whatever the outcome." Frankfurter had increasingly come to view Harlan as his true heir on the Court. After one case the previous term, Frankfurter wrote his friend Judge Learned Hand praising Harlan for "taking his blinders off in viewing the dubious — very dubious — qualities of Hugo and Douglas and the shoddy Brennan." In the middle of consideration of *Baker v. Carr*, Frankfurter wrote Harlan a note lamenting the Court's willingness to intervene in the case, which concluded, "Why do I bother you with this? I suppose to prove the truth of a German saying that when the heart is full it spills over. And so it spills over on you — who alone gives me comfort." Frankfurter began inviting Harlan's clerks to his annual dinner for Harvard Law School graduates, bestowing on them the rank of honorary alumni. He had given up on wooing Brennan's clerks altogether as a lost cause, and had long since stopped visiting Brennan's chambers with any frequency.

Like Frankfurter, Harlan worried about how far Brennan and his allies were willing to go. Yet his concerns did not interfere with his ability to maintain good relations with other justices thanks to a personality that earned him the nickname, "Frankfurter without mustard." Harlan's dealings with his colleagues, including Brennan, were free of the sort of intrigue that Frankfurter enjoyed. He and Brennan grew closer as friends, despite their disagreements. They talked so late into the night about cases when Harlan came over for dinner or Brennan and Marjorie visited his Connecticut summer home that their wives would give up in frustration. Brennan shocked his clerks in the 1961–62 term by greeting the patrician Harlan at a cocktail reception for visiting British judges by putting his arm around his shoulder and saying, "Hiya, Johnny Boy, how're you doing?" Harlan grinned ear to ear.

Even Frankfurter realized that Harlan was often a more effective advocate than he for the positions they jointly espoused. "I strongly believe," he wrote Harlan in one case, "that a memo by you, to which I append agreement, will carry with it the persuasiveness of your calm least discounted by my heat." As the justices took up *Baker v. Carr* for a second time at their October 13 conference, Frankfurter largely deferred to Harlan to make their case. Harlan spoke with intense emotion as he pleaded "against getting into these political contests."

Brennan, who spoke next, argued that there was simply no getting around the fact that the Tennessee apportionment was "a capricious and arbitrary denial of equal protection." He advocated for asserting jurisdiction in *Baker v. Carr* but not necessarily announcing a specific remedy. "I think that an assertion of power will cause the Tennessee legislature to act," he said. When it came time for Stewart to speak, he made clear that he agreed with Brennan's analysis. Stewart would vote to reverse, although he would go no further than agreeing that the district court had jurisdiction to hear the case. Stewart would not sign onto an opinion in which the Court directed any particular remedy and was not convinced that every district had to be drawn identically. He also suggested that voters who complained about unequal districts would have to bear a heavy burden of proof to show a violation of the equal protection clause.

The question of who should write the opinion was a delicate one, because the fifth vote, Stewart, was not willing to accept the kind of strict equality in numbers of voters in legislative districts that Black and Douglas favored. A broad opinion might lose Stewart outright; an opinion too narrow might prompt Douglas to fire off a concurrence that would alienate Stewart. Warren talked it over repeatedly with Black and Douglas, who reinforced his natural inclination to assign the case to Brennan. After Warren visited him early on October 22 to tell him the news, Brennan wrote Black to thank him for helping sway Warren.

Brennan's biggest challenge was how to explain the Court's intervention in this apportionment case without completely undermining the longstanding legal doctrine that the Court will not decide political questions. Brennan's solution was to do some gerrymandering of his own. He redrew the doctrine to emphasize that the Court should avoid cases that were largely political disputes between Congress and the executive branch, but he concluded that the Court need not restrain its involvement in apportionment disputes involving the states. To keep Stewart's vote, Brennan gave no hint of a remedy or what standards lower courts should employ to determine whether an apportionment came close enough to equal representation. He suggested only that judges could apply "well developed and familiar" equal protection criteria.

In fact, there were no "familiar" criteria as to what judicial standards might be applied by judges to decide a redistricting case under the Fourteenth Amendment's equal protection clause. Brennan's reasoning would come under heavy criticism. One professor labeled it "a judicial sleight of hand." One of the harshest critics of the opinion would later be Michael McConnell, who clerked for Brennan during the 1980–81 term and went on to a distinguished career as a conservative law professor and federal judge. McConnell pointed out years later that the equal protection clause had never been applied to a districting question before. McConnell wrote, "It is hard to avoid the conclusion that the fateful decision to shift ground to equal protection was made for no reason other than to avoid the appearance of a departure from" the Court's precedents that apportionment matters were not appropriate for federal court decision.

Brennan circulated a draft to Stewart, his intended audience of one, on January 22, 1962 — five days before he showed it to Black, Douglas, and Warren. Brennan was pleased when Stewart called to tell him he was satisfied. "There was a broad Irish grin on his face when he told me that the fifth vote was secure," Douglas recalled. For his part, Douglas thought the opinion was long and tedious. But all looked to be in place when Brennan circulated the opinion to the full Court on the last day of January before

departing for a ten-day judicial conference in Puerto Rico along with Warren and Clark. While he was gone, though, Harlan pleaded with Stewart to
hold off before formally joining Brennan's opinion. Stewart assured Harlan
the next day that he would "try to bring an open mind to it, although as of
now I find myself in agreement with Bill Brennan's opinion."

But by the time Brennan returned from Puerto Rico, Stewart had begun
to move away from his position. It was not Harlan's pleading but rather
the actions of one of his own allies that had started the trouble. As feared,
Douglas circulated a concurring opinion in which he wrote that the equal
protection clause required substantial equality in legislative districts. A
day later, Stewart informed his colleagues that Douglas's concurrence had
prompted him to decide to write too. Brennan, worried that Stewart was
drifting away, called him after strategizing with his clerks. After small talk
about his trip, Brennan tried assuring Stewart that he did not much care
for Douglas's concurrence either. Stewart promised only to circulate his
concurrence to the majority privately first.

Stewart circulated his concurrence, in which he drew a strict marker
on how far he would go, on February 13. He declared that the Court had
decided "three things and no more" — that the district court had jurisdiction to hear the claim by Tennessee voters, that they had standing, and
that the issue was not a political question that could not be adjudicated by
the courts. If Douglas insisted on going further, Brennan would lose Stewart's vote. Stewart was not satisfied even after Douglas made the changes
he requested, and hinted he might write separately that his vote was only
good for the current case, thus diminishing the decision's impact considerably. Brennan talked him out of that idea, although he drove home with his
clerk that night in a funk.

Matters remained uncertain for several weeks until an unexpected vote
switch. Brennan received a telephone call from Justice Clark, who said
he wanted to discuss the case right away. Despite a snowstorm, Brennan
volunteered to come over to Clark's apartment immediately. Brennan had
gotten some hint the day before that Clark was still thinking about his position when his clerk stopped by Brennan's chambers to ask for a copy of
the chart Brennan had circulated the previous October. Brennan's clerk
stayed in the car as snow fell and Brennan remained upstairs in Clark's
Connecticut Avenue apartment for more than an hour.

Brennan came back down in a jubilant mood: Clark had decided to switch his vote and join Brennan's opinion, which meant that Brennan would no longer have to worry about Stewart's shaky fifth vote. Despite the hint the day before, Clark's decision caught Brennan by surprise. He had not even talked with Clark about the case during their trip to Puerto Rico. Frankfurter, by contrast, had tried to firm up Clark's vote by suggesting he write separately about the other remedies available to Tennessee voters. Clark's research — which included a careful study of the charts Brennan had circulated earlier — convinced him that no such remedy existed. Clark was inclined to go much further than Stewart; he was willing to announce a remedy rather than merely hold that the district court had jurisdiction over the case. Clark informed Frankfurter that he was withdrawing from his dissent in a note he circulated that same day. "I am sorry to say that I cannot find any practical course that the people could take in bringing this about except through the federal courts."

Brennan now faced something of a dilemma: should he rewrite his opinion to go beyond what Stewart wanted, now that he no longer needed his vote? Stewart made clear that he would dissent from such a revised opinion. Although this still would have left Brennan with a majority, he stopped short, preferring to accomplish less rather than risk alienating Stewart. "That's the way Potter and I very often got together," Brennan recalled. "He didn't want to go as far as I wanted to go and I was content just to keep his vote to get a larger majority."

As Brennan explained to Black, Douglas, and Warren, "The changes represent the maximum to which Potter will subscribe." That decision disappointed Clark, who scolded the majority in his concurrence for the way "it refuses to award relief here — although the facts are undisputed — and fails to give the District Court any guidance whatever." The margin of victory turned out to be 6–2, since Whittaker ultimately did not participate in the case. He had been admitted to a hospital for treatment of exhaustion, and was to announce his retirement a few days later. The strain of being a Supreme Court justice had proven too much for the chronically indecisive Whittaker to bear.

The presence of several justices' wives in the audience — including Marjorie — signaled to close Court watchers that something momentous would be announced when the Court convened on March 26, 1962. Leaning forward in his green leather chair, Brennan began, "I have for announcement, No. 6 — *Baker v. Carr*," and continued reading for almost an hour until he had finished the entire fifty-four-page opinion. "Bill," Warren wrote in a note he passed along the bench, "it is a great day for the Irish" — crossing out Irish and replacing it with "country."

Both Frankfurter and Harlan lashed out in sharply worded dissents. Frankfurter warned of a looming "mathematical quagmire" and Harlan criticized the "abrupt departure that the majority makes from judicial history." As in *Cooper v. Aaron,* Brennan's prose in *Baker v. Carr* did not inspire, and looked all the more tepid in comparison to what Frankfurter and Harlan each wrote. A *Washington Post* editorial called his language "pallid and technical," noting, "Perhaps it was necessary to water it down and make it largely a review of what the Court had decided in previous cases in order to obtain substantial majority support." The *Post* said, "On the basis of legal scholarship, judicial tradition and forensic ability a jury would award victory to the minority."

Brennan's *Baker* opinion received far less criticism than most of the other landmark decisions he had previously joined or written, a fact he would later proudly recall. "There's nothing that the Court's done in my time that was so completely accepted as the whole result of the reapportionment fight," he said. While it is true that the result was widely accepted, Brennan's reasoning came in for a great deal of criticism among legal academics, who accused him of being fast and loose with precedent. Lucas "Scot" Powe, one of the foremost chroniclers of the Warren Court and a former Douglas clerk, labeled the case "a perfect illustration of Brennan's willingness to say virtually anything (or nothing) if a key member of his majority requested it, so long as the opinion reached the right outcome."

Reporters immediately picked up on the many questions left unanswered by Brennan's opinion. "In some sense what the court did not decide was almost as important as what it did," the *New York Times* declared. "The Justices did not say how bad districts would have to be before they would be deemed unconstitutional. In short, they laid down no standards for judging the validity of any particular state's districts." Also left unanswered was whether the same logic applied here to state legislative districts would also be applied to federal congressional districts. *Time* magazine observed, "Justice William J. Brennan's majority opinion is so vague in its implications that lawyers are not sure what it means, or even how important it is." When a reporter asked Republican congressman Thomas B. Cur-

· 8 ·

TRIUMPHANT

A T THE END of August 1962, Brennan stopped for a visit at David Bazelon's home on Cape Cod on his way back from his family's own two-month vacation on Nantucket. Brennan, Marjorie, and Nancy had first visited the crescent-shaped fourteen-mile-long island off the coast of Massachusetts a couple of summers earlier at the invitation of Robert Silvercruys, a former Belgian ambassador to the United States, and his wife.

It was Marjorie rather than Brennan who insisted on Nantucket. She had missed the beach ever since leaving Rumson, and was eager to return to Massachusetts, where the family had vacationed during the 1940s. Brennan was no beach person. He did not like the feel of sand between his toes, and his family was never even sure he knew how to swim. Over time Brennan, too, would come to enjoy these summers in Nantucket — he and Marjorie would return for two decades — but this August it is easy to imagine him relieved to take the ferry back the thirty miles to the mainland and drive to Bazelon's summer home, not far from the dock in Falmouth.

It was at Bazelon's that Brennan learned that Justice Frankfurter, who had remained hospitalized for two months after his April stroke, had finally submitted his letter of resignation to President Kennedy. Bazelon and Brennan turned on the television on the afternoon of Wednesday, August

29, having heard that Kennedy was about to announce Frankfurter's successor. They watched as the president named his fifty-four-year-old labor secretary, Arthur Goldberg, to replace Frankfurter in the Court's "Jewish seat."

According to Brennan, the news left Bazelon crestfallen. Bazelon almost certainly knew he was too liberal and controversial to win confirmation as a Supreme Court justice, and that two other prominent Jewish Washington lawyers with whom he was friends, Goldberg and Abraham Ribicoff, were closer to the president. Both Goldberg and Ribicoff — but not Bazelon — had appeared on published shortlists of potential nominees. Still, Brennan thought Bazelon had not entirely given up the dream of being tapped for the Court himself — not until the president named Goldberg, another self-made son of Russian Jewish immigrants from Illinois, five years his junior. Bazelon received a reasonable consolation prize: he would become chief judge of the D.C. Circuit in October after the staunchly conservative judge holding that post reached the mandatory retirement age of seventy. The announcement of Goldberg also disappointed Frankfurter, who would have preferred that Kennedy select a like-minded scholar such as Freund to replace him.

Brennan could not have been happier about Goldberg, an unabashed liberal labor lawyer who helped mobilize the union vote for Kennedy in the 1960 election. Brennan liked to greet his new clerks each fall by asking them what they thought was the most important thing they needed to know as they began their work in his chambers. The pair of stumped novices would watch quizzically as Brennan held up five fingers. Brennan then explained that with five votes, you could accomplish anything. Now, with Goldberg's nomination, Brennan's bloc would finally have a reliable fifth vote. The implications were not lost on reporters covering Kennedy's announcement. As the conservative *Richmond Times-Dispatch* lamented, "Mr. Goldberg's confirmation by the Senate would establish a solid majority of five, enabling liberalism 'to sound what stop she please.'"

Goldberg's swearing-in drew both President Kennedy and his brother Attorney General Robert Kennedy to the Court on the morning of October 1. (Warren had only recently moved up the Court's start time from noon to 10 A.M.) In the weeks that followed, Brennan did his best to tutor his new colleague, who had wavy gray hair and wore thick black-framed eyeglasses, about life at the Court. Goldberg, like so many new justices who had been in public life, found the transition difficult. "The Secretary's phone never stops ringing; the Justice's phone never rings — even his best friends don't call him," he complained.

Brennan made it a point to call on Goldberg, although he carefully avoided repeating Frankfurter's mistake of coming on too strong. He walked down the hall to Goldberg's chambers after his newest colleague circulated a memo to his fellow justices blaming a clerk for two incompatible paragraphs in an opinion that had been released to the public. Brennan gently advised Goldberg that whatever he said to his clerks inside his chambers was a private matter, but as far as the rest of the world knows, only justices make mistakes. Goldberg immediately circulated another memo taking responsibility for the error. When Goldberg, the sole Jewish justice, put up Christmas decorations, Brennan informed him that such displays were not customary at the Court. Goldberg did not understand why Brennan had not voted to consider a case involving a criminal-procedure issue he thought was ripe for change. Brennan, knowing that this was one of the rare instances where he and Warren disagreed, smiled and asked quizzically, "And where, Arthur, were you going to get the fifth vote?" Brennan operated with a light enough touch that Goldberg later could not recall a single instance of his fellow justice lobbying him while they served together.

Brennan had little success winning over President Kennedy's earlier appointee, Byron White, who had replaced Whittaker in April 1962 at the age of forty-five. Born in a small Colorado plains town of 550 with a view of the Rocky Mountains twenty miles to the west, White became the most famous college football player of his day at the University of Colorado, where he earned the nickname he came to detest: Whizzer. The all-American halfback deferred a Rhodes scholarship to play pro football with the Pittsburgh Pirates and then alternated semesters between the Detroit Lions and Yale Law School, where he still managed to rank first in his class.

White returned to practice law in Denver after a clerkship with Chief Justice Vinson. He brushed off efforts seeking to enlist him as a political candidate, but in 1959 signed on to help with the fledgling presidential campaign of an old acquaintance, John F. Kennedy. White had been a student at Oxford when he first met Kennedy in the south of France in 1939. They had crossed paths again a few years later in the Pacific when both served in the Navy during World War II. President Kennedy had tapped

White to be deputy attorney general under his brother Robert. And when Whittaker stepped down from the Court, White was the only person Kennedy seriously considered as his successor.

White joined the Court as the first clerk ever to return as a justice, and was disappointed to see that not much had changed in the intervening fifteen years. "The same issues that were here in 1947 are still here and Hugo [Black] still runs the Court," he complained. Although his hair had thinned in the interim, White, with his square jaw and running back's build, looked much the same as he had during his days as a clerk. Brennan and his allies immediately realized that White, the first Democratic appointee to the Court in thirteen years, would not join their liberal bloc. Throughout his first term, White voted on the side of restraint, filing dissents charging that the Court was deciding issues not presented, failed to defer to Congress, and wrote opinions too broad in scope. But Goldberg's arrival meant that Brennan did not need to accommodate White's concerns: the bloc had its fifth vote without him. After the very first Friday conference of the term, Brennan came back to his chambers with a look of triumph on his face — a look he would keep all term.

If there was one day when his new majority flexed its muscles, it came in the spring of that term, on March 18, 1963. The liberal bloc overturned four of the Court's long-standing precedents. It also set standards for Georgia legislative districts in one case and significantly enhanced the rights of criminal defendants in three others. "Perhaps on no other single day since the Civil War had states' rights taken such a beating," noted the *Washington Post*'s Supreme Court reporter. Brennan's bloc forcefully cast aside Frankfurter's legacy of judicial restraint just shy of the one-year anniversary of his stroke. It was a day of particular exultation for Frankfurter's main antagonist, Black, who had served long enough to see some of his most important dissents finally become majority opinions. Of greatest significance for Black was the decision he announced in the case of *Gideon v. Wainwright*, directing states to provide lawyers to indigent criminal defendants, nineteen years after he had first called for such a requirement in a 1942 dissent.

The *Gideon* case became the best known to the public of the quartet announced that day, thanks to the best-selling book *Gideon's Trumpet*, by *New York Times* reporter Anthony Lewis, and a 1980 Emmy-nominated television movie starring Henry Fonda. Less publicized or easily understood but equally far-reaching in its implications was the case announced by Brennan. His opinion for the Court in *Fay v. Noia* strengthened significantly the ability of state prisoners to challenge their convictions in federal court.

At issue was the use of petitions for writs of habeas corpus, a means by which prisoners can seek review of their detentions even after a full trial and direct appeal of their conviction. Twenty years had passed since a New York state court convicted Charles Noia and two codefendants of murder committed during a robbery, based solely on their signed confessions. Noia's two codefendants successfully challenged their life sentences on the grounds that their confessions were coerced and that the convictions thus violated the Fourteenth Amendment. But when Noia then asked the state court to review his conviction, he was rebuffed for having failed to appeal his conviction within the time frame allowed by the state court, as his codefendants had done. A federal judge similarly rejected Noia's habeas corpus petition on the grounds that he had not exhausted available remedies in state court, although the Second Circuit reversed and held in Noia's favor.

When *Fay v. Noia* reached the Court in 1962, Brennan and his fellow justices again faced the issue of how much access to federal courts state prisoners should have to challenge their convictions after the fact. The Court had wrestled with the question before. What had originally been deemed a mechanism to challenge pretrial detention or the convicting court's jurisdiction had expanded to include an examination of whether a defendant's constitutional rights had been violated during the trial. But that power to intervene was not particularly significant until the Supreme Court began applying more of the Bill of Rights to the states, thus expanding the constitutional rights prisoners could claim were violated during their trials.

As a state judge, Brennan had viewed habeas corpus petitions as a vehicle for meddlesome federal judges to unjustly intrude on their decisions in cases that had been given a full hearing. But Brennan's views on habeas corpus — and the proper division of labor between federal and state judges — had shifted dramatically since he joined the Supreme Court. Brennan had flipped through enough cert. petitions to realize that courts in other states were not quite as diligent about reining in police abuses as he and his colleagues were in New Jersey. He had seen enough to convince him that state courts — particularly those in the South — often required close federal court scrutiny. "Far too many cases come from the states to the Supreme Court presenting dismal pictures of official lawlessness, of illegal searches and seizures, illegal detentions attended by prolonged interrogation and coerced admissions of guilt, of the denial of counsel, and downright brutality," Brennan said in a 1961 lecture at New York University. "Judicial self-restraint which defers too much to the sovereign powers of the states and reserves judicial intervention for only the most revolting cases will not serve to enhance Madison's priceless gift of 'the great rights of mankind secured under this Constitution.'"

The Court had begun to apply the requirements of the Bill of Rights to the states piecemeal in cases such as *Gideon,* but these new rights would be meaningless without some way of ensuring that recalcitrant states actually applied them. Brennan believed prisoners' access to federal courts via habeas petitions could be the vehicle for ensuring that the states recognized defendants' new rights. "As the Supreme Court brings state criminal proceedings more and more within the protections and limitations of the federal Bill of Rights, federal habeas jurisdiction will correspondingly expand," Brennan predicted a year before the Court took up *Fay v. Noia.* No longer would states be able to use minor procedural defects to justify knocking out prisoners' appeals.

Any expansion of access to habeas corpus required rolling back several legal doctrines that served as barriers to such petitions. As it stood, prisoners could not file a habeas petition if they had waived their rights, failed to exhaust state remedies, or if a state conviction rested on grounds independent of any question under federal law. Harlan tried his best to convince his fellow justices that they should not blithely cast aside those limits. He warned in a thirty-nine-page memo he circulated on December 3, 1962, that the Court's decision in the case "will have far-reaching and lasting effects in this important field of federal-state relations."

Brennan retorted with a memo of his own a week later, taking particular exception to Harlan's analysis. "I submit with all respect that this argument is nothing more than a play on words," Brennan wrote. This, like obscenity, was one of the rare instances where Brennan and Warren did not see eye-to-eye. Warren, a former county prosecutor himself, still feared that expanding access to habeas corpus petitions would infringe upon local autonomy. Brennan devoted more time trying to convince Warren than in any case during their entire tenure together. He met privately with Warren several times with the goal of allaying his concerns that expanding habeas corpus might cripple local law enforcement. Those private conversations worked. At the justices' January 11, 1963, conference, Warren said he agreed with the analysis in Brennan's memo.

Assigned the case by Warren, Brennan produced an opinion that significantly opened federal courts to habeas petitions from state prisoners. Even if criminal defendants failed to follow a state procedural rule, they would not necessarily lose the ability to pursue their constitutional claims in federal courts. Brennan wrote that defendants only forfeited their opportunity to raise a claim in federal court if they had "deliberately bypassed" state procedures for adjudicating the claim. Brennan went out of his way to assert in his opinion that it was consistent with past precedent and modest in its potential impact. "Our decision today swings open no prison gates," he wrote. He dedicated much of the opinion to discussing the history of the writ, dating back to its English origins. Brennan asserted that "the nature and purpose of habeas corpus have remained remarkably constant," and that even in the early years of the nation's founding, "there was respectable common law authority for the proposition that habeas was available to remedy any kind of governmental restraint contrary to fundamental law." "Habeas corpus is one of the precious heritages of Anglo-American civilization," Brennan wrote. "We do no more today than confirm its continuing efficacy."

His draft opinion circulated January 31 largely satisfied the five other justices who joined, including both of the Court's newest members, White and Goldberg. "Your opinion in Fay v. Noia is another Brennan milestone," Goldberg wrote him on February 6. "Perhaps only Baker v. Carr outranks it in importance." A *Washington Post* editorial praised Brennan's work as "historic" and "a magnificent opinion." The opinion also elicited positive reviews from Huey E. Lee, an inmate at Kilby Prison in Montgomery, Alabama, who wrote Brennan to say, "I hope the Court will not permit its clarity and force to be mangled, obfuscated or ignored by judicial dogs."

But the opinion outraged the three dissenters — and Harlan in particular, who sharply disagreed with Brennan's assertion that his opinion was consistent with the Court's past precedent. "This decision, both in its abrupt break with the past and in its consequences for the future, is one of the most disquieting that the Court has rendered in a long time," Harlan wrote. He added, "The history of federal habeas corpus jurisdiction, I believe, leaves no doubt that today's decision constitutes a square rejection of long-accepted principles governing the nature and scope of the Great Writ."

As in *Baker v. Carr*, Brennan had suggested in his *Fay v. Noia* opinion more clarity than actually existed. It was not unusual for justices to insist that they were not changing the law significantly in an opinion that did just that. Brennan would admit years later that his opinion understated the case's significance and that "*Fay v. Noia* did completely revolutionize the whole law of habeas corpus." But Brennan, perhaps more than other justices, tended to write opinions that overstated the degree of clarity and masked the uncertainty about issues where history was not nearly as clear as he suggested. He almost certainly exaggerated when he suggested that the vindication of due process was the "historic office" of habeas. The debate over the original meaning of habeas corpus remains unsettled nearly half a century after Brennan's declaration in *Fay v. Noia*.

Brennan also played a vital behind-the-scenes role in a companion case released that same eventful day. In *Townsend v. Sain*, Warren held that federal courts could hold full evidentiary hearings when considering habeas petitions, thus opening up the possibility of what was in effect a second trial of the facts in a case. Warren's initial draft only barely addressed that central procedural question. Brennan and his clerks prepared a memo that Warren adopted nearly verbatim in several sections of his opinion. Brennan — both in his own opinion and the sections he quietly fed to Warren — had opened the doors to allowing federal district court judges, using habeas corpus jurisdiction to oversee local law enforcement and courts.

Not even Brennan's clerks realized the extent of their boss's triumph until the end of the term. Over morning coffee, something that had become a daily tradition in Brennan's chambers, Brennan asked his clerks to guess how many times he had dissented that term. Both guessed a dozen times. Brennan held up four fingers. That was the total number of times he had dissented among the 129 cases that term. The press took note of the Court's new direction. By the end of the term, the *Washington Post* would observe, "The Court is creating, is innovating, is intervening deeply in American life" and this "trend of creativity on the part of the Court shows no apparent signs of slackening."

Reporters also took note of Brennan's important role. The *Post* declared in April 1963 that Brennan was emerging as the leader of a new centrist bloc, having been in the majority in fifty-four of fifty-six cases decided so far that term. Similarly, a UPI wire service article that same month noted "the emergence of a kind of axis between Justice Warren and Justice William J. Brennan of New Jersey. They have voted together in all but two cases." That sort of recognition was a dramatic change from the kind of press coverage Brennan attracted just months earlier in the December 1962 issue of *Look* magazine. "At 56, Associate Justice Brennan is a chunky, hearty, informal jurist, and new acquaintances find it hard to use the traditional 'Mr. Justice' form of address." The *Look* article goes on to note, "He cusses moderately, dresses neatly, wears button-down shirts, smokes both pipe and filter-tip cigarettes, watches college and pro-football all autumn on television and loves to converse with friends about almost anything." Brennan, who preferred to be seen as a regular guy, could not have been more pleased.

FRANKFURTER WATCHED WITH dismay, if from a distance, as his first term on the sidelines in twenty-four years wound down. He wrote Harlan on May 28, 1963, lamenting "the atmosphere of disregard for law and to a large extent of the legal profession that now dominates the present Court and the Court on which I sat." The Court's direction troubled Harlan too, enough that he spoke publicly about it that August in Chicago at the American Bar Association's annual convention, which Brennan also attended. "Some well-meaning people apparently believe that the judicial rather than the political process is more likely to breed better solutions of pressing or thorny problems," Harlan said. "This is a compliment to the judiciary but untrue to democratic principle."

There was one place where the ailing Frankfurter and his marginalized heir, Harlan, triumphed over Brennan that summer. In the spring of 1963, Harvard Law School passed over Brennan and instead named Harlan, who had not attended the university, to its Visiting Committee. Appointment to the Visiting Committee, which provides advice on university governance and administration, is considered a singular recognition of professional success. Brennan had never viewed Harvard Law with the reverence that Frankfurter did. He often enjoyed recounting the story of his first appearance in a New Jersey courtroom as a young lawyer, when the judge mocked him for his Ivy League vocabulary. Brennan had not held it against his alma mater for rejecting his son Bill, who was still managing fine after attending Yale Law School, working at a white-shoe Wall Street law firm despite reservations from some quarters that Bill's ties would create conflicts of interest for Brennan with respect to cases headed to the Court. Brennan had taken it in stride when one Harvard Law professor, Henry Hart, attacked his opinion in the pages of the *Harvard Law Review* only months after he had spoken at the journal's anniversary dinner. Brennan accepted an invitation in 1962 to judge Harvard's moot court competition alongside his former colleague on the New Jersey Supreme Court, Nathan Jacobs, and he spoke at the law school's Legal Aid Bureau's fiftieth anniversary banquet the following year.

But even the usually unflappable Brennan could not forgive Harvard for this latest slight. Harlan had already emerged as Frankfurter's ideological torchbearer on the Court, and his carefully nuanced opinions made him a darling at law schools throughout the country. Frankfurter had anointed Harlan's clerks honorary Harvard Law graduates, and now the school was anointing Harlan himself at Brennan's expense. Dean Griswold later said no slight was intended; the school simply wanted to fill the Visiting Committee with men of "varied backgrounds." Brennan did not see it that way. Although he did not share his feelings with Griswold or anyone else on the Harvard Law faculty, he expressed his disappointment to his clerks. "Harvard in those days failed to acknowledge that Brennan was a son of Harvard," said Stephen Friedman, a recent Harvard Law School graduate who clerked for Brennan during the 1963–64 term. "It was a case of Harvard picking its ideological heir rather than one of its own sons."

Brennan would later contend that Harvard's action was not connected to his decision, but in April 1965 he informed Professor Freund that, after nine years, Freund's role — and Harvard's monopoly — in supplying his law clerks was coming to an end. "I now feel that graduates of some of the other fine law schools should share the opportunity with graduates of ours," Brennan wrote Freund in explanation. Freund wrote back a few days later saying, "I can understand, however regretfully, your decision to spread the opportunities of a clerkship more widely." Brennan enlisted former clerks and professors at Stanford, the University of Pennsylvania, the University of California at Berkeley, and Notre Dame to pick his clerks in upcoming years.

Brennan attributed the change to pressure from deans at those other law schools who urged him to spread out the coveted clerkships more widely. Robert O'Neil, one of his 1962–63 term clerks, recalled that Brennan, as the justice responsible for handling all emergency applications filed in the Third Circuit, felt guilty about not taking clerks from schools such as Rutgers and the University of Pennsylvania located within its bounds. Friedman, though, never entirely believed that the decision to look outward for clerks and Harvard's snub were unrelated. What is certainly incorrect is the version of events Brennan told the *New Yorker* two decades later when he suggested it was actually Freund's idea all along.

THE SUCCESS BRENNAN experienced at the Court during this time did not always extend to his home life. Marjorie had slowly made a life of her own in Washington, building a circle of friends both outside and within the city's elite circles, including their next-door neighbor, Gladys Harkness, nicknamed "Daz" for her dazzling personality. Her bridge foursome, which included Baroness Silvercruys, the wife of the former ambassador from Belgium, featured elegant French meals and was later the subject of an article in the *Washington Star*. Marjorie and Brennan frequently socialized with Justices Black and Douglas and their wives and with Judge Bazelon and his wife. The evenings often ended with everyone gathered around a piano, singing songs like "Show Me the Way to Go Home" or "When Irish Eyes Are Smiling." (Brennan was usually off-key.) Marjorie enjoyed hosting small dinner parties, where she served her new specialties: osso buco and chocolate soufflé. Marjorie fulfilled her social obligations as a Supreme Court wife, including embassy tours and the annual fashion shows organized by the Lawyers' Wives of the District of Columbia. Most Saturdays, she and Brennan watched whatever British comedy was playing at Georgetown's foreign movie house or stayed home for their favorite television show, the pioneering courtroom drama *The Defenders*.

But there were also serious problems. Marjorie's back injury in January 1961, coinciding with Kennedy's inauguration, had left her in terrible pain. An orthopedist diagnosed a grinding of two vertebrae. Life in Washington — and Hugh's troubles with both Roxey and the bottle — had been stressful for her. She had probably begun drinking excessively in Rumson, and the feelings of isolation and inadequacy she experienced in Washington only exacerbated the problem. Her friends and neighbors noticed that she occasionally slurred her speech after one too many martinis. That was not necessarily unusual in Washington in the 1960s, where the nondrinker stood out at cocktail and dinner parties. And if close friends noticed that Marjorie drank too much, they were likely to brush it off as signs of how upset she was about Hugh's annulment, or about being cut off from her first, and at that point only, grandchild. Unlike her husband, Marjorie maintained no contact with Hugh Jr.

Brennan would deny to his family — and even to himself — that his wife was an alcoholic, although he could readily acknowledge his father's and his son's troubles with alcohol. But the reality was that Marjorie was almost certainly exhibiting the symptoms of alcoholism by the early 1960s. Brennan came home each night to grim dinners in Georgetown, where he turned up the volume on the news radio station to fill the silence left by his sullen wife. No matter how hard Brennan tried keeping up appearances, his friends noticed the accumulated strain caused by caring for Hugh, before he sobered up and remarried, and now Marjorie. "You bothered me a little with (may I say this to a friend?) an air of anxiety or preoccupation," wrote Yale Law professor Fred Rodell. "I guess I know why, what with Marjorie (what a sweetie) Huey, etc. but I do hate to see you carrying them all on your shoulders, however broad." Brennan ignored Rodell's expression of concern when he replied to the letter. His prominence as a Supreme Court justice only increased the pressure he felt to keep family problems well hidden.

Brennan's admirers often marveled at his empathy. "He had the ability to see a case through the eyes of the people involved," said his clerk Richard Cotton, in a television interview on the night Brennan died. "He experienced their pain or experienced what they were litigating about." That ability to empathize proved harmful to his well-being at home, where he was unable to do any more to help his wife or son than he had been as a child to stop his father from overdrinking. Brennan's daughter, Nancy, later wondered whether he silently channeled all the worry and helplessness he felt about Hugh's and Marjorie's problems into his work. If he could not help those closest to him, Nancy theorized, perhaps he resolved all the more to help the defenseless and poor through his decisions.

Brennan's financial problems, too, had also only worsened since the move to Georgetown. In addition to his $500 in rent, Brennan paid $180 a month in salary to a maid and carried $9,200 in debt from refurbishing the Dumbarton Avenue home. He was struggling to cover the unexpected cost of simultaneously helping all three of his children with their school tuition. While he had put away money for his sons' education, Brennan had not anticipated the lag between Bill graduating Colgate and enrolling in law school, or that Hugh would drop out of college and enroll again later. Combined with Nancy's private school, the tuition bills had added up to almost $6,000 per year. And Brennan's salary had not increased from $35,000 since he joined the Court.

Making matters worse, Frank W. Ritchie, the friend who had lent him money three times in 1956, wrote him in January 1962 explaining he had suffered financial setbacks of his own and needed to be repaid. An embarrassed Brennan immediately wrote back to explain he did not have the money. "I've been at my wits end juggling loans," Brennan wrote. He assured Ritchie that his situation would improve once Bill finished law school and Hugh graduated college. Brennan wrote that he also planned to make "some very drastic" changes to improve his finances, including moving to a less-expensive apartment and making do without a maid. "In short, Frank, if it's at all possible, I'm asking you to bear with me while I get myself straightened out," Brennan pleaded.

There was certainly no hint of these troubles in the *Look* magazine profile published in December 1962 that declared, "Brennan is a man at peace with himself, in love with his family and his work." Accompanying the article was a picture of thirteen-year-old Nancy resting her head on Brennan's shoulder as Marjorie looked on with a smile. Yet not long before that article appeared, Marjorie's drinking had contributed to the decision to have Nancy live as a boarder at her prep school, Holton Arms, starting the following fall. Brennan and Marjorie did not explain the decision to Nancy, who knew nothing of her mother's troubles at the time and blamed herself. "I had the sense I was being banished because I was the problem," she recalled. Her departure in the fall of 1963 made Brennan an empty nester at the age of fifty-seven.

Living just a few miles from home, Nancy was extremely homesick. But she tried to put the best face forward in a letter home that first fall explaining her decision to put off a visit, at the advice of her history teacher. "She said that home was like an old shoe, more comfortable and more lovable and bording [sic] to some people was like a new shoe, stiff and hateful. But if you just wear it long enough it gets comfortable," Nancy wrote to her father. "But then if you go back to the old shoes for awhile, when you have to come back to the new ones, they are hateful again. Maybe I better not come home for a few weeks so I can try to wear in these darn new shoes."

Brennan offered Nancy no hint of problems at home during their regular Sunday telephone conversations or at a dedication of the school's new building in October 1963, where he thanked the administration and faculty with "heartfelt gratitude for the quality of the education our daughters are receiving at their hands." Concerned about Nancy's emotional well-being after she started losing weight, school officials soon suggested she return home. Marjorie insisted that her daughter, if she was going to live at home, do all the household chores. "She made it as unpleasant as a young teenage girl could experience it," Nancy said. The next semester, Nancy returned to school as a boarder.

9

DISARMING THE SOUTH

THE CIVIL RIGHTS struggle had expanded by the early 1960s from the doors of southern schools to Woolworth's lunch counters, Greyhound bus depots, and voter-registration tables in once-sleepy rural courthouses. Through spontaneous action and well-planned campaigns, young, newly assertive African Americans had channeled the nonviolent resistance preached by Martin Luther King Jr. into creative forms of protest. They joined Freedom Rides testing laws that prohibited segregation in interstate travel. They did not fight back as enraged whites beat them with pipes or Coca-Cola crates. In Birmingham, they sang spirituals, marched peacefully, and were taken off to jail in May 1963 in so many waves that Public Safety Commissioner Bull Connor ran out of paddy wagons. Connor then turned police dogs and water hoses powerful enough to knock bricks off mortar on protestors, some of whom were children as young as six years old.

Brennan would have seen the resulting pictures of police dogs biting into a teenager's abdomen and firemen aiming water hoses at children on the front page of the morning papers he read over breakfast in May 1963. He was confronted with the civil rights question more directly when he spoke with a group of Washington, D.C., junior high school students visiting the Court that spring. One student asked him whether the Court could intervene on behalf of African Americans trying to register to vote in Mississippi. Brennan explained that the lower courts would have to act first.

Brennan grew increasingly alarmed about the violence and did not hide where his sympathies lay. After the abduction and brutal murder of three civil rights workers in Mississippi the following summer, Brennan told a University of Pennsylvania audience that the "tragic deaths" of James Chaney, Andrew Goodman, and Michael Schwerner were "full cause for national mourning," adding that there was, however, "cause for satisfaction in the thousands of other students who worked for civil rights in many parts of the country all summer without physical harm — even if not without fear and anxiety at times." Brennan delivered a prescription for greater interracial understanding to a January 1963 Detroit audience. "Real tolerance means more than just colorblindness and impartiality," he said. "It means making an extra effort to get to know and understand your neighbor, whatever the color of his skin, or however strange the way in which he worships or the accent with which he speaks."

The circles in which Brennan himself moved, however, continued to be fairly homogeneous. An influx of African Americans had transformed his hometown of Newark since World War II. But the burgeoning slums where most African Americans in Newark lived were not included on Brennan's itinerary when he returned there for a black-tie gala celebrating the seventy-fifth anniversary of the city's public library in May 1963. Washington, D.C., had been majority black since 1957, but remained highly segregated, and Brennan of course lived in the all-white neighborhood of Georgetown. He no longer attended his integrated church on Dumbarton Avenue with any frequency. He sent his daughter, Nancy, to an exclusive private boarding school just across the border in Maryland rather than to Washington's public schools. Brennan could recall with some measure of righteous indignation a liberal friend who recoiled when his son got engaged to a black woman. "It was quite a lesson to me about how this great liberal could not overcome" his prejudices, Brennan recounted.

The prevalent social norms of his generation, which limited interaction among the races, extended to Brennan's day-to-day life as a Supreme Court justice as well. Until Thurgood Marshall joined the Court in 1967, the main personal interaction Brennan had with blacks was with two servants — his maid, Minerva, at home, and his messenger, Aloysius Hood, at the Court.

Some attendees cringed when Hood served their meals at Brennan's annual Sunday reunion brunch for former clerks. One said, "It was half a step out of slavery." Inside his chambers, Brennan treated Hood courteously, once rushing into the messengers' washroom to fan him after he fainted. Brennan's secretary, Mary Fowler, however, displayed the racial prejudices she soaked up while growing up in southern Maryland in her interactions with Hood.

Brennan's clerks were never quite sure whether Fowler, feisty and opinionated by nature, just enjoyed baiting them or meant it when she suggested she did not support the *Brown* school-desegregation decision. Brennan and his usually liberal clerks needled Fowler about her conservative politics over morning coffee. But the way Mary treated Hood when Brennan was not around troubled the clerks more. "There was always a plantation feeling between the two of them," said one clerk. "She was very short with him." Second-class treatment of black employees was typical at the Court, an institution that still did not practice what it preached when it came to racial integration. A decade later, blacks remained almost entirely limited to the Court's lowest-skilled and lowest-paying jobs, prompting journalist Nina Totenberg to write a 1974 magazine article in *New Times,* labeling the Court "the last plantation." Into the 1970s, Brennan regularly hired some of the Court's black workers to do manual labor around his house such as washing walls, waxing floors, and cutting grass. Although late in his career Brennan hired an African American clerk, his retirement ultimately prevented their working together.

Nonetheless, perhaps no justice deserves more credit for advancing the cause of the civil rights movement during the first half of the 1960s than Brennan. His opinions helped protect the NAACP and sit-in demonstrators, curbed the use of libel suits as a method of intimidating the press, and provided protestors greater access to appeals in the federal courts. None of these pivotal decisions proved as explosive — or as easy for the public to understand — as the *Brown* case. But taken together, Brennan's opinions sent a clear signal to lower courts that the law could no longer be employed as a bludgeon against the civil rights movement.

The Court had largely retreated from the issue of school desegregation after Brennan's bold declarations in *Cooper v. Aaron.* The justices were skittish about sparking any more confrontations along the lines of Little Rock or the University of Mississippi. James Meredith's attempts to become Ole

Miss's first black student in 1962 prompted a bloody overnight battle between rioters and a hastily organized force of federal marshals. When Alabama's new governor George Wallace ignored a federal court's order to integrate the University of Alabama in May 1963, the Supreme Court issued a terse order rejecting the state's motion for relief as not yet ready for consideration. But the justices could not entirely avoid civil rights cases as the protest movement grew and resistance to it stiffened. In December 1960 the Court prohibited segregation in waiting rooms and restaurants serving interstate bus travel, a decision that was the initial impetus for the Freedom Rides.

In August 1961 Brennan faced the first desegregation order in a northern school district to reach the Court. A federal district court found that New Rochelle, a suburb north of New York City, had shaped its zoning, transfer, and construction policies to maintain a segregated elementary school exclusively for black students. The school board petitioned the Court to delay implementation of the desegregation order until it had a chance to appeal the case. Usually, John Harlan, as the justice who oversaw emergency appeals that came to the Court from the Second Circuit of which New York is a part, would have considered the petition. But he was away for the summer. So it was Brennan who welcomed counsel in the case into his chambers for a rare in-chambers oral argument.

Brennan took off his suit coat and put it behind his chair before sitting down and urged the two lawyers to do likewise. He did his best to put the visibly nervous lawyer for the New Rochelle school board at ease, asking if he would like some tea or a tour of the Court for himself or his family. Brennan stepped in with sympathetic questions several times during the novice lawyer's ten-minute argument. He knew that the two seasoned lawyers for the NAACP Legal Defense and Educational Fund (LDF), Thurgood Marshall and Jack Greenberg, needed no such encouragement. He quickly interrupted with sharper questions after Marshall began to speak.

"Suppose you do have to wait a year for relief?" said Brennan. "What would be so terrible about that?"

Marshall looked downcast as he hunched forward in his seat and stared at his feet. He paused for a moment before finally responding. "Justice Brennan, my clients have been waiting a long time," Marshall said. "These other folks, won't hurt them if they have to hustle a little."

The argument soon ended and Brennan escorted the lawyers from his chambers. Out in the hallway, a discouraged Marshall told his colleague Greenberg, "Well, we lost that one."

Despite his dozens of prior appearances before the Court, Marshall had had little experience with Brennan beyond the oral argument in the Little Rock case. Marshall misinterpreted the kindness Brennan displayed for a lawyer appearing in the Supreme Court for the first time as evidence he was going to rule in New Rochelle's favor. Brennan quickly drafted an order denying the stay application. The full Court denied the city's petition for review a few months later.

Nor did Marshall realize that there, in Brennan's chambers, he had delivered his last oral argument before the Supreme Court on behalf of the NAACP. Only months later, President Kennedy nominated him to the U.S. Court of Appeals for the Second Circuit. It would be another year before the Senate confirmed Marshall, due to southerners' stalling. Brennan wrote Marshall in September 1962 to congratulate him. "I knew that old adage, 'This too shall pass,' applied to the ordeal you experienced, but that could not justify it," Brennan wrote. "What the Senate finally did expresses the regard and respect in which you are held all over the country. You know how sincerely I wish you all good health and happiness."

FOR EVERY CASE initiated by the NAACP that reached the Court, it seemed as if another bubbled up as a result of the South's use of the law to beat back civil rights movement leaders, protestors, and attorneys. Law — combined with violence and economic coercion — had long served as the South's bulwark for maintaining the institution of segregation. Southern laws kept the races apart in schools and playgrounds, hospitals and funeral homes, movie houses and marriages. Segregationists turned to ever more creative misuses of law as the civil rights movement began challenging those statutes in the courts and in the streets. Activists launching a voter-registration drive were charged with sedition — a capital offense. Martin Luther King Jr. became the first citizen in the state of Alabama ever charged with felony perjury regarding his state tax payments.

The NAACP's successful legal strategy against segregation made it the leading target of southern ire in the wake of *Brown*. Alabama judges did their best to drive the NAACP out of the state. The organization was sanctioned for failing to comply with registration requirements for out-of-state corporations and held in contempt for failing to hand over its membership lists. Alabama refused to back off for years even in the face of repeated Supreme Court orders to do so. Other states stripped the NAACP of its tax-exempt status. The practical effect was to blunt the NAACP's ability to operate in southern states or to recruit potential plaintiffs, who were often terrified of being publicly identified and subject to retribution.

In 1961 the Court took up a Virginia law targeting the NAACP's activities representing civil rights plaintiffs in the state as an improper solicitation of legal business. The law was neutrally written and did not name the NAACP specifically, but there was no question about its intended target and practical effect. The Court held over the case in the spring of 1961 after Whittaker resigned and Frankfurter became disabled. By the time the Court took up the case, *NAACP v. Button,* for a second time in the fall of 1962, Martin Luther King Jr.'s Southern Christian Leadership Conference, the Congress of Racial Equality, and the student-run Student Nonviolent Coordinating Committee had supplanted the NAACP as the most activist civil rights organizations. They were the ones leading the new protests. But southerners still blamed the NAACP for most of the troublemaking anyway.

Brennan immediately went to work on his two new colleagues, Goldberg and White, even before the Court took up the case again in the fall of 1962. He circulated an exhaustive sixty-three-page memo that detailed the activities of the NAACP and its Virginia branch. The memo described the ongoing school-desegregation suits in Virginia and emphasized the organization's vital role in protracted litigation that individual plaintiffs simply could not afford to undertake on their own. Brennan did not suggest striking down the law due to its discriminatory intent. Rather, he emphasized that Virginia's regulation of solicitation "has so broad and indefinite a sweep that a person who advised another that his constitutional rights were being infringed and urged him to consult a particular lawyer would run a grave risk of incurring criminal liability under the statute."

Brennan received the assignment after the justices' October 12, 1962, conference. He initially wrote a narrow opinion that rejected the Virginia law as overly broad, avoiding the underlying constitutional issue of whether the law interfered with freedom of association or speech. Black objected to that narrow approach, and Brennan rewrote the opinion to address the law's First Amendment implications. He emphasized that the First Amendment protected a lawsuit filed to redress grievances — just as much as if the plaintiffs had petitioned their government representatives. Litigation would be protected as a form of vigorous advocacy — "a means for achieving the lawful objectives of equality of treatment by all government, federal, state and local, for the members of the Negro community in this country." No longer could southern states target the NAACP's litigation as unlawful solicitation.

THE CIVIL RIGHTS movement continued to advance in fits and starts in the months after Brennan announced his opinion in the NAACP case in January 1963. Tragedy seemed to follow every hard-won victory. Footage of schoolchildren attacked by police dogs and fire hoses in Birmingham in May generated a new wave of sympathy and attention among horrified television viewers in the North. The next month, a sniper using a deer rifle fatally shot NAACP field organizer Medgar Evers in front of his Mississippi home as his three children came out to greet him. Hundreds of thousands of people on the National Mall and a huge national television audience watched King deliver his famous "I have a dream" speech in front of the Lincoln Memorial during the March on Washington in August 1963. Then, one Sunday in September, four African American girls were killed when a dynamite attack blew up part of their church in Birmingham.

Further terrible violence in Dallas jolted the nation two months later. The justices were sequestered as usual in their Friday conference on the afternoon of November 22 when a messenger interrupted with a typewritten note from Warren's secretary, Mrs. McHugh. The junior justice, Goldberg, took the note and passed it to Warren, who then read the grim contents aloud. Warren's voice broke as he informed his colleagues that President Kennedy had been shot while riding in a motorcade in Dallas. The extent of the president's injuries was not known.

The justices quickly adjourned, and several justices and clerks gathered in the outer room of Brennan's chambers to watch the news confirming President Kennedy's assassination, on an old black-and-white television a former clerk had given him. At the end of the day, after Brennan and Mary Fowler had both gone home early, Warren stopped by Brennan's chambers, perhaps seeking comfort over the loss of the president, whom he had considered a friend. Only Brennan's clerk was there to see a sad chief justice

216 · JUSTICE BRENNAN

turn his head away in disappointment when he saw that Brennan had already left. That night, White drove out to Robert Kennedy's house in Virginia, where he clasped his former boss's shoulder as he tried to console him. Lyndon Baines Johnson, who was administered the oath of office aboard Air Force One while it still sat parked on a Dallas airfield, called Goldberg later that night for advice about how to hold the country together.

Brennan, with no such ties to either president, mourned at home with his family that weekend. Always an avid television-news viewer, Brennan, like many other Americans, was transfixed throughout the weekend by the all-day coverage that included the live murder of assassin Lee Harvey Oswald. It all left Brennan worried that society was coming apart entirely. "I can't say that those of us here are fully recovered from the shock," Brennan wrote a friend back in New Jersey, Monsignor John Cain of St. Bartholomew the Apostle Rectory in Scott Plains. "The reaction seems to prove that we didn't fully appreciate our good fortune."

Just as Brennan stood on the periphery at Kennedy's inauguration, so too would he stand somewhat outside the inner circle as the capital mourned the murdered president. He joined his fellow justices in walking in the funeral procession through the streets of Washington. He sat in the chief justice's chambers when President Johnson's emissaries arrived to press Warren to chair the commission that would investigate the assassination. And he sat in the front row of the House Chamber as President Johnson addressed a joint session of Congress on November 27 and dedicated himself to carrying on Kennedy's legacy.

One particular element of that agenda — proposed civil rights legislation that would ban all discrimination in public accommodations — stayed at the forefront of Brennan's mind as the justices took up a series of cases that fall arising out of the student sit-in movement. What began in Greensboro, North Carolina, in February 1960, when four freshmen at North Carolina A&T State University sat down at the segregated lunch counter inside Woolworth's and demanded service, had quickly spread throughout the South in the months that followed. Onlookers beat the peaceful protestors or poured food on their heads. Southern police officers arrested demonstrators on charges such as disturbing the peace or trespassing, while letting those who attacked them go free.

The first sit-in case — involving a group of black college students at a Baton Rouge lunch counter convicted of disturbing the peace—had reached the Court in the fall of 1961. The justices, in an opinion by Warren and with no dissents, overturned the verdict on the narrow grounds that no evidence supported the convictions because there was no actual disturbance. But the Court was not as unanimous as it appeared. Brennan agreed with a broader approach suggested by Warren and supported by Douglas that would have found sit-ins to be a form of protected speech under the First Amendment. Frankfurter, at this point less than a year away from retirement, attacked as "extreme" the idea that the free expression of sit-ins outweighed the rights of property owners. The justices opted for the narrow decision, but all were aware that many similar cases would follow.

Five more sit-in cases were decided in the 1962–63 term, many centering on the difficult question of whether the Fourteenth Amendment governed conduct by private individuals such as the owners of luncheonettes. The Fourteenth Amendment says that "no state" may deprive persons of due process or equal protection, language generally interpreted by the Court to mean it applies only to action by the government. So whether the sit-in protesters would prevail on their claims that they were victims of race discrimination hinged on whether the Fourteenth Amendment even applied. The Court's results were mixed, with a majority pushing to overturn convictions of protestors but fighting over what grounds could be used. In all cases, the convictions were reversed and, in some, the Court found sufficient involvement by local police or state officials in enforcing separate lunch counters or local ordinances that the Fourteenth Amendment did apply.

In the fall of 1963, the Court faced another five sit-in cases arising from incidents stretching from Maryland to Florida. The justices had heard arguments in the cases on the first day of the term in October, and some unexpected divisions quickly surfaced at their October 18 conference. A majority at first voted to uphold the convictions in two of the cases on the grounds that they involved private action, not the sort of government action necessary to trigger the protections of the Fourteenth Amendment. Among those voting to affirm the two convictions—perhaps surprisingly—was White, who as deputy attorney general had organized a makeshift army of federal border-patrol agents and prison guards to protect civil rights demonstrators.

Joining White was Black—an early sign of his growing divergence from

218 · JUSTICE BRENNAN

the pro–civil liberties bloc he had anchored for two decades. Black was hesitant to extend civil liberties protections in the civil rights context as aggressively as Brennan and Goldberg. After pressing Brennan to extend free speech to include the NAACP's litigation, Black was pulling back. He was uneasy about treating physical protests as free speech — particularly protests on private property. Brennan recounted to his clerks that Black told the other justices he could not believe that his "pappy," who ran a general store in Alabama, lacked the right to decide whom he served. Douglas, by contrast, sought to interpret state action as broadly as possible to protect equal treatment of all citizens in public spaces.

Brennan agreed with Douglas that sit-ins were a form of protected speech, but nonetheless argued that the Court should avoid the "state action" problem entirely and overturn the convictions on narrow grounds. The key for Brennan was overturning the sit-in convictions and avoiding any decision that might complicate passage of the Civil Rights Act introduced by President Kennedy earlier in the year. He shared Goldberg's concern that any decision that upheld sit-in convictions could be used as ammunition by southerners seeking to defeat the legislation. A heated argument ensued at the conference, and Brennan recounted to his clerks that he threatened to do his utmost to delay the decision in the hopes Congress would pass the Civil Rights Act in the interim. Brennan exhibited keen awareness of a decision's potential political impact — something he had lacked during the controversial subversion and school-prayer cases earlier in his tenure. Brennan and his fellow justices in the minority requested that the Court postpone a decision until the United States could present its views. His threat of delay angered other justices, who viewed it as inappropriate gamesmanship.

Brennan saw just how tough a road ahead the civil rights bill faced in Congress as he flipped between CBS and NBC nightly news programs that spring. CBS's Roger Mudd reported from the steps of the Capitol each night on the status of a filibuster of the bill by southern senators that in the end would break the previous longevity record set in 1846. Brennan made note of the ongoing debate in Congress in the dissent he circulated to the other justices in May in the *Bell v. Maryland* sit-in case. "We cannot be blind to the fact," Brennan wrote, that this was a "most unfortunate time to commit the error of reaching out to decide the question." Black, too, nodded to the potential impact on Congress in his draft opinion for the Court in *Bell*. "The case does not involve the constitutionality of any existing or proposed state or federal legislation requiring restaurant owners to serve people without regard to color." Nonetheless, by springtime, Brennan abandoned his determination to delay a decision in the case. He conceded that Black's view would likely prevail. But he still viewed it as a mistake for either side to raise the question of the proper scope of state action.

Then the case unexpectedly turned in Brennan's direction when Clark announced at the justices' May 15 conference that Brennan's dissent had won him over. As in *Baker v. Carr*, a last-minute change of heart by Clark appeared to give Brennan the margin of victory. But Clark's decision outraged Douglas. Black, angry as well, proposed calling up one of the more recent sit-in cases that did not have the narrow grounds as an escape clause, which would have forced the Court to address the underlying state-action issue.

The multiple opinions announced by the Court on June 22, 1964, were exceedingly complicated, but the bottom line was that Brennan's view prevailed. Black congratulated Brennan and his clerks on how hard they had fought, even though he did not agree with the outcome. Douglas, by contrast, wrote a sharp attack on the Court's unwillingness to address the state-action question. Douglas eventually dropped his most caustic language accusing the Court of an "abdication of judicial authority." But he stormed out of town, leaving Goldberg and Black to deliver his opinion. For Brennan, it was yet another example of how difficult Douglas could be, and more evidence of how he limited his own effectiveness by refusing to be a team player. "His great mistake was his insistence — and he repeated it time and time again — 'I have no soul to worry about but my own,'" Brennan said. But Brennan was often forced to accept Douglas's behavior, because he needed his vote.

Twelve days before the Court announced its decision, the Senate ended a fifty-seven-day filibuster of the civil rights bill. Two weeks after the Court's decision came down, President Johnson signed the Civil Rights Act of 1964 into law. Brennan was relieved both at its passage and that the Court was finally getting some help from the other branches of government. The law banned race discrimination in schools, public accommodations, private employment, and programs receiving federal funds. For the first time, the new law authorized the Department of Justice to file suits to implement desegregation in public schools. The Court no longer had to carry the weight of advancing civil rights alone.

AT THE SAME time that the Court argued over the sit-in cases, the justices took up another even more important case for the civil rights movement — and for the press. In March 1960, one month after the sit-in protests began, a full-page ad appeared in the New York Times soliciting contributions for the "Committee to Defend Martin Luther King and the Struggle for Freedom in the South." The ad condemned the "unprecedented wave of terror" being unleashed on "thousands of Southern Negro students . . . engaged in widespread non-violent demonstrations." The advertisement was signed by celebrities such as poet Langston Hughes, the pioneering black major league baseball player Jackie Robinson, former First Lady Eleanor Roosevelt, and actor Marlon Brando as well as a separate list of southern ministers, including four from Alabama, who had not been consulted in advance about their names being used.

The advertisement had some minor factual errors. It incorrectly suggested that students at Alabama State College in Montgomery were expelled after singing "My Country, 'Tis of Thee" on the steps of the state capitol and that the school's cafeteria "was padlocked in an attempt to starve" students "into submission." Though the ad did not refer to any southern whites by name, L. B. Sullivan, a city commissioner in Montgomery, filed suit against the four local clergymen and the New York Times, claiming the ad's references to Alabama and the mistreatment of Martin Luther King Jr. by "Southern violators" defamed him. An Alabama jury awarded Sullivan $500,000 in damages after two hours and twenty minutes of deliberations. It was an enormous amount of money by any standard of the time. Alabama's governor, two other city commissioners, and Montgomery's mayor all followed suit. By the time Alabama juries were through, the Times faced millions of dollars in potential damages, a liability that called into question the paper's very survival.

Such enormous awards threatened to drive out of the South reporters from major media organizations — exactly the intended goal of those filing the suits. Keeping the press out would deprive the civil rights movement of the valuable media attention needed to fan northern outrage and increase political pressure. The *New York Times* had already pulled its correspondent out of Alabama for a year to avoid being served process as it sought to challenge the state courts' jurisdiction over the paper. All the better, southern politicians thought, if the libel judgments also forced the four ministers in the ad to give up their cars and property to pay the huge awards, drove some out of the state entirely, and forced their cash-strapped Southern Christian Leadership Conference to spend a fortune to appeal the decision.

The use of libel suits as a tool of intimidation had already spread beyond the one targeted at the *Times*. CBS faced a lawsuit of its own for a television program describing difficulties African Americans faced in registering to vote in Montgomery. By the time the *Times* case reached the Supreme Court, southern officials had brought millions of dollars in libel actions against the press. Brennan fully understood the implications of letting the verdicts stand when the Court took up the case in January 1964. If the Court did not impose some restraints, Brennan believed the progress toward desegregation that began with the Court's decision in *Brown* would be seriously set back.

The implications for the civil rights movement might have been obvious, yet the racial dimensions of the case, *New York Times v. Sullivan,* were downplayed at every step along the way at the Supreme Court. The *Times'* lead attorney, Herbert Wechsler, a fifty-two-year-old Columbia Law School professor, made only glancing reference to the racial issue in his brief to the Court. Instead, Wechsler emphasized in vaguer terms the potential impact "not only upon the press but also upon those whose welfare may depend on the ability and willingness of publications to give voice to grievances against the agencies of government power." He presented the Court with several possible theories for overturning such a libel verdict in the case of a public official criticized in the course of his official duties. Wechsler argued for an absolute freedom to criticize public officials as well as a more limited rule that did not protect instances where the speaker knew the offending statement was not true.

Wechsler recognized the many hurdles to getting the verdict overturned. Libelous utterances had long been considered beyond the protection of the First Amendment, as the Supreme Court had said as recently as 1952. Libel remained an area of law the Supreme Court had left entirely to the state courts, and the prevailing common-law rules were heavily weighted in favor of plaintiffs. Defamatory statements were presumed to be false, and those who published them carried the burden of proving they were true. It did not matter if the defamatory statement resulted from malice, negligence, or bad luck — motive was irrelevant. And the aggrieved parties did not have to prove they had suffered actual harm, unlike in suits for other kinds of injuries.

A majority of states did protect opinions commenting on public officials, as long as there were no factual errors, which was not the case here. "Taken together," Harry Kalven, a noted constitutional scholar, wrote, "the publisher of a serious criticism was, in effect, required by law to insure the absolute accuracy of what he said." That is inherently difficult in newsgathering, where factual errors can unwittingly make their way into print. The Supreme Court had shown little interest in offering any protections to the press and Wechsler could not be confident the justices were going to offer much in the way of relief here either.

If the justices wanted a reminder of the potential consequences of *New York Times v. Sullivan* as they gathered for oral arguments, they only needed to look out into the audience, where Martin Luther King Jr. sat among the spectators. Justice Goldberg abandoned any pretense of impartiality when he slipped the civil rights leader a copy of King's book *Stride Toward Freedom* for him to sign. Brennan was uncharacteristically vocal from the moment the oral argument began on January 6, 1964. To begin, he politely asked Wechsler to speak up, because he could not hear the argument.

Brennan and the other justices interrupted Wechsler with so many questions that he could only present his argument in favor of absolute immunity rather than presenting the alternatives, such as the actual malice standard. This was less a strategic attempt by any justice to avoid the airing of particular arguments than a reflection of the case's complexity. The attorney for the four ministers, whose case was being heard together with the newspaper's, presented their case the next day. Three days later, the justices gathered at their weekly conference, and all agreed that the libel verdict should be overturned, although they did not agree on the rationale for doing so. A majority favored reversal on the narrowest possible grounds: that Sullivan had not proven the ad was talking about him or had defamed him. Brennan suggested that a public official be required to prove each element of libel by a "clear, convincing and unequivocal" standard, as in expatriation cases, although there was no consensus among the justices on what standard to choose.

Brennan, as a matter of fact, harbored ambivalent feelings about the press. He was an avid consumer of journalism, reading at least two newspapers each morning and watching the evening news on television each night and he believed reporters played a vital role in a democratic society. "As money is to the economy, so the press is to our political culture; it is the medium of circulation," Brennan said in a 1979 speech. Marjorie had worked as a newspaper proofreader, and two of his three children would marry newspaper reporters.

Family members aside, Brennan did not particularly enjoy dealing with the press himself. He quickly came to regret the one time he had given an impromptu press conference during his February 1962 visit to Puerto Rico with Chief Justice Warren and Clark. Reporters asked whether a new statute that directed the Supreme Court to review directly the judgments of Puerto Rico's highest court — just as it did with the highest courts of each state — meant that Puerto Rico was a de facto state. Brennan gave a complicated answer about Puerto Rico's status as a territory, but front-page headlines in the island's newspaper the next day trumpeted his comments as an important endorsement of statehood. "I did put my foot in my mouth didn't I?" Brennan wrote Luis Blanco Lugo of the Puerto Rican Supreme Court upon returning to Washington. "Apparently, I should have followed my general practice of keeping quiet on such matters." And that is what he did in the years to come, declining all interview requests during his campus speaking engagements. He explained to one college administrator, "There is just too much risk of being misquoted or misunderstood."

A few days after the *Times* oral argument, Warren asked Brennan to write the opinion. Once again, the chief justice had turned to Brennan in a high-profile case where the justices might be unanimous on the ultimate goal, but did not agree about how to get there. Brennan had already carved out a niche in cases involving free expression and obscenity, which several justices viewed as a possible model for how to handle this one. Warren also knew that Brennan could build and hold on to a majority — a unanimous

224 · JUSTICE BRENNAN

one if possible — in a way that he or other justices could not. Compounding the challenge was that Warren's and Brennan's three most reliable allies, Black, Douglas, and Goldberg, all made clear at conference that they wanted an absolute bar against libel suits involving criticism of public officials. This case would prove to be another nail biter in which Brennan was not sure of the ultimate disposition of his allies until the very last minute. He and his clerks generated eight drafts in less than two months — an extraordinarily compressed and demanding schedule.

Brennan abandoned his usual practice of having one of his clerks sketch out a first draft after they talked through what he wanted; he opted to write it himself. He relied heavily on the brief submitted by Wechsler for his own reasoning. As in *Cooper v. Aaron,* Brennan's first draft was not as dramatic as the Court's ultimate decision, yet his initial structure and arguments survived largely intact. He embraced a standard that would bar libel actions by public officials against critics of their official conduct unless there was evidence that a story was published with a reckless disregard for the truth. Mere falsity or negligence did not suffice under this "actual malice" standard, which had been adopted by a minority of the states. Brennan concluded there was no evidence of actual malice in this case.

Years later, Brennan would incorrectly credit his clerks with unearthing the "actual malice" language and the Kansas Supreme Court decision he cited in his decision. In fact, that approach had been in Wechsler's brief all along. Stephen Barnett, Brennan's clerk at the time, later confirmed that is where they found it. Barnett did write the most widely quoted language in Brennan's opinion, which declared "a profound national commitment to the principle that debate on public issues should be uninhibited, robust, and wide-open, and that it may well include vehement, caustic, and sometimes unpleasantly sharp attacks on government and public officials."

Brennan circulated a second draft to the full conference on February 6 after going over his first one only with his clerks. Warren and White signed on quickly but his three other allies — Black, Douglas, and Goldberg — all made clear they believed he had not gone far enough. They still favored absolute protection for libel against public officials. But Brennan, ever the skilled and careful vote counter, knew that the absolute view simply could not command a majority even if he joined his trio of allies, since Warren and most likely White did not want to go that far. "In order to get a court for the conclusion we reached, I just had to make it clear that while it was a

First Amendment right here, there were other considerations that had to be taken into account," Brennan said.

More than pragmatism motivated his approach. While Brennan later admitted he had some sympathy for the more extreme view, he, too, was uneasy about absolute protections. He had repeatedly eschewed absolutes since joining the Court, favoring instead balancing tests that allowed him to weigh competing values. Brennan believed that "there are circumstances under which a government interest can override a First Amendment interest." In the context of libel, he thought that weight should be given to the reputation of the targets of criticism. As Brennan explained in a lecture the following year at Brown University, "At the time the First Amendment was adopted, as today, there were those unscrupulous enough and skillful enough to use the deliberate or reckless falsehood as an effective political tool to unseat the public servant or even topple an administration." It is likely Brennan had not forgotten the way his father was attacked in the newspaper by Prohibitionists. And the memory of Senator McCarthy ruining reputations and sparring with him personally at his confirmation hearing was fresh.

Without his usual trio of allies, Brennan had to pick up support for his approach from among Clark, Harlan, and Stewart, which proved difficult. The normal course would be for the Court to allow lower courts to apply a new legal rule to the facts of a case — in this case, the new rule being the barring of actions by public officials against critics, minus reckless disregard for the truth. But the justices had increasingly come to lose faith in recalcitrant southern judges. Harlan, usually an ardent defender of federalism, worried here that an Alabama court would simply apply the new rule, find actual malice, and reaffirm the damage award in the case. Brennan tried accommodating Harlan by adding language that he requested, but they eventually reached an impasse over additional changes. Harlan circulated a memorandum on March 3 that threatened to derail the Court's intended forceful showing of unanimity. Unlike the sit-in cases, where he held firm to his more absolutist position, Douglas joined Goldberg in offering to sign on to a more limited opinion, although Black insisted that he could not agree to an actual malice standard.

Clark provided more drama as he suddenly showed Brennan a sharp separate opinion he intended to circulate. As with Stewart's abrupt shift midway through *Baker v. Carr*, Brennan worried now that his majority was unraveling. But just as suddenly, Clark told Brennan the next morning that he would not circulate his separate opinion after all. All Clark asked Brennan to do was add language explaining that "effective judicial administration" explained why the Court was reviewing the evidence itself, rather than returning the case to Alabama for further consideration. And at the last minute, Harlan, too, backed down. He called Brennan at home on the night of March 8, one day before the Court was scheduled to announce the decision. He said he had decided to withdraw his dissent and join the majority opinion. The decision showed how different Harlan was from his intellectual forebear, Frankfurter. Despite their differences, Harlan cared greatly about the Court as an institution and did not want to do anything to detract from what he viewed as a great occasion for the Court and Justice Brennan.

The next morning, Brennan announced the decision for the Court, emphasizing its significance from the very first sentence. "We are required in this case to determine for the first time the extent to which the constitutional protections for speech and press limit a State's power to award damages in a libel action brought by a public official against critics of his official conduct," Brennan said. He emphasized that the rule applied by Alabama's courts did not sufficiently protect speech and press freedoms as required by the First Amendment. Once again, the Court had intruded into an area of law previously left to the states. Brennan did not speak for the entire Court. All the justices agreed about overturning the verdict. Yet his three usual allies, Black, Douglas, and Goldberg, all argued for absolute protection in their concurring opinions. Black, ever the southern gentleman, sent Brennan a gracious handwritten note. "You know of course that despite my position & what I wrote I think you are doing a wonderful job in the Times case and however it finally comes out it is bound to be a very long step towards preserving the right to communicate ideas."

The opinion Brennan announced fundamentally altered the nation's libel laws in virtually every state, and gave far greater protection to defendants accused of libeling public officials. It shifted the burden of proof in libel cases from defendants, who previously had to demonstrate the truth of statements, to plaintiffs, who would have to show that the defendants had published a falsehood and done so either knowingly or recklessly. Not surprisingly, the *New York Times* praised the decision as "a victory of first importance in the long—and never ending—struggle for the rights of a free press." Harry Kalven, the University of Chicago constitutional scholar, predicted it "may prove to be the best and most important opinion it has ever produced in the realm of freedom of speech."

The full significance of the opinion for freedom of speech only became apparent over time. The Court extended protections to statements of fact —rather than just doctrines or political opinion—and provided breathing room for journalists by protecting some erroneous statements. Those protections proved crucial as reporters began questioning the government's accounts of the Vietnam War and exposed the Watergate scandal that eventually led to President Nixon's resignation. The decision's impact on the civil rights movement was more readily apparent. "The case could have an immediate impact on press coverage of race relations in the South," the *New York Times* noted. The decision stood as one of the strongest defenses of freedom of speech ever by the Court, recognizing that even erroneous and reputation-damaging speech are part of the price the country must pay to facilitate the free exchange of ideas in a democracy.

But all sides in the case came to have a bit of buyer's remorse concerning the actual-malice standard on which Brennan relied. The standard was criticized for opening the door to examinations of the defendant's state of mind, and for failing adequately to take into account the potential harm to a plaintiff's reputation. Brennan himself came to regret using the term "malice" as too confusing, especially to juries, who associated the word with the idea of hatred or ill will. Brennan said later that he wished he had picked another term for the idea of knowing or reckless falsehood. "Oh well, you have to make some mistakes," he said later.

Brennan provided the civil rights movement a potent offensive weapon of its own the following term, while once again radically altering the balance of power between the federal and state courts. His opinion in *Dombrowski v. Pfister* made it easier for civil rights litigants to shift their cases from state to less-hostile federal courts. Louisiana had indicted James Dombrowski, executive director of the civil rights group the Southern Conference Educational Fund, for violating two Louisiana laws aimed at Communists and other subversives. Dombrowski sought an injunction against enforcement of those laws, charging state officials with using the laws to frighten potential members of the organization and to interfere with the organization's activities. A federal statute prohibited enjoining state prosecutions, and federal courts generally shied away from interfering in them.

Brennan and his allies abandoned such deference, overturning the lower-court decision dismissing Dombrowski's complaint, and holding that injunctive relief was clearly appropriate. The decision opened the doors of the federal courts to civil rights plaintiffs seeking protection from state prosecution. Implicit but unspoken by Brennan's majority, Harlan noted in his dissent, was "that state courts will not be as prone as federal courts to vindicate constitutional rights promptly and effectively." The *Dombrowski* case highlighted again the extent to which the justices had come to distrust southern courts and to turn the federal courts into a refuge for the civil rights movement. Not all of these innovations would survive. *Dombrowski,* for example, was sharply circumscribed in 1971. Yet, by then, the civil rights protest movement had faded and the most acute need for such a tool had passed.

BOTH BRENNAN'S BLOC and the civil rights movement seemed ascendant as the Court's term ended in June 1964. But it had proven a tough one in tactical terms for Brennan, and it was often his stalwart allies that made his job as coalition builder harder. Douglas and Black often went their own way, or would not budge from their absolutist positions, as they had shown in the sit-in cases and *New York Times v. Sullivan.* As Brennan tellingly confided to his friend Judge Stanley Weigel at the end of the term, "Both we and the Country could probably stand a respite."

On July 19, Brennan and his family arrived in Nantucket for a month's stay as usual in one of the small rented waterfront cottages on Old North Wharf. At the time, Nantucket had not yet fully transitioned from faded whaling outpost to the playground for the rich it became later. The growing number of summer visitors such as Brennan could still find plenty of solitude here.

Brennan put the term behind him as he set out each morning for a walk, just as he did in Georgetown. His companion was usually Robert Silvercruys, the retired Belgian diplomat who had first invited the Brennans to the island as guests. They headed out early for their favorite destination, the treeless moors filled with poverty grass, sweet fern, and wildflowers. Trees could not grow on much of Nantucket due to the harsh windswept winters, and the low vegetation covering the island made it look more like Scotland than nearby Martha's Vineyard. "To walk on the moors, though less than five miles from town, is to feel isolated in a landscape that has no end, particularly when not another human being besides us can be seen in any direction," Brennan later said with uncharacteristic near-eloquence. Their only company along the trails that "run like ribbons over the moors," Brennan said, might be quail, woodcock, or cottontail rabbits. Brennan, who came to Nantucket initially for Marjorie's sake, had started to come around. "Once bitten with the Nantucket bug," Brennan said, "one becomes a devotee of that 'fragile sandy mound.'" The Court — or the nation's racial problems — never seemed farther away.

Yet Brennan could not completely avoid reading about the trouble brewing elsewhere in the country when he picked up the newspaper at a Nantucket country store each morning. The day before Brennan arrived on Nantucket, an incident of alleged police brutality fueled a riot by blacks in New York's Harlem neighborhood. Similar urban disturbances followed in subsequent days in Rochester, New York, Philadelphia, and in a trio of northern New Jersey cities, Elizabeth, Jersey City, and Paterson, not far from where Brennan grew up.

There were hints of another kind of backlash among northern whites. Unexpectedly high numbers of whites in states such as Indiana, Maryland, and Wisconsin chose Alabama's segregationist governor George Wallace in the Democratic presidential primaries. The issue of race had begun to drive a wedge in the Democrats' New Deal coalition. That August, as the Brennans left Nantucket to welcome their second grandson and Bill Brennan's first child, William J. Brennan IV, Democrats held their national convention in Atlantic City. A fight erupted over whether to seat an integrated or all-white delegation from Mississippi. Strom Thurmond, the pro-segregation senator from South Carolina, abandoned the Democrats by announcing, "The party of our fathers is dead." Brennan noted the northern riots in a September 1964 speech at the University of Pennsylvania. "It is hardly my role to place the blame for these unfortunate outbreaks," Brennan said. But he warned that such disorder would "really put our values to the test."

10

CRIME & CRITICISM

B RENNAN AND HIS ALLIES on the Court were being attacked by the mid-1960s for encouraging racial mixing, coddling Communists, and trying to drive God out of public life. No one maligned the Court with greater fervor than the archconservative John Birch Society. Since its founding in 1958, the political advocacy group had made removing Chief Justice Warren from office a top priority. "Impeach Earl Warren!" billboards sprouted along American highways — and even at the Indianapolis Motor Speedway. Members carrying similar placards followed Warren at every public appearance, although impeachment was not punishment enough for the most ardent believers. One speaker at a 1961 Bircher event in Dallas suggested hanging him instead. Brennan was well aware of the anti-Warren campaign. He passed along to Justice Stewart a 1961 newsletter, the *Dan Smoot Report,* headlined "Impeaching Earl Warren," which accused the chief justice of being a socialist. "Thanks for letting me see this trash," Stewart wrote Brennan. "It's extraordinary."

Brennan observed the hostility directed at Warren firsthand every time he joined the chief justice at a Washington Redskins football game. Warren's friend, team co-owner Edward Bennett Williams, allowed the chief justice to drive his Cadillac right onto the field before each home game to park behind the goal posts. The car's arrival invariably elicited hearty boos from the crowds in the stands above. Without Warren as company, Brennan remained anonymous enough that he could escape such protests undetected. But after attending a legal conference in California in 1962, he joked in a letter that "there was plenty of time to take Nancy to Disneyland, to be picketed by the John Birchers and generally to do all right." So too could he shrug off the hostility in 1963 when five undergraduates at the Auburn University chapter of his fraternity, Delta Tau Delta, returned a picture he and fellow fraternity member, Justice Clark, had autographed. The five fraternity brothers wanted it known that they refused to display the photograph, because the Court's recent decisions "have greatly conflicted with the freedom-loving ideals of the populace."

But by the end of Brennan's eighth term on the Court in 1964, it was getting even harder to dismiss the Court's critics as merely a lunatic or immature fringe of what one writer in the *New Republic* called "segregationists and security mongers." Some of the nation's most eminent judges and law professors had begun second-guessing the justices too. Judge Learned Hand had fired the first shot in a series of lectures at Harvard Law School in 1958 when he warned against the Court acting as a "third legislative chamber." Hand said, "It would be most irksome to be ruled by a bevy of Platonic guardians." Alexander Bickel, a Yale Law professor and former Frankfurter clerk, stated in a 1962 book, *The Least Dangerous Branch,* that judicial review was a countermajoritarian force that thwarted the will of the peoples' representatives when it declared laws unconstitutional.

Surveying all the unprecedented changes wrought by the justices in such rapid succession, the press now as well began asking whether the Court was going too far, too fast. The *New York Times* took note of complaints in June 1964 that the Court "is taking too much joy in its own power, trying too boldly to fix up the wrongs of our system, feeling insufficiently cautious and modest about imposing on society the solutions — however honorably motivated — of nine men appointed for life and not subject to the voters." The issue was injected in that fall's presidential race too. The Republican nominee, Barry Goldwater, the first major presidential candidate to campaign against the Court in decades, accused the justices of exercising "raw and naked power." Senator Strom Thurmond aired ads in South Carolina that promised, "A vote for Barry Goldwater is a vote to end judicial tyranny."

Nonetheless, Brennan continued to take the criticism in stride. He repeatedly said in speeches at the time that he viewed negative assessments of the Court's work as inevitable. "Almost every decision is disapproved by somebody," Brennan told a conference of federal judges in Chicago in May 1965. It was harder for members of his family back in New Jersey, who were often approached in restaurants or the supermarket by hecklers who disapproved of the Court's decisions, to maintain the same level of dispassion. Nancy especially was disturbed by the harsh criticism directed at her father. She was home without a babysitter for the first time one night while her parents went off to visit friends when she heard Senator James Eastland on the radio slam Brennan and several other justices for favoring Communists in their decisions. Nancy called Brennan at their friends' house in tears. Brennan came home right away and sat on the edge of Nancy's bed, trying to comfort her. Brennan knew something about what she was feeling. He had been just a little older than Nancy when his father had been the target of Prohibitionist ire in Newark's newspapers. It was not personal, Brennan explained, just politics. He told Nancy it was perfectly OK to feel a combination of rage and shame, and that he felt that way sometimes too.

Brennan and his fellow justices were to pay a financial price for the opinions they wrote. Congress made its dissatisfaction with the Court known in 1964 by granting the justices only a $4,500 pay raise — while all other federal judges received a $7,500 increase. Brennan, who still relied almost exclusively on his judicial salary, could surely have used the extra money.

Congressional and public grievances varied, but they all coalesced around a single rallying cry against "judicial activism," a term that became the ultimate epithet hurled at judges in the decades to come. The phrase did not have a derogatory connotation when historian Arthur Schlesinger Jr. first coined it in *Fortune* magazine in 1947 as shorthand for contrasting the judicial approach of Black and Douglas, Murphy and Rutledge, with Frankfurter's model of judicial restraint. But by the mid-1950s, "judicial activism" was pejorative, a blanket term for many different complaints: focusing on results, ignoring precedent, invalidating arguably constitutional actions of the other branches, "amending" the Constitution, or inventing new rules as needed. Harvard government professor Robert McCloskey summed up that point of view in 1966 when he charged that the Warren

Court "has with more or less frankness, created Constitutional rules out of whole cloth."

Brennan insisted that he, too, objected to such an approach to judging. "The Court is not a council of Platonic guardians given the function of deciding our most difficult and emotional questions according to the Justices' own notions of what is just or wise or politic," he said in a 1963 speech at Maxwell Air Force Base in Alabama. He invoked the same line over and over throughout the 1960s, an apparent rebuttal to Judge Hand's 1958 speech at Harvard Law School. Brennan assured *Look* magazine in 1962 that "our government structure assigns to the people's elected representatives the function of making policy for handling the social and economic problems of state and nation" and that "the impropriety of a judiciary with life tenure writing its own social and economic creed into the Constitution is therefore clear." However, Brennan insisted, "judicial intervention becomes a duty when action of the political branches, or of the states, offends constitutional limitations. Where the Constitution is violated, judges have no choice but to say so." Of course, matters were not nearly as neat as Brennan suggested, particularly when justices redefined — as Brennan and his allies were doing — what the Constitution required contrary to the public's common understanding.

Brennan believed that the Constitution was a dynamic document, one open to interpretation in response to the realities of contemporary life. "Law is again coming alive as a living process responsive to changing human needs," he told the Jewish Theological Seminary in November 1964, using language he repeated in speeches throughout the 1960s. "The shift is to justice and away from fine-spun technicalities and abstract rules." To interpret the meaning of the Constitution, Brennan looked to underlying — and often unstated — values, such as social justice and, particularly, human dignity.

Brennan later offered his most expansive philosophical justification for judicial intervention in February 1969, in a speech at Princeton University. Too often, Brennan said, the choice had been between the Court confronting and solving a broad social issue or "no one doing it at all." "If the legislature simply cannot or does not act to correct an unconstitutional status quo, the Court, despite all its incapacities, must finally act to do so," he said. Brennan believed the courts had a special role as watchdogs to make sure the country was adhering to its highest ideals. "Just as an individual may be untrue to himself, so may society be untrue to itself," Brennan explained. "The Court's reviewing function, then, can be seen as an attempt to keep the community true to its own fundamental principles."

Brennan insisted that the Court's structure — and judges' training and the benefit they have of more time to make decisions — makes it "peculiarly well suited" to the watchdog task. In a clear rebuttal of the "activism" charge, he affirmed that "casting the Court as the guardian of enduring principle and as a check on overzealous legislatures depicts the Court as essentially a conservative rather than creative force in society." Eight months later, Bickel, the Yale Law professor, responded forcefully to Brennan's notion of the societal watchdog role for the judiciary in a speech at Harvard Law School. Bickel lamented that too many federal judges had come to believe they held a "roving commission as problem solvers and as charged with a duty to act when majoritarian institutions do not." Bickel warned that courts were too detached, slow moving, and ill-equipped to deal with complex problems of public policy. It was a warning judges failed to heed as they set out to reform — and even inject themselves into the operations of — an ever-expanding list of institutions in the coming years, including prisons, schools, and welfare departments.

IN SEPTEMBER 1965, Brennan attended the annual conference of the U.S. Court of Appeals for the Third Circuit in Atlantic City. This typically uneventful two-day gathering of lawyers and judges had become routine duty for Brennan as the justice responsible for handling emergency applications to the Court in cases emanating from the Third Circuit. He was accompanied this time at the oceanfront Shelburne by Chief Justice Warren, who planned to deliver a tribute to a Third Circuit judge being honored at dinner that night.

As circuit justice, Brennan took his seat in the front of the hotel conference room alongside the speakers as attendees settled in after lunch for two consecutive discussions. Warren had opted to sit in the back of the room, but moved up at the urging of the moderator, taking a seat beside Brennan. Both justices were thus just ten feet away as the panel's first speaker, Michael Murphy, a twenty-five-year veteran of the New York City Police Department who had just recently ended a four-year stint as commissioner, launched into a sharp attack on the Supreme Court's criminal-procedure decisions. "To impose upon us unreasonable standards and at the same time extend the constitutional safeguards surrounding the individual," Murphy said, "is akin to requiring one boxer to observe the Marquis of Queensbury rules and to permit his opponent to gouge, strike foul blows and use every unfair advantage as the referee turns his back." Murphy, who had graduated from Brooklyn Law School, singled out the Court's *Escobedo* decision of the previous year, which said police could not keep suspects' lawyers out of the interrogation room. Murphy accused the Court of issuing a series of decisions that "unduly hampered" police while "there is a vicious beast loose" on the streets.

The broadside against the Court — delivered in the presence of two of the Court's leading liberals — left many in the audience dismayed. Some coughed or squirmed in their seats uncomfortably and a few even gasped. Warren sat stone-faced during Murphy's attack, and Brennan looked equally impassive. Both lightened up considerably as another panelist, University of Michigan law professor Yale Kamisar, rose to defend the Court. "Crime is a terribly complex problem," Kamisar said. "We all know that. It is baffling. It is frustrating. When people can't solve something readily, they look for scapegoats." And since the 1950s, he said, "police spokesmen found the easy answer, the simple answer: the courts, especially the Supreme Court of the United States." He continued: "It is politically attractive to blame it on the courts. It doesn't cost any money to attack the courts. Nor do you buck any powerful lobbies." Brennan and Warren roared with laughter along with the rest of the crowd as Kamisar read magazine articles from "the good old days" earlier in the century when coerced confessions were admitted into evidence yet officials still laid the "crime crisis" to "coddling the criminals." Kamisar asked, "It sounds a lot like what we heard today, doesn't it?"

In an article about the incident, the *New York Times* noted, "As the Chief Justice and Justice Brennan demonstrated in Atlantic City, the Court can afford to maintain an impassive silence, for it is sure to have the last word." But beyond this Atlantic City hotel, Murphy's alarmism regarding criminal coddling rather than Kamisar's measured reason was already winning in the broader court of public opinion. Personal security had started to become as powerful a political issue as national security. The FBI's Uniform Crime Reports showed a rise in crime in each of the previous three years. A 1964 Harris Poll found that 73 percent of those surveyed felt crime in their neighborhood had increased in the previous year, whether they lived in cities, suburbs, or small towns.

For the first time, the specter of random violent street crime had become a theme in a major presidential candidate's campaign. At the 1964 Republican National Convention, former president Eisenhower warned, "Let us not be guilty of maudlin sympathy for the criminal who, roaming the streets with the switchblade knife and illegal firearm, seeking a helpless prey, suddenly becomes, upon apprehension, a poor, underprivileged person who counts upon the compassion of our society and the laxness of weakness of too many courts to forgive his offense." The party's presidential nominee, Arizona senator Barry Goldwater, made crime his signature domestic issue and linked the spike in crime to recent Supreme Court decisions. "Crime grows faster than population, while those who break the law are accorded more consideration than those who try to enforce the law," Goldwater warned in September 1964 in a typical stump speech in Arizona.

Goldwater overwhelmingly lost the 1964 election to President Johnson, but the notion that the Court was to blame for rising crime outlasted Goldwater's campaign and only grew more politically potent. After noting rising crime from New York to San Francisco, *U.S. News & World Report*'s March 1965 cover story, "Is Crime in U.S. Out of Hand?" declared, "The Supreme Court and lesser tribunals are grinding out decisions which stress suspects' rights — making it easier than ever for criminals to evade detection and punishment."

What if any role the Court's decisions played in the rise in crime remained a subject of debate a half century later. There were many invisible demographic factors at work, including the vast rural-to-city migration and the baby boomers' entrance into adolescence, which greatly expanded the population of people at the prime age for committing crimes. But what was most readily apparent to the public and press was the revolution engineered by the Warren Court in the rights of criminal defendants during police investigations and prosecutions.

During the 1960s, the Supreme Court applied almost all of the provisions of the Bill of Rights related to criminal procedure to the states. Defendants were entitled to lawyers, who could not be barred from police interrogation rooms. Police were required to warn suspects about their rights before they were taken into custody and interrogated. Defendants in state criminal cases would eventually be extended further provisions of the Bill of Rights that applied in federal cases, including the rights to be confronted by witnesses testifying against them in court, to have speedy trials, and to not be subject to double jeopardy.

During a March 1965 speech at Georgetown University, Brennan acknowledged, "I am aware that some of these decisions have aroused the concerns of state judges." He added, "It cannot be denied that the decisions do restrict the latitude of choice open to the States in this area. But that is the price which must be paid for recognizing and enforcement of guarantees deemed to have a place among those fundamental principles of liberty and justice which lie at the base of all our civil and political institutions." Brennan later privately admitted that if he were "a private citizen and someone escaped punishment because, say, an exclusionary rule barred the admission against him of evidence that guaranteed his conviction," he would conclude "that the law's an ass when it permits that sort of thing to happen." But as a judge, Brennan said, "I'd have to affirm the exclusion of the evidence because the Constitution would require it."

CRIME INCREASINGLY BECAME entwined with race as the 1960s progressed, with blacks in urban slums blamed for much of the problem. But if anyone symbolized the kind of unsavory defendant benefiting from the Warren Court's criminal-procedure decisions it may well have been Ernesto Miranda. In 1963 the twenty-two-year-old Miranda, a Mexican American man living in Phoenix, was charged with kidnapping and raping an eighteen-year-old woman. Miranda, who had a felony rap sheet dating back to the eighth grade, said he did not know he had any choice in the matter when two detectives asked him to get in their car for questioning at police headquarters. Miranda had no lawyer during the ensuing two-hour interrogation, in which he confessed to the rape. A jury convicted Miranda after five hours of deliberations and a judge then sentenced him to two concurrent twenty- to thirty-year prison terms. Miranda's lawyer appealed the case to the Arizona Supreme Court on the grounds police had improperly obtained his confession.

When the case reached the U.S. Supreme Court, Warren, a former prosecutor, proposed it as a vehicle to bar prosecutors from using any statements made by suspects during interrogations while they were in police custody unless they were adequately warned of their rights. Warren laid out with unusual specificity exactly what such a warning should include: that suspects had the right to remain silent and that any statement made by them could be used against them in court; and that they had the right to consult with an attorney and to have a lawyer provided if they could not afford to retain one. Defendants could waive these rights — but only if the waiver was made "knowingly and intelligently." The burden would be on the prosecutor to prove the waiver was sufficient. Questioning would have to cease at any point during an interrogation where the suspect requested a lawyer.

Brennan was uneasy when he read the draft opinion the chief justice circulated privately to him alone on May 9, 1966. He feared that Warren had adopted too rigid a solution and left too little room for state legislatures or Congress to devise alternative procedures. He believed the public would more likely accept the opinion if the Court left legislators greater flexibility in crafting the kind of warning police would be required to give to criminal suspects. Brennan took great care in drafting his reply memo to Warren. He crossed out the second sentence in a reply initially drafted by his clerk that read, "These suggestions are many in recognition that this will be one of the most important opinions of our time and I know that you want each of us to give you our views in full." Instead, Brennan inserted a more personal, apologetic appeal. "I feel guilty about the extent of the suggestions but this will be one of the most important opinions of our time and I know that you will want the fullest expressions of my views."

Warren followed Brennan's advice about changing the first sentence of the opinion from describing the root problem as "the role society must assume consistent with the federal constitution in prosecuting individuals for crime" to "the restraints society must observe consistent with the Federal Constitution in prosecuting individuals for crime." He accepted, too, Brennan's suggestion to emphasize the Fifth Amendment rather than the Sixth Amendment, and removed a reference to the race of the defendant. "I wonder if it is appropriate in this context to turn police brutality into a racial problem," Brennan wrote. "If anything characterizes the group this opinion concerns it is poverty rather than race." As in the *New York Times v. Sullivan* libel case, Brennan realized that emphasizing race would do little to help an opinion gain public acceptance.

Brennan recalled later that he and Warren talked more about this case than any other except the *Fay v. Noia* habeas case, in which Brennan had been the one needing to persuade Warren. This time, it was the other way around. Brennan even considered writing a concurrence in response to Harlan's dissent, suggesting that states should retain the flexibility to adopt their own alternative procedures. Brennan showed his draft concurrence to Warren before circulating it to the other justices. After the chief justice made clear his misgivings about a separate concurrence, Brennan agreed not to file it, a decision he was later relieved to have made. The standardized Miranda warning became familiar to viewers of every television police show in succeeding decades, in contrast to the confusing medley of fifty different state formulations his concurrence might have encouraged. "Obviously, it would have been just dead wrong," Brennan said. "Thank heavens I woke up."

The far-reaching *Miranda* decision, which upended police procedures throughout the country, generated a new round of law enforcement outrage. Boston's police chief warned, "Criminal trials no longer will be a search for truth, but a search for technical error." Los Angeles's police chief predicted that *Miranda* would lead to an end of confessions altogether. Arkansas senator John L. McClellan soon blamed the *Miranda* decision for freeing a Brooklyn man who confessed to killing his common-law wife and five children. "Some people think that you mustn't say any criticism of the Supreme Court. The hell with that," said McClellan, who complained the decision "serves to protect the robber, the murderer and rapist."

As *Miranda* illustrates, Brennan, who played a major role in much of the Warren Court's remaking of constitutional law, had a relatively minor role in the criminal-procedure revolution. He wrote none of the three other landmark decisions in the field during the 1960s. And his first major decision in criminal procedure, not written until 1964 when the movement was well under way, was one of the least controversial. The case of *Malloy v. Hogan* applied the Fifth Amendment privilege against self-incrimination to the states through the Fourteenth Amendment's due process clause. But by that point, the privilege against self-incrimination had gained widespread acceptance. Brennan's biggest contribution was providing the rationale for applying the protections afforded by the Bill of Rights to the states piecemeal via a process he called selective incorporation. The Court had been selectively incorporating the Bill of Rights as a limit on the states for several years already without explicitly saying so.

Brennan acknowledged what the Court was doing and he countered criticism that the justices exercised judicial authority unconstrained by any limitations.

For Brennan, moving one step at a time was the prudent thing to do. "We were plowing new ground—oh my, what new ground we were plowing," Brennan recalled. "And when you do that sort of thing, you make progress by stages. You don't do it in one fell swoop." But as with the First Amendment, Brennan insisted he also had substantive objections to a wholesale incorporation of the Bill of Rights. Unlike Black, Brennan said he did not believe that the right to indictment by a grand jury or the right to a trial by jury—including trials where only little money might be at stake—should be considered vital rights. To skeptics, Brennan's embrace of selective incorporation was just facile justification for cherry-picking the rights he preferred, and yet more evidence that he put outcomes above doctrinal consistency.

An opinion Brennan wrote in another criminal-procedure case announced one week after *Miranda* provided additional fodder for criticism about Brennan's apparent inconsistency. After joining his allies in protecting defendants such as Miranda against self-incrimination Brennan took a very different view in the case of Armando Schmerber, who was hospitalized after a driving accident. A police officer smelled liquor on Schmerber's breath, placed him under arrest, and directed a doctor to take a blood sample to determine his alcohol level. Prosecutors used the analysis of the blood test against Schmerber at his trial for driving while intoxicated. At conference, Brennan's usual four allies all voted to reverse his conviction. The other four justices voted to affirm. Brennan was undecided but indicated he was leaning toward affirming.

Clark, as senior associate justice in the majority, assigned the case to Brennan, who agonized over it and remained so undecided that he considered asking that it be held over and reargued the following term. But Brennan ultimately wrote an opinion that rejected Schmerber's self-incrimination claim, opening the door to all sorts of nontestimonial evidence to be admitted against defendants, including blood, hair, and handwriting samples. Unlike his usual allies, Brennan seemed persuaded that the case presented a very limited intrusion under carefully controlled circumstances and filled the opinion with notes of caution against any greater intrusions. The motivation for Brennan seemed similar to his concern in the never-published *Miranda* concurrence: the Court should do more to balance legitimate law enforcement needs against the protections of the Bill of Rights. But such departures remained relatively rare for Brennan. He usually struck that balance to favor the defendant.

EVEN AS BRENNAN provided the fifth vote for the criminal-procedure revolution, he never became a target of criticism as did his friend David Bazelon, whose views in this area of law made him a deeply polarizing figure both on and off the D.C. Circuit. "People are not neutral about Judge David L. Bazelon," Brennan acknowledged in a 1978 tribute speech. "He deeply pleases some. He deeply distresses others." The D.C. Circuit was unique at the time among the nation's intermediate federal courts because it functioned as the de facto state supreme court for the District of Columbia. That special status made it possible for judges on the D.C. Circuit to influence a broad swath of criminal law, a role Bazelon embraced as chief judge. He never shied away from being labeled a judicial activist. "In some circles, 'activist' is about the dirtiest name there is," Bazelon once said. "Activism for me means a willingness to try new approaches even though one cannot be sure that they will succeed."

No one ever doubted Bazelon's willingness to experiment, particularly at the intersection of crime and mental health that interested him most. In addition to landmark opinions regarding the insanity defense, Bazelon argued forcefully for the right to treatment for people in custody in mental hospitals and juvenile facilities, and wrote a novel opinion holding chronic alcoholism a defense to a criminal charge of public intoxication. He advocated what would be mocked by conservatives as the prototypical "bleeding heart" liberal view of criminals' broader social and psychological ills, ranging from broken families to drug addiction and alcoholism. He also questioned the wisdom of tough penalties. "Giving them more of the same — more punishment — is like giving harder and harder lessons in algebra to a student who has shown his inability to absorb even the basic lessons," Bazelon said in a February 1966 speech. One law professor denounced such views as "welfare criminology."

Some Court observers strongly suspected that Bazelon influenced his friends on the Supreme Court, including Brennan. Lawyers were said to load up their briefs with as many references to Bazelon opinions as possible in the belief that the justices would view that as a signal for how they should vote. That view exaggerates Bazelon's impact on Brennan in the area of criminal law. Brennan came to the Supreme Court with his own concerns about the need to bolster the rights of criminal defendants, which he had exhibited in New Jersey Supreme Court decisions. But it also is true that Bazelon likely influenced Brennan's approach to crime, exposing him to just the sort of sympathetic views of criminal suspects' socioeconomic problems that President Eisenhower had mocked at the 1964 Republican National Convention. Brennan read the speeches Bazelon sent him with care, underlining passages as he went along. He quoted them in his own speeches on crime, which often echoed Bazelon's message about the need to rethink how the criminal justice system treated defendants. "The issue," Brennan told the D.C. Circuit's annual meeting in May 1963, "really comes down to whether we should further whittle away the protections of the very people who most need them — the people who are too ignorant, too poor, too ill-educated to defend themselves."

Bazelon generated the kind of national headlines Brennan rarely attracted as a result of letters he exchanged in 1965 with Attorney General Nicholas Katzenbach. Bazelon was concerned about a proposal to allow police to question suspects scooped up in dragnet arrests for up to twenty-four hours after their arrivals in police stations without making any allowance for them to retain counsel. "These provisions would, in my experience, primarily affect the poor, and in particular, poor Negro citizen," Bazelon wrote. "I doubt that the police would, for example, arrest and question the entire board of directors of a company suspected of criminal anti-trust violations." Instead of sympathizing with his positions, as Bazelon expected, Katzenbach wrote back, "Your suggestion that police questioning will primarily affect the poor and, in particular, the poor Negro, strikes me as particularly irrelevant." The letters circulated widely among law professors and then wound up published in the *Washington Star* in August and eventually in several national publications. The exchange also prompted bipartisan questions at the confirmation hearing of Abe Fortas to replace Arthur Goldberg on the Court later that year. Fortas's appointment came after the president had persuaded Goldberg to replace Adlai Stevenson as UN ambassador in order to make room on the Court for his friend and adviser Fortas.

Bazelon's controversial views alone do not explain why he so infuriated colleagues on the D.C. Circuit, like Warren Burger, and Washington judges and lawyers more generally. As with Frankfurter, his abrasive personality played a role. Bazelon came into his court's conference meetings with his mind made up, and he rarely budged, seemingly lacking in the powers of persuasion Brennan employed so successfully. The contrast in styles between these two friends could not have been starker. Brennan prided himself on building coalitions and getting along with all of his colleagues. Bazelon almost seemed to enjoy stoking conflicts. Some of his colleagues on the D.C. District Court reciprocated Bazelon's open disdain. One told the *Washington Post* Bazelon was "one of the worst things that has ever happened to the administration of criminal justice in Washington." Mistrust ran so deep on his polarized court that some accused Bazelon of rigging who was assigned to the three-judge panels that heard cases, keeping the best cases for himself and his allies. The conservative and liberal judges on the District Court even sat at different tables during lunch, prompting one uncommitted jurist to eat at a nearby office building most days rather than have to choose sides.

Bazelon's principal opponent on the D.C. Circuit was Burger, a Minnesota-born judge and former official in Eisenhower's Justice Department who joined the court in April 1956, six months before Brennan came to Washington. Burger, one year Brennan's junior, was younger and more energetic than most of the court's other conservatives and eagerly took up the mantle of combat. Burger's contempt toward Bazelon dated back to his *Durham* decision redefining the criminal-insanity defense. Burger believed that decision downplayed the role of individual responsibility and left an opening for "the avant-garde of [psychiatrists] . . . 'fixing' to include a whole new batch of ailments under the name of 'mental disease.'" Burger privately mocked Bazelon in letters as "Baz" and called in Washington reporters for off-the-record conversations in which he dismissed his colleague as "misguided," "pathetic," and "a menace to society." Brennan heard all about the conflict from Bazelon. "It was a blood feud, there isn't any doubt about that," Brennan said.

Bazelon and Burger had more in common than either man would ever care to admit. Both grew up poor in the Midwest and were largely self-made. Burger had been admitted to Princeton but could not afford to attend, and wound up at the University of Minnesota. He had worked his way through the St. Paul College of Law by selling insurance for Mutual of New York. Both men were emotional and strong-willed. Neither showed much interest in the particulars of opinion writing, leaving that task to their clerks. One clerk who observed both described them as two "pompous peas in the pod taken in by the trappings of their offices," a marked contrast with Brennan, who struck almost everyone who met him as completely unassuming.

Burger's anger extended beyond Bazelon and the D.C. Circuit. He did not care much for the way the Supreme Court was handling criminal-procedure cases either. Burger's unease with the Supreme Court had only grown since he had written in 1957 to his friend Harry Blackmun in Minnesota, about its decisions during Brennan's first term. By 1960, Blackmun, too, was a federal circuit judge when Burger wrote him, "You can be thankful . . . that the 4 Leopards on the Sup. Court have not picked your jurisdiction as the 'laboratory' for new ideas." Burger wrote Blackmun once again in April 1961: "Things will need to get worse before they will get better in relation to those bastards on the Sup. Ct. who as Felix said, 'turn every criminal appeal into a quest for error.'" Two months later, Burger lamented in another letter, "The horrible thing is that the Eisenhower appointees are doing most of the damage."

That summer of 1962, Burger came face-to-face with one of those "bastards" on the Supreme Court when he joined Brennan as an instructor at a two-week seminar for appellate judges at New York University. Brennan had been serving as an instructor at the annual seminar since 1959, his dual experience as a state judge and Supreme Court justice making him a natural choice. Burger had previously attended as a student. Burger and Brennan found themselves at odds when the seminar discussion turned to criminal procedure. Brennan believed that Burger let his feud with Bazelon spill into the seminar, while Burger resented what he viewed as Brennan's attempts to proselytize to impressionable judges there. "Brennan was his usual attractive, plausible zealot-on-the-march self," Burger wrote Blackmun after the seminar had concluded, adding that "I do not underrate his appeal to a bunch of new younger judges."

Summer after summer as the 1960s progressed, Brennan and Burger exchanged sharp volleys before this small audience of state and federal judges from across the country about the Court's latest criminal-procedure decisions. The judges did not realize they were getting a sneak preview of the conflict that would play out on a larger scale when Burger succeeded Warren as chief justice in 1969. At New York University, Burger increasingly came to view himself as fighting Brennan for the hearts and minds of America's judges, and waging a noble defense against the ascendant liberal activists. "In the present context, if I were to stand still for some of the idiocy that is put forth as legal and constitutional profundity I would, I am sure, want to shoot myself in later years," Burger wrote Blackmun in 1967. "The question really comes down to this," Burger wrote. "Shall we let [judges such as Brennan, Douglas, and Bazelon] have the floor alone?"

There was at least one place in Washington where Brennan and Bazelon had the floor to themselves: Milton Kronheim's warehouse. By the mid-1960s, his cafeteria had become something of a clubhouse for the ascendant liberals on the Supreme Court and D.C. Circuit. Brennan and Bazelon continued to lunch there, as often as three times a week when the Court was not in session, so frequently that they would only call Kronheim to let him know when they could not make it. They occasionally brought along Douglas or Warren. More often, their lunch mate would be one of the most recent additions to the D.C. Circuit, J. Skelly Wright, a transplant from New Orleans. Bazelon and Brennan found a kindred spirit in Wright, five years younger than Brennan. Wright grew up Catholic, the second of seven children in a poor working-class neighborhood in New Orleans. He graduated from Loyola University and then taught high school English during the day while attending Loyola Law School at night. Wright worked as an assistant U.S. attorney and then as the U.S. attorney in New Orleans before Truman named him the youngest federal district court judge in the country at age thirty-eight in 1949 — the same year Bazelon joined the D.C. Circuit.

Wright later said he was not acutely aware of the injustice of racial segregation in New Orleans until, as U.S. attorney, he looked out his office window one Christmas Eve. He saw a bus unloading a group of African Americans arriving for a holiday party at the nearby Lighthouse for the Blind, who were led to a segregated entrance at the rear of the building. "They couldn't even see yet they made them walk into separate doors," Wright recalled decades later. "That sight still affects me." Even before the *Brown* decision, Wright ordered Louisiana State University to admit black students to its law school and then its undergraduate campus. He later ordered New Orleans's city buses and parks desegregated too. Wright's most controversial decision came as part of a three-judge panel that ordered the city's public schools desegregated, an opinion that made Wright the most hated man in New Orleans, shunned by friends and guarded twenty-four hours a day by federal marshals. Yet he harbored no regrets. Southern senators bottled up the Kennedy administration's attempt to elevate him to the Fifth Circuit. They were happy to see him leave the region when Kennedy, instead, appointed Wright to the D.C. Circuit in 1962.

Wright quickly emerged as an ally of Bazelon, who later appointed him to preside over the desegregation of the District of Columbia's schools. Wright joked that he was the only circuit judge in America liberal enough to call Bazelon a conservative. Their names became blurred together in time. Court observers often referred to Bazelon-Wright or Wright-Bazelon as a single entity. Wright had a more easygoing demeanor than Bazelon, a southern gentility that made him better liked personally by conservatives on the D.C. Circuit. But Wright, too, embraced the label of judicial activist. "When I get a case . . . the first thing I think of automatically is what's right . . . and then I look at the law to see whether or not you can do it," Wright later explained.

The Wrights quickly hit it off with the Brennans. Wright's wife, Helen, became one of Marjorie's closest friends. Brennan greatly admired the courage Wright had shown in New Orleans. "Here is a man, a Louisianan by birth and upbringing, who to a degree matched by few others courageously assumed the burden of explaining to his state and the nation why the deepest principles of law required, and continue to require, the often painful resolution of racial equality," Brennan wrote in a 1985 tribute. The warm feelings were mutual. Wright wrote Brennan early in their relationship, "Your work on the Court has been an inspiration to me, and I'm certain many others who labor in the judicial vineyards."

Brennan's original regard for Bazelon continued — the two thought of each other in glowing terms. But Brennan also believed it was important to handle himself publicly as independent from his friend. Bazelon felt no hesitation about sharing his displeasure when Brennan did so. After joining one particular bruising rebuke, Brennan remembered receiving an obscenity-laced call from Bazelon. He tried responding with reason, explaining that the last thing either of them needed was a reputation for being beholden to the other.

Bazelon and Wright were not just like-minded judges and lunch mates — they also served as Brennan's chief conduit for clerks. A clerkship with Bazelon or Wright became the gateway to one with Brennan. Bazelon came to use the enticement of a clerkship with Brennan as a way to lure the most coveted candidates to his chambers. Brennan still relied on law school deans and his former clerks sprinkled throughout academia for recruiting his clerks, and he eventually expanded his judicial farm team to include other judges throughout the country. But none would ever match the frequency with which Bazelon and Wright landed clerks in his chambers. Sadly, competition over placing clerks in Brennan's chambers later contributed to a falling out between Bazelon and Wright.

The bright young law school graduates who moved directly from Bazelon to Brennan's chambers were often surprised to discover how different these two best friends could be as bosses. Bazelon was described later by the *Washington Post* as a "demanding taskmaster who is brutally frank with his staff members." He played favorites among clerks, threw opinions down on their desks in disgust, and thought nothing about calling them at home in the middle of the night. (These clerks apparently never told Brennan about their difficult experiences in Bazelon's chambers, as he would express surprise to hear of it later.) Bazelon could also be remarkably generous, anonymously paying for one clerk's dinner on a special occasion with his wife at one of Washington's fanciest French restaurants and then insisting that Kronheim had footed the bill.

Brennan, by contrast, more strictly separated his personal life from his life at the Court. To be sure, he displayed tremendous warmth toward everyone at the Court, down to the secretaries and policemen, whom he would inevitably greet with a hearty "Hiya, pal." Displaying the physical intimacy of a skilled politician, he became famous for his handshake, known as the "Brennan Grip." Brennan grasped the target's arm and drew in his entire body. He was especially warm toward his clerks, whom he treated like long-lost friends from their first day in his chambers. Many clerks remembered their intimate morning coffees with Brennan as the highlight of their clerkships. Long after they had left his chambers, Brennan could instantly recall the names of their wives and children as he asked for updates about them.

For Brennan, making others the focus of his attention served another purpose: deflecting attention away from him. Beneath his genuinely warm exterior, Brennan maintained a core of privacy his clerks found just as difficult to pierce as had his colleagues at his Newark law firm. "He was a private person," observed Daniel O'Hern, one of Brennan's earliest clerks who grew particularly close to his former boss in subsequent years. "He rarely, at least with me, discussed his inner thoughts or why he did what he did." Unlike Bazelon, Brennan seldom took his clerks along to lunches at Kronheim's, where he felt most free to unwind. And even the conversations over morning coffee rarely moved beyond Court business or current events into his personal life. "So much of who he really was was covered up by the backslapping leprechaun exterior," recalled one clerk. Another clerk later looked back on his time in Brennan's chambers and wondered "if he was close to us or if it was an act perfected over thirty years. I don't know which it was."

· 11 ·

ANGERING THE LEFT

R ALPH GINZBURG SAW himself as a champion of the First
Amendment when he released the first issue of his new magazine
about love and sex, *Eros*, on Valentine's Day 1962. The thirty-
three-year-old New York publisher never expected that his high-end hardcover magazine would lead to a federal obscenity conviction, a five-year
prison term, and a $28,000 fine. Most surprising, perhaps, was that the Su-
preme Court would affirm this unusually harsh punishment in an opinion
written by Brennan, who dismissed Ginzburg as a crass peddler of smut.
The magazine's contents proved less objectionable than Ginzburg's mar-
keting techniques. He flooded the nation's mailboxes with promotional
flyers, prompting complaints from many of the millions of recipients, including a Boy Scout troop and a convent. Never one for subtlety, Ginzburg
had shipped the mailings from Middlesex, New Jersey, after first inquiring
about the mailing possibilities in two towns in Pennsylvania: Intercourse
and Blue Ball.

In his first decade on the Court, Brennan had sided with plenty of
unsympathetic, unsavory, or simply unpopular appellants: criminals and
Communists, atheists and agitators — and more than one pornographer.
Yet all the empathy for which Brennan would become famous seemed to
vanish when Ginzburg's case reached the Court in the fall of 1965. Brennan

upheld Ginzburg's punishment after laying out a new justification for an obscenity conviction: pandering by the seller. That surprising 5–4 decision announced in March 1966 prompted some of the first — and only — vocal criticism liberals directed at Brennan during his entire tenure on the Court. In fact, the only other notable incident of liberals criticizing Brennan came just a few months later, when he rescinded a clerkship offer to a recent law school graduate with alleged Communist ties. At the time, no one linked these two incongruous decisions by Brennan. Yet in each instance, some wondered why he would take an action that seemed so contrary to his convictions about freedoms of speech and association. Answering that question requires considering how far Brennan was willing to bend in order to accommodate the wishes of his friend and closest colleague, Chief Justice Earl Warren.

BRENNAN HAD GROWN ever closer to Warren as the 1960s progressed. Their weekly preconference meeting had become such a fixed event on Thursdays at 4 P.M. that one Brennan clerk made a mental note not to take catnaps when he knew the chief justice would inevitably walk into the chambers.

These private sessions were Brennan and Warren's little secret — or so they thought. Warren never told his secretary or his clerks where he was headed beforehand. Brennan's secretary and clerks knew about the meetings because they saw the chief justice arrive each week, but could only guess about what was discussed. Brennan's not telling his clerks what he and Warren talked about was a sharp departure from his practice on returning from the justices' private conference. He freely discussed all that transpired inside the conference, even handing clerks his notes when he was too tired to chat afterward. Brennan thought his discretion about his meetings with Warren ensured that none of the other justices knew about them — but it actually only fueled more conjecture. His secretiveness fed suspicions within his chambers that Brennan was telling Warren what to do. Word of the meetings spread to other justices too. Douglas described them as a "mock conference" in his autobiography. Others assumed the meetings had a more conspiratorial purpose. Harlan feared Brennan and Warren coordinated their positions during these sessions, turning the justices' conference that followed into something of a sham.

Brennan, who was always protective of Warren's reputation, categorically denied any suggestion that he ever told the chief justice how to vote or what to do. "People jumped to the conclusion that I must have been telling him how to decide cases because he did not have a reputation of being a very great intellect, that he'd been a good governor all right, but he was a politician and not an intellect," Brennan said. "Well, they're just dead wrong about that." He insisted that he did no more than serve as Warren's sounding board. "He'd come in and say, 'This is the way I feel about it, this is the way it looks to me on this and that and the other issue — what do you think?' And we'd talk about it." Brennan said that they did not talk about the cases the justices had agreed to hear, whether they had the votes for their view, or who might be the best justice to take an assignment in any given case during those Thursday-afternoon meetings. "He was just interested in how the case ought to come out," Brennan said.

The strategizing, Brennan insisted, was limited to trying to decide which cases might work best for incorporating the requirements of the Bill of Rights against the states. About once a month, Warren went further after conference, asking Brennan to come to his chambers or talk on the telephone about assignment decisions. "He'd just call and say, 'I've got in mind giving such and such to Potter — what do you think of that? And more often than not, I was quite able to agree with him." Brennan did not view himself as a better vote counter than Warren. "He was too shrewd and experienced not to have had that kind of sense," Brennan said. He thought Warren "was looking more for confirmation." When Brennan disagreed with him, as he occasionally did, he said Warren "more often than not" would "make the change." Brennan took pains to point out that he was not the only justice whom Warren sought out for advice about opinion assignments; Black was another.

As details emerged decades later about their working relationship, Brennan was described as Warren's alter ego, quarterback, or tactician. Brennan strenuously rejected any such characterization. But however much Brennan sought to minimize it, his close working relationship with Warren — and the degree to which Warren relied on him — had few precedents in the Court's entire history. Perhaps the only parallel was the reliance of John Marshall, a political genius who served as chief justice between 1801 and 1835, on the legal prowess of Justice Joseph Story during their twenty-four years together on the Court. In the century and a half since, no pair of justices had worked so closely together to accomplish such dramatic change in the nation's constitutional law. But Brennan, in his own mind, always remembered who was boss. Stephen Barnett, one of Brennan's 1963–64 term clerks, recalled that after Warren visited the chambers to ask for support in one case, Brennan said, "Who am I to say no to the Chief Justice of the United States?"

IN FACT, BRENNAN and Warren voted together so frequently that Brennan rarely had to worry about saying no to the chief. Obscenity remained the rare area of law where they did not see eye-to-eye. Neither man ever felt particularly comfortable looking at obscene books and movies. But, unlike Warren, that discomfort did not stop Brennan from protecting the sorts of materials he did not want to see. His *Roth* decision, written during his first term, had been applied by the Court in the following decade to protect from censorship more and more literature and films with serious literary or artistic merit. The Court also rejected state censorship boards that had banned movies and books or intimidated their distributors. By 1963, Anthony Lewis credited the Court in the pages of *Esquire* with "liberating this country from Puritanism." "The United States has moved from one of the most timid countries in dealing with sex in the arts to what many believe is now by far the most liberal in the Western World," Lewis wrote. "The nine no-longer-so-old men are responsible."

The seemingly liberalized law of obscenity remained a headache for Brennan and his fellow justices — as well as for the lower courts trying to apply their decisions. The heart of the problem remained the difficulty of defining exactly what should qualify as obscene. The Court had not provided lower courts much in the way of clarity in *Roth* or in a series of decisions that followed in which the Court overturned obscenity convictions without any detailed explanation. The justices themselves remained "hopelessly divided" about the definition, as Brennan himself noted in 1962. That is when the Court took up a case involving a post office determination barring the mail distribution of several magazines featuring naked pictures of men aimed at a homosexual audience. Harlan sought to clarify the *Roth* rule in the case, *Manual Enterprises v. Day.* He set forth a new additional requirement of "patent offensiveness." On that basis, Harlan concluded that the magazines were not obscene.

Brennan, however, advocated a narrower basis for overturning the conviction, which focused on the postal statute rather than the Court's constitutional obscenity standard. "I have no doubt that we must some day give further thought to the Roth test," Brennan wrote Harlan in a private note. But, Brennan added, "I lean to the idea that we ought let the widespread ferment continue a bit longer in legal periodicals and courts over the soundness and meaning of the Roth test before we re-examine it." Brennan was concerned that adding the "patently offensive" criteria might limit obscenity to only "hard core" pornography. Two years before Potter Stewart would famously declare "I know it when I see it" when it came to obscenity, Brennan wrote Harlan, "I have trouble defining 'hard core,' although no trouble at all recognizing it when I see it." The biggest problem for Brennan as vote counter was the disagreement among justices about how to proceed. "There appears almost no prospect of an agreement of five of us upon anything."

Nonetheless, in 1964, Brennan, too, attempted to clarify the Court's obscenity standard when the justices faced a pair of cases involving works of obvious artistic and literary merit. The first involved *Tropic of Cancer,* a 1934 novel by Henry Miller that wound up on the Modern Library's list of the fifty greatest books of the twentieth century. Its explicit descriptions of sexual encounters by the American expatriate narrator living in Paris explain why it was not published in the United States until 1961. The justices also took up a case involving the 1958 French film *The Lovers,* an account of an unhappily married woman balancing a husband in Dijon and a lover in Paris who falls for a third man who drives her home after her car breaks down. The film won a prize at the Venice Film Festival and landed on several American critics' best-of-the-year lists. But a single sex scene in the last reel of the film, which reveals little more than the paramours' naked backs, triggered the prosecution of Ohio movie theater manager Nico Jacobellis.

Six justices voted to reverse Jacobellis's conviction, but they would offer five different explanations for why they did so. Black and Douglas stuck to their absolutist position that any obscenity regulation violated the First Amendment, which Stewart came closest to joining in his separate concurrence. Brennan wrote a plurality opinion joined only by Goldberg in which he noted that "the proper standard for making" obscenity determinations "has been the subject of much discussion and controversy" since the Court's *Roth* decision. He admitted that the test "is not perfect," but argued the Court must make its own independent review of the facts in each obscenity case instead of relying on the lower courts' findings. The justices and their clerks were now gathering in a basement room, 22-B, to watch each of the movies at issue in obscenity cases.

Most controversially, Brennan suggested in his opinion in *Jacobellis v. Ohio* that the "contemporary community standards" against which obscenity should be judged was a national rather than a local one. While acknowledging "that local communities throughout the land are, in fact, diverse," Brennan nonetheless argued that a single national standard should apply in all of them: "It is, after all, a national Constitution we are expounding." Brennan suggested that *Roth* explicitly laid out this national approach, which in fact was not the case at all. In a rare break, Warren took exception to Brennan's approach in a dissent. "It is my belief that, when the Court said in *Roth* that obscenity is to be defined by reference to 'community standards,' it meant community standards — not a national standard." Warren wrote, "I believe that there is no provable 'national standard' and perhaps there should be none." Brennan's notion that the Court should make its own determination of a book or movie's obscenity also troubled Warren. Instead, he argued, the justices should defer to state and federal courts and only review the sufficiency of the evidence upon which the lower court made its decision. Warren warned against the Court establishing itself as "an ultimate censor."

The justices had completely fractured once again, but Brennan's position in the middle — between Douglas and Black's absolutism and the puritanism of Warren and Clark — made him the pivotal figure on obscenity, a fact noted by the press. In August 1964, the Associated Press declared Brennan "the Court spokesman on obscenity cases." A few days later, the *Newark Evening News* similarly reported that Brennan "has emerged as chief arbiter" of obscenity on the Court. "A combination of shifting philosophies and new appointees on the nation's high court have left Brennan the single most important justice in drawing what he has called 'the dim and uncertain line' between the obscene and the printable."

As the Court further narrowed limits on obscenity, critics accused the justices of fueling public immorality and crime. Goldwater had pointed to "a flood of obscene literature" as part of his broader attack on moral decay during his 1964 presidential campaign. A 1965 *Reader's Digest* story described several horror stories about the damage obscenity wrought, including the tale of a fifteen-year-old girl who confessed to selling sexual favors to local college students after reading several paperback novels glamorizing the lives of prostitutes.

Brennan's prominent position in the *Jacobellis* case made him a particular target of anti-obscenity groups. Operation Yorkville, a New York City–based campaign against obscenity founded by an ecumenical group of religious leaders, printed Brennan's home address in its November–December 1964 newsletter and suggested parents who received unwanted pornography in the mail forward the offensive material to him. "Perhaps enough mail of this sort would convince Mr. Justice Brennan that America's 'standards' are much higher than he believes them to be," the newsletter suggested. One man from Long Island, New York, sent the newsletter to Brennan, writing beside the justice's home address that "intelligent, God fearing people know what community standards are."

The criticism was particularly intense within the Catholic Church. A columnist in the Philadelphia Archdiocese's newspaper, the *Catholic Standard and Times,* declared, "Many Catholics may have winced when they read that Justice William Brennan of their faith had written the majority opinion." Archbishop Spellman, who had long battled obscene movies in New York, did not single out Brennan by name when he said the decision reflected "an acceptance of degeneracy and the beatnik mentality as the standard way of American life." Spellman's secretary of education in the New York Archdiocese, John Paul Haverty, went even further, calling the Supreme Court the "greatest evil in the country today." Joseph O'Meara, Notre Dame's civil liberties–minded law school dean and an acquaintance of Brennan's, rebuked Haverty in a letter. "Like other human institutions, the Supreme Court is helped by criticism," O'Meara wrote. "But those who undertake to criticize have an obligation to know what they are talking about. You did not fulfill that obligation."

Just because O'Meara scolded Haverty did not mean he agreed with Brennan's *Jacobellis* opinion. O'Meara did not mince words when he wrote Brennan a letter that June describing the problems he saw with a national obscenity standard. "In my opinion, Bill, you would impose upon the Court an absolutely impossible task — and I mean that literally," O'Meara wrote. Big cities, he noted, are more permissive than small towns and the Court simply could not apply the same standard to both. He concluded, "I hope you won't mind, Bill, if I say the situation is simply impossible. The Court's judgment can't stand." O'Meara turned his private critique into the draft of a law review article that he shared with Brennan a few months later.

Instead of being insulted, Brennan invited O'Meara to join him and Warren for lunch at the Court in November 1964. Brennan shared a copy of O'Meara's article with Warren in advance. "He flays me to a fare-thee-well about my view in Jacobellis and supports you to the hilt," Brennan wrote Warren lightheartedly. "There must be a violation of the Equal Protection Clause there somewhere!" Brennan continued his correspondence with O'Meara after the lunch. He shared his frustration that both academics such as O'Meara and many judges incorrectly assumed that Brennan did not realize his declarations about a national standard were a minority view on the Court. That view, Brennan wrote, "reflects the misreading of Jacobellis that I told you bothers me." Nevertheless, events would soon prove just how correct O'Meara was when he wrote in his law review article, "The sheer weight of the burden of deciding independently the issues in obscenity cases will drive the Court, sooner or later, to find some way of escape."

AS O'MEARA PREDICTED, Brennan and his fellow justices were beginning to chafe under the burden of examining each of the works that had been deemed obscene. On December 7, 1965, dubbed "dirty books day" by one journalist, the Court took up a trio of obscenity cases, including Ginzburg's. One of the other cases involved Massachusetts's ban of an eighteenth-century English novel, Fanny Hill, which described in vivid detail an innocent fifteen-year-old British country girl's descent into a life of ill repute. Fanny Hill did not offer a plot as much as an excuse to describe a variety of titillating scenes, including same-sex encounters for both men and women and the narrator enjoying her first whipping. Edward Mishkin, in a third case, had a more tenuous claim of literary merit for the bondage tracts he published. His own lawyer described them as "sadistic and masochistic." Nonetheless, the lawyers for all three appellants could arrive in Court that day at least somewhat confident about their clients' prospects. While no clear standard had emerged, the overall trend toward liberalizing the nation's obscenity laws seemed obvious to Court watchers. The Court had not upheld a single obscenity conviction since beginning to weigh in on the subject a decade earlier. The New Republic could predict in December 1965 that "most of the lawyers there knew that the Roth tests were way stations on the road to total abolition of obscenity sanctions."

Such optimism proved misplaced. Few outside the Court appreciated the degree of frustration building among the justices as they undertook to review these three cases. Over the course of a decade, Brennan had led the Court exactly into the morass Justice Jackson predicted in 1948 when he cautioned his colleagues against making themselves the "High Court of Obscenity." The Court had in fact become a de facto censorship board as the justices examined each book and movie that came before them to judge for themselves whether it was obscene. Warren had groused about that distasteful possibility in his *Jacobellis* dissent a year earlier. He now could not hide his frustration during the December 7, 1965, oral arguments. He was the most persistent questioner right from the start in Mishkin's case. Even the titles of the books peddled by Mishkin, including *Mistress of Leather, Bound in Rubber,* and *The Whipping Chorus Girls,* would probably have been hard enough for the famously prudish chief justice to read. "I'm sure this Court doesn't want to be the final censor to read all the prurient material in the country to determine if it has social value," Warren observed from the bench. "If the final burden depends on this Court, it looks to me as though we're in trouble."

It was not solely Warren's distaste for obscenity that gave him pause in these cases. Warren realized the Court had to pick and choose the areas in which it would run ahead of public opinion if it was to stave off congressional threats to prune its jurisdiction. He had no interest in wasting any of the Court's finite political capital on an area of law he found so distasteful. Harry Kalven, a prominent legal scholar at the University of Chicago, later theorized that, after years of reversing obscenity conviction after obscenity conviction, "The Court may have felt the need to reassure advocates of regulation that it was still possible to secure a conviction for obscenity. If so, Ginzburg may unwittingly have presented himself as the ideal candidate for sacrifice."

Ginzburg's interest in obscenity began when he was a copy boy at a New York newspaper that published an article on the retirement of Anthony Comstock's successor at the New York Society for the Suppression of Vice. Ginzburg set out to write a biography of Comstock and instead wound up publishing *An Unhurried View of Erotica,* which described the secret stores of erotic materials at famous libraries around the world. That book, published in 1958, sold 325,000 copies, which helps explain why Ginzburg could afford to live in an elegant thirtieth-floor apartment in Lincoln Towers and send his three children to private schools.

The book's success persuaded Ginzburg that there was a demand for a fine periodical about sex. Brennan's *Roth* decision convinced him he might publish such a magazine legally. Ginzburg and his wife and creative collaborator, Shoshana Ginzburg, set out the year Brennan announced his *Roth* decision to create their first-class quarterly magazine named after the Greek goddess of love. "Love and sex are beautiful," Ginzburg told *Playboy* magazine in 1966. "Mature people — everyone, as a matter of fact — ought to approach them without shame or fear." Ginzburg and his wife hired a leading typographer and art director and made the decision to publish in hardback in order to help justify the magazine's ten-dollar cover price. Compared to *Fanny Hill* or the sort of magazines that would soon follow — the first *Penthouse* was published in the United States in 1969 — *Eros* was decidedly tame. It featured a dictionary of vulgar words and engravings from the late eighteenth century as well as the works of more contemporary artists and writers. There was little inside its pages racier than photographs of male prostitutes in Bombay, an amorous interracial couple, and French postcards showing buxom nude women.

What got Ginzburg into trouble was the way he promoted his magazine. The 9 million direct-mail solicitations attracted 150,000 subscribers — and generated a furious backlash among anti-obscenity activists. Ginzburg had relied on mailing lists purchased from other magazines, but did not bother to cull, for example, St. Charles Convent and the Sisters of Mercy. The postmaster general received 35,000 letters of complaint. Congresswoman Kathryn E. Granahan, who chaired the House Post Office Operations Subcommittee, demanded in a furious fit of alliteration on the House floor in March 1962, three weeks after *Eros*'s debut, that "the presses of this pornographic pestilence . . . be stopped and its scabrous publisher smitten."

The Kennedy Justice Department initiated a criminal-obscenity prosecution against Ginzburg a few months later. He was indicted by a grand jury in Granahan's Philadelphia district for publishing *Eros* and two other publications. One was the book *The Housewife's Handbook of Selective Promiscuity*, which purported to be the sexual autobiography of an Arizona businesswoman and wife from the age of three to thirty-six, and a biweekly newsletter, *Liaison,* which offered off-color jokes, poems, and professionally written articles on sexual relationships. The experts testifying on Ginzburg's behalf at his five-day trial included doctors and psychiatrists who said they found *The Housewife's Handbook* helpful in their practice. U.S. District Court judge Ralph Body disagreed. He meted out an unusually stiff sentence after finding Ginzburg guilty and calling all three publications "dirt for dirt's sake and dirt for money's sake."

It was not only Ginzburg and his attorneys who thought the Supreme Court should overturn his conviction. He became a cause célèbre, with briefs filed on his behalf by the American Civil Liberties Union and a group of prominent artists ranging from singer Bob Dylan to novelist Philip Roth. Even the Justice Department appeared to view at least part of the conviction as wrong-headed. The brief filed by Solicitor General Thurgood Marshall — who was supposed to present the government's views — invited the Court to overturn the *Eros* and *The Housewife's Handbook* convictions, the two that resulted in Ginzburg being sentenced to prison. Paul Bender, a former Frankfurter clerk working in the Solicitor General's Office, was assigned to argue the case before the Court, but hardly delivered a rousing defense of the conviction. Bender told the justices that 75 to 90 percent of the material the government sought to suppress in other cases was more objectionable than Ginzburg's publications. Bender sensed he had unwittingly won over one vote to uphold the conviction when Warren complained about having to read this sort of material.

Ginzburg's showboating personality certainly did not help his cause. He seemed almost to be baiting the justices in his direct-mail postcard solicitations. One boasted, "The publication of this magazine which is frankly and avowedly concerned with erotica, has been enabled by recent court decisions ruling that a literary piece or painting, though explicitly sexual in content, has a right to be published if it is a genuine work of art." Then there was the seemingly intentionally provocative postmark, which Ginzburg insisted was coincidental. He claimed the mailing firms just happened to be based in Middlesex. In spite of Bender's sense that Warren was on his side, he left the oral argument convinced there still were not five votes to affirm Ginzburg's conviction. He certainly was not thinking about Brennan supporting the prosecutions.

But when the justices gathered for their conference three days later,

Brennan tersely indicated he agreed with Warren and would vote to uphold the obscenity convictions in all three cases without offering an explanation for why he was doing so. Brennan's unexpected course of action—particularly in *Fanny Hill*—alarmed the newest justice, Abe Fortas, who had joined the Court just two months earlier. Despite *Fanny Hill's* explicit contents, Fortas worried that a conviction in that case would give rise to a new round of the modern equivalent of book burning. "Contrary to my principles," Fortas said, he "went to work" trying to find a way to convince the justices to overturn the conviction in *Fanny Hill*. Fortas showed more of a willingness to uphold Ginzburg's conviction. He said he found *The Housewife's Handbook* not obscene, but was leaning toward joining an opinion that found *Eros* obscene.

After the conference, Warren focused on convincing Fortas to uphold Ginzburg's conviction. During several long conversations, Warren persuaded Fortas to join an opinion affirming the conviction using an approach that focused on Ginzburg's conduct rather than the content of his books. This theory of pandering had not been discussed during the justices' conference, but was not new. Warren had first raised the concept in his concurring opinion in *Roth* when he emphasized that the defendants in that case "were plainly engaged in the commercial exploitation of the morbid and shameful craving for materials with prurient effect." In a companion case, he had stressed, "It is the conduct of the individual that should be judged" rather than the quality of the book sold. However, Fortas would recall it was he who suggested the pandering formula to Brennan.

Once again, Warren handed Brennan the task of writing the opinions in these obscenity cases. Brennan ultimately decided to write an opinion reversing the *Fanny Hill* conviction in order to keep Fortas's vote to uphold Ginzburg's. No matter whether it was suggested by Warren or Fortas, Brennan adopted the pandering approach, despite resistance within his own chambers. Brennan later recalled that his clerk Peter Strauss "fought him tooth and nail" in the case. Nevertheless, Brennan's opinion condemned Ginzburg as being in the "sordid business of pandering" and using advertising material that displayed the "leer of the sensualist." In close obscenity cases, Brennan's approach made the conduct of the seller as important as what he sold. Brennan did insist on one limitation over Warren's objections, narrowing the pandering doctrine to cases where the sole emphasis was on the sexually provocative aspect of the material. Brennan, joined by

Fortas, insisted that using the word "sole" was necessary to prevent abuse of the doctrine by lower courts. Fortas also suggested changing the language to make it clear that it was Ginzburg's objective conduct — rather than his character or personal qualities — that were being judged.

To attract additional votes for his *Ginzburg* opinion, Brennan moved his new definition of obscenity further liberalizing the *Roth* standard to a brief opinion he wrote overturning the *Fanny Hill* conviction. This new test protected materials with even a modicum of social value. Brennan wrote a brief, straightforward opinion upholding Mishkin's conviction and attached an appendix listing dozens of suggestive titles he published. In all, the deeply divided justices would file an astonishing fourteen opinions in these three cases. Clark and White voted to uphold the convictions in all three, while Black, Douglas, and Stewart voted to reverse in all three. Warren and Fortas, who were the only justices who did not write at least one opinion for themselves, joined Brennan in reversing *Fanny Hill* and upholding the other two convictions.

Nothing seemed unusual to the audience inside the courtroom as Brennan began announcing the trio of decisions from the bench on March 21, 1966. He started with *Fanny Hill,* which continued the Court's liberalizing trend by suggesting that works with even a modicum of artistic merit would not qualify as obscene. That development was quickly obscured as Brennan announced the decision in *Ginzburg.* The outcome so shocked the lawyers from the Solicitor General's Office in the packed audience, they could not hide their surprise. Warren passed Brennan a handwritten note on the bench pointing out "the quizzical expression" on their faces. The chief justice, however, was entirely pleased with Brennan's handiwork. "You have made a great contribution to the jurisprudence of our Court and your announcement was superb," Warren wrote Brennan.

Bender, the attorney in the Solicitor General's Office who argued the case, was stunned when he learned of the decision back at his office on the fifth floor of the Justice Department's headquarters. When a federal prosecutor called to congratulate him, Bender cut him off by saying there was no grounds for celebration. Bender believed it was a "terrible decision," and would later write Ginzburg's parole board on his behalf seeking his early release from prison. Thurgood Marshall, whom President Johnson had named solicitor general the year before, joked with his staff that he had found the sure way to win at the Court. "Just send Bender up with instructions to lose." Brennan, too, would later joke with Bender that he could not even lose when he tried.

To Bender — and more so to Ginzburg — the outcome in the case was no laughing matter. The overconfident publisher was caught completely off-guard when his attorney called him with the bad news at *Eros*'s office in Manhattan. Ginzburg had prepared two statements, both of which assumed his conviction would be overturned. Ginzburg's outrage overflowed as he spoke with reporters at a press conference in front of the statue of Benjamin Franklin near New York City Hall. "Today's decision was worthy of a court in the U.S.S.R., not of the Supreme Court of the United States," Ginzburg said. He predicted, "I'll be regarded as a martyr in the future." Many in the press portrayed him as a martyr immediately. A sympathetic *New York Herald Tribune* profile noted that he supported not only his wife and three daughters but also his mother and a blind sister who it was said suffered a nervous breakdown at the start of the *Eros* case. *New York Times* columnist Russell Baker wrote that, after the *Ginzburg* decision, "It is obvious that the Supreme Court is in over its head on the smut issue."

As Warren had probably hoped, the press portrayed the Court as retrenching from the greater protections it had afforded obscenity. "These are dark days in the 'nudie' business," the *New York Times* observed. The *Los Angeles Times* noted that "the majority found its attitude much more in line with the popular attitude than in some recent cases," such as in school prayer. Prosecutors interpreted *Ginzburg* and *Mishkin* as a green light to go after obscenity; the *New York Times* predicted that the *Ginzburg* decision would result in "massive prosecutions across the country against book publishers, book sellers, and the movie industry." Adult-bookstore employees in Manhattan's Times Square scrambled to replace masochistic titles like *The Spankers' Monthly* with the works of serious fiction writers in dusty show windows.

Ironically, the new obscenity test Brennan laid out in *Fanny Hill* actually expanded free speech protections by keeping books or films with even the slightest literary or artistic merit beyond obscenity prosecutions. But that fact was overlooked as the press focused on the *Ginzburg* and *Mishkin* decisions. Outraged liberals criticized Brennan for turning his back on free speech. "It was a grim day in the temple of justice," the *New*

Republic declared. "There is little if anything to be said for Justice Brennan's opinion." And a *Nation* editorial entitled "Demeaning the Court" declared that "the silliness to which even wise men descend was vehemently expressed by Justice Brennan."

For once, Brennan found himself praised in letters from church groups and clergy, including E. Earle Ellis of the New Brunswick Theological Seminary, who thanked him for "drawing a line against the smut peddlers." And this time, liberals wrote Brennan to condemn him. "The Ginzburg case decision places an ugly blemish on an otherwise remarkable Supreme Court record," one angry correspondent scribbled atop a *New York Herald Tribune* editorial mailed to Brennan. "Is there anything you can do to correct this mistake?"

Anthony Lewis, who had by now left the *New York Times'* Supreme Court beat, saw only one possible explanation for Brennan's decision in *Ginzburg*. It was a view shared by Bender, who concluded that, "the Chief felt strongly and Brennan didn't feel like arguing." By the end of Brennan's tenure, Bender had come to believe he was one of the greatest justices ever to serve on the Court. But Bender also believed that *Ginzburg* showed that Brennan was "not the world's most principled person. He would change votes to get a result."

Yet it is possible that Brennan had come to his view independently of Warren. As he showed in the civil rights sit-in cases, Brennan was acutely aware of how the justices' decisions were received outside the Court. A few days after the *Ginzburg* decision was announced, Thurman Arnold, the Washington attorney and former judge, wrote Fortas, his former law partner, a letter praising the decision. "If the Supreme Court didn't do something about all this pornographic advertising which is flooding the country the storm which was raised over the prayer issue would seem like a minor breeze," Arnold wrote. Fortas forwarded the letter to Brennan, who wrote back, "It certainly reflects Thurman's profound wisdom."

Regardless of whether Brennan deviated from his previous decisions at the expense of Ginzburg because he viewed the conviction as correct or bent to the wishes of Warren, he did not look back. The same could not be said for Fortas, who almost immediately expressed regrets privately. He confided in a note to Douglas three weeks later, "I think I was wrong in Ginzburg." Fortas admitted, "I guess that subconsciously I was affected by

G's slimy qualities — but if I had it to do over again, I'd vote to reverse at least as to all except his publication of 'Liaison.' Well, live and learn."

BRENNAN ANGERED THE Left a second time less than four months later, and Fortas again played a central role. The cause was Brennan's decision to withdraw a clerkship offer to Michael Tigar, a student at the University of California at Berkeley's law school, whose alleged radical ties would become a subject of national controversy. That Tigar's selection might prove problematic seemed obvious from the start to the person who recommended him, Brennan's former clerk Robert O'Neil, then a law professor at Berkeley.

In 1965 Brennan had asked O'Neil to recommend a clerk for the 1966–67 term. O'Neil enlisted the advice of his colleague, Robert Cole, who had clerked for Justice Minton. Based on merit, they both thought Tigar, a twenty-four-year-old native of Glendale, California, was the obvious choice. Tigar had ranked first in his second-year class and served as editor of the law review. His ambition to become a lawyer began early — at age eleven. His father gave him a copy of *Clarence Darrow for the Defense* and told Tigar he should model himself on Darrow, a tireless defender of the poor and unpopular causes.

What worried O'Neil were Tigar's extracurricular activities as an undergraduate and law student at Berkeley. Tigar had led the American contingent to a youth festival in Helsinki, Finland, in 1962, and he wrote an article about the experience for the *People's World,* the West Coast organ of the Communist Party. Then, as a first-year law student, Tigar had spearheaded an effort to strip the loyalty oath from the application California lawyers needed to sign to be admitted to the state bar. "This wasn't 1955. This was 1965," O'Neil recalled. "The political climate was different than at the height of the McCarthy era but the Court was still politically vulnerable." Nonetheless, O'Neil and Cole decided after some agonizing to recommend Tigar, and informed Brennan of their choice in a telephone conversation. During the call, O'Neil tried to tell Brennan he ought to know about some aspects of Tigar's past. O'Neil made a veiled reference to Tigar's politics, but Brennan cut him off. "I don't want to know any more," O'Neil recalled Brennan saying. "If the two of you think he's the best person, then I'll take him."

Brennan extended the offer on June 16, 1965, and Tigar accepted immediately. That night, Tigar celebrated at home with his pregnant wife and a friend. He drank cheap rum, put on a Clancy Brothers record, and listened over and over again to their version of the traditional Irish song "Brennan on the Moor," which began,

Oh it's of a brave young highway man this story we will tell
His name was Willie Brennan and in Ireland he did dwell

Tigar, too, tried to warn Brennan a few weeks later in a letter. "Frankly, there may be a little stir in the press as reporters with long memories recall student politics in Berkeley a couple of years ago." Brennan ignored the warning in his reply, and a relieved Tigar returned to his state of bliss. He was about to enter his final year of law school with a prestigious Supreme Court clerkship and had a second child on the way. "The summer of 1965 had a magical quality," Tigar recalled later. Then came the fall.

The first hint of trouble appeared in the fall 1965 issue of *Tocsin*, an anti-Communist newsletter based in the Bay Area, which criticized Brennan's decision to offer Tigar a clerkship given his leftist leanings. The attention given his appointment only grew in the months ahead. Neither Tigar nor O'Neil — and least of all Brennan — had anticipated the degree to which the student protest movement at Berkeley would become a political issue in the 1966 California governor's race. The sit-in protests by a group known as the Free Speech Movement which began in the fall of 1964 had become a lightning rod for growing anger about student campus unrest and broader societal disorder. In May 1966, a California state senate committee issued a report charging that "disciplined members of the Communist movement" were "deep in the heart" of the student protests. That report would become campaign fodder for a leading Republican gubernatorial candidate, a fifty-four-year-old movie and television actor named Ronald Reagan. He demanded public legislative hearings on "charges of communism, sexual misconduct and near anarchy" on Berkeley's campus. The issue helped Reagan win the Republican primary on June 7, 1966.

A day after Reagan's victory, conservative columnist James J. Kilpatrick wrote about Brennan's decision to hire Tigar: "A remarkable thing it is, then, that with such a background he was able to get one of the coveted Supreme Court clerkships." Kilpatrick's syndicated column ran in papers throughout the country, including the *Chicago Tribune*, prompting an outpouring of outrage from both the public and members of Congress. Congressman William Tuck, a Virginia Democrat, entered the column into the *Congressional Record* and called Brennan's decision to hire Tigar "horrible and shocking." Congressman Charles Bennett of Florida wrote Brennan that he was "deeply grieved" when he read Kilpatrick's column, which he said had prompted considerable mail from the public. More attention from other conservative writers followed, with Tigar's associations described in increasingly menacing terms. A guest writer filling in for syndicated columnist Fulton Lewis warned of "a fiery young leftist whose radical activities are chronicled in Congressional files" in a column entitled "Radical Leftist Named Law Clerk for Supreme Court Justice Brennan."

The attention alarmed Brennan enough that he called O'Neil and requested that Tigar come to Washington immediately for their first face-to-face meeting. Tigar boarded a red-eye flight to the capital that very night, feeling understandably worried. He had already boxed up his family's belongings and rented a house in Washington. In an attack of nerves mid-flight, he rushed to the plane's lavatory in a cold sweat and vomited. After shaving and brushing his teeth in the airport bathroom, Tigar headed to the Court. Brennan greeted Tigar with his usual warmth and trademark handshake before ushering his guest into his chambers.

Tigar recalled that Brennan seemed bemused while showing him some of the angry mail he had received about his hiring. Then Brennan turned serious as he talked about the perennial attempts in Congress to strip the Court's jurisdiction. Tigar told Brennan that he would answer any of Brennan's questions in private but would not subject his private views to public scrutiny. Brennan asked him to write out a history of his political activities, including every organization he had ever joined.

Tigar returned to California that night and began typing the letter Brennan requested. "I am ready to enter into the obligation which is that of the clerk," Tigar wrote, "to accord your interests, and those of the Court as seen by you, primary and unswerving loyalty." But Tigar wrote that he had concluded that his resumé of experiences and activities should be for Brennan's eyes only — or those of his fellow justices. While Tigar said he understood if Brennan wanted to share the letter with other members of the Court, "I think it would place me in an untenable position . . . were the details of my political views and associations to become a matter for disclosure to the press or to a coordinate branch of the government." In the event of a congressional investigation, Tigar said he would refuse to answer questions regarding his political views or associations based on First Amendment grounds. The next morning, Tigar called Brennan at home as the justice had requested, and read him the two-page letter in its entirety. Brennan paused before saying, "You're my clerk!" Tigar thanked him and hung up. He wept in relief, convinced the matter was settled. He began packing his Volkswagen bus for a leisurely drive to Washington with his family, planning to stop at public campgrounds along the way.

TIGAR DID NOT know as he drove east that matters were not nearly as settled in Brennan's mind as their telephone call suggested. Brennan not only faced external pressure from members of Congress and the public, but was getting some from inside the Court too. Justice Fortas, his newest colleague, had come to his chambers with an ominous warning: if Brennan did not withdraw the offer to Tigar, members of Congress would launch a major offensive against him. Brennan knew that Fortas's warning probably represented more than idle chatter, given his connections within the Johnson administration. He had no idea at the time just how actively Fortas still advised Johnson, from helping write State of the Union speeches to passing along details of the justices' confidential deliberations. (Fortas even had a private line to the White House on his phone that lit up red when the president called.) But Brennan knew enough to be uneasy. The president had not erased Brennan's sense of Fortas's closeness to Johnson when he leaned over at a White House luncheon and drawled, "How do you like that fine judge I gave you." Brennan replied, "Splendid."

Brennan had good reason to suspect Fortas was acting as a go-between on behalf of Clyde Tolson, a top aide to FBI director J. Edgar Hoover. Brennan later insisted that Fortas was the only justice who approached him about Tigar and that he did not discuss the matter with any other colleague. "I never bothered them, never told them anything about it, handled it all myself," he recalled.

Still, as in the *Ginzburg* case, the question remains whether, despite Brennan's insistence to the contrary, Warren influenced his decision. Warren certainly knew about the controversy. California senator George Murphy had forwarded his letter of concern to Warren too. Warren wrote back that he considered the selection of law clerks "a matter personal to each of the Justices" and had referred his letter to Brennan. No matter how detached Warren tried to appear in that letter, he remained acutely interested in the issue, particularly given the state and the campus it involved. Like Tigar, Warren had attended both college and law school at Berkeley. He first confronted the purported Communist infiltration of Berkeley as governor when there were demands at the height of the Red Scare that all professors sign a loyalty oath. Warren insisted then that all state workers should sign one rather than singling out Berkeley's professors. He maintained his ties to the campus even after moving to Washington. His children studied there. There was a building on campus named in his honor, and he still visited the campus a couple of times each year.

Warren also remained keenly interested in California politics. He kept so close an eye on the state where he had served three terms as governor that one former clerk joked his boss was still running vicariously every four years. While Warren's position as chief justice precluded overt partisanship, he went on a widely publicized hunting trip with Democratic gubernatorial candidate Pat Brown in 1962 that made clear where his preferences lay in the race against Richard Nixon. Warren could barely contain his relief when Brown beat Nixon, which he assumed would end Nixon's political career for good. Warren now watched with alarm four years later as Reagan threatened to unseat Brown. Warren thought Reagan was a "boob," recalled his son, Earl Jr., who worked on the Brown reelection campaign. Warren underestimated Reagan, who later accomplished what he never could: using the governorship of California as a springboard to the White House.

Still, Warren likely realized how Tigar's selection provided Reagan the perfect vehicle to exploit the Communist-infiltration issue in the general election. That May, Reagan complained in a speech in San Francisco that "a small minority of beatniks, radicals and filthy-speech advocates have brought such shame to a great university." As Warren must have feared, the issues inevitably coalesced; the conservative journal *Human Events* ran a June 25 article titled "Brown, Berkeley, Brennan." Noting that Tigar was recommended by Berkeley professors, the article said, "Brown as head of the University of California's Board of Regents was in a key position to have protested the decision of the faculty." *Human Events* noted, "Even at this late date, he has a chance to make his feelings known. But the governor has always preferred to shield the radicals at the university rather than root them out."

What remains unclear is whether Warren shared his concerns with Brennan. Tigar later recalled that Owen Fiss, one of Brennan's two clerks that term, told him that Brennan said the chief justice instructed him to fire Tigar. Fiss said he had no recollection of Brennan ever saying such a thing when asked many years later. Regardless of whether the internal pressure came from Fortas alone or from both Fortas and Warren, Brennan felt deeply torn by the time he traveled to California in late June 1966. He delivered a speech in Los Angeles on "Progress and the Bill of Rights" before heading to the Bay Area. O'Neil recalled meeting with Brennan in a parking lot at Berkeley, where his former boss shared his growing reservations. Either Brennan requested or O'Neil suggested another meeting with Tigar in Washington. Word reached Tigar of this second summons to Brennan's chambers as he stopped to visit friends in Lawrence, Kansas. He immediately sped up his trip to Washington.

BRENNAN'S TONE WAS grave when he sat down with Tigar for a second time on July 11, 1966. The justice had returned from California to find a growing stack of critical letters from members of Congress. According to Tigar, Brennan asked him for permission to distribute his personal political history to anyone the justice chose as a condition of employment. Tigar asked for twenty-four hours to think it over, which Brennan granted.

Tigar and Brennan offered different accounts of what happened the next morning when Brennan called him at his Capitol Hill motel room. Tigar recalled that Brennan informed him of his unilateral decision — that no matter what Tigar had decided, Brennan had made up his mind to withdraw the offer. Brennan, however, recounted it as a joint decision. That same day, Brennan wrote Stanley Weigel, his friend and fellow federal judge in San Francisco, that he and Tigar "had a very long talk and today we decided that he should not come with me." (Brennan might have felt a particular need to explain himself to Weigel, who in 1949 had successfully defended thirty-nine Berkeley professors dismissed for refusing to sign a loyalty pledge — a case many other Bay Area lawyers had shunned.) Brennan altered his version of events slightly when he wrote Weigel a fuller explanation two days later. After giving Tigar a day to think over whether to release his personal history, Brennan wrote, "Overnight I decided that I could not possibly go through with the arrangement. Accordingly, I telephoned him the next day and said I'd relieve him of the necessity for deciding the disclosure question by telling him that I had decided we should not go through with the appointment." According to Brennan, Tigar "said that he himself had about reached the same conclusion." Brennan once again preferred to characterize a wrenching decision as an amicable parting of the ways.

After getting off the telephone with Tigar, Brennan called Attorney General Ramsey Clark and followed up with a letter to Clark and each member of Congress who had contacted him, informing them of his decision. He turned to his friend Skelly Wright for help replacing Tigar. Wright suggested one of his clerks, Abraham Sofaer, as a last-minute substitute. Tigar's name would not be uttered further in Brennan's chambers, except privately among his clerks. They came to believe, as did his secretary, Mary Fowler, that he had followed Warren's wishes in withdrawing the offer. Not that they believed Brennan would ever admit to doing such a thing.

AS WITH *Ginzburg,* Brennan's decision in what he described as "the Tigar matter" seems at odds with his principles. He had spoken out in 1954 against McCarthy for tarring people with guilt by association at a time when such criticism still carried risks. He voted against the government in nearly every subversion case he had heard as a justice. It is hard to disentangle with any certainty his motives regarding Tigar and whether he was acting at Warren's behest or according to what he sensed Warren wanted. It is probably not a coincidence that both times—with *Ginzburg* and with Tigar—he seemed to go against his principles, within months of each other, he did so in ways that comported with Warren's stated or unstated preferences.

But as with *Ginzburg,* Brennan also might have had independent grounds for concluding that he was making the right decision. He carried with him during his entire tenure a deep aversion to doing anything that might hurt the Court as an institution. It was a concern born during the *Jencks* subversion case his first term. That case did not change how he voted in subsequent subversion cases, but left him loath to act in a way that could threaten the Court's independence. "The notion that the Congress would convene an investigation and require us—Mike [Tigar] and me and everybody else—to appear, that was simply something I wouldn't put the Court through," Brennan recalled later.

Brennan remained particularly sensitive about touching on the raw nerve of Communism in America. By 1966, the Red Scare had faded away, but the fear of Communism had taken a new guise as United States involvement in Vietnam intensified. President Johnson had secretly begun the first major escalation of the war the year before by ordering the bombing of North Vietnamese targets and by sending Marines to guard the airfields housing the warplanes. A crowd of 100,000 protestors marched against the war in New York in October 1965. American troop levels in Vietnam would more than double, to 385,000, by the end of 1966. U.S. involvement in Vietnam would not peak for another two years, but 6,000 American servicemen would be killed in action there in 1966 — more than one and a half times as many as died during the first five years of the Iraq war four decades later.

Brennan later recalled opposing American involvement in Vietnam from the start. "I felt we shouldn't be there," he said. Brennan felt sympathetic for those who tried to avoid compulsory military service. "Ever since the Civil War we've had draft resisters and it's always been a difficult question to know whether you could force somebody [to serve]. You can't if they're conscientious objectors. But how do these kids who don't profess to be conscientious objectors really differ from them? It's hard for me to draw the line." While his own sons were too old to be drafted, Brennan unsuccessfully tried to help get his niece's husband transferred from an Army infantry unit slated for service in Vietnam. The young man wound up being wounded on patrol there in late 1968, and sent home to the United States to recuperate from a fractured skull. But when cases involving the war began reaching the Court, Brennan put aside those personal views. Only three months after rescinding Tigar's clerkship, Brennan was faced with the case of three Army soldiers court-martialed at Fort Dix in New Jersey for refusing to serve in Vietnam, a war they viewed as illegal. Brennan, acting alone in his capacity as Third Circuit justice, rejected their request for an emergency order to delay the start of their prison sentences.

The Vietnam War was the subtext of angry letters Brennan received from the public objecting to his hiring of Tigar. To employ a clerk perceived to be a Communist was to leave himself — and his fellow justices — vulnerable to charges of Communist sympathies in future cases. Not that withdrawing the offer put an end to such accusations. A year later, Brennan's opinion striking down a New York law requiring public teachers to sign an affidavit that they were not Communists, again prompted several

letters. Frederick S. Benson, chairman of the New York State Bar Association's Committee on Judicial Administration, wrote to ask him, "How can I
explain to my son fighting Communists in Vietnam the rationale of your
decision which would permit Communists to teach school children?"
Brennan received a far more threatening letter from another parent with a
son serving in Vietnam. "Of all the human scum balls you top the list of
their breed. To help give the deciding support to Communists gives me the
right to put a bullet through your skull. (Why?) Because my son is in the
front lines, fighting for bastards like you in Vietnam. I will take the opportunity to dispose of you when in Washington where I will be for a long
time. Farewell to a human rat." The letter alarmed Brennan enough that he
forwarded it directly to FBI director J. Edgar Hoover.

WORD OF BRENNAN'S decision about Tigar quickly reached reporters.
Both the *Washington Post* and *New York Times* published articles about it
on July 17, 1966. The stories generated angry and disappointed letters from
liberals. One of Tigar's fellow Berkeley law students lamented, "His appointment meant a lot to those of us who saw in it a reaffirmation of certain important and traditional features in the law and in our Republic for
which the Supreme Court has, under Warren, come to be identified." He
concluded, "PLEASE, RECONSIDER." The counsel for the ACLU's northern California chapter scolded Brennan: "The pressures you bowed to (in
violation of your own concept of freedom as expressed in your opinions
for the Court) were created by fear and could have been neutralized by
reason." Brennan found himself second-guessed inside the Court too.
Douglas, the justice famous for putting his own needs above all else, and
who later became a target of congressional investigations himself, could
not understand why Brennan would back down. "Go tell them, 'go fuck
themselves,'" Brennan recalled Douglas telling him.

Tigar, too, was angry. The father of two young children had just lost his
job, been tarred publicly as a radical, and then hung out to dry by Brennan.
But he kept those feelings largely to himself when he wrote an open letter
to friends, which he forwarded to Brennan later in July along with a short
cover letter. In the letter, Tigar wrote that he believed Brennan was "egregiously mistaken" about "what was required to save the Court." But Tigar
emphasized that "Justice Brennan is not a man without courage" as he recounted how he had stood up to McCarthy a decade earlier. He concluded,

"I feel a sense of obligation to the Justice at this point which is rather hard to define" and said he had no interest in speaking out against him publicly. He wrote Brennan, "Though both of us have been put to great and difficult choices, please accept my assurance that I walk away from this situation without bitterness or rancor." He also told Brennan that he had accepted a position in Edward Bennett Williams's law firm.

Brennan just wanted to put the whole incident behind him. He offered no apology or further explanation in his reply to Tigar. "I see nothing in the enclosure requiring comment," he wrote, adding, "I am delighted to know you have joined my good friend Edward Bennett Williams." Brennan told Weigel only two days after rescinding the clerkship that "I think probably [he] will wind up" at Williams's firm. One biographer of Williams suggested it was Brennan who first called Williams and "strongly recommended" Tigar; Brennan credited Douglas with convincing Williams to extend the job offer. (Tigar later recalled he first contacted Williams long before ever losing the clerkship.) Douglas later offered a clerkship in his chambers to Tigar, who declined. He, too, wanted to put the whole incident behind him.

Tigar went on to a distinguished career as a litigator and law professor, defending figures far more controversial than he himself had ever been. His clients would include 1960s radicals such as Angela Davis and the Chicago Seven as well as alleged Nazi war criminal John Demjanjuk and Terry Nichols, one of two men convicted for the 1995 bombing of the Oklahoma City federal building that killed 168 people. In June 1977, long after he had already argued three cases before the Supreme Court, Tigar decided to write Brennan after reading one of his dissents in a First Amendment case. He was surprised to receive a two-page handwritten reply from the justice two weeks later. "I'm deeply touched that you wrote me — far more than I can say," wrote Brennan, who noted he had followed Tigar's career with "keen interest" and invited him to come to the Court for lunch. Tigar accepted, and they dined together in Brennan's chambers in early 1978. The closest they came to discussing the clerkship was when Brennan rattled off a list of his former clerks who had gone on to work at Williams's firm and added, "There's you, you're my clerk."

They saw each other again several more times in the years to come. When Brennan prepared a speech for the dedication of Georgetown University Law Center's library, named in Edward Bennett Williams's honor, he called Tigar in for advice. Tigar later asked Brennan for an autographed picture, which he provided in February 1989 with an inscription, "To Mike Tigar whose tireless striving for justice stretches his arms towards perfection." By that time, Brennan had confided, "I wish to hell maybe that I'd had guts enough to tell them all to go to hell and then taken them on. It'd all have blown over, of course, if I had." He made a similar admission to Nat Hentoff for a profile in the *New Yorker* published in 1990. By that time, the Berlin Wall had fallen and the fear of Communism that was so pervasive in 1966 had become passé.

Tigar carried his own regrets. After Brennan retired, Tigar wrote him to say, "I behaved arrogantly and self-centeredly" when they'd met in 1966. "I carried my anger and arrogance around all these years, when I should simply have looked you in the eyes and apologized for that." Only in hindsight, Tigar said, did he realize, "You are, as you tried to remind me that morning, a Supreme Court Justice with significant institutional responsibilities. I apologize now." Brennan replied a few days later. "That morning in June 1966 is a date I shall never forget. I've often wondered whether I overreacted. I must say in all candor that, given the circumstances, I probably did." He concluded, "I hope we shall always remain the friends we have become."

GINZBURG, FOR HIS PART, remained forever as unforgiving about his conviction as on the day Brennan upheld it. Time would prove that Ginzburg's case was the high-water mark against obscenity on the Court. Within a year, the Court's interest in trying to define obscenity had begun to wane. The justices, or at least their clerks, continued to go to room 22-B in the Court's basement to watch many of the movies deemed obscene that came before them. But in future decisions they largely limited themselves to keeping such materials away from children and nonconsenting adults. Brennan eventually gave up on trying to define obscenity altogether, and voted to vacate every criminal-obscenity conviction that came before the Court.

None of that helped Ginzburg, who finally went to prison in 1972 after years of drawn-out litigation over his sentence. He served eight months at the Allenwood minimum-security prison in Pennsylvania and wrote about the experience in a tiny thirty-five-page book titled *Castrated: My Eight Months in Prison*. Except for the title, it makes for bland reading. For once,

Ginzburg avoided controversy during his time in jail, resolving to become a model prisoner in order to get out as quickly as possible. That rare self-restraint ceased as soon as Ginzburg left prison. He held a press conference outside its gates, where he read a statement titled "In Contempt of the Supreme Court." He accused the justices of "high crimes and treason, namely, of mocking the Constitution, trammeling Freedom of the Press, and playing fast and loose with one man's liberty — mine."

Ginzburg resumed his publishing career, this time sticking to safer territory by starting a cheeky consumer newsletter called *Moneysworth*. He went on to a successful second career as a photographer, selling his pictures to New York newspapers and magazines. Ginzburg never gave up his flair for the dramatic, donning disguises, including the garb of a clergyman, to enter events where he lacked proper credentials. Nor did he ever forgive Brennan for a decision that he believed thwarted his potential for an even greater publishing career. Ginzburg wrote a 1988 *New York Times* op-ed piece in which he noted a recent book that suggested Brennan subsequently regretted the decision. "My regret, of course, is that you did not see it sooner," Ginzburg wrote. "That could have spared me eight months in Federal prison, four years and four months of probation, Draconian fines, a half million dollars in legal costs, emotional torment for my family, disgrace before my professional colleagues and the public and the near ruination of my career." Ginzburg made sure to mail a copy of his column to Brennan's biographer with a note saying, "I thought you might like to know about this."

Even after Ginzburg published his open letter in the pages of the *New York Times,* Brennan never felt compelled to apologize, although he remained touchy about the matter. Journalist Nat Hentoff later asked Brennan whether he felt any regrets about the case during an interview toward the end of his tenure on the Court. Hentoff recalled that Brennan "was uncomfortable at the question and snapped, 'You haven't seen the decision quoted by any other judge, have you?' Ginzburg died in 2006 at the age of seventy-six, leaving Shoshana, his wife of forty-nine years, the repository of his grievances against Brennan. "Had he made the decision you would have expected from the justice, the whole case would have gone the other way," she said in 2007. "He may have been a First Amendment champion in his other decisions but in this case he dropped the ball."

PASSAGES

JOINING THE COURT at the age of fifty meant that each time Brennan completed a decade of service as a justice, he also marked a new decade in his life. In 1966 Brennan celebrated both his first decade on the Court and his sixtieth birthday. He remained in good health ten years after his doctor had expressed concern about his heart, thanks to his morning walks and the care Marjorie took in watching his diet. Having a daughter still in high school might have made him feel younger than other men his age. Nancy was finishing her junior year at boarding school that spring.

But Brennan could not escape the recent reminders that time was passing. At sixty, he was now three years older than the age at which his father had died. His mother had passed away in October 1964 at the age of eighty-six, having spent the last five months of her life in a Montclair, New Jersey, nursing home. As her mind failed her, Agnes had begun speaking in Gaelic, the language she had been ashamed to speak as a young immigrant. Brennan's professor and former colleague, Felix Frankfurter, had died four months later, in February 1965, at the age of eighty-two, after suffering a final stroke.

It was right around the time Brennan turned sixty in April 1966 that he began to reconcile with Harvard Law School. His alma mater provided an unexpected and unintentional sixtieth birthday present by finally inviting him to serve on the school's Visiting Committee. "Your counsel and assistance would prove most valuable," wrote Paul Reardon, an associate justice on the Massachusetts Supreme Judicial Court who was then chairing the committee. Reardon added a handwritten postscript at the bottom that Dean Griswold "would be delighted by your acceptance." Word of Brennan's disaffection with the school had reached the sixty-two-year-old dean, who knew the law school as well as anyone. Griswold graduated from Harvard Law three years before Brennan, started as a professor there in 1934, and had been dean since 1946. A lifelong Republican, Griswold was uneasy about the Warren Court's activism, but did not want one of the school's most prominent alumni feeling alienated. Griswold decided to take what he described as "cautious but not too obvious" steps to make Brennan feel more appreciated. Soon after Reardon's invitation, Griswold wrote Brennan directly to ask him to speak at the school's 150th anniversary celebration scheduled for the following year. "It is the best, albeit inadequate, way we have of recognizing the honor you have brought to the Law School, and you have much to contribute to the occasion," read Griswold's invitation, which was hand-delivered by Archibald Cox, the former solicitor general who had rejoined the Harvard Law faculty. "I am greatly honored by the invitation and am most happy to accept it," Brennan responded.

Griswold also joined in the tributes offered Brennan on the occasion of his tenth anniversary on the Court in October 1966. Griswold, who even in his private letters to Brennan usually mixed criticism with praise, offered only kind words for the justice he characterized as the Court's pragmatist. Griswold wrote in the *Harvard Law Review*, "Brennan has more often functioned as the balance wheel, standing in the center and working out the uneasy compromises and accommodations necessary for the Court to get on with its work." He noted, "It cannot be an easy task, and at times the resulting opinions have earned academic criticism for lack of logical purity or the absence of consistent policy. It is the role of the critics to help the law work itself pure, but the first necessity of the Court's work is that it must function if it is to be a court at all."

Warren wrote his own *Harvard Law Review* tribute. He drafted it himself in longhand on ten sheets of paper. "In the entire history of the Court, it would be difficult to name another Justice who wrote more important opinions in his first ten years than has he," wrote Warren, the man responsible for most of those assignments. "As a colleague, he leaves nothing to be desired. Friendly and buoyant in spirit, a prodigious worker and a master craftsman, he is a unifying influence on the bench and in the conference room." There were other tributes as well that fall. One of Brennan's former clerks, Stephen Friedman, put together a compilation of some of Brennan's most important opinions that was published as a book, *An Affair with Freedom.*

Brennan's life at the Court had settled into a comfortable rhythm that would remain largely fixed for the remainder of his tenure. He still welcomed each new pair of clerks every summer by raising five fingers to stress the importance on the Court of five votes. Convinced he was the better equipped to identify promising cases, he read all cert. petitions himself, but assigned his clerks more of the first drafts of opinions. Starting in the early 1960s, he directed his clerks at the end of their year in his chambers to prepare a history detailing cases he had had a major role in during their term. Brennan came up with the idea of maintaining term histories after asking his former colleague, Stanley Reed, about a case. Brennan watched as Reed riffled through a file cabinet and pulled out a card containing a short history of the case. Brennan saw the merits of having such a reference tool, and set about creating his own.

Brennan arrived at the Court early each morning before sitting down for coffee with his clerks at eight or nine o'clock. Brennan's secretary, Mary Fowler, almost always sat in during the morning coffee. After a decade in Brennan's chambers, Fowler had become a fixture there, far more so than the clerks who came and went each year. Fowler and Brennan had developed a genuine rapport, despite their vastly different politics. She still enjoyed teasing Brennan and his clerks about their liberal views, and was not shy about making sure everyone knew when she disagreed with a decision. But Fowler had grown fiercely loyal to her boss. She knew that Brennan was skittish about confrontation, so she was the one to pass along the word when a clerk did not measure up to expectations. Fowler did not have children and had never remarried after a 1948 divorce, so her boss — and the Court where she had now worked for a quarter century — were the center of her life. Like a proud parent, she cut out and pasted into a scrapbook every newspaper or magazine article about Brennan, including those in foreign languages when he traveled abroad.

By the time he celebrated his tenth anniversary as a justice in October 1966, Fowler's scrapbooks were starting to include the first smattering of stories noting Brennan's central role on the Court. Sidney Zion, then a reporter for the *New York Post,* devoted an entire article in his five-part series on the Supreme Court in 1965 to Brennan, whom he described as "the most important man in the majority bloc." "Hugo Black may be the spiritual leader, Douglas the most brilliant, Goldberg the most promising, Warren the face of the Court given to the world, but time and time again decisions get written the way Brennan wants them written." Zion credited Brennan's influence to his philosophy, "which, except in criminal cases, is the most moderate within the majority." The same themes were echoed in a story in the *New York World Telegram* that ran a few days later under the headline "Brennan: Core of Liberals." A friend back in New Jersey, William H. Borden, mailed Zion's article to Brennan, who had not seen it yet himself. Brennan objected to Zion's conclusions. "Mr. Zion is very flattering but I am appalled at the idea that the Chief Justice and Justices Black, Douglas and Goldberg goose step to my tune," Brennan wrote back. "Believe me, Bill, it just ain't so."

NO MATTER HOW much Brennan tried to downplay it, he had in fact become what one academic observer would later call "the center of gravity" on the Supreme Court by his tenth anniversary in the job. In the previous four terms since Goldberg provided a reliable fifth vote, Brennan had dissented only fifteen times and voted with the majority an astounding 97 percent of the time. Those statistics tell only part of the story, because Brennan exerted much of his influence beyond public view. There were the preconference meetings he had with Warren. And there were also the opinions that he helped craft even when his name did not appear on them as author. There was no better example of the silent hand of Brennan shaping an opinion during this period than the case of *Griswold v. Connecticut,* a 1965 decision on contraception that laid the foundation for a constitutional right to privacy.

Connecticut legislators, swept up in the fervor of Anthony Comstock's anti-obscenity crusade, had passed a statute outlawing contraceptives in 1879, and it still stood as an anachronistic relic in the 1960s. Other states might still have banned the advertisement or manufacture of birth control, or the sale of same, as in the case of the next-strictest state, neighboring Massachusetts. But none besides Connecticut barred the use of contraceptives — as well as banning doctors from counseling patients about their use. The law had rarely, if ever, been enforced. Connecticut pharmacists sold contraception openly, although under the guise of preventing disease rather than avoiding pregnancy. Nonetheless, the law stood; and it had proved impervious to at least two-dozen challenges in both Connecticut's legislature and courts since 1917.

The Catholic Church's support for the law did much to ensure its longevity. While most religious denominations softened their stance against contraception starting in the 1930s, the Church had become more vocal in its opposition. Pope Pius XI came out forcefully against birth control in a 1930 encyclical that called all forms of artificial contraception "intrinsically against nature." Catholic clergy and lawmakers in both Connecticut and Massachusetts took the lead against repealing the anticontraception laws. William Kenealy, the dean of the Jesuit-run Boston College's law school, testified at a 1948 legislative hearing in Connecticut that birth control was no better than "mutual masturbation" and constituted "pleasure by means of an unnatural act."

Opponents of the contraception law set their sights once again on the courts in the mid-1950s. Their goal: to get a state judge to declare that the law harmed women who faced medical risks due to their pregnancies. The new assault was led by Estelle Griswold, the executive director of Planned Parenthood of Connecticut, and C. Lee Buxton, a physician who headed Yale's infertility clinic. Their legal strategist was Yale Law professor Fowler Harper. The son of an Ohio minister, Harper had become a respected legal scholar as well as an unrepentant leftist and defender of controversial causes. Among the plaintiffs recruited for the birth control lawsuits were Elizabeth and David O., known in their case, *Poe v. Ullman*, by the pseudonyms Pauline and Paul Poe, whose three severely abnormal children all died within days or weeks of their births. (Abraham Ullman was the state prosecutor in New Haven.) A Connecticut judge rejected their suit in 1958, a decision affirmed by the state's Supreme Court in 1959.

When Harper appealed the case to the United States Supreme Court in 1959, he included a novel argument in his jurisdictional statement laying out his reasons for why the Court should hear it: "When the long arm of the law reaches into the bedroom and regulates the most sacred relations between a man and his wife, it is going too far." Harper asserted his clients' marital privacy was "mercilessly invaded by these laws" and that "the normal and voluntary relations of spouses in the privacy of their homes is regarded as beyond the prying eyes of peeping Toms, be they police officers or legislators." Harper certainly could not point to any explicit language in the text of the Constitution to support his argument. At best, an interest in protecting privacy could be inferred to underlie provisions that prohibited the quartering of soldiers in private homes in the Third Amendment or unreasonable searches and seizures in the Fourth Amendment.

The notion of privacy accepted by American courts in the country's first decades did not extend beyond a right to enjoy one's property without unwanted intrusions. But technological advances in the late nineteenth century such as telegraphs, telephones — and, particularly, photography — presented challenges to the traditional conception of privacy defined in terms of physical space. In 1888 Thomas M. Cooley coined the term, the "right to be let alone." Two years later, a writer in *Scribner's Magazine* invoked a "right to privacy" against salacious newspaper articles. Future Supreme Court justice Louis Brandeis and a fellow Boston lawyer, Samuel Warren, did much to advance a notion of a right to privacy in an 1890 article in the *Harvard Law Review.* Brandeis invoked a right to privacy thirty-eight years later as a Supreme Court justice, when he dissented from a Court decision upholding the conviction of a bootlegger whose smuggling operation was wiretapped without a warrant. Brandeis asserted, "The makers of our Constitution . . . conferred as against the government, the right to be let alone."

In his *Poe v. Ullman* appeal, Harper invoked Brandeis when he wrote that his clients "want to be left alone in the bedroom." Fowler returned to the same argument in his brief after the Court agreed to hear the case. The privacy argument took up just a page deep inside Harper's sixty-two-page brief but was at the very core of the amicus brief submitted by the ACLU and its local Connecticut affiliate.

Those arguments did not sway a majority of the justices, who voted to dismiss the case in March 1961. The opinion, written by Justice Frankfurter, held that there was no actual case or controversy, since the law had rarely, if ever, been enforced. Dissenting was Douglas, who wrote in June of that year, "This is an invasion of the privacy that is implicit in a free society." Justice Harlan offered a far lengthier dissent in which he, too, invoked privacy. "I believe that a statute making it a criminal offense for married couples to use contraceptives is an intolerable and unjustifiable invasion of privacy in the conduct of the most intimate concerns of an individual's personal life."

Brennan initially appeared willing to join Douglas's opinion invoking a right to privacy. But he changed his mind, paradoxically at Douglas's urging. Without Brennan's vote, Frankfurter might have trouble keeping a majority. That would likely delay the end of the term — and Douglas preferred to get out of town rather than pick up an extra vote for his opinion. "Stick to Felix so we can get this case decided and get out of here," Douglas told him. Brennan followed Douglas's advice, writing a concurring opinion that seemed almost to invite another legal challenge to the Connecticut law. "The true controversy in this case is over the opening of birth control clinics on a large scale; it is that which the State has prevented in the past, not the use of contraceptives by isolated and individual married couples," Brennan wrote. "It will be time enough to decide the constitutional questions urged upon us when, if ever, that real controversy flairs up again."

Brennan raised the case when he spoke to a group of British barristers shortly after the 1960–61 term ended. "We must indeed find difficulty in imagining a more indefensible invasion of privacy than an invasion of the marriage chamber by government," he said. But, Brennan explained, the Court had not addressed the constitutional issue, "since apparently the plaintiffs were not truly caught in an inescapable dilemma and actually were seeking invalidation of the Connecticut statute in the interest of the opening of birth control clinics." Privately, Brennan made clear to his clerks that he would vote to overturn the Connecticut statute should the Court ever reach the merits.

Only days after the Court announced its decision, the Planned Parenthood League of Connecticut publicized plans to open a birth control clinic for married couples in New Haven. Executive Director Estelle Griswold invited reporters to a November 2, 1961, press conference where she announced that the first ten consultations had occurred the night before at the new clinic at 79 Trumbull Street in New Haven. As intended, police detectives soon arrived. Griswold and Lee Buxton, the medical director of the clinic, were subsequently convicted of violating the Connecticut statute and fined $100 each. Harper invoked both Douglas's and Harlan's dissents in the earlier case as evidence of judicial recognition of a "right to be let alone" and a constitutional protection of a right to privacy, but the Connecticut Supreme Court nonetheless rejected his appeal in the spring of 1964. Harper renewed the privacy argument once again in his appeal seeking U.S. Supreme Court review in September 1964, as would Thomas Emerson, the Yale Law professor who replaced him when Harper entered a New Haven hospital with terminal cancer that December, six days before the Court agreed to take up the law once again in the case of *Griswold v. Connecticut.* Connecticut's law seemed all the more archaic by the time it reached the Supreme Court. Four years had passed since the Food and Drug Administration first approved the sale of birth control pills. More than 2 million American women were taking oral contraceptives by the end of 1963.

Warren expressed reservations about using privacy as the basis for overturning the law when the justices met in conference to discuss the case on April 2, 1965. Brennan, by contrast, argued for reversing the convictions because the statute infringed on the "realm of privacy." The votes were there for finally overturning the Connecticut law although the justices had not agreed on the basis for doing so. Warren assigned the case to Douglas, who had already argued for rejecting the statute in *Poe.* Douglas dashed off his first draft by hand on a yellow legal pad within ten days. Rather than invoking a right to privacy as he had in his *Poe* dissent, Douglas relied almost entirely on a right of association. While Douglas noted that "marriage does not fit precisely any of the categories of First Amendment rights," he argued, "it is a form of association vital in the life of a man and or woman as any other, and perhaps more so." Douglas circulated the five-and-a-third-page draft opinion to Brennan on April 23.

Brennan and his clerk, S. Paul Posner, were not impressed by what they read. Brennan never doubted Douglas's brilliance, but thought little of his colleague's work ethic. Douglas did not hide the fact that he had never entirely given up on his dream of being president. He had come tantalizingly close to being named Franklin Roosevelt's running mate in 1944. Had he been chosen, rather than Harry Truman, he might have become president upon Roosevelt's death the following year. Truman twice offered Douglas the job of interior secretary and tried to convince him to be his running mate in 1948, although Douglas declined because he wanted the presidential nomination himself. "He didn't really care about the job," Brennan recalled later. "He was slipshod in what he did."

The same day Douglas's draft arrived, Posner drafted a long letter for Brennan suggesting substantial revisions. Brennan sent along Posner's memo nearly verbatim, making only minor changes in pencil to soften up the tone. Brennan wanted it to sound more like a suggestion than a critique. "While I agree with a great deal of it," Brennan gently wrote to his prickly colleague, "I should like to suggest a substantial change in emphasis for your consideration." He noted, "I hesitate to bring the husband-wife relationship within the right to association we have constructed in the First Amendment context." Brennan suggested that "any language to the effect that the family unit is a sacred unit, that is unreachable by the State . . . may come back to haunt us . . ." He warned that such an expansive definition of advocacy could wind up protecting any advocacy group calling itself an association. "It seems to me," Brennan continued, "that we are really interested in the privacy of married couples quite apart from any interest in advocacy."

Brennan suggested using association as an analogy. He noted that the Court had invoked the First Amendment to protect association even though it was "not literally within its terminology of speech and assembly, because the interest protected is so closely related." He indicated that the same could be done for other protections afforded by the Bill of Rights. "Where fundamental rights are concerned, the Bill of Rights guarantees are but expressions or examples of those rights, and do not preclude application or extensions of those rights to other situations unanticipated by the Framers." Using that logic, and applying the same argument invoked by the lawyers for Planned Parenthood in their filings with the Court, Brennan concluded that the Connecticut statute would "run afoul of a right to privacy" created out of the Fourth Amendment and self-incrimination clause of the Fifth Amendment together with the Third. "Taken together, those amendments indicate a fundamental concern with the sanctity of the home and the right of the individual to be let alone."

Douglas quickly recast his opinion and had it back to Brennan within two days after receiving his colleague's input. He largely adopted Brennan's approach, employing a right to association as an analogy, one illuminating how a right to privacy extends beyond the rights actually laid out in the Bill of Rights. Douglas did recast the idea in his own words, writing that "other specific guarantees in the Bill of Rights also have a penumbra, reflecting emanations from those guarantees that help give them life and substance." This time, Douglas's draft was well received in Brennan's chambers. "This is a signal victory," Posner wrote Brennan that same day. But Douglas's talk of penumbras and emanations evoked a mixture of laughter and scorn in other chambers. Critics of the *Griswold* decision cited that single sentence as embodying all that was wrong with the Warren Court's willingness to invent new rights as they went along.

In his dissent, Black rejected any rights not specifically delineated in the text of the Constitution. He dismissed the notion that "many good and able men have eloquently spoken and written, sometimes in rhapsodical strains, about the duty of this Court to keep the Constitution in tune with the times." Goldberg, too, was somewhat uneasy with Douglas's approach, and, spurred on by Warren, he filed a concurrence written by his clerk, Stephen Breyer, who would become a Supreme Court justice in 1994. Brennan also joined Goldberg's concurrence, obscuring all the more his role in helping shape Douglas's majority opinion.

In hindsight, Brennan would perhaps claim more credit than he deserved at the time for the final shape of the opinion, when he suggested he gave Douglas the idea of relying on a privacy argument. In fact, what Brennan had done was redirect Douglas back toward an idea Douglas had already embraced. Still, there is no denying that Brennan played a substantial role in shaping one of the most significant opinions issued during his tenure.

Brennan did not create the notion of finding a right to privacy implicit in provisions of the Bill of Rights. The intellectual parentage belongs, perhaps, to Douglas for his dissenting opinion in *Poe v. Ullman*, or perhaps to the briefs filed in *Poe* by Harper and others. But the always-pragmatic Brennan perceived that expanding the legal concept of freedom of association to include marital association might undermine the strength of that constitutional right. He understood as well that the idea of association would not provide the strongest foundation for a right to personal privacy. With this ability to see the bigger picture, he successfully shifted the focus of the Court's reasoning by persuading Douglas to take a different approach.

It was not any fear of a backlash from within his Church that led to Brennan's staying behind the scenes in *Griswold*. Unlike in the school-prayer cases a few years earlier, he did not have to worry about getting excoriated by the Church hierarchy if he voted in favor of contraception. The

Court's consideration of the case coincided with what appeared to be a broad rethinking about contraception at every level of the Catholic Church. Laity and theologians openly questioned the Church's opposition, on television and in the pages of the nation's newspapers. There was enough dissent on the issue that not all priests felt they could tell parishioners they faced in confessional that the ban on contraception was a Church teaching beyond doubt. Pope John XXIII had quietly convened a papal commission to review the Church's traditional teachings about contraception in 1963, and expectations that change was in the offing were widespread among American Catholics when word of the commission was made public in 1964. The nation's foremost Catholic theologian, John Courtney Murray, wrote a famous 1965 memo on contraception to Boston's Cardinal Cushing in which he argued against Church opposition to the Massachusetts contraception law. The liberal Catholic magazine *Commonweal* praised the *Griswold* decision as "long overdue" although legally "muddy."

Brennan's quiet maneuvers behind the scenes in cases such as *Griswold* were typical, and explain why even the closest Court watchers could still overlook or underestimate his central role. Yale Law professor Fred Rodell, for example, wrote a cover story for the *New York Times Magazine* in March 1966 on "The Warren Court" that makes no reference to Brennan at all. Not much had changed since Brennan attended a Pennsylvania Bar Association meeting in Pittsburgh in 1960 where he was completely overshadowed by the nation's most famous fictional lawyer, Raymond Burr, who played Perry Mason on television. Burr "was never free of a mosquito-like cloud of autograph seekers," the *Pittsburgh Post-Gazette* noted then, while "Mr. Justice Brennan came unheralded. He left unfollowed." Apparently, Brennan harbored no hard feelings. Burr appeared in Court one day when Marjorie sat in the audience. Brennan passed her a note from the bench that read, "Honey — sitting behind you and Ethel [Harlan] is Perry Mason in the flesh." And when Burr — now the admirer — wrote him in 1966 asking for an autograph, Brennan happily obliged.

Only rarely — and reluctantly — did Brennan accept special treatment. After he got caught speeding on his way to New Jersey, a police officer directed him and a group of other offenders to the local courthouse for processing. The local magistrate, casually clad in short sleeves, instantly recognized Brennan. After disappearing into another room where he changed into a jacket and tie, the magistrate insisted that Brennan quietly exit out the back door. Brennan at first refused but eventually did so at the magistrate's insistence. Marjorie enjoyed teasing him about the incident. "Equal justice under the law, ha!" she joked.

Although never quite as humble as he liked to portray himself, Brennan was not someone who needed public recognition for his contributions at the Court, and actually enjoyed his low profile. He took a certain puckish delight in strolling the sidewalks around the Court and innocently asking tourists what they thought went on inside its walls. He could laugh it off when a student heading home for Thanksgiving dropped a bag at his feet in the line for tickets at Union Station and asked Brennan, "Hey buddy, would you hold my place in line?" His low profile would cost him what modest success and supplemental income he enjoyed as a campus speaker during the 1960s. When Brennan wrote his agent, Harry Walker, in 1968 about why his speaking engagements seemed to have dried up, one of Walker's subordinates wrote back to explain that students wanted a more flamboyant personality than Brennan's.

WARREN HAD COME to rely on Brennan even more as the 1960s progressed, particularly as Hugo Black's tack to the right cost the Court's liberal bloc its fifth secure vote. His shift to a more conservative voting pattern had been evident since the sit-in cases in the early 1960s. Black, who turned eighty-one in February 1967, seemed increasingly out of step with his onetime allies. He believed the civil rights movement had won what it needed when the Court had knocked down the barrier of segregation. Similarly, he grew uneasy about just how assertively the Court was expanding the rights of criminal defendants. While he would continue to support civil liberties claims that arose in traditional contexts in areas such as the First Amendment or subversion, he increasingly broke with the bloc when it came to the actions of civil rights demonstrators or the extent of criminal defendants' protections.

Black might also have suffered from a bit of a bruised ego. He may well have resented that Warren got all the credit for the triumph of many principles such as incorporation of the Bill of Rights that he had fought to adopt for decades. Brennan told Black's biographer that Warren was aware of Black's hurt feelings. "[Warren] didn't talk about it being called the 'Warren Court' . . . [he] thought the naming of the Court after the Chief was inappropriate." Black did not hide his disdain for the Court's newest member, Abe Fortas. Black thought both Brennan and Fortas went too far in some of their decisions, and he may have also resented Brennan for supplanting him as the liberal bloc's key player. Being at odds at the Court, though, did not ruin their friendship. Black still could praise Brennan's work, as he had done in the sit-in and New York Times v. Sullivan libel cases, even when he did not agree with the outcome. When Justice Black celebrated his tenth wedding anniversary with his second wife in September 1967, Brennan offered the first toast, which Elizabeth Black called "dear and sincere." But as Black moved away from the bloc, he grew closer to Harlan. Their clerks remembered the sight of Black, shrunken with age, and Harlan, nearly blind, walking together to conference.

Black's drift toward the right became acutely obvious during the 1966–67 term, particularly when it came to criminal-procedure cases. Black cast the deciding vote in all six cases decided against criminal defendants that term by a 5–4 margin. In each of those cases, Black abandoned Brennan, Warren, Douglas, and Fortas to provide the fifth vote to Harlan, Stewart, Clark, and White. That is not to say that Black completely deserted the liberal bloc in criminal law or that the Court suddenly swung to the side of law enforcement. The justices ruled in favor of criminal defendants in twenty-four cases that term, compared to fifteen cases against them. But Black was the crucial vote in close cases decided by a 5–4 margin, voting against defendants five times and in their favor twice. Black's change in direction during that term attracted reporters' attention. The New York Times' Fred Graham noted what he called Black's "defection" from the liberal bloc in an article reviewing the term in July 1967. He attributed the Court's "newly cautious stance" to Black. The nation as a whole seemed to be moving to the right along with Black. Democrats suffered significant losses at every level in November 1966. Ronald Reagan, who won in California by almost one million votes, was one of eight new Republican governors. Republicans also picked up forty-seven House seats and three seats in the Senate.

Black's change of heart led to new friction among old allies. When Douglas objected to Black's plan to hand down an opinion in a case until he had a chance to dissent, Black testily complained to the conference about the delay. Brennan noted Black's change in direction with concern. When Black affirmed a conviction of civil rights demonstrators, Brennan wrote Douglas that the decision could have a "'chilling effect' on legitimate protests" on public property.

Brennan shared his concerns with Warren and Douglas about how Black had changed — and even aired them publicly. "Hugo of today is not Hugo of five years ago," Brennan told a reporter in 1968. Brennan found himself dissenting more than any time since Frankfurter had retired in 1962. Faced with a faltering majority, Warren turned to Brennan, assigning him eleven decisions decided by a 5–4 margin during the 1966–67 term. One of those decisions, in the Keyishian v. Board of Regents subversion case, prompted the threatening message that Brennan forwarded to FBI director J. Edgar Hoover.

But without Black, Brennan could not prevail in every close case. He wound up venting his frustration in a dissent in one of those defeats, Walker v. Birmingham. The case arose from a 1963 protest in Birmingham led by Martin Luther King Jr. A city ordinance prohibited street parades or protests without a permit, but King and the other protest leaders went forward with the demonstration after the city rejected their permit application. Birmingham officials then obtained an injunction in state court, and King and other leaders were jailed for criminal contempt. A state court rejected their claim that the permit ordinance and injunction violated the protestors' First Amendment rights. At a March 24, 1967, conference, there was a 5–4 majority to affirm the conviction, with Black abandoning the liberal bloc. That outcome greatly concerned Warren, Brennan, and Douglas, each of whom wrote his own dissent. Of the three, Brennan wrote the sharpest, most uncharacteristic dissent. It was particularly unique for the degree to which it directly suggested that the majority was swayed by outside political considerations. "I expect that this decision reflects only sensitivity to today's transitory shift in political and social attitudes towards the civil rights movement," Brennan wrote.

After Brennan had warned in the fall of 1964 that urban disorder would test the national commitment to civil rights, violent riots had spread through the North in subsequent summers. The riots in the Watts section of Los Angeles, televised live in 1965, would sear the phrase "Burn, baby, burn" into the national psyche. No section of the country escaped the violence, and each summer's riots seemed worse than the last. Riots broke out in 1966 in Dayton, Des Moines, and Omaha. Martin Luther King Jr., too, had turned his attention northward in 1966 to Chicago. The protests King led against Chicago's residential segregation and slum conditions sparked violent resistance as hateful as in the South. Calls for "Black Power" by younger African American militants eclipsed King's pleas for nonviolence. Efforts to address northern school desegregation — including proposals to bus students between black and white schools — further inflamed white anger. The riots, the new militancy, and the war in Vietnam all divided the civil rights movement, its strength and the sympathy it had generated among northern whites ebbing together.

Brennan addressed such concerns directly in his draft dissent in *Walker v. Birmingham*. He noted that this case arose from events "before 'Black Power' and 'Long Hot Summer' became part of the jargon of the civil rights movement." That language was too much for Warren, who told Brennan he would not join his dissent if those references to current events remained. Brennan tempered his language enough so that Warren felt comfortable signing his dissent, but it still attracted much press attention when the decision was announced on June 12, 1967. "We cannot permit fears of 'riots' and 'civil disobedience' generated by slogans like 'Black Power' to divert our attention from what is here at stake," Brennan lamented in the final paragraph of his dissent. Exactly one month later, on July 12, that summer's riot season began in Brennan's hometown of Newark.

Newark had become a twenty-three-square-mile microcosm for all the troubles afflicting urban America: shuttered factories and staggering tax rates, a shrinking white population and sprawling slums where most of the city's blacks lived amid poverty and disease. Incompetence and corruption permeated the city government and police force that Brennan's father had once led. By 1967, Newark had the highest percentage of substandard housing and the highest infant mortality rate in the country. So it is not surprising that an incident of alleged police brutality would spark five days of rioting inside the city's black ghetto. Rioting and looting caused $10 million in damage. Twenty-six people died, most killed in a fusillade of indiscriminate shooting by National Guardsmen and state police. The riots did not reach Brennan's old neighborhood of Vailsburg, one of Newark's last white enclaves, still home mostly to municipal employees. Vailsburg was saved by an unnatural barrier — the Garden State Parkway — which separated it from the rest of Newark. But the riots only accelerated the process of white flight. In the days that followed, only real estate agents fielding calls from panicked white residents looking to flee Newark did better business than the gun shop in a neighboring town where frightened citizens sought protection against future violence.

BRENNAN TOOK A short break from a term characterized by the struggle to preserve narrow majorities in order to attend his annual clerk reunion in April 1967. The tradition had begun seven years earlier when his first seven clerks organized a Saturday-night dinner at the University Club in Washington, timed to coincide with his birthday. That annual Saturday dinner had continued each year since, usually inside a private dining room at the Occidental Restaurant. Brennan spoke so candidly over dinner about how the votes were lining up in pending cases that his former clerks felt for one night like they had never left his chambers. Brennan had complete trust that none of them would betray his confidence by repeating what he said. As the clerks married and had children, they had added a Sunday brunch for their growing families at Brennan's Georgetown home. Brennan enjoyed mixing bloody marys for the adult guests, and left his clerks marveling at how he remembered the names of everyone's wives and children.

For the eighth reunion, in 1967, Brennan and his clerks relocated to Cambridge, Massachusetts, for the unveiling of his portrait to be hung at Harvard Law School, another part of Dean Griswold's effort to make amends with Brennan. Griswold had approached Frank Michelman, the first of Brennan's clerks to join the school's faculty, looking for a way to honor the justice. They settled on the idea of commissioning a portrait by Cambridge portrait specialist Gardner Cox, an artist who had also painted Frankfurter's portrait. The Harvard Law School Association paid for half the cost while Brennan's clerks contributed the rest. The weekend unveiling celebration began with a dinner at the Harvard Faculty Club on Friday night, where Brennan encouraged students to enter the field of poverty law. He addressed a huge crowd of law students Saturday in the school's Ames Courtroom, and met privately with his clerks at a local restaurant for lunch before the evening dinner at the law school's Harkness Commons. His portrait sat covered on an easel, awaiting the formal unveiling.

Dean Griswold spoke first after dinner, surprising Brennan's clerks with his praise for the *Baker v. Carr* reapportionment decision many Harvard Law faculty still held in disdain. When it was Brennan's turn to speak, he first joked about how, when his professor, Zechariah Chafee, sat for a similar portrait, a friend had told him, "I hope the artist is doing you justice." Chafee replied, "I don't want justice, I want mercy." Then Brennan turned serious. "I simply cannot command words sufficient to express to my law clerks, the council, and the law school the gratitude I feel." Professor Freund spoke last, ending the night with warm words of his own about Brennan, despite having been cast aside as his law school classmate's exclusive supplier of clerks. The next morning, Brennan, his clerks, and their families all gathered at Michelman's house in Lexington for brunch, where the host gave Brennan a break from mixing the bloody marys.

Brennan returned to campus a few months later as a featured speaker at the law school's 150th anniversary celebration. "The school has not been content to rest on memories of a Golden Age — an age of giants, now legendary," Brennan said. "After 150 years, I sense no lessening of vitality. Indeed, I am confident that the school's greatest days are still before it."

TWO WEEKS AFTER the Newark riots, on July 29, 1967, Brennan, Marjorie, and Nancy set sail aboard the SS *Santa Mercedes* on their way to a seven-country tour of South America. He left behind a country still racked by violence. In the previous week, federal troops had been called in to quell the latest riot in Detroit, and President Johnson had established a commission chaired by Illinois governor Otto Kerner Jr. to probe the causes of urban disorder. "Fear of the darkened city streets has become a fact of urban life," *Time* reported in its issue of July 28, 1967. Brennan's schedule on this month-long trip on behalf of New York University's Inter-American Law Institute read like the itinerary of a visiting head of state. He was scheduled to meet the presidents and high court justices of most of the countries on the continent.

Yet as he prepared to board the 546-foot cruise ship, Brennan confessed to the friends who were seeing the family off that he was most excited about meeting a fellow passenger on the ship: the president of Notre Dame, Theodore Hesburgh. "Father Ted," as everyone had called him, had worked tirelessly to build the academic reputation of the Catholic university in South Bend, Indiana, a football powerhouse, since becoming its president in 1952, at the age of thirty-five. It was in that capacity that Hesburgh had written Brennan in 1960, asking him to consider Notre Dame graduates for his clerkships. This was during his arrangement with Professor Freund, and Brennan wrote back explaining almost apologetically that his clerks came exclusively from Harvard. Brennan had visited the Notre Dame campus in 1965 to deliver an address and had come to greatly admire Hesburgh, probably in part for his activities beyond Notre Dame. Hesburgh had become a leading champion of civil rights ever since President Eisenhower appointed him to the new U.S. Commission on Civil Rights in 1958.

Brennan wound up on the same cruise ship as Hesburgh purely by happenstance. Marjorie's fear of planes explains why they had opted for a boat ride to South America. They would do enough flying once they arrived. Hesburgh, who traveled frequently to South America, had chosen this Grace Line ship because the owner, J. Peter Grace, was chairman of Notre Dame's board of trustees. Grace treated Brennan and his family like VIPs too. He arranged for a local agent and driver to meet them at every port: Kingston, Jamaica, Cartagena, Cristobal, Panama, Balboa, Bogotá, and Quito. During the thirteen-day voyage, Hesburgh and Brennan, both avid readers, found themselves looking for quiet spots to enjoy their books on the top deck. Hesburgh recalled he and Brennan shared "a number of good, long talks" during the cruise. For Hesburgh, counselor to presidents and popes, a man who was well on his way to visiting 131 countries and becoming America's most beloved priest, it was merely a pleasant way to pass the time aboard ship.

These deck-side chats meant more to Brennan, who, never one to court powerful figures in Washington, went out of his way to befriend Hesburgh. Brennan was no longer a particularly observant Catholic, but he continued to find comfort in kinship with priests both famous and obscure. The Brennans' friend Alice Knight, who saw them off at the dock, recalled Brennan saying there was no one in the entire country he wanted to meet more than Hesburgh. Upon returning to Washington, Brennan would write to "Father Ted," full of gratitude for the leisurely days they had spent together.

The time with Hesburgh meant just as much to Brennan's daughter, Nancy. Brennan had persuaded the State Department to allow Nancy to join them before she started college at his alma mater, the University of Pennsylvania. He argued that her high school Spanish classes qualified her to serve as their interpreter. (She managed to teach him just two phrases in Spanish: "Very glad to meet you" and "Just a minute, my daughter.") Nancy's brief flirtation with becoming a nun had long since faded away. Still, the time she spent with Hesburgh during the trip, including a visit to a slum in Panama, affected her deeply. By the time she arrived at the University of Pennsylvania, she told the alumni magazine that she planned to study South American history and Spanish. Brennan gave Hesburgh Nancy's telephone number and college address, and he promised to call when he visited Philadelphia. She maintained a correspondence with Hesburgh throughout her years at the university.

The Brennans eventually went their separate way from Hesburgh as they began their whirlwind tour, mixing official duties and sightseeing. In three weeks, the Brennans flew from Peru to Chile and Argentina, then on to Brazil and Venezuela. Photographers snapped pictures of Brennan's arrival on the tarmac at several stops, and local reporters chronicled his every move. "Before I finished I'd had audiences with the Presidents of Peru, Chile and Argentina, conferences with the Supreme Courts of those countries and of Brazil and Venezuela, with law school deans in uncounted numbers, gave lectures (not short enough), dodged the press everywhere (not always successful) and generally rode an unstoppable merry-go-round," Brennan wrote Hesburgh. In between, he and his family took in all the sights they could. They attended an opera in Buenos Aires, dined at a São Paolo racetrack, took a boat cruise on the bay near Rio de Janeiro, and attended many dinners in their honor organized by American ambassadors. Marjorie loved it all. Nancy even convinced her mother to accompany her in a bathing suit to the beaches of Rio. Brennan's memories of the trip would only grow warmer, as he looked back and realized it would be the last time he traveled abroad with his wife and daughter.

AS BRENNAN WRAPPED up his Latin American tour with a visit to Caracas on August 30, 1967, back in Washington, the United States Senate voted on the nomination of Thurgood Marshall for the Court's newest addition, replacing Justice Tom Clark. Neither old age nor ill health had prompted sixty-seven-year-old Clark to leave the bench at the end of the Court's term in June. As he had in engineering Goldberg's replacement by Fortas, President Johnson managed to create a vacancy on the Supreme Court, this time by elevating Clark's son, Ramsey, to the post of attorney general in February 1967. That appointment presented Justice Clark with an insurmountable conflict of interest, since he could not possibly recuse himself from every case argued by the Justice Department run by his son.

So Clark left the Court, although he stayed active as a judge, becoming the first person ever to serve on all of the U.S. circuit courts of appeal before his death in 1977. In Clark's place, Johnson chose Marshall, the first African American nominated to the U.S. Supreme Court. Marshall, still serving as solicitor general at the time, enjoyed a close relationship with Johnson. They traded gossip in the White House over glasses of bourbon and Dr Pepper in the months leading up to his nomination in June.

Marshall's five days of confirmation hearings that July proved less difficult than those for his appointment to the Second Circuit. Southern senators directed most of their fury at the sitting justices rather than the nominee. When the full Senate finally voted to confirm Marshall on August 30, the tally would be 69–11. Another twenty senators, afraid of angering white constituents, did not vote at all. On September 1, the day Brennan flew back to the United States from Caracas, Justice Black, a former Klansman, privately administered the constitutional oath to the nation's first African American justice. Johnson nominated Harvard Law School's dean, Erwin Griswold, as Marshall's successor as solicitor general.

In the weeks to come, Brennan took Marshall under his wing and tried to help ease his transition, just as he had done with Goldberg. Brennan had watched Marshall argue many cases before the Court, first for the NAACP and then as solicitor general, for much of the previous decade. He had gotten to know Marshall outside the Court too, since Marshall had moved to Washington. Marshall and his wife, Cissy, invited Brennan and Marjorie to dinner at their Washington apartment. The Brennans reciprocated in Georgetown. As a justice, Marshall aligned quickly with Brennan. They would vote together 95 percent of the time during his first two years on the bench. Having a secure fifth vote made Brennan's job easier again. Brennan and Warren no longer had to worry as much about how to rustle up a majority when Black went his own way. Their bloc never seemed more secure.

· 13 ·

TUMULT

ON THE NIGHT of April 4, 1968, Martin Luther King Jr. was assassinated as he stood on the balcony outside his room at the Lorraine Motel in Memphis, Tennessee. So began a tumultuous spring not only for the nation, but for the Court and for Brennan himself.

Transistor radios carried by pedestrians at the corner of U and Fourteenth streets in the heart of Washington's black ghetto broadcast the first bulletins of King's death. An angry crowd demanded nearby shops close in King's honor, and within an hour, a brick crashed through the window of a Peoples drugstore. Looters soon carried away television sets, liquor, and suits from nearby shops, and the first fires destroyed a pair of neighborhood food markets after midnight.

The rioting had quieted down by the time the justices met for their regular Friday conference the next morning. They took up a school-desegregation case they heard earlier in the week before adjourning early to head to a memorial service for King at the National Cathedral. Five days earlier, King himself had stood at the cathedral's elevated Canterbury Pulpit, preaching to a crowd of four thousand people about the Poor People's Campaign he planned to lead to Washington that coming spring. "I don't like to predict violence," King warned at a press conference afterward. "But if nothing is done between now and June to raise ghetto hope, I fear this summer will not only be as bad, but worse than last year." That same night, President Johnson shocked the nation by announcing, at the end of a televised address on Vietnam, that he would not run for reelection.

Now, Brennan, seated just a couple of pews behind Johnson, watched as clergy of all denominations honored the slain civil rights leader from the same pulpit of the high-vaulted, unfinished Gothic church at which King had so recently spoke. Among the audience of high government officials, civil rights leaders, and members of the public, including a stonemason in dusty overalls, the justices of the Supreme Court looked particularly old. "Hugo Black more than any, but even the energetic Douglas looked played out and Warren, he seemed drained of his friendly vigor," the *Washington Post* reported. Brennan, invisible as usual, did not even merit a mention. As the forty-five-minute service ended and the cathedral's tower bell tolled mournfully, a group of youths spontaneously began singing the civil rights anthem "We Shall Overcome." By the time Brennan and the other dignitaries filed out of the church, the rioting and looting had started up again along U Street, and had spread closer to downtown along Seventh. Panicked whites clogged the roads as they fled the city. Brennan, who lived just two miles down Wisconsin Avenue from the cathedral, returned across town to the Court.

Brennan told his two clerks to go home early. One of them, Raymond Fisher, looked in his rearview mirror as he drove away from the Court and saw smoke from some of the five hundred fires set that day, making it seem as if the entire city were in flames. Brennan headed back to Georgetown, a part of the city left unscathed except for isolated plundering. The most visible signs of the riot observed there was the shiny new Lincoln parked in one driveway with the words "soul brother" soaped by the owner on the rear window. Brennan frantically tried to reach Nancy at her University of Pennsylvania dorm in Philadelphia. Her roommate did nothing to calm Brennan's worries when she mentioned that Nancy had gone off as usual to tutor a black teenage boy in South Philadelphia. It would be several more anxious hours until she returned, after the student's mother insisted the teenager escort Nancy back to her dorm. He had stood between Nancy and an angry crowd drawn to what must have been one of the last whites still out on the ghetto streets, and he stayed in her dorm that night because it was not safe for him to walk home.

Back in Washington, the first troops of the Army's Third Infantry Division crossed the Potomac River by nightfall in their jeeps and olive-colored trucks. Soldiers surrounded the White House and mounted machine guns on the steps of the Capitol. A total of 13,600 federal troops and National Guardsmen poured into the city over the next thirty-six hours, a different crowd of visitors than the one anticipated for the Cherry Blossom Festival scheduled for that weekend. Rioting broke out in dozens of American cities in the wake of King's murder, although Washington suffered the heaviest damage, particularly in black neighborhoods, home to most of the 645 destroyed buildings. Still, the Court opened on Monday, April 8, for business as usual. The justices resumed handing down decisions as if Army troops with fixed bayonets and armored personnel carriers were not stationed outside in the biggest military occupation of an American city since the Civil War.

BRENNAN SPOKE OF King's murder and the riots that followed in a series of unusually anguished speeches he delivered in subsequent weeks. He asked a gathering of lawyers in New York on May 1 why "excesses of protest have seemingly become the rule rather than the exception?" He rejected any notion that "by nature we are a violent people." "Rather," Brennan said, "we should ask ourselves, whether, while we increasingly acknowledge that we have denied 20 million of our citizens rights and opportunities to which they are entitled, we have in fact done anything as yet actually to afford them those rights and opportunities." While the riots further undermined many white Americans' support for the civil rights movement, Brennan remained unyielding. "A great society above anything else keeps its promises," Brennan said. "Our engagement in Vietnam is concrete evidence that we keep our promises abroad. But where is that evidence at home?" Brennan returned to the same themes in a May 19 speech to the Talmudical Academy of Baltimore, condemning both violence and any backlash it generated against the civil rights movement.

> However just the cause, however devoted and dedicated its proponents, those who resort to violence to further it must be made to understand that they defeat their own ends, for society cannot, and will not suffer violence, however noble the ends sought to be attained. At the same time, the rest of us cannot avoid our

responsibility to redress the wrongs of centuries out of fear or impatience with the course events have taken.

Such pleas increasingly fell on deaf ears in much of the country, a fact made dramatically evident during President Johnson's State of the Union address in January 1968, when his calls for new civil rights laws to ensure fair jury trials and to enforce equal employment opportunity and open housing were met with silence. The only standing ovation came when Johnson declared that "the American people have had enough of rising crime and lawlessness in this country." *Time* magazine predicted that same month that only Vietnam would surpass crime "as the nation's prime pre-occupation in Election year 1968." The specter of urban riots combined with fears of street violence and dismay about antiwar protestors were encapsulated in a single phrase: law and order. And it seemed that everyone put the courts on the top of the list of those to blame.

No one proved more adept at exploiting the issue than Richard Nixon, rising from the ashes of his failed 1960 presidential candidacy and 1962 bid to become California's governor. "Some of our courts in their decisions have gone too far in weakening the peace forces as against the criminal forces in this country," warned Nixon during his August 1968 acceptance speech for the Republican presidential nomination. Alabama governor George Wallace, who had also launched a repeat presidential bid, this time as an independent, was equally alarmist in his stump speeches. And the U.S. Senate had taken up a crime bill that included provisions designed to curb the Court's jurisdiction over cases involving crime. Sponsor John McClellan, the Arkansas Democrat and longtime Court critic, displayed a chart on the Senate floor that showed rising crime rates and the dates of Court decisions. "The Supreme Court has set a low tone in law enforcement and we are reaping the whirlwind today!" McClellan said.

Brennan was aware of that political context as the Court considered a case, *Terry v. Ohio,* beginning in December 1967, involving a defendant who was subject to a widely employed police practice known as the "stop and frisk." A Cleveland police officer became suspicious of a pair of men he watched walk up the street about a dozen times, look inside a store, and then walk back down the street to confer with a third individual. Concerned that they were casing the store for a possible robbery, the officer approached the three men. He patted them down, removing fully loaded automatic handguns from two of the men's coats. Both were subsequently convicted of carrying a concealed weapon.

The Court had taken up the case of one of the men who appealed his conviction, John Terry, in December 1967. During the justices' private conference discussion of *Terry,* Brennan helped move his colleagues toward the view that any stop and frisk had to be supported by probable cause, as if there were an arrest and search being carried out. Because of his active role at the conference, Brennan was concerned when Warren decided to write the decision rather than assigning it to him.

Brennan was further disappointed when Warren circulated his draft in January; it focused largely on the frisk rather than the initial question of whether the officer had justification to stop the suspect. Brennan sent Warren a long memo raising the concern that it would be difficult to control police conduct at the stage of the frisk, especially in a case in which a weapon was found, and that a probable-cause standard had to be imposed to justify the initial stop of an individual. Other justices weighed in, and Warren's redraft did little to clarify the problem. Then Brennan took the highly unusual step of taking the comments of various other justices and Warren's draft and quietly writing his own version of the opinion. Despite the long, easy working relationship between the two men, Brennan was quite solicitous when he sent his version privately to Warren in mid-March, noting, "I hope you won't think me presumptuous to submit my thoughts in this form."

Two aspects of Brennan's new draft stood out, most of which Warren used as the core of the final opinion. First, Brennan expressed a deep concern that the tone of Warren's original drafts would encourage police to stop and frisk individuals freely, and so inflame civil rights passions against the police. As Brennan's law clerk Raymond Fisher later wrote in the annual term history, the chief justice's opinion was "written in a rhetoric almost embarrassingly sympathetic to the plight of the policeman." Brennan felt this approach would be likely to compound "the 'crime in the streets' alarms being sounded in this election year in the Congress, the White House and every Governor's office," as he wrote Warren.

Brennan also notably abandoned the use of probable cause as the required threshold for police to stop and frisk. Instead, he turned to the first clause of the Fourth Amendment, which prohibits "unreasonable searches." He said that the reasonableness standard was the right measure, because probable cause was intended to provide an independent assessment by a judge prior to police activity; this was simply not a feasible approach to the immediacy of the stop-and-frisk situation.

The requirement that an officer have only "reasonable suspicion" and not probable cause for a stop and frisk became the rule adopted by the Court in the *Terry* case. It is one that remains controversial, since it gives law enforcement considerable leeway to justify stopping, questioning, and searching individuals on the street. Indeed, Brennan foresaw the controversy in his March 14 letter to Warren, but apparently viewed it as the more practical alternative. "In this lies the terrible risk that police will conjure up 'suspicious circumstances' and courts will credit their versions," Brennan told Warren. Injecting the dimension of contemporary civil rights strife, Brennan added, "It will not take much of this to aggravate the already white hot resentment of ghetto Negroes against the police — and the Court will become the scapegoat."

While *Terry* may be the most formidable example of Brennan ghostwriting a Warren opinion that term, Brennan influenced the chief justice's direction in at least one other major case that spring. The case, *United States v. O'Brien*, stemmed from David Paul O'Brien's burning of his draft card on the steps of the local South Boston, Massachusetts, courthouse in 1966. O'Brien was convicted under a 1965 federal amendment that made anyone who "knowingly destroys, knowingly mutilates" a draft card subject to criminal prosecution. But the U.S. Court of Appeals for the First Circuit ruled that the federal law violated the free speech guarantee of the First Amendment.

It was clear from the outset that the Supreme Court would disagree with the appeals court and affirm O'Brien's conviction. However, Chief Justice Warren's first draft of the Court's opinion suggested that O'Brien fell into a narrow circumstance in which his conduct did not involve verbal expression and therefore was outside the First Amendment. Brennan was concerned that this attempt by Warren to make the O'Brien case seem like a narrow First Amendment exception would backfire and undermine protection for freedom of speech. Working patiently behind the scenes with warren, he persuaded the chief justice to recognize that O'Brien's actions included some aspects of free speech, but that the government could still prevail because its "compelling" interest in draft registration outweighed the interference with freedom of speech. Warren accepted Brennan's approach in an opinion that established a new test for government regulation of symbolic speech. The government must have an important interest unrelated to suppressing free speech, and the restriction could not be greater than essential for furthering that interest. The test was also subsequently used to analyze whether laws that seem content-neutral on their face, in fact infringe on free speech.

THE ARMY SOLDIERS had long since withdrawn by May 1968 when the Poor People's Campaign that King had intended to lead arrived in Washington. Along the National Mall, demonstrators set up a settlement of tents and shacks they named Resurrection City. But King's vision of massive civil disobedience bogged down in the rain-soaked mud and participants' disparate causes. Four hundred of the demonstrators descended on the Court on May 29 to protest a decision upholding the conviction of twenty-four Native Americans for violating a state regulation barring net fishing of salmon. Protestors let out war whoops, smashed windows, swarmed over the statue of Athena, and splashed around in the pools of water in front of the Court. Brennan's clerk Raymond Fisher emerged from one of the basement pornography viewings to hear protestors banging on the great bronze doors that had been shut and locked. Brennan himself exaggerated the extent of the incursion when he later recalled it as the time protestors "raided" the building and "came in through the windows."

That was perhaps an understandable elaboration given Brennan's sense that the rule of law had broken down completely — not just on the Court's front steps but also on his own front lawn. On a Sunday morning in May of that year, Marjorie had looked out the window of their second-floor bedroom and seen a red tag lying in a bank of ivy in the front yard. She went outside to remove the tag, noticed it was tied to some kind of case, and called for Brennan. Together they opened the case and discovered a Browning 12-gauge shotgun inside. Brennan called the city police, and responding officers found thirty-one shotgun shells on the lawn, wrapped inside a blanket. The discovery unsettled Brennan, coming so soon after King's assassination and the subsequent riots, and on top of his own history of receiving threatening letters. He pleaded with police officers to keep quiet about the incident, not wanting to attract any media attention.

Nonetheless, articles about the gun found on Brennan's property appeared in at least one newspaper, the *Orlando Star*. That May 27 article prompted a Florida woman to mail Brennan a typed letter care of the White House that reached him at the Court on June 3. "It is too bad that the guns found on your premises were not used on you and your family," wrote Evelyn Brown, in a rage about the Court's school-desegregation cases. That letter alarmed Brennan enough that the next day, June 4, he asked Fortas to contact the FBI on his behalf. J. Edgar Hoover's second in command, Cartha "Deke" DeLoach, sent agents to interview Brennan that same day. If the FBI's involvement eased Brennan's worries, the sense of renewed security was short-lived. The next morning, Brennan woke to discover that Senator Robert Kennedy had been shot at a Los Angeles hotel shortly after midnight after celebrating his victory in the California presidential primary. Kennedy would die the next day. The FBI later determined that the gun found on Brennan's lawn had been stolen from a neighbor's home and dropped by thieves unaware of who lived there.

KENNEDY'S MURDER WEIGHED heavily on Brennan as he prepared to speak at Harvard Law School's graduation exactly one week later. His reconciliation with the school now complete, he was also to receive an honorary degree at the university-wide graduation ceremony, an honor of enough significance that he requested tickets to the event for two of his children. When Harvard's news office requested an advanced copy of his speech, Brennan wrote back, the day after Kennedy's death, to say that that would not be possible. "In light of the tragic assassination, I am making substantial revisions," Brennan wrote. He arrived in Boston with Marjorie on an overnight train on the morning of June 12 and headed to Cambridge, where signs of the turbulent times permeated the Harvard campus. More than 140 members of the graduating class signed a letter to the *Harvard Crimson* student newspaper calling the war in Vietnam "unjust and immoral" and pledged that "as long as the United States is involved in this war, I will not serve in the armed forces."

Brennan was supposed to have shared billing on campus that day with Martin Luther King Jr., the scheduled speaker at Harvard College's Class Day. Instead, King's widow, Coretta, spoke three hours after Brennan's noontime speech. Beneath a downpour, Brennan began on a somber note. "Unhappily, the joy of the occasion has been saddened by the tragic events of the last week," Brennan said. "Each of us recoiled with horror upon awakening a week ago and learning of the assault on Senator Kennedy. His assassination, like the assassination of Dr. King and earlier President Kennedy, was a shocking, profoundly depressing act. It almost seems that events in this country have reached a state where we can no longer retire at night secure in the knowledge that we can awake without facing headlines announcing a new and violent tragedy."

Robert F. Kennedy's murder had also deeply shaken Earl Warren, who predicted in early June that Kennedy could win the election. His assassination, Warren now believed, made it all the more likely that Nixon would instead be elected president. That conclusion lent new urgency to the seventy-seven-year-old chief justice's consideration of his own future. A week after Brennan asked Fortas to contact the FBI on his behalf, Warren approached him with a sensitive request of his own: that Fortas discreetly arrange a meeting with President Johnson. Fortas had no trouble getting his friend, the president, to agree. So, as Brennan attended Harvard's June 13 graduation ceremonies, where he was to receive an honorary degree, Warren went to the White House to meet with Johnson in the Oval Office. Warren carried with him two letters. The first, a single sentence long, stated his "intention to retire as Chief Justice of the United States effective at your pleasure." Warren disclosed his reasons in a second letter. After fifty years of continuous public service, he cited a duty "to give way to someone who will have more years ahead of him to cope with the problems which will come to the Court." Warren made no reference to his desire to have Johnson, rather than Nixon, should he win the election, name his successor.

Warren returned to the Court that day and told at least some of the other justices about his decision. Mrs. Black noted in her diary that night that "Hugo told me the C.J.'s secret (confidentially)." Brennan had no idea of Warren's resignation until he returned to Washington from Boston on an overnight train the following morning. Warren for once had not consulted in advance with his closest colleague on the Court. Brennan recalled being "absolutely stunned" when he heard the news. "We all were," he said. The man who had led the Court for Brennan's entire thirteen-year tenure and had become his closest friend there was leaving. Shortly afterward, Warren confided his wish that Brennan succeed him. "You know I'd love to see you Chief Justice," Brennan later recalled Warren telling him. "But you know you can't be, Bill. The only one who can be is Abe Fortas." Brennan was mentioned as a possible successor by journalists after Warren's letters were made public a week later, although he later insisted he never had any interest in the job. Nor did he think it was even a remote possibility. The expectation that Johnson would pick Fortas, his close friend and adviser, was shared widely at the Court.

When the Court convened on June 17 for the last session of the term, the justices and their families believed they were witnessing the last time Warren would preside as chief. All the wives except Mrs. Harlan attended, Elizabeth Black noted in her diary, and the chief justice's wife and daughters looked particularly sad. She observed that Douglas looked weak, drawn, and pale after having undergone surgery to have a pacemaker inserted. Black had begun mulling his own retirement. As she studied Black, Douglas, and Warren, Mrs. Black "thought fate might decree none of the three would be there next year. Truly the end of an era." It was the end of an era — but not in quite the way Mrs. Black or Brennan now expected.

EVERYTHING SEEMED TO go wrong after Warren made known his intention to retire — starting with Johnson's plans to replace him. As expected, Johnson announced on June 26, 1968, his intention to elevate Fortas and replace him with Homer Thornberry, a fellow Texan and judge on the Fifth Circuit. Thornberry first met Johnson as a young page in the Texas state legislature and later succeeded him in the House when Johnson moved across the Capitol to the Senate in 1949. This time, unlike with Johnson's machinations over the appointments of successors for Justices Goldberg and Clark, all the scheming by LBJ did not work out as he anticipated.

Publicly, Brennan had nothing but good things to say about Fortas. *Time* magazine quoted him in an article announcing the nomination as calling Fortas "an utterly delightful companion." Privately, Brennan harbored deep reservations about the prospect of Fortas becoming chief justice. "I don't believe I could ever have worked with Abe Fortas as I worked with Earl Warren," Brennan later recalled. "As a matter of fact, I'm inclined to think I would never have tried it because I wouldn't have trusted him." Brennan blamed what he considered Fortas's outsized ego. "You couldn't work with him. Abe had to be the greatest and everybody had to kowtow to him. He could be very mean."

President Johnson, the old master of the Senate, overestimated how much clout he retained now as a lame duck three months after announcing he would not run again. Fortas and Thornberry encountered a surprisingly hostile reception on Capitol Hill. Resentment over LBJ's overbearing style and the Court's liberal direction had festered for years among conservative southern Democrats. Republicans saw a chance to save the appointment for a president of their own party. Johnson's choice of two men who were both viewed as his cronies did not help. Nor did the wording of Warren's retirement letter, making it effective "at your pleasure," seen by some as evidence that he was colluding with the president. Brennan was surprised by the reception Fortas encountered when they both attended the American Bar Association's annual convention that August in Philadelphia. "I must say the opposition to confirmation has been much greater than I had anticipated," Brennan wrote Douglas on August 5, 1968. After watching Fortas deliver what he described as "a truly splendid address," Brennan noted the nominee "seemed quite somber." Nonetheless, Brennan predicted, "I still believe it will all come out all right in the end."

Fortas had not done himself much good when he testified before the Senate Judiciary Committee in July, the first nominee for chief justice ever to do so. He faced hostile questions about Warren Court rulings — particularly those involving obscenity and criminal procedure — and his links to the president, which he downplayed. Details soon emerged of his role writing Johnson's 1966 State of the Union address — several months after joining the Court — as well as a substantial payment he had received for a summer seminar at American University. In this era, well before C-SPAN televised Senate floor proceedings, Brennan asked his two clerks to attend the debate on Fortas's nomination in late September. He wanted them to gauge just how much trouble Fortas was in. One of the clerks, Robert Weinberg, had spent the summer prior to arriving in Brennan's chambers at Fortas's old law firm, Arnold & Porter, culling through materials as part of an effort to rehabilitate Fortas's image. Weinberg and his fellow clerk, Joseph Onek, reported back that things looked grim. Senate Minority Leader Everett Dirksen had switched from supporting Fortas to "neutral," and Republicans and southern Democrats joined together in offering lengthy, searing attacks against the Warren Court during a five-day-long filibuster.

As the Senate prepared to vote on whether to end the filibuster on October 1, Brennan was in New York delivering a speech at New York University. He stressed how much was left to be done in order to ensure justice for all "who do not partake of the abundance of American life," including the poor, minorities, and the criminally accused. He added, "We are surely nearer the beginning than the end of the struggle." The speech was almost entirely a retread of one he had given at the ABA convention two months earlier in Philadelphia. Here in New York, he ended his speech, as he did so many, with his favorite line from the Irish poet William Butler Yeats, to make the point that in service of the goal of equal rights, the Fourteenth Amendment, although one hundred years old, is never outdated, but "like the poor old woman in Yeats' play." Brennan quoted:

> "Did you see an old woman going down the path?" asks Bridget.
> "I did not," replied Patrick, who had come into the house just after the old woman left it. "But I saw a young girl and she had the walk of a queen."

Brennan's usual outsized optimism was all the more poignant — and misplaced — this day. The Senate's failure to end the filibuster all but doomed Fortas's chances of becoming chief justice. The next morning, Fortas asked Johnson to withdraw his nomination. No elevation meant that there was no vacancy for Thornberry, whose nomination died too. In spite of Brennan's strong — if, at the time, unstated — reservations regarding Fortas, the outcome disappointed him. Brennan followed the 1968 presidential campaign quite closely, even correctly predicting to his clerks that Nixon would pick Spiro Agnew as his running mate. He knew that Nixon looked increasingly likely to defeat Vice President Hubert Humphrey and Alabama governor George Wallace, and thus to pick Warren's successor. As much as Brennan did not want Fortas taking the job, he liked the idea of Nixon picking the next chief justice even less.

Six days after the Senate vote, the Court's new term began with Fortas still an associate justice and Warren back as chief. It was a bittersweet return, made all the more bitter when Nixon was elected on November 5. As the television networks began showing election returns that night, a clearly disappointed Brennan, watching at home, announced to his family that he was going to bed early. Brennan shared his disappointment about the election returns with his clerks and privately spoke about Nixon in uncharacteristically harsh terms. "He thought he was an evil man," said Abner

Mikva, a Democratic congressman from Chicago whom Brennan later befriended when Mikva was a judge on the U.S. Court of Appeals for the District of Columbia. Apparently, the ill will was mutual. Nixon's secret White House tapes later recorded the president calling Brennan "a jackass Catholic."

One day that fall, Brennan's former colleague Arthur Goldberg asked to meet him for breakfast at a hotel in downtown Washington. Brennan had kept in touch with Goldberg sporadically since he had left the Court to become the U.S. ambassador to the United Nations in 1965. Goldberg had more free time since resigning from his UN post in April 1968 without having even come close to achieving the purported mission for which Brennan believed Johnson had lured him away from the Court: bringing peace to Vietnam. After leaving the UN, Goldberg had joined Paul, Weiss, a New York law firm to which his name would be added. As they now sat down for breakfast, Brennan sensed that Goldberg was almost desperate to return to the Court. He asked Brennan to try to convince President Johnson to name him to replace Warren as chief justice. Perhaps Brennan had given Goldberg false hope in a note Brennan had written back in June, after Goldberg had left the UN: "I needn't tell you that I'd been hoping against hope that the Chief's leaving would mean that you'd join us again. As a matter of fact, I've not yet given up hope." Goldberg had already approached Warren with a similar plea, to no avail. "He was so desperate to get back that he'd ask anybody," Brennan later remembered. "I told him I couldn't do it."

Brennan at the time was not entirely sure the president had given up on Fortas, and later came to believe that Johnson would never have subjected himself to another potential humiliating defeat in the Senate over reinstating Goldberg. The former justice left the breakfast with a deepening disappointment that would never dissipate. He went on to serve as president of the American Jewish Committee, ran unsuccessfully for governor of New York against Nelson Rockefeller, and eventually moved back to Washington, where he opened his own law office. Two decades after leaving the Court, Goldberg would still regret giving up his seat.

A sense of foreboding hung over the 1968–69 term, as if anything left unfinished might be lost under the new undesignated chief. Brennan's clerks recounted in their term history their unsuccessful attempts to convince Douglas's clerks to change their boss's mind concerning one particular case, using the argument that they could not afford to wait. Brennan and his allies had no better success in affirming a lower court's decision regarding welfare benefits, which they wanted to consider without briefs or oral argument out of fear that the case would be held over for the next term and lost. "There just wasn't a thing you could do," Brennan said, recalling his feeling of helplessness. "Not a thing."

BRENNAN'S WORRIES THAT fall extended beyond the direction of the country or the Court, to two of his children.

Nancy was scheduled to testify at the trial of a college friend facing murder, manslaughter, and arson charges for starting a fire at a University of Pennsylvania fraternity that killed three people. Nancy had attended a holiday party at the fraternity house shortly before Christmas, 1967, at the invitation of the friend, a sophomore named Richard Noble. She had already left when Noble, who admitted to having drunk at least fifteen glasses of champagne and some liquor, started playing with matches. He accidentally set fire to holiday decorations that included a ten-foot-high paper snowman. The fire quickly engulfed much of the house, where two students and a teenage friend died while trying to escape.

An ambitious young Philadelphia district attorney and future U.S. senator named Arlen Specter aggressively prosecuted Noble, and a grand jury indicted him on eleven counts. His trial was to begin in October 1968, and Nancy volunteered to be a character witness on her friend's behalf. Brennan, fearful that one or both sides would try to use the daughter of a Supreme Court justice as a pawn, worried about her testifying. Brennan hired a prominent Philadelphia attorney to represent his daughter, although that proved unnecessary. Nancy testified without incident before a jury of seven men and five women, the only reference to her father made by journalists in the next morning's newspapers. Her testimony did little to help Noble, who was found guilty of involuntary manslaughter two days later.

Two months later, back in New Jersey, Brennan's son Bill found himself enmeshed in a controversy of his own making. Bill had left his Wall Street law firm and gone to work for New Jersey's attorney general Arthur Sills the previous year. Around the same time Nancy testified in Philadelphia, Bill took over the state's organized-crime inquiry at the behest of Sills. It was not long before Bill grew uncomfortable with the extent of mob influence. On December 11, 1968, in a speech before the local chapter of a society of journalists in New Jersey, Bill warned that organized crime had infiltrated every facet of life in the state, including the state legislature. He charged that "three state legislators were entirely too comfortable with members of organized crime." The speech provoked a political firestorm in the state capital, Trenton, where the governor and legislators demanded Bill name names. The story dominated the headlines of New Jersey's largest papers, including the *Newark Star Ledger*, where his wife, Georgie, worked as a reporter.

So it was an unusually tense time as the family arrived for their traditional Christmas at Brennan's home in Georgetown that December. Bill, the former Marine, did not worry about his safety, although Georgie and Brennan feared possible mob retribution. Brennan also knew enough about how New Jersey politics worked to see that his son was about to be thrown overboard as a political sacrifice. Bill was scheduled to testify before a specially created committee of the state legislature just a few days after Christmas. One of the three lawmakers Bill accused had already called for his ouster. Bill's December 30 testimony was front-page news throughout New Jersey as well as in the *New York Times*. Although Brennan was proud of how his son had handled himself throughout the controversy, few others seemed impressed with what he had to say. One member of the special legislative committee predicted, "I think young Mr. Brennan is finished here." Even the state ACLU chapter chimed in against Bill, criticizing him for unjustifiable accusations based on guilt by association. An ally of Bill's tried defending him. "He's new at this game and is obviously more than a little naïve. But he's a tough Irishman, like his old man, and he'll overcome." A week later, Bill was relieved of his job as head of the Mafia investigation.

Vindication was not long in coming. In January 1969, a special legislative committee criticized two of the legislators Bill had identified and referred the case of the third to a grand jury. Forty people would soon be indicted, and the U.S. attorney in New Jersey warned — just shy of one year after Bill's speech — that the mob was taking over the state. After mulling a run for state attorney general and working on a New Jersey gubernatorial campaign, Bill settled into a small but well-respected law firm in Princeton, where he built a successful corporate practice focused on aviation, product liability, and insurance law. Like his father before him, the contro-versy had soured Bill on politics for good.

BRENNAN SKIPPED THE rainy inauguration ceremony, sending Nancy in his place on January 20, 1969, when Earl Warren administered the oath to Richard Nixon as president of the United States. Two weeks later, Bren-nan began a weeklong series of speeches defending the Warren Court's legacy of judicial activism and insisting once again that its work was not done. Brennan noted the "passionate protests against the Court" and their "almost hysterical character" as he launched into a February 4 speech at Princeton University. At Notre Dame on February 8, he warned that much sacrifice was still needed to ensure real equality. "Are we willing to pay sub-stantial higher taxes necessary to make up for past legal deprivations and create a truly just and equitable society?" And he largely repeated that same speech six days later at the midwinter meeting of the National Asso-ciation of Attorneys General, where the Associated Press reported he "de-fended the 'social activism' of the Supreme Court and said it was just be-ginning to make a dent on inequality." Coming so soon after the election of a president who won by promising personal security rather than equality, it all sounded more than a bit out of step with the times, more a wish or la-ment about lost opportunities than a promise of what lay ahead.

Brennan's worst fears about the new administration were soon con-firmed. On March 12, Brennan's secretary answered a telephone call from Jack Landau in the Justice Department's Public Information Office. Bren-nan knew the thirty-five-year-old journalist from his previous job as a le-gal reporter for the Newhouse chain of newspapers. Landau had written one of the stories in 1966 highlighting Brennan's influence, and then asked Brennan to write a recommendation for the prestigious Nieman Fellow-ship for journalists at Harvard University. Brennan had seen Landau a couple of times since, but had not realized he had taken a job with the new administration as the Justice Department's press secretary. Mary Fowler informed Brennan of Landau's request for a meeting that day, and Brennan immediately agreed. Landau arrived within minutes, and Brennan quickly realized it was not a social call.

Landau had come to discuss the Court's ruling in a trio of cases involv-ing government wiretapping that had been announced two days earlier.

The Court had rejected the government's attempts to forestall release of wiretap transcripts by arguing that information obtained from illegal surveillance wiretaps was not used in the prosecutions. The Court had sent the defendants' appeal back to the district court for further consideration. What made the Justice Department nervous was that the Court still had a dozen other cases on the docket involving similarly sensitive and potentially embarrassing surveillance of everyone from boxer Muhammad Ali to Teamsters president Jimmy Hoffa to alleged Russian spies. Landau told Brennan that the attorney general and other top officials feared that the Court's decision meant that the government would have to turn over to defense attorneys transcripts of conversations from illegal electronic surveillance. The CIA and FBI were particularly concerned about turning over transcripts of surveillance on foreign embassies, a practice that had not been publicly disclosed.

Much discussion had ensued among top Justice Department officials about how to discreetly get word to the justices that intelligence agencies were eavesdropping on every foreign embassy in Washington. They had ruled out a visit to the chief justice by Attorney General John Mitchell or Solicitor General Erwin Griswold, and finally settled upon Landau as the messenger via Brennan, since the two already knew each other. Brennan and his clerks were in fact already aware of the sensitivity of the surveillance cases. Brennan's clerks had written a memo to him that "wiretapping is going to be a major pastime of the Nixon administration . . . and this Court should deal with the problem carefully." Even so, Brennan was utterly shocked by Landau's highly unusual mission to deliver information to the Court in the hopes that it would influence the decision in pending cases. What was even more troubling was the veiled threat that Landau transmitted from Mitchell: the attorney general would do whatever he could to help the Court avoid congressional reaction on this issue, which might include a constitutional amendment or new legislation aimed at stripping the Court's jurisdiction. Mitchell appeared to be warning the Court to expect retribution should it limit government surveillance.

Brennan suggested that they visit Warren's chambers directly, so that Landau could repeat his message to the chief justice, which Landau did with trepidation. Warren recalled in his memoirs that he told Landau the pending cases would be decided based only on the public record rather than anything they were hearing from the Justice Department from this sort of secret back channel. After Landau left, Warren discussed with Brennan what he characterized later in his memoir as "this outrageous attempt to influence a Court action." Warren called a conference with all the other justices in which he relayed the substance of his and Brennan's conversations with Landau. Brennan then wrote up a memo laying out the incident in great detail, which he forwarded to Warren to create a permanent record. On March 24, the Court released its opinions in the other cases — opinions that reached the same conclusion as the earlier ones had.

Brennan, who usually told his clerks about everything that transpired in chambers, mentioned nothing to them about Landau's visit. It was a troubling first interaction with the Nixon administration, as Douglas observed in a memo to his files on March 17: "It seems pretty apparent that [Deputy Attorney General Richard] Kleindienst and perhaps Mitchell himself has a cause and the cause is to give the Court as much trouble as possible. So this is probably the opening salvo on a long and intense barrage." (This was not the only visit in 1969 from an outsider trying to influence a case. In October 1969, Tommy "the Cork" Corcoran, a well-known Washington lobbyist and power broker, asked Brennan during a visit to his chambers to vote to rehear a case. Brennan later remembered all but throwing Corcoran out, and the justices voted unanimously against rehearing the case.)

TWO DAYS AFTER Landau's visit, Brennan received what must have seemed like the first good news in months. On Friday, March 14, 1969, a telegram arrived from Father Hesburgh, the president of Notre Dame with whom he had so enjoyed the boat cruise to Latin America two years earlier. The telegram brought word that Brennan had been selected as the 1969 recipient of the school's Laetare Medal, the highest honor bestowed upon a Catholic layperson in the United States. "We take great pride in welcoming you to the select circle of extraordinary Catholic men and women who, by achievement and personal example, have brought glory to the Church and our beloved country," Hesburgh wrote in the telegram. The official announcement came two days later: "In a year in which dissent and violence loom large in our national life and a time when Americans are sensitive as never before to the imperative of justice for all, Mister Justice Brennan is a particularly felicitous choice for the Laetare Medal," Hesburgh stated. The congratulations piled up from Catholic clergy, including Washington archbishop Patrick Cardinal O'Boyle. Even President Nixon was a well-wisher.

Brennan would receive countless awards and honorary degrees in the course of his Court tenure—but none meant more to him than this one. It was a symbol of acceptance by his Church, bestowed by a man, Father Ted, he respected above almost anyone else. "I am just completely overwhelmed," Brennan wrote Hesburgh the same day he received the telegram. "I tried to reach you by telephone when I received your wire, and perhaps it's just as well I did not. I am afraid I would have been too emotional about it." It was no exaggeration when Brennan later wrote Hesburgh, "Nothing has given me, or ever can, greater satisfaction."

Another surprise visitor—not, this time, from the Attorney General's Office—awaited Brennan that spring inside his chambers. Brennan was just about to sign a stay delaying a death sentence when Mary informed him that Nancy's boyfriend, Tim Phelps, was there to see him. Brennan put aside his work and welcomed Phelps, a University of Pennsylvania senior and grandson of a former New York governor and justice on the state's highest court. Brennan did not see Nancy, who remained hidden in the anteroom. Phelps informed Brennan he had proposed to his daughter. Brennan, perhaps recalling the shotgun marriage of Hugh at a young age, grew suspicious.

"Why?" he asked.

"Because I love her," Tim explained.

That was enough to satisfy Brennan, who went back to his paperwork, relieved. Brennan liked Tim. He had written a friend at ABC News a few weeks earlier to help him get a summer job in journalism, Tim's intended career. When that friend told Brennan he had recommended Tim for a job at the UPI newswire, Brennan wrote back, "This will not only make Timothy happy but Nancy too. And from where I sit, that's even more important." After the engagement, soon announced in the *New York Times,* Brennan also made inquiries on Tim's behalf to find him a slot in the Coast Guard or reserves in order to avoid active duty military service and a likely tour in Vietnam.

Still, the idea of marrying off his daughter, now finishing up her sophomore year at the University of Pennsylvania, probably took some adjusting for Brennan, even with the planned nuptials two years off. Nancy seemed determined to have both a career and a family, a goal at odds with Brennan's — and particularly Marjorie's — notions about her future. They were proud she was attending college at her father's Ivy League alma mater. But they viewed education as an achievement in its own right for their daughter, rather than as a steppingstone into a profession. They expected Nancy to forgo a career in favor of staying home and raising a family. His private views about his daughter's future were at odds with what Brennan said publicly. In an October 1963 speech delivered at her boarding school, Holton Arms, Brennan had dismissed the notion that "marriage was the only career which attracted girls," assuring Nancy and her classmates that "no field of endeavor is closed today to the qualified woman, whether business, the professions, the arts or government."

The Brennans' traditional vision of a girl's proper future explains why Marjorie put aside her distaste of Washington society and made sure Nancy attended the Washington Debutante Ball during the fall of her freshman year of college in December 1967. Nancy stood at the receiving line inside the Mayflower Hotel's ballroom alongside the daughters of Senator Harry Byrd, former deputy secretary of defense Cyrus Vance, and William McChesney Martin Jr., chairman of the Federal Reserve Board. "I have had to relearn the waltz," Brennan confessed to the *Washington Post*. Nancy was pictured in the next day's paper with what the *Post* labeled the other "happy debutantes," each clutching her own bouquet of flowers.

Nancy, now well past her debutante season, had become convinced after a 1968 summer job at the Smithsonian that she wanted to pursue a career in museums. She was not alone in challenging the traditional notions of a woman's role her parents still held. Five years had passed since Betty Friedan published her groundbreaking book, *The Feminine Mystique*, which detailed the quiet desperation of housewives devoting their lives exclusively to their husbands, children, and domestic duties. "Vacuuming the living room floor — with or without makeup," Friedan warned, "is not work that takes enough thought or energy to challenge any woman's full capacity."

Gender consciousness in the United States had also grown due to a 1963 presidential report on the status of women filled largely with tepid recommendations but detailing the inequalities women faced in the workplace, and after the Equal Pay Act passed by Congress that required women doing the same work as men receive the same compensation. Congress further raised women's expectations by adding a ban on sex discrimination to

Title VII of the 1964 Civil Rights Act. Those laxly enforced laws did little to improve women's economic status. Three-quarters of the nation's 28 million working women remained at the bottom of the workforce pay scale when, in 1966, the newly formed National Organization for Women called for "a fully equal partnership of the sexes." By the time Tim proposed to Nancy in the spring of 1968, an even more assertive wave of feminists were demanding a revolution in the treatment of women.

Nancy gave Brennan an earful about the ideas emanating from the new women's movement as he picked her up at the end of the workday during her summer internship at the Smithsonian. Brennan never took the bait during these car rides home, when Nancy said things like, "Society would be better off if women were running it." Nonetheless, Nancy recalled, "He was making a mental shift in how he saw me." It was not easy for either of her parents. Brennan had only one working woman in his family as a guide, his sister Katherine in New Jersey. "He was really conflicted," Nancy recalled. "He didn't know what was best. He really did not have a road map." It was harder still for Marjorie. She looked askance at Bill's wife, Georgie, who continued to work as a reporter after getting married. "She believed the best thing for me was to marry a good person, raise children, and not work," Nancy recalled.

ALMOST EXACTLY TWO months after Landau's appearance, another visitor from the Justice Department came calling at the Court. Attorney General John Mitchell, a longtime confidant of Richard Nixon, personally delivered the message to Warren that Abe Fortas had to go. Two days earlier, *Life* magazine published a story detailing a $20,000 payment Fortas received from a foundation run by Louis Wolfson, a Las Vegas financier and industrialist. Fortas kept the money for eleven months even after Wolfson had twice been indicted. The payment was widely interpreted as a bribe. Now, Mitchell had word that the IRS had discovered a contract in which Wolfson had promised to pay Fortas $20,000 a year for life. "He can't stay," Warren told his secretary. Fortas met with his colleagues on May 13 and resigned the next day. Fortas's humiliation would continue. Arnold & Porter, the law firm his name once graced, would not take him back.

Brennan felt more anger than sympathy toward his colleague. Scrupulous in his own professional behavior, he cared deeply about the Court's image and about the ethics of lawyers more generally. "There is no profession, save perhaps the ministry, in which the highest morality is more necessary than that of law," Brennan declared in an October 1956 decision disbarring a New Jersey attorney. Brennan was so furious that he at first refused to invite Fortas to Nancy's wedding.

He was just as angry about what Fortas's departure meant for the Court's future. Fortas single-handedly managed to hand Nixon two seats during the new president's first year in office, a fact noted by the press. "Fortas' departure, coupled with the scheduled retirement of Chief Justice Earl Warren, will mean two fewer votes for the activist policies that developed during the Warren Court's 16 years," the *Washington Post* observed. "It is a political windfall for Mr. Nixon." Looking back two decades later, Brennan would still spin out a lengthy string of "what ifs." If Johnson had not "seduced" Goldberg into leaving the Court to make room for Fortas; if Fortas had not exposed himself to the criticism he deservedly got for teaching a seminar at American University financed by former clients; if Fortas had not been appointed for the first time until Warren retired. Then, Brennan theorized, Fortas might have been confirmed as chief justice and Goldberg might still be a justice. "The whole face of the nation" — or at least the Court — Brennan lamented, might have been different.

Fortas surely hurt his prospects of becoming chief justice and doomed his chances of staying on the Court. But in blaming Fortas for the changing face of the Court, Brennan was sidestepping his own responsibility and that of his allies. To be sure, Brennan and his allies did not start the Vietnam War or the protests that followed. Their criminal-procedure decisions alone did not explain the rapid uptick in crime. They did not launch President Johnson's Great Society social programs, which many disenchanted white voters blamed for rewarding minorities who engaged in criminal behavior during urban riots.

Still, their decisions — particularly on crime and race — had provided conservative politicians such as Goldwater, Reagan, and Nixon with the ammunition, or at least the rhetorical tools, that helped peel away northern urban ethnic Catholics and southern white voters from the Democratic Party. Nixon, in particular, successfully exploited the anger and anxiety the Court's decisions fueled to break apart the old Roosevelt New Deal coalition. It was a frustration best summed up by the white father from North Carolina who wrote his senator, "I'm sick of crime everywhere. I'm sick of riots, I'm sick of 'poor' people demonstrations . . . I'm sick of the

U.S. Supreme Court ruling for the good of a very small part rather than the whole of our society." For Brennan, it was easier to blame Fortas than to admit that the entire liberal consensus to which he subscribed was coming undone right before his eyes — and that he may well have played a role in making it happen.

One immediate consequence of Fortas's resignation came in an important free speech case, *Brandenburg v. Ohio,* involving an Ohio Ku Klux Klan leader charged with advocating violence. Fortas had circulated a draft decision in mid-April, but it had not yet been announced when he resigned. Brennan took over the opinion and made a few important modifications before the decision was released as an unsigned per curiam opinion on June 9, 1969. Fortas wrote that advocacy of illegal action could not be prohibited "except where such advocacy is directed to inciting or producing imminent lawless action and is attended by present danger that such action may in fact be provoked." Brennan changed the second half of the test to read, "and is likely to incite or produce such action." He wanted the new test to be a clean break from the past and significantly more protective of speech than the earlier "clear and present danger" test that had defined the First Amendment for fifty years.

Nixon announced his nominee to replace Warren one week after Fortas's resignation. With his deep baritone voice and flowing mane of white hair, Warren Burger certainly looked and sounded the part of a chief justice. The selection of Burger, the D.C. Circuit judge with whom Brennan often sparred at the annual New York University summer seminars, could not have been worse in his eyes, although it was not much of a surprise. Burger first met Nixon at the 1948 Republican convention and had curried Nixon's favor more recently with speeches criticizing the Court's criminal-law rulings. Burger's appearance as the only lower-court judge at an April 23, 1969, White House dinner held in Warren's honor signaled he was being considered as a potential successor. Just as with the appointment of Goldberg, which launched the Warren Court's high years, Brennan and Bazelon were together when they heard news of the nomination that seemed certain to end it.

Brennan was distressed, although few outside the Court knew of the depth of his concerns. Their previous history of ill will at the New York University seminars remained unknown beyond the judges who attended. The lack of public awareness of the Brennan-Burger exchanges explains why one of the most insightful Court watchers, Lyle Denniston of the *Washington Star*, could predict after Burger's nomination that Brennan might retain his influence under the new chief. "There are reasons to suggest he would find it convenient to use Brennan's talents as a judicial playmaker," Denniston wrote that June. Brennan, though, had no such illusions about his likely influence under Burger. Still, ever the optimist, Brennan told his clerks he wanted to give Burger the benefit of the doubt. Burger seemed less inclined toward good will. "What can one man do to stop the nonsense?" he wrote his friend Blackmun on March 31, 1969, before Fortas announced his resignation. "[Richard Nixon] can only straighten that place out if he gets four appointments."

CONSERVATIVE MEMBERS OF Congress seemed intent on creating as many openings for Nixon as possible. Scrutiny immediately shifted to the liberals left on the Court. Senator Strom Thurmond suggested "Douglas is next," although in fact Brennan emerged as the next target. On May 15, 1969, one day after Fortas's departure, Louisiana congressman John Rarick inserted into the *Congressional Record* a detailed description of four real estate partnerships set up by Charles E. Smith in which Brennan invested along with Fortas, Bazelon, Goldberg, and Wright. "We have the responsibility to our people not to permit ourselves to be pacified by the departure of one — Abe Fortas — while there remain in the federal judiciary others with similar interests damaging the solemnity of the judiciary," Rarick said. That same day, a professor suing Catholic University sought to disqualify Brennan from hearing his case because Bazelon and Wright had participated. The *New York Times*, several Washington papers, and the *Chicago Tribune* all published stories about the real estate deals or the Court's decision to deny the motion to disqualify Brennan.

Those stories helped persuade Brennan to take extreme measures aimed at heading off the controversy. On May 23 he resigned from teaching at the New York University seminar — and from every other outside activity in the days that followed. He quit the Visiting Committee at SUNY Buffalo, and informed Harvard Law School he could not serve on its Visiting Committee after all. He canceled every upcoming speech after the college commencement season ended, even those he delivered for no fee. He resigned from the ABA and the New Jersey Bar Association, which he had first joined in 1934. He would no longer even agree to speak to classes visiting the Court or attend the dedication of new state supreme court buildings. Brennan liquidated his investments with equal haste. He sold off the AT&T stock his mother left him when she died and severed his connection with Smith's real estate investments. From now on, he would hold no investments except federal bonds.

Brennan told his clerks about his decision to cut off all ties with every organization except the Court and the Catholic Church. "Have you written the pope?" Onek joked. For selfish reasons, his clerks were relieved they did not have to write any more speeches during the waning months of their tenure in his chambers. But they knew how much Brennan enjoyed those speaking engagements, and concluded that he had overreacted. No other justice went as far. Warren had convinced the Judicial Conference, the federal judiciary's policymaking body, to enact a ban on compensation from outside activities for district and circuit court judges after promising that the Supreme Court would take up a similar proposal. But when Warren raised the issue in June, his fellow justices voted to postpone any decision until the next term. Three other justices told Warren they would voluntarily give up outside income. Douglas, who relied heavily on his income from books and other outside sources to pay alimony to his three ex-wives, did not join them. Friends and fellow judges pleaded with Brennan to reconsider, but there was no turning back. As with his decision to revoke Michael Tigar's clerkship, Brennan here displayed a tendency to overreact impulsively when faced with a crisis.

Brennan offered his most extensive explanation of his decision to Father Hesburgh in a handwritten letter that June. "It's a decision Marjorie and I reached after long long hours of discussion," Brennan wrote. "It's simply not possible to draw a line because, on one basis or another, someone can always find impropriety in any activity or any investment. And because this institution can't exist without absolute confidence in its members and that confidence has been sorely tried by events, we've decided not to do or have anything that can provoke criticism." Brennan explained, "I'm simply cutting out everything and from now on will do nothing except my Court work. If you disagree—think this goes too far—I should tell you you have plenty of company, including all of my colleagues. But we feel it's best for us. I wanted you particularly to know why."

Brennan's withdrawal cost him financially. Never rich, he cut off a substantial, albeit declining, source of outside income by forgoing future speaking engagements. Money problems continued to plague Brennan as he now paid the last of the family's college bills, although a boost in the associate justices' salary from $39,500 to $60,000 in 1969 certainly helped. It had taken Brennan eight years to repay his friend Frank Ritchie for the three loans, and he did so only after receiving another pleading letter from Ritchie. "I seem fated to remain continuously on the debit side of the ledger," Brennan lamented in his letter to Ritchie that accompanied his final payment of $5,082.99 in 1964. Brennan had never moved into a more modest apartment, as he had told Ritchie he would. He and Marjorie stayed in Georgetown, where he relied on the below-market rent charged by his landlord and friend Richard Harkness. Marjorie often shouldered the burden of making ends meet. The family certainly never went wanting, although she struggled to keep up appearances living among neighbors with considerably more money to spare. She shopped at a Georgetown resale shop for the dresses she wore to society events. She went overboard with her spending only on Christmas presents. As a joke, one year she wrapped an old radio of Brennan's that she had had repaired, to prove she could be frugal at Christmas too.

Still, Brennan recalled, she completely supported his decision. "We're getting on all right," he remembered her saying. Only time would prove just how much a sacrifice Brennan had made. He had already fallen far behind his former law firm colleagues such as Donald Kipp, who called on Brennan's modest summer Nantucket rental in a yacht. Now, he would watch his fellow judges — including Bazelon — who maintained their investments with Smith grow even wealthier. Brennan never discussed his financial struggles with his clerks. But after leaving his chambers, several would make it a habit in the years to come of treating him to lunch at some of Washington's finest restaurants, the kind of places they knew he could not afford on his own.

BRENNAN HAD HOPED the controversy over his real estate deals had died down as he prepared for a ceremony to receive the Laetare Medal from Notre Dame. Notre Dame gave him great discretion in deciding where and when to hold the ceremony. He told Hesburgh he wanted it to take place at the Court before Warren retired. They settled on a modest ceremony on June 9, 1969, in the Court's East Conference Room. Brennan chose this occasion, meant to honor him, as the venue where he would publicly pay tribute to the chief on the eve of his retirement. Brennan had already organized a private retirement party three days earlier aboard the presidential yacht, the *Sequoia,* for the justices and their wives. Brennan, as usual, did his work behind the scenes. Black served as master of ceremonies once they sailed from the Navy Yard at 6:30 P.M. Douglas presented Warren, an avid hunter, with a custom-made Winchester shotgun with the justices' signatures engraved on a silver plate on the stock, for which Brennan had collected the contributions. A more public tribute was to follow on the National Mall on June 29 attended by twelve hundred people.

Brennan wanted to deliver his tribute to Warren surrounded by 150 family members, colleagues, and friends inside the Court, where their relationship blossomed. On this, the same day Warren's successor was confirmed by the Senate, the departing chief justice sat listening to Brennan in the front row alongside Hesburgh, who was dressed in his clerical collar. Pictures of that day show Brennan with his hands resting on the podium, the medal mounted on a wooden base displayed on a small table beside him. Although there is no record of Brennan's remarks at the ceremony, the speech was almost certainly the first of what would be many such efforts by Brennan, giving Warren the credit he thought was due him. "Your wonderful remarks about the Chief were both well taken and wonderfully generous," Hesburgh wrote him a few days later. All Brennan's son Hugh would remember about the ceremony in his father's honor that day was the depth of feelings he expressed for Warren. Brennan never passed up an opportunity in the years ahead to praise Warren, whom he often said belonged in the "pantheon of our greatest judges." Twenty years later, a member of a visiting high school group would ask Brennan if he still missed Warren. "Every day," Brennan replied.

Despite his best efforts to make Warren the focus of the event, the latest news about Brennan's finances overshadowed the tribute. That morning, the *New York Times* reported on his decision to cut back on most off-the-bench activities. The *Times'* story — rather than Brennan's praise of Warren — was on the minds of the Supreme Court reporters attending the ceremony. Afterward, Brennan smiled as Barry Schweid of the Associated Press approached him in a crowd of well-wishers. Brennan recognized

Schweid as one of the six reporters who sat on the side of the courtroom between the justices' bench and the counsels' tables. Brennan's smile disappeared when Schweid asked him about the *Times* article. He cut him off by saying, "Go ahead . . . beat it," and then gave Schweid a nudge to the chest. Schweid recounted the incident in a dispatch he filed for the AP wire.

Brennan recalled the incident differently. He remembered shoving Schweid but, as with other confrontations, he misremembered the details, suggesting he reacted so strongly because Schweid had asked him a question about Douglas. Schweid was not the only reporter who incurred Brennan's wrath over the issue. The *New York Times*' Fred Graham said Brennan was so "livid" about his articles that the justice stopped returning his telephone calls. The champion of press freedom admitted later that he refused to talk to Graham for years. He blamed Graham for the *Times*' coverage of his son's remarks about mob influence in New Jersey, rather than his coverage of Brennan's investments. In fact, Graham had not written a single story about Brennan's son.

AFTER THE HARDEST year of his tenure on the Court, Brennan and Marjorie both particularly looked forward to their two-week-long summer vacation in August 1969. They stopped first at the summer home of Justice and Mrs. Harlan in Westport, Connecticut, before heading to a lakeside resort in New Hampshire, rather than to their regular destination of Nantucket. The family of Nancy's fiancé, Tim, had often vacationed at the Rockywold-Deephaven camp on Squam Lake, and Nancy had persuaded her parents to give it a try. The setting did not agree with the Brennans. The camp featured a communal dining hall, where other vacationers felt free to approach Brennan. This did not suit the justice, who was there to get away from the Court, not to talk about it with strangers. The weather did not cooperate either. "It's a camp in the woods with nothing to do but sail, fish, swim or read and doubtless delightful when the sun shines," Brennan wrote his friend Judge Weigel. "But the sun came out only four of the fourteen days."

To make matters worse, Marjorie kept complaining about a terrible pain in her ear. It kept her up at night and did not go away during their stay. When they returned to Washington, Marjorie went to see a doctor.

Her friend Helen, the wife of Judge Wright, tried to calm her nerves over lunch before the doctor's appointment by saying it was probably just a sore throat. Brennan worried that it was something more serious. And when Marjorie's doctor called Brennan's chambers, his worst fears were confirmed. The diagnosis was advanced throat cancer.

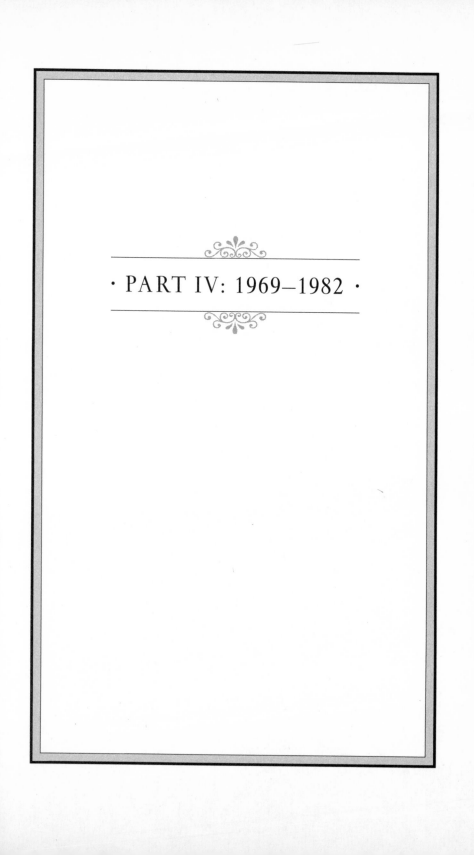

· PART IV: 1969–1982 ·

14

NEW CHALLENGES

B RENNAN FACED TWO major challenges on the eve of the Court's 1969–70 term: a new chief justice and his wife's potentially terminal cancer, and the early signs for both were not encouraging.

It had not taken long for Burger to irritate Brennan and some of the six other justices. (The ninth seat remained vacant, awaiting Senate consideration of President Nixon's nominee to replace Fortas, Judge Clement Haynsworth of the Fourth Circuit.) Word reached them during the summer recess that Burger intended to put their conference room to his personal use, as a ceremonial office to host visiting dignitaries. The justices, already dispersed around the country, gossiped about the news from afar. Surprisingly, none seemed angrier than Harlan, the gentlemanly justice not usually prone to outbursts. He called Black from his Connecticut vacation home to vent his fury.

Brennan was less angry than troubled about what the conference room appropriation foretold about Burger's view of his status as chief justice. Brennan had greatly admired Earl Warren, who had seemed embarrassed to be the only justice provided with a government car, for seeing himself as merely first among equals. Brennan appreciated that Warren vigorously opposed increasing the supplement in pay the chief justice received from $500 to $2,500. Now, Warren's successor was unilaterally trying to turn the justices' inner sanctum into his personal annex. The grumblings among his new colleagues prompted Burger to back off, but only partway. He still moved an antique desk into the conference room for his own use.

Nonetheless, Brennan kept trying to give the new chief justice the benefit of the doubt. When his clerks said anything disparaging about Burger over morning coffee, Brennan defended the new chief. Similarly, he returned from lunch at Kronheim's and told his clerks that Bazelon was exaggerating how awful his former colleague could be. Brennan started out treating Burger quite formally, relying on written memos rather than personal chats. But after a few weeks of beginning his letters to Burger "Dear Chief Justice," Brennan reverted to the more familiar "Dear Chief," the same term he had used with Vanderbilt and Warren.

Burger, for his part, showed little early warmth toward Brennan. He happened to stop by Brennan's chambers one day over the summer and found the justice absent. While chatting cordially for a few minutes with Robert Weinberg, who was wrapping up his clerkship that summer, Burger caught a glimpse of the chambers' outer room. Brennan's clerks had hung a poster of African American athletes raising their fists in a Black Power salute during a medal ceremony at the 1968 Olympics; a rubber-mask caricature of President Nixon worn by protestors at an inaugural demonstration earlier in the year was also on display. Brennan's secretary, Mary Fowler, had not much cared for these decorations, and had dragged Brennan out of his chambers to object. Brennan had just shrugged and muttered something about the First Amendment. For Burger, the fact that Brennan would sanction such displays probably only reinforced his fears about his new colleague's liberal leanings.

Forming a relationship with the new chief justice was an issue overshadowed by Brennan's worries about Marjorie. In the weeks since her initial diagnosis, Marjorie's doctors warned they might need to remove part of her jaw in order to excise the cancer lodged in her salivary glands. She was scheduled to undergo surgery on October 23. Brennan had told family members, friends, and colleagues at the Court about the diagnosis. But he did so in the understated way he always shared difficult news, one that betrayed none of the depth of his own concerns. Contrary to his public image as the stereotypical happy Irishman, Brennan was a worrier, particularly when it came to his family. Now he feared that his wife of forty-one years might lose part of her face—or not survive at all. He was loath to burden his clerks with his fears, although they could not help but notice him popping antacids to calm his stomach.

On the day of her surgery, Brennan paced anxiously in the hospital waiting room. He had given up one potential distraction. Doctors were not sure what had caused Marjorie's cancer, but Brennan suspected her long-time smoking habit was a factor, and he quit his own habit cold turkey almost immediately after her diagnosis. The surgery went better than Brennan feared. Marjorie's doctors did not have to remove any part of her jaw. Justice Black's wife, Elizabeth, after getting a report from Mary Fowler, wrote in her diary, "They were reasonably hopeful they got it all. Praise the Lord!"

WHAT BRENNAN DID have to distract him from Marjorie's surgery was his work on the Court, which continued that day without him. Burger made note of Brennan's absence but did not offer any explanation as the justices took up an emergency appeal by fourteen Mississippi school districts seeking to delay a federal judge's order to desegregate their classrooms immediately.

What constituted the proper pace and extent of school desegregation was a question the Court had largely sidestepped in the decade since Brennan's bold declarations in the Little Rock case. Southern schools had proven endlessly creative in the intervening years as they sought to forestall the mixing of black and white students. The justices had knocked down the most flagrantly obstructionist tactics during the early 1960s: closing public schools entirely or funding all-white private schools.

For the most part, though, the Court seemed content to leave the burden of ruling on most other delay tactics to lower federal court judges. Those judges varied widely in their response to the Court's desegregation edict in *Brown*. The Fifth Circuit, which then considered cases emanating from Alabama, Florida, Georgia, Louisiana, Mississippi, and Texas, pressed vigorously for desegregation under the leadership of Chief Judge Elbert Tuttle. But the Fourth Circuit, which encompassed Maryland, North Carolina, South Carolina, Virginia, and West Virginia, had embraced a view that the Constitution forbids discrimination but does not require integration. The Fourth Circuit gave its blessing to so-called freedom of choice plans as an acceptable means to desegregate. Theoretically, these plans allowed black and white students to attend any school in a district that had room for them. The reality was that black parents, who feared losing their jobs — or worse — as retribution, felt very little freedom to choose to enroll their children in predominantly white schools.

The seemingly glacial pace of school desegregation began to pick up only after the passage of the 1964 Civil Rights Act. The law empowered the Justice Department to bring lawsuits against segregated school districts and to strip them of federal funding. The passage of a major elementary and secondary school education act the following year, which included significant funding for schools, had given that threat real teeth. But the guidelines adopted by the Department of Health, Education, and Welfare for what constituted acceptable desegregation remained quite lax. By 1968, a full decade after the Little Rock case, Brennan and his fellow justices were growing exasperated with foot-dragging among many southern judges.

Brennan gave voice to that frustration in 1968 when the Court had considered the case of *Green v. County School Board of New Kent County*, which finally addressed southern "freedom of choice" plans. New Kent County was a rural district just east of Richmond, Virginia, accused of segregating its two schools. The county's population of forty-five hundred included roughly equal numbers of whites and blacks who lived interspersed with one another, yet students were assigned according to their race to separate schools that housed both elementary and high school classes. The county school board, fearing loss of federal funding after being sued, adopted a freedom of choice plan that allowed students to decide which school they attended. But in three years, not a single white student chose to attend the all-black school. And although 115 African Americans enrolled at the white school, 85 percent of black students still attended the all-black school.

The justices happened to have heard the case the day before Martin Luther King Jr.'s assassination, and voted on it the morning after, by which time the rioting had begun in Washington. Brennan wrote a forceful opinion that left little doubt where the justices stood. Adopting a freedom of choice plan was not enough. School districts had to take affirmative steps now to desegregate their schools. For extra emphasis, Brennan chose to italicize the word "now" at the suggestion of his clerk that term, Raymond Fisher. As in the Little Rock case, however, Brennan studiously avoided using the word "integration." Brennan's decision particularly pleased Warren, who had written the *Brown* opinion. "When this opinion is handed down, the traffic light will have changed from Brown to Green. Amen!" Warren wrote him. The South immediately grasped the decision's significance. Georgia governor Lester Maddox lowered state flags to half-mast and ordered an official day of mourning.

In rural New Kent County, where blacks and whites were spread throughout the community and there were only two schools, Brennan's decision in *Green* could lead immediately to action. As Brennan suggested in a footnote, the district could simply divide the county into two geographical zones or designate one school for elementary students and the other for high school students. Desegregating schools became more complicated in urban settings, where whites and blacks often lived far apart in segregated neighborhoods. Mixing black and white students in residentially segregated cities would require busing students to schools outside their own neighborhoods. Some northern liberal college towns such as Berkeley, California, had started busing students as a means to integrate in the mid-1960s without incident. But the prospect of involuntary busing of students elsewhere sparked furious protests among parents. In March 1968, a bomb was thrown through the window of an elementary school in Chicago's all-white Northwest Side two hours before 249 African American elementary school students were to start being bused to eight schools in the area.

Brennan got a sense of how much resistance court-mandated busing could generate in the North in August 1969. Federal judges had approved desegregation plans in Denver and Oklahoma City that would require the busing of thousands of students when classes began that fall. Both school districts appealed, and the U.S. Court of Appeals for the Tenth Circuit blocked the plans. Brennan wound up handling both cases, instead of Byron White, the justice who normally would have done so since he typically handled appeals from the Tenth Circuit. That fall, the *New York Times* noted that "the school bus has come to represent for thousands of people the stupid, clumsy, inept attempt by a heavy-handed bureaucracy to force school integration, a problem they believe only time can solve." But Brennan, fearful that the momentum for desegregation was slowing, viewed busing as a reasonable solution. He issued orders reversing the Court of Appeals' rulings, setting the stage for busing to begin in both cities. Repeating his admonition to school boards fifteen months earlier in *Green,*

Brennan wrote in the Denver order, "The burden on a school board today is to come forward with a plan that promises realistically to work and promises realistically to work *now.*"

A few weeks later, with Brennan absent for Marjorie's surgery, the justices faced another attempt to delay a desegregation order, this time back in the South. The fourteen Mississippi school districts seeking relief found an ally in the White House. President Nixon had won election one year earlier in part by denouncing forced school busing and tacitly promising the South to slow the pace of desegregation. Nixon administration lawyers persuaded the Fifth Circuit to delay implementing the desegregation order until at least December by arguing that "chaos and confusion" would result if integration occurred immediately. That argument was not well received by Justice Black, who considered the case first, as the justice who heard emergency appeals from that circuit. Black wrote, "There is no longer the slightest excuse, reason or justification" for delay. He was in favor of the full Court considering the NAACP Legal Defense Fund's argument that the request should be rejected.

Alexander v. Holmes County Board of Education was the most important case the Court had heard since Burger became chief justice. It presented him an opportunity to influence an area of law considered his predecessor's most enduring contribution. Brennan saw the case as yet another opportunity to make clear the Court would not accept further delays in desegregation, even if encouraged by the Nixon White House. And although Brennan missed the oral argument due to Marjorie's surgery, he had no intention of absenting himself from the case. During the unusually long two-hour oral argument, Burger noted that Brennan would participate in the case on the basis of the transcript. The next day, as Marjorie recovered in the hospital, Brennan returned to the Court to attend the weekly conference.

A majority of the justices agreed that they needed to reverse the Court of Appeals' ruling, but the question remained how much time to give the schools. At one extreme, Black made clear he would never again join an opinion that used the phrase "all deliberate speed." Douglas and Brennan were ready to be a little more flexible, giving the school districts additional time to implement whatever the Court of Appeals approved. At the other end of the spectrum was Harlan, who found support among the other justices for the idea that they needed to take note of the practical difficulties involved in desegregating immediately. The conversation ended without any consensus and Burger said he would prepare a draft himself.

The result, delivered to the home of each justice the next day, on Saturday, troubled Brennan. It was more than the fact that Burger indicated in his cover letter that he had privately consulted with Harlan and White. Brennan, the former chief justice's confidant, had been frozen out of Burger's inner circle during their first major case together. "It was clear he wasn't the quarterback anymore," one of Brennan's clerks recalled. Even more problematic was the substance of Burger's opinion, which seemed to leave the school districts too much wiggle room by setting an indeterminate deadline of "at the earliest possible time." On Sunday morning, Brennan called Black about a potential response, and then started drafting a revision in longhand on a lined pad. After reiterating that desegregation must occur now, Brennan directed the Court of Appeals to enter an order "immediately" by October 30 and barred the District Court from interfering. Brennan read the resulting draft over the phone to Black's secretary, and Black soon circulated a draft that afternoon to the other justices' homes that incorporated most of Brennan's suggestions.

Burger presented his own revisions when the justices met Monday morning. He suggested that the schools had a duty to desegregate "forthwith" but did not go far enough in Brennan's view in repudiating "all deliberate speed." The next version Burger circulated that afternoon proved even more unpalatable. Brennan thought Burger wasted too much space stating the facts. Brennan had made that same beginner's error in his first draft in the Little Rock case. He thought Burger's opinion still lacked a concrete deadline and further undermined its finality by referring to "interim" relief. Other justices also had concerns about Burger's product, which gave Brennan a chance to step in with a more palatable alternative. The question was how to do so. A year earlier, he would have avoided the appearance of undercutting Warren's authority by sharing his concerns in private. Now, he had to act even more gingerly. He sent his draft to Burger along with a cover letter that explained he hoped to "remove the impression of HEW and the Justice Department that the standard of 'all deliberate speed' retains some vitality." "I fear," Brennan wrote, "that message is obscured by your proposed opinion." Brennan's preamble plainly stated that "all deliberate speed" was no longer the applicable constitutional standard. He set no specific deadline but said compliance had to be "immediate and final."

Other justices would circulate alternatives, but five would soon indicate support for Brennan's version.

With the votes lining up behind Brennan, Burger visited his chambers that afternoon to talk face-to-face. He agreed on a revision that largely incorporated Brennan's language. The six-paragraph opinion directed the school districts to "begin immediately to operate as unitary school systems." Burger circulated the result the next morning on October 29. "In some respects, it resembles the proverbial 'horse put together by committee,' with a camel as the end result," Burger wrote. What he did not say was that the final result looked more like Brennan's blueprint for a camel than his own. The first major case of Burger's tenure had come out Brennan's way. It proved to be the first of many instances where Burger was unable to marshal a court for his position, leaving room for Brennan to fill the resulting leadership void. As in the Little Rock case, no one outside the Court had any idea of what had transpired.

The Court issued a per curiam opinion that listed no individual author. In *Green* and now *Alexander,* the Court had spoken clearly and unambiguously: delay was no longer an option. The Court did not explain how far school districts needed to go in integrating their schools, what constituted sufficient ratios of white and black students, and whether they were liable if government policies did not cause segregation. The united front in school-desegregation cases first established by Warren in *Brown* had begun to fray within the Court, although, this time, all the justices signed on despite their reservations.

BRENNAN FELT UNDERSTANDABLY relieved when Marjorie finally left the hospital in mid-November. But while she had not required radical surgery, her recovery proved more difficult than expected. She could still eat only with a feeding tube. "It was an ugly business," Brennan confided to the Weigels in a November 17, 1969, letter. "There will be an extensive period of convalescence and I am afraid of much travail for her." As for a prognosis, Brennan wrote that her doctors "would only say there was a 'reasonable probability'" that she would recover. Brennan kept distracting himself with work, although he spent less time at the Court. He started leaving for home in the later afternoon in order to be with Marjorie. Brennan could not entirely hide from his clerks the toll his wife's illness was taking on him. "He did not take his eye off the ball after his wife got sick but the exuberance was gone," said Robert Weinberg, who clerked for Brennan during the 1968–69 term.

Nancy and her fiancé, Tim Phelps, in part due to Marjorie's precarious health, decided to squeeze their wedding between his completion of Army basic training and the start of his study at the Army's language school in Monterey, California. They set the wedding for December 27, 1969 — about a year and a half ahead of their original plan. With Marjorie so weakened by illness, the burden of planning this last-minute affair fell entirely on Nancy and Brennan. Marjorie joined them only to pick up Nancy's cream-colored gown. Nancy selected the music and the venue. She chose to hold the ceremony at Epiphany Church, the modest Catholic church where Brennan took Nancy to watch the annual blessing of the animals when she was a little girl. The reception would follow at Anderson House, an elegant nineteenth-century Beaux Arts mansion near Dupont Circle. Brennan was responsible for the flowers and decided whom to invite.

Following Marjorie's wishes, the family planned a big wedding, the kind of affair she did not have when she eloped at roughly the same age. The guest list ran to thirty-five pages. In addition to family, the Brennans invited close friends in Washington like the Bazelons and Kronheim, and clerks and colleagues past and present. Nancy and Tim convinced Brennan to overlook his lingering anger and invite Fortas. There were also legal luminaries such as Erwin Griswold, the former Harvard Law School dean, who was now solicitor general, and Washington dignitaries such as Clark Clifford and General Maxwell Taylor. "This was not a family occasion," said W. Taylor Reveley III, one of his clerks that term. "It was a high society event." On the wedding day, everything went off without a hitch — except for the weather. A massive snowstorm dumped several inches of snow on the nation's capital and more than a foot on the suburbs. The storm closed airports and roads from Washington to New York, preventing Brennan's brother Frank and sister Betty as well as former justice Goldberg from attending.

After the wedding, Nancy and Tim headed for a truncated honeymoon in California before he began his language training in January. Nancy opted to stay with him in Monterey rather than returning to the University of Pennsylvania for her junior year of college. She planned to finish her last two years of study at the Monterey Institute of Foreign Studies. So she would be three thousand miles away in January 1970 when Brennan learned that Marjorie would require yet another round of surgery. Brennan called Marjorie's friend Alice Knight, an artist who lived in Westport, Connecticut, and asked her to come down to Washington to be with her before the surgery. Knight arrived in Washington braced for the worst. No one expected Marjorie to survive much longer. Still, she was shocked by the sight of Marjorie drinking vodka through a tube in her throat to ease the pain. The cancer diagnosis and the aftereffects of surgery, which left her unable to eat normally, had not ended Marjorie's drinking. Brennan, watching helplessly as his wife suffered, did not feel he was in any position to stop her. "I don't think he liked it but there was nothing he could do about it," Knight recalled.

BRENNAN DID NOT realize it at the time, but as 1970 began, he was on the verge of announcing what he would later consider perhaps the proudest achievement of his entire tenure on the Court. At issue in the case, *Goldberg v. Kelly*, was what kinds of protections government agencies must afford welfare recipients before cutting off their benefits. Several cases aimed at expanding the rights of welfare recipients had reached the Court in recent years due to the efforts of a new cadre of poverty lawyers. These lawyers, based at Mobilization for Youth (MFY), a social service agency on Manhattan's Lower East Side, and at the Center on Social Welfare Policy and Law at Columbia University, looked to the NAACP Legal Defense Fund as a model for using law as an instrument of social change. Their concerted litigation strategy was developed at a time of broad rethinking of how best to help the poor. For the first time, President Johnson's Great Society began funding legal services for the poor in noncriminal cases through the Office of Economic Opportunity. Welfare recipients, mostly African American women, organized themselves and began asserting their rights too.

Instead of helping just individual recipients, the poverty lawyers at MFY and the Center on Social Welfare Policy set out to target a broad range of welfare-agency practices designed to detect fraud or ineligibility. Such welfare polices stripped recipients of their privacy and sense of security by threatening the sudden suspension of benefits. One of the most egregious practices in some states was the midnight raid on the homes of recipients of Aid to Families with Dependent Children (AFDC). The premise was that the presence of a man in the home of a woman receiving

AFDC payments cast doubt on her need for financial assistance. Raiders rarely had search warrants, but recipients were advised that if they did not open their doors, their benefits would be terminated. The poverty lawyers at the Center on Social Welfare Policy sought to protect recipients against that kind of search as well as to protect their freedom to move between states. The most ambitious lawyers envisioned eventually establishing a constitutional "right to live," guaranteeing that every American receive a minimum level of support.

The first case to reach the Supreme Court involved rules barring the presence of men other than a father in a recipient's household. The justices unanimously rejected that rule in 1968. The following year, the Court addressed the question of whether a state could require recipients to have lived in the state for a minimum period of time before qualifying for welfare benefits. The case, *Shapiro v. Thompson,* involved a nineteen-year-old pregnant mother of a young son who moved in 1966 from Massachusetts to Connecticut to be with her mother. She was denied aid due to Connecticut's one-year residency requirement. Brennan wrote an opinion for the Court rejecting such residency requirements as violating the Fourteenth Amendment's equal protection clause. Brennan said the effect of the waiting period was "to create two classes of needy resident families" indistinguishable except for how long they lived in the state. "On the basis of this sole difference, the first class is granted, and the second class is denied, welfare aid upon which may depend the ability of the families to obtain the very means to subsist — food, shelter, and other necessities of life."

Brennan had inserted into the draft written by his clerks the phrase "very means to subsist," insisting on keeping it there even after his clerks warned it might cost them the votes of other justices. The language was an important recognition by Brennan and the Court that the issue was not simply about public charity, handouts, or government benefits, the pejorative terms used to describe welfare programs; rather, Brennan recognized, the issue was about basic subsistence — the ability of individuals to survive. Framing the issue that way, which built on the arguments of the welfare-rights lawyers, made the stakes greater. Because the regulation touched "on the fundamental right of interstate movement," Brennan applied a higher level of scrutiny, which required that a government regulation could be upheld only if it promoted a compelling state interest. Simply deterring an indigent from moving did not satisfy that test, he wrote, given the historical value placed on the freedom to travel (although no such right to travel is mentioned expressly in the Constitution). Critics suggested that the decision created incentives for migration to benefit-rich states, which eventually prompted those states to reduce their benefits in order to curb the inflow.

The poverty lawyers next sought to expand the procedural protections welfare recipients must receive before their benefits are terminated. In the mid-1960s, federal law and federal and state regulations required that welfare recipients receive a "fair hearing" when they were turned down for benefits or were thrown off the welfare rolls for alleged ineligibility. Yet few social service administrators knew recipients were entitled to a hearing. Even when a recipient received one, benefits had usually already been discontinued, leaving recipients with no money for food or shelter for weeks or months. In New York, state law required no proof of notice or hearing prior to the suspension of benefits. If the state subsequently found it had made a mistake and payments were reinstated, the state would only pay up to two months of benefits retroactively, even in cases where the suspension period had lasted substantially longer.

Welfare benefits had traditionally been treated as a gift or privilege rather than something anyone was entitled to as a right. The welfare-rights lawyers needed, then, to find some legal basis for arguing that government agencies had violated recipients' constitutional rights by depriving them of a hearing. The attorneys balked at arguing for a "right to live" that might require the federal government to guarantee a minimum standard of living to all. Instead, they decided to focus on convincing judges that once eligibility is established, welfare benefits must be dispensed in accordance with the protections afforded in the Constitution. In making the case for formal notice and hearings, welfare lawyers argued that denying welfare recipients violated the constitutional protections afforded by the Fourteenth Amendment's due process clause. But that clause only applied where a state deprived an individual of "life, liberty or property." If government benefits continued to be treated as a privilege, the requirements of due process would not apply. Judges would need to accept the still-novel idea that welfare constituted a form of property.

The idea of classifying welfare as a form of property had just begun to gain currency in legal academia. In 1964 Charles A. Reich, a Yale Law School professor, argued in a widely read article in the *Yale Law Jour-*

nal that government benefits, from licenses to welfare checks, should be viewed as private property. "It is time to see," Reich wrote, "that the 'privilege' or 'gratuity' concept, as applied to wealth dispensed by government is not much different from the absolute right of ownership that private capital once invoked to justify arbitrary power over employees and the public." Brennan — or at least one of his clerks who helped write his speeches — clearly read Reich's article. A year later, Brennan cited Reich in an address at George Washington University Law School in which he argued for an updated conception of property. Brennan noted that much had changed from a century earlier when "freedom and dignity found meaningful protection in the institution of real property." In modern America, Brennan said, "to a growing extent, economic existence now depends on less certain relationships with government — licenses, employment, contracts, unemployment benefits, welfare and the like." He also expressed concern about "arbitrary action by government officers, especially when it is camouflaged in bureaucratic complexity, as is so often the case." He urged the law students present to get involved in legal-assistance efforts, since "we all know that claims to be made before agencies are apt to be won or lost at the level of the first bureaucrat."

Brennan, in retrospect, insisted he was acutely concerned by the late 1960s about the termination of welfare benefits without a hearing. "Once they lost these checks, they were really in a desperate way," Brennan recalled. "I thought that was unfair unless they had both an opportunity to be heard and . . . an explanation of why." Brennan remembered looking for the ideal vehicle for addressing the issue as he culled through the cert. petitions arriving at the Court. In late 1967, lawyers at MFY and the Center did not know about Brennan's concerns but began watching for clients to enable them to file just the kind of case he was awaiting. The lawyers targeted New York, based on the theory that its state and city officials would concede that the due process clause applied and the issue would simply be how much due process welfare recipients should receive.

On January 24, 1968, John Kelly, a twenty-nine-year-old African American living on the street, arrived at MFY's East Third Street office in Manhattan seeking help. He was greeted by a young Volunteers in Service to America (VISTA) volunteer named Peter H. Darrow. As Kelly began to tell his story, Darrow recognized he might have found just the sort of sympathetic plaintiff they needed. Kelly was the victim of a hit-and-run accident that had left him disabled, frequently hospitalized, and unable to work. He began collecting welfare in August 1967, receiving an $80.05 check every two weeks, which he used to pay for a room at the Broadway Central Hotel in lower Manhattan.

The once grand hotel itself had fallen on hard times. Occupied mostly by welfare recipients, it collapsed six years later in an accident that left four dead. But Kelly's welfare caseworker at the New York City Department of Social Services ordered him to move to even worse accommodations nearby at the Barbara Hotel, which was a notorious haven for drunks and drug addicts. Kelly had no choice but to follow his caseworker's dictates. Within a few days, Kelly found his new residence so uninhabitable that he moved in with a friend, leaving the Barbara Hotel as his mailing address so he would continue to receive his welfare benefits there. The welfare checks quickly stopped coming, and on January 8, 1968, Kelly learned from the hotel desk that his caseworker had terminated his benefits. The caseworker had also instructed the hotel to return a special check issued to Kelly for the purchase of a winter coat. Kelly was twice denied an interview when he visited the welfare office.

Darrow's supervisor at MFY, David Diamond, quickly realized this was not the case of someone trying to abuse the welfare system. During the next two days, Diamond lined up six equally sympathetic clients, including one man cut off for mismanagement of funds after he was robbed of twenty dollars and a woman whose aid for herself and her four nieces was terminated due to an erroneous report that she had failed to disclose earned income. This woman and her nieces wound up in a hospital emergency room after eating spoiled food. Five days after Kelly had first arrived at the MFY office, the lawsuit was filed in federal District Court in Manhattan.

As hoped, the city and state did concede that recipients should receive a review prior to their benefits being terminated. But the two levels of government disagreed about what they must offer welfare recipients. In the middle of the lawsuit, state officials adopted new regulations that required an administrative hearing prior to the termination of benefits. New York City opted for a more modest procedure due to concerns about the costs of hiring hearing officers, stenographers, and clerks. Recipients would receive seven days' notice and get a chance to submit written evidence under the city plan, but not receive a hearing where they could be heard or present their case orally. In November 1968 a three-judge U.S. District Court issued a unanimous opinion that upheld the state procedure but said the New York City plan violated the Fourteenth Amendment's guarantee of due process.

New York City appealed the decision and the case went directly to the Supreme Court during the spring of 1969. Brennan later recalled that he flagged the case while reading through the cert. petitions as one that presented the issue exactly as he hoped. When the case was first reviewed by the justices in April 1969, Brennan advocated the unusually truncated approach of affirming the District Court opinion without briefs or hearing oral argument. That was because this was during the period after Fortas's failed nomination as chief justice. Brennan likely knew that if they heard the case it would almost certainly be held over to the next term under the new chief to be named by President Nixon. He would readily have accepted the less significant value as precedent of a brief order summarily affirming the lower court's opinion instead of gambling on finding five votes for a full-blown discussion of the issue the following term. But four other justices did vote to hear the case, which was not surprising given its potential significance. The case was held over for the 1969–70 term.

The eight-person Court heard oral arguments in the case on October 13, 1969, along with a related case from California, and the justices discussed them both together four days later at their weekly conference. Burger argued that existing procedures were adequate and that the local government deserved some leeway. He found support for his position from Black and Stewart. A majority of five sided with Brennan in voting to uphold the District Court's opinion, although they disagreed about how far to go. Douglas argued that welfare deserved the full protections afforded other forms of property, comparing it to a radio or television license. Harlan argued it was an entitlement rather than a gratuity, but he did not think recipients should be given all the procedural protections afforded during a trial.

Brennan suggested that welfare recipients should receive more due process than Harlan wanted, including a right of confrontation. White and Marshall seemed inclined to support Harlan's more limited hearing requirements. With Burger in the minority, it fell to Douglas as the senior associate justice to assign the opinion. He passed Brennan a note during conference on October 17 asking him if he would take the assignment. Despite his interest in the issue, Brennan was reluctant at first, for strategic reasons. "I'd have to write it more narrowly than you and I might like," Brennan wrote back on the bottom of Douglas's note. "Maybe it would be best to let John [Harlan] do it + leave us free to join him + write more broadly." Douglas disagreed, assigning the decision to Brennan to craft something that could hold their majority together.

Brennan and his clerks needed to find a way to classify welfare benefits so that due process applied but without losing Harlan and White, who were not prepared to treat government programs fully like other property. The first draft written by Brennan's clerks included a footnote that read, "It is probably unrealistic today to deny that welfare entitlements constitute 'property.'" But that language was toned down by the time Brennan circulated his draft to other chambers, to read, "It may be realistic today to regard welfare entitlements as more like 'property' than a 'gratuity.'" The footnote also quoted from Professor Reich's law review article for support.

Brennan trimmed but did not entirely excise a passage written by his clerk, W. Taylor Reveley III, which blamed the plight of the poor on larger societal forces that they could not control, including technological change and economic policy. Reveley asserted that the manner in which society was organized virtually compelled the sacrifice of a segment of the population and that welfare was not charity but rather the means "for treating a disorder inherent in our society." As a result, he argued, government "has an overriding interest in providing uninterrupted assistance to the eligible, both to help maintain the dignity and well-being of a large segment of the population and to protect against the societal malaise that may flow from a widespread sense of unjustified frustration and insecurity." Brennan did not write that language and had never suffered from that kind of poverty growing up. This was another area of law, like race, where personal experience did not fuel his empathy. Still, the passage written by his clerk comported with the economic worldview of Brennan's father, what Brennan himself had seen in Depression-era Newark, and the importance he placed on protecting people's human dignity.

When Brennan circulated the opinion to other justices on November 24, 1969, both White and Harlan objected to its discussion of poverty. Harlan labeled it "offensive," and White made clear he could not accept it. After talking privately with White, Brennan circulated a new version focused less on societal blame and more on the importance of values of self-sufficiency and patriotism. Welfare could "help bring within the reach of the poor the same opportunities that are available to others to participate meaningfully in the life of the community." The new language sounded more like White than Brennan, although the original reference to dignity did survive. The changes satisfied White, who wrote Brennan on December 2 to say he would join the opinion. Douglas and Marshall had joined a week earlier, while Burger and Black both indicated they planned to dissent. That left Brennan with only two possibilities for picking up a fifth vote: Stewart or Harlan. Neither seemed particularly enthusiastic. But Brennan had long experience successfully accommodating both in big cases.

Harlan laid out his concerns in a two-page single-spaced letter requesting five changes. He was particularly wary about language indicating that the Court was ruling only on the procedural fairness required by the due process clause, rather than on whether there might be a substantive due process right to receive welfare. Even this passing allusion to the right to receive welfare left Harlan uncomfortable. He had good reason. In the years to come, many of Brennan's colleagues learned to watch for the seemingly innocuous casual statement or footnote — seeds that would be exploited to their logical extreme in a later case. Brennan would have been delighted to lay the groundwork for recognizing a substantive due process right to receive welfare benefits if it was essential for the recipients' survival. But that was less important than achieving his bottom-line goal of recognizing that the due process clause protected welfare recipients. Brennan also worked to address Harlan's concerns about repeated references to due process requiring a "trial-type" hearing. Brennan substituted the more vague term "evidentiary hearing," which was one of Harlan's suggested alternatives. By December 16, Brennan had accommodated Harlan enough that he agreed to join the opinion.

Brennan had his fifth vote for a ruling laying out much of what he wanted, in an opinion that afforded welfare recipients substantial new rights. After being given fair written notice, they had to be provided a chance to be heard in person by "an impartial decision maker," and to cross-examine witnesses testifying against them. They had the right to bring a lawyer to the hearing, although, unlike criminal cases, the government was not required to provide one for them. After the hearing, the decision makers had to put their rulings in writing and provide the reasons for cutting off benefits.

Brennan could do nothing to win over Black, his erstwhile ally and the justice who had grown closest to Harlan as the two aging men's health continued to deteriorate. Black was in a high state of agitation about the case as he neared his eighty-fourth birthday that December. He underlined much of Brennan's draft in pencil as objectionable and filled the margins with angry comments. Black woke up two nights in a row, a dissent forming in his mind. Brennan's opinion only reinforced his belief that the remaining members of his old bloc of allies went too far in interpreting the Constitution in line with their preferences. They were too willing to find rights that did not exist or to extend existing rights to situations they did not really cover. He was so riled up he needed a drink to fall back asleep. The old fire was back in his belly, his wife observed. Black wrote out his dissent over his Christmas vacation in Florida and circulated it to his colleagues after returning to Washington in January. "It is obvious," Black wrote, "that today's result does not depend on the language of the Constitution itself or the principles of other decisions but solely on the collective judgment of the majority as to what would be a fair and humane procedure in this case."

Getting that dissent off his chest did not ease Black's fury. Brennan and his clerks suspected Black held up the announcement of the decision for another month because he disliked the result so intensely. Finally, Black relented, and the result was announced on March 23, 1970. It was an important enough occasion that Black's wife as well as Marjorie were in attendance. Black was still furious when he read his dissent from the bench, departing from the text to declare extemporaneously that welfare is a "gratuity" that is "nice for those who do not work but receive payments from the government." The conservative columnist James J. Kilpatrick praised Black's dissent and noted with some satisfaction how much Black was sounding like his old foe, Frankfurter.

The decision was front-page news in both the New York Times and Washington Post, both of which noted its broad potential impact throughout the country. It received less favorable coverage in the New York Daily News, which catered more to the city's blue-collar workers. As one New York City steelworker told journalist Pete Hamill in 1969 before the decision came down, "I pick up a paper and read about a million people on welfare in New York . . . or some fat welfare bitch demanding you know — not asking — demanding — a credit card at Korvette's . . . You know you see that and you want to go out and strangle someone." The gap separating Justice Brennan from the sort of working-class Irish Catholics among whom he grew up would only widen as the 1970s progressed.

Public dissatisfaction about welfare continued to fester for another quarter century, but critics could not continue to blame the Court. Brennan's decision quickly proved to be the high-water mark for the welfare-rights legal campaign. Only two weeks later, the Court upheld the practice of setting a ceiling on benefits, no matter the size of a family or its particular needs. The Court also upheld the authority of welfare agencies to conduct unannounced inspections of recipients' homes without a warrant and to pay different benefits to different categories of recipients. The Court proved equally parsimonious about granting due process rights to those challenging the termination of other forms of government benefits or jobs. The protections of due process would be required before revoking a driver's license essential to a person's livelihood, terminating parole, or evicting residents from a public housing project. But the Court, over Brennan's dissent, declared that no hearing was necessary before cutting off disability payments, firing federal civil service workers, or terminating an untenured assistant professor at a state university.

Nonetheless, in the years to come, interest in Brennan's decision only grew as the implications resonated in areas of law well beyond welfare. In academic circles, the ruling had a life of its own, igniting a prolific debate about the meaning of both property and due process under the Constitution. "This deceptively simple decision turned out to be a critically important one," Justice Stephen Breyer wrote in a 1997 tribute to Brennan. "Its holding, based on easily understandable facts, suddenly brought into focus an entire field of administrative law." Fans praised the decision for sparking a due process revolution, although one of those who inspired the movement, Charles Reich, reflected in 1990 that "twenty years later, we must confront the fact that the road opened by *Goldberg v. Kelly* has not been taken. Instead there has been retreat." Judge Henry Friendly decried the "due process explosion" *Goldberg* helped spark. Critics argued that the continued vitality of the decision did more harm than good, adding expense to the welfare system. Money required to administer the hearings, some complained, came out of funds that might otherwise go toward benefits.

At the time he announced *Goldberg v. Kelly,* Brennan thought the *Sha-*

piro decision striking down minimum residency requirements would prove to be far more significant. "I had no idea [*Goldberg*] was going to be . . . probably the most important thing that came out of these chambers from me," Brennan recalled. Brennan himself would touch off a new round of debate about his decision in 1987 when he delivered a speech to the Association of the Bar of the City of New York, in which he described the decision as a triumph of passion over reason. "From this perspective," he said, "*Goldberg* can be seen as injecting passion into a system whose abstract rationality had led it astray."

NO MATTER HOW hard Brennan tried to give Burger the benefit of the doubt, the new chief justice kept giving new cause for concern early in 1970. He showed every indication of being a martinet, more focused on the minutia of managing the Court than on the cases the justices heard. A February 7, 1970, memo he circulated to the conference about print shop overtime read: "I wonder if a large part of this is not attributable to our own habits and whether as to much of it, a slight change in our habits might not eliminate most of the overtime. There are many uses for that $19,818.00."

But it was the unyielding manner in which Burger handled even minor cases that really gave Brennan the most pause. That January, the Court took up a challenge by several direct-mail marketers to a statute that allowed people who received sexually provocative mail to request that the postmaster general block the senders from mailing anything else to their address. The justices unanimously agreed to uphold the statute. But when Burger circulated his draft opinion, it included language asserting that parents had an "absolute" right to control or censor their children's mail. Brennan worried that such sweeping language, raising an issue not presented in the case, might allow parents to control even the political or religious literature their teenage children received. Harlan shared similar concerns and wrote Burger to share his "distaste for absolutes." Burger adjusted the language slightly, but not enough to satisfy Brennan. "It may be that I'd agree that parents should have this authority if we had a case presenting that question but I'd rather not pass on that until the issue is directly before us," Brennan wrote Burger.

Rather than yielding further ground on a minor point that had drawn strong objections from two of his colleagues, Burger instead grew more insistent. "I think it is essential to the opinion and if the holding doesn't mean that, it doesn't mean anything," Burger wrote. Brennan tried speaking with Burger in person, which did not help matters. He returned to his chambers and told his clerks that Burger insisted that parents ought to have the right to exercise tight control over their children. Brennan concluded that this issue tapped into a deeper issue for Burger than postal regulations; for Burger, it was a way to strike back against the kind of parental permissiveness that he felt fueled excesses among the counterculture generation of 1960s college students. Brennan believed Burger was simply misconstruing the statutory language. And when Burger announced the opinion on May 4, Brennan made his point by filing a concurring opinion joined by Douglas. He wrote, "I understand the Court to leave open the question of the right of older children to receive materials through the mail without governmental interference," and also made clear that the Court had not ruled on whether the statute could be applied to all materials and all children under the age of nineteen. Brennan's clerks felt free to sharply criticize Burger's handling of the case in the annual term history they wrote at the end of their tenure, and Brennan did not feel any compulsion to remove the criticisms.

Brennan had additional reason for concern that spring: President Nixon had nominated Burger's childhood friend to fill the vacancy open since Fortas's resignation. Nixon turned to sixty-one-year-old Harry A. Blackmun after the Senate rejected his first two nominees, Clement Haynsworth and another conservative southerner and federal appeals court judge, G. Harrold Carswell. As he read newspaper accounts of the nomination, it was easy for Brennan to see why reporters soon took to calling Burger and Blackmun the "Minnesota Twins." Growing up blocks from each other on the east side of St. Paul, they had first met at the age of five and then attended the same grade school and Sunday school.

The friendship survived when they went to different high schools and even after Blackmun headed off to Harvard for college and law school while Burger stayed behind in St. Paul. The two friends picked right back up when Blackmun returned home to Minnesota in 1932 to clerk for an Eighth Circuit judge before joining a prestigious Minneapolis law firm. Burger, as reporters liked to point out in their confirmation profiles of Blackmun, had even chosen the nominee as his best man at his 1933 wedding. (Reporters did not know that Blackmun had wired Burger twenty dollars a few days later when Burger ran out of money on his honeymoon.)

Blackmun went on to serve as the counsel for the Mayo Clinic before succeeding John B. Sanborn Jr., the Eighth Circuit judge for whom he had clerked a quarter century earlier, in 1959. Brennan could not have felt any better as he read the *New York Times'* conclusion that Blackmun "appears strikingly like Mr. Burger in judicial philosophy." Blackmun tried to distance himself a bit during his April confirmation hearing, assuring senators that he would have "no hesitation whatsoever" in disagreeing with Burger — and that the chief justice felt the same way.

Brennan could draw upon a far more modest shared history with Blackmun. Although Brennan and Blackmun did not know each other at Harvard Law School, from which they graduated a year apart, Blackmun, too, had enrolled in Professor Frankfurter's Public Utilities course. Blackmun cited Frankfurter as a model for his own judicial philosophy during his confirmation. Brennan met Blackmun when he attended the New York University summer seminar in 1960, one year after joining the Eighth Circuit as a judge. Brennan noted that shared experience when he sent Blackmun a warm congratulatory letter, although he waited to write until the day in May when Blackmun actually got confirmed by the Senate.

Brennan joked to his clerks that he was concerned that the good wishes he sent earlier to Haynsworth and Carswell immediately after their nominations were announced might have jinxed their chances. Blackmun later blandly recalled that he initially viewed Brennan as a "very pleasant, outgoing, wonderful Irish personality." Blackmun might have drawn a very different conclusion based on the letters Burger had mailed him full of criticism of Brennan for more than a decade. Blackmun and Brennan exchanged several more letters over the summer as the newest justice prepared to move to Washington and join the Court for its 1970–71 term. "Please bear with the new recruit as he struggles," Blackmun wrote. "I shall need all the instruction possible."

TWO DAYS AFTER the term ended in July 1970, the Brennans and their closest friends gathered at Justice Black's federalist-style house in Alexandria, Virginia, to celebrate Marjorie's birthday. Black and Brennan's sharp exchanges over the welfare case that winter had not affected their friendship. The Blacks had helped the Brennans celebrate their forty-second wedding anniversary in May. And now Black delivered a touching toast and said he hoped Brennan would remain on the Court for years to come.

That Marjorie was still alive at all to celebrate their anniversary and now her birthday was remarkable. She had lived long enough to see the Brennans' fourth grandchild, Bill's daughter, Alexandra, born in May. Nancy was pregnant with their fifth. Yet the months since her second surgery had provided little relief. In early May, she had begun eight weeks of cobalt treatments. Marjorie was so frightened about the treatments that Brennan took her to the hospital each day. The treatment left her so exhausted she could only get out of bed a few hours a day.

Now, nearing the end of her treatments, Marjorie stood among her friends at the Blacks' home. There were reminiscences and jokes, which gave the occasion the feel of a premature Irish wake for someone assumed to have very little time left to live. Marjorie, whose diet was now restricted to soft foods, was unable to partake of much of the fare served in her honor. Mrs. Black found it difficult to write a toast for someone she believed had only a 10 percent chance of surviving, but she managed to pen a poem in tribute to Marjorie that Justice Black read aloud. Then it was Brennan's turn to speak. He told the guests he had married Marjorie when she was twenty, and now she was sixty-three. "I love her more now than I did then," Brennan said.

15

FRUSTRATION RISING

B Y THE SPRING of 1971, Brennan did not feel much need to suppress the frustration and anger building inside his chambers. Every
new opinion seemed to confirm the fears he and his clerks shared
that the Warren Court's gains had begun to slip away.

First, Burger penned a majority opinion affirming that prosecutors
could use evidence police obtained from suspects before issuing a Miranda
warning to impeach the credibility of the suspects if they testified on their
own behalf. The opinion appalled Brennan, who feared it rewarded police
misconduct and represented just the first step in chipping away at Warren's
Miranda opinion. He wrote a dissent with uncharacteristically sharp language, declaring, "It is monstrous that courts should aid or abet the law-
breaking police officer."

Next came an opinion by Black upholding a Louisiana state law that
blocked illegitimate children from receiving a share of a parent's estate.
One of Brennan's clerks, Richard Cotton, suggested the justice quietly tell
Black how strongly he disagreed with the opinion. Brennan, who had always prided himself on compromise and had so consciously avoided pro-
voking his colleagues during the Warren years, was now in no mood to be
conciliatory. "Let's blow them out of the water," Brennan directed Cotton.
It was a pattern that would repeat itself in the years to come: Brennan and

his clerks egging each other on, rather than the justice moderating his clerks' impulses toward excess as he had done in the past. Cotton drafted just the sort of fiery dissent Brennan had in mind, accusing the majority of upholding "the untenable and discredited moral prejudice of bygone centuries which vindictively punished not only the illegitimates' parents, but also the hapless, and innocent, children." Brennan went so far as to suggest that "today's decision cannot even pretend to be a principled decision."

Then, to top it all off, Blackmun circulated a majority opinion that spring which said that the children of American citizens born abroad could lose their citizenship unless they lived continuously in the United States for five years between the ages of fourteen and twenty-eight. The opinion enraged another one of Brennan's clerks, Loftus Becker, who decided to vent his anger by writing up a sarcastic paragraph-long parody dissent for the benefit of Brennan and his fellow clerks. "Since the Court this Term has already downgraded citizens receiving public welfare and citizens having the misfortune to be illegitimate," Becker wrote, "I suppose today's decision downgrading citizens born outside the United States should have been expected." Becker left the mock dissent — formatted to look like a real one — on Cotton's desk, where Brennan discovered it the next morning. When Becker arrived, he was surprised to hear Brennan direct him to send it to the printer. Becker tried to explain he intended it as a joke for internal consumption only. "Is there anything wrong with it?" Brennan asked. When Becker said no, the dissent went off to the printer unchanged.

The unusually harsh tone of Brennan's dissents that spring was bound to catch the attention of the Supreme Court press corps. "Justice Brennan now appears to be angry, and lately has had trouble containing his hot feelings," Lyle Denniston wrote in the *Washington Star* in April 1971 after reading Brennan's dissent in the illegitimate-children case. The *New York Times*' Fred Graham singled out Brennan when he noted "the increasingly vinegary statements by justices who were mainstays of the Warren Court's liberal wing," while the *Chicago Tribune* noted that Brennan's dissents "have an angry bite to them."

The trio of contrary opinions that spring reflected Brennan's growing frustration over finding himself in the unhappy role occupied for years by Harlan: dissenter. Brennan's combined seventy-two dissenting votes in the 1970–71 and 1971–72 terms exceeded the sixty-seven he cast during the entire 1960s, and the number per term would only rise as the decade progressed. Where a decade earlier Brennan would triumphantly hold up four fingers to show his clerks the number of times he dissented in one term, now he mournfully tabulated a growing roster.

Brennan tried his best to keep his anger to himself and to stay optimistic, reluctant to give his clerks the sense that the tide had completely turned. But he did not always succeed in hiding his feelings. He often returned to his chambers after the justices' Friday conference looking noticeably deflated. Brennan liked building majorities; he harbored no ambition of becoming the Court's great dissenter. Yet in time he would grow more comfortable with his insurgent role and eventually came to enjoy the notoriety it attracted. No longer tasked by the chief justice with corralling majorities, Brennan adopted more cutting rhetoric and extreme positions, particularly on two issues about which he and Warren had disagreed: the death penalty and obscenity. His stridency sometimes undercut his own effectiveness, alienating the moderates who increasingly came to hold the balance of power.

In the spring of 1971 Brennan had good reason to feel particularly dispirited. Marjorie's cancer had returned that April, requiring a new round of radiation treatment. She was hospitalized yet again after the radiation ulcerated the wall of her larynx. For the next six months, she could eat only through a feeding tube, and her weight fell to under ninety pounds. She was in constant pain and slept so fitfully that Brennan moved to their spare bedroom in order to get a full night's rest. Marjorie rarely complained and did her best to maintain a normal life. She continued playing bridge and inviting close friends like the Bazelons over for dinners she prepared, even though she was unable to enjoy the meals herself. But she did not get out as much anymore. Even sitting through a movie could be an ordeal for her. She relied more on the telephone to connect with friends and family. The only good news was the birth of the Brennans' grandchild, Hugh's son Andrew, in early January, their third in less than a year. Hugh and his wife, Mary, lived in the Washington, D.C., area with their children, Marianne and Andrew. Bill, Georgie, and their children Billy and Alexandra lived in Princeton, New Jersey, while Nancy and her husband, Tim, and their daughter, Connie, lived in Florida. Noting that the number of their grandchildren had doubled in little more than a year, Brennan joked in a letter to the Crawleys in Ireland that, "It's a trend that I hope has now stopped (at least for awhile)."

Unable to do much to alleviate Marjorie's agonizing pain, Brennan felt compelled to spend all the time that he could with her. Having already cut off his nonwork commitments, Brennan now further constricted his hours at the Court. He no longer headed to his chambers on Saturdays, although he still worked at home that day. He allowed himself just one escape: weekday lunches at Kronheim's cafeteria, although even that spot did not feel the same anymore. What was once a clubhouse where Brennan and his fellow liberals like Bazelon and Wright basked in their victories now felt more like a last refuge. Bazelon and Wright, too, were under siege at their courthouse. Angered by their liberal criminal-procedure rulings, Congress in 1970 had stripped the D.C. Circuit of much of its jurisdiction over the District of Columbia's criminal docket, and Nixon appointees threatened their liberal majority.

Declining health proved a cause for concern at the Court that spring as well. There was no denying that Black was fading at the age of eighty-five, just a year shy of what was then the record for a justice's longevity. He suffered from chronic headaches and had grown increasingly cranky, derisively referring to his former allies Brennan, Douglas, and Marshall as the "three musketeers." Even though they disagreed more often than in the past, Brennan certainly did not welcome the prospect of Black's departure. The center of gravity seemed to shift farther from Brennan with each seat President Nixon filled.

Blackmun already appeared to be living up to his billing as Burger's "Minnesota Twin." In their first full term together, Blackmun and Burger voted the same way in sixty-nine of seventy-two of the Court's non-unanimous cases, including all but one of the criminal-procedure cases. "President Nixon has already succeeded in large part in his expressed goal of reshaping the Court," the *New York Times* noted in June 1971. Nixon would soon have the opportunity to recast the Court even further, with Black and Harlan deteriorating rapidly. The two ailing friends wound up in adjacent rooms at Bethesda Naval Hospital in the summer of 1971. Black suffered from inflamed blood vessels; Harlan from terrible back pain. Black would retire on September 17; Harlan did so six days later after learning he had cancer, delaying his announcement so he did not detract from the attention focused on his old friend. Not that Black knew of the gesture: he had suffered another stroke and lapsed into a coma before dying on September 25.

Their often-sharp disagreements on the Court in recent years did not stop Brennan from visiting Black in the hospital over the summer. He also helped Black's family plan the funeral. Given their close relationship, Brennan's son-in-law, Tim Phelps, could not understand why Brennan and Douglas joked throughout the car ride he shared with them to Black's funeral. Only later did Phelps conclude it was Brennan's way of masking the mixture of grief and concern that Black's death precipitated. Douglas, nearly seventy-three, was now the last justice who had been on the Court longer than Brennan. Harlan's health continued to deteriorate for the rest of 1971. One side of his body was paralyzed and the other racked by pain. Brennan was shocked to see how gaunt his old colleague looked when he visited Harlan's hospital room around Christmas. Two days before the year ended, Harlan died at age seventy-two.

The departures of Black and Harlan provided Nixon the extraordinarily rare opportunity to fill four seats on the Court in less than three years in office. Nixon and Burger, his handpicked chief justice, seemed poised to upend the entire Warren Court legacy. Brennan — along with most Court watchers — assumed it was only a matter of time before the conservatives captured the Court. *Time* confidently predicted in October 1971 that the Court "will turn more sharply away from the activist, innovative role as practiced under Chief Justice Earl Warren and toward a limited and cautious translation of the Constitution." And yet, as time would tell, the counterrevolution that Brennan so dreaded never entirely materialized. To be sure, the rapid advances of the Warren years in many fields of law had ended. Some would even get rolled back, much to Brennan's frustration. But the core holdings of the Warren Court would survive. What is more, Brennan would experience more new victories in areas of law such as civil rights and women's rights than he could ever realistically have expected.

Brennan's relative success during the 1970s became evident only later, but two key factors emerged early in the decade: Burger's utter ineffectiveness as chief justice, and the unexpected signs of independence by Blackmun. At the time, though, Brennan primarily experienced an overarching sense of anger about the mounting losses — and fear of worse to come — interspersed with some satisfaction over the occasional and often surprising victories. The public glimpsed Brennan's frustration with his trio of angry dissents in the spring of 1971. What those outside the Court did not learn about was his role behind the scenes in another case that term that typified the other aspect of Brennan's experience during the Burger years. Brennan helped engineer another school-desegregation victory, at the new chief justice's expense.

BRENNAN HAD BEEN visiting his daughter, Nancy, then six-months pregnant with her first child, in August 1970 when a telegram arrived from Burger. The chief justice had written each of his colleagues asking whether they wanted to interrupt their summer vacations for a special session to consider what to do about a desegregation order pending against a North Carolina school district. The justices opted not to return to Washington early, but could not avoid the case — *Swann v. Charlotte-Mecklenburg Board of Education* — or the thorny issue it presented. When the new term began in October, they almost immediately took up for the first time the question of how to desegregate a major urban area, in this case involving an enormous school district that spanned some 550 square miles. Only 2 percent of the twenty-one thousand black students in the city of Charlotte studied in schools whites attended; two-thirds were concentrated in twenty-one schools that were at least 99 percent black.

The case had followed a now-familiar pattern since being filed five years earlier. The school district had unsuccessfully tried to head off the lawsuit with a "freedom of choice" plan. The home of Julius L. Chambers, the black lawyer who filed the suit, was bombed and his office later burned down. James B. McMillan, the federal judge who ordered the busing of a quarter of the school district's students in order to achieve racial balance, was hung in effigy and denounced from church pulpits. Bomb threats and boycotts followed when the desegregation plan went into effect on the first day of school on September 9, 1970. Charlotte-Mecklenburg was hardly alone in instituting court-ordered desegregation that fall. Spurred in part by the Court's previous pronouncements in its *Alexander* and *Green* decisions, desegregation of southern schools had finally begun in earnest. The number of black students attending integrated schools in the South more than doubled, from 18 percent in 1969 to 38 percent by the spring of 1971, far exceeding the rates in the northern and western United States. At issue in *Swann v. Charlotte-Mecklenburg Board of Education* was how to desegregate a city and surrounding suburbs where blacks and whites lived in separate areas, unlike in rural communities where they were often interspersed. Simply reassigning all students to their neighborhood schools was not an option here. Neighborhood assignment would result in virtually no desegregation.

As in *Alexander,* Burger set out once again to shape the Court's decision from the start. And once again, he failed spectacularly in his attempt to build consensus around his preferred approach. Several of the justices — including Brennan — pushed back, determined not to let Burger prevail. Even before *Swann,* Burger's management style had begun to turn off many of his colleagues, who often experienced the chief justice as sneaky and heavy-handed. They had grown tired of his rambling pronouncements during conference, particularly in criminal cases, which contrasted with Warren's crisp presentations. He seemed sloppy with assignments, providing incorrect tallies of how the justices voted and assigning cases to justices who had been in the dissent. More problematic was the way he tried to manipulate assignments. Brennan had noticed he seemed willing to stay with the majority or even switch his vote solely for the purpose of keeping a case out of Brennan's hands.

Where a year earlier Brennan might have cut off clerks who badmouthed Burger, now he returned to his chambers from the weekly conference complaining about Burger's latest missteps and even parodied the chief justice for their benefit. Brennan also expressed frustration about colleagues whom he believed were trying to curry favor with the chief justice. Brennan did appreciate the more thoughtful, social side Burger often displayed. The chief justice and his wife, Vera, occasionally visited the Brennans' home to see Marjorie during her illness, bringing flowers, wine — or Burger's own homemade jams. But as with Frankfurter, Burger's kindnesses could not counterbalance the trouble he caused at the Court.

Burger's machinations in the *Swann* case began at a special conference he called on an October Saturday to discuss the case. Burger asked his colleagues to dispense with their usual practice of conducting a vote in favor of a freewheeling discussion. Seven justices spoke in favor of the desegregation order; only Burger and Black spoke against it. Nonetheless, Burger tried to take control at a subsequent discussion of the case, offering to draft an opinion that reconciled the justices' views. The result, which Burger circulated on December 8, was not well received in Brennan's chambers. Brennan viewed the opinion, which remanded the case rather than expressly affirming the District Court judge's ruling, as too sympathetic to southern school districts. He objected to language in Burger's draft such as, "It may well be that some of the problems we now face arise from viewing *Brown I* as imposing a requirement for racial balance, i.e., integration, rather than a prohibition against segregation."

Brennan believed that Burger needed to go much further in emphasizing the need to eliminate the stigmatizing effect of racial segregation. Brennan had come a long way in his thinking since the Little Rock case in 1958, when, at the advice of his neighbor, he so conscientiously avoided using the word "integration" in school-desegregation cases. Now, as Brennan explained in a memo to Burger, he had concluded that "the only way to dismantle a dual school system and remove the stigma of racial separation is to achieve substantial integration." Brennan here was following in the footsteps of John Minor Wisdom, a Fifth Circuit judge who, in a 1966 opinion, had explicitly rejected the position adopted in the Fourth Circuit that *Brown* forbade discrimination but did not require integration. Wisdom had argued that undoing the effects of past segregation required converting dual school systems "to a unitary, nonracial system — lock, stock, and barrel." Brennan believed that lower-court judges should have the discretion to determine what methods to employ to achieve integration, whether it meant gerrymandering neighborhood school districts, busing students, or changing where schools were located.

Burger knew he could expect opposition from Brennan and his liberal allies Douglas and Marshall. What proved even more significant were the concerns expressed by other justices, particularly Stewart. Now in his thirteenth term, Stewart at age fifty-six remained one of the youngest justices and perhaps the most difficult to pigeonhole. He was not guided by any deep-seated judicial philosophy and bristled at ideological labels. Stewart preferred narrow opinions that respected precedent and laid out practical standards. Yet he was also enough of a closet iconoclast to invite the leader of a group of Vietnam veterans who opposed the war to sit in the justices' reserved seats, an invitation that appalled Blackmun. Brennan always got along with Stewart, although he rarely relied on his vote. Stewart, in turn, came to view Brennan as too reflexively liberal.

But Brennan and Stewart shared a growing antipathy toward Burger. Stewart took issue with the sloppy manner in which Burger assigned cases.

As in the *Alexander* case, Stewart thought little of Burger's draft and worked up his own alternative, which he labeled a memo rather than a draft out of concern that he might anger Burger. Stewart privately circulated copies of his memo to both Brennan and Douglas, who urged him to circulate it to the full conference as a draft. They thought Stewart was in a better position to rally other justices such as Harlan and White. Stewart demurred, hesitant about being seen as dividing the Court or undercutting Burger. After years of getting less than choice assignments under Warren, Stewart had no interest in alienating the new chief justice.

During the course of four months and six drafts, Brennan and his colleagues gradually forced Burger to recast his opinion as an explicit affirmation of the desegregation order. It was largely a team effort, although Brennan proved most persistent in pressing his recommendations. On Brennan's sixty-fifth birthday, after announcing the opinion from the bench in April 1971, Burger sent a note thanking him for helping "get a solid Court" in the desegregation cases. Once again, the result looked far more similar to what Brennan sought than what Burger had ever intended. The final product was the Court's first ringing affirmation of busing as a desegregation tool. It reaffirmed the need to dismantle dual school systems where students were divided by race, and upheld the broad power of federal courts to use remedies such as busing, teacher assignment, and even statistical formulas, as long as they were not quotas.

The Court's decision in *Swann* focused on a southern school district, but its impact extended northward as judges there applied the same rationale in ordering citywide busing. For the first time, as the new school year began in August 1971, a substantial amount of school desegregation was scheduled to begin in cities outside the South and border states. The focal point of resistance to school desegregation moved northward, too, as compulsory busing became a national issue. Bull Connor, the Birmingham, Alabama, public safety commissioner, may have embodied resistance to desegregation in the 1960s. But in the 1970s the symbols of resistance were northerners like Boston's Louise Day Hicks, who helped lead the fight against desegregation. The most iconic image of racial strife from the decade proved to be a picture of a black attorney being attacked with the staff of an American flag on the plaza outside Boston's City Hall in the midst of court-ordered desegregation there.

Busing proved extremely unpopular, particularly among whites.

Seventy-seven percent of those polled in February 1972 disapproved of busing as a method of racially balancing schools. The next month, President Nixon proposed a temporary halt in busing, and it was a Republican congressman from New York named Norman Lent—rather than a southern segregationist—who took the lead in sponsoring a constitutional amendment barring it permanently. Busing became a major issue in the 1972 presidential primaries that spring, propelling Alabama governor George Wallace to victory in the Democratic primaries in both Florida and Michigan.

One month before the November 1972 presidential election, the Court took up its first northern desegregation case, one centered on Denver's schools. The issue in *Keyes v. School District No. 1* was far trickier than what the justices had previously faced. Colorado's capital and largest city had never officially segregated its schools by law, the way southern cities and states had done. The segregation in Denver involved only one neighborhood, Park Hill, rather than the city as a whole. The plaintiffs in the case had a more difficult task of proving the city's school board had promoted school desegregation in its decisions about where to build schools and how to draw neighborhood school boundaries. A federal district court judge had concluded that the school district's actions had contributed to the segregation of schools in Park Hill.

But in addition to ordering busing of students in that neighborhood, the judge also ordered busing of students in a broader swath of Denver to achieve at least some mixing of black and white students in all schools, even though there was no proof government action had caused segregation there. The U.S. Court of Appeals for the Tenth Circuit upheld the order regarding Park Hill but rejected the broader desegregation of the entire city. The case had enormous potential national implications. Residential segregation could be found in almost all northern cities, and many school boards had made at least some decisions designed to keep blacks and whites in separate schools. If northern school boards had to eliminate the direct consequences of their past discrimination and also counteract the effects of residential segregation, almost every major city would eventually have to desegregate all of its schools. That goal could only be accomplished via massive busing.

The Court's membership had undergone two important changes in the year since it heard the Charlotte school-desegregation case. President

360 · JUSTICE BRENNAN

Nixon had replaced Black and Harlan with Lewis F. Powell and William H. Rehnquist, who both joined the Court in January 1972. Brennan believed he had good reason to worry about Rehnquist, a youthful-looking forty-seven-year-old Wisconsin native who had first worked at the Court two decades earlier as a clerk for Justice Robert Jackson after graduating first in his class at Stanford Law School. Brennan had not forgotten about the 1957 article Rehnquist wrote in *U.S. News & World Report* describing how clerks' liberal biases — including an "extreme solicitude for the claims of Communists and other criminal defendants" — influenced the Court's decisions.

What emerged about Rehnquist after his nomination gave Brennan new grounds for concern, particularly about how he might vote in school-desegregation cases. As a clerk for Jackson, Rehnquist wrote a memo in which he suggested that the 1896 *Plessy v. Ferguson* decision upholding the "separate but equal" doctrine was "right and should be affirmed." After moving to Arizona to begin his legal career, Rehnquist had opposed a public-accommodations law in 1964 and written letters to the editor against an integration plan for Phoenix's schools. As head of the Justice Department's Office of Legal Counsel, Rehnquist had emerged as one of the Nixon administration's leading critics of both the civil rights movement and the Warren Court. He had spoken out in favor of government surveillance of American citizens and of reversing the *Miranda* decision. "So when he was appointed, I was alarmed to say the least," Brennan recalled later. The distrust was mutual. Rehnquist's clerk assured his boss in another case the Court heard early in 1972 that he would read over Brennan's circulation "with an eye for any omissions or unfair phraseology."

Based on resumé alone, Brennan might have had just as much reason to fear how his other new colleague, Powell, might vote in school-desegregation cases. This sixty-four-year-old could claim roots in Virginia extending back to the original Jamestown settlement. He grew up in Richmond, the former capital of the Confederacy, and attended both college and law school at Washington and Lee University in Lexington, Virginia. Powell ventured beyond the South to enroll at Harvard Law School for an extra year of study the fall after Brennan graduated, although he then turned down a job offer at a Wall Street law firm and returned home to work in Richmond. Like Brennan, he rose through the ranks of his hometown's leading law firm and eventually saw his name added to it. Also like

Brennan, he gravitated toward public service. Powell had served eleven years on Richmond's school board beginning in 1950 — including eight as chairman — and then another nine on the state board of education. During his tenure, Richmond made almost no progress in desegregating its schools. And Powell stayed mostly silent on the subject of desegregation.

Brennan had gotten to know Powell through his work for the American Bar Association, of which Powell became president in 1964. Even though Powell emerged as a national critic of the Warren Court, Brennan had come to respect him during their interactions at bar association events. So, too, did President Nixon, who first considered nominating Powell to the Court in 1969 and again two years later. Powell accepted only reluctantly, fearful he was too old and likely to suffer the same fate as Haynsworth, his friend and fellow southerner whose nomination was rejected by the Senate. In fact, Rehnquist attracted much of the fire from liberal critics, and Powell's age wound up helping him, since everyone assumed he would not serve too long anyway. Despite the objection of black lawmakers about Powell's role on Richmond's school board, his nomination sailed through the Senate.

In the Denver case, Powell approached desegregation from the perspective of a southerner. He objected to the distinction between two kinds of segregation. De jure segregation is codified into law, as was the case in the South. In contrast, de facto segregation results from other causes such as housing. That is what predominated in the rest of the country. Powell saw no point to a distinction that held the current generation of southerners responsible for the sins of their fathers in enacting segregation statutes, while no such responsibility was imposed outside the South, where the schools remained equally segregated. He was also concerned by the extent of busing unleashed in the *Swann* decision, which in some places might require elementary school-age children to travel up to twenty miles each day. "In my view there is not the slightest justification in the Constitution or any rational basis for such a travesty," Powell privately confided in a memo to his clerk. Still, Powell worried about giving voice to such opinions out of concern it would be labeled "'southern' bias, if not indeed southern 'racism.'"

After oral arguments in the Denver case in October 1972, Brennan was among the five-justice majority, and Douglas assigned the opinion to him. It was one of the best assignments Brennan had received in the three years since Burger had become chief justice. The key, Brennan knew, would be holding onto Blackmun, who had shown signs since joining the Court of being plagued by indecision. A vote by Blackmun in conference did not guarantee he would ultimately sign on to the final opinion. The loss of Blackmun's vote would flip Brennan's 5–3 majority into a 4–4 deadlock and the Circuit Court's decision would stand. (White recused himself since his former law firm represented the Denver school board.)

Brennan would have been delighted to eliminate the de jure–de facto distinction as Powell preferred but knew that Stewart objected to the idea and shelved it rather than risk losing one of his votes. Blackmun seemed reluctant to go beyond the Swann decision and did not accept the argument that a problem in one part of a school district "permeates the entire system." Brennan initially drafted a narrow opinion but soon cast that aside in favor of a more aggressive approach. He proposed that, if a substantial part of a school system was found to be purposefully segregated, then the entire school system would be required to desegregate. Where a school district could be divided into separate identifiable units, purposeful segregation in one unit would shift the burden of proof onto school authorities to prove that they did not segregate in other units.

Douglas, Stewart, and Marshall joined the opinion within a week of his November 30, 1972, circulation, giving Brennan four votes. Powell initially indicated he would hold off on committing one way or the other and then later signaled plans to concur on different grounds. Rehnquist announced his intention to dissent, a rarity in desegregation cases. Blackmun, though, remained silent for a month and then indicated in a note to the conference that he would delay making a decision pending further circulations in this and two other pending school-desegregation cases. Blackmun's unwillingness to join his opinion frustrated Brennan. He worried that Blackmun might join Powell's concurrence, which argued for eliminating the de jure–de facto distinction. So Brennan circulated a memo indicating he would drop that distinction if the majority favored doing so, although he stressed he would not do so in a way that might free schools of the "affirmative duty to desegregate."

The waiting game continued until the end of May 1973, when Burger suggested holding over the case for consideration along with a Michigan District Court's desegregation order that would require the busing of students between the city of Detroit and surrounding suburban school districts. The proposal infuriated Brennan, who believed Burger was trying to prevent him from announcing a decision in the Denver case. Brennan immediately dashed off a reply to Burger that he shared with the full conference, in which he wrote, "I most strenuously oppose" any delay and suggested the two cases were not "even remotely connected."

If anything, Brennan's opinion of Burger had fallen further since the *Swann* case. The shift was evident in his clerks' term histories, which were increasingly sprinkled with digs at the chief justice's opinions. Brennan had occasion to vent some of his growing frustration with Burger publicly, albeit in an indirect fashion, a few days before Burger circulated his memo suggesting they hold the Denver case. One of the few exceptions to Brennan's four-year-old self-imposed ban on public speeches and out-of-town appearances was speaking to the annual conference of judges in the First Circuit, for which he served as circuit justice. He used the occasion of his speech at the judges' May 23, 1973, gathering in New Hampshire to criticize a proposal by a committee appointed by Burger to reduce the Court's workload by creating a new national court of appeals that would prescreen cases. Brennan viewed culling through potential cases as a critically important part of his role as a justice, in part because it was the means by which he flagged promising strategic opportunities. He had refused to join the "cert. pool" recently established by several other justices so that their clerks could work together to screen the petitions. Brennan told the First Circuit judges that the idea of a new national court of appeals was "fundamentally unnecessary and ill-advised."

Burger and Brennan continued their heated exchange over the Denver case, but Blackmun made it moot when he circulated a memo indicating he planned to join Brennan's opinion. Brennan's clerks suspected Blackmun was put off by Burger's heavy-handed attempts to hold over the case. The press immediately picked up on the potential significance when, three weeks later, Brennan announced the decision, which Burger had ultimately decided to join. Brennan viewed the decision as an important victory.

But the forward momentum on school desegregation that began with *Brown* two decades earlier soon came to an end. And again, Blackmun's vote proved decisive. When the Court considered the Detroit case, *Milliken v. Bradley*, the following term, Blackmun joined the 5–4 majority, which held that suburban school districts could not be forced to participate in a desegregation plan with an adjacent city absent some proof that they had participated in the segregation. Given the extent of white flight to the suburbs during the previous decade, achieving any sort of racial balance would be impossible without such city-suburban busing. But the idea of suburb-to-city busing absolutely enraged parents who had fled cities in large measure so that their children could attend higher-quality schools in the suburbs. Brennan joined the dissent written by Marshall who, angry about the first setback on desegregation since *Brown,* accused the majority of sacrificing the education of urban black children for the convenience of white suburbanites. The decision did not eliminate the possibility of inter-district plans entirely, but did usher in a two-decades-long period of retrenchment and eventually abandonment of school desegregation. What intermittent victories Marshall and Brennan achieved in school-desegregation cases as the decade progressed usually required Blackmun's support.

The national outcry over busing began to ease after the Court pulled back in the Detroit case, but the northern battles over desegregation did not entirely cease. The worst northern busing crisis yet exploded a few months later in Boston, where an Irish Catholic federal District Court judge, W. Arthur Garrity Jr., had ordered the pairing of schools in the city's African American neighborhood with its most insular working-class Irish Catholic enclaves. Garrity was hung and burned in effigy, just like so many southern judges before him. Protestors bombarded him with threatening calls and hundreds staged a rally outside his house in Wellesley, an affluent Boston suburb, that October. Senator Edward Kennedy also became the target of working-class Irish Catholic rage generated by Garrity's order. Protestors pelted Kennedy with eggs and tomatoes and even punched and kicked him when he tried to address a protest rally at Boston's City Hall Plaza in September 1974.

These lawmakers and judges were excoriated as "limousine liberals" who, in the words of one antibusing leader in Boston's Roslindale neighborhood, enjoyed the security of "good jobs and big houses in snobzoned localities" while forcing "the public school workingman to face the moral crisis of our time." It was an argument echoed by conservative intellectuals such as Harvard's Nathan Glazer, who questioned why the leading advocates of busing escaped its consequences by sending their children to private schools.

That critique applied with equal strength to Brennan, given where he had chosen to live and send his children to school. And Brennan, who did more than any other Irish Catholic to facilitate school desegregation and busing, never faced the kind of protests that Kennedy — and particularly Garrity — endured. Brennan's cloistered life in Georgetown and the fact that his family back in New Jersey had long ago moved out to the suburbs, meant that he lacked the sort of long-standing ties to neighborhood and parish that bound working-class Catholics to a place like South Boston. Any frustration Garrity experienced over being put in the predicament of micromanaging the desegregation of a city's schools with too little guidance from the Supreme Court could not have been more appropriately directed than at Brennan. Yet, after all the death threats and ostracism, Garrity expressed only admiration for Brennan, whom he got to know as the justice overseeing cases coming out of the First Circuit. "I feel indebted to you every time I enter my chambers," Garrity wrote him a few years later.

ON THE DAY that Brennan, thanks to Blackmun's support, announced his majority opinion in the Denver desegregation case in June 1973, he suffered a defeat in another case of great interest because he could not win over the Minnesota Twin. The issue was the one that had bedeviled Brennan and his colleagues ever since he had joined the Court: obscenity. Since 1967, the justices had stuck mostly to issuing short summary reversals of obscenity convictions, banning only hard-core pornography. In the process, they had avoided having to address in a full opinion the fact that they still lacked anything resembling a consensus approach for dealing with obscenity. Brennan had more than once passed up the opportunity to support the liberalization of obscenity explicitly. In 1969, while a majority opinion held that a right to privacy protected the possession of obscene materials at home, Brennan instead joined Stewart's opinion grounded in the Fourth Amendment's limitations on searches and seizure. And as late as 1971, Brennan declined to be the fifth vote for liberalization and instead joined a narrow reading of that earlier decision limiting its holding to the private use of obscenity.

More recently, though, Brennan had begun to rethink the Court's approach to obscenity, just as term after term of his clerks had been unsuccessfully urging him to do for years. He had come to believe that it simply was not possible to define obscenity specifically enough so that individuals might know in advance whether they were committing a crime. Brennan concluded that his *Roth* opinion and all that followed just did not work. It is certainly worth noting that Brennan had softened his position only after the retirement of Warren, who so vehemently disliked obscenity. Brennan's rethinking came not long after a national commission appointed by President Johnson and Congress recommended lifting limits on consenting adults' access to obscene materials and maintaining restrictions only to minors and on public displays. Those surprising recommendations were poorly received by President Nixon and Congress.

Brennan first shared his change of heart with his colleagues in the spring of 1972 after the justices took up the case *Miller v. California.* The defendant in that case was convicted in a California state court of mailing unsolicited brochures full of sexually explicit pictures advertising a movie and four books. Burger proposed giving states tremendous discretion in devising their own tests to regulate obscene materials. In a May 22, 1972, memo to his colleagues, Brennan rejected Burger's proposal, arguing that it would "worsen an already intolerable mess." "I've been thinking for some time that only a drastic change in applicable constitutional principles promises a way out," he explained. Brennan indicated that he planned to write an opinion stating "in effect that it has proved impossible to separate expression concerning sex, called obscenity, from other expressions concerning sex, whether the material takes the form of words, photographs or film."

In June Brennan circulated a more detailed thirty-one-page memo, which began, "I think that the time has come when the Court should admit that the standards fashioned by it to guide administration of this Nation's obscenity laws do not work, and that we must change our constitutional approach if we are to bring stability to this area of the law." Brennan concluded that obscenity could not be "wholly suppressed," since it could not be defined with sufficient specificity to prevent encroachment on protected expression. Instead, Brennan suggested sanctioning only those laws "precisely drawn" to control its dissemination to unwilling individuals and children without parental consent. There would be no resolution in the case that spring, since the justices voted to hold it over for the following term and consider it along with several other obscenity cases.

Brennan was not optimistic as he renewed his effort to convince his colleagues to rethink the Court's approach to obscenity when the new term began in October 1972. He thought he could count on support only from Douglas, Marshall, and Stewart, who had revealed himself to favor liberalizing obscenity law in the years since 1964 when he famously declared, "I know it when I see it." That left Brennan once again in the position of searching for a fifth vote. Rather than focus on the California case held over from the previous term, he opted to concentrate his efforts on another obscenity case the justices took up that October, which had more favorable facts.

While Miller, the defendant in the California case, had mailed obscene brochures to people who had not solicited them, *Paris Adult Theatre v. Slaton* involved the prosecution of two Atlanta theater owners charged with showing obscene movies to a willing audience. Brennan knew that some of his colleagues were uneasy about the availability of obscenity to juveniles and nonconsenting adults; this case focused on the availability of sexually explicit materials to consenting adults. The only sign outside the theater said, "Atlanta's Finest Mature Feature Films" and one posted on the door warned, "Adult Theater — you must be 21 and able to prove it." Burger set the tone for consideration of the case at the justices' October 24 conference, where he compared obscenity to filth in the streets that needed to be cleaned up and deposited in garbage dumps.

As in the school-desegregation case, it soon became apparent that Blackmun was the key undecided vote. In a November 20 circulation, Blackmun indicated that Brennan's suggested new approach "has a distinct appeal," since it would "relieve the courts of much of the pornography burden." On the other hand, Blackmun wrote, "I am not certain that the Constitution requires that commercial exploiters of pornography may rot an unwilling community." After Brennan circulated a draft in early December, Blackmun replied a month later that he considered it "exceedingly well done" and that his proposed solution remained "a tempting one." But Blackmun added, "I am not certain . . . that pressures upon the judicial institutions, which you stress throughout your opinion, is to be regarded as a persuasive factor." Blackmun was leaning toward a more restrictive approach, although he indicated he would await other circulations until casting his vote.

Brennan discovered that his change in thinking about obscenity came with a price. As he moved away from the center on the issue, he ceded his ability to shape the Court's approach as he had done since 1956. Unlike so many of the earlier obscenity cases during his tenure, Brennan was essentially marginalized here. Burger corresponded extensively with White, Blackmun, and Powell about the case during the term, which Brennan would only learn later. In the early days of 1973, when Burger circulated a draft with a reconfigured test for obscenity, he replaced Brennan's permissive formulation that defined obscenity as "utterly without redeeming social value" with the potentially more stringent test that it "lacks serious literary, artistic, political or scientific value."

Burger's approach satisfied White, leaving Blackmun as Brennan's only possible fifth vote. So when Brennan circulated his next draft in March he aimed it squarely at Blackmun, so much so that White joked with Brennan that he should have captioned it "Dear Harry." Brennan considered Blackmun's likely reaction before each circulation that spring. He opted against circulating a memo criticizing Burger's opinion out of concern that he might wind up pushing Blackmun away. Brennan had his clerks check with their colleagues in Blackmun's chambers. They brought back word that, yet again, Blackmun had not made up his mind and that there was a small possibility that he might still join Brennan's opinion. But in the course of the term, Burger had managed to remove much of what Blackmun found most problematic about his opinion. On May 15, Blackmun circulated a memo indicating he planned to join Burger.

A month later, Burger publicly announced the Court's newest obscenity standard, one that on its face seemed to favor regulation. The standard appeared to tighten obscenity regulation by emphasizing local standards and by more narrowly defining what constituted socially valuable material. But Burger's opinion also made clear that individuals would be subject to prosecution only for materials that depicted "patently offensive 'hard core' sexual conduct" as specifically defined by state law. Brennan wrote a short dissent in *Miller* and saved his longer explanation of his change of position on obscenity for *Paris Adult Theatre*, released the same day. Absent distribution to minors or nonconsenting adults, he concluded that "the First and Fourteenth Amendments prohibit the State and Federal Governments from attempting wholly to suppress sexually oriented materials on the basis of their allegedly 'obscene' contents."

THE TELEGRAMS CAME first—by the hundreds. Then the letters started arriving at a rate of two thousand or three thousand a day, so many that boxes of unopened mail stacked up in the hallways of the Court. They came typed or handwritten in neat script on postcards or flowered stationery—more of them directed at Blackmun and Brennan than any of the other justices. Some included death threats and at least one warning that the Court had unleashed the wrath of God upon America. What prompted this avalanche of angry mail burying the Court in the winter of 1973 was the opinion authored by Blackmun and joined by Brennan and five other justices declaring women had a constitutional right to choose whether to have an abortion.

Even more so than in other cases, Brennan worked quietly behind the scenes in *Roe v. Wade,* reluctant to push Blackmun too hard and perhaps a bit reluctant to come out front and center on the issue of abortion. In fact, he worked so quietly that for some time it remained difficult to determine exactly how influential a role he played.

In the years since the justices had knocked down Connecticut's restrictive contraception law in their 1965 *Griswold* decision, reformers had turned their attention to extending access to legal abortions beyond women whose lives were at risk. A handful of states had added additional exceptions allowing doctors to perform "therapeutic" abortions in cases where a pregnancy resulted from rape and incest, a mother's health was at risk, or a child was very likely to be born severely mentally or physically defective. But doctors and hospital administrators continued to be the ones who decided who had abortions, and the number of legal abortions remained low. With a push from women's rights groups, reformers shifted their goal to repealing abortion regulations and giving women more control over the decision. While four states had passed some kind of repeal measures, the reform drive had stalled by 1971 in the face of strong opposition from the Catholic Church. The most promising avenue for change became litigation rather than legislative repeal.

In December 1971 the justices considered a pair of cases—*Doe v. Bolton* and *Roe v. Wade*—challenging the abortion laws of Texas, which allowed abortions only to save the life of the mother, and of Georgia, which had additional exceptions. Federal district court judges had struck down Texas's law and invalidated Georgia's statute, although they had left in place the latter's elaborate procedural requirements before an abortion could be performed. After the December 15 conference, the lineup of the justices' votes remained somewhat murky, at least to Burger, who assigned the opinion to Blackmun. Douglas vigorously objected, asserting he had the power to assign the case as the senior associate justice in the majority.

From the outset, Brennan believed a "right to privacy" should be the basis for granting women broader access to abortion. In a late-December memo to Douglas, Brennan offered a detailed explanation of how he conceived of that right as derived from three groups of "fundamental freedoms," one of which he described as a "freedom of choice in the basic decisions of life," such as marriage, procreation, contraception, and education. For support, Brennan invoked a contraception opinion he was working on at that very moment.

A month before the abortion oral argument, the justices heard the case of William Baird, a thirty-three-year-old former medical student convicted under a Massachusetts law barring single people from being given contraceptives for the purpose of preventing pregnancy. Baird had passed out lists of abortion providers and packages of vaginal contraceptive foam after a lecture to an overflow crowd at a Boston University auditorium in April 1967. Brennan was assigned the majority opinion. After mulling a narrow decision, he opted to use the case, *Eisenstadt v. Baird,* as a vehicle for extending to unmarried people the right of privacy he had helped Douglas propound in *Griswold* for married couples.

In his memo to Douglas, Brennan wrote, "Incidentally, Eisenstadt in its discussion of Griswold is helpful in addressing the abortion question." Douglas subsequently joined that opinion, which Brennan announced in March 1972. The potential significance for the abortion decisions was not lost on lawyers and journalists when they read Brennan in the *Eisenstadt* opinion: "If the right of privacy means anything, it is the right of the individual, married or single, to be free from unwarranted governmental intrusion into matters so fundamentally affecting a person as the decision whether to bear or beget a child." In his opinion for the Court in *Roe,* Blackmun would ultimately cite both *Griswold* and *Eisenstadt* before concluding that the "right of privacy . . . is broad enough to encompass a woman's decision whether or not to terminate her pregnancy." In the future, even some liberals would question the basis of the *Roe* decision. Some, like Ruth Bader Ginsburg, wondered why the Court did not build in a sex-discrimination discussion under equal protection. Others wondered why Blackmun relied on an undefined notion of privacy instead of using the guarantee of liberty protected by due process in the Fourteenth Amendment. But Brennan insisted that relying solely on due process was never an option strategically. "Bill Douglas never would've gone along on due process."

Brennan did not share with Blackmun his thoughts about how best to approach the abortion cases, at least not directly. Going out of his way to avoid alienating the justice, he held back his criticism when Blackmun circulated what he considered two disappointing drafts in May 1972. Instead, he gently encouraged Blackmun to go further and address "the core constitutional question." When Blackmun urged his colleagues to hold over the two cases until the following term, with the Court back at full strength, Brennan objected only tepidly. And when Blackmun renewed his efforts at drafting an opinion for the Court after the October 11, 1972, reargument, Brennan opted to let his clerks relay his proposals to their counterparts in Blackmun's chambers rather than communicate directly with his colleague. "He didn't want to make it look like he was telling Blackmun how to write the opinion," recalled Brennan's clerk William Maledon, who worked closely on the abortion cases in the 1972–73 term.

Blackmun eventually sought Brennan's help, although on theological rather than legal matters. As he circulated a new draft in November 1972, Blackmun wrote Brennan a note asking him to pay "particular attention" to a portion of the opinion invoking canon law and the position of the Catholic Church. "I believe they are accurate factually, but I do not want them to be offensive or capable of being regarded as unduly critical by any reader," Blackmun wrote, leaving unstated the fact that Brennan remained the Court's sole Catholic sixteen years into his tenure. "Your judgment as to this will be most helpful." There is no record of a reply by Brennan, although he undoubtedly resented being cast in the role of house Catholic. The previous term, Brennan vented his irritation to his clerks when reporters noted his religion in stories about his opinion in the *Eisenstadt* contraception case.

Brennan was certainly aware of the Catholic Church's vigorous opposition to abortion. The brief Vatican II–inspired moment of openness regarding contraception when the justices had taken up the *Griswold* case had long passed. When New York debated a legislative reform bill in 1967, the head of all eight of New York's dioceses issued a first-of-its-kind letter of opposition read at every pulpit in the state. Catholic legislators in the state faced intense pressure when they took up a reform bill in 1970. And the Catholic governors of Hawaii and New Mexico voiced anguish in trying to decide whether to veto reform bills passed by their respective state legislatures in 1969 and 1970. Both governors ultimately let the bills become law after first explaining that they did not personally support abortion.

Given the vocal opposition of the Church, it is easy to understand why Brennan might have preferred to stay behind the scenes in the abortion case. Brennan privately admitted later that he had his own misgivings about the issue. "I wouldn't under any circumstances condone an abortion in my private life," Brennan said privately in 1987. "But that has nothing to do with whether or not those who have different views are entitled to have them and are entitled to be protected in their exercise of them. That's my job in applying and interpreting the Constitution." Brennan recalled that, by the time the Court addressed the abortion question, he had long since thought through the issue and experienced no anguish, particularly in regard to his religion. "It never crossed my mind — never, nót the slightest — that my faith had a damn thing to do with how I decided the abortion case," Brennan said in 1987. But his clerk William Maledon later recalled it was not quite as easy for Brennan as he preferred to remember. "He was obviously troubled by the issue," recalled Maledon, a twenty-six-year-old graduate of Loyola University Chicago and Notre Dame Law School. Maledon experienced some discomfort of his own, having written an article for the *Notre Dame Lawyer* arguing that unborn children had an unalienable right to life.

IN HIS DECEMBER 1971 memo to Douglas, Brennan had predicted the "critical question" in the case would be at what point a state's interest in protecting the health of the mother or life of the fetus outweighed the rights of the mother. Blackmun admitted he found the issue "difficult and elusive." Blackmun had fixed the decisive moment after which the government could regulate abortion as the end of the first trimester, which he confessed to his colleagues was "arbitrary." "But perhaps any other selected point, such as quickening or viability is equally arbitrary," Blackmun wrote. In a private letter to Blackmun, Powell indicated that he preferred viability, which would have delayed the point at which the state could regulate abortion from twelve to after twenty weeks.

Blackmun replied in a private note to Powell that even though he had "no particular commitment" to the first trimester, he preferred it, since it was more likely to command a court and it allowed states to "draw their own medical conclusions" between the first trimester and viability. Blackmun soon followed up with a note to all his colleagues asking for their thoughts. Douglas indicated he preferred the first trimester, while Marshall wrote back one day later expressing a preference for viability, since "the opinion's present focus on the end of the first trimester would lead states to prohibit abortions completely at any later date." Marshall suggested it might be best to state explicitly that between the end of the first trimester and viability, "state regulations directed at health and safety alone were permissible."

Brennan weighed in with his views in a December 13 memo he sent solely to Blackmun. Like Powell and Marshall, Brennan expressed a preference for moving the "cutoff" point after which the state could regulate abortion past the first trimester, but questioned if viability was the proper marker. Brennan argued that since the compelling state interest justifying regulation was the health of the mother, it seemed "technically inconsistent" to set as the demarcation point viability, which was associated more with the fetus than the woman. Instead, Brennan advocated setting as the threshold "that point in time where abortions become medically more complex," which he suggested usually occurs between sixteen and twenty-four weeks. "The exact 'cut-off' point and the specifics of the narrow regulation itself are determinations that must be made by a medically informed state legislature," Brennan suggested.

The combined suggestions of Powell, Marshall, and Brennan prompted Blackmun to revise his approach. In a December 15 memo to the conference, Blackmun proposed replacing the single threshold with two. "I have in mind associating the end of the first trimester with an emphasis on health, and associating viability with an emphasis on the State's interest in potential life. The period between the two points would be treated with flexibility." He circulated an updated draft several days later with a cover letter attached in which he explained, "I have tried to follow the lines suggested by Bill Brennan and Thurgood." In his new draft, Blackmun divided the pregnancy into three phases: Until the point of viability, Blackmun suggested that physicians in consultation with their patients were "free to determine, without regulation by the State" whether a pregnancy should be terminated. After the first trimester, the state could adopt regulations aimed at protecting maternal health, while after the point of viability, when the state's "interest in the potentiality of human life" became compelling, "it may go so far as to proscribe" all abortions except when medically necessary "to preserve the life or health of the mother." Within a week, Douglas, Marshall, Stewart, and Brennan all joined Blackmun's opinion. Burger ultimately joined the opinion, too, while White and Rehnquist circulated dissents, making it 7–2.

Brennan felt a strong enough sense of ownership in the *Roe* and *Doe* opinions that his clerks included them in the bound volume of his opinions for the term that Brennan maintained for his own use. The accompanying note explained that the opinions "were substantially revised in response to suggestions made by Justice Brennan." Unlike in *Griswold*, where Brennan later claimed a bit more credit than he deserved, Brennan accurately recalled that he "was involved" in helping formulate the trimester approach. Blackmun gave Brennan far less credit than he was due when he later asserted that Brennan "made no suggestions whatsoever." After reading a 1993 article in *Washingtonian* magazine suggesting that Brennan played a key role in the case, Blackmun wrote, "This is hogwash" on a copy he saved in his files. Blackmun's recollections reflected both his deep sense of ownership of his *Roe* opinion as well as the fact that Brennan had taken such care in minimizing his efforts to shape the final product. As best as can be discerned, Brennan's contribution in *Roe* was twofold. He helped lay the groundwork in the form of prior precedent for the constitutional right to privacy that was at the center of the decision. And he was one of several justices who helped shape Blackmun's trimester framework under which women could obtain abortions subject to varying degrees of regulation.

One contribution by Brennan is beyond dispute. Anticipating tremendous public interest in the case, Blackmun drafted an announcement he intended to deliver from the bench that he also envisioned distributing to reporters. The next day, Brennan advised Blackmun against issuing such a statement. "Our practice in the past has always been not to record oral announcements of opinions in order to avoid the possibility that the announcement will be relied upon as the opinion or as interpreting the filed opinion," Brennan explained. "I think that policy is very sound, and important as the Abortion Cases are, I do not think we ought to depart from that policy." Blackmun dropped the idea after Douglas, Marshall, and Stewart all indicated they agreed with Brennan.

The decision — announced on January 22 — was shunted to the bottom of many newspapers' front pages, overshadowed by the death that same day of former president Johnson. The fiercest condemnations, as expected, came from within the Catholic Church. John Cardinal Krol, the archbishop of Philadelphia and president of the National Conference of Catholic Bishops, called it "an unspeakable tragedy," while Washington's archbishop Patrick Cardinal O'Boyle accused the Court of producing "another Dred Scott decision," a reference to the 1857 ruling denying slaves citizenship. One newspaper columnist, Lester Kinsolving, held up Brennan's supposed Catholic renegadism: "Notably, one of these 'few men' who sanctioned what his Eminence described as 'grave sin' is one of O'Boyle's very own archdiocesan flock," Kinsolving wrote.

Brennan, like all of the other sitting justices, skipped the annual Red Mass held five days after the *Roe* decision was announced. Speakers at the Red Mass in St. Matthew's Cathedral purposely made no reference to the decision, although Archbishop O'Boyle had asked priests throughout the archdiocese to preach against it in their Sunday sermons. Outside St. Matthew's, a half-dozen picketers carried placards calling for Brennan's excommunication, a demand soon echoed in at least two small conservative Catholic publications. Maledon sensed Brennan was saddened to be singled out by members of his church and perhaps even wished there was a way he could explain that *Roe* did not reflect his personal views.

Clerks for both Brennan and Blackmun noticed a pattern as they started opening up the huge volume of letters that quickly began arriving at the Court. Big batches would come from particular parishes or Catholic schools where a local priest had asked parishioners to write en masse. Unlike Blackmun, who read through many of the letters and preserved a large sampling in his files, Brennan looked at few and saved none in his papers. The only letter in response to *Roe* that Brennan's clerks chose to quote in their term history came from a correspondent in Australia who wrote "to congratulate you on your courage and to assure you that . . . at least one

Catholic lawyer who, believing that he has deeply considered these implications, fully sympathizes with your point of view."

As the often hateful mail continued to flood the Court, Brennan drew
upon his long experience to offer Blackmun some measure of comfort.
This was not the first time and would not be the last a Court opinion
sparked public outrage, Brennan explained. It just came with the territory. But neither Brennan nor Blackmun could imagine the intensity and
longevity of the anger the *Roe* opinion generated. Unlike so many of the
heated but brief public outcries Brennan had experienced after his controversial decisions about school prayer and Communist subversion, opposition to *Roe* only seemed to grow more intense over time. A grassroots
movement of evangelical Protestants later supplemented Catholics as foot
soldiers in the battle against legalized abortion. Protestors began trailing
both justices at most of their public appearances, although Blackmun bore
the brunt of the scorn at first, since Brennan so rarely spoke in public anymore. Blackmun turned to Brennan to commiserate, particularly when he
was targeted by Catholics. When Catholic University revoked a speaking
invitation, Blackmun shared the news with Brennan. So too did Blackmun
tell Brennan when a Catholic bishop wrote him to say his pending commencement appearance at the University of North Dakota filled him "with
anguish and travail."

No one in the Catholic Church hierarchy ever endorsed the sporadic
calls for Brennan's excommunication or tried barring him from accepting
Communion, a punishment later proposed for elected officials who had
endorsed abortion rights. Still, Brennan began feeling even more uncomfortable attending church — or even socializing with priests he did not already know well. He feared they were judging him based on the decision.
Brennan continued to correspond with Father Ted Hesburgh, the president of Notre Dame, but it seems inconceivable that he would have received the university's prestigious Laetare Medal in the wake of *Roe*. Brennan seemed most taken aback by antiabortion protestors who appeared
outside subsequent Red Masses he attended, carrying signs that accused
him of murdering babies. Brennan said these graphic protests never made
him regret his vote in *Roe*. But his clerks got the sense he was perfectly satisfied to avoid writing any abortion decisions beyond those dealing with
access for poor women who relied on government funding.

•

EVERYONE AT THE Court knew where to find Brennan around July 1: on the ferry to Nantucket. Although the Brennans had been visiting Nantucket since 1960, that reservation — booked like clockwork each February — had become almost sacred since 1971. Marjorie had rebounded from her latest cancer relapse during their stay on Nantucket that summer. She remained weak, and the damage to her throat left her unable to eat anything other than meals liquefied in an electric blender. Still, both Brennan and Marjorie had come to associate her fragile well-being with their six weeks on the island. Here, they could briefly recapture the life lost when she had first become ill in 1969. So Brennan would not let anything get in the way of his ferry reservation. Not an invitation from the president of Israel's high court to visit during the summer of 1973, which he declined by explaining that they planned "to spend another quiet summer on Nantucket Island where [Marjorie] seems to do particularly well." Not even the Arab oil embargo could stop him. When it looked as if he might miss his ferry reservation later in the 1970s due to gas shortages, clerk lore has it that Brennan ignored the possibility that his fuel tank might rot — or his car explode — and gassed up with jet fuel.

Brennan's daily routine on Nantucket had not changed much after a decade vacationing on the island. He still started each morning with an hourlong walk on the moors. Afterward, he retreated to the Wharf Rat Club, a men's club housed in a small cedar-shingled waterfront shanty, whose motto carved onto a wooden sign above the door fit Brennan perfectly: "No Reserved Seats for The Mighty." Brennan, whose rental cottage was just steps away on Old North Wharf, blended right in among the local fishermen and summer visitors who traded true stories and tall tales for a couple of hours each morning. The conversation and male camaraderie around the potbellied stove provided a perfect substitute for the lunches he so enjoyed at Kronheim's during the Court term.

Nantucket's appeal proved strong enough to the family that Bill, Georgie, and their two children, Billy and Alexandra, began joining Brennan and Marjorie on the island, renting a nearby cottage each summer. Except for occasional contact with some of Nantucket's summer notables, including author David Halberstam, Brennan kept his customary low profile. His friends at the Wharf Rat Club knew to plead ignorance about his whereabouts any time a reporter showed up looking for an interview. Brennan, who traded in his judicial robe for the island's ubiquitous summer uniform of khaki pants and a fisherman's cap, wouldn't have been easy to single out, in any case. In the afternoon, he parked himself in one of the deck chairs behind his modest two-story wood-shingled rental, reading history books for pleasure or just watching boats sailing the inlet. "We've developed an amazing capacity to forget what's going on in the world," Brennan wrote Blackmun. "Nantucket does that to people."

In the summer of 1974 Brennan left Washington as usual for Nantucket, but he could not prevent the Court's business from intruding on his summer vacation. The justices had finally gotten involved in a two-year-old scandal that threatened to bring down the Nixon administration. In June 1972, five burglars had been caught breaking into the Democratic National Committee headquarters at the Watergate, a luxury apartment and office complex in Washington. Despite White House denials, two *Washington Post* reporters, Bob Woodward and Carl Bernstein, soon began to reveal the links between those burglars and President Nixon's reelection campaign.

Separate investigations by a special federal prosecutor, Archibald Cox, and a Senate committee chaired by Sam Ervin, a North Carolina Democrat, slowly unraveled details about the break-in, a larger pattern of political espionage dating back years, and a cover-up involving payoffs, perjury, and the destruction of evidence perpetrated by some of the president's closest advisers. In televised testimony before the Senate committee, Nixon's former White House counsel, John Dean, charged that the president knew about the break-ins and had directed the cover-up. A former White House aide and appointments coordinator offered a way to corroborate Dean's allegations a few weeks later when he revealed the existence of a secret White House taping system installed at Nixon's direction for recording nearly all of the president's conversations and telephone calls.

When Cox and senators demanded Nixon turn over portions of those tapes, the White House initially refused, citing executive privilege. Even after the D.C. Circuit ruled that the Nixon administration had to release the tapes, the White House offered only select, edited transcripts. When the special prosecutor held that the transcripts would not suffice, Nixon ordered Cox fired, in October 1973. Both Attorney General Elliot Richardson and his deputy, William D. Ruckelshaus, quit rather than fire Cox, in what became known as the Saturday Night Massacre. The next most senior official at the Justice Department, Solicitor General Robert Bork, wound up carrying out the order. The resulting firestorm prompted Nixon to relent and release some of the tapes. Cox's successor as special prosecutor, Leon Jaworski, subpoenaed tapes of an additional sixty-four conversations in April 1974, following the indictment of seven senior Nixon aides for conspiracy to obstruct justice. Again, Nixon offered only edited transcripts of some of the tapes. A month later, John Sirica, the federal District Court judge in Washington presiding over the Watergate prosecutions, ordered the White House to release the tapes. When Nixon's lawyers appealed, Jaworski asked the Supreme Court to invoke a rarely used power to bypass the circuit court and to hear the case directly.

Brennan was not surprised when the case of *United States v. Nixon* reached the Court in May 1974. He had followed news accounts of Watergate closely and often talked with his clerks about the latest developments over morning coffee. Brennan had expected that the justices would have to get involved ever since Judge Sirica ordered the president to turn over the first batch of tapes a year earlier. The stakes had only gotten higher since. The House Judiciary Committee had begun investigating the possibility of impeaching Nixon. Although the tapes were intended only as evidence in the trial of Nixon's aides, the Court's decision could provide new ammunition for impeachment — or take the steam out of the effort entirely. It also remained unclear whether Nixon would even comply with the Court's decision. Nevertheless, Brennan felt strongly that the justices should grant cert. After two years of the Watergate scandal, he believed the nation should have access to the evidence most likely to reveal the truth. When the justices gathered to discuss whether to take the case on May 31, Brennan persuaded many of his seven colleagues participating in the case to agree to hear it on an expedited basis. Rehnquist, who had served as an assistant attorney general in the Nixon Justice Department, recused himself. On May 31, the justices announced their decision to hear the case. Oral argument was scheduled for July 8.

Brennan had less success convincing his colleagues to heed another one of his suggestions. In order to underscore their unanimity, he argued that all eight of the justices participating in the case should individually sign the opinion as they had done in the Little Rock school-desegregation case sixteen years earlier. Brennan felt so strongly about this approach that, before leaving for Nantucket, he visited each of his colleagues' chambers to lobby them face-to-face. Douglas, Marshall, and Stewart seemed agreeable. White was skeptical. Powell and Blackmun were somewhat open to the idea, although Blackmun thought that he should get the assignment. He believed it was important that the task fall to one of Nixon's Republican appointees; under that logic, he was the only possible candidate, since Powell was a Democrat, Rehnquist had recused himself, and Burger might wind up presiding over a Senate impeachment trial. Only Burger, whom Brennan approached last, definitively opposed a jointly signed opinion. Burger believed his name alone should appear atop the opinion.

Brennan brought the briefs filed by Nixon's lawyers and the special prosecutor with him to Nantucket along with the memos his clerks prepared. After only a week of vacation on their island retreat, he left Marjorie behind on Nantucket and returned to Washington on July 6 to prepare for the oral argument scheduled to begin two days later. Brennan, as usual, asked few questions during the three-hour oral argument. Reporters speculated, based on the other justices' questions, that three of them — Burger, Blackmun, and White — might support the president's position. But when the justices gathered together in conference the next day it became apparent that none did. They voted unanimously that Nixon must turn over the tapes. Brennan renewed his argument on behalf of a joint opinion, motivated largely by concern about the possibility that Burger might wind up in control. Brennan believed that Burger too often proved unwilling to change opinions he drafted and that he lacked the finesse needed to steer the opinion toward a middle view. Brennan suggested that each chambers could take charge of drafting a different section of the opinion. Burger once again made clear his belief that, as chief justice, the responsibility for writing the opinion rested on his shoulders alone.

After the conference, Brennan and Douglas headed to Georgetown University Hospital, where Earl Warren had been hospitalized for a week with congestive heart failure. Warren had been in and out of the hospital since May, but the eighty-three-year-old former chief justice did not want to talk about his faltering health. Brennan and Warren had continued their friendship since the chief justice's retirement. Brennan regularly stopped by Warren's chambers, where the former chief justice kept office hours. Warren also joined his former colleagues for occasional lunches in the justices' dining room. Warren on such occasions made it a habit of not asking too many questions about pending cases, fearful of overstepping what he viewed as the proper bounds for a retired justice. On this day, Warren violated his own rule about not inquiring too much about current Court business. He could not resist asking whether Nixon would have to release the tapes. Yes, Brennan explained, the justices had voted unanimously to require him to do so. The news clearly pleased Warren. "Thank God," he said. By 5 P.M., Brennan and Douglas left, reluctant to tire out the former chief justice any further. Just three hours later, Warren died with his wife at his side.

Brennan and his colleagues and three of the four living former justices lined the marble steps of the Court two days later as Warren's flag-draped casket was carried inside, where he would lie in state overnight. The funeral service the next day at the National Cathedral included the curious spectacle of the justices sitting near President Nixon, whose fate they would now determine. Warren's death left Brennan profoundly saddened, although he either did not show his grief that day — or reporters did not notice. The *New York Times* noted that both Douglas and Marshall "appeared particularly moved and near tears" during the service. As at the memorial service for Martin Luther King Jr. held at the National Cathedral six years earlier, Brennan did not attract press attention despite being the justice who was closest to Warren. Brennan offered Warren his ultimate tribute later that year in the pages of the *Harvard Law Review*. He labeled his friend "the Super-Chief" as if to set him further apart from Burger.

The Nixon tapes case that coincided with Warren's death provided even more proof to Brennan of just how much less effective Burger was as chief justice. In the course of the next two weeks, Brennan and his colleagues rejected much of what the chief justice drafted, and ended up doing what Brennan had suggested all along: dividing up sections among themselves. This was an unusual coalition: Blackmun, Brennan, Douglas, Marshall, Powell, Stewart, and White all worked together — and at times met together in small groups — to hash out their individual parts. Burger became aware of what was happening after he inadvertently walked in on some of his colleagues during one of their small-group sessions. (Brennan missed that meeting, having flown back to Nantucket for the weekend).

Burger seemed particularly put off by Blackmun's objections. Yet the chief justice seemed unable — or unwilling — to grasp the depths of his colleagues' concerns about his approach. Several justices objected that

Burger seemed to propose that a subpoena to a president had to meet a higher-than-usual standard of justification, something most other justices rejected. They also felt that Burger did not properly support the Supreme Court's power to decide the *United States v. Nixon* case over objections by the president's lawyers that it was merely an internal political dispute over which there was no Court jurisdiction.

Burger wrote his colleagues in frustration on July 15 that "my effort to accommodate everyone by sending out 'first drafts' is not working out." He suggested in a huff that no more circulations would be forthcoming until he was ready. When Burger did finally circulate a full draft, he had incorporated wholesale sections prepared by the other justices. On July 24, Burger announced from the bench the Court's decision squarely rejecting Nixon's executive privilege claim. Brennan was impressed by Burger's delivery and how they had reached the outcome, what his term history characterized as "a collegial product in the best sense of that term." Eight hours later, fears about how Nixon would respond proved unfounded when the president announced he would fully comply with the Court's decision.

Nixon's presidency unraveled quickly in the days that followed. Three days after the Court released its opinion, the House Judiciary Committee adopted the first of three articles of impeachment against Nixon, charging obstruction of justice in the cover-up of the Watergate scandal. On August 5, Nixon released a transcript of a conversation he had with H. R. Haldeman, his then chief of staff, which showed the president had obstructed justice by ordering the FBI to end its Watergate break-in investigation. The release of that transcript undercut what little support Nixon had left among Republicans, and three days later he announced in a televised address that he would resign the presidency at noon the next day, August 9, 1974. By then, Brennan had returned to Nantucket. A written postscript Burger offered to his colleagues a few weeks later read: "All of us know that from the day of our conference on July 10 we were in accord on every major point and that our only differences (and few they were) related to semantics and detail, not substance." That account was completely at odds with what Brennan and his clerks had experienced.

Looking back, Blackmun recalled the Nixon tapes case as pivotal for him. It marked a turning point in his relationship with his friend since childhood, Chief Justice Burger. Their relationship had already clearly deteriorated since Blackmun joined the Court. In a parallel to the disappointment Frankfurter experienced about Brennan, Blackmun had proven more independent-minded than Burger had anticipated. Burger had unleashed his frustration even before the Nixon tapes case, Brennan recalled. Burger had yelled at Blackmun about his vote with such ferocity in one case the previous term that Blackmun asked his old friend to leave his chambers. It is possible, as with Frankfurter and Brennan, that there was no single moment when the two men's relationship chilled. Rather, things may well have built up over the five years they served together on the Court, as mutual grievances festered.

Whatever the turning point, by the time the justices returned from their abbreviated summer vacation in 1974, Brennan had begun an assiduous courtship of Blackmun. Brennan's clerks soon noticed how their boss returned from conference with his arm draped around Blackmun's shoulder. Brennan wrote notes effusively praising opinions by Blackmun — opinions that his clerks considered subpar. When Blackmun called Brennan one day and mentioned that he was having difficulty rewriting an opinion, Brennan went straight to Blackmun's chambers. Brennan's clerk Edward Leahy peeked in and saw his boss standing behind Blackmun's desk with one arm around him, pointing at the opinion. Blackmun would recall later, "I had no feeling that I was being wooed by him in any way." But Blackmun privately told clerks over breakfast he was well aware of Brennan's transparent courtship. Still, Brennan always treated Blackmun better than Burger did. The chief justice acted like his old friend owed him his vote and got angry when Blackmun showed any signs of independence.

Brennan could use every vote he could get, particularly after Douglas suffered a debilitating stroke in December 1974 while vacationing in the Bahamas. Brennan found himself in a difficult position. He remained close to Douglas and his fourth wife, Cathy. Brennan was the first person she invited to visit Douglas at Walter Reed Hospital in January 1975 after he was airlifted back to the United States. Even before Douglas's illness, Brennan had to carry more than his share of the administrative burden usually taken up by the senior associate justice — at this point Douglas. For years, Brennan had resented the way Douglas had imposed on him to cast his votes when he left early each summer for vacation out west in Goose Prairie, Washington. Now the justice who once enjoyed marathon-length hikes sat slumped to one side in his chair, his face horribly gaunt and sallow.

Brennan did his best to moderate Douglas's growing petulance and impulsivity. He also felt increasingly uncomfortable about passing along Douglas's votes, which did not always make sense. In one case, Douglas voted to reverse at conference but sent a dissent from his hospital bed that made the same argument as Brennan's majority opinion did. Brennan had to sort it out with Douglas's clerks and eventually converted the dissent into a concurring opinion. And so, while Brennan certainly did not relish the idea of losing one of his two remaining liberal allies, he went along with the decision to stop assigning majority opinions to Douglas. The justices conspired to ignore Douglas's vote if it was the fourth to grant cert., and to hold over cases where his vote was decisive. Brennan had agonized over that decision, which he considered "horribly difficult," but ultimately decided it was the right thing to do. Around the same time Brennan voted to cut off Douglas's assignments, he and Marjorie hosted Douglas and his wife, Cathy, for their annual October 16 dinner to celebrate Douglas's birthday and Brennan's nineteenth anniversary on the Court. "One frequently reads about the 'court family,'" Cathy wrote in a thank-you note. "It is truly a family." A month later, Douglas submitted his letter of resignation to President Ford, making Brennan the Court's senior associate justice.

16

PEDESTALS & CAGES

IN DECEMBER 1972 a young attorney named Ann Torregrossa, just a couple years out of Villanova Law School — and just a few weeks from giving birth — stood up to argue her first case before the Supreme Court. The novice public interest attorney and her lawyer husband, Joe Torregrossa, represented a group of Philadelphia prisoners seeking a way to vote in the city's mayoral election. The two had alternated argument duty at every step of the appeal. Now, as the case reached the nation's highest court and Torregrossa entered the ninth month of her pregnancy, it was her turn. Torregrossa later stated that she became so nervous as she waited to present her case, she started to have contractions, causing the baby to kick so hard, she could see the front of her maternity dress move up and down.

Brennan looked at the pregnant Torregrossa, not much older than his own daughter, and worried she might go into labor right there in the courtroom. He had by now a well-developed habit of jumping in on behalf of attorneys arguing his side of a case with helpfully leading questions. Here, he tried deflecting another justice's tough query. When Torregrossa answered the next question with ease, Brennan patted the shoulder of one of his neighbors on the bench with satisfaction. "He was so in my corner, I can't tell you," recalled Torregrossa, who named her son Brennan in appreciation when he was born in January. Days later, Brennan announced a 9–0 decision in Torregrossa's favor.

Many other women would express their gratitude to Brennan in the years to come, as he authored several landmark gender-equality decisions, beginning the same term as Torregrossa's appearance. Ruth Bader Ginsburg, the attorney who led the legal attack for gender equality and later became a Supreme Court justice herself, would hail Brennan as "the Court's clearest, most constant speaker for women's equality." Nina Totenberg, National Public Radio's Supreme Court reporter, marveled, "When it comes to sex discrimination, well, he 'gets it.'"

Yet, in the early 1970s, another recent female law school graduate had a very different view of Brennan's attitudes toward women, particularly in his own workplace. Alison Grey was one of the top recent graduates from the University of California at Berkeley's Boalt Hall Law School when two Brennan clerks turned professors there, Stephen Barnett and Robert O'Neil, called in late 1970 to tell her they intended to recommend her for a clerkship in Brennan's chambers. The opportunity excited Grey, then working as an associate at a prestigious Washington, D.C., law firm, Covington & Burling, but she asked for a couple of days to think it over.

Although she had been first in her class, Grey had given up on the idea of a Supreme Court clerkship after a professor told her that the faculty would not waste a nomination on a woman. She had already clerked for a Fourth Circuit judge and liked her law firm job. Yet she knew that a coveted Supreme Court clerkship would improve her chances of achieving her ultimate goal of becoming a law professor, a career track few women had penetrated. So she called Barnett back and accepted the nomination. But when one of the professors called Brennan to offer their recommendation, he did not get much beyond saying Grey's first name before Brennan cut him off. "Send me someone else," Brennan said, making it perfectly clear that he meant a male clerk.

A quarter century had passed since Douglas had hired the Court's first female clerk; that was during World War II, when male law students were in scarce supply. Black and Fortas hired the second and third in 1966 and 1968. Brennan showed no inclination at the time to follow his allies' lead. When Yale Law School dean Louis Pollak wrote him in September 1966 to say that he would begin looking for "the appropriate young man (or woman)" as his clerk, Brennan replied, "While I am for equal rights for women, I think my prejudices are still for the male." His refusal to consider women had consequences. At that time, women accounted for less than 4 percent of lawyers overall and 1 percent of federal judges. A Supreme Court clerkship could provide a young woman lawyer rare entrée to the profession's most elite jobs, particularly in academia, where a Court clerkship was then often a prerequisite at top schools. It was just the sort of disparity that angered women joining the burgeoning women's rights movement. A month after Brennan wrote Pollak, the National Organization for Women was launched in Washington, D.C., demanding the government stop discriminating against women in all areas of public life.

Brennan, who was so attuned to the civil rights struggle a decade earlier, seemed slow to grasp the connection between his actions and the feminist movement pushing for equality. By 1970, he could not have avoided newspaper and magazine stories detailing protests by increasingly vocal feminists of his daughter's generation, many disillusioned with the sexism they encountered in both the civil rights and antiwar movements. Behind closed doors, women around the country gathered in small consciousness-raising sessions to discuss their common experiences with sexism.

Since Nancy had begun to educate him about women's rising expectations during their car rides home together while she interned in Washington in the summer of 1968, Brennan had slowly begun to come to accept her professional aspirations. By the fall of 1970, when women accounted for 10 percent of law school students, he still had great difficulty accepting the idea of any of these young female attorneys sharing his workplace.

Even Warren, fifteen years his senior, had employed women attorneys in senior positions when he was a district attorney and governor. But Brennan, who turned sixty-four in 1970, had little or no experience working alongside any women other than secretaries. His Newark law firm did not employ any female attorneys during his tenure there. None served alongside him as judges on New Jersey's courts. Brennan had not entirely adjusted to the presence of women acting as advocates at the Court, either, as suggested by his excessive solicitousness of the pregnant Torregrossa. A decade earlier, Brennan and Harlan liked to joke about Beatrice Rosenberg, one of the few female attorneys who argued before the Court. The two justices both viewed Rosenberg, who argued more than thirty cases before the Court, as a gifted litigator and physically unattractive. She also happened to have graduated Barringer High School in Newark with Brennan. After she showed Brennan a copy of their yearbook, Harlan used to tease him about her being his high school sweetheart, the sort of juvenile jokes they did not make about male attorneys who argued before the Court.

Brennan simply felt more comfortable around men. He liked to joke — sometimes crassly — with his friends and fellow judges in the private-club atmosphere of Kronheim's liquor distributorship over lunch. In the summer, he found similar all-male camaraderie at the Wharf Rat Club on Nantucket. At the Court, he salted his stories with the occasional profanity. Brennan confided to his clerks over coffee during the 1968–69 term that he worried about having to watch what he said if a woman clerk worked in his chambers. He did not feel he could have the same sort of relaxed rapport with a female clerk or colleague. If a woman ever got nominated to the Court, Brennan predicted, he might have to resign. "It's a strange kind of sexism," his friend Abner Mikva later observed. "He had [women] on such a pedestal he couldn't have their ears sullied by four-letter words." Ironically, this is one thing about which Brennan and Burger agreed entirely. In 1971 Burger warned President Nixon he would resign if a woman was named to the Court.

Brennan's reaction to their recommendation of Alison Grey surprised Barnett and O'Neil. When O'Neil had recommended Tigar four years earlier, he knew in advance that the nominee's leftist affiliations might prove problematic. This time it had not even occurred to O'Neil that Brennan would veto a woman out of hand. They did not try to argue with him. His vehemence left them both too surprised and perhaps skittish about doing anything that might cause him to cross off Berkeley permanently from the list of schools that supplied his clerks. They agreed instead to approach their second choice, Paul Hoeber, who had graduated first in his class at Boalt and was then clerking for a Ninth Circuit judge. They called Grey and rescinded the offer. Barnett tried to explain that Brennan did not feel he could have a woman in his chambers.

A stunned Grey could not understand why the professors did not stick up for her. It was true that she had grown accustomed to second-class treatment because of her gender. As an undergraduate at Harvard, she could not enter the main undergraduate library or qualify for the most prestigious academic prizes. Her law school would not nominate her for a Supreme Court clerkship. But this direct rebuff, at the hands of one of the

Court's leading liberals, hurt even more. She drafted a letter to Brennan protesting his decision, first showing it to a fellow attorney at her law firm who had clerked at the Court, to make sure she was not too strident. Grey mailed off the letter and, as she expected, never received a reply from Brennan. "Of course, what could he say?" she later said. Grey would never clerk for the Supreme Court, although a few years later, her brother did. She kept quiet about the incident, not out of any sense of loyalty to Brennan but to protect herself. She feared being tainted as some sort of rabble-rouser when she sought a job as a law professor. "So I just wrote my letter and went about my business and had a very low opinion of the justice for the rest of my life," said Grey, who went on to a distinguished career as a UCLA law professor.

HAD GREY PUBLICLY discussed Brennan's decision at that time, few women might have understood her experience better than Ruth Bader Ginsburg, then a thirty-seven-year-old law professor at Rutgers University. This Brooklyn-born daughter of a struggling haberdasher had graduated as the top-ranked woman in her class at Cornell in 1954. Yet Harvard Law School's Dean Erwin Griswold asked how she justified taking up a slot rightfully belonging to a man when she enrolled as one of nine women in her class of more than five hundred. Not wanting to seem overly assertive, Ginsburg mumbled that studying law might help her understand the work of her husband, Martin, who was beginning his second year there. (She made the *Harvard Law Review;* her husband did not.) After transferring to Columbia Law School when her husband took a job in New York, she graduated tied for first in her class. But no New York law firm offered her a job. Nor would any Supreme Court justice hire her as a clerk. Frankfurter, to whom she was recommended, worried she might wear pants instead of dresses. Edmund Palmieri, the federal District Court judge in New York who eventually hired her, at first balked, too, worried about the propriety of working alongside a woman late at night.

Even Brennan's fear of cursing in front of a female clerk would have sounded familiar to Ginsburg. The judge she clerked for often gave a ride home to the aging Judge Learned Hand while Ginsburg sat in the back seat. During one car ride, Ginsburg asked Hand, who refused to hire female clerks because of his colorful vocabulary, why he felt so free to curse in the car in her presence. "Young lady," Hand replied, "here I am not looking you in the face." For her next job, assisting a Columbia Law professor's study of international civil procedure, Ginsburg learned Swedish in order to observe that country's courts firsthand. She was struck during her time there by how far women had progressed in Sweden's workplaces.

Ginsburg wound up teaching at Rutgers University's law school in Newark in the early 1960s, the second female law professor there — and one of the first twenty in the entire country. She felt so insecure about her standing as a woman on the faculty that she wore her mother-in-law's baggy clothes to hide her pregnancy from the dean. When she set out to research a potential course on sex discrimination, she found little written about the subject. One widely used property law casebook, she discovered, declared, "Land, like woman, was meant to be possessed." She volunteered to help the ACLU's New Jersey affiliate with gender-discrimination cases, representing teachers who lost their jobs when they got pregnant and a campus gardener who could get a tuition waiver for his son but not his daughter.

In early 1971 Ginsburg offered to assist the ACLU's national office in preparing a Supreme Court brief on behalf of an Idaho woman, Sally Reed, who discovered that state law favored her ex-husband as administrator of her sixteen-year-old son's estate after he shot himself with his father's hunting rifle in 1967. A state trial judge ruled in Sally Reed's favor but the Idaho Supreme Court reversed. The ACLU persuaded her Boise lawyer to let it help with the appeal to the U.S. Supreme Court. Ginsburg wrote ACLU legal director Melvin Wulf to inquire whether he might like a woman co-counsel in the case, an offer he readily accepted.

Ginsburg and Wulf could not find much encouragement in the Court's prior precedents as they set out to write their brief in *Reed v. Reed*. The Court had never rejected a law on the grounds that it treated men and women differently. In considering whether a law violates the Fourteenth Amendment's equal protection clause, the Court applied two different standards. If a law was deemed to involve a "suspect classification" such as race, alienage, and nationality, or to affect a "fundamental right" such as voting, the Court applied strict scrutiny and would only let it stand if legislators were promoting a "compelling state interest." Where there was no suspect classification or fundamental right at issue, the Court applied a more lenient "rational basis review," allowing legislators to treat groups differently while advancing a general public purpose.

The Court had always applied the more lenient standard when faced with laws treating women differently. Among the laws upheld were those exempting women from poll taxes or barring them from bartending except at establishments owned by their fathers or husbands. Most recently, the justices had unanimously rejected a 1961 challenge to a Florida state law that exempted women from jury lists unless they took the initiative to register. Writing for the Court, Justice Harlan concluded it was perfectly permissible for a state to conclude that a woman should be relieved from jury duty, since the "woman is still regarded as the center of home and family life." (That opinion incensed Harlan's secretary enough that she almost refused to type it.)

Nonetheless, Ginsburg pressed for an unusually aggressive approach in *Reed*, devoting much of the brief to arguing that sex is a suspect classification and that laws that distinguish on that basis should be subject to strict scrutiny. The Warren Court had shown a willingness to broaden the category of suspect classifications, and had expanded the roster of fundamental rights that triggered tougher scrutiny to include travel. Some lower courts had begun to treat classifications based on gender as suspect too. In May 1971, one month before Ginsburg filed her brief, the California Supreme Court rejected a law limiting where women could work as bartenders. As an alternative, she suggested tougher language from an obscure 1920 decision that required a classification to have "a fair and substantial relation to the object of the legislation, so that all persons similarly circumstanced shall be treated alike." Commentators sometimes refer to this test as rational basis plus or rational basis with "bite" or "teeth."

Ginsburg did not think the justices would actually treat sex as a suspect classification in this case. Ever the law professor, she saw herself as embarking on a long-term education project, in a courtroom rather than a classroom. She wanted to rid the justices of the widely held paternalistic view among men of their generation that women benefited from laws that treated them differently. Ginsburg knew that many men believed women had the best of both worlds: they could work if they wished and stay home if they chose, while remaining shielded from the worst aspects of life that men encountered. She filled the ACLU's brief with references to a variety of nonlegal disciplines including biology and philosophy, all in an effort to help show the justices that even laws intended to help women were grounded in unfair and harmful stereotypes. She compared gender to racial classifications, both of which were "once thought normal, proper and ordained in the 'very nature of things.'" Sex discrimination, too, the brief predicted, "may soon be seen as a sham." She included a two-page excerpt of the recent California Supreme Court decision that most colorfully declared, "The pedestal upon which women have been placed has all too often, upon closer inspection, been revealed as a cage."

Ginsburg watched silently from the audience as Sally Reed's Boise attorney argued the case before the Court in October 1971. A month later, Burger announced a short unanimous opinion holding that the Idaho statute violated the equal protection clause. The Court did not apply strict scrutiny as Ginsburg suggested, but the outcome was still a victory for her cause. For the first time, the Supreme Court had invoked the equal protection clause to void a law that distinguished between the sexes. Although the justices did not explicitly say so, the Court appeared to be employing a less deferential form of "rational basis" review than in the past. If the justices had employed a traditional rational-basis test, the statute should have survived. After all, it could be seen as rational for state legislators to conclude that men were better equipped in business affairs than women. Burger's opinion cited the 1920 equal protection case Ginsburg had invoked in her brief that employed a tougher formulation of the rational-basis standard.

The *Reed* victory helped convince the ACLU's board of directors to make women's rights a top priority. A few months later, Ginsburg cofounded the ACLU's Women's Rights Project, which she would help lead while also teaching at Columbia University as its first tenured female law professor. As a model, Ginsburg looked to Thurgood Marshall and the NAACP Legal Defense Fund. Ginsburg, who stood barely five feet tall, did not quite measure up physically to the tall stocky civil rights lawyer turned justice. She was as quiet and reserved as Marshall was outgoing and brash. And yet, she was no less steely or savvy a legal strategist. She envisioned employing a strategy similar to what the NAACP Legal Defense Fund had used successfully to dismantle the "separate but equal" doctrine. Gradually, she hoped to challenge laws that embodied the stereotype of man as breadwinner and woman as homemaker, and to guide the Court toward accepting heightened scrutiny of gender-based differences. She discovered plenty of targets, helped in part by an appendix the Solicitor General's Office included in one filing with the Court laying out hundreds of provisions of the U.S. Code that differentiated based on sex.

To challenge those laws, she purposely sought out cases "with a strong human appeal," aware that justices would not naturally relate to a woman's experience. She looked for sympathetic plaintiffs, including men who found themselves disadvantaged by a gender classification. Female military officers proved another potentially sympathetic class of plaintiffs. Ginsburg was particularly hopeful about a case involving an unmarried female Air Force officer involuntarily discharged after getting pregnant. The military took no action against the father, who was also an Air Force officer. But that case became moot when the Air Force lifted the discharge.

Instead, Ginsburg focused on the case of Air Force lieutenant Sharon Frontiero, a twenty-six-year-old physical therapist at Maxwell Air Force Base in Alabama, who had unsuccessfully sought an increase in her housing and medical benefits after getting married. Such increases came automatically for newly married male service members, but women had to prove their husbands depended on them for more than half of their support. Her husband, a student at a local college who received GI benefits for veterans, did not qualify. Two Alabama civil rights lawyers, Joseph J. Levin Jr. and Morris Dees, founders of the Southern Poverty Law Center, took Frontiero's case. After a three-judge panel of District Court judges rejected her claim, the attorneys asked the ACLU for help in appealing to the Supreme Court. Ginsburg had assumed she would take the lead if the Court agreed to hear the case, but quarreled with Levin over strategy and who should handle the oral argument. Ginsburg wanted to follow her approach in *Reed* and advocate strict scrutiny. Levin preferred emphasizing a less-demanding standard.

Unable to agree on an approach, Ginsburg wrote a separate amicus brief, which reiterated her earlier argument in favor of strict scrutiny. But, as a fallback position, she also urged that the justices scrutinize the law closely under an intermediate standard of review. She was influenced in part by a 1972 article written by Stanford Law School professor Gerald Gunther in the *Harvard Law Review*. Gunther analyzed fifteen cases from the Court's previous term and concluded that there was growing discontent with the rigid two-tier approach to equal protection. The Court, Gunther concluded, seemed ready to intervene using equal protection without resorting to strict scrutiny. Ginsburg recycled much of her history of sex discrimination from the *Reed* case, and similarly included a lengthy excerpt from the California Supreme Court decision depicting the pedestal on which protective laws placed women as "upon closer inspection . . . a cage." She also emphasized the harmful effects of seemingly "benign" classifications. "Presumably well-meaning exaltations of woman's unique role as wife and mother has, in effect, denied women equal opportunity to develop their individual talents and capacities and has impelled them to accept a dependent, subordinate status in society."

Ginsburg appeared before the Court for the first time as oral advocate when the justices took up the *Frontiero* case on January 17, 1973, although she was relegated to speaking second after Levin. Ginsburg prepared for her debut with great care. "It had to be kept very simple and nonthreatening," Ginsburg later recalled. She carefully avoided doing anything that might cause the justices to take even the slightest offense, something she would continue to do during each of her future appearances. She always watched how she dressed. She rejected her students' suggestion that she request a change to her Supreme Court bar admissions card that listed her name as "Mrs. Ruth Ginsburg," even though she did not in fact go by "Mrs." Years later, after many appearances before the Court, she still bit her tongue when Justice Rehnquist asked her why women were not satisfied with their status considering that Susan B. Anthony's face now graced the front of a coin. She quashed the impulse to reply, "No, your honor, tokens won't do."

As she looked at the justices arrayed before her, Ginsburg could see at least one familiar face. She had met Brennan in 1966 when he visited Rutgers for the dedication of a new law school building along with Chief Justice Warren and Justice Fortas. The trio of justices had encountered protestors circling the block, and the nervous law school dean wondered whether to call in the police. Brennan had left a good first impression on Ginsburg when he suggested leaving them undisturbed. "They are just exercising their First Amendment rights," she remembered Brennan as saying. The justices peppered Levin with questions during his sixteen-minute argument based on rational-basis review, but when Ginsburg rose to argue for strict scrutiny, Brennan and his fellow justices did not ask her a single question. For ten minutes, she spoke from memory without interruption in a slow and steady cadence that belied how nervous she felt. The lack of questions puzzled Ginsburg and left her wondering whether the judges were merely indulging her.

Two days after the oral argument, the justices discussed the case in their Friday conference. Seven of them, including Brennan, agreed that the statute violated the equal protection clause, while Rehnquist and Burger voted to uphold it. Most of the justices seemed inclined to let *Reed v. Reed* govern and to once again sidestep the question of whether sex constituted a suspect classification justifying strict scrutiny. Douglas, as senior associate justice in the majority, assigned the case to Brennan. As Ginsburg surmised, Brennan's initial instinct was to stick with the middle ground laid out in *Reed,* an approach certain to hold a majority. He directed his clerk, Geoffrey Stone, to declare, "We need not, and therefore do not, decide whether classifications based upon sex are 'suspect,'" since the statute at issue "cannot pass constitutional muster even under the more 'lenient' standard of *Reed v. Reed.*" But Stone found that approach intellectually dishonest. If the Court was going to subject classifications based on sex to a higher level of scrutiny, Stone thought the justices should come out and say so. He decided also to draft an alternative opinion explicitly declaring sex a suspect classification.

Brennan later recalled arguing with Stone about the merits of that approach over the course of several days. Stone, by contrast, remembered leaving the alternative drafts on Brennan's desk, expecting to hash it out the next morning. But when Stone came in the next day, on February 14, Brennan had already circulated his first opinion to the other justices along with a cover note in which he told his colleagues that "the case would provide an appropriate vehicle for us to recognize sex as a 'suspect criterion.'" Whether Brennan debated the issue with Stone or was convinced by his draft opinion alone, this was clearly an instance where a clerk heavily influenced Brennan's thinking. Providing additional impetus was a memo circulated the previous week by Potter Stewart in a different case in which he suggested that he, too, might be amenable to recognizing sex as a suspect classification. "In light of Potter's memo," Brennan wrote, "perhaps there is a court for such an approach. If so, I'd have no difficulty in writing the opinion along those lines."

Justice White almost immediately indicated that he interpreted *Reed* to apply greater than a rational-basis test. Douglas said that he favored strict scrutiny. Marshall and Blackmun did not reply at all. Powell indi-

cated he would join the opinion as originally drafted but saw no reason to consider whether sex was a suspect classification. Weighing on his
mind was a proposed constitutional amendment pending before the states,
which declared in its entirety, "Equality of rights under the law shall not
be denied or abridged by the United States or by any state on account of
sex." Some version of the equal rights amendment had been percolating in
Congress since 1923, but this was the first time it actually advanced beyond
Capitol Hill. The House of Representatives passed it in 1971 and the Senate followed suit in March 1972. In the ten months since, twenty-two of
the thirty-eight states needed for ratification of this constitutional amendment had done so. Powell was not the first to mention the ERA during
consideration of the case. The briefs of both the ACLU and the government had invoked the amendment's pending ratification in the states in
support of their respective positions. Powell indicated he wanted to wait to
confront the equal protection issue "until we know the outcome of the
Equal Rights Amendment."

Still, Brennan and his clerks remained confident they could win over
Marshall and perhaps even Blackmun, given some of his surprisingly liberal recent votes. They would have been buoyed had they seen a memo
Blackmun wrote to himself during the consideration of *Reed* in October
1971. "All in all, I am inclined to feel that sex can be considered a suspect
classification . . . There can be no question that women have been held
down in the past in almost every area." Even without any such hint from
Blackmun, Brennan was confident enough about his chances of attracting
a majority that he circulated a second draft on February 28 arguing that
sex was a suspect classification.

The opinion followed the reasoning of Ginsburg's brief, agreeing with
Frontiero's contention that "classifications based upon sex, like classifications based upon race, alienage or national origin, are inherently suspect
and must therefore be subjected to strict judicial scrutiny." Brennan wrote
that departing from traditional rational-basis review was "clearly justified"
by the nation's "long and unfortunate history of sex discrimination." Borrowing a phrase from the California Supreme Court without attribution,
he noted, "Traditionally, such discrimination was rationalized by an attitude of 'romantic paternalism' which, in practical effect, put women not on
a pedestal, but in a cage." Brennan observed that, while the position of

women had improved markedly in recent decades, "women still face pervasive, although at times more subtle, discrimination in our educational institutions, in the job market and, perhaps most conspicuously, in the political arena."

Brennan soon received "join" letters from Douglas, Marshall, and White, meaning he had four votes for strict scrutiny. But he remained one justice short of a majority. Powell made clear on March 2 that he could not accept Brennan's approach, again expressing concern about preempting the ERA ratification process. He questioned "the desirability of this Court reaching out to anticipate a major political decision which is currently in process of resolution by the duly prescribed constitutional process." Blackmun raised a similar concern about entering "the arena of the proposed Equal Rights Amendment" when he wrote on March 5 to say he did not think they should declare sex a suspect classification. Brennan took a very different view of the amendment's prospects. He noted in a March 6 circulation to his colleagues that eleven states had already voted against the ERA and four more were expected to do so in the near future. "Since rejection in 13 states is sufficient to kill the Amendment, it looks like a lost cause," Brennan wrote. "I therefore don't see that we gain anything by awaiting what is at best an uncertain outcome."

As Brennan suggested, the ERA did in fact face uncertain prospects in early 1973. After a burst of twenty states ratified it in the first three months after Senate passage, only two states had done so in the last six months of 1972. A well-financed lobby, Stop ERA, led by conservative activist Phyllis Schlafly, had sprung up in opposition, successfully attracting support with the argument that the ERA would abolish legal safeguards that protected women's place at home. In an article headlined "Trouble for ERA," *Time* magazine warned in February 1973 that "it now seems dubious whether the 38 ratifications can be won this year" and "if the issue drags on into 1974, the prospects may become even dimmer."

Brennan's willingness to act in the face of a political process that had not yet played itself out was quite an about-face from a decade earlier when he had seemed so concerned about the Court stepping out in front of Congress. Then, he had urged his colleagues not to do anything that might jeopardize passage of the 1964 Civil Rights Act. Here, Brennan seemed intent on forging ahead, no matter the consequences. "The 'suspect' approach is the proper one," Brennan urged his colleagues. "Now is the time, and this is the case, to make that clear." His sense of urgency did not sway any more of his colleagues. Stewart indicated the next day that he would concur in the result on the grounds that the "statutes before us work an invidious discrimination in violation of the Constitution," but he would not vote for making sex a suspect classification. The unusually aggressive gambit had failed. Brennan had run out of possible fifth votes. Uncharacteristically, for someone who had built a reputation inside the Court for near-wizardry in cobbling together five-vote majorities, Brennan would have to settle for a plurality opinion.

Powell circulated a concurrence on March 14 that declared, "It is unnecessary for the Court in this case to characterize sex as a suspect classification with all the far-reaching implications of such a holding." Blackmun joined that same day. Sensing a potential opportunity, Rehnquist and Burger said that they would join, too, if Powell could convince Stewart, which would prevent Brennan from having a plurality. Stewart approached Brennan with an offer: if he reverted to his original language, Stewart promised to join Brennan in a future case holding that *Reed* and *Frontiero* implicitly meant that sex was a suspect criterion. Stewart said that if Brennan went ahead with the more aggressive version, it would be harder to join such a holding later, since it would make him look inconsistent. Brennan rejected Stewart's offer, which he viewed as a quid pro quo. Even without Stewart, Burger opted to join Powell's opinion on May 8, while Rehnquist dissented. When the decision was announced on May 14, the Court had overturned the statute but was divided four to four on the question of whether sex was a suspect classification. That division explains why the *New York Times* concluded, "The decision fell just short of a major triumph for the women's rights movement."

Upon hearing news of the decision, Sharon Frontiero and her husband jubilantly predicted it would give a lift to the feminist movement. Publicly, Ginsburg put the best face on the decision. "Brennan's opinion is a joy to read," she wrote a fellow attorney on May 15.

She told an audience of lawyers later that year that the implications of the case were "far more spectacular than the decision in *Reed*." Privately, though, Ginsburg was disappointed that Brennan had adopted the very position she had advocated. Brennan had surprised her. Ginsburg thought he should have settled for more incremental progress and waited for a broader victory down the road. The outcome, Ginsburg predicted, would only make her job more difficult.

SEVEN MONTHS AFTER Brennan announced his landmark opinion in *Frontiero*, Barnett, his former clerk turned Berkeley law professor, prepared to recommend a female law clerk to him for a second time. Even in late 1973, after Brennan had decried the nation's "long and unfortunate history of sex discrimination," Barnett remained understandably concerned about how Brennan might react. He held off on telling the candidate, Marsha Berzon, another top-ranked student, until after he spoke with Brennan. Barnett decided to make the recommendation in person during a December 1973 visit to Washington instead of talking about it over the telephone. But Barnett proved no more persuasive face-to-face. As with Grey, Brennan rejected Berzon on the basis of her gender alone. Without offering any explanation, he once again requested Barnett recommend a male candidate instead.

If Brennan's refusal to hire a female clerk had seemed odd in 1970, it was now all the more inexplicable three years later. Brennan had proven to be Professor Ginsburg's most eager pupil, forcefully condemning discrimination against women and calling for strict scrutiny of sex-based classifications. Attention to gender inequalities in legal hiring had only intensified in the intervening years. A group of female law students attracted media coverage with their 1971 lawsuit against ten New York law firms alleging discrimination against women in hiring. Yet Brennan apparently did not think twice about continuing to discriminate against women in his own chambers. His fear of his own potential discomfort and of sullying the ears of women prompted Brennan to put them on the very same pedestal he had denounced in *Frontiero*.

Brennan might not even have recognized the profound disconnect between his judicial opinions and this personnel decision. He strictly compartmentalized his Court opinions and his life, often taking positions in opinions that were far more liberal than his own personal views. Conservative critics of judicial activism accused liberal judges such as Brennan of reading their own personal values into the Constitution. That was not necessarily true of Brennan. He had endorsed a constitutional right to abortion even though he remained personally uncomfortable with abortion. He advocated for press freedoms, but no one could enrage him more than reporters. This disconnect on the issue of hiring women clerks was far more problematic, given that he was arguably violating law he had helped establish. Yet this compartmentalization perhaps explains how Brennan could condemn gender discrimination while continuing to practice it in his own chambers.

Barnett told Berzon she did not get the clerkship but not the reason why. But this time, instead of silently accepting Brennan's decision without complaint, he opted to share his concerns with Brennan in a letter. "Mr. Justice, I don't believe you realize how serious this matter is. For one thing — looking only at the pragmatic side — I am very much afraid that the subject will come out in the open and embarrass or threaten you. Your blanket refusal to accept a woman clerk is not just 'sexist,' and not just contrary to government policy; it seems to me that it is literally unconstitutional, under the decisions" that Brennan had joined or written himself. Barnett warned Brennan of the "militancy with which the growing numbers of women in law school today view sex discrimination." He enclosed an article from Harvard Law School's student newspaper detailing the growing attention given to the paucity of female law clerks. Barnett predicted that "it is only a matter of time" before someone brought a lawsuit against a Supreme Court justice alleging discrimination in clerk selection. "You would be a prime target for such an attack," warned Barnett, who added that, if subpoenaed, he would have to tell the truth.

Even more troubling, Barnett confided, was how at odds Brennan's policy was with his own principles. "I can't believe you would want your daughter or granddaughter, say, who had excelled in law school and in lower-court clerking to the point of being considered the best person available by whoever was doing the choosing, to be denied an opportunity to clerk for the Supreme Court — and all the subsequent opportunities that flow from that — because the Justice in question simply refused to hire a woman. With all the admiration I have for you and what you stand for, I just cannot believe that, on reflection, you will continue a policy that is both unconstitutional and simply wrong, and is so much at odds with your great principles."

It was a remarkable rebuke for Brennan at the hands of one of his own former clerks. To his credit, though, instead of getting angry, Brennan called Barnett after receiving the letter and admitted he was wrong. "Steve," Brennan said, "you must win all your cases." Barnett hung up the telephone with Brennan both relieved and impressed. "He was big enough to change his ways and recognize his error," Barnett recalled. Barnett called Berzon, then clerking in San Francisco for a judge on the Ninth Circuit, with the news that she would be clerking for Brennan after all beginning in the fall of 1974. He did not mention that she would be Brennan's first female clerk. Five days after receiving Barnett's letter, Brennan wrote Berzon to formally offer her the clerkship starting in July 1974. Before she left the Bay Area for Washington, Barnett mentioned nothing about the circumstances surrounding her hiring or Brennan's earlier rejection of Grey. He warned Berzon only that she should be careful about how she handled Brennan's secretary, Mary Fowler. Berzon did not feel quite as out of place as the women clerks at the Court who came before her. In the wake of *Frontiero,* several justices either saw the light — or the potential public relations problem that might result from hiring only men. Women clerks also went to work that term in the chambers of Justices Blackmun, Marshall, and Powell.

Brennan admitted to his clerks that he felt uneasy about the pending arrival of his first female clerk in the weeks before she arrived. But once she started working in his chambers, neither Berzon nor her male colleagues noticed any difference in the way Brennan treated her. In fact, Berzon actually felt most uncomfortable attending Brennan's clerk reunions, where she was the sole female attendee. Berzon was charmed when what she called Brennan's "generational chivalry" prompted him to insist she sit at his side. As Barnett warned, the adjustment proved more difficult for Fowler. Although Berzon did not have any problems with her, a clerk in a subsequent term recalled Fowler confiding after a visit by Berzon how hard she had found it to understand this younger woman.

Berzon made an unlikely connection with Brennan, given his ideas about gender roles. Berzon brought her two-year-old son, Jeremy, with her to Washington when she began her clerkship and left each day to pick him up from daycare. In fact, Brennan faced some unexpected childcare responsibilities of his own that fall after his daughter, Nancy, and her husband, Tim, divorced. Nancy moved back to her parents' home on Dumbarton Avenue with Connie, who was four years old, while she earned a master's degree in museum education at George Washington University. Their presence delighted Brennan, although Marjorie's illness meant he took on more of the burden of helping Nancy care for Connie. He and Berzon wound up leaving the Court at the same time each day to pick up the children from daycare.

Brennan exhibited great affection for all his grandchildren — as well as his step-grandchildren after Nancy later remarried. He still exchanged letters and sent presents to Hugh Jr. in Arizona. When this grandson wrote Brennan at the age of thirteen in 1970 expressing interest in the Air Force Academy, Brennan wrote back an encouraging reply. But he formed a particularly close bond with Connie that year they lived under the same roof. They even became roommates when Connie took to sleeping in the second bed in the backroom he had moved into since Marjorie's illness. She so enjoyed waking her grandfather in the morning that, if he got up first to go for his morning walk, he got back into bed and pretended to be sleeping again for her benefit. Then Brennan would make her breakfast, as he had done two decades earlier with Nancy. Connie played ball at the Court with clerks and police officers, just as her mother had done. Once Brennan even enlisted his clerks to scour the city, looking for Minnie Mouse ears for her.

Brennan and Connie shared a conspiratorial sweet tooth. She once caught him sneaking one of the cookies he had hidden in the kitchen, pleading with her not to tell Marjorie, who still carefully watched his diet. One summer morning on Nantucket, he took Connie along on one of his morning walks and then shared an ice-cream sundae with her at the general store where he bought his newspapers. The catch: he insisted that she still had to eat a full breakfast when they got back to their summer house so Marjorie would not get suspicious. And he worried about Connie as much as he had about his own children. Brennan once left the Court to get a haircut on a day when Connie stayed home sick with Marjorie. He received a call at the barbershop that Connie had gone missing. Fearing that perhaps someone had kidnapped her, Brennan bolted from the barbershop with a half-finished haircut and headed home to Georgetown. He called out for Connie around the house and frantically searched the neighborhood without success. Then, after returning home, he heard noises upstairs. He discovered Connie hidden under the bed playing a one-person game of hide-and-seek. "You're not supposed to come out, even if people are calling you," Connie explained.

As she grew up, though, Connie found it no easier to get her grandfather to reveal himself to her than his clerks did. Despite her best efforts, he would not talk much about his childhood beyond impersonating his father's Irish brogue and joking about how his mother ran their house. An unintentionally revealing moment came one day when Brennan babysat Connie while Marjorie took a nap. Brennan gave her a legal pad and pencil to draw while he worked at the dining room table. Connie showed Brennan her drawing of a stick figure standing behind bars with gigantic tears and told him that is what he did: put people in jail. "That is not what I do!" Brennan said sharply before launching into a complicated discourse about his role as a judge. At the time, Connie did not understand why he had gotten so angry and thought he just disliked her picture. Only later did she realize how important it was to Brennan that his granddaughter did not think of him as someone who imprisoned people for a living.

HALFWAY THROUGH THE TERM, the justices took up a case involving a man burdened by unexpectedly heavy childrearing responsibilities. Stephen Wiesenfeld found himself the sole caretaker for his newborn son, Jason, after his wife of seventeen months, Paula, died during childbirth in 1972. Wiesenfeld, a self-employed consultant in New Jersey, had always intended to stay home with the baby while Paula, the family's primary breadwinner, continued teaching high school math and pursuing a Ph.D. After her death, Wiesenfeld applied for Social Security survivors' benefits for both himself and his son that would cover his wife's lost income and ensure he could still stay home. His son qualified for the payments but Wiesenfeld was told only women could obtain survivors' benefits for themselves. The law assumed men were the primary wage earners and did not need survivors' benefits.

Ginsburg learned of this potential case after a friend who taught at Rutgers read a letter to the editor in a New Jersey newspaper that Wiesenfeld had written about his situation. It was just the sort of counterintuitive situation inverting traditional gender roles that Ginsburg, still at Columbia, found ideal. The case showed clearly how a gender-based classification could harm both men and women. Ginsburg called Wiesenfeld in December 1972 and, after he agreed to be a plaintiff, filed suit on his behalf in New Jersey's federal District Court two months later. A special three-judge panel followed Brennan's reasoning in *Frontiero*, subjecting this provision of the Social Security Act to strict scrutiny and ruling that it unconstitutionally discriminated against women wage earners.

Still, Ginsburg had little grounds for optimism as she prepared to argue before the Supreme Court for the third time on January 20, 1975, on Wiesenfeld's behalf. As she had feared, momentum had stalled in the wake of the Court's *Frontiero* decision two years earlier. Just five days earlier, the Court had handed down the latest in a trio of setbacks upholding statutes challenged as discriminating on the basis of sex. This one upheld a Navy rule that required male officers twice passed over for promotion to retire — but gave women officers a guarantee of thirteen years total service before they had to retire after being passed over. The Court had also upheld a California law that barred women absent from work due to normal pregnancies from receiving payments from the state's disability insurance program, and a Florida statute that provided a $500 property-tax exemption to widows — but not widowers.

Ginsburg had argued the Florida tax exemption case before the Court, even though she would never have appealed the case to the Supreme Court if the local ACLU lawyers had bothered to consult her. Still, she tried her best, avoiding the strict-scrutiny argument, which now seemed like a losing one after *Frontiero*. Instead, Ginsburg called for "heightened scrutiny" in her brief. Brennan, though, had not abandoned strict scrutiny. In each of the three cases, he wrote a dissent maintaining, as he had in *Frontiero*, that classifications based on sex were suspect and should be subject to strict scrutiny.

Brennan had treated Berzon enough like her male fellow clerks that she did not think it odd when he asked her to write a first draft of the opinion in *Weinberger v. Wiesenfeld*. In hindsight, she would conclude he had purposely assigned the case to the young mother in his chambers. Berzon sidestepped the question of whether gender was a suspect classification but nonetheless rejected the Social Security provision as an "archaic and overbroad" generalization that earnings of women wage earners do not contribute to their families. Without saying so, Brennan employed some form of heightened scrutiny here, since in the past even the mere mention of a compensatory purpose had proven sufficient to satisfy the more lenient rational review. In his opinion, Brennan had made clear that "the mere recitation of a benign, compensatory purpose is not an automatic shield which protects against any inquiry into the actual purposes underlying a statutory scheme." With Justice Douglas absent due to ill health, all eight justices voted to reject the statute. Four joined Brennan's opinion for the Court. Powell, Burger, and Rehnquist concurred on narrower grounds.

The *New York Times* called the decision a "major victory for supporters of equal rights for women," noting that "it was the first time the Court had insisted on equal treatment in a sex discrimination case when such a ruling would be very expensive to the Government." In an editorial a few days later, the *Times* noted that the ERA's fate remained in doubt, and predicted that "the route to full legal equality for women may lie in a broadened interpretation by the Supreme Court of its own precedents on equal protection." The outcome pleased Ginsburg. "Wiesenfeld gets us back on track," she wrote a fellow law professor. When a friend wrote to tell her that tears filled her eyes as she read the decision, Ginsburg wrote back, "I cried too!" It was not Brennan's experience helping care for his granddaughter that changed his approach to sex-discrimination cases; he had already embraced strict scrutiny. But it had perhaps forced him to reconsider his traditional views about family and gender roles.

In the wake of the *Wiesenfeld* decision, Ginsburg received word about a sensitive matter involving Brennan from one of her former Columbia Law students. Ginsburg wrote to invite the former student, Lynn Hecht Schafran, now clerking for a New York federal judge, to a victory party to celebrate the *Wiesenfeld* decision. In response, Schafran recounted a rumor she had heard about how Justice Brennan rejected the recommendation of a woman clerk for the 1974–75 term and had ultimately reconsidered under pressure. Rumors about Brennan's refusal to hire women soon were circulating widely. A 1976 law review article about the ACLU Women's Rights Project mentioned it too.

Three decades later, Ginsburg, who by then was a Supreme Court justice herself, did not remember receiving that letter or knowing at the time about Brennan's unwillingness to hire women. But Brennan's hesitance certainly did not surprise Ginsburg — nor did she hold it against him. "He was a man brought up in a certain age," Ginsburg explained. It reminded her of her own experience after law school when so few judges wanted to hire her as a clerk and Judge Hand worried about cursing if he had to look at her face-to-face. They were "uncomfortable dealing with a woman. That's the way things were." Brennan, she said, like so many men of his generation, "had to wake up."

It took Brennan longer to wake up than many of his colleagues. Between 1973 and 1980, thirty-four women served as Supreme Court clerks. Brennan employed just one of them. However smoothly Berzon's clerkship might have gone, another seven terms would pass before he hired another woman clerk. Brennan later blamed that on a lack of female candidates being recommended to him. "Believe me, it ain't for gender-discrimination reasons," he insisted.

The subject of female clerks remained a sensitive one inside his chambers in the intervening years. During the 1978–79 term, Brennan and his clerks enjoyed watching a television show based on the novel and movie *The Paper Chase*, which chronicled the experiences of a stern and demanding Harvard Law School professor named Kingsfield and his students. Every Wednesday, Brennan and his clerks discussed the latest episode during their morning coffee session — that is, until the episode that aired that December, where the plot focused on a noisy protest by a group of Harvard Law students during the visit to campus of a Supreme Court justice who had never hired a female clerk. The plot bore uncanny similarities to the scenario Barnett had warned Brennan about five years earlier. A fictional professor, who had recommended women clerks for years, tells the fictional justice that he may have been preaching equal justice in his opinions, but he did not practice it himself. After lamenting, "It's what I'm comfortable with," the justice says, "I assumed my philosophy and my opinions on women's rights would be enough." No one uttered a word about the episode to Brennan the next morning.

GINSBURG DID NOT think much of one of the two gender-discrimination cases the Court heard on October 5, 1976. In what she derisively labeled the "beer case," two underage fraternity brothers and the female co-owner of a Honk-N-Holler convenience store challenged an Oklahoma law that allowed eighteen-year-old women to purchase 3.2 percent beer containing half the alcohol of regular beer while men could not do so until turning twenty-one. Ginsburg got involved in the case, *Craig v. Boren,* after a three-judge federal district court ruled in favor of the state in 1975. Ginsburg considered the case frivolous, involving a "non-weighty interest pressed by thirsty boys," but the Supreme Court agreed to take the case in January 1976.

Once again, Ginsburg found herself tangling with the local counsel over the best approach. She urged them to avoid arguing in favor of strict scrutiny. "We don't have 5 votes for suspect classification so play that down," Ginsburg advised. "Urge instead, 'heightened scrutiny.'" That's what she did in the amicus brief she filed separately after the local lawyers resisted her entreaties to combine efforts. Ginsburg was equally vague about the proper standard of review when she rose that same day on October 5 to argue what she considered the more substantial gender-discrimination case, a challenge to another provision of the Social Security Act that limited the benefits widowers could receive.

Brennan, as senior associate justice, assigned himself both cases after the justices discussed them at their weekly conference. In the Oklahoma beer case, *Craig v. Boren,* Brennan had a shaky majority of five. Both Stewart and the newest justice, John Paul Stevens, who replaced Douglas, seemed unwilling to go any further than an amorphous endorsement of heightened scrutiny. But as in *Frontiero,* Brennan opted to go further than the majority's apparent consensus, hopeful that although he was out on a limb he could win over Blackmun and Powell. This time, he did not try to go as far as strict scrutiny. Instead, in a strategic retreat, Brennan laid out for the first time an explicit formulation of heightened scrutiny. He characterized the standard of review as requiring that classifications based on gender "must serve important government objectives and must be substantially related to achievement of those objectives." The term "important government objectives" fell somewhere between the "compelling" requirement of strict scrutiny and the looser "legitimate" requirement of rational basis.

Brennan circulated the opinion on November 2, and nine days later Blackmun indicated his willingness to "go along" with much of it. White and Marshall joined. Four justices concurred, with both Powell and Stevens criticizing Brennan's middle-tier approach. Powell made clear he did not welcome a further subdivision of equal protection analysis. Stevens similarly took issue with the new standard. "There is only one Equal Protection Clause," he wrote. All the concurrences sowed confusion about the opinion's significance. It would be another two and a half months before Brennan announced his opinion in *Califano v. Goldfarb* — the other case argued that same day — which Ginsburg had assumed would be more significant. She liked the result in that case enough that she joked that she had an urge to kiss Brennan. But it was the beer case that proved more impor-

tant in the long term. Brennan had surprised her once again, finally pro-
nouncing an intermediate level of scrutiny in a case with such an inconse-
quential issue at stake. Her goal of heightened scrutiny had finally come to
fruition in a case she had dismissed as "an embarrassment."

During the course of the 1970s Ginsburg wrote briefs in numerous
gender-discrimination cases before the Supreme Court and argued six
of them herself. She won five — of which Brennan wrote the opinions in
three. Her arguments before the Court came to an end in 1980 when President Carter nominated her to a seat on the U.S. Court of Appeals for the
D.C. Circuit. She would return to the Supreme Court in 1993 as the nation's
second female justice. Brennan had retired by then, but his absence did not
diminish her appreciation and gratitude toward him. "First he was my hero
and now he's my colleague," she said on a 1996 public television documen-
tary. When Ginsburg wrote a landmark gender-discrimination decision of
her own in 1996, she delivered Brennan a signed copy of her bench announcement inscribed, "Dear Bill, See how the light you shed has spread!
With appreciation, Ruth." As she handed it to Brennan, she said, "Without
you this would not have been possible."

· 17 ·

DEATH & DIGNITY

B RENNAN SAT AT the far end of the justices' conference table on April 2, 1976, and announced to his colleagues that he would never again vote to sustain a death sentence. "I'm absolutely convinced that it's 'cruel and unusual,'" he later recalled saying. "And that's where I'm going to be from now on." Brennan proved good to his word. From that point forward, he would issue a dissent in every case upholding a death sentence, noting his view that "the death penalty is in all circumstances cruel and unusual punishment prohibited by the Eighth and Fourteenth amendments." Joined by Marshall, he would also begin a practice unprecedented in the Court's history of dissenting every time their fellow justices declined to hear an appeal brought by a death row convict.

That decision to vote against the death penalty in all circumstances was the culmination of a lifelong evolution in Brennan's thinking. The resulting absolutist position he adopted severely restricted his influence in death penalty cases. It was a sharp break from his first twenty years on the Court when he so often drafted the compromise approach that held together majorities in landmark cases. Only Marshall shared his belief that the death penalty was unconstitutional under all circumstances, an issue that bound them together in the public mind and further solidified their standing as heroes of the Left. But their sustained dissents raise troubling questions about just how far justices should go in questioning a decision in the face of settled precedent. And the death penalty proved to be the source of some behind-the-scenes friction between these two close allies, feeding the disappointment Brennan quietly harbored regarding his last remaining liberal colleague.

BRENNAN LATER TRACED his opposition to the death penalty back to his earliest days as a lawyer in Depression-era New Jersey, when he took criminal-defense assignments from a Newark judge as a way to supplement his relatively meager earnings as a junior law firm attorney. The judge assigned him to help represent a woman charged with killing her husband after she caught him in their bed with another man. The more experienced defense attorney whom Brennan was assisting feared that a jury might regard her act of going into the kitchen and getting a knife, which she then used to stab her husband, as sufficient evidence of premeditated intent to kill him, rather than the murder being a sudden act of passion. That could have resulted in a death sentence, which meant electrocution in New Jersey. Although death sentences remained relatively rare — particularly for women — they were common enough in the early 1930s that Brennan could not discount the possibility altogether.

Brennan's early life coincided with a fall and rise in the death penalty's prevalence in the northern United States. Nine states abolished capital punishment between 1907 and 1917, and bills outlawing the death penalty advanced in several other state legislatures, including New Jersey. But the abolition drive ceased during World War I. And many of the states that had outlawed executions brought back the death penalty during the 1920s. By the time Brennan began practicing law in 1931, the number of death sentences nationally and in his home state had started rising again. New Jersey judges handed down on average about five death sentences per year, spiking to sixteen in 1930. Nationally, the number of executions peaked in 1935 when 199 convicts were put to death.

The increasing prevalence of death sentences explains why Brennan felt a sick sensation in his stomach as he went to the prison where his female client was being held. For the first time in his life, Brennan came face-to-face with someone who could realistically face a death sentence. Brennan's client avoided that outcome by agreeing to plead guilty to manslaughter in exchange for ten years in prison, but the experience of coming so close to the death penalty with a client was something that never left him.

Brennan would come up against the issue again when he became a New Jersey judge. By that time, the number of death sentences in New Jersey had begun to wane again, falling to twenty-eight statewide in the 1940s. The drop reflected a trend toward fewer executions in much of the northern United States. Juries seemed increasingly inclined to choose prison over death as the appropriate sentence. While Brennan did not impose any death sentences during his brief tenure as a trial judge, he did sit on a small number of murder appeals as a justice on the New Jersey Supreme Court, some involving death sentences. In the first such case, he voted in dissent to overturn a murder conviction, finding fault with the judge's jury instructions; the defendant was executed a few months later. In some other cases, he rejected defendants' appeals, although the legality of the death penalty itself was never at issue. "I was always sort of sick and troubled by it," Brennan recalled. "But there wasn't anything in those days you could do about it."

Up to that point, no American court — state or federal — had struck down the death penalty as unconstitutional. While the Eighth Amendment included a prohibition on "cruel and unusual punishment," other provisions of the Constitution treated the legality of capital punishment as a given. In the nineteenth century, the Supreme Court upheld both firing squads and electrocution as execution methods, holding that the cruel and unusual punishment clause pertained only to punishments involving torture or lingering death. That was still the state of the constitutional law surrounding the death penalty when Brennan joined the Supreme Court.

To be sure, notions about what sorts of crimes merit a death sentence and what are acceptable means and circumstances for executions had changed over time. The American colonies had followed the English practice of making death the default punishment for crimes ranging from murder and treason down to arson, counterfeiting, and theft. But eventually prison replaced execution as the main method of punishing criminals, and northern states ceased executions for most crimes other than murder or treason, a trend that was all but complete by the time of the Civil War. Once-popular public executions fell into disfavor as the nineteenth century progressed, and by the time Brennan was born many states had retired the hangman's noose altogether in favor of electrocution and the gas chamber. But it was elected officials rather than judges who had made those changes.

IF, AS BRENNAN insisted later, the death penalty troubled him long before he arrived in Washington, he appears to have kept such concerns to himself. Daniel Rezneck, who clerked for Brennan during the 1960–61 term, recalled that he had no trouble voting against hearing the appeal of two Kansas death row inmates convicted of the brutal murder of a farmer and his family, a case vividly depicted in Truman Capote's bestselling book In Cold Blood. By that time, several other justices had publicly expressed personal misgivings about the death penalty's propriety, even though they made clear they thought it was constitutional. Brennan lectured extensively during the 1960s about criminal procedure and the rights of defendants, although his prepared remarks include no references to the death penalty. The closest Brennan came to airing his reservations was in 1965, when he wrote a private letter to Norman Redlich, a New York University law professor who represented the New York Committee to Abolish Capital Punishment. Brennan said the group's successful efforts to get rid of the death penalty in that state "are gratefully encouraging."

At this time, Brennan associated the death penalty most closely with an unwelcome personal intrusion. Brennan was in a San Francisco hotel room with his family in August 1962 while attending the American Bar Association's annual convention when the phone rang and Nancy picked it up. The caller was a lawyer for Elizabeth "Ma" Duncan, who faced an imminent death sentence in California for hiring two men to kill her son's wife. California's governor had already denied Duncan clemency, the state Supreme Court had rejected her habeas petition, and the U.S. Supreme Court had refused to review the case too. Unable to reach Justice Douglas, who usually heard emergency petitions from the Ninth Circuit, Duncan's lawyers tried desperately to convince Brennan to agree to hear another last-minute stay request. Brennan recalled that Duncan's lawyer gave up after Brennan made clear on the phone that he would hear no such request. Brennan's brother Frank, who joined them for that trip to San Francisco, remembered the incident even more dramatically. Frank arrived at the hotel to find Brennan and his family visibly shaken after Duncan's lawyers had barged into their hotel room. Brennan shouted at them to leave. Duncan was executed a day or two later.

A turning point in Brennan's thinking about the death penalty came in the fall of 1963. Arthur Goldberg, just beginning his second term on the Court, was troubled by a sense that the death penalty was being unfairly imposed, and directed one of his incoming clerks to research a memo about its constitutionality. In the resulting memo, Goldberg condemned "as barbaric and inhuman the deliberate institutionalized taking of human life by the state," which he concluded was cruel and unusual punishment under the Eighth Amendment. Even if the justices were not willing to consider that larger question, Goldberg urged his colleagues to address the narrower issue of whether executions for certain types of crimes or certain offenders might violate the ban on cruel and unusual punishment.

Given the common understanding that the death penalty was constitutional at the time of the Eighth Amendment's adoption, Goldberg had to build an argument that a punishment considered acceptable then might no longer be so now. For support, Goldberg turned to two Court precedents. In 1910 the Court had struck down as cruel and unusual the punishment of a U.S. government officer convicted of falsifying a public document. The officer was sentenced under the Filipino penal code to at least twelve and a half years of bound imprisonment (chains around the ankles and wrists), hard labor, and the loss of many civil liberties. The Court in that case, *Weems v. United States,* held that the cruel and unusual punishment clause "is not fastened to the obsolete, but may acquire meaning as public opinion becomes enlightened by a humane justice." Goldberg also invoked *Trop v. Dulles,* a 1958 opinion by Chief Justice Warren that struck down denaturalization as a cruel and unusual punishment for wartime desertion by a soldier. Warren had argued in that case that the meaning of cruel and unusual punishment should be determined by "evolving standards of decency that mark the progress of a maturing society." Goldberg did not discuss the fact that Warren had also made clear in that opinion that the death penalty "cannot be said to violate the constitutional concept of cruelty."

When he circulated his memo in October, most of Goldberg's colleagues rejected his suggestion that executions for some crimes violated the ban on cruel and unusual punishment. Warren later told Goldberg he preferred to let the matter "sleep for a while," given all the recent attacks on the Court for its decisions in other areas of law. Black, who read the Constitution's text literally, entirely rejected the notion of "evolving standards of decency." Brennan, though, proved more receptive.

Goldberg's memo convinced Brennan that the Court would eventually have to take up the question of the death penalty's constitutionality. Already leaning privately against the death penalty, he now welcomed this opportunity to go public with his concerns. Brennan's position surprised his clerks, given how little he had talked about the death penalty. But Brennan seemed reluctant to get too far out in front of Warren's position. So when Goldberg decided to draft a rare dissent from the denial of cert., in one of the cases, Brennan suggested framing it as a brief series of questions rather than as an argument for why the death penalty was unconstitutional. Goldberg followed that approach in his dissent, raising several questions, including whether imposing the death penalty in a rape case was cruel and unusual. Brennan, along with Douglas, joined this unusual dissent.

GOLDBERG'S UNORTHODOX DISSENT was read with particular interest at the offices of the NAACP Legal Defense and Educational Fund (LDF), where litigators interpreted it as an invitation to target the death penalty in court. The LDF's lawyers viewed the death penalty as inextricably linked to the issue of race. Blacks accounted for a disproportionate share of defendants sentenced to death, a trend most apparent in but not exclusive to the South. A study of the death penalty in Brennan's home state of New Jersey revealed that blacks accounted for 58 percent of those sentenced to death between 1937 and 1961, although they made up only 8 percent of the state's population. But as the number of death sentences in the North fell faster, southern states accounted for a rising proportion of the nation's executions. And it was in the South that the death penalty was still imposed for the crime with the most glaring racial disparity in its application: rape. Nine out of ten of those executed for the crime between 1930 and 1967 were black.

The LDF lawyers opted against a frontal assault on the death penalty's constitutionality, which still seemed premature. Instead, they decided to begin modestly by challenging the legal procedures employed in capital cases. The goal was to build upon some of the Warren Court's recent decisions in other areas of criminal procedure that benefited defendants. They targeted three particular practices: excluding potential jurors who had reservations about the death penalty, allowing the same jury to determine simultaneously both a defendant's guilt and whether to impose a death sentence, and the lack of legal standards to guide jurors in their decision. Incremental victories on these questions might have the added benefit of forestalling executions, since any new procedures would likely require states to first retry or resentence death row inmates.

The death penalty lawyers, including Anthony Amsterdam, a former Frankfurter clerk then teaching at the University of Pennsylvania Law School, ultimately adopted a strategy of trying to block every execution in the country, no matter the state, the crime, or the defendant's race. Sets of briefs called "Last Aid Kits" were distributed to lawyers around the country and contained every conceivable constitutional claim they could make against the death penalty. The strategy succeeded, aided by the greater access to federal courts that Brennan had helped provide state inmates by making it easier for them to file habeas corpus petitions. As legal challenges increased, the number of executions nationwide fell from forty-two in 1961 to two in 1967. That year, as successful legal challenges to the death penalty mounted and as public support for executions declined, states one by one stopped imposing capital sentences or stopped carrying them out, creating an unofficial moratorium as they awaited guidance from the Supreme Court.

As the first of these procedural challenges reached the Supreme Court in the late 1960s, death penalty opponents scored a few modest victories. In 1968 the justices struck down a provision of the Federal Kidnapping Act, which authorized death sentences in cases tried before a jury, but not those tried by a judge or where the defendant pled guilty, on the grounds that it penalized a defendant who sought a jury trial. That same term, the justices also accepted one of the LDF's three central arguments, rejecting the practice in many states of excluding people who are uneasy about the death penalty from "death qualified" juries. But the justices continued to sidestep the question of the death penalty's constitutionality. Even when lawyers directly challenged the death penalty as violating the Eighth Amendment in an Alabama robbery case during the 1968–69 term, the justices opted to strike down the verdict on narrower grounds.

Opponents had no idea at the time how close they had come to an important victory in another case the justices heard in March 1969. William

L. Maxwell, a twenty-one-year-old African American, had been sentenced to death in Arkansas for the rape of a thirty-five-year-old white woman. In his initial petition to hear the case, Amsterdam had presented statistical evidence of how differently death sentences were applied to black defendants in rape cases. The justices opted to ignore the race question entirely and instead focus on two narrower issues: the propriety of having "unitary trials" where a single jury considered both defendants' guilt and punishment, and whether juries had too much discretion — and too little guidance — in imposing death sentences.

After much debate, a majority of the justices seemed to agree that submitting the question to a jury of whether to impose the death penalty without providing jurors standards to guide their decision violated due process. Douglas drafted the opinion for the Court. Brennan wrote a concurrence in which he argued that "the most elementary requirement of due process is that judicial determinations concerning life or liberty must be based on pre-existing standards of law and cannot be left to the unlimited discretion of a judge or jury." But the case was held over after Fortas resigned. When the case was reargued in 1970, the justices opted to issue a short per curiam opinion on narrow grounds rather than addressing the constitutional due process issue.

By the time the issue came up again for a full airing the following term in another case, a majority of the justices declared that state statutes that gave juries absolute discretion to impose a death sentence without any standards to guide them did not violate the Constitution's due process requirement. Brennan, who had been part of the majority the first time, now found himself in a three-justice minority in *McGautha v. California* along with Douglas and Marshall. The justices considered this case in the spring of 1971, the same period when Brennan was issuing his trio of angry dissents that generated press attention. Here, too, Brennan wrote a stinging dissent emphasizing the importance of rigorously regulating the death penalty, and accusing the Court of "an unguided, unbridled, unreviewable exercise of naked power." But even though Chief Justice Warren was no longer a possible constraint on Brennan's approach to the issue, he did not argue that the death penalty constituted cruel and unusual punishment.

Although Brennan gave no hint of it in his *McGautha* dissent, where he stuck to the due process issue, by this time he had come to believe that the death penalty should be abolished altogether. The way Brennan explained it at the end of his career, what had begun as a private sense of unease in the 1930s had slowly deepened into the conviction that all executions were unconstitutional, no matter the circumstances. Although the Catholic Church had not yet come out forcefully against the death penalty, Brennan recalled talking about the issue with a friend and judge he had known back in New Jersey who had since left the bench and joined a Jesuit order. In their term history, his clerks from the 1969–70 term explained his position in a trio of cases by writing, "Justice Brennan's position was dictated in no small measure by his abhorrence of the death penalty." Clearly he had begun to share his increasingly strong views about the death penalty with his clerks too.

Brennan suggested that he also shared his death penalty thinking with some of his allies, although he did not press the point with either Black or Warren, a reticence he later regretted. He had good reason to be pessimistic at the time. It was not until after his retirement that Warren said he had found the death penalty "repulsive" his whole life. And, while Warren had been willing to vote for requiring standards for jurors, he seemed dead set against ruling that the death penalty as a whole was unconstitutional. "Maybe they might have been persuaded," Brennan said later. "This is a big, big 'maybe.' Sitting here now and recalling how rigid they were about it, I kind of think I would have gotten absolutely nowhere."

BRENNAN WAS FINALLY ready to declare the death penalty to be cruel and unusual punishment under the Eighth Amendment in the spring of 1971. By that point, several of his potential allies on the issue had left the Court. And now that the Court had rejected the due process challenge, attacking the death penalty as cruel and unusual punishment was the only major avenue left for declaring it unconstitutional. Brennan expressed his view about the "cruel and unusual" strategy in conference as the justices discussed several other cases held over until *McGautha* had been resolved.

As the only justice to hold that position, Brennan suggested that the Court should deny cert. in these other cases and that he would append a short dissent stating his view. But Black argued that the Court should take up these other cases and decide the question of the death penalty's constitutionality once and for all, an approach that a majority of the justices supported. They ultimately agreed to consider the cases of four highly unsympathetic defendants: Earnest J. Aikens Jr., convicted of two rape-mur-

ders in Ventura County north of Los Angeles; William Furman, convicted
of the accidental shooting death of a homeowner during a burglary in Sa-
vannah, Georgia; Lucious Jackson Jr., a prison escapee convicted of raping
a woman after breaking into her home in southeast Georgia; and Elmer
Branch, convicted in Texas of raping an elderly woman.

Toward the end of the term in the spring of 1971, Brennan directed Loftus Becker, who was soon to finish a clerkship in his chambers, to write
a memo laying out arguments for why the death penalty was cruel and
unusual punishment. Among the arguments Becker included in his memo
was that the Eighth Amendment clause "serves to protect society as a
whole from the inevitably brutalizing, dehumanizing impact that results
from society's deliberately treating any human beings in ways that deny
that person's essential dignity and humanity." Becker was well aware that
Brennan considered the idea of human dignity particularly important. No
justice would become as closely identified with the concept in the years
ahead as Brennan. By the end of his tenure, Brennan would cite human
dignity as "the basic premise on which I build everything under the Constitution."

Some of Brennan's clerks later questioned whether human dignity was
less a guiding principle than a rationalization he adopted after the fact to
justify how he had reached desired outcomes. In fact, Brennan had been
talking about human dignity even before he joined the Supreme Court. In
1954 Brennan placed "simple human dignity" along with "justice and fair
play" as the values "which have made our land what it is" in his Saint Patrick's Day speech to the Irish Charitable Society in Boston. And in a 1961
Newark speech titled "The Essential Dignity of Man," Brennan cited "the
dignity and worth of the individual" as the "supreme value of our American democracy" as he called for better treatment of criminal defendants
and prisoners. His invocations of the term in speeches only grew in frequency as the 1960s progressed.

It is not possible to identify what exactly inspired Brennan to embrace
human dignity, a concept employed by both liberal Enlightenment thinkers such as Immanuel Kant in the eighteenth century and, more recently,
by Catholic social thinkers. Pope Leo XIII invoked human dignity in his
1891 encyclical on capital and labor (*Rerum Novarum*) to argue that individual workers should not be treated as mere commodities in industrial

economies. As discussed earlier, Father John A. Ryan, the American Catholic social thinker, referred to human dignity on the first page of his 1906 book arguing that all workers deserved a living wage. More recently, the 1948 Universal Declaration of Human Rights enshrined every individual's dignity as the foundation for all human rights. And the drafters of the German constitution of 1949 incorporated human dignity in the very first article, later to be interpreted as the supreme value underlying all other rights.

There is nothing to suggest that Brennan read the writings of either Kant or Ryan; his notion of human dignity aligns more closely with the liberal conception emphasizing autonomy and independence. In his speeches during the 1960s, Brennan — at times sounding somewhat Kantian — expressed concerns that the move from agrarian to industrial society had left many Americans "without any real prospect of the dignity and autonomy that ownership with real property could confer." But Brennan usually drew upon a broad amalgam of sources — ranging from the Old and New Testaments to the Universal Declaration of Human Rights — when he talked about human dignity.

Where the concept of "human dignity" does not appear is in the text of the United States Constitution — or in many Supreme Court decisions prior to the 1940s. That changed as Frank Murphy, Brennan's Irish Catholic predecessor on the Court, periodically employed it, including in his dissent from the decision upholding the internment of Japanese Americans during World War II. So too did Black and Douglas begin to refer to individual dignity in the 1950s in decisions condemning coerced criminal confessions and improper police searches. Warren invoked dignity in his 1958 *Trop v. Dulles* decision. Warren did so again in *Miranda*, describing the interrogation environment in the case as "destructive of human dignity." Human dignity would come to be invoked in cases in discussions of at least seven different constitutional amendments, although rarely with any specificity about what is meant by the term.

By the time the 1971–72 term began, no one had been executed in the United States in nearly four and a half years due to the unofficial moratorium. But more than seven hundred inmates remained on death row in the forty states that still had the death penalty. These inmates would have to wait a little longer to find out whether the Supreme Court intended to overturn their death sentences. The justices postponed the oral argument, originally scheduled for October, for three months, until the appointments of Powell and Rehnquist restored the Court to full membership.

Brennan gave no hint of his position during the unusually long four hours of oral arguments on January 17, 1972, in the three cases consolidated as *Furman v. Georgia* and in a separate California case. He listened silently as death penalty attorney Anthony Amsterdam argued that, as notions about acceptable forms of punishment evolved, the death penalty had been "repudiated and condemned by the conscience of the country." Further, Amsterdam argued, the death penalty had been applied so infrequently that it had become an unusual punishment, and society would not tolerate executions even if they were administered evenly and without discrimination. Nor did Brennan ask any questions as the attorneys representing California, Georgia, and Texas argued that the word "cruel" in the Constitution referred to torture rather than the death penalty and that the Court could not strip away the states' power to make the death penalty available absent a constitutional amendment.

As usual, Brennan was more forthcoming when the justices met privately four days later at their weekly conference. He made clear to his colleagues that he would reverse all four convictions. He cited Goldberg's 1963 memo and echoed Amsterdam's arguments that the death penalty was susceptible to infrequent, selective use and that it was cruel when interpreted according to contemporary standards. Burger, Powell, and Rehnquist indicated that they favored upholding the death sentences. Blackmun abstained after explaining that he was personally opposed to the death penalty but believed it was a decision best left to legislators. Four other justices joined Brennan in speaking in favor of reversing, although for different reasons. Douglas focused on statistics that showed the death penalty was being imposed primarily on minorities. He argued that such discrimination qualified as "unusual" punishment under the Eighth Amendment. Stewart and White emphasized the infrequency and arbitrariness by which death sentences were imposed. Marshall provided the fifth vote for what Brennan knew was a particularly fragile majority.

Each justice seemed inclined to go his own way rather than sign on to a single opinion. Nevertheless, in the weeks that followed, Brennan and his clerks worked on a draft aimed at winning over some of the least commit-

ted justices. Brennan began with the central premise he had announced
the previous spring: the death penalty was unconstitutional under all circumstances. His argument largely tracked the logic of the LDF in its brief
that the death penalty had always been cruel and was now unusual because
it was so rarely and arbitrarily imposed. To support the proposition that
the cruel and unusual punishment clause should be interpreted according
to evolving standards of decency, he cited *Weems* and *Trop v. Dulles,* Warren's 1958 decision. For evidence of society's growing unease, Brennan, like
the LDF, pointed to how infrequently death sentences were being imposed.
"It is tolerated only because of its disuse," Brennan wrote. He privately
circulated the draft opinion, which he labeled a memorandum, to Stewart
and White in March and to the full conference two weeks later.

As expected, Brennan's memo did not win over any of his colleagues.
Powell remained unconvinced that the Constitution forbade the death
penalty or that the Court had any justification for intervening. He circulated an opinion in which he seemed to pick up the mantle of judicial restraint from Harlan, arguing that outlawing the death penalty would show
"a basic lack of faith and confidence in the democratic process" and that
they should leave it to legislators to fix any defects in its administration.
Blackmun, too, insisted that the Court should leave the issue to state legislators despite his belief that capital punishment "serves no useful purpose."
He added, "I yield to no one in the depth of my distaste, antipathy, and indeed abhorrence for the death penalty."

Stewart and White remained the two justices who had not laid out their
positions with any specificity. Stewart began the term convinced that the
Constitution did not bar capital punishment, but the idea that hundreds of
people might die if the justices upheld it weighed heavily on him. He had
concluded that a narrower approach was needed in order to keep White in
the majority. Stewart and White worked together privately in early June to
find some mutually agreeable approach. Brennan found out what they had
done on June 13 only when Stewart's clerk delivered both of their draft
opinions to Brennan's chambers.

As Brennan sat down and began reading their opinions out loud, he
was surprised to find that Stewart had stopped short of declaring the death
penalty unconstitutional. Instead, Stewart wrote that it could not "be so
wantonly and so freakishly imposed." White went out of his way to empha-

size that he believed the death penalty was constitutional in some circumstances and that some system of capital punishment could comport with the Eighth Amendment.

ONE DAY AFTER reading Stewart and White's opinions, Brennan circulated his own opinion, defining a cruel and unusual punishment as one that "does not comport with human dignity." That still left the question of what did comport with human dignity. For an answer, Brennan turned to four principles Stewart had suggested to him in April. A punishment could not be too severe, arbitrarily inflicted, unacceptable to contemporary standards, or excessive. Brennan interpreted each of these principles in terms of what he believed human dignity demanded, applied each to the death penalty, and, not surprisingly, found capital punishment failed on every score.

Like those who invoked human dignity before him, Brennan did not offer many details about what he meant. Brennan believed that human dignity's meaning and what it required was self-evident. But human dignity is an amorphous concept, whether employed in the context of ethics, law, or religion, one subject to widely different interpretations. Brennan's conception of what human dignity required aligned with the Catholic Church's later call for "a need for a consistent ethic of life" when it came to the death penalty. In fact, Brennan invoked human dignity to condemn the death penalty earlier than any prominent figures within the Church. But while Brennan and the Catholic Church agreed about what human dignity demanded with regard to the death penalty, the same would not be true in other contexts. Opposition to the death penalty soon became overshadowed by antipathy to abortion in official Church thinking. As a result, Brennan, as a signatory of the *Roe* decision, would get little credit within the Church for his early advocacy against the death penalty.

Brennan could talk vaguely about the demands of human dignity in speeches. But putting such an undefined concept at the heart of a legal standard that lower-court judges would have to apply required far more specificity than he provided here. The reality is that Brennan had a very weak foundation of precedent on which to build. The text of the U.S. Constitution did not include any reference to human dignity, and no extensive body of precedent subsequently defined exactly what the concept meant. *Trop v. Dulles* provided the only precedent for his invocation of human dignity in the context of the Eighth Amendment. His defenders argued that it is no more difficult to discern the standards for applying human dignity than for the Fourteenth Amendment's due process requirements, which had been accomplished by other justices in the past.

In the years ahead, critics of Brennan's jurisprudence would single out his use of human dignity as his most egregious act of judicial activism. The lack of supporting precedent later led Raoul Berger, a noted Harvard legal historian and critic of the Warren Court, to write, "Respect for 'human dignity' clearly is spun out of thin air." To his critics, Brennan was laying out a moral vision rather than a legal standard. One law professor cited human dignity as an instance where "Brennan's humanistic activism runs amok."

Brennan, in turn, rejected as "utterly groundless" suggestions that his conception of human dignity was too subjective or lacked standards. His assertion that the aim of law was to vindicate human dignity only grew stronger in his opinions over time and in the face of criticism. Speaking in 1986, Brennan would say, "If the interaction of this justice and the constitutional text over the years confirms any single proposition, it is that the demands of human dignity will never cease to evolve." And the contexts in which he would invoke the concept only seemed to broaden. He asserted that both gender bias and refusing to offer redress to a man whose name and photograph had been improperly included on a flyer identifying shoplifters deprived individuals of their dignity. He looked back on his welfare rights decision, *Goldberg v. Kelly*, and later declared it a triumph of human dignity too.

BRENNAN WAS JUST one voice among many when the justices finally released the death penalty decision on the last day of the term, June 29, 1972. All nine justices wrote their own separate opinions, filling 233 pages, making it the longest decision in the Court's history to that point. The nine separate opinions were tied together by only a one-paragraph per curiam opinion which tersely explained that, by a 5–4 vote, the Court had found that the death penalty as carried out in these three cases constituted cruel and unusual punishment.

Anyone trying to determine a rationale or discern a governing rule of law in the finding had to wade through the separate opinions written by each of the five justices who constituted the majority. Only Brennan and Marshall asserted that the death penalty was impermissible in all circumstances. Douglas left open the possibility that executions might be constitutional if no longer applied disproportionately against minorities. The other two members of the majority — Stewart and White — explicitly avoided the question of whether the death penalty was unconstitutional under all circumstances. Stewart expressed concern for the procedures in the current cases that allowed the death penalty "to be so wantonly and so freakishly imposed." White emphasized that the death penalty was so infrequently imposed that it could not serve any purpose as an effective deterrent.

The opinions of Stewart and White controlled the outcome and suggested to states that they could rewrite their death penalty laws to make the punishment less random and less subject to the unguided discretion of juries. In reviewing future state laws, White and Stewart could join the four dissenters to uphold new laws or vote to strike down those laws; their view would thus tip the majority one way or the other. The ruling was far from what Brennan had hoped, but for now at least there would be a stop to executions.

ON THE NIGHT of the day on which *Furman* was announced, the ninety-six occupants of Florida's death row happened to be watching the movie *Dirty Harry* inside Florida's Raiford State Penitentiary. The film features Clint Eastwood as Inspector Harry Callahan, a rogue San Francisco police detective who bristles at the sorts of rules imposed by the Warren Court as he hunts for a serial killer who had kidnapped a teenage girl. In one scene, the suspect pleads for his rights as Callahan points a gun at him, stepping on his wounded leg until he confesses to where he buried the girl. In the next scene, the district attorney excoriates Callahan for his actions, which made prosecution of the killer impossible. The movie struck a chord with audiences around the country; many viewers jeered during the scene in which the suspect pleads for his rights.

After the movie ended, inmates learned of the Supreme Court's decision in *Furman*. Jubilant convicts laughed, hollered, and shook the doors, a reaction common that day on death rows around the country. In Georgia, Lucious Jackson was lying on his bunk when a fellow inmate shouted the news. "I've been thinking about nothing but death for a long time," Jackson said. "Now I can think about living."

Beyond death row, the Court's decision was considerably less well received. In making his case for abolishing the death penalty, Brennan had argued that "our society has, in fact, rejected this punishment," a premise supported by some evidence prior to the *Furman* decision. Public opinion polls indicated that only half the public supported the death penalty, no execution had taken place in years, and a growing roster of foreign countries had abolished it altogether in the 1960s. But on the eve of the decision, forty states still had death penalty statutes and supporters still outnumbered opponents. Events quickly proved how profoundly Brennan had misjudged Americans' attitudes toward capital punishment.

Support for the death penalty spiked rapidly in the wake of the decision. That uptick might have occurred absent the Court's ruling. As audience response to *Dirty Harry* suggested, the public remained deeply fearful about crime. Violent crime rose 25 percent during the 1970s. But the *Furman* decision at the very least sped up that shift in attitudes toward capital punishment. Many Americans came to view the decision as yet another instance of the Court protecting criminals at the expense of public safety. If, as Brennan argued, "evolving standards of decency" determined the death penalty's constitutionality, then it now appeared they were evolving in favor of capital punishment.

Brennan's conclusion that society had rejected the death penalty was both wishful thinking and a function of his growing isolation. Alabama's lieutenant governor, Jere Beasley, reacted to the decision by suggesting that a majority of the justices had "lost contact with the real world." In the case of Brennan, that was actually true. His self-imposed exile from outside engagements meant that he no longer spoke on college campuses or participated in the New York University summer conference, where he had once heard feedback from state judges at the receiving end of the Court's decisions. He had further cut himself off due to Marjorie's illness and did not even go to the movies much anymore. He was surrounded mostly by like-minded liberals at his one regular social outlet, Kronheim's cafeteria. He had even given up on lunching with his Court colleagues, preferring to eat at his desk. And his clerks tended to be just as liberal as he was. As a result, it is easy to see how Brennan could become increasingly out of step with the national mood on issues such as the death penalty and school desegregation without fully realizing it. Of course, had Brennan understood the degree of his isolation, it might not have changed his positions on the hot-button issues that came before the Court. He believed that the Court had to view the Constitution in a way that protected the rights of the minority — whether it was death row inmates or black schoolchildren — against the rule of the majority.

Legislators wasted no time in responding to the Court's decision. Rather than abandoning the death penalty, thirteen states enacted laws to bring capital punishment back within a year of the decision. Similar measures were pending in sixteen other states. Lawmakers took a variety of approaches to address the concerns Stewart and White expressed about arbitrariness. Instead of leaving jurors with complete discretion, some of the new laws specified the aggravating and mitigating factors that could count for or against a death sentence. Other states, such as Louisiana and North Carolina, made the death penalty mandatory for particular crimes such as first-degree murder or aggravated kidnapping. The nation's death rows already had sixty-four new occupants by the spring of 1974. By 1976, thirty-five states and the federal government had put new capital punishment statues into place. But executions could not resume until the Supreme Court had ruled on the constitutionality of the new sentencing schemes.

FOUR YEARS ELAPSED between the *Furman* decision and when the justices heard challenges to the new death penalty statutes adopted in its wake. On March 31, 1976, the Court heard arguments regarding five different state statutes that encompassed all iterations of the new sentencing schemes. It was at the justices' private conference two days later that Brennan announced to his colleagues that he would never again vote to sustain a death sentence. Only Marshall joined him in arguing that the death penalty was unconstitutional in all circumstances. Like Brennan, Marshall abhorred the death penalty, in part based on his own experience as a young lawyer. Marshall had felt so badly about losing a case involving a former high school classmate accused of robbery and murder that he had decided to attend the execution himself. He ultimately stayed home after a reporter warned him about the grisly nature of the proceedings.

In the face of a strong public backlash, Brennan and Marshall felt no compulsion to back off. Their absolutist position left them on the margins as it became clear that there were not enough votes to strike down any of the five laws. The rest of their colleagues favored allowing capital punishment to resume, at least in some circumstances. Convinced that the new statutes had adequately addressed his concerns about arbitrariness, White joined Blackmun, Burger, and Rehnquist in voting to uphold all five states laws. The outcome would be determined by the trio of justices in the middle: Stewart, Powell, and newcomer John Paul Stevens, who had joined the Court in December 1975.

Brennan missed his first opportunity to meet his newest colleague when he skipped a November 24, 1975, White House dinner that President Ford hosted for the federal judiciary. The fifty-five-year-old Chicago native was among at least seven potential nominees who attended the dinner, along with all sitting justices except Brennan. Four days later, Ford announced that Stevens was his choice. Unlike many of Nixon's nominees, this mild-mannered moderate provoked little controversy. Stevens had graduated with the highest grade point average in the history of Northwestern University Law School and then clerked for Justice Rutledge. He turned down an offer to teach at Yale in favor of practicing antitrust law in his hometown. His work investigating a political scandal on the Illinois Supreme Court brought Stevens to the attention of Illinois senator Charles Percy, who recommended him to President Nixon as a potential judicial nominee. He was tapped for the U.S. Court of Appeals for the Seventh Circuit in 1970. His fellow Chicagoan Edward Levi, who served as Ford's attorney general, recommended him as Douglas's successor, and he easily won confirmation by a 98–0 margin. Brennan welcomed Stevens with the usual warm letter and excessive praise for some of his early opinions. But when it came to drafting the death penalty decision, Brennan had no influence over Stevens or the other two members of his trio.

Even more so than in *Furman*, Brennan remained out of the loop as Powell, Stevens, and Stewart crafted their opinions. They were willing to uphold the Florida, Georgia, and Texas statutes, which set out aggravating factors to guide jurors regarding the death penalty, but not the Louisiana and North Carolina laws, in which certain crimes triggered mandatory death sentences. In his opinion in the lead case, *Gregg v. Georgia*, Stewart noted the degree to which "developments during the four years since *Furman* have undercut substantially" the argument that the country had decisively rejected capital punishment according to evolving standards of decency. "It is now evident that a large proportion of American society continues to regard it as an appropriate and necessary criminal sanction," Stewart wrote.

Brennan opted to write his solitary dissent himself, which was unusual at this point in his tenure when he typically left the initial drafting to his clerks. Brennan broke no new ground in the resulting five-page dissent. He quoted from his *Furman* opinion at length. The opinion seemed almost perfunctory, as if he had given up trying to persuade his colleagues. One of the central arguments against the death penalty in *Furman*—that public attitudes had evolved to the point where it had come to be viewed as abhorrent—had been dramatically repudiated. But unlike Marshall, who also dissented, Brennan did not even attempt to address how the upsurge in public opinion polls and the rush of states to enact new death penalty statutes undercut his argument.

Brennan did add one rhetorical flourish, a quote at the end from the French philosopher Albert Camus' book against the death penalty, *Reflections on the Guillotine*, which summed up Brennan's feelings about the death penalty's resumption. "Justice of this kind is obviously no less shocking than the crime itself, and the new 'official' murder, far from offering redress for the offense committed against society, adds instead a second defilement to the first." Marshall added an unintentional but even more dramatic flourish soon after reading his dissent from the bench on the day the decision was announced, July 2, 1976. That weekend, he suffered a heart attack.

It was clear that Brennan and Marshall had become increasingly lonely voices on the death penalty. For the next two decades, the level of support for capital punishment would remain between 66 and 76 percent of those surveyed, a degree of support higher than at any time since the first such polls were taken in the 1930s. On the Court, too, Brennan had marginalized himself over his death penalty position, in the same way that Black and Douglas had done by adhering to an absolutist position on free speech. Brennan would write just two majority opinions in death penalty cases during the rest of his tenure, both of which were narrow opinions that applied prior precedent. But Brennan did not back down in the face of strong public opinion and a solid Court majority in favor of capital punishment. His resolve only deepened.

Four days after announcing the decisions upholding the death penalty statutes, the justices announced they would not hear five other appeals by death row inmates. At the end of each one, separate similarly worded dissents by Brennan and Marshall appeared. Brennan's read:

For the reasons stated in my dissenting opinion in *Gregg v. Geor-gia* . . . the imposition and carrying out of the death penalty in this case constitutes cruel and unusual punishment in violation of the Eighth and Fourteenth Amendments.

I would therefore grant certiorari in this case and vacate judgment in this case insofar as it leaves undisturbed the death sentence imposed.

This was no onetime protest. Brennan and Marshall appended the same language three more times to orders issued on the first day of the new term in October 1976. And they would do so again every time the Court voted against hearing a death penalty appeal or stay application for the rest of their tenure on the Court together. Sometimes they wrote separate boiler-plate dissents, but most of the time they would sign a single joint dissent, which they appended to a remarkable 1,841 different cases. Less frequently, Brennan — or, more usually, Marshall — wrote a more lengthy dissent lay-ing out why he believed the Court should have heard that particular case. They also dissented when the justices agreed to hear a capital punishment case and subsequently upheld the death sentence.

Neither Brennan nor Marshall could have ever realistically expected that the Court would actually take up every capital case. That would have completely overwhelmed the Court's docket and left little time for anything else. Their sustained dissents were a form of persistent protest that transmitted their belief that the imposition of death should never be considered routine. In the years to come, Brennan would file similar stock dissents in cases involving double jeopardy, obscenity, and the Eleventh Amendment.

Their supporters praised Brennan and Marshall for taking a brave stand. One law professor described them as conducting "a kind of vigil against the death penalty, even virtually a silent vigil — closer to the tradi-tion of civil disobedients who see themselves as prophets in a wilderness." One day after Brennan's first stock dissent was published, his friend Judge Stanley Weigel wrote him, "In my book and that of countless others, many of your dissents — including particularly that in the chief capital punish-ment case — will live long after the majority decisions have once again, with the swinging of the pendulum, been overturned." To his critics, Bren-nan was displaying the worst kind of judicial arrogance, dissenting in the face of settled Court precedent and ignoring public opinion. It seemed hypocritical that Brennan became so indignant when his colleagues over-turned what he considered well-settled Warren Court precedent but re-fused to accept precedents less to his liking.

Brennan addressed such criticisms when he delivered his most detailed defense of these dissents in a 1985 speech at Hastings College of Law. Brennan acknowledged that he adhered to his death penalty dissents even though "this is an interpretation to which a majority of my fellow justices — not to mention, it would seem, a majority of my fellow countrymen — do not subscribe." He conceded that many viewed it as "simply contrary, tiresome, or quixotic" at best, or at worst "a refusal to abide by the judicial principle of stare decisis, obedience to precedent." But Brennan explained that he believed "the unique interpretive role of the Supreme Court . . . de-mands some flexibility with respect to the call of stare decisis." He said, "In my judgment, when a justice perceives an interpretation of the text to have departed so far from its essential meaning, that justice is bound, by a larger constitutional duty to the community, to expose the departure and point toward a different path."

To Brennan, such a persistent dissent was not meant as merely an at-tempt to offer an alternative analysis. "That could be done in a single dis-sent and does not require repetition," Brennan said. "Rather, this type of dissent constitutes a statement by the judge as an individual: 'Here I draw the line.'" In general, Brennan conceded that judges must acquiesce to the rulings of their court. "But it would be a great mistake to confuse this un-questioned duty to obey and respect the law with an imagined obligation to subsume entirely one's own views of constitutional imperatives to the views of the majority."

THE DEATH PENALTY dissents helped feed the public perception that Brennan and Marshall shared a special bond. "Their names are almost al-ways spoken together," the *Washington Post* observed a few years later. "They generally vote together on major social issues. They dissent together and concur together. They often socialize as well." Brennan's hometown of Newark, New Jersey, renamed its municipal courthouse the Brennan Marshall Justice Complex. *People* magazine, the chronicler of American celebrity culture, later profiled their shared "battle to keep liberalism alive at the U.S. Supreme Court." Looking back, Marshall's son, Thurgood Jr.

— named "Thurgood William Marshall" in Brennan's honor — observed, "More than my father's best friend, Justice Brennan was his perfect ally in the fight for freedom."

It is certainly true that Brennan and Marshall were close allies, particularly after Douglas's retirement left them the Court's last two liberals. So too did they share a deep mutual respect and heartfelt affection. Marshall would joke they were "soul brothers," and liked to greet Brennan by teasing, "You dumb bastard, don't you think you should do something to earn your pay?" It was the same sense of humor that could leave Marshall's colleagues in stitches during conference. But they were not as close friends as those outside the Court assumed. Beyond lunching at Kronheim's, they did not socialize much or share the kind of professional kinship Brennan had had with Warren. Their clerks were surprised to find how seldom they talked over cases.

Few understood just how much Marshall's performance on the Court came to disappoint Brennan. It was a topic Brennan did not like to talk about with anyone. Brennan believed that Marshall had never gotten his due for all he had achieved as the NAACP LDF's chief lawyer. He still considered Marshall one of the most gifted litigators he had ever heard argue before the Court. Brennan worried about fueling the sort of racism that explained why white lawyers refused to acknowledge Marshall's greatness as an attorney and why a reputation for laziness had dogged him since he served as solicitor general. Brennan bristled at any suggestion that Marshall was his pawn. (Perhaps it is not a coincidence that the nation's second African American justice, Clarence Thomas, would face similar criticism about his silence during oral arguments and perceived reliance on his conservative colleague Antonin Scalia.)

Still, Brennan privately wondered what had come of the skilled lawyer who so dazzled him at oral arguments. "What the hell happened when he came on the Court, I'm not sure, but he doesn't seem to have had the same interest," Brennan said. "He has some areas where he does and when he really gets involved with a case . . . he just does an absolutely superb job. But when he's not interested, whatever I do, that's all right with him." As best as Brennan could tell, Marshall had simply given up, convinced that all he had worked for as a civil rights lawyer was now coming undone. Marshall became suspicious of his colleagues' motivations, concluding that many of the justices simply did not understand the nation's race problem. His jokes could take on a dark edge during conference in cases involving race, where he would address other members of the Court as "massa" in a deep slave dialect. Where Brennan was naturally optimistic, Marshall's work as a civil rights lawyer in the Deep South had left him understandably pessimistic about human nature.

But another factor helped explain Brennan's and Marshall's divergent outlooks. Brennan had had the benefit of a lengthy stretch in the majority, which allowed him to take a longer view now that he was in the minority. He had watched as Black had his dissenting opinions vindicated and he himself had rammed majority opinions down the throat of dissenters like Harlan. Marshall, by contrast, had only been on the Court for a single term when Warren announced his retirement, and he saw his majority bloc quickly shrivel after Fortas resigned. Marshall could not draw upon memories of the pendulum swinging once again in his direction for comfort.

Making matters worse, a series of health problems intermittently kept Marshall off the bench throughout the 1970s. Marshall's body began failing him after years of eating, drinking, and smoking too much. He had been hospitalized for a month with a serious respiratory infection in 1970 and then required an appendectomy the following year. He suffered from another serious bout of pneumonia in early 1975 and a series of three heart attacks following the *Gregg* death penalty decision in 1976. By that time, Marshall weighed at least 231 pounds and smoked two packs of cigarettes a day. As his health failed, he seemed to grow more reclusive and grumpy. He rarely appeared in public, not even to attend his teenage sons' sports games.

Historians and journalists sought Brennan's help in getting Marshall to consent to interviews, which Marshall usually refused, much to Brennan's regret. Event organizers also turned to Brennan for help in trying to coax Marshall into attending ceremonies. "I'm afraid it's beyond my powers to persuade my friend Thurgood to accept this high and distinct honor," Brennan wrote the organizers of an event to mark the hundredth anniversary of the admission of the first black student to the University of Pennsylvania. In his biography of Brennan, Hunter R. Clark wrote that Brennan "resented Thurgood's 'deification.'" In fact, even when Marshall refused to appear, Brennan happily attended many ceremonies in his honor out of a sense that his colleague was receiving some overdue and well-earned recognition. Marshall boycotted a 1980 ceremony at the University of Maryland, where the law library was named in his honor, angrily brushing it off as an attempt to "salve its conscience for excluding" black students — including himself — for so long. Over Marshall's objections, Brennan attended anyway. In his speech, Brennan said, "Perhaps no advocate of our time has more profoundly altered the course of our national development."

Brennan did resent Marshall for not carrying his share of the workload as they fought to preserve the gains of the Warren Court. The death penalty was one of the few areas of law where Marshall was still engaged and displayed some of his old passion. Yet here, too, Marshall disappointed Brennan. He came to believe that Marshall diluted his voice by too often writing full opinions in death penalty cases. While he never tried to dissuade Marshall from dissenting, Brennan favored holding their fire for when a new issue appeared before the Court. "My way of approaching is to pick out some major things and write them, but don't just dissent for the sake of dissenting. It is sufficient simply to adhere to your view." Nonetheless, when the facts in a case were particularly gruesome, such as a murder involving a child, Brennan might nevertheless join Marshall on a dissent he did not think was necessary. "I don't like to see him out there all by his lonesome," Brennan said. "It isn't the easiest damn thing to stick to this position."

UNEXPECTED ALLY

B RENNAN BEGAN 1976 — the year he turned seventy and celebrated his twentieth anniversary on the Court — having just recently marked two other significant milestones. He became the
longest-sitting justice when Douglas departed in December 1975 a year after a debilitating stroke. That same month, Brennan and Marjorie moved
out of their home on Dumbarton Avenue, where they had lived for eighteen years. They relocated about three miles north to an apartment on De-
vonshire Place in Washington, not far from the National Zoo. If Brennan
felt sorry to leave the place he had called home for the longest stretch of
his entire life, he hid it well. "We wonder why we didn't do it earlier," Brennan wrote a friend. If nothing else, moving out of a two-story home with
two additional flights of exterior steps made it easier for Marjorie to get
around.

Marjorie's health continued to fluctuate, but she felt well enough to join
Brennan for a trip to New Jersey in May 1976 for a celebration at the New
Jersey Bar Association's annual convention honoring his birthday and anniversary on the Court. Brennan had agreed to this rare break from his
self-imposed exile from public life, although he found the setting a bit unusual. Playboy's Great Gorge Resort Hotel occupied 585 acres of hilly coun-
tryside an hour northwest of Newark in McAfee, New Jersey. Playboy had

refashioned the hotel's image to attract more families and conventions since the bar association held its last conference there the previous year. But the carpet in the lobby was still patterned with the company's signature bunny logo and cocktail waitresses bedecked as bunnies still served drinks in the Playboy Club.

The black-tie affair on the evening of Saturday, May 22, 1976, began with a private gathering in Brennan's honor inside the hotel's presidential suite. Guests moved on to a cocktail reception, where Marjorie, looking outwardly healthy in a flower-print dress, posed with their son Bill and his wife, Georgie. Then Brennan and Marjorie took their seats on a two-tier dais in the main ballroom before a crowd of six hundred lawyers, judges, and their spouses. Every judge in the state seemed intent on catching a glimpse of Brennan, given how rarely he appeared in public. With his gray thinning hair and skin sagging a bit around the neck, Brennan must have looked older to most than when he had attended such events in the past.

Brennan seemed genuinely touched by the efforts made by Joe Nolan, the bar association's president whom Brennan had hired as a young lawyer at Pitney Hardin, to make this a special occasion. The evening featured a local Emerald Society band playing bagpipes in his honor, a multitier cake with sparklers on top, and the unveiling of a portrait of Brennan painted by a New Jersey artist. The portrait was presented to the New Jersey Supreme Court two days later in its courtroom in Trenton at a ceremony attended by Brennan's family, friends, and colleagues from every phase of his career in the state.

Brennan was understandably in a reflective mood when he finally stood up that night at the worn wooden tabletop podium. "Reaching the biblical summit of three score and ten seems to be the occasion — or the excuse — for looking back," Brennan began. "Forty-eight years ago I entered law school and forty-four years ago was admitted to the New Jersey Bar." Brennan did not mention that, had he remained on the New Jersey Supreme Court, he would have been attending this dinner as a retiree, since he had now reached that court's mandatory retirement age. Brennan's last surviving former colleague on the New Jersey court, Nathan Jacobs, had retired the previous year for that reason. Brennan then turned to the substance of his speech: a passionate plea for state courts to take up the mantle of protecting constitutional rights he believed his colleagues on the Supreme Court had abdicated. "State courts no less than federal are and ought to be the guardians of our liberties," Brennan said. He had come prepared to cite more than a dozen recent cases where he believed his own Court had interpreted the Bill of Rights too narrowly and a few instances where state courts, including New Jersey's, had stepped into the breach.

Maybe it was all the drinks and festive bagpipe music. Maybe the audience had already sat through enough speeches and just wanted the dancing to start. Or maybe Brennan had simply chosen the wrong venue for such a serious speech. Whatever the reason, he noticed that the crowd, which had already begun to dwindle, did not seem to have much interest in what he had to say. So after delivering only a third of his speech, "I said the hell with it [and] just quit," Brennan recalled. He quietly went back to his seat without anyone in the audience realizing he had cut the speech short.

The irony is that this speech — which he did not deliver in its entirety and to which the audience paid little attention — became the most famous and widely quoted of his entire career when later republished in the January 1977 Harvard Law Review. Brennan would be credited with helping to launch or at least jump-start a renaissance in state constitutional law. But the movement had already begun gathering steam in recent years. A handful of state justices had rested their decisions upon state constitutional grounds, and the trend had caught the attention of both litigants and journalists. One month before Brennan's speech, Stanley Mosk, a justice on the California Supreme Court, had called attention to the trend and predicted a coming "phoenix-like resurrection of federalism" in the constitutional works of state courts. Two weeks before Brennan delivered his speech, the Los Angeles Times noted that "reform-minded lawyers, who once clamored to bring ground-breaking cases before the Supreme Court, now do their best to avoid it," preferring instead to "concentrate on state tribunals."

What triggered Brennan's interest in the idea was a 1975 decision by the New Jersey Supreme Court, which had held that failing to tell the subject of a criminal investigation that he could refuse to consent to a search violated a provision of the state's constitution. In a similar case, the U.S. Supreme Court had earlier held that such an omission did not violate the U.S. Constitution. Brennan read about this New Jersey case at a time when he was increasingly convinced that the long-dreaded rollback of the Warren Court's criminal-procedure precedents had finally begun in earnest.

Of acute concern to Brennan was evidence that his fellow justices seemed intent on limiting access to courts of individuals seeking redress against government abuses of power. He was particularly troubled by how the majority of his colleagues handled the case of a photographer, arrested for shoplifting but never prosecuted, who nevertheless found his picture on a flyer of active shoplifters that police in Louisville, Kentucky, distributed to local merchants. The majority upheld the lower-court decision dismissing his civil rights lawsuit. Brennan filed a dissent accusing the majority of "dissembling" and perpetrating "a saddening denigration of our majestic Bill of Rights."

In another case that troubled Brennan, the Court held in December 1975 by a 6–2 margin that police had not violated a criminal suspect's Miranda rights when they questioned him about a murder two hours after he had declined to discuss an unrelated robbery. "Today's distortion of *Miranda*'s constitutional principles can be viewed only as yet another step in the erosion, and, I suppose, ultimate overruling, of *Miranda*'s enforcement of the privilege against self-incrimination," Brennan complained in his dissent. But Brennan found a more constructive outlet for his anger in that opinion. He invited state courts to reject the approach taken by his colleagues in the majority: "It is appropriate to observe that no State is precluded by the decision from adhering to higher standards under state law." He picked up the same theme in other dissents in the months leading up to his speech to the New Jersey Bar Association, a trend noted by the *Washington Star*. "What a frustrated William J. Brennan is failing to do in Washington a hopeful William J. Brennan expects to see happen in places like Trenton, Sacramento, and Des Moines."

Among those who did not appreciate the significance of Brennan's speech as delivered at the Great Gorge Resort Hotel was Stewart Pollock, a New Jersey lawyer and former federal prosecutor. Pollock, who was serving on the New Jersey Board of Public Utilities, had not been thinking much about constitutional rights up to that point. But Brennan's message started resonating with him after he was appointed to the state Supreme Court in 1979.

During a period when the Burger Court was curbing protections afforded by the Warren Court, Pollock says he realized that Brennan "in effect suggested an end run: look to your own constitution." "We grasped onto that," Pollock affirmed. Pollock cited Brennan's article in several opinions he wrote and became one of the state judges around the country most closely identified with what became known as the "new judicial federalism" movement. In a tribute, Pollock later described Brennan's article as "the Magna Carta of state constitutional law." State judges invoked provisions of their constitutions that were often identical to those in the U.S. Constitution's Bill of Rights, to put stricter limits on police searches and seizures. The ripples were felt beyond criminal procedure in cases involving school finance, exclusionary zoning, privacy for gay and lesbian people, and protections for news reporters. Three decades after Brennan's speech, a handful of states looked to their own state constitutions to legalize gay marriage.

Not everyone celebrated the trend. "Like the fox in Aesop's fable, the wily Brennan cajoled whole flocks of jurists into dropping their reserve," Harvard Law professor Mary Ann Glendon wrote in 1994. Long after Brennan's retirement, corporate lawyer Mark Pulliam lamented in a guest column on the *Wall Street Journal*'s editorial page how Brennan's article had helped inspire a wave of liberal activism on state courts. "Brennan may have lost his activist majority on the Supreme Court, but he gained 50 junior Warren Courts in the process," Pulliam wrote. "Call it Brennan's revenge." Critics complained there was something almost unseemly in the way Brennan had blatantly invited state judges to circumvent his own court. Skeptics had good reason to question Brennan's newfound devotion to federalism, given how little respect he had shown for state autonomy in many of his past decisions. One law professor labeled Brennan a "false prophet" who embraced federalism only to achieve the results he could no longer obtain on his own court. While it is true that his underlying goal of protecting individual rights had not changed, this sudden about-face on federalism suggested sheer opportunism.

THE TONE OF Brennan's dissents grew only more shrill as the 1975–76 term progressed. Brennan and his clerks seemed to goad each other into using overwrought language. The word "eviscerate" became their term of choice, appearing in six different dissents to describe how the majority ignored or swept aside precedent. One of Brennan's clerks that term, Barry Simon, displayed a particular penchant for writing fiery dissents. Simon, then twenty-six, arrived in Brennan's chambers with typically sterling credentials: magna cum laude at both Harvard College and Harvard Law

School, editor of the *Harvard Law Review,* clerkship with Judge Wright on the D.C. Circuit. His intense combative style later helped make him one of the top criminal defense attorneys in Washington, D.C. Simon acted the same way during his clerkship with Brennan, going at every case as if it were warfare. Instead of toning down these opinions, Brennan encouraged Simon to employ an "acid pen," just as he had done with his clerks in the spring of 1971.

The sharp tone of Brennan's dissents once again attracted reporters' attention. "The impression that comes through these days when reading his many dissenting opinions is that Supreme Court Justice William J. Brennan Jr. is an angry, frustrated and somewhat saddened man," a UPI story noted in early June 1976. Two weeks later, the *Washington Star* quoted one unidentified justice, in a rare public swipe, as suggesting Brennan and Marshall both felt "beleaguered" after Douglas's departure and another as commenting disparagingly on the angry dissents: "You don't go around chasing rabbits. You don't need to answer every flag they run up."

It was not just criminal-procedure decisions that raised Brennan's ire. He filed one of his sharpest dissents in a case raising the question of whether the Tenth Amendment limited the federal government's ability to apply minimum-wage and maximum-work-hour regulations to state and local governments. Congress did not initially apply the Fair Labor Standards Act to state employees when it was first enacted, but amended the law in 1961 to extend its provisions to certain state workers. After the Supreme Court had upheld that limited extension in 1968 and suggested it could be applied to even more public workers, Congress again amended the law in 1974 to cover all state and city employees. Cities and states then filed suit challenging the new regulations, but the lower court upheld the amended law, citing the earlier Supreme Court case, *Maryland v. Wirtz.*

Brennan initially appeared to have a majority for upholding the law when the justices discussed the case, *National League of Cities v. Usery,* at conference in March 1976, but lost it after Stewart switched his vote and came out in favor of explicitly overruling the Court's 1968 precedent. Burger then assigned the majority opinion overturning the law to Rehnquist, still the youngest justice at fifty-one, then in his fourth full term. Rehnquist's sideburns and long hair made him the "hippie" of the Court, in the words of one newspaper profile, but only in appearance. Rehnquist had established himself as Brennan's polar opposite in his first three and a half terms on the Court, described by the *New York Times* in 1974 as "a one-man strong right-wing." This term, Rehnquist was the justice with whom Brennan agreed with least often, in only a third of cases. Rehnquist was on the opposite side in every case in which Brennan dissented, and Rehnquist wrote the majority opinion in six of them.

Rehnquist was no stranger to dissenting. He wound up in the minority so often that his clerks gave him a Lone Ranger doll that he placed on his mantel. Even when he was not writing solitary dissents, Rehnquist found life at the Court isolating. He later compared it to working in a monastery. Rehnquist tried his best to make the Court more collegial, suggesting a coffee hour after oral arguments where justices and their clerks could socialize. Burger rejected the idea. Rehnquist had more success organizing a skit at the Court's Christmas party gently spoofing Burger, Douglas, and Brennan.

Brennan might have appreciated Rehnquist's efforts to make the Court a friendlier place, but he also recognized he had emerged as the most committed opponent to Brennan's vision of the Constitution. Rehnquist invariably ruled for the government over the individual and for limiting federal court jurisdiction. As Rehnquist explained in a speech at the University of Texas just days after the oral argument in *National League of Cities v. Usery,* he was deeply suspicious about the idea of a "living constitution" or decisions based on human dignity. While Rehnquist did not single out Brennan by name, there can be little doubt he had his senior colleague in mind when he suggested judges had no business issuing themselves "a roving commission to second-guess Congress, state legislatures, and state and federal administrative officers concerning what is best for the country."

Despite their deep philosophical differences, Brennan got along with Rehnquist far better than he did with Burger. Rehnquist was much more easygoing than the chief justice, and did not take himself or his work too seriously. He started off one opinion with a limerick and diffused differences with his colleagues with humor. "I shall soon circulate a short pungent dissent from your opinion," Rehnquist wrote Brennan in one case. Brennan also respected Rehnquist as a worthy adversary. During a 1978 visit to Brennan's chambers, Harvard Law School professor Milton Katz noted that Rehnquist scored several hits in his dissent to a Brennan opinion. Brennan grinned in ungrudging admiration and replied, "Wasn't Rehnquist good!"

Rehnquist viewed *National League of Cities v. Usery* as the perfect vehicle for starting to roll back the expansion of federal power he believed came at the expense of the states. He wrote a decision for the Court that held the amendment to the Fair Labor Standards Act exceeded the power of Congress and violated the essential "attribute of sovereignty attaching to every state government." This was the first time since the New Deal that the Supreme Court employed the notions of state autonomy to strike down a federal law based on the rationale that Congress had overstepped the permissible boundaries of federalism. While the Tenth Amendment, which preserves power for the states that is not specifically delegated to the national government, has sometimes been interpreted to support this view, Rehnquist relied more on the structure and general principles of the Constitution.

Brennan, with some justification, feared Rehnquist's opinion was just the beginning of a wider campaign to rein in federal power. But instead of writing a reasoned dissent that might win over other less-committed justices, Brennan adopted an almost apocalyptic tone. He accused the majority of a "patent usurpation of the role reserved for the political process," manufacturing an "abstraction without substance," and exercising "raw judicial power." He charged that parts of the majority opinion were "absurd," and that its author had engaged in "sophistry." The majority, he wrote, dealt a "catastrophic judicial body blow to Congress' power under the Commerce Clause." And he warned of "an ominous portent of disruption of our constitutional structure implicit in today's mischievous decision." Brennan wrote, "I cannot recall another instance in the Court's history when the reasoning of so many decisions covering so long a span of time has been discarded in such a roughshod manner." After its release, a generally sympathetic *Washington Post* editorial labeled Brennan's dissent "as caustic as any written in recent decades."

If Brennan hoped his forceful language might attract wavering colleagues, the effort backfired. When Blackmun's clerk wrote him a memo that described the first two pages of Brennan's opinion as "unnecessarily emotional," Blackmun scribbled "25" — the length in pages of the whole opinion, suggesting he found the entire dissent over the top. Rather than join Brennan, Blackmun opted to file a separate, more limited concurrence to Rehnquist's majority opinion. Brennan's opinion also proved unpalatable to his newest colleague, Stevens. "Although I agree with your analysis and think you have written an excellent and persuasive opinion, I am reluctant to join it only because I am not sure that I completely share some of your extremely strong criticism of other decisions of the Court," Stevens wrote Brennan in a private note. "Perhaps if time were available, I could review those cases and join you, but believe I will simply rest on the brief dissent which I have prepared."

Brennan's clerks, dispatched to find out what Stevens found objectionable, reported back that he simply did not want to alienate any colleagues so early in his tenure. Brennan, who always prided himself on accommodating his colleagues' concerns, stuck to the language that had so repelled Stevens. In their term history, Brennan's clerks were almost cavalier about the loss. Rehnquist had won, they noted, but Brennan "did get some satisfaction out of having given him a run for his money."

Brennan had greater success working with his colleagues in the 1975–76 term when they considered a case involving congressional reform of federal campaign funding. The case of *Buckley v. Valeo* involved several complicated facets of the Federal Election Campaign Act of 1971. Brennan felt it was important to have consensus among the justices, and proposed a single opinion signed by all nine justices as had happened only once before — in the Little Rock schools case. But his colleagues rejected the idea, as they had in the Nixon tapes case. The end result was an unsigned opinion for the Court with sections written by Burger, Stewart, Brennan, Powell, and Rehnquist, and then five separate opinions concurring in part and dissenting in part by Burger, White, Marshall, Blackmun, and Rehnquist. When the votes were tallied, deciding on an astonishing array of issues concerning campaign funding, the Court had invalidated limits on how much a campaign could spend, voided limits on independent expenditures by individuals, and struck down a restriction on how much candidates could give to their own campaigns. The justices had also OK'd public financing of presidential races — the section Brennan wrote — and approved of public reporting and disclosure requirements.

Brennan made it clear to his clerks that he did not entirely agree with the Court's approach. His chief concern was that the Court relied on a distinction, one that he rejected, between speech and conduct. The Court upheld limits on giving campaign contributions, which was characterized as conduct, but struck down limits on campaign expenditures as a form of speech. Brennan recognized the important First Amendment interests in both contributions and expenditures but believed the government interest in avoiding the corrupting influence of money justified upholding the limit on contributions. He also found the restriction on a candidate's contributions to his or her own campaign justified, but he nevertheless went along with the Court's decision to invalidate that provision. Finally, Brennan thought the restriction on independent expenditures by individuals who were not part of the campaign was too vague to meet First Amendment standards, and he would not have reached the Court's conclusion that the rule interfered with too much political advocacy.

BRENNAN QUICKLY CAME to regret the tone of some of his dissents that 1975–76 term, which he later described as "much too sharp and acid." In subsequent terms, Brennan and his clerks made a conscious effort to de-escalate. Over morning coffee they talked about how the hyperbole had proven counterproductive inside the Court and beyond. They concluded that the shrill dissents only magnified the significance of the majority opinions, and had the unintended consequence of providing lower-court judges an excuse to go even further in the direction Brennan opposed. "Telling the lower courts that the majority opinion was, however wrong, narrow was a better strategy than telling them that the majority had written the Bill of Rights out of the Constitution and the sky was falling," said Gerard Lynch, a 1976–77 term clerk who later became a federal judge himself. Brennan and his clerks came to realize that screaming dissents did nothing to win over the key justices in the middle: Blackmun, Powell, Stevens, and Stewart. "These were not people who thought stridency was appropriate to the institution," said Whit Peters, a clerk during the 1977–78 term.

That was particularly true of Powell, a southern gentleman who chose his words with great care and expected his colleagues to be equally courteous. Powell was quick to take offense on his own behalf or others when Brennan's dissents turned strident. "This is garbage!" Powell wrote atop one of Brennan's draft dissents in which Brennan referred to language in Stevens's majority opinion as "transparently fallacious." "No doubt you have read Bill Brennan's dissent in which he pays his 'respects' to my dissent as well as the Court's opinion," Powell wrote Blackmun in June 1978. "Perhaps you will not wish to be associated with an opinion said to display 'acute ethnocentric myopia,' 'a sad insensitivity' and 'a naïve innocence of reality.'" In his reply, Blackmun resisted any temptation to pile on Brennan, chalking it up to late-term exhaustion. "I am convinced things would not be so strident if the present circulations were making their rounds in October or November." Powell was less inclined to forgive Brennan's rhetorical excesses. "No one is kinder or more generous than WJB until he takes up his pen in dissent," Powell later observed in a handwritten note atop his copy of another Brennan dissent.

Powell did not much care for ideological or expansive opinions, no matter who was the author. A cautious lawyer by nature, he had come to fill the role on the Court previously occupied by Harlan: a moderate conservative who believed in following precedents, even if he did not necessarily agree with them. This meant that Brennan benefited greatly from the unwillingness of Powell and other colleagues to overturn precedents he had earlier established. Powell, for his part, had learned to watch out for seemingly innocuous language Brennan might try to plant in opinions to harvest in subsequent cases. He directed his clerks to pay close attention to Brennan's circulations. "I know from experience that WJB has a demonstrated ability (that I admire) to shape future decisions by the inclusion of general language unnecessary to the present opinion but apparently free from serious objection," he warned his clerk in a note dated April 21, 1978.

Despite these concerns, by the 1977–78 term Powell was beginning to be a key and unexpected partner for Brennan, a relationship that proved pivotal in the years to come. Brennan and his clerks took great pains to accommodate Powell's views in a case during the 1977–78 term, *Monell v. New York City Department of Social Services,* addressing whether civil rights plaintiffs could recover monetary damages from local governments for constitutional violations. A group of New York City schoolteachers and social workers sued to challenge a policy that required pregnant city employees to take unpaid maternity leave before they were medically required to stop working. They wanted to recover damages for the salaries they would have received had they not been forced to take the leave. In 1961 the Court held municipalities enjoyed absolute immunity against liability in civil rights cases, although the justices had subsequently allowed lawsuits to proceed against school boards in desegregation cases. Powell was initially disinclined to overrule this earlier decision in *Monroe v. Pape.* But he wound up joining Brennan's 7–2 majority opinion expressly overruling the earlier decision. Brennan convinced his colleagues that

Douglas had misinterpreted the relevant statute. Brennan's opinion limited the circumstances under which plaintiffs could recover to situations where a wrong resulted from the "official policy" of a municipality and not simply instances where the municipality employed the person who violated the plaintiff's rights. Over many drafts, Brennan managed to overcome the concerns of several of his colleagues, including Powell.

The ruling in *Monell* became a powerful tool for civil rights plaintiffs in the years ahead, establishing the idea that you can sue City Hall. It became a major vehicle for lawsuits against abusive police practices and for many other rights violations. For Brennan, it was an important step in his evolving view that government should be accountable to the people — not merely through popular elections but also through the courts — and that it should be held liable for the harms public officials cause.

The interplay between Brennan and Powell proved particularly pivotal when the Court took up the issue of affirmative action in the fall of 1977. Three years earlier, Allan Bakke, a thirty-four-year-old white engineer and Vietnam veteran, sued the University of California at Davis Medical School, challenging its admissions policy that reserved for minority applicants sixteen of one hundred entering slots. Bakke had been twice rejected from the medical school, although lower-scoring minority students had been admitted. The California Supreme Court sided with Bakke, ruling that the admissions policy violated the state constitution, the Fourteenth Amendment's equal protection clause, and Title VI of the Civil Rights Act of 1964, which prohibits racial discrimination in programs receiving federal funds. Although a legal showdown over affirmative action was inevitable, the justices had dodged an earlier challenge to the admissions policy at the University of Washington Law School. Brennan, who preferred ruling on affirmative action in a case with better facts, would have preferred to avoid hearing this case too. He feared that a majority of his colleagues would be unsympathetic to the fixed number of slots for minority students set aside by Davis. Over Brennan's objections, though, the Court voted to hear the case.

Not surprisingly, the case attracted tremendous public interest. Affirmative action had supplanted busing as the nation's most prominent and polarizing racial flashpoint by the late 1970s. As with busing, affirmative action forced the nation to confront the question of how far it was willing to go to redress discrimination, particularly when the whites now being disadvantaged were not themselves responsible for past injustices. President Kennedy had had a limited definition of affirmative action in mind when he first invoked the phrase, in a 1961 executive order creating the Equal Employment Opportunity Commission, to explain what was needed to root out job discrimination. The 1964 Civil Rights Act had subsequently outlawed discrimination in education, employment, and housing. But as President Lyndon Johnson argued in a commencement address the following year at Howard University, merely outlawing discrimination was not necessarily enough. "You do not take a person who, for years, has been hobbled by chains, and liberate him, bring him up to the starting line of a race and then say, 'You are free to compete with all the others,' and still justly believe you have been completely fair."

Under Johnson and his successors, the federal government began to require contractors who accepted federal money to set concrete numerical timetables and goals tied to the percentage of minorities in the local workforce. Universities, too, began consciously considering race as they sought to expand the number of minorities attending their colleges and graduate schools. All had concluded that "colorblind" selection in university admissions or hiring would not narrow the enormous racial gap in educational and employment opportunities. While black college enrollment had doubled between 1966 and 1976, so had black unemployment, and black median income seemed stuck at around 60 percent of what whites earned. Even so, giving candidates an advantage merely because of their race, ethnicity, or gender seemed to many to be at odds with American ideals of equal opportunity and of measuring people based solely on ability. From the start, affirmative action had raised charges of "reverse discrimination" and complaints about unfair quotas. Whites overwhelmingly opposed any affirmative action program that set aside a fixed percentage or specific number of jobs, school admissions, or government contracts for minorities.

The dozens of amicus briefs pouring into the Court from all sides in the debate highlighted how this issue, like busing, had driven a wedge among traditional New Deal allies. Many groups representing white ethnics, such as the National Italian American Foundation and the Polish American Congress, lined up against affirmative action. So did all the major Jewish organizations, whose members still remembered a time when quotas were used to limit the number of Jews admitted into Ivy League schools. Jews, who occupied a disproportionately large share of the student bodies at elite universities, stood to lose the most under affirmative action. The issue also divided the Carter administration. Attorney General Griffin Bell argued that the Davis admission plan was an artificial quota system, while some of Carter's White House advisers and Joseph Califano, secretary of the Department of Health, Education, and Welfare, advocated defending it.

The central legal question in the case was how to analyze whether affirmative action programs satisfied the demands of the Fourteenth Amendment's equal protection clause. Bakke's lawyers argued that the same strict scrutiny applied to racial classifications designed to disadvantage minorities should also be applied to plans that gave them an advantage. Such strict scrutiny under the Fourteenth Amendment's equal protection clause required government to show a compelling state interest to justify the classification. If the Constitution were truly colorblind, they argued, then it should not matter what a person being disadvantaged looked like. The university's lawyers, however, argued that strict scrutiny should be reserved for classifications that disadvantage "discrete and insular" minorities, a formulation dating back to a footnote in the 1938 Supreme Court decision laying out a foundation for modern equal protection analysis. Instead of the strict scrutiny, the university argued for a less exacting standard that required that the state only prove some rational basis for the policy.

While the justices avoided a formal vote after the October 12, 1977, oral argument, it soon became clear that there were three votes to reject Davis's policy and three in support of affirmative action. Stevens lined up with Burger and Rehnquist against affirmative action. That trio did not necessarily agree about whether to strike it down as unconstitutional or rely on narrower statutory grounds as violating Title VI of the Civil Rights Acts of 1964. White, whose voting record on civil rights remained liberal even as he drifted rightward in other areas, stuck with Brennan and Marshall in support of the university. The key undecided votes were Blackmun, Powell, and Stewart.

Powell did appear a likely ally for Brennan at the outset. Powell believed universities could take race into account but should never set aside a fixed number of places in an incoming class. Powell laid out his position in a November 22 memo to his colleagues. He endorsed applying strict scrutiny to Davis's programs and found no compelling government interest that would justify setting aside a fixed number of slots for particular types of applicants. But Powell did not rule out the use of race entirely in admissions. As an example of what he believed could pass constitutional muster, he pointed to Harvard College's admission program. While "race or ethnic background might be deemed a 'plus' in a particular applicant's file," he noted that Harvard's undergraduate program "specifically eschews quotas." If a favorable stance toward race-conscious admissions seemed an unusual position for this son of the South, it was also in keeping with his character as a pragmatist who had come to believe that this strategy was the only way to enroll significant numbers of minorities.

Brennan circulated his own memo the next day that showed how far apart he was from Powell. Brennan argued that not all racial classifications were forbidden by the Constitution. "Short-term race consciousness is a necessary and constitutionally acceptable price to pay if we are to have a society indifferent to race," Brennan wrote. He argued that only racial labels that insulted or stigmatized must be barred. "Government may not on account of race, insult or demean a human being by stereotyping his or her capacities, integrity or worth as an individual." That was not the case here, where Brennan believed the classification was benign. As for what kind of test to apply, instead of the strict scrutiny favored by Powell, Brennan suggested a "reasonableness" test.

Despite their considerably different views, Brennan initially hoped he might be able to persuade Powell to uphold the Davis program. He saw the difference between the Davis and Harvard admissions programs as largely a matter of form; Davis was just more explicit about its goal. Brennan, like many of his colleagues, was less enthusiastic than Powell about holding up as a model one of the nation's most elite educational institutions. Not every college and university had the luxury of adopting multifactor admissions policies. Still, Brennan had no intention of undermining Powell's endorsement of the consideration of race. Over morning coffee, Brennan and his clerks talked about how to find common ground with Powell.

The justices gathered for what proved to be the pivotal conference in the case on December 9 with one colleague missing. Blackmun, sixty-nine, had traveled back home to Minnesota to undergo treatment for prostate cancer at the Mayo Clinic, where he had served as legal counsel. Blackmun urged his colleagues to continue the discussion without him. When it was Stewart's time to speak, he indicated that he favored affirming the California decision striking down Davis's program. That made it all but impossible to uphold affirmative action, particularly if Powell took a similar position. Powell said he, too, intended to affirm. At that point, Brennan spoke up and asked Powell whether based on his view of the case he might consider affirming in part and reversing in part. After all, Brennan argued, the California court ruling did not seem to leave room for any consideration of race, while Powell had endorsed some consideration of race in his discussion of Harvard's admissions program. He proved persuasive. Powell agreed that, insofar as the lower court's judgment prohibited Davis from taking race into account, it must be reversed.

Brennan once again had displayed the skills that had made him such an able tactician on the Court in the past, but had more recently seemed to elude him. Brennan did not talk Powell into doing something his colleague did not want to do. Rather, he suggested a mutually beneficial vehicle by which Powell could accomplish what he seemed to endorse in his November memo: preserve some kind of consideration of race. In the process, Brennan had preserved the chance to snatch some measure of victory from the jaws of defeat. Even if the Court struck down Davis's program, Brennan had preserved the possibility of upholding some less rigid consideration of race in college admissions and affirming affirmative action as constitutional. Brennan here was paying particularly close attention to how the case would be perceived by the public. As his clerks noted in their term history, "If the case were to come down as a partial reversal, public attention was more likely to be focused on the positive aspect of the decision: that the principle of affirmative action was being upheld."

EVER SINCE THAT spring of 1977, Brennan could not seem to shake a sore throat that left him hoarse much of the time and depleted his usual high energy level. He had gone to see an ear, nose, and throat doctor at Bethesda Naval Hospital recommended by Powell, and had consulted another specialist at Yale Medical School. No one could quite figure out the cause of the swelling until Brennan finally underwent a laryngoscopy on December 13. A biopsy the next day revealed a malignant tumor on his left vocal cord. Just like Marjorie, Brennan had been diagnosed with cancer, although his was less virulent. His doctors ordered seven weeks of radiation treatments scheduled to begin three days before Christmas. "I am advised that after three weeks the soreness of my throat will make speaking somewhat difficult," Brennan wrote his colleagues on December 16. "Since the end of that 3 week period coincides with the January conference and argument session, I very much doubt my ability to participate in the session although I shall make every effort to do so."

Blackmun, still recovering from his own cancer treatment, immediately dashed off a note. "You are in my thoughts. Please let me know what I can do. We have talked about this before, so please don't hesitate to ask." Powell and his wife, Jo, sent Brennan flowers along with a copy of Leon Uris's novel *Trinity*, detailing Ireland's struggle for independence. Powell explained that he and his wife were reading it together at night. "We find it a rather fascinating — and shocking story," Powell wrote. "As Presbyterians, we can't believe that Uris is 'telling it like it was.' If so, we hope you good Catholics will forgive us."

Brennan remained engaged in his work even as he absented himself from the Court on days he underwent the radiation treatments at Bethesda Naval Hospital. Still, his clerks noticed how unusually weak and uncharacteristically upset he seemed. For once, Brennan let down his mask and revealed himself more fully to some of his associates. In an unfortunate coincidence, one of his clerks, Steven Reiss, had been diagnosed with bladder cancer a few weeks earlier, and they often talked about their treatment one-on-one. Another clerk, Carmen Legato, recalled how despondent Brennan seemed as he drove the justice to the hospital one day for treatment. Brennan feared that if the radiation treatment failed he might need surgery and even an artificial voice box. He worried less about the impact of the first serious illness of his life on himself than about how he would be able to care for Marjorie. When Brennan missed the first oral argument of 1978, the Court released a statement announcing his condition and revealing he would be absent for ten days.

Another downturn in Marjorie's health soon overshadowed his own. Doctors discovered a swollen sac pressing on her lung, which required risky thoracic surgery. Given Marjorie's weakened condition, the prospects looked grim. If she survived the surgery, she would need weeks of recovery in intensive care. Brennan faced the strain of shuttling between his treatments and her convalescence at Georgetown University Hospital. For the first time in his tenure on the Court, he gave serious thought to retiring. He did not explicitly mention the possibility to his clerks, although they

Brennan accepts the Laetare Medal from the president of Notre Dame, Reverend Theodore Hesburgh, 1969.

Brennan and Marjorie
outside their rental
cottage on Old North
Wharf, Nantucket, 1975

Brennan and Marjorie on the beach in Nantucket

The Wharf Rat Club, Nantucket. Although the picture was taken in 2007, the club looks much the same as it did in the 1970s when Brennan stopped in on summer mornings.

The Burger Court meets with President Ronald Reagan. Seated in front, left to right: Thurgood Marshall, Brennan, Warren Burger, Reagan, Byron White, Harry Blackmun. Standing, left to right: John Paul Stevens, Lewis Powell, William Rehnquist, Sandra Day O'Connor.

Justices Marshall and Brennan enjoy a laugh at the dedication of a Baltimore courthouse, 1985.

Justices Brennan and Blackmun walk arm-in-arm down the Supreme Court's
hallway to the justices' conference, 1983–84 term.

Brennan and Mary Fowler, whom he married after Marjorie's death

Brennan speaks at the Loyola Law School graduation on June 1, 1986, where he was the subject of an anti-abortion protest. The photograph is a composite.

Justice Brennan with his successor, Justice David Souter, 1996

PILLARS OF JUSTICE

BRENNAN OPINIONS

1956-1990

©1990 HERBLOCK

Justice William Brennan Jr. lies in state in the Supreme Court's Great Hall, July 28, 1997. Standing with their backs to the camera are, left to right, Justice Harry Blackmun (retired); Assistant to the Chief Justice James Duff; Justice John Paul Stevens; Justice Ruth Bader Ginsburg; Mrs. Thurgood Marshall; Justice Clarence Thomas; Justice Byron White (retired).

picked up on his thinking as Brennan talked about wanting to resolve the affirmative action case before any vacancy occurred.

But the night before Marjorie's scheduled surgery in mid-January, an X-ray revealed the growth had shrunk on its own. Surgery would not be necessary after all. Marjorie's doctors slowly began removing the tube from her throat. Brennan finished his radiation treatments on Valentine's Day, although his throat remained sore and his voice quit on him if he spoke too long. "It's a tremendous relief to have the treatments behind me and even a greater one to have the doctors say it seems to have worked," Brennan wrote his brother Frank on February 23. "Marjorie too is definitely on the mend, so things look much brighter." Brennan soon booked their usual ferry reservation to Nantucket, ceased any talk of retirement, and got back to work on the *Bakke* case.

BRENNAN FOUND HIMSELF in a familiar position after finishing his radiation treatments: waiting for Blackmun. As usual, Blackmun was taking his time in announcing his position, one that was likely to prove pivotal in an important case. With four justices lined up against affirmative action, three in favor, and Powell in the middle, Blackmun's vote meant the difference between a split decision and a loss for Brennan. Since returning from the Mayo Clinic, Blackmun had wrestled with his own position as he struggled with a more difficult than expected recovery and a backlog of other cases. Blackmun, like Brennan, had not wanted to hear the case initially, although for different reasons. He hoped that, given enough time, the country would come to accept that applicants should be judged "according to ability and promise of accomplishment" and that racial classifications "may be abandoned as outmoded tools," as he wrote himself in an August 1977 memo. "But the Court in its wisdom granted certiorari and chose to plunge once more into what essentially is an issue of social policy and the case must be decided," he lamented.

But by the eve of the oral argument, Blackmun's position had softened considerably. In a handwritten outline of a possible opinion, he seemed willing to approve of the Davis program in which "race is used to enhance the fairness of the system." "We have seen that mere neutrality is often not enough," Blackmun wrote. He was not impressed when Burger privately circulated a draft opinion to him along with Stewart, Rehnquist, and Stevens in late December. "I could not join this," he wrote to himself.

In February, Blackmun had still not provided any hint of his views to his colleagues, much to their exasperation. One of Brennan's clerks suggested their boss try to approach Blackmun about the case. Brennan immediately rejected the idea, convinced it would only drive Blackmun away. Brennan took great care in how he handled Blackmun all spring, out of fear of alienating him. He was torn when Blackmun asked for the assignment in another case. According to his clerks' term history, Brennan believed that Blackmun had mishandled opinions in two other cases and he worried he might do likewise in this case as well. On the other hand, Brennan feared irritating Blackmun on the eve of a discussion of the *Bakke* case scheduled for the March 6 conference. So Brennan ultimately relented and assigned the other opinion to Blackmun. It was not until May 1 that Blackmun finally revealed his position in a memo to his colleagues. He explained that he believed "the Davis program is within constitutional bounds, though perhaps barely so. It is free of stigma. I am not willing to infer a constitutional violation."

With the votes now lined up four on each side and one in the middle, Brennan's hopes for a partial victory hinged on Powell. Brennan suggested to Burger the idea of a joint assignment to Powell, in which he would write the opinion of the Court and each group of four would join different parts. Powell agreed to the arrangement. Brennan and his clerks remained hopeful that he might be able to join an opinion written by Powell. But after their clerks talked over the areas of disagreement, Powell's clerk Robert Comfort was pessimistic when he reported back to his boss about the likelihood Brennan would join them.

Powell did not agree with Brennan's notion that racial classifications could be divided into stigmatizing and nonstigmatizing categories. Nor did Powell agree with Brennan that correcting broad societal discrimination rather than actual instances of past discrimination was a compelling state interest that could overcome the strict scrutiny test. So it was not a surprise in Powell's chambers when Brennan balked at joining the opinion Powell circulated on May 9. In a memo to Powell the next day, Brennan explained that the views of the four justices in his camp "differ so substantially from your own that no common ground seems possible." Brennan reluctantly concluded that his foursome would have to write separately while concurring with Powell as much as possible.

Brennan had earlier mulled assigning the *Bakke* opinion to White. He recognized White had had scant opportunity to write such a historical opinion during his fifteen terms on the Court. White had developed a reputation as gruff and distant outside the Court, although he and Brennan had a warm rapport. White had sat next to Brennan on the bench since joining the Court, and they frequently traded quips. White seemed incapable of whispering, much to the annoyance of Blackmun, who complained to their colleagues about the noise. Off the bench, White occasionally stopped by Brennan's chambers for substantive conversations about cases. He felt free to tease him too: White crowned Brennan "deputy prime minister," because he thought Brennan in at least one case was acting more like a member of another branch of another government.

But Brennan now decided to keep the assignment for himself, convinced that no one else could hold together his fragile coalition with Marshall, White, Powell, and Blackmun. He feared that the more fragmented the opinions of those favoring a partial reversal, the more precarious affirmative action's legal status would appear to the public. Brennan had good reason for concern, particularly when it came to Marshall. This was an emotional issue for Marshall, as Brennan well understood. Over lunch one day, Brennan asked Marshall whether he thought a medical school admissions committee should accord his son special consideration if he ever applied. "Damn right, they owe us!" Marshall replied.

Far more so than Brennan, Marshall had been characteristically pessimistic about the prospects for preserving affirmative action from the start of the term. He was always suspicious about how little his colleagues — particularly Powell, the lone southerner — understood about the state of race relations. He believed they blithely overestimated how much progress blacks had achieved. In April, Marshall handwrote an angry draft opinion in which he dismissed the notion that American society was colorblind. "We are not yet all equals, in large part because of the refusal of the Plessy court to adopt the principle of color-blindness," Marshall stated, referring to the 1896 Supreme Court decision upholding "separate but equal" legalized segregation. "It would be the cruelest irony for this Court to adopt the dissent in Plessy now and hold that the University must use color-blind admissions." Blackmun credited Marshall's statement with helping sway his vote. But Marshall had also alienated another potential member of their coalition. At the December conference where Brennan had prompted Powell to split his vote, Marshall suggested that blacks might still need special preferences for another hundred years. It was a conclusion that left Powell speechless, highlighting the gap that separated him from his liberal colleagues who seemed comfortable with the idea of generations of racial preferences.

For several weeks, Brennan worked to try to keep Blackmun, Marshall, and White onboard, a task that proved difficult, particularly when it came to laying out a standard of review. Brennan eschewed strict scrutiny in favor of a new standard of review, requiring an "important and articulated purpose." He needed to align it with the standard applied in gender cases in order to keep Blackmun, and he had to avoid using the language employed by Powell in order to avoid offending Marshall. On June 8, he privately circulated the first of several drafts to the other members of his quartet plus Powell. White responded by noting he still preferred strict scrutiny and also objected to the tone of Brennan's opinion. "I am inclined to keep the decibel level as low as possible," White wrote Brennan on June 13. "We won't accomplish much by beating a white majority over past ills or by describing what has gone by as a system of apartheid." Nevertheless, all three ultimately signed on to his opinion, while also writing separately.

Brennan provided one last source of disagreement by inserting language in his opinion declaring that "the central meaning" of the *Bakke* decision was that "government may take race into account when it acts not to demean or insult any racial group, but to remedy disadvantages cast on minorities by past racial prejudice." Brennan was very consciously trying to shape how the public — and particularly lower courts — perceived the case. He wanted to put the emphasis on the fact that generally the Court had upheld racial preferences rather than on what it had rejected. Eventually Powell concluded that Brennan had taken liberties in his interpretation of the case's central meaning, and he wrote Brennan to say so. "In terms of 'judgment,' my opinion is limited to the holding that a state university validly may consider race to achieve diversity," Powell wrote. However, Powell indicated he did not intend to object to Brennan's language, "as I have thought you could put whatever 'gloss' on the several opinions you think proper."

Brennan continued his effort to shape the public perception of the case when the decision was announced on June 26, 1978. The wives of several of the justices — including Marjorie — sat in the audience that day in a sign of its import. Brennan spoke third after Powell and Stevens in a slightly gravelly but still strong voice that give little hint of his battle with throat cancer just months earlier. His eighteen-minute statement was almost as long as the two that preceded his, combined. He emphasized "the signal importance of today's decision on the constitutional question," which he described as whether "race conscious programs are permissible under the equal protection clause." Then he repeated his formulation of the "central meaning" in the case. In the days that followed, the case received the kind of press attention Brennan might have hoped. "No Quotas — But Race Can Count," read the headline on the cover of *Newsweek*. Two months later, Bakke started class at Davis's medical school guarded by plainclothes police officers as one hundred noisy demonstrators protested outside. Four years later, Bakke quietly graduated not long before his forty-second birthday and went on to practice medicine at the Mayo Clinic in Rochester, Minnesota, where his patients later included Justice Powell.

For Brennan, the more important outcome was that affirmative action had survived. From what looked initially to be an almost certain defeat, he managed to salvage a partial victory. The case showed Brennan at his best: working cooperatively with his colleagues to build consensus rather than writing fiery dissents that alienated them. While the justices were not nearly as fragmented as in their first landmark death penalty decision, they had shown themselves to be as divided on the issue of affirmative action as the rest of the country, and much remained unsettled. The justices had provided some sense of what might be allowed in university admissions, but had not addressed the context of employment at all. A year later, the justices took up the question of whether private employers could establish voluntary affirmative action programs. Brennan authored a 5–2 opinion upholding an agreement between the Kaiser Aluminum company and the steelworkers union to reserve for minorities 50 percent of the slots in a training program for skilled jobs. Neither Powell nor Stevens participated in the case. But their support would prove vital to Brennan as the Court considered the legality of affirmative action in other contexts, including setting aside a proportion of government contracts to minorities or shielding them from layoffs.

· 19 ·

DARKEST YEARS

BRENNAN GATHERED TOGETHER with nearly all of his former clerks on October 20, 1979, for their first reunion in three years. The Saturday-night dinner was held at the International Club in downtown Washington, D.C. Spouses and children would join them as usual the next day for brunch at the Court. Much had changed since the first such reunion nineteen years earlier. Brennan's current family of sixty-two clerks had long since outgrown the more intimate backroom of a Washington restaurant where early reunions had taken place. Brennan had served so long that his first clerks were now old enough to be the fathers of the current ones — and the justice himself could be their grandfather. Many of the attendees had not seen the justice since the last reunion, and noticed how much more frail he looked now at the age of seventy-three.

Brennan had prepared what he intended to say this night with great care. He had written out his speech in longhand with some difficulty on eight and a half pages of a legal pad. "Over 23 terms," he began, "This assembly has produced 902 opinions." He went through some more detailed statistics that summarized his tenure, as he often liked to do in these reunion speeches, although this time it all seemed more somber than celebratory. Then, term by term, he singled out which clerks had served and what opinions they had crafted together. "That brief review will give you the reason why I am so deeply indebted to each and every one of you," he said. Finally, Brennan explained he had another reason to want to review his record on the Court. "I've been considering retirement," he explained. The announcement elicited audible gasps of "No!" from the crowd of clerks, who were nonetheless not entirely surprised. The Supreme Court press corps had started calling Brennan's chambers the previous spring after learning he had not yet hired clerks for the following 1980–81 term.

Brennan told his clerks that he had started thinking about retirement the previous year, when Marjorie's health took another turn for the worse and he was undergoing treatment for throat cancer. More recently, as Brennan and Marjorie had left Nantucket in early September, she had fallen ill again on the ferry back to Woods Hole. They checked into a nearby motel rather than driving to their son Bill's house in Princeton, New Jersey, as planned. Brennan started feeling sick, too, but was so concerned about Marjorie's health that he ignored the numbness in his right arm and hand. It was only when they finally reached Princeton a few days later that a doctor diagnosed a possible stroke. Brennan returned to Washington, but was admitted to Bethesda Naval Hospital for three days of observation. He returned to work part-time in mid-September but had not yet regained full use of his right hand. So all of Brennan's clerks attending the reunion understood why he had greeted them by shaking hands awkwardly with his left hand.

Whether it was the lingering effects of the throat cancer and stroke "or just old age," Brennan admitted to his clerks "that things don't come as easily as they once did, and I fatigue more quickly." He explained that he would wait until December to decide whether to hire clerks for the following term, or announce his retirement at the end of the current term in the spring of 1980. "I . . . thought you ought to know what's on my mind," Brennan said. "I would, however, appreciate your help in keeping it within the family until I've made my final decision and announced it."

Much to Brennan's surprise, the *Washington Post* ran a front-page story three days later reporting that he had told his clerks he was "giving serious consideration to retiring." The story, which ran without a byline, cited "several close associates" of Brennan. He had no doubt that one or more of his clerks had been the source, a suspicion shared by some of his clerks.

The disclosure deeply disappointed Brennan, who had always spoken candidly at his reunion dinners because of his absolute faith that nothing he said would leave the room. Now at least one of his confidants had breached that trust. But Brennan later stated, "I've never tried to find out [who it was] and don't really want to know."

Following the *Post* article, many of Brennan's admirers and friends wrote urging him to reconsider. His correspondents included Powell, who sent Brennan a typed note the same day the article appeared calling it "most unwelcome news." "I am sure that Marge's health is a major factor in your thinking," Powell wrote. "But please do not make any premature judgment. You are in full vigor mentally and adequate health physically. Your leaving the Court would be an irreparable loss to the Court as an institution, and certainly to each of us as your friends."

Yet events in the days that followed only seemed to confirm that it was the right time to retire. Marjorie broke her nose, left kneecap, and a couple of ribs in a serious fall. Her leg was so swollen that several days would pass before doctors could even put it in a cast. "It is to be a six to eight weeks business and she'll have to get around with a walker," Brennan wrote a friend on October 30. "But life goes on." That letter's stoic tone masked the depth of Brennan's concerns. He feared that Marjorie might never walk again. And even if she did, he could not bear the thought of not being there the next time she fell.

Brennan's powers of persuasion failed him when he tried to convince Marjorie and their children that he should tend to her full-time. Beyond looking after his wife, he had not actually given any thought to what he would do in retirement, although he could finally afford to stop working. Having served twenty years on the Court, Brennan was now entitled to a full pension. His contemporaries were already easing out of full-time work. Bazelon had taken senior status just a few months earlier, although he still heard a reduced load of cases.

Likely but left unspoken was the guilt Brennan harbored about bouncing back from two serious health crises with such ease while Marjorie began her second decade of suffering from cancer and its consequences. "Oh, how she suffered," Brennan would say in a deeply pained voice whenever his biographer asked about her. Her illness only added to the misgivings Brennan still occasionally felt about uprooting Marjorie from the life she loved in New Jersey. These feelings help explain why Brennan continued to avoid addressing Marjorie's drinking, even when, over lunch in his chambers one day in the mid-1970s, Nancy told Brennan she thought her mother had a drinking problem. She asked her father whether he agreed and whether there was anything she could do to help. The ever garrulous Brennan seemed to stop breathing as he stared down at his napkin. He sat there silently for what felt to Nancy like ten minutes. Finally she got up, apologized, and left. "I was really sorry," she later recalled. "I assumed I was wrong and disappointed him." Nancy remembered that Brennan and her brother Hugh actually discouraged attempts to do anything about the problem. "My dad the protector and Hugh the sober alcoholic said, 'This is one of her few pleasures. Let her have it.'" Referring to Marjorie's tendency to mix her drinks with Clamato, Nancy says their rationale was, "Let her have her vitamins that way."

Marjorie felt significant guilt of her own. "She was always so worried during the long bout of illness that she was holding him back," recalled her friend Adrian Barth. During one summer visit to Nantucket, Marjorie confided to another friend that she thought Brennan deserved a younger, healthier wife, saying, "He's so active and has so much energy and I've been sick all these years." She certainly did not want to be the reason for Brennan having to retire from the Court early.

Brennan's sons pleaded with him not to quit. They argued that the last thing that their mother needed—or even wanted—was to have him fretting over her all the time. As his family knew well, Brennan defined himself by his work. He had close friends and a loving family but had given up on most of his interests beyond reading during Marjorie's illnesses. Bill and Hugh felt that any benefit to Marjorie would be outweighed by the toll retirement would take on his well-being. "Pop without his work ain't pop," his son Hugh later recalled. "So maybe an upbeat pop three hours a day is a lot more than a downbeat pop eight hours a day." Into November of 1979, Brennan debated what to do, until Marjorie finally had the last word. "She thought it would be a terrible mistake and that I shouldn't under any circumstances because of her illness even think of doing it," Brennan later recalled. By the end of November, the New York Times reported that Brennan had hired four clerks for the 1980–81 term. (The number of clerks in each justice's chambers had grown from two to three and then four during the 1970s.) "I finally decided there was no good reason to leave," he wrote his former clerk Daniel Rezneck that December.

NO SOONER HAD Brennan decided to stay on the Court than he had new reason to feel betrayed by his clerks. The spark was *The Brethren*, a book by Bob Woodward and Scott Armstrong that offered a behind-the-scenes look at the Supreme Court during Burger's first seven terms as chief justice.

Brennan had known for more than a year that the Supreme Court had become the latest investigative target for Woodward, whose reporting on Watergate for the *Washington Post* had helped bring down President Nixon. For many months, Brennan's clerks reported back to him as Woodward approached them for interviews. Brennan left it to them to decide individually whether to talk. He asked only that his current clerks not discuss pending cases. Brennan insisted that he never cooperated with the authors himself, although that did not stop him from gossiping about the book, like everyone else at the Court. "Rumor has it that Woodward's book will be out fairly soon," he had written publisher Alfred Knopf in April 1979. (Hugo Black had introduced Brennan to Knopf in 1963 and they continued to correspond and socialize occasionally in subsequent years.) Word of the book's progress slowly leaked out. *Legal Times*, a weekly Washington newspaper, reported in June that Woodward and coauthor Armstrong had "accumulated a staggering amount of unpublished information" and noted that Brennan "has been aggressively abrupt in turning down Woodward's interview requests."

The months of anticipation finally ended on Sunday, December 2, 1979, as excerpts of *The Brethren* began appearing in newspapers around the country, including in the *Washington Post*, where Woodward was now an editor. The first excerpt began with Burger's selection in 1969 and chronicled his ineffectual leadership during the *Alexander* school-desegregation case that first term. The particularly unflattering portrayal of Burger in the excerpt troubled Brennan less than the accompanying news story on the *Post*'s front page. Brennan was shocked to read in the *Post* that among the "unprecedented accumulation of secret court materials" obtained by Woodward and Armstrong were some of his own term histories. The *Post* described them as "the private journals of Justice William J. Brennan Jr., who used his clerks to keep detailed accounts of what was going on in other justices' chambers." The *Post* also revealed that *The Brethren* quoted Brennan as privately calling Burger a "dummy." The most explosive allegation regarding Brennan previewed in the *Post* story was that he refused to overturn a prison sentence in 1972, even though he believed the defendant, "Slick" Moore, was unfairly convicted. "His motive, the book says he told clerks, was the appeasement of Justice Harry Blackmun, who Brennan hoped to bring into line on unrelated abortion and obscenity cases."

That night, Woodward and Armstrong appeared on the CBS television news magazine *60 Minutes*. When asked whether Brennan was *The Brethren*'s "Deep Throat," a reference to Woodward's secret Watergate source, Armstrong replied, "I think we'd rather not answer that." Armstrong later explained he was simply trying to avoid questions about their sources. But that answer enraged Brennan, who thought it intentionally left the impression that he had cooperated with the two authors. (Woodward later revealed that his key source on the Court had actually been Potter Stewart, but not until after the justice had retired and died.) Pounding his hand down on the table, Brennan yelled, "I will never vote for the First Amendment again!" His angry response shocked Tim Phelps, Nancy's ex-husband, who was a journalist himself and happened to be watching the program with his former father-in-law that night in the Brennan apartment. Phelps had known Brennan for more than a decade, but had never seen him so irate.

As he made clear in his *New York Times v. Sullivan* opinion establishing a high bar for libel suits against public officials, Brennan believed strongly in the need to protect what he viewed as the press's vital role in a democratic society. He remained an avid consumer of newspapers and the television networks' evening news programs. Yet journalists managed to infuriate Brennan like no one else. That had been most acutely evident a decade earlier when he had shoved an Associated Press reporter at the Laetare Medal ceremony. He still refused to speak with Fred Graham, who had moved onto CBS News from the *New York Times,* for articles he incorrectly believed Graham had written in the 1960s about his son. Brennan also continued to decline almost all interview requests, making no exception even for Anthony Lewis, with whom Brennan became friendly after the writer moved off the Supreme Court beat.

Brennan thought it best to let his opinions speak for themselves. That does not explain why the characteristically gregarious justice could be sharp when reporters attempted even simple gestures of good will. As a new reporter at the Supreme Court, Nina Totenberg had sent Brennan a note with a free subscription to her publication, the *National Observer*. Brennan replied tartly that he did not accept gifts. He even avoided photojournalists trying to take his picture. In 1973 a photographer on assignment for *Time* magazine approached him as he left for his morning walk and asked whether he was Justice Brennan. "No," Brennan said. "Never heard of him." Only when Brennan was out of camera range did the photographer realize he had been tricked.

The irony that journalists' greatest defender on the Court avoided — and occasionally raged against — the press was not lost on those close to him. Peter Harkness, who grew up next door to Brennan in Georgetown, remembered attending a dinner where Brennan exploded about an article that had appeared in the *Washington Post*. "Here is the icon of the First Amendment and he is just lambasting this newspaper," said Harkness, who went on to a career in journalism. "I'm certain he'd rule in their favor the next day if the case was presented but I was shocked at the anger."

Three days before the clerk reunion at which he broached his possible retirement, Brennan had occasion to scold the press publicly, during a speech at Rutgers University. After noting the press's vital role, Brennan expressed concern that "in the heat of the controversy the press may be misapprehending the fundamental issues at stake, and may be consequently failing in its important task of illuminating these issues for the court and the public." What prompted his comments was a decision by the Court a few months earlier holding that the Sixth Amendment's guarantee of public trials did not protect a right of trial access for the general public or reporters. The ruling had led dozens of judges to close proceedings and it sparked a wave of outcries from media outlets across the country. A *Los Angeles Times* editorial warned that the Court had taken the country "down the ominous path to secret trials," while a *Minneapolis Star Tribune* columnist condemned the justices for giving trial judges "a free hand to lock courtroom doors against the public and journalists who are the citizens' surrogates." That sort of rhetoric prompted unusual public rebuttals that summer from four justices who insisted the decision held no such thing.

In his Rutgers speech, Brennan distinguished between two different ways of thinking about the role of the press. He contrasted the "speech" model under which the press "requires and is accorded the absolute protection of the First Amendment" with a "structural" model in which "the press' interests may conflict with other societal interests and adjustment of the conflict on occasion favors the competing claim." Brennan argued that the tendency on the part of the press to confuse these two models explained much of the recent acrimony in press-court relations. "The press has reacted as if its role as a public spokesman [was] being restricted, and as a consequence, it has on occasion overreacted," Brennan said. "The press can be of assistance only if bitterness does not cloud its vision, nor self-righteousness its judgment."

Despite the harsh tone of the speech, Brennan's status as a protector of free speech meant that his comments attracted serious press consideration. In an editorial titled "Justice Brennan Tells Off the Press," the *Washington Post* noted Brennan's "hard words" should have "sent quivers through" newsrooms around the country, since they came "from a friend on whose support, in judicial circles, the press has come to depend." The *Post* praised Brennan for providing "a fascinating and highly useful analysis of what the Court has been doing in recent years" and said, "Unlike most criticisms of the press, it provides a theory whose wisdom the press and the judges can debate without engaging in outrageous rhetoric."

Two months after the Rutgers speech, Brennan's tolerance for the press was put to the most profound test yet by *The Brethren* and its embarrassing details about the Court. Many believed, the authors did not get everything right. Woodward and Armstrong could be faulted for an omniscient narrative style that did not reveal sources, and for relying too heavily on the perspective of those who did speak, especially the law clerks. The book set off a debate over whether the revelations might chill candid conversation within chambers and between justices. Nevertheless, Woodward and Armstrong accomplished a remarkable reporting feat that, as promised, pierced the absolute secrecy that usually surrounded the justices' deliberations and showed how the Court was beset by the same backbiting and petty intrigue as any other workplace. Whatever its shortcomings, *The Brethren* proved enormously popular. A public increasingly distrustful of once-vaunted government institutions in the wake of Watergate snapped up more than six hundred thousand hardcover copies.

The Brethren's depiction of Brennan was ambiguous enough that some reviewers concluded he came off well, while others considered the portrait devastating. Brennan, depicted as the Court's "most energetic advocate," had far less to complain about than some of his colleagues. "He cajoled in conference, walked the halls constantly and worked the phones, polling and plotting strategy with his allies," Woodward and Armstrong wrote of Brennan. "He was thin and gray-haired, and his easy smile and bright blue eyes gave him a leprechaun's appearance as he sidled up and threw his arms around his colleagues."

The book's depiction fed the public perception that Brennan operated in the Court like a savvy Irish ward boss, a notion that he always resented. During the second interview with his biographer, in 1986, Brennan asked that he "kill off that silly notion of an amiable Irishman going around cajoling and maybe seducing colleagues — that just doesn't happen." While Woodward and Armstrong might have exaggerated by depicting Brennan as the Court's retail politician, the justice himself understated his role as a political operator. Brennan tried to portray himself as someone who remained completely detached in his chambers, relying on formal memos to communicate with his colleagues. But he regularly deployed his clerks as a diplomatic corps to gather information and to act as middlemen with other chambers. And, as legal historian Mark Tushnet has observed, Brennan was a successful politician in a deeper sense: "Like all good political leaders, Brennan structured the process of decision and gave his colleagues reasons for doing what he understood to be the right thing."

Still, publication of the book proved particularly traumatic for the justice in several ways. The conflict-averse Brennan was mortified that Burger would read about the derogatory names he privately called the chief justice. Brennan went out of his way to appear friendly with Burger publicly as they emerged laughing and chatting after the Court heard oral arguments one day after the first excerpt ran in the *Washington Post*. After intentionally trying to distance himself from abortion cases, Brennan certainly did not welcome Woodward and Armstrong's depiction of him as a key behind-the-scenes player in the *Roe* case, which sparked a new smattering of condemnation in Catholic publications. The D.C. Bar launched an ethics investigation of Tommy "the Cork" Corcoran after *The Brethren* revealed he had visited Brennan's chambers to ask that a case be reheard. (The investigation was dropped after Brennan told the D.C. Bar that he had "no independent recollection" of the incident in a January 1980 letter.) And he was outraged by the suggestion that he might have traded his vote in a case to curry favor with Blackmun, which he labeled a "damnable lie" and "canard" in a letter to one law professor: "I would hope that after 31 years on the Bench and votes in over 100,000 cases, it would not be necessary for me to affirm that I have never cast a vote against my conscience."

Brennan was particularly bothered by Armstrong and Woodward's intimation that he might have been one of their sources. When Woodward told the *Oakland Tribune* that Brennan had not provided copies of his term histories regarding the Nixon tapes case, Brennan wrote a former clerk, "I only wish the skunks would make a more public acknowledgement." Brennan also resented how the authors trumpeted his term histories as the product of a secret intelligence service he operated inside his chambers. All the focus on his histories — which many of his colleagues were now hearing about for the first time — fed the perception both inside the Court and beyond that Brennan must have willingly helped the authors. Brennan, who prided himself on his collegial relations with the other justices, was greatly troubled by their suspicions.

Equally galling was the way columnists mischaracterized and condemned his case histories as some sort of sordid diary or "gossip file." William Safire, in his *New York Times* column, accused Brennan of misusing federal employees — his clerks — "to edify or enrich his posterity." Syndicated columnist James J. Kilpatrick demanded Brennan resign if he had voluntarily provided the histories to Woodward and Armstrong. "So gross a breach of the court's tradition of confidentiality cannot be condoned," Kilpatrick wrote. What stung worse was lawyer-author George V. Higgins's column in the *Boston Globe*'s Sunday magazine. "Brennan appears so to dislike Burger that he made notes of conferences of the judges, and condoned their delivery along with the products of snooping by his clerks — i.e., gossip — to the reporters," Higgins wrote. "Justice Brennan and I share a fondness for Nantucket, but this behavior of his is contemptible." Brennan confided in a letter to professor Walter Murphy, "My daughter and granddaughter live in Boston and this has hurt them deeply."

The publicity built a lasting aura of mystery around Brennan's term histories, which no one outside his chambers had ever seen before. Their contents — offering the richest details of the Court's internal byplay ever assembled inside its walls — remained tantalizingly out of reach in the future, too. Produced in the Court's print shop, the histories physically resembled the justices' opinions in appearance and style. To be sure, these accounts cannot be relied on as a definitive historical record or as Brennan's personal memoir. Although many were written in the first person, the clerks did nearly all the drafting, usually with little overt instruction or input from Brennan in advance and scant editing upon completion. The resulting products vary greatly in length, quality, and detail. Many were colored by the biases of clerks who wrote them or a desire to please their boss.

Nevertheless, the histories are a valuable subjective chronicle of what Brennan and his clerks directly observed and how they perceived events. The histories often provide the only record of private meetings and conversations between justices such as John Harlan's Sunday-night call in 1964 to tell Brennan he would withdraw his separate opinion and join *New York Times v. Sullivan*. The history from the 1981–82 term reveals that Rehnquist referred to illegal immigrants as "wetbacks" — a comment that upset Marshall — during one of the justices' conference discussions of a case involving a law that permitted school districts to exclude illegal alien children.

The histories make it possible to track changes in Brennan's tactics and strategies — and his impressions of colleagues — over time. Brennan's clerks describe his unsuccessful attempts to convince his colleagues to have opinions signed jointly by the whole Court in major cases in the 1970s, including the Nixon tapes and *Buckley v. Valeo* campaign-finance cases, an approach he had resisted in the 1958 Little Rock school-desegregation case. Descriptions of minor cases are often equally revealing. In an otherwise unmemorable 1970 case involving postal service regulation of direct-mail marketers, Burger's insistence on including what Brennan believed to be extraneous language about parents' "absolute right" to control their children's mail showed how the chief justice alienated Brennan early in his tenure. Criticism of Burger in the term histories grew sharper the longer they served together. The chief justice's opinions and statements at conference were characterized in term histories as "an embarrassment," "an unqualified disaster," and "a long and incoherent series of rambling non-sequiturs."

Understanding these limitations, Brennan had not originally intended them for wide external consumption. He considered destroying the case studies after publication of *The Brethren*, though ultimately changed his mind and granted access to a handful of journalists and historians. The decision to share the histories suggests that Brennan came to view them as a means to help shape how history would view his tenure, even if he had only commissioned them as a reference tool for use within his chambers. Though Brennan bristled at any suggestion he was a secret source for *The Brethren*, he felt no qualms about later revealing the inner workings of the Court to his biographer.

While Brennan, like all of his colleagues, stayed publicly silent about *The Brethren*, he felt compelled to try to correct the record with select friends and law professors. In what became a standard response to letters inquiring about whether he cooperated, Brennan would write, "I have never met either Woodward or Armstrong. I have never talked to either of them, by telephone or in person. I have not personally delivered or authorized any person to deliver to them any documents or other materials from my files or chambers or anywhere else." Brennan became more emotional when his friend Alfred Knopf joined the list of major publishers inquiring whether he might want to turn his "diaries" into a memoir. After explaining that he had prepared the case histories as "reference materials," Brennan wrote Knopf, "The hype that preceded the book referred to these as 'memoirs' or 'a diary.' They are neither, as I said, and I have no intention of writing either 'memoirs' or 'a diary.'"

Brennan did not want to believe that any of his clerks might have actually provided any of his histories to Armstrong or Woodward. As one clerk explained, it would be to Brennan as if those closest to him "had raided the holy relics." He preferred to theorize, on at least one occasion, that perhaps the authors had paid off a maintenance man to steal them from the bottom right-hand drawer of his desk, where he kept them close at hand for easy reference. (A second set was locked securely inside a safe in the outer office of the chambers behind his secretary's desk.) But Brennan could not completely deny the very likely fact of his clerks' complicity. Woodward almost certainly obtained the histories from former clerks who had taken home drafts of the ones they had prepared — or from current clerks who had copied the larger set held in Brennan's unlocked drawer.

It would have been difficult for the young clerks in any of the justices' chambers not to be flattered and a bit starstruck if approached by the nation's most famous newspaper reporter. Woodward's notoriety had only grown after Robert Redford portrayed him in the 1976 movie version of his book about Watergate, *All the President's Men*. Some of the clerks, whose intelligence was exceeded only by their self-confidence, naïvely assumed they could help shape the book's contents, and wound up revealing much more than they ever intended. Other Brennan clerks insisted the authors had misled them about the nature of the project or distorted what they said. In a law review article about *The Brethren*, Brennan's 1976–77 term clerk, William A. Fletcher, wrote, "The authors said only that they were writing a book on decision making in Washington, of which the Supreme Court would form only a part, and that prospective sources would be asked to violate no confidences." Some of Brennan's clerks wrote him confessional letters in the weeks after publication admitting they had spoken to Woodward. "I did so partly out of curiosity and partly out of a desire to communicate to him my belief that, with all its imperfections, the Court is perhaps the most honorable institution of government yet devised by man," wrote Geoffrey Stone, a 1972–73 term clerk. No clerks admitted to Brennan having supplied the term histories.

The idea that his clerks betrayed his confidence hurt Brennan deeply. "I've always worked closely with my law clerks and feel a sense of sadness and deep disappointment that any of them should have breached the essential confidence of our relationship," Brennan wrote in a letter to Erwin Griswold. He thought back to the recent reunion where he had discussed possibly retiring, and the undeniable evidence that at least one clerk had immediately called the *Washington Post*. He now concluded that it must have been Woodward who wrote the resulting story without a byline. But in his typically conflict-averse way, Brennan swallowed his anger when replying to his clerks' confessional notes and explained he had no intention of responding publicly. "I've personally come to the conclusion that there are so many misstatements, knowingly so or not, that nothing is to be gained by denials," Brennan wrote three of his former clerks in December 1979. "It would only get into a shouting match which would prove nothing."

Brennan certainly did not mind when his clerks and a friendly journalist sought to challenge the book's most damning charge against him: that he switched votes to curry favor with Blackmun. Four clerks who served during the term of the case at issue involving Slick Moore wrote a letter to the editor of the *Post* denouncing *The Brethren's* account as false. Journalist Anthony Lewis followed up with an investigation of his own that ran in the *New York Review of Books* in February 1980. Lewis accused Woodward and Armstrong of "hit-and-run journalism." That prompted a lengthy rebuttal from Woodward and Armstrong in which they stood by their story. Brennan privately thanked both his clerk Paul Hoeber and Lewis for their efforts. "I can't adequately tell you how much your response means to me," Brennan wrote Lewis.

The furor over *The Brethren* eventually died down. Unlike Byron White, Brennan did not respond by becoming less forthcoming in the future to those working beside him in his chambers. He would eventually reveal to his clerks the discomfort the disclosures had caused him at a subsequent reunion. But his anger about the book — and particularly toward its authors — did not fade with time. Having heard how furious Brennan was about the book, Woodward later approached Judge Bazelon and his wife, Mickey, in an effort to arrange a meeting with the justice. Brennan said he would think about the offer when Mickey mentioned it. But he never raised the subject again. "Nor did I ask him to," Mickey later recalled. "I had to tell Bob that it didn't look like he would ever give him the privilege of speaking with him directly and privately." When a law student visiting the Court asked him a question about the book in March 1990, he labeled it "pure fiction." Brennan used less delicate terms when his biographer made reference to the book while asking about a case from that period. "I don't want anything [from] that Goddamn shit sheet," Brennan exploded. "We'll have to rely on what I can remember."

SYNDICATED COLUMNIST CURTIS GANS offered Brennan some unsolicited career advice in July 1980 as the presidential election approached. He suggested that both Brennan and Marshall resign to allow President Carter, who had not yet had a chance to nominate anyone to the Court, to name their successors. Gans expressed fears "that their three decades of accomplishment may be vitiated and overturned should Ronald Reagan be elected President and empowered to appoint their successors."

Democrats had good reason for concern as the election grew closer. Carter appeared to be the first incumbent elected president since Herbert Hoover at risk of being cast out of the White House. Watergate had fed a false confidence among Democrats, who had picked up dozens of seats in the 1974 midterm congressional elections and retaken the White House two years later. Republicans had seemed in full retreat in the mid-1970s. Yet, behind the scenes, conservatives had quietly laid the groundwork for resurgence. New grassroots organizations and think tanks such as the

Heritage Foundation sprung up, thanks to generous funding from foundations controlled by conservative businesspeople. "Neoconservative" — as they were newly known — intellectuals agitated against affirmative action and the threat of Soviet aggression. Social conservatives mobilized around a cluster of issues such as abortion, gay rights, and school prayer, often in response to Court decisions they disliked. Minister Jerry Falwell and social organizer Paul Weyrich called for a return to "traditional moral values" when they founded the Moral Majority in 1979. These disparate strains of conservatism coalesced around Reagan, the sixty-nine-year-old former actor and two-term governor of California making his third run for the presidency in 1980. The New Deal Democratic coalition, meanwhile, seemed exhausted and beset by division. Its disarray was best symbolized by Senator Edward Kennedy's primary challenge against Carter and his refusal to shake the incumbent president's hand onstage at the party's August 1980 convention in New York.

Brennan harbored a low opinion of Reagan even before the campaign began. Warren had always made clear how little he thought of his fellow California governor. And Brennan still resented how, with Reagan targeting the University of California at Berkeley during the 1966 gubernatorial run, the clerkship offer to Michael Tigar had become so fraught. During the 1980 campaign, Reagan made clear he opposed many of the policies made possible by Brennan's opinions. While it was hardly a major campaign issue, Reagan's occasional rhetoric about judicial appointments and the role of the courts gave Brennan additional reason for concern. Reagan did not disavow language in the GOP platform suggesting that opposition to abortion might be a prerequisite for appointment to the federal bench. Through the fall, the opinion pages of the *New York Times* were filled with dire warnings about what a Reagan victory might mean for judicial selection. Floyd Abrams, the noted First Amendment lawyer, warned, "We can only despair as to the likely caliber of his potential Supreme Court appointments."

In a landslide victory, Reagan swept 489 electoral votes compared to Carter's 49. Republicans picked up thirty-three seats in the House and a dozen in the Senate, where liberal stalwarts such as George McGovern, the party's 1972 presidential candidate, went down to defeat. Exuberant Republicans crowed about a watershed political realignment the likes of which had not been seen since the New Deal era first began in 1932. Reagan managed to win every northeastern state except Maryland and Rhode Island in part because he successfully attracted white working-class — and often Catholic — voters, dubbed Reagan Democrats. The Court's decisions championed by Brennan throughout the 1970s on issues such as welfare, busing, and affirmative action had helped feed these voters' perception that the Democratic Party cared more about the poor and minority voters than it did about their working-class aspirations.

REAGAN STILL CONSIDERED Washington alien territory when he arrived there on November 17, 1980, two weeks after the election, for his first visit as president-elect. Fresh off a vacation at his mountaintop California ranch, Reagan set out to introduce himself to official Washington. He went first to the Capitol, where he managed to disarm even the most skeptical Democrats. "I liked him very much," confessed House Speaker Thomas P. "Tip" O'Neill Jr. On the second day of his visit, Reagan stopped by the Supreme Court, where Brennan came face-to-face with the president-elect for the first time. Reagan and George H. W. Bush, the vice president–elect, first met privately with Burger and then posed with all eight justices present as news photographers snapped their picture in the justices' conference room. (Burger groused about there being too many photographers.) Then Burger led them all to the justices' private dining room.

Over coffee, tea, and white wine, Reagan introduced himself to the Court. Standing in the background during the meeting was forty-nine-year-old Edwin Meese III, who had been a top Reagan aide since 1966. The six-feet-tall Californian with the cherubic smile and ruddy complexion had been passed over for campaign manager — and was about to be passed over again for White House chief of staff. But Meese, who was both fiercely loyal and conservative, would nevertheless come to play a key role in the administration as part of a troika of top White House aides.

Brennan went into the meeting skeptical about Reagan, but left less so. No newly elected president had paid such a courtesy call on the Court in decades, and Brennan appreciated the gesture. He came away convinced that Reagan was not nearly as bad as so many liberals portrayed him. (Working such a conversion was typical for Reagan, who liked to say that even his fiercest adversaries realized after meeting him that "he didn't have horns.") Brennan liked Reagan personally much better than Nixon or even Johnson, a president with whom he politically had much more in common. Only five years separated Brennan from Reagan, whose seventieth birthday fell seventeen days after his inauguration, but the age difference seemed much greater when the two men stood side-by-side. Reagan retained the striking good looks that made him a movie star. He still stood above six feet and had a full head of wavy dark hair. The diminutive Brennan, shriveled a bit with age, his thinning hair having long since gone gray, barely reached Reagan's neck.

Yet, as between Tip O'Neill and Reagan, there was a genuine connection. "The two of them are Irish pols in the best sense of the words," Brennan's son Bill later noted. "Reagan is a man my father would have had a hard time disliking." Brennan made a point of attending Reagan's inauguration, unlike Nixon's, which he had skipped. And it struck Brennan's liberal clerks, who had no love for the new president, how upset he became when Reagan was shot and seriously wounded outside a Washington hotel in March 1981. Still, they hardly became friends. Beyond the occasional formal function at the White House or Court, Brennan did not see much more of Reagan than any of the other presidents who preceded him.

Liking the president as a person did not mean Brennan had any intention of rolling over as Reagan and his conservative administration set out to undo much of his legacy. During that brief postelection victory lap, neither Reagan nor Meese, who would become Brennan's chief antagonist, appreciated the degree to which Brennan and O'Neill — two old Irish liberals sitting atop the other branches of government — would thwart their agenda. (Another younger Irishman, Ted Kennedy, played a similar role in the Senate.) Brennan and O'Neill would probably not have believed it either at the time, given all the momentum building behind the Reagan Revolution. In that first year, Reagan seemed unstoppable, successfully pushing through Congress deep tax cuts and a budget that slashed federal spending for the poor. He fired eleven thousand air traffic controllers, breaking their union in the course of a strike and grievously wounding organized labor's morale in the process.

While Reagan took little interest in legal matters, his attorney general, William French Smith, laid out the administration's ambitious agenda for rolling back what Brennan had tried to achieve. Smith, sixty-three, was a Los Angeles corporate lawyer who had been Reagan's longtime personal lawyer and political adviser. In a May speech, Smith signaled a major departure from decades of civil rights policy, declaring that the Justice Department would no longer vigorously pursue mandatory busing or support the use of racial quotas in employment discrimination cases. Smith delivered an even bolder statement of the Reagan administration's legal agenda later that year. "The groundswell of conservatism evidenced by the 1980 election makes this an especially appropriate time to urge upon the courts more principled bases that would diminish judicial activism," Smith declared. He promised that the Justice Department would "play an active role in effecting the principles upon which Ronald Reagan campaigned," including new legislation "that would help to redress the imbalance between the forces of law and the forces of lawlessness." He promised to select appointees to the federal bench "who understand the meaning of judicial restraint."

Reagan almost immediately had an opportunity to nominate his first addition to the Supreme Court. Most Court watchers had expected the first departure to be one of the five justices in their seventies. Instead, the first to step down was sixty-six-year-old Potter Stewart, who quietly passed word in the spring of 1981 to his friend and fellow Yale graduate Vice President Bush that he intended to retire at the end of the term. Stewart kept the decision to himself at the Court until the last minute. Over lunch just two weeks before he wrote his colleagues about his plans to resign in June, Stewart told Brennan's clerks how enthusiastic he remained about the job. Powell, who had grown closest to Stewart and his wife, took his departure particularly hard. Brennan, who had watched his colleague grow more conservative with time on the Court, had never developed a close bond with Stewart. He fully expected any successor named by Reagan would pull the Court even further to the right.

On July 7, 1981, Reagan announced his nominee, a little-known fifty-one-year-old judge on Arizona's intermediate appellate court named Sandra Day O'Connor. The selection, which fulfilled a campaign pledge to add the first woman to the Supreme Court, was well-received among women's groups. But the Moral Majority took issue with O'Connor's past positions on abortion and the equal rights amendment. What appealed to Reagan was O'Connor's nontraditional legal background and upbringing in the western United States. Sandra Day had grown up on her family's cattle ranch in Arizona, the Lazy B, before enrolling in Stanford University, where she stayed for law school and met both her future husband, John O'Connor III, and a lifelong friend, William H. Rehnquist.

As with Ruth Bader Ginsburg, in O'Connor's case top grades and law review membership were not enough to overcome prospective employers' biases against women. The only job offer she received from a law firm was for the position of legal secretary. After moving to Phoenix, she opened her own small law office and became involved in Arizona Republican politics while raising her three sons. Her friendship continued with Rehnquist, who had also settled in Phoenix. Their families socialized regularly, and she organized a campaign on his behalf when Rehnquist was nominated to the Court. She served in the state senate and rose to majority leader at the age of forty-two. But with her sons reaching their teenage years and her parents' health fading, she had given up her state senate seat and opted instead to run for superior court judge. In 1979 Arizona's Democratic governor tapped her for a seat on the Arizona Court of Appeals.

Brennan, like most of his colleagues and the rest of the country, knew nothing about O'Connor, although she had enough connections to two of the Court's conservatives to raise concerns. Reporters made note of O'Connor's ties to Rehnquist. Given how off-the-mark early predictions about the Minnesota Twins had proven to be, reporters were more skeptical about drawing facile conclusions this time. "Legal scholars doubt that O'Connor will become a clone of the Court's leading conservative," *Time* magazine noted. "They do not expect a pair of 'Arizona twins' to develop and hang together any more consistently than have the now-splintered 'Minnesota Twins' Burger and Blackmun." More troubling was a short item in the *Wall Street Journal,* one Brennan clipped, that reported Burger was "positively cooing" over the nomination of O'Connor, whom he had met "at social outings, including a cruise on Lake Powell on the Utah-Arizona border and a visit to England."

Brennan, who prided himself on getting along with all of his colleagues, would recall that O'Connor's arrival in the fall of 1981 went completely smoothly. "She ceased immediately to be 'the first woman Justice' and became just another Justice, and quite a fine one," Brennan told an interviewer in 1986. "Moreover, she is delightful." The experience proved less delightful for O'Connor than Brennan suggested.

Nor was this an easy time for Brennan, then thoroughly distracted by Marjorie's latest health crisis. Marjorie had been diagnosed with cancer in her left breast and undergone a radical mastectomy after returning home from Nantucket in August 1981. On the day O'Connor was sworn in, September 24, Marjorie was still convalescing at Georgetown University Hospital. "She has certainly had more than her fair share over the past ten years," Brennan wrote his relatives in Ireland. "And she faces some painful therapy before she'll have the full use of her left arm — and, as you know, she's left handed." He arrived at the Court each day by 6:30 A.M. in order to leave by midafternoon.

Still, Brennan remained engaged in his work, working again painstakingly with Powell to produce a majority in the case of *Plyler v. Doe*. *Plyler* involved a Texas law that permitted school districts to exclude illegal alien children from public school classrooms. From the outset, Brennan saw the case as being about the denial of a basic education to thousands of children who were the victims of discrimination because of their immigration status. Brennan believed that this exclusion violated the Fourteenth Amendment's equal protection clause and should be subject to the most demanding judicial scrutiny, requiring compelling justification by the state. But while Brennan found a Court majority who shared his outrage at depriving children of an education, Powell, in particular, kept Brennan on narrower ground in the reasoning of the Court's decision.

The case triggered strong feelings within the Court. Brennan recounted to his clerks that Rehnquist referred to the children as "wetbacks" during the conference discussion. Marshall had taken offense, and when Rehnquist defended it as a term still in use out west, Marshall said that under that theory he used to be known as a "nigger." Tempers cooled, and Brennan went to work on a Court opinion. To try to muster a majority, Brennan took what he described as "the unusual step" of sending the first draft only to Powell and the others on his side — Marshall, Blackmun, and Stevens. Such private circulations were more frequent among Brennan's allies during Warren's tenure, but he had employed them less frequently in recent years as his reliable bloc of allies shrank.

Three months of negotiations between Brennan and Powell ensued, with Powell threatening to concur only in the result and to refuse to join Brennan's opinion. Powell felt that Brennan, who saw the educational discrimination as inherently suspect, just like racial bias, went too far in protecting a class of illegal immigrants. He believed there was a valid basis for treating them less favorably than legal aliens, since adult illegal aliens had broken the law when they entered the United States. He wanted to focus solely on the innocence of the children. He also believed that Brennan was overstating the constitutional status of education, which the Court had ruled nine years earlier was not a fundamental right.

By this point, Powell and Brennan had developed a close working relationship. Powell felt comfortable writing or even occasionally calling or visiting Brennan in person to tell him what bothered him about his circulations, which Brennan then tried to accommodate. Drafts went back and forth between them, accompanied by solicitous cover letters, and the two finally agreed on raising the level of equal protection scrutiny to something like the intermediate approach used in gender-discrimination cases. But as they closed in on final agreement, Burger tried to derail their approach. Burger wrote privately to Powell that he was "profoundly troubled by the developments in this case," meaning the giving of equal protection recognition to illegal alien children.

But Powell remained consistent in his support. When Brennan announced the decision on June 15, 1982, Powell sent him a handwritten note the next day thanking him for the "painstaking and generous" accommodation of his views. Powell wrote, "Your final product is excellent and will be in every text and case book on Constitutional law." It was a satisfactory outcome for both of the two friends and increasingly frequent allies. Powell got what he wanted, a more cautious approach to protecting the illegal alien children in Texas without opening up new frontiers of constitutional law. Brennan, although more narrowly than he might have hoped, was able to expand the reach of the Fourteenth Amendment's equal protection clause and to sow seeds that he might be able to use in future cases.

But, while he put enormous effort into the *Plyler* case with Powell, his truncated workday left little time for Brennan to play his traditional role of orientation counselor to his newest colleague. Thrown into the job without any direction, O'Connor felt completely overwhelmed as the cert. petitions piled up on her floor. Into the breach stepped the gentlemanly Powell, who seemed to compensate for the loss caused by the retirement of his friend by helping Stewart's successor. O'Connor would recount with gratitude how much Powell went out of his way to assist her, letting her hire away his second secretary, and even lining up an apartment for her to rent temporarily at the Watergate.

O'Connor's selection happened to coincide with the arrival of Brennan's second female clerk. It had now been more than a decade since he had mused to his clerks that the presence of a woman justice might prompt his retirement, and seven years since Marsha Berzon had worked in his chambers. He had hired Mary Mikva, the daughter of his friend Judge Abner Mikva. Mark Campisano, another Brennan clerk that term, recalled having heard stories about awkward interactions during Berzon's clerkship, but had no sense that Brennan treated Mikva any differently, beyond extending to her conventional courtesies.

Mikva, though, remembered noticing that Brennan had not entirely gotten used to the presence of a woman in his chambers. "You could sense that he was less comfortable with a professional woman," Mikva later recalled. "With me, the kidding was more paternal, not quite as friendly." Mikva joked with her father at the time about how Brennan carefully edited himself to avoid telling stories or uttering curse words he still viewed as inappropriate in the presence of women. "He couldn't even say 'damn' around her," Judge Mikva later recalled. "It cramped his style." Whatever discomfort her presence caused, Brennan went out of his way to note his pleasure with Mikva's work. Brennan, who rarely if ever commented on his clerks' contributions in communications with other justices, pointed out in a cover letter to his colleagues in December 1981 that "you may be interested in the attached memorandum of my clerk Mary Mikva on that question."

Brennan seemed to have more difficulty getting his bearings around O'Connor, having to adapt his usual expressions of male camaraderie — linking arms in the hallway and vigorous handshakes — in her presence. For someone who had previously gone out of his way to win over new colleagues, Brennan seemed utterly tone-deaf to the ways his actions might alienate her. Shortly before the Court's Christmas recess, O'Connor had proposed dispensing with oral arguments in some cases and relying on written briefs as a way to address their growing caseload. Some of the justices endorsed the idea and others were tentative. Brennan responded with a letter vehemently opposing her proposal. He cited his experience in New Jersey where almost all cases were decided on written briefs alone and the resulting opinions were of low quality. But instead of suggesting they talk about the idea further, he tacked on a threat: "I feel so strongly about this that I must publicly dissent if the rule is changed." It was a far different reaction than when he gently tried to correct Goldberg's rookie errors two decades earlier in ways that avoided causing the new justice any embarrassment.

Brennan's lashing out was once again a gauge of his sense of diminishing influence. He had begun the term hopeful that O'Connor might be an independent-minded swing vote. But he became increasingly frustrated by what he viewed as her reflexive conservatism and unwillingness to vote on the opposite side of Burger, Rehnquist, and Powell. His frustration with O'Connor came to a head in February when O'Connor circulated her second majority opinion in a habeas corpus case that term. As Brennan had almost thirty years earlier, O'Connor came to the Court with the perspective of a state appellate judge. She was in fact the first state judge to join the Court since Brennan. She looked askance at the way federal judges used habeas corpus as a way to intervene in state criminal proceedings. She had even published a law review article in 1981 before joining the Court that noted state judges' frustration about the extent of federal judges' intervention. In the first habeas case, *Rose v. Lundy,* O'Connor wrote a majority opinion that directed federal judges to dismiss habeas petitions that mixed both unexhausted state and new federal claims. Brennan dissented from O'Connor's opinion, which he believed would make it harder for prisoners to reach federal court.

Then, just a few weeks later, O'Connor circulated her majority opinion in the second habeas case, *Engle v. Isaac,* on February 9, 1982. The issue in the case was whether three state prisoners could challenge jury instructions as part of a habeas claim even though they had failed to do so at the time of the trial as required by state law. O'Connor held against the prisoners, noting that such "federal intrusions may seriously undermine the morale of our state judges." O'Connor's opinion infuriated Brennan, author of the Court's seminal habeas decision two decades earlier. As he had shown throughout the 1970s, Brennan reacted particularly strongly when he saw the Court cutting back on rights for criminal defendants expanded by the Warren Court. Brennan believed O'Connor was helping the conservative majority further curtail prisoners' access to the federal courts and misapplying her own opinion that she had written just weeks earlier. He directed his clerk, Mark Campisano, to write a scathing dissent.

Campisano, more conservative in his politics than Brennan but not one by nature to mince words, did as requested. He wrote a draft dripping with anger and filled with acerbic asides. "Today's decision is a conspicuous exercise in judicial activism — particularly so since it takes the form of disregard of precedent scarcely a month old," the opinion began. The dissent referred to O'Connor's decision as "incomprehensible," suggested it contained "several pages of tortuous reasoning" and "sentiments in reasons' clothing." As was the practice in Brennan's chambers at the time for all opinions, Campisano circulated the draft to his three fellow clerks for their sign-off. Two of Campisano's fellow clerks expressed concerns about the tenor of the opinion and suggested toning it down.

But, echoing his tactics from the spring of 1971 and the 1975–76 term, Brennan egged on Campisano rather than tempering his language. "I really like this," Campisano recalled Brennan telling him. "It's got some ginger to it." Brennan even added a rhetorical flourish of his own, drawing upon his years of Latin at Barringer High School. In a not-so-subtle nod to the habeas case from just weeks earlier, *Rose v. Lundy,* he penciled in the words "sic transit Gloria Lundy!" — a play on the Latin phrase "sic transit Gloria mundi," which translates as "nothing on earth is permanent." As if that was not enough, the next sentence carried the pun further. "In scarcely a month, the bloom is off the Rose." When the other clerks pointed out the dissent might upset O'Connor, Campisano recalls Brennan replying, "She has to learn to play in the big leagues." Just a few years after regretting the sharp tone of his earlier dissents, Brennan failed to stop and reflect about whether this sort of language might again prove counterproductive.

Brennan insisted later that he had not intended a personal attack on O'Connor. In fact, several of the justices exchanged a number of unusually pointed barbs throughout the term, prompting the *Wall Street Journal* to question whether "the Supreme Court is losing its cool." In one dissent circulating around the same time, Rehnquist accused Brennan and his colleagues in the majority of "sophism" and "judicial wizardry." But even in a term full of sharply worded opinions, Brennan's dissent stood out when he distributed the finished product to his colleagues on March 24. Blackmun wrote "WOW!" at the top of his copy and penciled in exclamation points next to the choicest passages.

Brennan's dissent particularly appalled Powell. "No one is kinder or more generous than WJB until he takes up his pen in dissent," he wrote atop his copy. He underlined Brennan's reference to "judicial activism" in the first sentence and asked, "Who's calling who what!?" To Powell, this burst of outrage rang all the more hollow given Brennan's selective dedication to following precedent. A few months later, Powell would circulate a memo to his colleagues saying, "I wonder if we are not doing the Court it-self an injustice by some of the language we use, particularly in dissents."

O'Connor incorporated a comparatively reasoned response to Brennan in a footnote, criticizing his views as "incomprehensible" and carrying "more rhetorical force than substance." She was aware of the strain Marjorie's illness was causing and suspected that Brennan's clerks — rather than the justice himself — had drafted the most inflammatory language. The incident reinforced her sense that Brennan had grown disengaged, leaving the heavy lifting of opinion writing to his clerks. But she was nevertheless offended that he did not have the good sense to remove it. Having long ago learned to swallow her anger in such situations, O'Connor said nothing about the opinion's tone directly to Brennan and remained pleasant in their interactions. The only reference she made to the incident was an offhanded aside on her way out of conference one day. Brennan told his clerks that O'Connor said, "I've got to go put the bloom back on the rose."

O'Connor seemed to have forgotten the contretemps entirely in a note she wrote him at the end of the term "to express my appreciation for your kindness during my first Term on the Court." (She sent a similarly gracious note to Blackmun, with whom she also sparred that term.) Nevertheless, Brennan's clerks quickly realized the damage they had caused. In reference to another case later in the term, Brennan's clerks wrote — in the first person, as if Brennan penned it himself — "I had little expectation that I would be able to enlist Sandra in any opinion I wrote. She had not joined a single opinion of mine since the circulation of my angry dissent in Engle v. Isaac."

IN RETROSPECT, IT was a bad omen when Brennan found himself priced out of Nantucket in the summer of 1982. Brennan had already mailed off his $1,000 deposit for his usual rental property when he received a letter from the Old North Wharf Company that explained rents had gone up substantially. The bucolic island Brennan had slowly grown to love was becoming a retreat for the rich, as wealthy investors from New York and beyond began buying up properties there. The rental agent assured Brennan that the new price included a discount reflecting his age and lengthy tenure on the wharf. Nevertheless, Brennan wrote back a few days later, "We do thank you for your considerate effort but our budget simply does not have room for even the discounted rental." After two decades on the island, Brennan could no longer afford to summer in the place they had come to associate so closely with Marjorie's convalescences.

Instead, Brennan and Marjorie headed to Cape Cod along with their eleven-year-old granddaughter, Connie. All three returned to Washington in August with severe fevers and were diagnosed with Lyme disease. Brennan and Connie, who seemed the worst stricken, soon started feeling better thanks to daily doses of penicillin. But Marjorie's health continued to deteriorate. The Lyme disease diagnosis distracted Marjorie's doctors from the fact that her cancer had metastasized and spread to her other breast, kidney, and liver. She was soon confined to Georgetown University Hospital once again, and her doctors concluded they could do little else to help her.

Brennan further constricted his life at the Court that fall as he maintained a bedside vigil at the hospital. He asked his clerks to screen the cert. petitions for him and directed them to write bench memos to help guide him at conference, since he did not have much time to prepare. On days the justices heard oral arguments, Brennan left for the hospital by 6 A.M. and stayed at Marjorie's bedside until shortly before the Court convened at 10 A.M. Even on the bench, he remained distracted.

"I just received the bad news that Marjorie's sedimentation rate has risen to 110 from 91," Brennan wrote Blackmun in a November 3, 1982, note on the bench. "The doctors are switching from Keflex to Tetracycline to find out if that may be more effective."

"I am with you on these very difficult days," Blackmun wrote Brennan on November 29. Brennan responded on the bottom of the note, "You know how deeply I appreciate this. It helps so much."

Before her hospitalization Marjorie had managed to attend one oral argument at the Court early that fall of 1982. She looked terribly thin and sick, Brennan's clerk Edward Kelly recalled, but when Brennan saw her in the audience his face lit up. On November 21, Brennan took a rare break from his bedside vigil to speak at Connie's private school in Baltimore. As he often did, he ended with his favorite passage from Yeats's poem about the old woman walking down the path. This time, he almost certainly was thinking about Marjorie when he quoted the line "I saw a young girl and she had the walk of a queen." The strain of both continuing his work and caring for Marjorie proved too great for Brennan, now seventy-six, and he again seriously considered retiring. He confided his plans to one of the

Brennans' friends, but not to Marjorie, whom he knew would try to talk him out of it again. By the end of November, Brennan had missed several oral arguments and had all but put aside his work.

Marjorie's friends prayed for an end to her suffering; they sensed she was ready to let go. She started calling close friends and relatives to say goodbye from her hospital bed. But Brennan was not ready for her to die, holding her hand tightly in the dark late into the night. On the night of Tuesday, November 30, Brennan received a call at home from Marjorie's doctor, who said she was not likely to make it much past morning. He rushed back to the hospital and, unlike what had happened with his father, was there when Marjorie died at 10:55 A.M. on the morning of December 1, 1982. Her funeral followed two days later at Memorial Chapel at Arlington National Cemetery, where she was buried in a plot just below the gentle slope of a hill where both John F. Kennedy and his brother Robert were interred. Just two rows away was Justice Douglas, who had died in 1980.

Of all the condolences Brennan received, the one that might have meant the most came from Father Hesburgh, Notre Dame's president with whom he and Marjorie had traveled on their last trip abroad fifteen years earlier. "I will offer Mass here at Notre Dame for the repose of her good soul," Hesburgh wrote. "She suffered enough in recent years to have a quick trip to heaven." Brennan replied with a handwritten note. "Marjorie often reminisced about that wonderful trip we had with you — wistfully, because she could not repeat it . . . She was indeed a gallant lady throughout the 12 years she was ill."

After the funeral, Brennan returned to his empty apartment accompanied by his son Hugh, and broke down in tears. "How can I live without her?" he cried. Hugh looked at his father, who had never seemed so pale or thin, and thought of the stories he had read in the newspaper of widowers who die from heartbreak. Brennan remained equally despondent the next day, when his granddaughter Connie came to visit. Sitting on the couch, he turned to her forlornly and said, "I'll be joining your grandmother very soon."

· PART V: 1983–1997 ·

20

REBIRTH

B RENNAN'S LAW CLERK John Schapiro was surprised to find the lights off in the chambers when he came to work on the morning of March 10, 1983. Brennan's sudden disappearance the previous day had already alarmed Schapiro, and his boss's failure this morning to arrive first as usual only heightened his concerns. Once inside, Schapiro discovered an envelope on his chair addressed to all four law clerks. So soon after Marjorie's death, it was natural to suspect the envelope contained Brennan's resignation letter.

With a grim face, Schapiro shared the contents of the note with his fellow clerks as they arrived; they were all stunned by the news. But the note, surreptitiously delivered by Brennan early that morning, did not bring word of his resignation. Instead, Brennan informed them that he had married his secretary, Mary Fowler, the day before, and had already departed for a honeymoon in Bermuda. Brennan had slipped similar notes under the doors of his eight colleagues' chambers. By the time the newlyweds got on their plane in Baltimore, the entire Court was abuzz. Brennan had dropped off one additional letter before dawn that morning: Mary's letter of resignation after nearly twenty-six years as his secretary. The news so startled clerks in some other chambers that they suspected it had to be some sort of prank. But they soon realized this was no gag. Indeed, Brennan had been working on getting Mary to marry him for more than a month.

IN THE DAYS after Marjorie died in December 1982, now four months earlier, Brennan found himself living alone for the first time in his entire life. His family, friends, and colleagues did their best to help him fill the void. Friends stocked his freezer and invited him out to dinner and Nancy and Connie came down from Baltimore regularly, but everyone could not help but notice how despondent he remained. He resumed his work at the Court almost immediately, but his clerks had a nagging sense he might retire at any time. Brennan confided his feelings when Marsha Berzon, his first female clerk, came to visit his chambers that winter. "It's no fun to live alone," he told her.

Brennan had always relied heavily on Mary to manage his affairs inside his chambers, and that dependence extended into his personal life as he mourned for Marjorie. Mary took charge after the funeral, directing the flow of mourners in his apartment. In the weeks that followed, Brennan and Fowler had dinner together a few times. Then they went to the movies. By the end of January, when Brennan's son Hugh invited his father over to watch the Super Bowl, Brennan asked to bring Mary along. The 27–17 victory of Brennan's beloved — and long-suffering — Redskins over the Miami Dolphins was not the only thing that stood out that night. "We could see all over that something had come back into his life, his face was slightly lit up," Hugh recalled. A few days later, as the Court entered its February recess, Brennan and Fowler headed for separate Florida vacations. Brennan visited Bazelon's condominium on Longboat Key near Sarasota on the west coast, while Fowler stayed with friends 170 miles away in Titusville on the Atlantic coast near Cape Canaveral.

Brennan arrived in Florida still in a state of mourning, wearing a black suit, coat, and hat. But within a couple of days, he started asking the Bazelons about evening plans, eager to go out. From the first morning of the vacation, Brennan began calling Fowler, who was initially puzzled by her boss's attention. They quickly settled into a pattern in which she called Brennan promptly at 10 A.M. as he waited by the telephone as nervous as a smitten teenager. Brennan soon confided to the Bazelons that he wanted to marry Fowler. Bazelon, his usual blunt self, seemed taken aback. "You're out of your fucking mind," Mickey Bazelon recalled her husband saying.

But Mickey could tell Brennan was serious. "He was like a little kid in love."

When they returned to Washington, Brennan proposed to Fowler. The liberal justice who wanted everyone to like him and his conservative secretary with a blunt edge were an odd pair in many ways. She had no intention of ever swallowing her own opinions for his sake as Marjorie had done. But he felt entirely comfortable around her. They had developed an easy rapport while working alongside each other for a quarter century. And he certainly did not have any doubt about how she felt about him. Brennan said Mary admitted during the brief courtship that she had harbored romantic feelings for him for much of the time she worked in his chambers, but had never acted on them. Without a husband or children, Fowler had come to see taking care of Brennan as her life's calling. Yet she wanted to wait to marry, thinking too little time had elapsed since Marjorie's death. There were also practical problems: she was a divorced Catholic and was not supposed to remarry in the Church, and he was a Catholic and was not supposed to marry a divorcée. But Brennan did not want to wait.

On March 9 — the day before the notes were delivered — Brennan had given no hint of anything unusual afoot, but had disappeared from his office so suddenly and without explanation at 2 P.M. that Schapiro peeked in to Brennan's private bathroom to make sure he had not passed out in there. Brennan and Fowler had been picked up by Judge Bazelon's driver and taken to Bazelon's twelfth-floor apartment at the Watergate. Three more years would pass before the couple could have their marriage sanctioned by the Catholic Church. Bazelon stood at a lectern in front of the window in his living room and performed the civil wedding as Brennan and Fowler looked out at the Potomac River below. With Mickey out of town, the only guest was Bazelon's cousin, who took pictures. Brennan grew impatient as Bazelon read from his prepared notes on a sheet of paper. "For Christ sakes, David, get on with it," Brennan said. That evening, the newlyweds dined at the Four Seasons Hotel in Georgetown with Bazelon and their close friends Milton Kronheim and Arnie Shaw.

As Brennan and his new wife honeymooned in Bermuda over a long weekend, his colleagues digested the news. None had been there long enough to recall the Court precedent for such a marriage, which had occurred in the 1950s. Justice Black, whose wife had died while he was on the

Court, had also married his secretary, although not nearly as abruptly. Powell wrote "Wow!" atop the copy of the note Brennan slipped under his door. Chief Justice Burger considered, somewhat awkwardly, whether the justices should purchase a collective gift, and then wrote back to his colleagues that he opted instead to leave it to their individual discretion.

The marriage generated mixed reactions among Brennan's children and friends. None voiced any suspicions that the relationship predated Marjorie's death. But Bill thought Brennan should have waited a while, out of respect for Marjorie — and for the sake of appearances. Hugh and Nancy greeted the news more enthusiastically, welcoming anything that might lift Brennan out of his deep sadness and help him resume an active life. Some close friends of Brennan and Marjorie's felt that the marriage to Fowler was beneath him and the social place he had come to occupy in Washington. Brennan showed he was not naïve about how the marriage would be received. When Mildred "Vergie" Ching, the widow of his longtime friend Cyrus Ching and a good friend of Marjorie's, wrote to congratulate him, she recalled that he wrote back, "I knew you were one person who would understand."

EVEN BY THE often cloistered standards of the Court, Brennan had led an unusually isolated life since Marjorie's first illness in 1969. He had exiled himself from almost all commitments outside the Court and rarely socialized. But in the weeks and months after marrying Mary, Brennan underwent a sudden and dramatic transformation. "When they came back from the honeymoon, he was a transformed person," recalled Perry Dane, one of Brennan's clerks that term.

Brennan quickly resumed traveling, beginning with a homecoming of sorts at the New Jersey Supreme Court in April 1983 to mark the dedication of a new courtroom and to help present an award named in his honor by the state's federal bar association. Brennan sat with the New Jersey justices behind their mahogany bench. He began accepting other speaking engagements around the country and even traveled abroad, mixing lectures with sightseeing. In Washington, Brennan and Mary drew the attention of reporters as they started attending black-tie affairs and even a reception for Prince Charles and Princess Diana at the National Gallery of Art. "Brennan is his ebullient former self — working the crowd at a reception, dancing the night away at a party, traveling to Europe and around the country," the *Washington Post* observed in 1985. "His face shows new color; his frame, his handshake and his voice, new robustness." Mary deserved much of the credit for helping spark Brennan's reawakening. "His entire existence had been the Court and his home," Brennan's clerk Dane noted. "Mary wanted to change all that with travel, giving speeches, doing moot courts. He did seem to get younger in that process."

Marjorie had always discouraged Brennan from thinking of himself as anything more than a regular guy with a job. Mary, who felt insecure about her status in Brennan's family — knowing that Bill had doubts about the timing of the marriage did not help — had to adjust her perhaps overinflated expectations of what it meant to become the justice's wife. After all the years of toiling in obscurity in his chambers, Mary expected she might finally get some recognition. The Brennan family shared a joke about Marjorie that proved apt for Mary, too. Marjorie once chewed out the grocer for delivering poor-quality produce, opening the conversation by saying, "This is Mrs. Justice Brennan." Marjorie learned, and now Mary had to learn, as well, that there is no such title or position as "Mrs. Justice."

Brennan did his best to be sensitive to Mary's adjustment. He did not talk about Marjorie in her presence, even with his children. His first wife became the only topic Brennan was reluctant to discuss with his biographer, out of fear of offending Mary. He also left behind parts of his life most closely associated with Marjorie. He had already booked the Nantucket ferry and rented his cottage on Old North Wharf for the summer of 1983, most likely a present from his son Bill, who took over the reservation after the wedding. Brennan and Mary instead made plans to jet off to Hawaii. Brennan would honor Marjorie's memory in his own private way. He put her wedding ring in the upper-right-hand drawer of his desk, where he kept his most precious possessions, including the letter his brother Charlie had sent him from Leyte shortly before his death.

There was also the question of where to live. Mary was in Virginia. Brennan still lived in the apartment near the National Zoo in Washington he had shared with Marjorie since 1976. Arnie Shaw, Brennan's friend through Kronheim and Bazelon, suggested that Brennan ask Charles E. Smith, the real estate magnate, about buying a condominium in his Crystal Gateway apartment complex in Arlington, Virginia. The Virginia location suited Mary, and the proximity to downtown Washington was convenient for Brennan. Brennan and Mary bought and moved into an eighth-floor condominium that spring, the first home he had owned since moving to Washington twenty-five years earlier. They soon opened their new home to guests, hosting his clerks for lunch and then inviting Justices Marshall, Blackmun, and Powell over for dinner.

Brennan's travels only intensified the following year, a remarkably frenetic pace for a seventy-eight-year-old man who had rarely left Washington in fifteen years. In the summer of 1984, for example, he attended the Aspen Institute in Colorado for two weeks in July, before embarking on a weeklong cruise to Juneau, Alaska. Then he returned to Colorado for a stay at the Keystone Resort. After only eight days back in Washington, Brennan and Mary flew to the Tenth Circuit Judicial Conference in Jackson, Wyoming, touring Yellowstone National Park along the way with a U.S. marshal as their tour guide. That fall, he spoke at Mercer University Law School in Macon, Georgia, and traveled to London to join his son Bill, who was presiding over the winter meeting of the New Jersey Bar Association.

All this travel represented more than an opportunity for Brennan to see the country and the world after so many years of being shut in at home. It was a chance to enjoy genuine adulation for his role on the Court. This was a new phenomenon. In the 1960s, when he gave speeches and appeared on programs, he carefully deferred to the leadership of Chief Justice Warren. Brennan was now the most visible remaining embodiment of that bygone era, since Marshall seldom appeared in public. Large audiences of law school students and professors, lawyers, and judges eagerly lionized Brennan and all he symbolized. "You made history here," U.S. Court of Appeals judge Ruggero Aldisert wrote him after a 1986 appearance at the University of Pittsburgh. "No one has ever provoked so overwhelming an audience and enthusiastic a reception." Brennan discovered he enjoyed the fawning attention and Mary helped him to accept the accolades.

Brennan's public reemergence coincided with a new reassessment of his role on the Court among legal scholars. The rethinking was prompted by a book published in 1983 that chronicled the life and Court tenure of Chief Justice Earl Warren. Written by Bernard Schwartz, a New York University law professor, *Super Chief* documented the inner workings of the Warren Court. Schwartz had gained unusual access to internal memos and written drafts. But the 853-page book's dense prose made it far less readable or widely read than *The Brethren*. Virtually unacknowledged in the book was that Brennan had provided Schwartz with much of the book's best material, including access to his case files and many of the term histories covering the Warren Court. Brennan said he granted Schwartz that access to help detail Warren's role as "Super Chief," the name Brennan used to refer to Warren. He was not pleased with the result. "I must say I had expected something better," Brennan wrote in a June 1984 letter to Aldisert, the Third Circuit judge, who criticized *Super Chief* in a book review.

Ironically, the book did more to reveal Brennan's significant influence and contributions behind the scenes on the Warren Court than it did to enhance Warren's reputation. While Woodward's *The Brethren* provided a glimpse of Brennan's behind-the-scenes role in the early Burger years, *Super Chief* was the first to document fully how quietly influential he was during Warren's tenure. Brennan's central role would later be taken for granted, but at the time it was a true revelation. Another New York University law professor, Stephen Gillers, picked up on the theme of Brennan's centrality in a September 1983 article in the *Nation* magazine. "It is increasingly clear that he deserves much of the credit for fashioning the legal theories that could support the progressive decisions of the last quarter century, and for then persuading a majority of his colleagues to accept them," Gillers wrote.

Another law professor, Dennis J. Hutchinson of the University of Chicago, made the point even more succinctly in his review of *Super Chief* in the *Michigan Law Review*. "Schwartz's argument belies his subtitle: it was 'the Brennan Court.'" Hutchinson concluded, "If any single justice deserves to be identified with the constitutional revolution engineered by the Supreme Court in the last generation, it is William J. Brennan and not Earl Warren." Brennan responded with the same modesty as he had when articles in the 1960s first focused on his role. When his friend Norman Dorsen, a New York University law professor and the ACLU's national president, sent him a copy of Gillers's article, Brennan wrote back, "He was extremely generous in his appraisal but you know as I do that no single hand molds opinions in this forum."

EVEN AS BRENNAN basked in the glow of his admirers' praise for his past accomplishments, he faced an uphill climb holding onto those earlier victories as the 1980s progressed. From federalism to affirmative action to privacy, Brennan and his clerks felt as if they were constantly playing defense, trying desperately to hold back the Court's conservatives. He shared his frustration with his clerks about having so few big cases to write. A sense of foreboding hung over Brennan's chambers as he and his clerks waited for the dam to break and the conservatives to sweep away his quarter century of precedents.

Nowhere did Brennan suffer more losses than in the area of criminal procedure. In June 1983, he denounced the 6–3 majority's abandonment of the Court's test used to determine the reliability of police informants whose information provided the basis for probable cause for a search or seizure. Brennan was bitterly disappointed when the Court adopted a "good faith" exception to the exclusionary rule in *U.S. v. Leon*. The new rule allowed the use of illegally obtained evidence against a criminal defendant if police acted with a good-faith belief that they were operating with a valid search warrant that later turned out to be faulty. "It now appears that the Court's victory over the Fourth Amendment is complete," Brennan decried in dissent. He accused the majority of an "impoverished understanding of judicial responsibility in our constitutional scheme." The defeat could not have surprised Brennan; conservatives had long opposed the "exclusionary rule." But that did not ease the sting for Brennan of watching as his fellow justices undid another piece of the Warren Court's legacy of expanding the rights of criminal defendants.

Brennan had not helped his cause any by alienating O'Connor during her first term. He came to realize, albeit too late, how much offense O'Connor had taken at his snide dissent in the habeas corpus case. Brennan confided his regrets to his clerks during the 1982–83 term. He went out of his way that term to be nice to O'Connor, as if paying penance. Not that his charm offensive helped much. His inviting O'Connor to lunch at Kronheim's, his bastion of male camaraderie, backfired. The rare appearance of a prominent woman merited coverage in the *New York Times,* but O'Connor had no interest in returning to the boys' club. Brennan had more success relating to O'Connor's husband, John J. O'Connor III. After attending a dinner together, the justice's husband had sent Brennan a packet of speeches, jokes, and cartoons, including one in which a male lawyer says to a female judge, "I hope the court will not consider it sexist to preface my motion with a reference to Your Honor's charm and grace." John O'Connor enclosed a mock bill requiring Brennan to provide a free lunch in his chambers, and Brennan responded two days later with a lunch invitation.

Brennan tried his best to work with O'Connor and to accommodate her concerns. His notes to her took on a particularly obsequious tone as he sought to win her vote in *Karcher v. Daggett,* a case the Court took up in the spring of 1983 involving New Jersey's plans for redrawing its congressional districts. Brennan, who had helped develop the Warren Court's reapportionment principles, felt it would be an important step forward for him to declare that New Jersey had failed to make a "good-faith effort" to eliminate the relatively small variances in the size of its districts. "Thank you for commenting so promptly on the first draft I sent you," Brennan wrote O'Connor. "I am pleased that you think you will be able to concur at least in part of the opinion and I am hopeful that we can work out whatever differences we have so that you might consider joining all of it." When she wrote back with more suggestions, Brennan replied praising them as "quite to the point and I appreciate them greatly." O'Connor astonished Brennan and his clerks by eventually joining Brennan's full opinion, providing him the decisive fifth vote. Until the day Brennan finally announced his decision, though, he expected her to change her mind and withdraw.

But it was not often that Brennan could win over O'Connor, who voted the same way as he did only half the time. And even when she joined Brennan's opinions, she remained distrustful about his motives. Brennan's clerks shared the news from their counterparts in O'Connor's chambers that his opinions received the closest scrutiny of any justice's. That mistrust was evident during an important victory for Brennan in July 1984, when he wrote that a Minnesota civil rights law applied to the Jaycees, a civic group, which required them to admit women, did not violate the constitutional rights of the group or its members. Brennan managed to satisfy Powell's concerns, but was unable to sway O'Connor. Brennan wrote O'Connor that he hoped she would find the changes he made for Powell acceptable. Illustrative of her distrust, however, O'Connor wrote back the next day, "I continue to have some concerns in this case because of its implications in so many future cases." She joined only parts of his opinion.

O'Connor had taken to heart Powell's warnings that Brennan planted "time bombs" in his opinions. She had learned to watch for those seemingly offhand, throwaway phrases that he exploited in later cases. She viewed Brennan's attempts at accommodation as entirely self-serving, and thought he tended to give her the cold shoulder unless he needed her vote. After O'Connor's retirement, two journalists who covered her closely at the Court asserted in separate books that Brennan's efforts at persuasion completely backfired, driving her toward the conservatives. Only after Brennan retired, they posited, did she move closer to the Court's center. O'Connor rejected any notion that Brennan repelled her in that manner but admitted that she never entirely trusted him either.

Brennan tried not to get too dispirited even as he found himself on the losing side in many big cases. He certainly still had more perspective than his clerks, who had not been at the Court for the good years. He still held up five fingers when orienting his new clerks to the importance of commanding a majority on the Court. His marriage to Mary did much to help reinvigorate his naturally optimistic spirit. During the 1983–84 term, his clerks noticed that Brennan would occasionally go home discouraged at the end of the week, but come back on Monday resilient as ever. "He was fired up to keep on going and win when he could," recalled John Savarese, one of his 1983 clerks.

Still, even Brennan found it difficult to remain perpetually optimistic after so many years in the minority. He began airing his frustration with the direction of the Court publicly, starting with a December 1983 speech at a judicial conference in Puerto Rico. "Under the banner of the vague, undefined notions of equity, comity and federalism," Brennan lamented, "the Court has condoned both isolated and systematic violations of civil liberties." In February 1984 he delivered the same message to the Palm Beach County Bar Association in Florida, adding that his colleagues on the Court were "crippling" federal judges in their ability to protect civil rights and civil liberties. "With federal scrutiny diminished, state courts must respond by increasing their own," he said. These were not new themes for Brennan. It was in 1976 that he first suggested that state supreme courts must safeguard individual rights if the U.S. Supreme Court no longer did so. But, since he had spoken publicly so infrequently in the years since, his message sounded new to many.

Surprisingly, Brennan was still winning more battles than he could realistically have expected. By 1984, seventeen years had elapsed since a Democratic president last appointed a justice to the Court. That justice, Thurgood Marshall, remained his most reliable ally. Marshall voted with

Brennan at least 80 percent of the time and in the 1984–85 term, they agreed in 100 percent of the cases. Marshall joked that he liked to disagree with Brennan once or twice a term "just to make it look right," although when he did so, his wife "gives me hell." Jokes aside, that remarkably similar voting pattern masked tensions between the two chambers. And Marshall alone could not guarantee a majority. Brennan owed whatever continued success he achieved to the unexpected voting patterns of three Republican appointees: Blackmun, Stevens, and particularly Powell.

Blackmun, who had first drifted away from Burger in the 1970s, voted with Brennan more than ever in the early 1980s. The 1981–82 term proved to be a breakout year, the first in which they voted together more than 70 percent of the time. That proportion would hold steady for the remainder of their tenures together. A symbol of that collaboration would become etched in the minds of many Brennan clerks. Each time their boss left his chambers for the courtroom, he would stop first for Blackmun and, a few paces later, Marshall would emerge from his chambers as well. Together, the three septuagenarians walked down the hall with Brennan in the middle, his arms linked with Marshall and Blackmun.

Stevens, too, increasingly aligned with Brennan beginning in the early 1980s. They would vote together between two-thirds and three-quarters of the time each term. Brennan, though, always found it hard to pin down how the notoriously independent-minded Stevens might come out in any particular case. "It has to be trial and error," Brennan said in 1988. "I just have to write the damn thing and wait. And if John reacts against something, he very quickly lets me know." By the end of the 1985–86 term, the *Washington Post* would note that both Blackmun and Stevens, "once considered part of the traditional center, found themselves firmly in the liberal camp."

A signal collaboration came in February 1985, when Blackmun provided the key vote to uphold the application of federal minimum-wage and overtime laws to a local transit system in San Antonio, Texas. Brennan asked Blackmun to write the opinion, which expressly overruled a major federalism decision by Justice Rehnquist, *National League of Cities v. Usery*. Rehnquist's decision said that Congress could not impose minimum-wage and overtime guarantees on states that were engaged in "traditional governmental functions." Blackmun had cast the deciding vote in Rehnquist's 5–4 decision, which had infuriated Brennan and prompted him to write one of the angriest dissents of his entire tenure on the Court. But in the years since, Blackmun found it difficult to apply Rehnquist's definition of "traditional governmental functions." By 1984, encouraged by Brennan, Blackmun was ready to abandon as unworkable the Rehnquist attempt to define federalism protections for state and local governments.

THE DIFFERENCE BETWEEN victory and defeat for Brennan often rested in the hands of Powell. The conservatives could usually count on Powell's vote on criminal-procedure or federalism issues. But in many other areas, Powell's voting record was moderate or even liberal. Being the pivotal vote gave Powell leverage, sometimes to the annoyance of Brennan and his clerks. "When in that position, Powell can occasionally become difficult," Brennan's 1984–85 term history noted.

The degree to which Powell could determine the outcome was evident in church-state cases. Powell sided with the conservatives in upholding the practice of a chaplain leading an official prayer at the start of Nebraska legislative sessions. Two decades earlier, Brennan had come close to endorsing that very outcome in one of his decisions striking down official prayer and ceremonial Bible-reading in the public schools — a fact he noted in an unusual footnote in 1983: "Nevertheless, after much reflection, I have come to the conclusion that I was wrong then and that the Court is wrong today." A year later, Powell once again joined the conservative majority, which found that a nativity display in a public park in Pawtucket, Rhode Island, did not violate the establishment clause.

To maintain the separation of church and state, Brennan had become the leading defender of a three-part test adopted by the Court in 1971 known as the *Lemon* test. Under the test, for a government practice that involves or implicates religion to meet constitutional standards, there must be a secular purpose, an effect that neither advances nor inhibits religion, and an avoidance of excessive entanglement between government and religion. The test was hanging by a thread by 1984. In the legislative-chaplain case, the Court did not use the *Lemon* test at all. In the Pawtucket crèche case, the Court applied the *Lemon* test but found that the nativity display had a secular purpose of marking the Christmas holiday season. Brennan said that the Court had undermined the purposes of the establishment clause and misused the history of religious freedom in the United States to support the conclusion. "Indeed, our remarkable and precious religious diversity as a nation . . . which the Establishment Clause seeks to protect, runs directly counter to today's decision," Brennan wrote.

And yet Powell would also provide the key fifth vote to the liberal bloc in two important church-state decisions in subsequent terms. In one, Brennan ruled that a New York City practice of paying public school teachers to provide remedial teaching in religious schools violated the establishment clause. In the other, Brennan struck down a Grand Rapids, Michigan, program that offered enrichment and remedial classes to private school students in classrooms at religious schools that are leased at public expense. In both cases, Powell's vote gave Brennan a narrow majority; Powell informed Brennan of his intention to join his decision at a surprise party for Brennan's seventy-ninth birthday in his chambers, and Brennan thanked Powell for a "splendid birthday present." In the Grand Rapids decision, O'Connor and Burger ultimately joined Brennan's result, making it 7–2. In a third ruling, Brennan assigned Stevens to write the opinion striking down an Alabama law that provided for a moment of silence for meditation or "voluntary prayer." Stevens's analysis embodied Brennan's skepticism that the law's purpose was to advance prayer in school; Alabama schools already had a moment of silence, but the legislature wanted to add the term "voluntary prayer" to the law. Powell and O'Connor both joined the majority, making it 6–3.

Powell came to regret his decision to cast the deciding vote contrary to Brennan's view in one case, *Bowers v. Hardwick,* the consideration of which proved unusually confusing. Michael Hardwick had been arrested on charges of sodomy when a police officer allowed to enter his home regarding an unrelated matter observed him engaging in a sex act with another man. The U.S. Court of Appeals for the Eleventh Circuit had ruled for Hardwick, an outcome with which Brennan agreed. Nevertheless, Brennan discussed with his clerks whether it might be a good idea to vote to hear the case as a vehicle to recognize the rights of gays and lesbians before the Court got even more conservative. He ultimately decided against voting to consider the case, which fell short of the four votes needed to grant review.

But Brennan's clerk Larry Kramer, assuming incorrectly that Brennan had wanted to hear it, sent a letter joining White's draft opinion dissenting from the decision to deny certiorari. When Brennan inadvertently became the fourth vote needed to hear the case, Marshall followed his lead and also joined White's dissent. Blackmun, who was apparently concerned that the case might be a vehicle for undermining abortion rights, convinced Brennan to switch his vote. But Marshall let his vote stand and so the case was slated for decision. The Court went on in *Bowers* to decide that there was no right of privacy that protected homosexual sodomy. The 5–4 ruling, written by White and joined by Powell, was a bitter defeat for Brennan and the Court's liberals, who hoped to expand the right to privacy under the Constitution. Brennan's clerks very much wanted to keep the dissent within his chambers, but he heeded Blackmun's request to write it.

Affirmative action remained the area where Powell retained the most influence. Powell never dissented in a single affirmative action case during his entire tenure on the Court, and usually he sided with Brennan. Of the six major affirmative action cases, he would vote to uphold four plans and reject two. Powell seemed willing to allow some — but not too much — affirmative action. Powell could accept using affirmative action as a basis for hiring — but not in firings. Both plans he rejected involved the discharge of veteran white employees while less-senior African Americans had retained their jobs. So Brennan would find himself on the losing side when the Court reviewed a policy enacted by the Jackson, Michigan, school board that used race to lay off some senior white teachers while protecting the jobs of African American teachers with less seniority. Powell did not attract a majority for his opinion, which focused on the harm that using race in determining layoffs would impose on specific individuals because of their race.

But Brennan would prevail in another pair of affirmative action cases at the end of the 1985–86 term that upheld the power of federal courts under Title VII of the Civil Rights Act of 1964 to force the adoption of affirmative action plans benefiting a larger group than just those who were specific victims of past discrimination. In both cases, Brennan, Powell, and their law clerks spent many hours exchanging memos and negotiating language to try to reach common ground. In the end Powell joined one decision entirely, as did O'Connor, making it 6–3 to uphold an affirmative action plan to hire more minority firefighters in Cleveland. In the other case, Powell joined much of Brennan's opinion, despite concerns he shared privately with his clerks that it was "outrageously long" and contained "too many statements that in future cases can and will be read out of context." The resulting opinion upheld an affirmative action plan and contempt fines imposed on Local 28 of the Sheet Metal Workers for engaging in race discrimination in recruitment, training, and union membership. But the Court was so divided that Brennan took the unusual step of adding up the votes from different justice's opinions in the Local 28 case to summarize what the Court had done based on their points of agreement.

Brennan was elated with the outcome in these two affirmative action cases and seized the opportunity he had as senior associate justice in the majority to assign the cases to himself. That decision did not go over well in Marshall's chambers, where his clerks believed that Brennan was hogging the best assignments. Even some of the Brennan clerks thought at least one of the cases should be assigned to Marshall. Brennan's decision was in part a strategic one. He knew after the discussion at the Court's conference that the cases would hinge on Powell. And Brennan believed he was better able to work with Powell to resolve differences in their approaches to affirmative action.

It was not quite a revival of his old bloc of liberal allies during the Warren Court, but by the mid-1980s Brennan, Marshall, Blackmun, and Powell circulated privately to one another with some regularity. But the quartet could not hold out forever. By 1985, all four of them — as well as Burger — were at least seventy-six years old. Ronald Reagan's landslide 1984 reelection victory ensured no younger reinforcements would relieve the aging liberals anytime soon. Not that Brennan and the other three justices completely stood out in Washington — this was a year when the president turned seventy-four and the Speaker of the House was seventy-three. One newspaper columnist labeled it rule by "gerontocracy." The justices, too, could joke about their age. Blackmun circulated copies of a political cartoon depicting Brennan, Marshall, Powell, and Blackmun running in gym shorts and tank tops when Reagan comes up beside them and says, "Don't you think it's time to retire? You're up in your seventies." Blackmun took to referring to himself, Brennan, and Marshall as "three old goats."

A frightening reminder of their mortality had come in December 1984, when Powell underwent surgery for prostate cancer at the Mayo Clinic and experienced dangerously heavy bleeding during the operation, which lasted five hours longer than intended. Powell came out of surgery severely weakened and remained hospitalized or confined to a nearby hotel for the next five weeks. Brennan was alarmed about his friend's condition — and the possibility that Powell might retire. He sent his clerks on an intelligence-gathering mission, desperate to find out the true state of Powell's health. Powell did not return to the Court for nearly three months, and reentered the Mayo Clinic for a follow-up procedure in July 1985.

NO ISSUE THE Court addressed affected Brennan more deeply — or generated more tension among the justices — than the death penalty. By the early 1980s, it had been several years since the 1976 *Gregg* decision cleared the way for the resumption of executions. In the intervening years, states had worked out procedures for their new capital punishment laws. The number of death-penalty cases reaching the Court kept rising along with the number of executions: from one in 1981 and two in 1982 to five in 1983 and twenty-one in 1984.

There were typically at least one and often two or more appeals filed at the Supreme Court before a death penalty sentence was carried out. Since many states carried out their executions late at night, the Supreme Court's review of these cases frequently occurred after regular Court hours. The justices conducted tense conference calls from their homes or talked to their clerks on open lines. These cases took a toll on Brennan, who turned visibly more grave and taciturn as an execution approached. "You could tell it was tearing him up," said Donald Verrilli, one of his 1984–85 term clerks. Brennan and Marshall remained committed to their view that all executions were cruel and unusual punishment, although they had no success in convincing any of their colleagues. Brennan recounted to his clerks how the justices' discussions of death penalty cases were full of bitter recriminations and accusations.

One source of deep division in the Court was the question of whether to grant interim delays to death row inmates while they asked for Supreme Court review of a lower court's denial of their habeas corpus petitions. Some conservative justices, including Rehnquist, believed these stays of execution unnecessarily delayed lawful executions. Others, like Justice Stevens, believed that the Court had to grant a stay until it decided whether to hear a defendant's underlying habeas petition; to deny the stay would be to shorten the time the law allowed for the filing of that first petition for review. The Court's voting procedures further complicated matters. It takes only four votes to agree to hear a cert. petition, but five votes are required to grant a stay. Thus, it was conceivable that four justices might want to hear a case but be unable to find a fifth vote to delay the execution while the appeal was being heard.

This disconnect in the Court's voting requirements played out during the appeal of James Autry, convicted in Texas of the 1980 murder of a convenience store clerk. The Court initially denied his request for a stay of execution by a 5–4 vote, although by law and Court rules he still had time to file a petition for cert. on his habeas corpus claims. In October 1983, Texas officials proceeded with plans for his execution, strapping him to a gurney in the death chamber and inserting the needles in his arms in preparation for administering the lethal injection. While this was occurring, he had a second habeas petition and request for a stay pending in the Supreme Court. Justice White, who handled emergency applications from the U.S. Court of Appeals for the Fifth Circuit, which included Texas, granted the stay just minutes before Autry's execution. A few months later, however, Autry's appeals ran out and, with only Brennan and Marshall voting for a stay, he was executed in March 1984.

Another case that term proved even more divisive. James Hutchins was convicted in 1979 in North Carolina of murdering three policemen. As his habeas petitions worked their way through the courts, the U.S. Court of Appeals for the Fourth Circuit granted a stay of execution. Instead of awaiting further court proceedings, North Carolina officials asked the Supreme Court to throw out or vacate the stay and to allow the execution to proceed. After an extraordinarily acrimonious conference, the justices voted 5–4 to vacate. Justice Powell voiced the view of the increasingly impatient majority: "A pattern seems to be developing in capital cases of multiple review in which claims that could have been presented years ago are brought forward — often in a piecemeal fashion — only after the execution date is set or becomes imminent. Federal courts should not continue to tolerate — even in capital cases — this type of abuse of the writ of habeas corpus." Hutchins was executed two days after Autry.

Brennan's frustration over the death penalty cases may have reached its peak in the 1984–85 term in the case of Alpha Otis Stephens, convicted in Georgia in 1979 for shooting a man to death. At the time Stephens's habeas petition reached the Supreme Court, the U.S. Court of Appeals for the Eleventh Circuit had already granted a stay to several other death sentences to consider whether there was a pattern of race discrimination in death sentences. But by a 6–6 tie, the Eleventh Circuit had refused to grant Stephens a stay. Six judges maintained that he had never raised the race-discrimination issue. In December 1983 the Supreme Court granted Stephens a stay by a 5–4 vote, with Brennan, White, Marshall, Blackmun, and Stevens voting for the delay. The race-discrimination issue was still pending in the Eleventh Circuit when the justices took up the case at an October 1984 conference. But the justices nevertheless voted 6–3 against hearing a petition for certiorari by Stephens, instead of granting the petition and holding it until the Eleventh Circuit ruled. White and Blackmun changed sides, voting against the petition although they had voted for the stay. Neither offered an explanation.

Brennan held up the announcement of the Court's action while he wrote a dissent. In the draft he circulated to colleagues, he concluded that the Court's action "is at best an example of result-orientation carried to its most cynical extreme. At worst, it is outright lawlessness." The reference to "outright lawlessness" offended Burger, and Brennan ultimately deleted the language before the order denying Stephens's petition was released on November 26, 1984. Stephens's attorneys filed one more habeas petition and stay application in December. Blackmun provided the fourth vote to grant a stay, apparently stung by a *New York Times* article excoriating the Court's "reckless pursuit of efficiency."

But Brennan was still one justice short. He circulated another dissent, pressing the point that "a person should not be executed while the constitutionality of his sentence is in doubt." A lawyer for Stephens made one last try, leading to another, final round of late-night telephone calls between justices and law clerks. As it turned out, while there were four votes for Stephens, which should have been enough to grant a petition and force a stay, according to Brennan, both Blackmun and Stevens did not want to grant Stephens's petition. They were only willing to vote for a stay, which fell one vote short. When Stephens was executed in the Georgia electric chair just after midnight on December 12, 1984, the first volts through his body did not kill him, and he sat strapped in the chair, struggling to breathe, for eight minutes before a second round of electric volts was successfully administered.

AS PRESIDENT REAGAN began his second term in 1985, more than one top official at the Justice Department might well have sympathized with

President Taft, who lamented in 1909 of the Supreme Court, "These old fools hold on with a tenacity that is most discouraging." Reagan's brash young aides had come to Washington four years earlier intent on finally casting aside the Warren Court's activist legacy. But they had come to realize they had severely underestimated Brennan and another equally proud old Irishman atop the other branch of government, Tip O'Neill, the Democratic Speaker of the House. In 1984 O'Neill announced his intention to retire at the end of Congress's term in January 1987. Brennan had no such plans.

Changing the direction of the Supreme Court and the lower federal courts became a top priority at the Justice Department after Reagan appointed as attorney general Edwin Meese, his top adviser and close friend. When Meese's aides set about screening potential judicial nominations, Brennan was the very archetype of the kind of justice they wanted to avoid appointing. So too would Brennan become the leading target as conservatives sought to articulate what was wrong with the Supreme Court. "Brennan was the most articulate and consistent activist," recalled Gary McDowell, a top Meese adviser and speechwriter. "Brennan was pretty much our guy [to target]."

In 1984, two conservatives justified targeting Brennan in an article facetiously titled "The Mind of Justice Brennan: A 25-year Tribute" published in the conservative magazine *National Review*. It was authored by Alfred Regnery, a Justice Department political appointee, and Stephen Markman, who was then serving as the chief counsel to the Senate Judiciary subcommittee on the Constitution. Markman came to play a leading role in judicial selection when he became head of the Justice Department's Office of Legal Policy during Reagan's second term. "There is no individual in this country, on or off the Court, who has had a more profound and sustained impact upon public policy in the United States for the past 27 years," the two wrote. Unlike some other recent writers, these two conservatives did not intend that as praise. They blamed Brennan for "the transformation of the federal judiciary from its traditional status as a body that interpreted the law into a 'super legislature' where the judges' own policy choices become supreme law." Rather than being insulted, Brennan enjoyed the attention. It made him feel relevant at a time when his brand of liberalism seemed so out of fashion in Washington.

Attorney General Meese saw himself as engaged in a war of ideas over how to interpret the Constitution. He bulked up the Justice Department's public affairs department, which hosted regular internal seminars on constitutional interpretation attended by leading conservative thinkers. Meese and his deputies also wanted to spark a broader public debate about interpreting the Constitution and about the proper role of the unelected Court in a democratic system. Since the 1950s conservatives had criticized Brennan and his Warren Court allies for reading their policy preferences into the Constitution, but they had not yet offered a coherent alternative model of constitutional interpretation to limit judicial power.

Beginning in the 1970s, many conservative legal thinkers began coalescing around the idea that the Constitution could only properly be interpreted by determining the original intent of the framers. Brennan had consistently rejected the idea of trying to discern the founders' "original intent." As he argued in a 1983 case, "The Constitution is not a static document whose meaning on every detail is fixed for all time by the life experience of the Framers." For Brennan, the Constitution was a living document that should be interpreted to reflect fundamental underlying principles such as "human dignity" as well as the values of a given era that might not be expressly stated in the Constitution. The merits of originalism had been the subject of debate in law schools since the 1970s, but had garnered little public attention.

Meese and his aides wanted to bring the debate into the open, and chose as their platform the annual convention of the American Bar Association in Washington, D.C., in July 1985. In a speech titled "Jurisprudence of Original Intention," Meese criticized the Supreme Court for "a drift back toward the radical egalitarianism and expansive civil libertarianism of the Warren Court." Instead of relying on the text of the Constitution, Meese accused the justices of interpreting the Constitution to mean whatever they wanted. As Meese's advisers hoped, the attack received significant press coverage.

Well before Meese's speech, Brennan had accepted an invitation to speak at an October 1985 symposium at Georgetown University where different public leaders would discuss how a particular text had affected their lives. At the urging of his law clerks, Brennan chose the Constitution. The clerks began work on his speech in June 1985, several weeks before Meese addressed the ABA. Brennan's clerks waded through his prior speeches on the Constitution, culling statements that they could use to show his relationship to the text. Rather than offering new reflections on the Constitution's meaning, Brennan intended to show how the text had influenced him in the past. Recycling his past reflections on the Constitution seemed the most obvious way to show how the text had influenced his thinking and his work. Brennan did not expect to garner much public attention; no one considered the subject of "texts" in different walks of life a controversial topic.

Brennan told his Georgetown audience that attempting to "find legitimacy in fidelity" to the intentions of the framers was "little more than arrogance cloaked as humility." "It is arrogant," Brennan said, "to pretend that from our vantage we can gauge accurately the intent of the Framers on application of principle to specific, contemporary questions." Brennan said that advocates of originalism underestimated the difficulty in parsing the founders' intentions, given the sparse records of the ratification debates and ambiguous evidence of their intentions. What's more, he warned, "our distance of two centuries cannot but work as a prism refracting all we perceive."

Brennan insisted that "current justices read the Constitution in the only way we can: as twentieth-century Americans." He conceded that they looked to the history of the time of framing and to the intervening history of interpretation. But, Brennan said, "the ultimate question must be: What do the words of the text mean in our time?" Using language identical to what he said in speeches for two decades, Brennan claimed, "For the genius of the Constitution rests not in any static meaning it might have had in a world that is dead and gone, but in the adaptability of its great principles to cope with current problems and current needs." Turning to the meaning of the Constitution, Brennan reiterated his long-held view that the Constitution's goal is to recognize and protect individual human dignity. He ended his speech with a focus on the death penalty, the most glaring example, Brennan said, of where the nation continued "to fall short of the constitutional vision of human dignity."

Whole chunks of the speech had been recycled from Brennan's earlier talks. But because Brennan had been outside the public eye for so many years, listeners generally heard it as a brand-new attack. What's more, Brennan and his clerks had spiced up the speech with provocative new phrases, accusing advocates of originalism of practicing a "facile historicism." As a result — and in spite of Brennan's denial, a claim his clerks corroborated — reporters interpreted the speech as a counterattack directed at Meese. It became front-page news in the *New York Times,* and the subject of an approving editorial in the newspaper two days later, which praised Brennan's "impressive survey of constitutional thinking; the provocation and the rare response deserve attention." Similarly, the *Los Angeles Times* editorialized, "It is highly unusual and not without risk for judges — much less Supreme Court justices — to get into a political debate. But Brennan's integrity and propriety are unquestioned, and what he said needed saying."

Some commentators took a different view. Stuart Taylor, a *New York Times* reporter at the time, wrote in an article for the *New Republic* titled "Meese v. Brennan," that Meese had raised issues that needed attention. "For all his fumbling," Taylor said, "Meese has spotlighted some of the real problems with the freewheeling judicial activism sometimes practiced by people like Brennan. Among these is a tendency to 'find' in the Constitution rights (such as abortion rights) and social policies that can honestly be found neither in the language of the document, nor in the records left by those who wrote it, nor in any broad national consensus that has evolved since then." As an example, Taylor cited Brennan's assertion that the death penalty was unconstitutional, saying that Brennan knew the due process clauses of the Fifth and Fourteenth Amendments contemplated capital punishment but that Brennan preferred to elevate his own "moral convictions" over the choices made by elected representatives.

Verrilli, the law clerk who had worked on the Georgetown speech during the summer, called Brennan and apologized profusely for having created such an unintended stir. Brennan was not upset at all. He may not have set out to take on Meese, but he nevertheless liked the publicity that resulted when everyone else thought he had. As had the critical *National Review* article a year earlier, all the attention made Brennan feel relevant in the central constitutional debate of the time. Justice Stevens kept the debate alive with a speech of his own ten days later before the Federal Bar Association in Chicago. He took on the attorney general directly, mentioning him by name twenty-eight times.

The debate reignited the following year. William Bradford Reynolds, then serving as assistant attorney general in charge of the Civil Rights Division, criticized Brennan in a speech at the University of Missouri Law School in September 1986. Reynolds was a staunch conservative and close adviser to Meese and clearly was carrying the message of the Justice Department when he said, "Justice Brennan thus prefers to turn his back on text and historical context, and argues instead for a jurisprudence that rests, at bottom, on a faith in the idea of a living, evolving Constitution of uncertain and wholly uninhibited meaning." In an October 1986 speech at Tulane University, Meese did not mention Brennan by name, but singled out language written by him in the opinion signed by all nine justices in the 1958 *Cooper v. Aaron* decision declaring that the Supreme Court's opinion was the "supreme law of the land." Brennan remained unapologetic about engaging the conservatives in such a public debate. He told his biographer in October 1986, "The whole approach of the extreme right I just think is dead wrong in light of our history and what it is we're all about and I hope we continue to be about."

21

TWILIGHT

BRENNAN EMERGED FROM the justices' private conference on October 15, 1986, to find a mysterious trail of handmade white placards laid out on the carpet leading all the way back to his chambers. The first sign read, "Brennan landmarks: The first 30 years," and each one that followed featured the name of a single important decision Brennan had written. It was his clerks' way of marking his thirtieth anniversary on the Court that day. They could hear Brennan as he stopped to admire each placard, bellowing out the name of the case as if it were an old friend.

Unbeknownst to Brennan, his newest colleague, Antonin Scalia, was walking the hallway only a few steps behind him. The conservative Scalia stopped at each placard and studied the names of Brennan's achievements with a less approving eye. Scalia arrived in Brennan's chambers moments after Brennan did with a mischievous grin on his face. "My Lord, Bill, have you got a lot to answer for," Scalia quipped.

This quiet hallway anniversary celebration was a modest postscript to the huge surprise birthday party Brennan's clerks from the previous term had thrown him on April 24, 1986, the day before his eightieth birthday. For an invitation, Brennan's law clerks had prepared a mock Court opinion, titled "In re The 80th Birthday of Justice William J. Brennan Jr." It fea-

tured a footnote overruling *Gregg v. Georgia,* the 1976 decision that reinstated the death penalty over Brennan's dissent, and four other opinions
involving issues on which Brennan regularly dissented. Getting into the
playful spirit, Justice O'Connor sent a reply saying she joined the entire
opinion, except for the footnote.

Some two hundred people — justices, law clerks, and Court staff, whom
he always treated so warmly — crowded into the ceremonial East Conference Room awaiting his arrival. Brennan was genuinely surprised as he
entered the room with his secretary, Mary Elmore, who had taken Fowler's
place in 1983. She had successfully coaxed him out of his chambers with a
cover story about talking to a group of visiting students. Brennan worked
the room thanking his guests, who drank champagne and ate pieces of a
giant sheet cake emblazoned with an image of the Supreme Court Building. Senator Edward Kennedy sent Brennan a note wishing him "health
and life to you" in Gaelic along with a fifty-year-old bottle of Jameson Irish
Whiskey. (Kennedy apologized that he could not find an eighty-year-old
vintage.)

Just before his eightieth birthday, Brennan made a conscious decision
to raise his public profile. Having already started delivering public speeches
again, he now consented to speak with the many journalists who requested
interviews in the months leading up to his birthday. His media blitz began
during a trip to Alabama in February 1986, to celebrate the hundredth anniversary of Hugo Black's birth. While in Alabama, he sat for an interview
with NBC News Supreme Court reporter Carl Stern. Brennan believed that
for the sake of fairness, if he agreed to one interview he should grant them
all. So in the months to come, he spoke to virtually every major news organization in the country, emphasizing how much he still enjoyed the job.
It was around the same time that Brennan also agreed to participate in a
series of tape-recorded interviews with the *Wall Street Journal* reporter he
had selected as his biographer.

Brennan became something of a celebrity, at least compared to his
often-reclusive colleagues, who teased him good-naturedly. "How's my
movie star this morning?" joked Blackmun, who had done his own string
of interviews a few years earlier with media organizations, including a new
cable television news station called CNN. Brennan's heightened media
profile was all the more striking, given how strictly he had rejected all in-

terview requests for so long. Now Brennan worried that he might become overexposed. In fact, Brennan was still largely unknown to the public, as he found out during a lengthy layover at Heathrow Airport in London. An American woman approached him in the boarding area looking to strike up a conversation.

"What do you do?" she asked.

"I'm a lawyer," Brennan replied.

"What sort of law?" she asked.

"General practice," Brennan said, at which point her eyes turned to scan the boarding area for more interesting conversation partners.

Brennan faced questions in most media interviews about whether he might consider retiring. He developed a stock answer. "My intention is to stay as long as I think I can continue to do the job and to quit the day I think I can't," he told NBC's Carl Stern. Brennan also came up with a one-liner he invoked in speeches: "Insofar as the suggestions contemplate my voluntary departure, like Mark Twain's reported death, the rumor is grossly exaggerated." Privately, his wife, Mary, began urging him to consider retiring. "You've done enough damage," she joked with Brennan. Mary wanted him to leave the Court while he was still healthy enough for them to travel and perhaps resettle in a warmer climate. But Brennan had no intention of stepping down any time soon.

Brennan remained in good health and maintained a vigorous schedule, particularly for an octogenarian. He woke up every morning at 5:30 A.M., rode an exercise bicycle for thirty minutes, read the morning newspapers over breakfast, and left his Arlington, Virginia, condo for the Court by 7:15 A.M. He read through his mail and cert. petitions, which he still screened himself, before his clerks and secretary arrived and then joined them for morning coffee. "He had that irrepressible delight and joy that I think made it obvious why he would not want to retire," recalled Mark Haddad, one of his 1986–87 term clerks.

His clerks marveled at the way Brennan could still swivel around in his chair to pull out the volume of *U.S. Reports* containing the case he was talking about — and then open the book to the exact page on which it appeared. But there were signs that he was not the vibrant justice he'd once been. He had gotten into the habit of reading from prepared statements during the justices' conferences rather than speaking off the cuff as he had done in the past, a practice that particularly annoyed Rehnquist. "Bill is usually thorough but as often as not he sounds like someone reading aloud a rather long and uninteresting recipe," Rehnquist confided in a January 1985 letter to Powell.

Brennan continued a demanding travel and speaking schedule. He gave at least eleven speeches in 1986, as many as during the term in which he joined the Court, from New York to the University of Kansas. He often recycled entire speeches, or at least the same ideas he had been talking about for years, rather than presenting new ones. He once again denounced the death penalty when he delivered the prestigious Oliver Wendell Holmes Jr. Lecture at Harvard Law School on September 5, 1986. Two months later, he renewed his call for state supreme courts to turn to their own state constitutions as a source for protection of individual liberties when he delivered the James Madison Lecture at New York University Law School, twenty-five years after his first Madison Lecture. One speech stood out as fresh. In May 1987, he delivered an address to the American Law Institute about what legal regimes should govern human settlements on the Moon and Mars.

Even as Brennan clung to his job, his friends provided unwelcome reminders of mortality. In June 1986 Father Theodore Hesburgh, Brennan's junior by eleven years, announced plans to retire as president of the University of Notre Dame. When Brennan wrote to congratulate him, Hesburgh explained in his reply that he believed it was time to "get some younger blood in the saddle." Brennan's closest friend, David Bazelon, had already retired in 1985 at the age of seventy-six, an occasion heralded by reporters as an end of an era of judicial activism. Bazelon had exhibited symptoms of Alzheimer's disease the previous term but stayed on the bench as long as he could, enlisting clerks with medical degrees in his final term.

Brennan's other longtime lunch mate, Skelly Wright, also began to show signs of dementia and took senior status in 1986. After years of feuding, Bazelon and Wright poignantly renewed their friendship at an adult daycare center in Washington. But the group's lunches were a thing of the past by the time their host, Milton Kronheim, died in September 1986 at the age of ninety-seven. Brennan visited Bazelon regularly at his Watergate apartment along with Abner Mikva, another D.C. Circuit judge who filled some of the void created as their mutual friend declined. Watching their friend fade was hard on both Brennan and Mikva, but Bazelon and his family greatly appreciated their visits.

As he aged, Brennan grew closer to Bill, the oldest and most politically conservative of his three children. Just as Brennan had chosen not to follow his father into politics, Bill opted against following Brennan onto the bench. He had seen the financial sacrifices Brennan had to make and turned down offers to be a state or federal judge. Bill enjoyed the fruits of his successful New Jersey legal practice, including his own twin-engine Beechcraft airplane. At least once a month, Bill flew down to Washington, D.C., for Sunday visits with Brennan and Mary.

Soon, Brennan was getting regular visits from another William J. Brennan. Bill's son, William J. Brennan IV, known to his family as Billy, began stopping by Brennan's chambers for regular lunch dates after he graduated from Georgetown in 1986 and went to work on Capitol Hill for Newark congressman Peter Rodino. These lunches continued later when Billy enrolled at Georgetown University Law Center. Billy had the startling experience of reading his grandfather's opinions or even being called on to discuss them in class. Brennan thought it was endearing when Billy asked if it was OK if he left off his middle initial and went by the name "William Brennan" in order to attract less attention.

FATHER JACK O'HARA saw a new but familiar face as he looked out at the small crowd of parishioners attending Mass at St. Rita Catholic Church one Saturday evening in 1986. Sitting anonymously in the half-full pews in this nondescript church in Alexandria, Virginia, named in honor of the patroness of "impossible causes," were Brennan and Mary. When the 5:15 P.M. Mass ended, the thirty-six-year-old priest went over to greet his famous guest. Brennan asked whether O'Hara knew who he was. Yes, explained O'Hara, who had grown up in the Washington area and been a priest for six years, he recognized Brennan from television and newspaper photos. Brennan invited O'Hara to visit the Court the next week, an offer he readily accepted.

The two men soon became friends — and Brennan and Mary became regulars at the Saturday-evening Mass. They blended right in among all the other senior citizens. Few in the regular crowd of 100 to 150 people in the increasingly Latino parish had any idea that the apparent retiree who slipped in the side door from the parking lot was actually a Supreme Court justice. That anonymity suited Brennan perfectly. Unlike his visits to Epiphany Church in Georgetown, at St. Rita he never felt as if all eyes were upon him as he sat in the pews or received Communion. Nor did he have to worry about antiabortion demonstrators like those who had protested his appearance at the seventy-fifth anniversary of Rutgers Law School a couple of years earlier by holding placards that compared him to Hitler or Stalin for his role in *Roe v. Wade.*

Brennan's presence never inhibited O'Hara, who felt free to preach on any subject he chose. They chatted regularly after Mass, and O'Hara visited Brennan at the Court, sometimes accompanied by his mother. O'Hara showed up one time by himself and explained that his mother was sick. Before he even made it back to the church, Brennan had already had flowers delivered to her. Brennan did not talk much about his faith with O'Hara. Still, it was obvious how much comfort Brennan took from his friendships with priests.

While it was undoubtedly the more devout Mary who initiated their regular Mass attendance, Brennan unquestionably welcomed this opportunity to make peace with his church. After so many years of disaffection with Catholicism, it felt like a return home. During an interview with National Public Radio's Nina Totenberg broadcast in January 1987, Brennan proudly pointed out that he attended Mass every Saturday night and described himself as "a devout Roman Catholic." Even attending the annual Red Mass at St. Matthew's Cathedral in Washington, the site of Marjorie's blowup with the bishop so many years ago, seemed to get a little easier. The day after one Red Mass, Blackmun slipped Brennan a note on the bench asking him how it went. "Much less disconcerting than in the past," Brennan wrote in reply.

ONLY ONE RETIREMENT in 1986 had come as good news. Brennan was sitting at his desk a few minutes before 2 P.M. on June 17 when a messenger delivered a sealed letter from Chief Justice Burger and requested Brennan's presence in the justices' conference room. On the way, Brennan read Burger's retirement letter. He arrived in the conference room and found most of his colleagues watching a televised press conference where Rehnquist stood beside President Reagan in the White House briefing room. That is when Brennan first realized that Reagan intended to nominate Rehnquist as the new chief justice. Standing on the other side of the president was Scalia, the fifty-year-old judge on the D.C. Circuit whom Reagan tapped to fill Rehnquist's seat as associate justice.

Nino, as he was known, was the first-ever Italian American and first Catholic nominee to the Supreme Court since Brennan thirty years earlier. Born in Trenton, New Jersey, Scalia was the son of a deeply religious professor of Romance languages from Sicily and a first-generation Italian American schoolteacher. He grew up in a middle-class neighborhood in Queens, New York, and graduated at the top of his class from Xavier High School, a Catholic military academy in Manhattan, as well as from Georgetown University and Harvard Law School. After six years at a top Cleveland law firm, Scalia switched to academia. He became a respected legal scholar with a conservative bent at the University of Virginia and then the University of Chicago, mixing in service in the Nixon and Ford administrations. His specialty was administrative law and regulatory reform, and he was not vocal in debates over the hot social issues of the day. President Reagan appointed him to the D.C. Circuit in 1982, where he earned a reputation as an aggressive conservative, but one even liberal colleagues like Mikva viewed as unusually affable, brilliant, and skilled as a writer. He became closely connected to the conservative movement as a former fellow at the American Enterprise Institute and mentor to the Federalist Society, a new networking group for conservative law students and attorneys. Scalia also was a vocal critic of judicial activism, accusing courts of going too far in discovering new rights in abortion, busing, and death penalty cases.

While the press focused on how much more conservative the change in personnel might make the Court, Brennan envisioned a Court run more fairly and efficiently by the new chief justice. And although Brennan did not say so publicly, he was privately pleased to have outlasted the seventy-nine-year-old Burger. Brennan and Rehnquist still rarely agreed about cases, but the two had developed a warm rapport and enjoyed making each other laugh. Rehnquist wrote the majority opinion in a 1985 case involving a drug smuggler who had swallowed ninety-nine cocaine-filled balloons. When Rehnquist periodically inquired about the status of Brennan's dissent, Brennan replied, "Bill, I'm on the forty-ninth balloon now"; "I'm up to sixty"; "Only twelve to go." Brennan finished his dissent right before the last conference of the term and had his clerk deliver a copy to Rehnquist's chambers with a large deflated orange balloon attached. Rehnquist brought the balloon with him to conference, eliciting laughs from everyone. When Brennan celebrated his seventy-ninth birthday in 1985, Rehnquist had led three of his clerks in singing "Happy Birthday" inside his senior colleague's chambers. As Rehnquist later explained, "We're not great buddies, we don't go out to lunch together regularly or anything, but we like each other." Rehnquist generally respected Brennan's advice. When Brennan suggested removing language characterizing the Orthodox Jewish custom of wearing a skullcap as an idiosyncrasy in a case decided in March 1986, upholding a military regulation barring their use, Rehnquist readily agreed.

Brennan was not happy about attacks Democratic senators directed at Rehnquist in the run-up to his confirmation hearing. He genuinely wanted Rehnquist to succeed, even though it might come at Brennan's expense. He felt that, unlike Burger, Rehnquist — who laughed the first few times Brennan called him "Chief" — was not pursuing a hidden agenda and did not let the position go to his head. Brennan was flattered that Rehnquist consulted with him about administrative and personnel problems. He appreciated how efficiently Rehnquist ran the conference and conducted the Court's business and genuinely meant it when he later told the National Association of Women Judges, "The present chief is just ideal."

Brennan hoped Rehnquist might moderate his own views in order to build majorities. But in his first term as chief justice, Rehnquist seemed unwilling to abandon his own conservative principles in order to achieve consensus. He dissented in thirteen of his first forty-two cases as chief justice. Brennan, as senior associate justice in the majority, got to assign every one of those opinions. "I'm afraid his place in history may suffer because he simply will not do anything to mass a court," Brennan said in May 1987. The result was a string of victories for Brennan. He wrote a 7–2 opinion ruling that Louisiana's law requiring equal time for the teaching of creationism with evolution in biology classes violated the establishment clause. Brennan found that there was no secular purpose to the law, which he said was intended to undermine the teaching of evolution. At the height of the AIDS epidemic, he wrote another 7–2 opinion holding that federal laws banning discrimination against handicapped persons applied to victims of contagious diseases.

In both of those cases, the sole dissenters were Rehnquist and Scalia, although in the early months of his tenure, Scalia actually agreed with Brennan more often than anyone expected. Scalia had provided Brennan the critical fifth vote to strike down portions of a 1971 federal election campaign law as a violation of the First Amendment. By March 1987, conservatives were publicly expressing concern that Scalia had become a bit too friendly with the Court's liberals. Scalia had predicted such an outcome in a November 3, 1986, letter to Brennan shortly after his arrival at the Court. "I think we will be agreeing, you and I, more often than the world expects. And I am sure that, even when disagreeing, we will be the best of friends."

Brennan and Scalia did in fact get along remarkably well at first. During walks together through the corridors of the Court, Brennan was struck by how much they had in common. Scalia, known for his mischievous sense of humor, once quipped that the family of his Irish Catholic wife, Maureen, with whom he had nine children, considered her decision to wed an Italian American a form of intermarriage. Brennan was flattered when Scalia sought him out for advice about questions such as whether to accept a particular speaking engagement. "He is an uncle," Scalia said. "He's very avuncular. I am sure he would not steer me wrong." Midway through Scalia's first term in March 1987, Brennan privately confided, "I'm bold enough to say he regards me as a friend. I certainly regard him as one."

But Brennan, along with many of the other justices, was somewhat taken aback by Scalia's aggressive style on and off the bench. Right from the start, Scalia often dominated oral arguments by frequently interrupting with tough questions. As the *Washington Post*'s Al Kamen noted in December 1986, Scalia's "adroit grilling" made the "often excruciatingly dull" oral arguments more entertaining for the audience, although it took some getting used to for some of the older justices like Brennan, who tended to ask fewer questions. Brennan and his clerks joked about "Ninograms," the short, sharply worded memos Scalia circulated to his colleagues laying out his view of the cases. Scalia's assertive manner was somewhat reminiscent of the last professor with whom Brennan served — Felix Frankfurter — and Brennan occasionally called him "the professor" in private. And although Brennan found Scalia open-minded in some areas, there were other issues, such as affirmative action, in which Scalia bluntly told him, "There's no sense in you and I trying to persuade one another. We can't."

With Scalia in dissent, Brennan wrote the Court's first decision upholding affirmative action for women in *Johnson v. Santa Clara Transportation*

Agency in 1987. A male employee filed suit against a county transportation agency that had given the job of road dispatcher to a woman, claiming a violation of Title VII of the 1964 Civil Rights Act. He won at trial but lost on appeal. In the Supreme Court, Scalia and Rehnquist sided with the Reagan Justice Department, which had interceded as a friend of the court against Santa Clara's affirmative action efforts. Brennan argued that Title VII clearly permitted voluntary efforts to break down discriminatory barriers, whether based on race, as he had written in a 1979 ruling, or on gender. Brennan's view picked up the expected support of Blackmun and Marshall, but also the more unexpected votes of Stevens, who had dissented in the 1979 case, and of Powell, who continued to take a cautious, case-by-case approach to affirmative action. O'Connor felt Brennan went too far in permitting affirmative action that was not specifically tied to remedying past wrongs, but she nevertheless voted in favor of the affirmative action plan.

Brennan also wrote a majority opinion in *United States v. Paradise* upholding a lower-court order requiring the Alabama State Police to set aside half of its promotions for the immediate future for qualified black state troopers to make up for past discrimination. The Justice Department challenged the lower-court ruling as unconstitutional race discrimination. Brennan, joined by Blackmun, Powell, and Marshall, said the record of discrimination was so long-standing and egregious that using what amounted to a racial quota to correct the problem satisfied even the most demanding standard under the equal protection clause. Justice Stevens, their fifth vote, used a different analysis in upholding the plan.

These victories explain why reporters who had started the 1986–87 term predicting Scalia and Rehnquist would push the Court rightward were writing stories noting a "pronounced shift to the left" by early 1987. "It is Justice William J. Brennan Jr., the Court's senior liberal, who has been in charge so far," Stuart Taylor Jr. wrote in the *New York Times* in March. Even James J. Kilpatrick, a conservative columnist who usually had little good to say about Brennan, had to grudgingly admit in a column headlined "It Was Bill Brennan's Term" that "the 81-year-old justice had one helluva time."

But Brennan certainly did not end up in the majority in all major cases that term. As usual, a defeat in one death penalty case, *McCleskey v. Kemp,* stung most. Powell wrote a 5–4 majority decision rejecting the use of a statistical study to invalidate the capital punishment statute in Georgia and potentially other states because of alleged systematic race discrimination. Lawyers for Warren McCleskey, an African American convicted of killing a police officer, introduced as evidence a statistical study designed to show race discrimination in administration of the death penalty. The study revealed that defendants who killed whites were more likely to be executed than those who killed blacks. To overturn McCleskey's death sentence, the evidence would have to show purposeful discrimination against him in the imposition of the death sentence, and Powell, writing for the Court, said the evidence failed to prove intentional racial bias against McCleskey. The outcome was a major defeat to Brennan: if a majority of the Court had accepted the study as proof of racial bias in the death penalty, it would likely have invalidated the death penalty in numerous states.

IF THE LOSS in *McCleskey* was a blow to Brennan, what happened two months later when the term drew to a close on June 26, 1987, was even more distressing. Powell informed his colleagues that he was retiring. The news was not entirely surprising, given the difficulties Powell had experienced since prostate cancer surgery in 1985, but was nevertheless greeted with sadness by many at the Court. O'Connor was particularly devastated by the loss of the justice with whom she had established the closest bond.

Powell's retirement also upset Brennan, who was losing both a friend and a vital ally. President Reagan would have an opportunity to replace Powell, the Court's key swing vote, with a more conservative successor. The potential consequences for Brennan were noted by the press. A *Newsweek* story about Brennan titled "Renaissance of an Octogenarian Liberal" accompanying its coverage of Powell's retirement, asked, "Was it springtime for Brennan or Indian summer?"

The struggle to replace Powell provoked an epic battle, one that Brennan followed closely. President Reagan's nomination of Robert Bork, a conservative legal scholar and U.S. Court of Appeals judge, generated unprecedented resistance from liberal activists and Democratic senators. Edward Kennedy set the tone for what followed when he took to the Senate floor within minutes of the nomination laying out a dystopian vision of "Bork's America" in which police would knock down doors and women would again resort to back-alley abortions.

The intensity of the opposition caught the White House and Republican senators off-guard. They had assumed Bork's distinguished career as a law professor, solicitor general under two presidents, and as an appellate judge would assure his confirmation. But Bork's lengthy paper trail full of provocative writings provided his critics with plenty of ammunition, and the nominee did not help himself with his gruff demeanor and untelegenic appearance before the Senate Judiciary Committee.

Brennan had no illusions about what Bork's presence would mean for the Court's balance of power, but insisted at the time he would not have minded having him as a colleague. "I'd just have one more with whom I'd probably not always agree," Brennan said privately on October 28, 1987, just a few days after Bork's defeat. Brennan was troubled more by the nasty confirmation battle, which came to resemble a political campaign, complete with a television attack ad narrated by actor Gregory Peck. "I think they rather demean the process and give it the appearance of an ordinary ward fight in Chicago, or something like that."

In truth, Brennan's influential tenure on the Court helped spark the judicial confirmation war that so appalled him. By making the courts an agent for social change, Brennan had helped to create a role for the Supreme Court that virtually ensured that the judicial nomination process would come to be seen as a political battleground. With so much at stake, conservatives did not want to repeat the mistake of appointing another Brennan — or a Blackmun or a Powell, for that matter — who had proven so costly. Similarly, liberals could not afford to let such a conservative, although undeniably competent, nominee such as Bork replace the Court's swing justice.

After the Senate rejected Bork's nomination by a 58–42 vote, President Reagan chose Douglas Ginsburg, another judge on the U.S. Court of Appeals for the D.C. Circuit. But his nomination was withdrawn when Ginsburg admitted to smoking marijuana while he was a young Harvard Law School professor. President Reagan next turned to Judge Anthony Kennedy, a fifty-one-year-old judge on the U.S. Court of Appeals for the Ninth Circuit, whose candidacy was promoted by several young conservatives in the Reagan administration who had been his former law clerks. The mild-mannered California native had earned his law degree at Harvard Law School five years after Brennan joined the Supreme Court and then returned to Sacramento to take over his father's law and lobbying practice. He became friends with Edwin Meese in the mid-1960s, when Meese was advising then California governor Ronald Reagan. Kennedy helped draft legislation for the governor. In 1975 President Ford nominated Kennedy to the Ninth Circuit at Reagan's suggestion, and he continued to teach constitutional law at McGeorge School of Law in Sacramento.

Kennedy's selection disappointed conservatives, who considered the nomination a capitulation to the left. Kennedy came across as much less strident or rigidly doctrinaire than Bork. He told the Senate Judiciary Committee that he agreed with the existence of an implied right of privacy found in *Griswold v. Connecticut*. Kennedy was confirmed by the Senate, 97–0, and took his seat in the middle of the Court term on February 18, 1988. Brennan should have been pleased at the prospect of having Kennedy as a colleague. Unlike with Bork, there was no expectation that Kennedy would be an intellectually forceful conservative leader. Brennan had some reason to hope he might also be more open to persuasion, and predicted at the time of his arrival that Kennedy would prove to be "increasingly independent." But Kennedy seemed to arrive at the Court with the same skepticism about Brennan that O'Connor had developed. Their first interactions were strained, due largely to a case that dragged on for more than fifteen months.

Just eleven days after he joined the Court, Kennedy and his new colleagues heard argument in the case of *Patterson v. McLean Credit Union*. The case involved a lawsuit by Brenda Patterson, a black woman in North Carolina who said she was harassed on the job, denied a promotion, and then fired, all because of her race. Among her legal claims, she said the employer's actions violated a Reconstruction-era civil rights statute, known as section 1981, which guarantees all individuals the "same right" to "make and enforce contracts" that "is enjoyed by white citizens." Perhaps the most contentious issue for the Supreme Court was whether on-the-job harassment was even covered by section 1981. The lower federal courts said that Patterson could not bring the harassment claim because it did not relate to the creation or enforcement of her employment contract. The argument in *Patterson* was premised on a 1976 ruling, *Runyon v. McCrary*, in which the Supreme Court ruled 7–2 that the Reconstruction-era statute section 1981 applied to prohibit private discrimination in contracts, not just discrimination enforced by state laws or state action.

When the justices gathered to discuss the case at their conference on March 2, 1988, Brennan was prepared to argue that the federal law was violated whenever employment conditions depended on race. Brennan knew he could count on the votes of Marshall, Blackmun, and Stevens but was totally unprepared for what followed. The provocateur was White, who was seen as having drifted to the right over time but still sometimes joined Brennan on cases involving race. When it was White's turn to speak after Brennan, he remarked that he would favor overruling *Runyon* and returning to the view that the law applied only to actions by government entities rather than private parties. White picked up the support of Rehnquist, O'Connor, and Scalia, and then Kennedy. Counting five votes, Rehnquist quickly announced that the case would be scheduled for reargument to address whether to overrule *Runyon*.

The outcome should not have come entirely as a surprise, given the changes in the Court's composition since *Runyon*. But Brennan nevertheless returned to his chambers "crestfallen and virtually speechless." This was the first time in Brennan's entire tenure that his colleagues had proposed overruling a decision that significantly advanced civil rights. The potential outcome also upset Blackmun and Stevens, who wrote highly unusual dissents arguing against rehearing the case. They suggested that the main reason for considering overruling *Runyon* appeared to be changed personnel on the Court, not changed legal principles. Blackmun ended his dissent with a thinly disguised reference to what might lie ahead for *Roe v. Wade*. "Is this an omen of other similar moves to come?" Blackmun deleted that line after asking Brennan, "What do you think? Should the last sentence be omitted?"

The case was reargued on October 12, 1988, and discussed again at conference two days later. This time, the justices voted unanimously to reaffirm *Runyon*. Kennedy was among the five justices who argued that *Runyon* was correct; four others said it was wrong but should not be reconsidered. The conference then voted 5–4 that section 1981 covered racial harassment. Kennedy made a surprising fifth vote, arguing that the evidence of harassment was so extensive, it was clear that Brenda Patterson's employer had not entered into an employment contract in good faith. Stevens believed Brennan should have assigned the case to Kennedy, but Brennan opted to keep it for himself. Anxious to hold on to the fifth vote, Brennan sent a draft privately to Kennedy in early November. The Court's longest-serving member and its newest justice negotiated over language in the draft for several weeks. Brennan made numerous changes before Kennedy advised him in early December that he expected to be able to join the opinion. But Kennedy wanted to wait and hear what other justices had to say. Brennan circulated the opinion to the rest of the Court, picked up a number of other supporters, but did not hear from Kennedy again for nearly five months, until late April 1989.

In the interim, Kennedy had changed his mind. He circulated a proposed opinion that rejected application of section 1981 to racial harassment on the job. Brennan had lost his majority, and Rehnquist assigned Kennedy to write the Court's opinion. A disappointed Brennan remade his opinion into a dissent that opened angrily with, "What the Court declines to snatch away with one hand, it steals with the other." The opinion took a dig at the Court's "fine phrases" about eliminating race discrimination that "count for little in practice." Kennedy complained privately about the tone to Brennan. "Do we really need to do this to each other?" Kennedy asked in a handwritten note to Brennan. Brennan changed the word "steals" to "takes" so that the first sentence read, "What the Court declines to snatch away with one hand, it takes with the other." But when Brennan refused to make other changes, Kennedy circulated a new footnote criticizing the use of "barbs about our respective sensitivities." The escalating exchange between the two men prompted Stevens to ask Brennan to drop his most critical passages. "I am sufficiently troubled by it to be thinking of joining [Kennedy's] footnote response," Stevens wrote. Brennan agreed to drop the "fine phrases" dig and some other wording before the decision was announced, and Kennedy dropped his footnote criticizing Brennan. But the experience left both men leery of each other.

AS THE OUTCOME in the *Patterson* case suggests, Kennedy's presence made it more difficult for Brennan to replicate his success during the 1986–87 term in subsequent years. There were some signs that Rehnquist was willing to set aside his rigid conservatism in order to build consensus. He wrote an 8–0 opinion for the Court in *Hustler Magazine v. Falwell* holding that public figures suing publishers for intentional infliction of emotional distress had to meet the same high standard that Brennan established in *New York Times v. Sullivan* for libel cases. But more commonly Brennan found himself in dissent, as in another First Amendment case in which the majority held that school officials could censor high school student newspapers. By the spring of 1988, Brennan lamented privately that he wished Powell had stayed on the Court for just one more year. "It would have been a very, very different term," Brennan said.

Brennan tried to be philosophical about the Court's direction. He was not entirely convinced the conservatives would form as cohesive a bloc as he had enjoyed under Chief Justice Warren. But if they did, he took some comfort in knowing the pendulum was bound to swing back in a direction more to his liking at some point in the future. "The big strength of this society is we don't remain one way or the other forever," he said in May 1988. Mary, who had been at the Court when Brennan's bloc reigned supreme, tried to comfort him by saying, "You had your day. Now they have theirs." "Yes," Brennan replied. "But I'm right." Years of dissenting had taken a toll on Brennan's enthusiasm for his job. It was not nearly as exciting as when he was regularly in the majority, particularly during oral argument, which he now considered "boring as hell." He asked fewer questions than ever and admitted in October 1989, "I'm probably thinking about maybe the Redskins . . . or when we are going to get this damn day over with so we can go home."

The situation only got worse in the 1988–89 term, when Rehnquist was in the majority in twenty-seven of the thirty-three cases that split 5–4. The acrimony seemed particularly deep among the justices' clerks, who were divided into ideological factions, including one group of conservatives who called themselves "the cabal." Brennan largely ignored the clerks' melodrama but returned from the justices' conferences looking increasingly dejected. "Now I know how John Harlan felt," Brennan said. Brennan cast fifty-two dissenting votes in 133 decisions, including in two hard-fought death penalty cases in which Brennan found himself in dissent as the Court rejected the broad assertions that neither the mentally retarded nor teenagers could be executed consistent with the "cruel and unusual punishment" prohibition of the Eighth Amendment. By the end of the term, a frustrated Brennan mused privately about retiring. He wondered, "What's the point of staying around and getting kicked?"

A string of health problems corresponded with his setbacks on the Court. On the advice of Blackmun and Powell, who had both been diagnosed with prostate cancer, Brennan checked into the Mayo Clinic in August 1987 for a round of tests on his prostate, which had been giving him trouble. Blackmun wrote him a typically meticulous three-page, single-spaced letter, laying out every detail of the itinerary he had arranged, including a hotel reservation and restaurant recommendation. The tests did not reveal any serious problems, and Brennan resumed his regular routine, including a December 1987 trip to Jerusalem and Bethlehem. Brennan "had more stamina than the rest of us," recalled Peter Fishbein, a former clerk who accompanied him on the trip. But upon returning from the Middle East, Brennan developed a painful case of shingles that forced him to abandon his stationary bicycle and more than a dozen speaking engagements.

Brennan recovered fully, but his worries about his health lingered. A pain in his lower back in February 1988 was a sure sign in Brennan's mind of a kidney stone or organ failure. He frantically tried reaching his doctor, who diagnosed a pulled muscle caused by a coughing fit the night before. Brennan was embarrassed when he fell out of bed in June 1988 and hit his head on the edge of a glass table, which required thirteen stitches. He asked Powell for help drawing up a living will in August 1988. That same month, he delivered a eulogy for Skelly Wright at the Washington Cathedral, which might have been what he envisioned for his own. "He was a man of principle, and a wholly compassionate complete human being who never lost sight of the human dimensions of the great problems that confront society," Brennan said.

On December 8, 1988, Brennan went to the office of the Capitol's attending physician complaining of fever, chills, and a noticeable tremor in his hands. His doctor there, Robert Krasner, diagnosed pneumonia and sent Brennan by ambulance to Bethesda Naval Hospital. When Brennan responded quickly to antibiotics, his doctors reconsidered the diagnosis and soon recommended removing his gallbladder. President Reagan and his wife, Nancy, who happened to be at the hospital for routine checkups, visited Brennan there. Reagan even recited an Irish poem. Senator Kennedy stopped by the next day. Brennan enjoyed all the attention, but the prospect of surgery frightened him. He was nearly the same age at which his mother's health declined rapidly after undergoing surgery herself in 1962. The night before his operation, Brennan mused nervously about how hard it would be on his clerks and secretary if he died. The surgery was a success and he was released from the hospital on December 17.

Although Brennan had to abandon his exercise bicycle permanently, he was able to resume his hectic pace of speeches and travel in the spring and summer of 1989. After visiting England and Scotland, Brennan sailed back to the United States on the *Queen Elizabeth II* luxury liner. He had a chance encounter onboard with the aunt of his oldest grandson, Hugh, whom he had not seen in nearly thirty years. That prompted Brennan to extend an invitation to Hugh to visit him at the Court, which his grandson accepted. The first thing Brennan did after shaking the thirty-two-year-old's hand was to point out the painting of Nancy that Hugh's mother, Roxey, had given him as a Christmas present in 1956, which still hung over the mantel in his chambers. Brennan gave Hugh a tour of the Court and then took him to dinner and a performance at the Kennedy Center. Hugh, who had gone to work for the postal service in Arizona after six years in the Air Force, enjoyed the heady tour of Washington but was struck most by his grandfather's vitality. "It was a marvelous experience," Hugh later recalled.

Brennan remained remarkably active for a man in his eighties, but he seemed noticeably less engaged in his work than in the past. He talked less when his clerks gathered to discuss cases before oral arguments and gave them less direction about how to write opinions. He relied more heavily on the memos they prepared about cases in advance of the justices' conference. He had become such a light editor that it made some of his clerks nervous. Blackmun noticed that Brennan's clerks were doing more of the writing and thought what they produced was often too long. Brennan's chambers seemed to run on autopilot. His enormous body of opinions guided his clerks except in the rare instances when a new issue arose. Even if Brennan was not as focused on the details as in the past, he remained the commander in his chambers and decisively determined how he wanted to approach virtually every case. The guiding principle was not to contradict his prior opinions. When his clerks became too vigorous in advocating a position contrary to his own, Brennan cut them off by reminding them it was his name on the appointment on the wall.

Being in dissent so often made writing the occasional important majority opinion all the more special. One of these, though, sparked yet another unexpected public outcry. Gregory Johnson was convicted and sentenced to prison and fined for burning an American flag in front of Dallas City Hall during the 1984 Republican National Convention where Reagan was renominated for a second term. The Texas Court of Criminal Appeals threw out the conviction and the state appealed. When the justices voted on the case, *Texas v. Johnson,* at their March 22, 1989, conference, the lineup was unusual. The six justices who agreed with Brennan that flag burning was a form of expressive conduct protected by the First Amendment included O'Connor, Kennedy, and, perhaps most surprisingly, Scalia.

Despite the initial signs of agreement in the early months of his tenure, Scalia had proven a stalwart conservative, prompting Brennan to privately grouse that he "followed the party line rather more than I would have supposed he would." While free speech remained one area of common ground, Scalia agreed so rarely with Brennan that a few months after joining Brennan's majority in the flag-burning case, he joked with a Washington audience that, "Bill and I always vote together. They call us the New Jersey twins." Nevertheless, Scalia respected Brennan's skills and willingness to accommodate his colleagues even if he disagreed with the results. "In my experience, he is the most skillful 'general' on the Court," Scalia said. "He is the epitome of skill, subtlety, and yet tenacity and he's always going somewhere."

Determined to hold on to his votes, Brennan assigned himself the majority opinion in the flag-burning case. He wrote a narrow opinion ruling that expression cannot be prohibited simply because it is offensive. "If there is a bedrock principle underlying the First Amendment, it is that the government may not prohibit the expression of an idea simply because society finds the idea itself offensive or disagreeable," Brennan wrote. "The way to preserve the flag's special role is not to punish those who feel differently about these matters," he continued. "It is to persuade them that they are wrong."

Rehnquist circulated a dissent filled with dramatic passages from Ralph Waldo Emerson's poem "Concord Hymn," John Greenleaf Whittier's poem "Barbara Frietchie," and Francis Scott Key's "The Star-Spangled Banner." O'Connor, despite voting at conference to strike down the statute, decided without further explanation to join Rehnquist's dissent. Stevens also filed an emotional dissent, citing the way "the ideas of liberty and equality have been an irresistible force in motivating leaders" from Patrick Henry and Susan B. Anthony to the "soldiers who scaled the bluff at Omaha Beach" during the invasion of Normandy in 1944. "If those ideas are worth fighting for—and our history demonstrates that they are—it cannot be true that the flag that uniquely symbolizes their power is not itself worthy of protection from unnecessary desecration."

Even after thirty-three years on the Court and countless backlashes, Brennan was still unprepared for what followed, as the public and politicians rose up in outrage. At the urging of a conservative radio talk-show host, listeners inundated Brennan's chambers with flags of all shapes and sizes. The Senate passed a resolution condemning the Court's ruling, 97–3. Congress quickly enacted new protections against flag burning despite warnings from legal experts that the law was unconstitutional. President George H. W. Bush called for a constitutional amendment to protect the flag, the first time in the nation's history that altering the Bill of Rights was seriously contemplated.

Brennan stayed silent as protestors singled him out for criticism. A year earlier, Brennan had attended a ceremony renaming in his honor the Hudson County courthouse, where he first sat as a trial judge. Now, veterans groups tried to convince the county governing board to remove his name. His son Bill rose up in his defense, invoking Brennan's service in the Army, his brother Charlie's combat death, and his brother Frank's capture after being shot down during World War II. "I really don't think any of those birds up there can tell my family what patriotism is," Bill told the *Wall Street Journal*. Bill also spoke out against the proposed constitutional amendment at the American Bar Association annual meeting in Hawaii in July 1989. "We pay the Court to call the hard ones," Bill told the ABA House of Delegates. "And that's just what the Supreme Court did. It called a hard one." Closer to home, one of Brennan's condominium neighbors draped an American flag over his door and kept it there for several days, so Brennan would see it whenever he stepped off the elevator on their floor. Brennan was surprised by the intensity of the reaction but he remained unfazed by it. A year later, he wrote the 5–4 opinion of the Court striking down the newly enacted Flag Protection Act of 1989.

BRENNAN WAS AT the center of another protest in 1989 sparked by a more predictable subject of controversy: abortion. He had agreed the previous year to accept an honorary degree from Spalding University, a small Catholic women's college in Kentucky where his wife's sister, Sister Charlotte Fowler, had once been president. But by the time he was to attend the commencement ceremony in May 1989, an important abortion case,

Webster v. Reproductive Health Services, was pending before the Court. The outcome in the case, in which Missouri had defended numerous abortion restrictions and urged the Court to overrule *Roe,* was being closely watched by all sides in the abortion debate. It was the first abortion case in which Kennedy would weigh in on the issue. A few days before Brennan was to travel to Kentucky to receive the honorary degree, right-to-life activists announced plans to picket the ceremony. Then the local archbishop, Thomas Kelly, announced that he would not be present at the college's commencement for the first time in several years. Kelly refused to link his decision to Brennan's appearance, but acknowledged that Brennan had "bitterly disappointed" many Catholics with his position on abortion.

Brennan had become accustomed to protestors at his public appearances and to denunciations from religious figures for his role in the *Roe* decision. While Catholic Church leaders had recently taken to task Catholic elected officials, including New York governor Mario Cuomo, for their positions on abortion, the most vitriolic criticism directed at Brennan in recent years had come from evangelical Protestants. When Brennan delivered a commencement address at Loyola Law School in Los Angeles on June 1, 1986, the Fundamentalist Baptist Tabernacle church chartered a plane that circled overhead at the start of the ceremony, trailing a banner that read, "Pray for death: Baby-killer Brennan." The church also held a special prayer service calling for Brennan's death. "It's always a last resort to pray against a leader," explained J. Richard Olivas, the church's associate pastor. "But we have prayed now for thirteen years for this law to be changed and it appears that William Brennan is recalcitrant and does not want to change." Brennan's brother Frank sent Brennan an outraged note and enclosed a story about the incident from his local newspaper in northern California. "I know you can roll with the punches when things like this happen, but it's still a rotten shame," Frank wrote. Brennan replied reassuringly, "From the mail I have been getting the Baptist spectacle has no supporters. We're not really worrying about it and don't you."

Spalding's trustees refused to withdraw their invitation to Brennan. But as the outcry over his appearance and the threat of protests grew, Brennan decided to cancel the trip. A former Kentucky governor and federal judge, Bert Combs, accepted the degree on Brennan's behalf and had the last word when he spoke at the commencement ceremony. "It offends my sense of fair play and good manners," Combs said, "that a man who has served with distinction on this country's highest court for more than thirty years cannot visit an institution of higher learning in Kentucky without being publicly embarrassed by a few who disagree with his vote on one case." Once again, Brennan said nothing publicly about the incident, but sent a thank-you note to a Catholic lawyer in Louisville who wrote to say, "I am proud that you are a Catholic."

Being the target of antiabortion protests remained a not entirely welcome source of kinship for Brennan and Blackmun, who still bore the brunt as author of the *Roe* opinion. Blackmun continued to receive death threats, including a typewritten letter in 1985 in which the writer threatened to "blow the justice's brains out" and then "laugh" at his funeral. In February 1985, a bullet crashed through the window of Blackmun's third-story apartment in Arlington, showering his wife with shattered glass. The FBI concluded it was a random shooting, a conclusion Blackmun found difficult to believe.

Blackmun and Brennan were also linked in the minds of fans. They were greeted like heroes when they appeared together at a celebration of Harvard's 350th anniversary in 1986. In 1989 the artist Richard Serra titled a giant T-shaped sculpture *Blackmun and Brennan* because, as he explained to the *New York Times*, he admired the two justices. The newspaper's reviewer interpreted the sculpture as "a kind of heroic figure with out-stretched arms, holding up the walls as if straining to hold back the forces of conservatism." Blackmun forwarded a copy of the review to Brennan, along with a joking note: "It is a good likeness, don't you think?"

Ever since *Roe*, Brennan had avoided writing in abortion cases other than those involving the issue of public funding for abortion procedures. He was perfectly happy to lie low and defer to Blackmun, who took such a sense of ownership for the issue that had caused him so much trouble. But in *Webster*, Brennan considered writing separately in addition to joining Blackmun's dissent. Brennan wanted to explore the possibility of using the equal protection clause to attack abortion restrictions as a form of gender bias. But he ultimately abandoned the idea, apparently at the request of Blackmun, who did not want to leave the impression that there were any differences of opinion among the four dissenters: Brennan, Marshall, Blackmun, and Stevens. In the end, the *Webster* case did not become a major showdown over abortion because O'Connor would not yet go along with Rehnquist's effort to abandon *Roe*'s trimester framework.

Brennan again deferred to his allies the following term when the Court took up two state laws requiring minors to provide parental notification before obtaining abortions. The Court upheld an Ohio law requiring notification of one parent before a minor can have an abortion, and struck down portions of a Minnesota law that required notification of two parents but upheld the state's single-parent notice. Brennan joined opinions by Blackmun and Marshall finding that the state laws failed to adequately protect the rights of minor girls who were capable of making their own decisions.

While Brennan tended to defer to Blackmun on abortion, he was still actively trying to influence his colleague's approach to death penalty cases. Brennan believed that Blackmun would come around to opposing the death penalty as unfairly administered in all circumstances, and Brennan made a point of assigning the lead dissenting opinion to Blackmun in several capital punishment cases in the 1989–90 term. Indeed, when Blackmun wrote strong dissenting language in one case, he asked Brennan if the criticism of the majority went too far. Brennan replied, "Hit them harder," although Blackmun eventually toned down the dissent at the request of Marshall and Stevens.

AS HIS EIGHTY-FOURTH birthday neared in the spring of 1990, Brennan conducted another round of media interviews. He continued to assure reporters that he had no intention of retiring any time soon. "I so love what I'm doing here, that I don't want to stop doing it until I absolutely have to," Brennan told *Irish America* magazine. His resolve had only seemed to harden after Reagan's vice president, George H. W. Bush, defeated Democrat Michael Dukakis in the 1988 presidential election. But Brennan had privately been thinking more about retirement than he acknowledged publicly. He remembered how an enfeebled Douglas had stubbornly clung to his seat after a stroke. He also recalled the stories he heard as a young attorney at Pitney Hardin about how Mahlon Pitney, the brother of one of the firm's founders, similarly stayed on the Court after suffering a debilitating stroke. "It's always stuck in my mind that if anything like that ever happened to a justice, then God, he just owes it to the nation and the Court to recognize it and turn it over to somebody else," Brennan said privately on May 2, 1988. Mary had only grown more insistent that he should give up his seat. She wanted to resettle in a warmer climate, perhaps San Diego or Arizona. On the other hand, Brennan worried about the impact of his retirement on his secretary and clerks and found it difficult to imagine life as a retiree. "I'd go crazy," Brennan confided.

For advice, Brennan turned to his friend Timothy Healy, a Jesuit priest who had recently left the presidency of Georgetown University to head the New York Public Library. "The appointment to the Court, while it is for life, doesn't call for your death as part of its honorable keeping," Healy wrote Brennan on April 16, 1990. Healy reminded Brennan of an earlier offer to teach at Georgetown's law school that he described as a "gentler, better paced" alternative. Brennan did not retire, but the Georgetown offer provided him considerable comfort, since he had little interest in living anywhere but Washington, D.C.

The health of Brennan and his aging colleagues had become the butt of jokes for political cartoonists. Brennan remained far from the senile old fool portrayed in one cartoon sitting in an oversize chair and hunching over a desk with a juice box labeled "Fruit of the Prune." The cartoon shows Brennan writing a living will in his shaky penmanship that says, "I, William J. Brennan Jr., being of sound mind, willfully and voluntarily make known my desire that all means — heroic, artificial or otherwise — be used to keep me alive, so long as there is a Republican in the White House." Directly underneath was the signature of Thurgood Marshall, who wrote, "the declarer has been personally known to me, and I believe him to have all his marbles."

Brennan was surely in better shape than Marshall, who was badly overweight, wheezed heavily when he walked, and had trouble reading regular-size print. Marshall appeared hopelessly lost during one oral argument in October 1989. But Brennan's physical stamina had also noticeably ebbed. He still arrived in his chambers early each morning, but without the same boundless energy. He shuffled when he walked and looked physically shrunken. Some of his clerks took to calling him Yoda, an affectionate reference to the wise and shriveled old alien with protruding ears in the *Star Wars* movies. Brennan grew fatigued by midafternoon and occasionally required a brief nap. Rehnquist noticed him dozing off during oral arguments. Kennedy wondered whether walking arm in arm with colleagues to conference was now more about unsteadiness than charm.

Brennan knew his memory had slipped some. He forgot details about telephone calls or scheduled meetings and he no longer could instantly recall the correct names of past cases. He also found it more difficult to bounce back from illnesses. In March 1990, Brennan came down with what seemed to be flu, but turned out to be a more serious, prolonged bronchial infection. Doctors had difficulty identifying the right medication for him. On the advice of his doctors, who said he was wearing himself out, he canceled a number of speeches and plans to visit Ireland and to teach in Austria. Asked to deliver a tribute for Justice Arthur Goldberg at the Labor Department in April 1990, Brennan recycled whole passages from a 1975 eulogy he had given for his friend Robert Silvercruys.

But Brennan could still marshal his strength and skills when he put his mind to it. As he recovered from his bronchial infection in late March, 1990, the Court considered *Metro Broadcasting Inc. v. FCC,* which consolidated challenges to a pair of affirmative action policies adopted by the Federal Communications Commission. In one, the U.S. Court of Appeals for the District of Columbia Circuit upheld the FCC's policy of giving preference for broadcast licenses to minority-owned companies. Although Congress did not originate the policy, the Appeals Court was persuaded that Congress had approved of it in a series of actions after the fact, including by barring the FCC's efforts to reconsider the minority-preference policy in 1988. In the second appeal, a different three-judge panel of the D.C. Circuit held unconstitutional an FCC affirmative action policy. The policy allowed broadcast companies that face revocation of their licenses to avoid total loss by selling their stations in a distress sale to a minority-owned business. The Appeals Court said the policy violated the guarantee of equal protection implicit in the Fifth Amendment.

Brennan had good reason to be pessimistic about the likely fate of the FCC's programs. In the 1988–89 term, the conservative majority succeeded in requiring that affirmative action plans adopted by state and local governments meet the "strict scrutiny" test, the highest level of scrutiny under the Fourteenth Amendment's equal protection clause. That ruling, in *City of Richmond v. J. A. Croson Co.,* was a significant setback for affirmative action, requiring a compelling interest to justify plans that set aside a percentage of public contracts for minority-owned businesses. By a 6–3 vote, the Court ruled in an opinion by O'Connor that Richmond had not adequately justified the need for its 30 percent set-aside of subcontracts for businesses awarded city contracts. Brennan joined dissents by Marshall and Blackmun.

The prospects for Brennan looked equally bleak in this pair of FCC cases. The Reagan administration looked with disfavor at this sort of set-aside policy first adopted by President Carter. Although the Supreme Court had upheld Congress's authority to designate that 10 percent of a federal works program be set aside for minority contracts, Congress had only ratified the FCC program after the fact rather than authorized it by statute. And while a majority of the Court in the *Croson* case appeared to say that set-aside programs had to be narrowly targeted to help specific, well-documented victims of past discrimination, the FCC had used broadcast diversity rather than remedying past discrimination as the rationale.

Brennan believed the FCC policies should be upheld no matter what level of scrutiny was applied, since they were aimed at correcting the long-standing underrepresentation of minorities in the broadcast field, as well as at promoting programming diversity. His clerks thought Brennan would find it difficult to convince four other justices to agree, although he remained optimistic. He returned to his chambers after the justices' March 30 conference and went right into his office to have lunch alone at his desk, as he did most days, without providing his clerks any clues about what had transpired. Brennan was in a playful mood when his law clerks went in after lunch to be debriefed. He told them that the decision was 5–4 but refused to tell them which way. After much teasing, Brennan finally revealed that the majority had voted to uphold the FCC policies. As Brennan recapped the conference events to his clerks, he revealed that the pivotal vote was White.

White had passed initially, but then broke a 4–4 tie, saying that although it was a "tough" case for him, Congress and the FCC had acted within their authority. That meant Brennan, White, Marshall, Blackmun, and Stevens all favored upholding the FCC policies, while Rehnquist, O'Connor, Scalia, and Kennedy voted against. The chief justice's dissent meant that Brennan, as senior associate justice in the majority, would decide who should write the opinion. The law clerks strongly urged Brennan to assign the opinion to White, the least committed justice. Brennan, however, was just as adamant; he intended to keep the opinion for himself. He wanted to stem the damage to affirmative action caused by the *Croson* decision and thought he could best accommodate White. He also realized that his opportunities to write important majority opinions were waning.

Brennan dispatched his clerks to learn what kind of opinion might satisfy White and then directed them to draft the opinion accordingly. In his first circulation on May 31, Brennan indicated he was prepared for the first time to accept that the use of racial classifications must be subjected to "strict scrutiny," the most rigorous test under the equal protection clause, even when the purpose of the classification is benign rather than discriminatory. This was a reluctant concession to the *Croson* decision, since strict scrutiny is a high bar to overcome. Brennan had little choice, since both White and Stevens had joined the *Croson* majority. While he had emphasized the remedial nature of affirmative action in previous decisions, in *Metro* Brennan emphasized that "the objective of enhancing broadcast diversity" is sufficient to satisfy the strict-scrutiny test.

While Marshall immediately joined Brennan's opinion, White notified his colleagues on June 5, "I await further writing in this case." Brennan again dispatched a law clerk to see if he could learn anything about White's intentions. The clerk reported back that White might prefer a lower standard of review, something less rigorous than strict scrutiny. Brennan responded with a private memo he circulated only to White proposing to uphold the FCC programs under a lesser legal standard. When White received Brennan's note, he went to see Brennan in person. Brennan recounted to his clerks that White was worried less about what standard of scrutiny they applied than that the opinion explain more fully that the FCC had tried unsuccessfully to increase diversity through neutral, rather than racial, means. White wanted the decision to reflect his view, which he had expressed in a 1969 decision, *Red Lion Broadcasting Co. v. FCC*, that the FCC had a legal duty to promote diversity in broadcast programming to serve the public interest. This posed a problem for Brennan, who believed that the First Amendment limited the FCC's power to achieve this goal by meddling in the content and programming decisions of broadcasters.

BUT BRENNAN WAS determined not to squander this opportunity to further cement the validity of affirmative action. Concerned that White might decide to draft his own opinion and deprive Brennan of his majority, Brennan had his clerks go to work quickly on a new draft. They scrapped the strict-scrutiny standard and substituted a less demanding test. The new draft also included a lengthy discussion of how diversity benefits all "members of the viewing and listening audience" rather than just minorities. O'Connor complained in a June 18 memo that she would need time to rewrite her dissent because of Brennan's "surprisingly extensive" changes.

On June 18, Marshall and Blackmun both said they supported Brennan's second draft. Stevens also weighed in that day, asking Brennan in a memo to make clear that Congress had the power to adopt race-based programs for a range of benign reasons, even when the aim isn't to remedy past discrimination. With this change readily made, Stevens joined on June 19 and Brennan had four votes. Later that day, White also joined Brennan's opinion, making a majority. Brennan was jubilant, recognizing the significance of having five justices all sign a single affirmative action decision that limited the scope of the *Croson* decision. "So we got Byron," he exclaimed, marching into the part of his chambers where his law clerk Jonathan Massey sat. Brennan gave two of his law clerks money to splurge and buy doughnuts to celebrate the next day over morning coffee.

With just a few days left until the end of the 1989–90 term, patience was wearing thin among the tired justices and law clerks, as is often the case in June. O'Connor aggravated Brennan by making several out-of-town trips in mid- and late June, asking that the *Metro Broadcasting* decision not be announced until the last day of the term, June 27, instead of June 25 when it was originally scheduled. O'Connor, in turn, appeared unhappy at the wholesale changes Brennan had made between his first and second draft, especially regarding the level of scrutiny. She circulated a second draft of her dissent on June 21, concluding that the FCC programs could not withstand even the reduced level of scrutiny outlined by Brennan. That same day, Kennedy told his colleagues that he planned to write his own dissent.

Kennedy likened the majority's support for "benign" policies based on race to South African apartheid, the internment of Japanese Americans during World War II, and the doctrine of "separate but equal" facilities endorsed by the Supreme Court until the *Brown v. Board of Education* decision in 1954. When Brennan saw Kennedy's dissent, one clerk recalled, he felt the analogy was "ludicrous" and that he should not let Kennedy get away with it. But since Brennan had the votes, he opted to respond with only a footnote: "We are confident that an examination of the legislative scheme and its history will separate benign measures from other types of racial classifications," he wrote. One day later, on June 27, Brennan surprised Court watchers with what soon proved to be his last victory.

22

"SO LONG, BILL"

B RENNAN WAS EXHAUSTED and ready for a vacation when his thirty-fourth term on the Court ended on June 27, 1990. He had heeded his doctors' advice and canceled a two-week teaching engagement at Innsbruck, Austria, and instead booked passage on a less physically taxing Scandinavian cruise with Mary. But as they prepared to board their flight to Copenhagen at Newark International Airport on June 30, Brennan fell and hit his head. They managed to get on the plane with the help of airline staff. But Brennan remained weak during their two-day stopover in Copenhagen and he spent much of the two-week cruise in bed in his cabin. By the time the cruise ended in England, Mary told a friend who met them at the airport there, "Bill is going to be coming off the Court."

Brennan, who had ended the term intent on returning to the Court in the fall, remained undecided when he spoke to his son Bill upon returning to Washington on Tuesday, July 17. But two days later, his doctor, Capitol physician Robert Krasner, warned Brennan that the fall in Newark was probably caused by a mild stroke and that more strokes were likely if he did not slow down. The stark message left Brennan badly shaken: he could preserve his health or stay a justice but he could not do both. Early the next morning, on Friday, July 20, Brennan called his three children and told them he felt he had little choice but to retire. He then headed to the Capitol with Mary for another consultation with his doctor to make sure he really did have no other option.

The mood was somber when Brennan returned to his chambers to mull when to announce his retirement. His four new clerks—including the first African American clerk he had ever hired—were scheduled to begin work three days later, and he wanted to give them the news himself. He decided to keep his decision a secret over the weekend and to make the announcement on the Monday after he could meet with his new clerks face-to-face. Brennan prepared a brief statement for the media and drafted a letter to President George H. W. Bush, which he intended to sign on Monday. He opted not to inform any of his colleagues, except for Thurgood Marshall, whom he called at home on Friday. The news bitterly disappointed Marshall, who shocked Brennan by hanging up on him. Fittingly, the last vote Brennan cast had been with Marshall the previous day—a dissent from the Court's refusal to stay the execution of Richard Boggs, who had died Thursday night in Virginia's electric chair.

Brennan went home Friday afternoon hopeful that his announcement would remain a secret until Monday. But a *Washington Post* reporter soon called the Court's public information director, Toni House, asking about Brennan's plans. His clerks suspected the leak came from someone at the Senate Judiciary Committee, where Marshall's son, Thurgood Jr. (Goody), worked as an attorney. Later that afternoon, National Public Radio's Nina Totenberg called Brennan at home.

The fact that Totenberg was on the line did not surprise Mary, who answered the telephone. Despite his initial aloofness in the 1970s, Brennan and Totenberg had developed a close friendship. She had invited Brennan and Mary to her house for dinner, and he had recommended her for membership in one of Washington's elite social institutions, the Cosmos Club. Brennan visited Totenberg's husband in the hospital when he was sick, and when Brennan had his gallbladder removed in 1988, she wrote him a note saying, "We all have been feeling as if a member of the family were sick." As Totenberg later characterized their relationship in a tribute to Brennan, "It's not an easy friendship because each of you must recognize that the other has a job to do that may well be at odds with yours." That Friday, Mary had thought she was talking to Totenberg as a friend when she confided in her about Brennan's fall, his meetings with his doctor, and his decision to retire. So Mary was upset when Totenberg indicated she was going on the air to report his retirement, even after they implored her to wait until Monday.

The leaks left Brennan scrambling to move up his announcement. Two of his law clerks — Evan Caminker and Jonathan Massey — headed to his Arlington, Virginia, apartment with a new version of his retirement letter dated for that day, Friday, July 20, and then struggled to find someone at the White House willing to take the signed copy from them. Brennan cited the "strenuous demands" of the job in his resignation letter. President Bush, traveling back from a trip to Montana and Wyoming, received Brennan's letter aboard Air Force One. Bush called Brennan to accept his resignation and to thank him for his service. Brennan had less success reaching all of his new clerks. Several learned of his retirement via media reports, as did Brennan's fellow justices, who were scattered around the country and across the globe for their summer vacations. Blackmun heard the news on the radio while driving in northern Wisconsin and spent the rest of the ride pondering the impact of Brennan's departure on the Court.

The tributes began pouring in immediately from friends, fellow judges, and lawyers, and the public at large. Massachusetts senator Edward Kennedy said Brennan "earned an extraordinary place in American history and American constitutional law." Newspaper editorials praised Brennan as among the most influential justices of the twentieth century. The *San Francisco Examiner* labeled him as "one of the greatest justices ever to grace the United States Supreme Court, the Oliver Wendell Holmes, Jr. of his time." (Not all the press was positive: *National Review* groused, "The damage that William Brennan did may never be undone.") No one sounded more anguished about Brennan's retirement than Marshall. During an interview with ABC News in his chambers a few days later, Marshall lamented, "Brennan cannot be replaced."

By Monday, the spotlight had already shifted away from Brennan as President Bush announced that he intended to nominate as his successor David Souter, a little-known former state judge. Souter, a Rhodes scholar and graduate of Harvard Law School, had been New Hampshire's attorney general and a justice on the state Supreme Court before recently being named to the U.S. Court of Appeals for the First Circuit. The reality of retirement became harder for Brennan to accept as he slipped off the front page so quickly. Within days, he wondered aloud if he had made a mistake.

That sense of regret only intensified as time passed and the Court seemed to grow more conservative, although his deteriorating health made any thought of having continued as a justice increasingly unrealistic.

WHEN THE COURT'S new term began on October 1, 1990, Brennan sat in the audience for the first time since his swearing-in ceremony thirty-four years earlier, an experience he later described as heartbreaking. His colleagues honored him in the traditional ways, chipping in to buy him the leather chair he had sat in on the bench. Byron White and his wife organized a black-tie dinner in his honor on the eve of the new term in the Court's East Conference Room. But Brennan had to give up his first-floor chambers, and was relegated to a smaller, more isolated office on the second floor.

The invitations and honors continued to pile up. Many came from organizations such as the ACLU and the National Coalition to Abolish the Death Penalty, from which he could not accept honors during his tenure, since they were involved in issues that came before the Court. Brennan accepted an honorary degree from University College Dublin at a ceremony at the Irish Embassy attended by Senator Kennedy. (Brennan was soon to meet for the first time over lunch the other Irishman who had helped thwart the conservatives' advance of the previous decade, Tip O'Neill.) Nearly all of his 108 clerks — whose ranks eventually included several federal judges and deans of the nation's top law schools as well as a corporate CEO and a Republican cabinet member — gathered for his first postretirement reunion at the Court in January 1991. This time, the clerks did the talking, doing their best to avoid becoming too melancholy.

Brennan received invitations from several law schools to serve as a guest lecturer, which helped fill his otherwise empty schedule and augment his pension. He chose to begin his career as a part-time professor at the University of Miami in March 1991, thus fulfilling, at least partially, Mary's wish of retiring to a warmer climate. The school's dean, Mary Doyle, rolled out the red carpet for Brennan and Mary, providing an apartment in Coconut Grove, a car and driver, and nightly dinners. Brennan led a small seminar for a select group of students two times a week along with assistance from a member of the school's faculty and invited guests. Brennan also accepted the long-standing invitation from Georgetown University Law Center and lectured there in the fall of 1991. His old friend Charles E.

Smith, a real estate developer, helped further secure Brennan's financial future by forgiving $120,000 remaining on the mortgage to his condominium.

Brennan's cumulative health problems took an increasing toll. He had trouble keeping up with his teaching when he returned to the University of Miami in the winter of 1992 and relied more heavily on guest lecturers, such as his former clerks turned law professors, Owen Fiss and Frank Michelman. He sat as a judge just a single time, on a panel of the D.C. Circuit on November 22, 1991. Even on good days, his mind raced ahead of his ability to speak, and his memory was increasingly spotty. Brennan would not recall having talked to Nat Hentoff for an interview that ran in *Playboy* magazine. He developed a slow-growing form of prostate cancer, although his doctors opted against operating because the treatment risks were greater than the threat of the disease.

Brennan's decline was hard on Mary, who had never given up on her visions of an active retirement and plenty of travel. She had difficulty accepting that his stroke had left him weakened and occasionally confused. After decades of venerating Brennan the justice, she now found fault easily with Brennan the aging husband. They fought more often, occasionally requiring his son Bill's intervention. Having never had children, she had little experience as a caretaker and was not suited temperamentally for the role of tending to an aging, needy man. She had health problems of her own, undergoing treatment for cancer in 1993. To carve out some time for herself, she would prod him to go to the Court. After a few hours with little to do in his new chambers, he would call Mary and ask if he could come home yet. She usually told him to stay an hour or two longer.

While his marriage proved challenging after his retirement, Brennan developed an unexpectedly close friendship with his successor, David Souter. Souter, who had never met Brennan prior to his nomination, first wrote him in August 1990 to say he hoped to do so soon. He promised to "try to act with the integrity of principle that you have brought to the Court since the days when I was a boy in high school." Brennan wrote back a few days later, "I do hope that you will not hesitate to ask me for any help that I may be able to give you."

Souter had made a lasting impression on Brennan when the newest justice was asked about his predecessor's legacy during his confirmation hearing in September 1990. Souter predicted Brennan would be remembered as "one of the most fearlessly principled guardians the Constitution has had or will have." When they met for the first time in October after his confirmation, Souter expected a warm handshake and instead got one of Brennan's typically warm bear hugs. "Justice Brennan just threw his arms around me and he hugged me and hugged me and went on hugging me for a very, very long time," Souter recalled in a 1992 speech honoring Brennan.

As Souter emerged as a reliable vote for the Court's liberal wing, some wondered whether Brennan had brought his considerable powers of persuasion to bear one more time to cast some sort of liberal spell on his successor. Brennan and Souter certainly did develop an unusually warm bond. The two lunched together periodically, and Brennan came to look forward to regular visits with his more junior colleague as his health faded. While the public perception of Souter, a lifelong bachelor who returned each summer to his family's New Hampshire farmhouse, was that of a recluse, Brennan got to know him as a dedicated, thoughtful friend. But Souter insisted Brennan had little influence on his jurisprudence. "As fond as I was — and I was immensely fond of Bill Brennan — I did not take him as my model for how judging ought to be done," Souter said in 2007. Instead, Souter claimed as his inspiration one of Brennan's former colleagues, John Marshall Harlan.

What may have actually driven the friendship was Souter's deep appreciation of history. He did not have to agree with Brennan's general approach or his specific decisions to appreciate the enormity of his predecessor's impact. It was not empty praise when Souter inscribed a photograph of them both in 1991 by saying, "With a journeyman's homage to a master." As Souter said of Brennan's opinions at a 1992 tribute organized by the Harvard Club of Washington, "Their collective influence is an enormously powerful defining force in the contemporary life of this republic." He added, "The fact is that the sight and sound and thought of our contemporary world is in great measure the reflection of Justice Brennan's constitutional perceptions."

Brennan's admirers on the Court included another newcomer, Ruth Bader Ginsburg. When she was nominated by President Bill Clinton in 1993 to succeed the retiring Justice White, Brennan wrote her on June 15, 1993, "The President could not have made a better choice." She wrote back, "Dear Bill, I love you! Pray for me, Ruth." When Ginsburg wrote an impor-

542 · JUSTICE BRENNAN

tant gender-discrimination decision, she made sure to drop off a copy at
Brennan's chambers. So too did Blackmun come to see Brennan four days
before he announced a decision in February 1994 declaring, "From this day
forward, I no longer shall tinker with the machinery of death." Just as Brennan predicted, Blackmun had finally come around to the view that the
death penalty could never be constitutional. By then, Brennan was the last
surviving member of the Warren Court's liberal bloc. Thurgood Marshall
had died in early 1993, within a month of Brennan's other longtime ally and
friend, David Bazelon. After Marshall's funeral at the National Cathedral,
Brennan and Mary returned to the Court and paid one last poignant visit
to Marshall's chambers.

BRENNAN WAS LARGELY wheelchair-bound by the time he attended
his ninetieth birthday party at the Court on April 27, 1996. The event was
organized by the newly established Brennan Center for Justice, an activist
nonprofit organization founded at New York University thanks to contributions from his clerks. Brennan found it difficult to stand up to greet his
guests and required a few minutes' rest in his chambers during the celebration. His son Bill read his speech, which included another passionate invocation of "the constitutional ideal of human dignity," and one more plea to
abolish the death penalty. The speech, reprinted the next day on the op-ed
page of the New York Times, concluded, "If I have drawn one lesson in my
90 years, it is this: 'To strike another blow for freedom allows a man to
walk a little taller and raise his head a little higher. And while he can, he
must.'"

Seven months later, Brennan moved into a nursing home in Arlington,
Virginia, after falling and breaking his hip. His list of regular visitors
included Souter, Ginsburg, and Totenberg, whose singing Brennan particularly enjoyed. Brennan was still trading jokes with guests when his secretary Mary Elmore, his law clerk Paul Washington, and Carl Stern, the
former NBC Supreme Court reporter visited him on July 22, 1997. Two
days later, he died at the age of ninety-one with his wife, Mary, at his side.

On July 28, his flag-draped casket was carried up the front steps of the
U.S. Supreme Court past an honor guard of twenty-seven of his former
clerks into the Great Hall, the ornate atrium outside the courtroom. Sixty-
seven years after his father had lain in state in Newark's City Hall, Brennan's casket came to rest on the same catafalque that once held the body of

Abraham Lincoln. Justices Blackmun, Ginsburg, Stevens, White, and Clarence Thomas attended a private viewing before the doors were opened for the crowd of thousands waiting to pay their respects. Asked by a reporter why she stood in line, Tiffany Graham explained, "I am a woman. I am black. What more can I say?" Graham, a Justice Department paralegal about to start law school that fall, added, "I wouldn't have the advantages I have now. He was truly an American hero." That night, family members and former clerks gathered in one of the Court's ceremonial conference rooms for a private courthouse wake.

The next morning, a long list of dignitaries led by President Clinton filled St. Matthew's Cathedral in downtown Washington for Brennan's funeral. While many of the justices interrupted their summer vacations and returned to Washington for the occasion, neither O'Connor nor Chief Justice Rehnquist attended. In his introductory remarks, Brennan's friend Father Milton Jordan said that Brennan had ordered him not to let his funeral get too depressing. "Remember, I'm Irish," Jordan recalled Brennan telling him. Brennan's friend Father Jack O'Hara delivered the homily, and his son Bill, President Clinton, and Souter offered eulogies. "How do we say farewell to the man who made us out to be better than we were?" Souter asked. "I can only say it the way I learned it from him. When I'd see him in his chambers and it was time to go, I'd turn when I got to the door and look back. He'd say, 'So long, pal,' and I'd give him a wave and say, 'So long, Bill.'"

Outside St. Matthew's, a small group of antiabortion demonstrators protested against Brennan being allowed a Catholic funeral Mass. Even in death, Brennan could not escape criticism for his decision in *Roe*. Some mourners might have been upset at the interruption, Ginsburg later observed, but she concluded that Brennan would have replied, "Let him speak."

After a three-gun salute, Justice Brennan was buried later that day next to Marjorie at Arlington National Cemetery, in a plot near Thurgood Marshall and William Douglas. Hugo Black, Earl Warren, and Arthur Goldberg also found their final resting place at Arlington.

UNTIL THE END, Brennan maintained a modest public posture when talking about his accomplishments. In a speech delivered by his son Bill at his ninetieth birthday, in 1996, Brennan insisted, "There is no 'Brennan legacy' that can be teased out and considered on its own merits," and, "the strides we made on the Court during my tenure we made as a team."

Brennan was more candid in private, confidently predicting he had built up a considerable legacy that would be difficult to undo. "They're not going to unstitch the extension of the Bill of Rights against the states — that is the most important thing I can guess will not happen," Brennan said in 1988. "They're not going to unstitch Baker and Carr . . . They're not going to unstitch affirmative action." As for *Roe v. Wade*, Brennan predicted, "I think it'll be cut back a good deal, but I do not think it'll be overruled. Now let's see how good a prophet I am."

Brennan proved prescient about the durability of many of the most significant decisions he authored or helped craft behind the scenes. To be sure, some were subsequently chipped away. Both the Court and Congress, for example, have moved away from Brennan's vision of habeas corpus as a means to provide meaningful review of state criminal justice systems. The wall he helped erect of separation between church and state is no longer as high. The trend toward making it more difficult to use race as a factor in government decision-making only accelerated after Brennan's death, and the Court has all but abandoned its attempts to desegregate the nation's schools. And although the Court subsequently imposed some limits on the death penalty, Brennan's ultimate goal of abolishing it as cruel and unusual punishment remains elusive.

Nonetheless, a remarkable number of his landmark decisions remain intact and at the core of many areas of constitutional law. "The extent to which the Brennan legacy remains a force in American life and law after so many years" was something that *New York Times* Supreme Court reporter Linda Greenhouse labeled "quite remarkable" shortly after Brennan's death in 1997, and still held true more than a decade later. Because of Brennan, the government remains more accountable both at the ballot box and in courtrooms, where citizens can sue for wrongs committed and damage caused. Brennan's decisions continue to protect vigorous — and sometimes unpopular — free speech such as flag burning. He expanded the scope of the Bill of Rights, a permanent legacy, by helping apply most of the provisions to the states. And he helped redefine the meaning of equality under the Fourteenth Amendment's equal protection clause. Brennan took the Preamble to the Constitution's "We the people" and, in the words of Ruth Bader Ginsburg, made the "'we' an ever larger group" by expanding the rights of minorities and women. Even Antonin Scalia, not a fan of much of what Brennan accomplished, called him "probably the most influential justice of the century."

Brennan was the right person at a particular moment in the history of the Court and the nation. He was young and Catholic at a time when President Eisenhower most sought those characteristics in a Court nominee. He was a progressive centrist and well-suited temperamentally to the role of strategist at a time when Earl Warren was looking for a judicial partner to help bring about a revolution in constitutional law and American society more generally. Brennan served at a time when a solid bloc of justices and most liberals around the country were comfortable with the Court creating new rights and vigorously inserting itself into the nation's schools and police interrogation rooms — and ejecting itself from the bedroom.

Brennan was extraordinarily successful in building coalitions — even if that sometimes meant sacrificing clarity in the process — by accommodating his fellow justices' concerns. But he could not have created those coalitions without colleagues willing to be persuaded. Even the master tactician Brennan could not have accomplished much if he had shared the bench with eight Antonin Scalias. And although he retained his skills as a master strategist and consensus builder long after his closest allies had retired, he was also at times shortsighted and self-defeating in dissent. He clung to extremist positions that alienated centrist colleagues and, as in the case of the death penalty, generated a public backlash that resulted in the opposite of the outcome he wanted.

As with so much of Brennan's success during his tenure, the endurance of his precedents owes much to the unexpected voting habits of his colleagues. He benefited from Sandra Day O'Connor's drift toward the center in the years after his departure and from Anthony M. Kennedy's brooding moderation. (Brennan might also have been surprised to discover that Kennedy succeeded him as the leading invoker of human dignity.) Whether he drifted leftward or the Court moved toward the right as he stood still, John Paul Stevens emerged as a key liberal during a tenure that ultimately lasted longer than Brennan's. Brennan's successor, David H. Souter, also stood firmly in the Court's liberal bloc.

Brennan remained a focus of liberal nostalgia when Souter retired in 2009. Liberals pined for a justice with Brennan's passion and powers of persuasion who could counterbalance the Court's most assertive voices on the right. Conservatives, in turn, continued to invoke Brennan as the kind of nominee they feared most. But although Brennan remained the very embodiment of a liberal justice across the ideological spectrum, there was a growing sense even among his fans that his unabashedly activist approach to judging belonged to a bygone era.

His notion of a living constitution to be adapted flexibly to contemporary circumstances seemed increasingly anachronistic. Conservatives had gained the upper hand in the public debate over the proper method of constitutional interpretation, although the originalism that Attorney General Edwin Meese advocated a quarter century earlier in his public debate with Brennan never took hold. Everyone, it seemed, had become an advocate — although perhaps not a practitioner — of judicial modesty. Many liberals openly questioned the wisdom of relying so heavily on the courts to bring about social change. They groped for a new way of talking about constitutional interpretation that could effectively counter conservatives' talk of judicial restraint.

No one better embodied the liberal ambivalence about Brennan's style of activism than President Barack Obama. As a candidate, Obama cited Brennan — along with Thurgood Marshall and Earl Warren — as "heroes of mine" but immediately added the caveat, "That doesn't mean that I think their judicial philosophy is appropriate for today." As president, Obama emphasized empathy — a characteristic so closely identified with Brennan — as something he wanted his nominee to possess. Yet Obama's first pick for the Court, Sonia Sotomayor, felt compelled, like all other recent nominees, to distance herself from Brennan's philosophy at her confirmation hearing.

A small reminder of Brennan's enduring significance came shortly after Sotomayor's arrival, when he was one of four justices honored posthumously by a new postage stamp series in September 2009. One of the other honorees that day was his professor and former colleague Felix Frankfurter, an irony that Brennan, although not necessarily Frankfurter, would have enjoyed. Brennan's two surviving children and three of his grandchildren attended the ceremony at the Court. (Brennan's widow, Mary, died in 2000 at the age of eighty-three, and his eldest son and namesake, Bill, died in 2004 at the age of seventy-one.) But if there comes a time when Brennan's name fades from memory, that, too, might have been fine with Brennan.

Brennan may well have offered his best insight about how he would like to be remembered before he joined the Supreme Court. It came at the end of his February 1954 Saint Patrick's Day speech in Boston, recalled later for its veiled attack on McCarthyism. Brennan recounted a story once told by a nineteenth-century Scottish comedian, Harry Lauder, of sitting at his window before the advent of electricity. Lauder watched as a lamplighter worked his way down the street, climbing his ladder to light each lamp before moving on to the next one. Eventually, the lamplighter was no longer visible, and the storyteller could see only the lamps he had lit. Brennan concluded his speech by saying:

> So it is, my friends, with you and me of Irish blood. As we go through life, may we be found lighting the lamps of truth and justice and righteousness, even as our Irish forebears before us, so that as time passes and we move from the scene of action, our own children and their children after them, though we be lost to view, may tell the way we went by the lamps we lighted along life's pathway.

Authors' Note

I F THIS BOOK had a midwife, it was Abner Mikva, the federal judge and former congressman whom Stephen Wermiel got to know while covering the Supreme Court for the *Wall Street Journal*. Over breakfast in early 1986, Mikva asked whether Steve had ever thought of writing a book about the Supreme Court, and suggested he might be able to convince Justice Brennan to cooperate in a biography. That led to a meeting with Brennan in April, shortly before his eightieth birthday, where the justice expressed interest and suggested meeting again toward the end of the Court term.

Steve expected he would have to sell Brennan on the idea of participating in a biography when they met a second time in June 1986. But Brennan had already made up his mind that he wanted to cooperate with a biographer, and he liked the idea of working with a journalist-lawyer, who he hoped could make the resulting book accessible to a broad audience. So Brennan readily agreed to what would be the first of more than sixty recorded interviews conducted in his chambers over the course of the next five years.

The project was a secret at first, since Brennan said he did not want it to affect his working relationship with his colleagues on the Court. Steve told only his editors at the *Wall Street Journal* about the project. Knowing that

Brennan arrived early at the Court, Steve arranged to visit his chambers at 7:30 A.M. before the building opened for the day. Some days Brennan sat for an interview, but on many others Steve sifted through tens of thousands of pages of records in the justice's office. On a few occasions, Steve sat in when Brennan met with his law clerks in the morning over coffee and when he prepared for oral argument by going over the cases with his clerks.

Brennan granted Steve unrestricted access to his case files, including draft opinions and memos exchanged among the justice as well as his speeches, articles, and personal correspondence. Brennan facilitated access to the thousands of files he had donated to the Library of Congress, and later gave Steve copies of the narrative term histories, or case studies, prepared by his law clerks. Brennan encouraged members of his family and law clerks to cooperate, and more than 100 of the 108 clerks who served in his chambers while he was a sitting justice agreed to be interviewed.

Although this may be considered an "authorized" biography, Brennan promised not to exercise editorial control over the content, and he never tried to do so. Brennan did express a desire that the book not be published during his lifetime without his OK, to avoid potential conflict with other justices.

Steve asked Brennan for some advanced warning if he planned to retire. But he, like so many others, did not find out about Brennan's abrupt decision until the morning of the announcement in July 1990. While Steve tried to retain an arm's-length approach to his personal relationship with Brennan, he did help the justice draft a retirement letter and statement in July 1990, and he agreed to serve with a Brennan family member as coexecutor of the Brennan papers at the Library of Congress.

In subsequent years, Steve continued conducting research and completed a few draft chapters of the book as well as some encyclopedia entries on Brennan and law review articles on his selection as a justice and conception of human dignity. But he largely put the project aside in the years after Brennan's death in 1997.

Steve sought out another journalist-lawyer to coauthor the book, and Seth Stern joined in that capacity in 2006. Seth spent a year organizing and taking notes on the massive amounts of material Steve had accumulated and conducting additional research. He explored new archival materials not accessible at the time Steve began working on the book, including the papers of Justices Harry Blackmun and Lewis Powell and Ruth Bader Ginsburg's files from her tenure at the American Civil Liberties Union.

Seth reinterviewed many of Brennan's clerks and members of his family and conducted additional interviews while pursuing new angles. Seth conducted most of the interviews after 2006 that are cited in the book. He and Steve conducted joint interviews with Justices Ruth Bader Ginsburg, Sandra Day O'Connor, and David Souter, whom they interviewed in the justices' chambers at the Court, and with Father Jack O'Hara. Seth turned to writing in 2007 and is responsible for drafting most of the chapters.

Wherever possible, we have tried to confirm the version of events Brennan offered in his interviews with Steve with other sources and we have noted where those accounts differ. We have used the term histories prepared by Brennan's clerks judiciously; while they are a rich source of detail, the histories also have shortcomings as history, a fact that we discuss in the book.

Acknowledgments

WHILE WE CANNOT acknowledge individually everyone who agreed to be interviewed for this book, we would particularly like to thank the thirteen Supreme Court justices, the more than one hundred Brennan clerks, and the many members of Justice Brennan's family whose insights and recollections made this book possible.

To the many professors who provided tutorials on questions about law, the workings of the Supreme Court, the ins and outs of judicial biography, Catholic social thought, the concept of human dignity, and the history of the Irish in America: Terry Anderson, Stuart Banner, Harlan Beckley, Davison Douglas, Mary Doyle, Lee Epstein, Richard Fallon, Jo Renee Formicola, Eric Freedman, James Gardner, David Garrow, John Garvey, Michael Gerhardt, Maxine Goodman, Leslie Griffin, Rick Halperin, Richard Hasen, Morton Horwitz, Dennis Hutchinson, Gregory Kalscheur, Kevin Kenny, Michael Klarman, Donald Kommers, Sanford Levinson, Goodwin Liu, Jeffrey Lubbers, Paul Marcus, Richard McBrien, John McGreevy, Michael Meyer, Paul Moreno, Michael Naughton, Bruce Nelson, Burt Neuborne, Gary Orfield, Barbara Perry, Justin Poche, Nelson Potter, Scot Powe, Dermot Quinn, Mary Radford, Neomi Rao, Ira Robbins, Robert Schapiro, Fred Schauer, Reva Siegel, Michael Solimine, G. Alan Tarr, Leslie Woodcock Tentler, Mark Tushnet, Melvin Urofsky, John Wefing, Robert F. Williams, Wendy Webster Williams, and David Yalof.

A special thanks to Diane Dunnigan for her assistance in locating Brennan family genealogical records and for her knowledge of the history of County Roscommon. For help in learning more about Newark and the stationary firemen: Liz Del Tufo, George Francisco, Thomas P. Giblin, Edward Lewinson, Brendan O'Flaherty, Terri Seuss, and Brad Tuttle. And a special thanks to Michael Steinhorn for a tour of Rumson and Annie Von Arx for a tour of Brennan's former home there.

We benefited from assistance from many librarians and archivists including Jane Eigenrauch at the Red Bank Public Library, George Hawley at the Newark Public Library's Charles F. Cummings New Jersey Information Center, the reference staff of the Catherwood Library at Cornell University's School of Industrial and Labor Relations, Regine Heberlein at Princeton University's Seeley G. Mudd Manuscript Library, John Jacob at the Washington and Lee University School of Law, Mark Frazier Lloyd at the University of Pennsylvania's Archives and Records Center, Peter Lysy at the University of Notre Dame Archives, William Peniston at the Newark Museum, Edward Small at the Newark Public Library's Vailsburg branch, Jordon Steele at the University of Pennsylvania Law School, David Warrington of the Harvard Law School Library, the District of Columbia Public Library's Washingtoniana Division, the Harvard University Archives, and particularly the staff of the manuscript room of the Library of Congress, including Daun van Ee, David Wigdor, the late Mary Wolfskill, and Jeff Flannery. In addition, the staffs of the law libraries at William and Mary Law School, Georgia State University Law School, and American University Washington College of Law provided invaluable help.

At the Court, the Public Information Office was also helpful, especially the late Toni House, Kathy Arberg, and Ed Turner. The Supreme Court Police and the Marshal's Office assisted with the logistics of access to Justice Brennan's office. Court aide Ron Thongtavee also helped whenever he could. Jennifer Carpenter, Catherine Fitts, Franz Jantsen, and Lauren Morrell at the Supreme Court Curator's Office helped us find pictures of Justice Brennan.

Others who were instrumental in tracking down materials include Suzanna Artetta at the Harvard Legal Aid Bureau, Jan Cookerly at the University Club of Washington, D.C., Susan Lehman at the Brennan Center for Justice, Deborah Markowitz and Ginny Colbert, Cynthia Pellegrino at the New Jersey State Bar Foundation, Judge Joseph H. Rodriguez, Harry Sandick, Susan Travis, and Magistrate Judge Douglas Arpert of the U.S. District Court for the District of New Jersey, and Wendy Turman at the Jewish Historical Society of Greater Washington.

Seth would like to thank his editors at *Congressional Quarterly* — particularly Susan Benkelman, Anne Hoy, Mike Mills, and Mike Riley — for allowing him leave time to start writing and for the flexibility needed throughout this project. He also thanks Adeen Postar and the Washington College of Law's Pence Library for providing a workspace and research support.

Steve thanks Judge Abner Mikva, who took the first steps to make this book possible and provided much encouragement. Justice Brennan sat patiently for many hours of interviews, opened his office, staff, and files, and facilitated the cooperation of his many law clerks, who also shared memories, and of his second wife, Mary Fowler, and other family members. Justice Brennan's secretary, Mary Elmore, made access easy to all things Brennan and was never too busy to help, even in the most hectic moments of a Supreme Court term.

This effort was supported by Steve's editors at the *Wall Street Journal*, including former Washington bureau chief Al Hunt and former editor Norman Pearlstine. Bruce Sanford assisted in the formulation of the concept for the book. The book was encouraged by Tim Sullivan when he was dean of William and Mary Law School and Rod Smolla when he ran the Institute of Bill of Rights Law. Georgia State University Law School provided helpful research support. The Woodrow Wilson International Center for Scholars provided a valuable research year. And at American University Washington College of Law, Dean Claudio Grossman was consistently enthusiastic and supportive, and Program on Law and Government Director Jamin Raskin provided steady encouragement. The audiovisual staff at the Washington College of Law patiently burned numerous photographs onto disks.

Steve would also like to thank students and others who helped with research, transcribing interviews, and other projects related to this book. Most recently, Washington College of Law students Julia Altum and Scott Wise did yeoman's work making sure that the endnotes were accurate and in proper form. The full list, with apologies for any omissions, is: Cathy

Beckley, Pamela Corley, Kim Dammers, Diana Danzburger, Chris Davison, Samantha Dillon, Ashlea Ebeling, Karen Froslid, Arlene Griste, Jennifer Harmon, Linda Howell, Elizabeth Hyman, Karen (Hassinger) Milne, Nina Morrison, Donna Piccirillo, Jamie Richardson, Ann Robinson, Danielle Schonback, Daniel Scialpi, Sonya Spielberg, Glenn Verdi, and Alex Wohl.

For reading the manuscript in part or its entirety, John Bicknell, Laura Blinkhorn, Richard Carelli, Liriel Higa, Dennis Hutchinson, Ken Jost, Dan Marcus, Robert O'Neil, Keith Perine, Jim Rowley, Greg Stohr, Philippa Strum, and Mark Tushnet.

Gail Ross of the Gail Ross Literary Agency believed in this project and got us together with Deanne Urmy, our editor at Houghton Mifflin Harcourt, who was a supportive, enthusiastic, and sensitive editor. Nicole Angeloro kept many important details on track.

Seth Stern and Steve Wermiel
January 2010

Sources

BRENNAN PAPERS

Primary-source materials where the source is not otherwise identified were obtained from the papers of William J. Brennan Jr. Stephen Wermiel was granted access to all of Brennan's papers while they were housed in his chambers at the Supreme Court. Most draft opinions, memoranda between justices, and other case materials cited here are part of the Brennan papers open to the public at the Library of Congress. But some portions of Brennan's papers — including his personal correspondence — will remain closed until 2017. In addition, there are some other materials Wermiel had access to in Brennan's chambers that were not subsequently given to the Library of Congress by the justice and his family. Those materials are designated "WJB personal files." The designation "WJB scrapbook" refers to newspaper articles about Brennan pasted into a large scrapbook by Mary Fowler while she worked as Brennan's secretary. Wermiel photocopied the scrapbook.

The term histories prepared by Brennan and his clerks are identified by the nomenclature used at the Court to identify a term. So, for example, Brennan's final year on the Court, 1989–90, is formally referred to as October Term 1989; references in notes to the term history would be described as "OT '89 Term History," followed by the page number.

BRENNAN INTERVIEWS

Between 1986 and his retirement in 1990, Brennan sat for some sixty hours of interviews with Stephen Wermiel. These interviews are identified with Brennan's initials, the date, and the page number of the resulting transcript, so, for example, "WJB interview, Nov. 21, 1986 (6-26)" is interview six on November 21, 1986, with the cite referring to page 26 of the transcript. Copies of the transcripts remain in the possession of the authors.

OTHER PAPERS

Other papers are cited using the following shorthand (papers at the Library of Congress are housed in the Manuscript Division in Washington, D.C.):

Adams: Sherman Adams papers, Rauner Special Collections Library, Dartmouth College, Hanover, NH

AF: Abe Fortas papers, Sterling Memorial Library, Yale University Library, New Haven, CT

AG: Arthur Goldberg papers, Pritzker Legal Research Center, Northwestern University Law School, Chicago, IL

ATV: Arthur T. Vanderbilt papers, Wesleyan University, Middletown, CT

Bazelon: David L. Bazelon papers, Biddle Law Library, University of Pennsylvania Law School, Philadelphia, PA

DDE: Dwight D. Eisenhower Presidential Library, Abilene, KS

EW: Earl Warren papers, Library of Congress

FF: Felix Frankfurter papers; portions housed at Harvard Law School and Library of Congress are designated HLS and LOC, respectively.

Freund: Paul Freund papers, Harvard Law School, Cambridge, MA

Griswold: Erwin Griswold papers, Harvard Law School, Cambridge, MA

HAB: Harry A. Blackmun papers, Library of Congress

Hesburgh: Theodore Hesburgh papers, Hesburgh Libraries, University of Notre Dame, South Bend, IN

HHB: Harold H. Burton papers, Library of Congress

HLB: Hugo L. Black papers, Library of Congress

JMH: John Marshall Harlan, Seeley G. Mudd Manuscript Library, Princeton University, Princeton, NJ

LFP: Lewis F. Powell papers, William C. Hall Law Library, Washington and Lee Law School, Lexington, VA

RBG: Ruth Bader Ginsburg ACLU papers, Library of Congress

TC: Tom Clark papers, Tarlton Law Library, University of Texas Law School, Austin, TX

TM: Thurgood Marshall papers, Library of Congress

WOD: William O. Douglas papers, Library of Congress

OTHER SHORTHAND

In addition to the initials used in the notes to identify justices' papers, the following shorthand references are used for other justices:

AMK: Anthony M. Kennedy

AS: Antonin Scalia

BRW: Byron R. White

DHS: David H. Souter

JPS: John Paul Stevens
PS: Potter Stewart
SOC: Sandra Day O'Connor
WEB: Warren E. Burger
WHR: William H. Rehnquist

NEWSPAPER ABBREVIATIONS

BG: Boston Globe
CT: Chicago Tribune
LAT: Los Angeles Times
NEN: Newark Evening News
NPL collection: articles obtained from newspaper clip files maintained by the Charles F. Cummings New Jersey Information Center at the Newark Public Library where dates, bylines, and page numbers were sometimes unavailable.
NYHT: New York Herald Tribune
NYT: New York Times
RBR: Red Bank Register
WP: Washington Post
WSJ: Wall Street Journal

Notes

PROLOGUE: LAST SURPRISE

xi largely unchanged: Tony Mauro, "With Remarkable Swiftness, an Era Ends," *Legal Times*, Aug. 6, 1990.
might have looked: Lynn Rosellini, "The Most Powerful Liberal in America," *U.S. News & World Report*, Jan. 8, 1990, 27.

xii The six decisions: the other cases decided that day were five in which Brennan dissented: *Lewis v. Jeffers*, 497 U.S. 764 (1990), *Lujan v. Nat'l Wildlife Fed'n*, 497 U.S. 871 (1990), *Maryland v. Craig*, 497 U.S. 836 (1990), *United States v. Kokinda*, 497 U.S. 720 (1990), and *Walton v. Arizona*, 497 U.S. 639 (1990); and one in which Brennan was in the majority, *Idaho v. Wright*, 497 U.S. 805 (1990).
upholding the constitutionality: *Metro Broadcasting Inc. v. FCC*, 497 U.S. 547 (1990).
severely limited: *City of Richmond v. J. A. Croson Co.*, 488 U.S. 469 (1989).

1. BILL'S SON

3 estimated forty thousand: *Newark Star-Eagle*, "Whole City Mourns at Brennan Funeral," May 17, 1930; *NYT*, "Planes Drop Flowers on Brennan Cortege," May 18, 1930; *NEN*, "Newark Pays Last Honors to Brennan," May 17, 1930.
rushed home: WJB interview, Dec. 14, 1987 (26-4).

4 "Dad's reputation": Daniel J. O'Hern, *Brennan and Weintraub: Two Stars to Guide Us*, 46 Rutgers L. Rev. 1050 (1994).
Born on: Frenchpark Roman Catholic Parish Records, vol. 1, entry 538.

5 Trouble in: John T. Cumbler, *A Social History of Economic Decline: Business, Politics, and Work in Trenton* (New Brunswick, NJ: Rutgers University Press, 1989), 2; pottery

industry: John H. Sines, *A History of Trenton 1679–1929* (Trenton, NJ: Trenton Historical Society, 1929).

boosted the city's population: John T. Cunningham, *Newark* (Newark: New Jersey Historical Society, 1966), 199.

crowded into: William D. Price, *The Ironbound District* (Newark, NJ: Neighborhood House, 1912).

6 ascend toward: Rudoph J. Vecoli, *The People of New Jersey* (Princeton, NJ: Van Nostrand, 1965), 86–87; Kevin Kenny, "Labor and Labor Organizations," in *Making the Irish American*, ed. J. J. Lee and Marion R. Casey (New York: New York University Press, 2006), 358–60.

licorice factory: *Newark Sunday Call*, "Chips of the Old Blocks," Oct. 22, 1939. A 1957 profile incorrectly reported that the licorice factory was located in Trenton. Jack Alexander, "Mr. Justice from Jersey," *Saturday Evening Post*, Sept. 28, 1957.

Bill boarded: Elizabeth McFadden, "Brennan's Rise Included War Service," *NEN*, Feb. 10, 1952.

alternative account: Alexander, "Mr. Justice from Jersey." Brennan recounted the former version of the story in a 1990 interview. Sean O. Murchu, "Lone Justice," *Irish America*, June 1990, 27.

7 poorly run: Charles L. Whipple, "The Brennan Family Story," *BG*, Oct. 7, 1956.

displayed the qualities: "We Mourn Our Loss," 30 Firemen and Oilers' J. 1 (1930).

flagged down: Whipple, "The Brennan Family Story."

three different rentals: *Newark, City Directories of the United States* (Woodbridge, CT: Primary Source Microfilm).

8 playful postcard: provided to authors by Brennan family.

sat behind: Senate Committee on Finance, *Hearings on H.R. 4412: An Act to Promote Reciprocal Trade Relations with the Dominion of Canada*, 62nd Cong., 1st sess. (1911), 907 (statement of Mr. Timothy Healey, President of International Brotherhood of Stationary Firemen).

acutely aware: WJB interview, July 16, 1986 (1–11).

Willie Brennan: Herman Albert to WJB, Jan. 12, 1978. Albert recounted living on the same street as Brennan as a child.

bookworm: Katherine Brennan (WJB's sister) interview, Feb. 21, 1987.

only sparingly: WJB interview, Nov. 22, 1988 (47-1 to 47-2).

9 "He'd get himself": Ibid., pp. 4–5.

inches of slush: *NEN*, "Result of Parade Is Four Recruits," Apr. 10, 1916.

Union men retaliated: *Newark Star-Eagle*, "Nab Outsider for Hurling Stone at Car," Mar. 28, 1916; *NEN*, "Some Disorder Marks Course of Car 'Strike,'" Mar. 28, 1916.

finally granted: *Newark Star-Eagle*, Apr. 4, 1916, NPL collection.

secretary of the strike committee: *Newark Star-Eagle*, "Result of Parade Is Four Recruits."

elected president: *Newark Star-Eagle*, "Brennan New Head of Trades Council," Apr. 29, 1916.

bitter lesson: In his biography of Brennan, Kim Eisler writes that Brennan "witnessed his father being carried into the house by union brothers, bloodied and beaten by city police" during the trolley workers' strike and that "few events in his childhood affected him more." Kim Isaac Eisler, *A Justice for All: William J. Brennan, Jr., and the Decisions That Transformed America* (New York: Simon & Schuster, 1993), 19. There is no reference to such an attack in newspaper coverage of the strike and Brennan did not recall any such incident when asked in 1994. WJB interview, June 21, 1994. Nor did his sister Betty, who was born in 1913, remember ever hearing about such an incident while growing up.

palatable choice: Paul A. Stellhorn, "Depression and Decline: Newark, New Jersey: 1929–1944" (Ph.D. thesis, Rutgers University, 1982), 39.

10 overwhelmingly voted: *NEN,* "Newark Declares for Commission by Vote of 19,069 For, 6,053 Against," Oct. 10, 1917.

He pledged: *NEN,* "Vicious Saloons Must Go — Brennan," Jan. 6, 1918.

public drunkenness: *NEN,* "Won't Stand for Drunken Police," Jan. 1, 1918.

driving infraction: *NEN,* "Patrolman Arrests Motorist He Later Finds Is Brennan," Nov. 20, 1922.

chauffeur-driven car: In 1918 the city-owned car in which he was riding back from a New York dinner party struck and killed a forty-eight-year-old laborer, the father of a ten-month-old. The victim's widow sued Bill, along with the car's manufacturer and the driver, for $50,000, though the suit against him was dismissed. "Driver of Car in Fatal Accident Out on Bail," Mar. 1918, NPL collection; "Wife of Man Killed by Auto Sues Raymond and Brennan," Oct. 18, 1918, NPL collection. Kim Eisler writes, "Some believed that Brennan himself was at the wheel." Eisler, *Justice for All,* p. 21.

11 "A square deal": *NEN,* "Another Brennan Club Is Formed, Lithuanian Society for Brennan," Feb. 26, 1921; *NEN,* "Murray and Brennan Present Municipal Views," May 5, 1925.

earned the respect: William M. Ashby, *Tales without Hate* (Newark, NJ: Newark Preservation and Landmarks Committee, 1980), 87–88.

1906 book: John A. Ryan, *A Living Wage: Its Ethical and Economic Aspects* (New York: Macmillan, 1906).

"This was only": "No Apologies for Raising Pay in Department, Brennan States," Mar. 1921, NPL collection.

suppress the sale: *NEN,* "To Seek Ordinance as Magazine Curb, Brennan Declares," Mar. 12, 1925.

national crackdown: *NEN,* "Raid Approved by Brennan," Feb. 1929, NPL collection.

insult to the American flag: "Flag Insult Intolerable, Brennan Warns Police," Feb. 24, 1921, NPL collection.

William Z. Foster: American Civil Liberties Union, *Free Speech in 1924,* annual report (New York: ACLU, 1925), 25.

forbade a protest: *NEN,* "Brennan Forbids Meeting as Sacco-Vanzetti Protest," Nov. 28, 1921.

prohibited the showing: *NEN,* "Brennan Bans Hygiene Film," Oct. 14, 1926.

won praise: *NEN,* "Brennan Bans Hygiene Film."

12 issued an injunction: *Public Welfare Pictures Corp. v. Brennan,* 134 A. 868 (N.J. Ch. 1926).

place apart: John T. Cunningham, "Vailsburg Section of Newark Had Its Roots in the Ironbound," *Newark Sunday News,* Feb. 27, 1949.

newcomers were city workers: John T. Cunningham, "Vailsburg Section Is Home of City's 'White Collar' Workers," *Newark Sunday News,* Mar. 6, 1949; *Newark Sunday Call,* "Vailsburg Marks Twenty Five Years of Progress," Dec. 29, 1929; *Newark Sunday Call,* "City Employees Find Vailsburg Ideal for Home," Dec. 29, 1929.

Bill subscribed: Murchu, "Lone Justice," p. 27.

papal infallibility: Judi Brennan interview, Apr. 18, 2009. Judi is the daughter of Brennan's brother Frank.

Agnes bought: Murchu, "Lone Justice," p. 27.

closely associated: Margaret Lynch-Brennan, "Ubiquitous Bridget: Irish American Women in Domestic Service in America, 1840–1930," in *Making the Irish American,* ed. Lee and Casey, p. 333.

13 "the kind of family": WJB interview, Apr. 7, 1990 (60-27).

"an agony": WJB, oral history interview by Anthony Lewis, May 14, 1992. Federal Judicial Center.

happier memories: Ibid.

big ambitions: One of Brennan's classmates was Joseph Weintraub, the son of Russian Jewish immigrants, who succeeded him on the New Jersey Supreme Court and later became chief justice.

spending money: *BG*, "Justice Never Tough, Yet Never Hedges," Oct. 11, 1956.

developed a taste: Helen Brennan Mott (WJB's sister) interview, Feb. 21, 1987.

14 remembered reading: Jean Campbell, "Irish Roots in Jersey Soil," *Suburban Life*, Oct. 1959, 45; the statement was made by Betty Kirkwood Brennan, who married Brennan's brother Frank.

She cooked: Betty Brennan Buerck (WJB's sister) interview, Feb. 21, 1987.

torch-lit parades: *NEN*, "Parades and Much Noise Set Record for Celebrations of Eve of Primary," Apr. 20, 1921.

man of the people: Brad R. Tuttle, *How Newark Became Newark* (New Brunswick, NJ: Rivergate Books, 2009), 96.

hosting picnics: *NYT*, "Picnic Holds Up Traffic," Sept. 9, 1928.

bought ads: Stellhorn, "Depression and Decline," p. 41.

also reached out: *Pittsburgh Courier*, "Newark NJ," Jan. 31, 1925.

15 assured a gathering: *NEN*, "Liquor Interests Are Not Dejected," Jan. 21, 1918.

proved unpopular: Stellhorn, "Depression and Decline," pp. 37–38.

rooftop sign: Cunningham, *Newark*, p. 276.

insinuating that: *NEN*, "Asserts 'Higher Ups' Balk Newark Police," Jan. 23, 1925. One Anti-Saloon League leader told a YWCA audience that Commissioner Brennan "feels more at home in the saloon than anywhere else."

heckled Bill: *NEN*, "Brennan Asks Time on Demand to Quit," Feb. 2, 1922.

16 "I saw what": WJB interview, May 30, 1990 (63-10).

most American Catholic students: Thomas J. Shelley, "Twentieth-Century American Catholicism and Irish Americans," in *Making the Irish American,* ed. Lee and Casey, p. 595.

Bill had other ideas: WJB interview, June 6, 1988 (39-4 to 39-5); Alexander, "Mr. Justice from Jersey," incorrectly asserts "there was no dispute about colleges."

side of Wall Street: WJB interview, June 6, 1988 (39-4 to 39-5).

convinced Bill: Charles L. Whipple, "How Bostonians Played Part in Career of New Justice," *BG*, Oct. 9, 1956.

designed to evoke: George Erazmus Nitzsche, *University of Pennsylvania: Its History, Traditions, Buildings and Memorials* (Philadelphia: International Printing Company, 1918).

17 yearbook picture: U.S. Supreme Court Office of the Curator's photo collection.

custom-made suits: WJB interview, June 10, 1987 (18-6).

a cotillion: WJB interview, May 27, 1987 (16-6). Marjorie recalled that they met that December at a tea dance at the Washington Restaurant; see Josephine Bonomo, "Mrs. Brennan Up in Clouds," *NEN*, Oct. 7, 1956.

struck by lightning: *NYT*, "Hugh Leonard Killed," July 10, 1914.

an orphan: Alexander, "Mr. Justice from Jersey."

18 writing Marjorie: None of those letters survived in Brennan's files.

She visited Philadelphia: WJB interview, May 27, 1987 (16-8).

seemed uncomfortable: Katherine Brennan interview, Feb. 21, 1987.

nowhere to be found: Nancy Brennan interview, July 20, 2009.

father encouraging: *Newark Sunday Call*, "Chips of the Old Blocks," Oct. 22, 1939.

heavily influenced: WJB interview, June 6, 1988 (39-7).

Roughly a third: Arthur E. Sutherland, *The Law at Harvard: A History of Ideas and Men, 1817–1967* (Cambridge, MA: Belknap Press of Harvard University Press, 1967), 248.

19 "Why aren't you": WJB interview, May 27, 1987 (16-4).

roughly seven hundred: Harvard University, *Report of the President and the Treasurer of Harvard College, 1928–9*, 183.

case method: Donald L. Smith, *Zechariah Chafee, Jr., Defender of Liberty and Law* (Cambridge, MA: Harvard University Press, 1986), 121; and Sutherland, *Law at Harvard*, pp. 174–75.

20 They knew Marjorie: Bill Lord to Robert Rockhill, Dec. 3, 1958; provided authors.

was invited: Tilford E. Dudley to WJB, Sept. 27, 1930, WJB personal files.

"compassionate aspects": WJB (speech, Harvard Legal Aid Bureau, Cambridge, MA, Feb. 13, 1963).

21 "wanted no part": WJB interview, Apr. 7, 1990 (60-29).

Shaken by: Smith, *Zechariah Chafee, Jr.*, p. 13.

first thought seriously: WJB interview, Dec. 17, 1986 (7-9).

Chafee was praising: Ibid., p. 6.

"Continued Prosperity": Tuttle, *How Newark Became Newark*, p. 104; Stellhorn, "Depression and Decline," p. 56.

decline steadily: Stellhorn, "Depression and Decline," p. 67.

22 surgery to repair: *NEN*, Jan. 1930, NPL collection.

kidney stones: *Newark Star Eagle*, "Brennan Taken to Hospital As Illness Grows," May 13, 1930.

"pull through": Ibid.

Lord drove him: Bill Lord diary, provided authors.

Bill had died: *Newark Star-Eagle*, "Brennan Dies in Coma of Double Pneumonia," May 14, 1930.

bought parcels: Tuttle, *How Newark Became Newark*, pp. 109–10.

23 Bill's mother: *NYT*, "Mrs. Elizabeth Brennan," June 17, 1930.

Bill had left: *NEN*, "Brennan Estate Left to Widow," May 27, 1930.

founded the firm: Edward Quinton Keasbey, *The Courts & Lawyers of New Jersey 1661–1912* (New York: Lewis Historical Publishing Company, 1912).

Congleton, had intervened: WJB, interview by John Gibbons, June 27, 1988, Historical Society of the United States District Court for the District of New Jersey. Brennan recalled that the partner who Congleton approached was William L. Morgan. Relying on such connections was not unusual. The father of one of Brennan's Harvard Law classmates, Donald Kipp, intervened on his son's behalf with another partner, John Hardin. Kipp, a graduate of Princeton, at least had the right college pedigree. "Presentation of the Portrait of Honorable William J. Brennan Jr.," 69 NJ XXXVIII, May 24, 1976; Donald B. Kipp, *A Personal History of the Firm* (self-published, 1983).

"as a rugged": Ward to ATV, Jan. 31, 1952, ATV papers.

obtained a scholarship: *Newark Star-Eagle*, "WM J. Brennan Jr. Wins Scholarship," Oct. 24, 1930.

24 manufacturers had fallen: Stellhorn, "Depression and Decline," pp. 67, 80.

"The Case of": Ernest J. Brown, *Professor Frankfurter*, 78 HARV. L. REV. 1523 (1965).

Brown, a Harvard Law School alumnus and professor, took the course the same year as Brennan and relied on his class notes to describe the course in this tribute to Frankfurter.

"quasi-religious": Walter Isaacson and Evan Thomas, *Wise Men: Six Friends and the World They Made* (New York: Simon & Schuster, 1997), 88.

25 Dean Acheson: Ibid., p. 89.

intimate seminars: *Conversations with Morris M. Schnitzer,* 47 RUTGERS L. REV. 1391, 1433 (1995). Schnitzer, a Newark lawyer, graduated Harvard Law School soon after Brennan.

The trouble started: WJB interview, May 27, 1987 (16-5).

2. LAWYER

26 rank of counselor: *NYT,* "144 in Jersey Pass Bar Examinations," July 13, 1935.

27 serving notices: Donald B. Kipp, *A Personal History of the Firm* (self-published, 1983), 90–91.

"It's a dog's life": WJB to John Pashgian, May 16, 1932, WJB personal files.

felt pressed: WJB interview, June 10, 1987 (18-4).

bumped up his salary: WJB, interview by John Gibbons, June 27, 1988, Historical Society of the United States District Court for the District of New Jersey. He said it was $161 in WJB interview, June 10, 1987 (18-4).

A 1931 survey: Paul A. Stellhorn, "Depression and Decline: Newark, New Jersey: 1929–1944" (Ph.D. thesis, Rutgers University, 1982), 82.

attorneys struggled: Barbara Gotthelf, *Brennan's Career in N.J. Showed Little Liberalism,* N.J.L.J. 1 (1997).

earned extra money: WJB interview, July 5, 1989 (51-8).

later enjoyed recounting: Brennan told the story at a *Yale Law Journal* banquet on April 13, 1957, and was still telling it almost exactly thirty years later at the *Harvard Law Review*'s hundredth-anniversary dinner on April 11, 1987.

28 heavily courted: WJB interview, Mar. 13, 1987 (11-8).

Highland Avenue: "Meet Bill Brennan Junior, Who's Not in Politics — Yet," NPL collection.

mother pleaded: WJB interview, Mar. 13, 1987 (11-8).

Brennan volunteered: "Meet Bill Brennan Junior."

29 "I guess": Ibid.

Ledger praised: Editorial, "Another William J. Brennan!" *Newark Star-Ledger,* May 6, 1933.

garnered more ink: *Newark News,* "William J. Brennan 3d Born," Apr. 4, 1933; *Newark Star-Ledger,* "Brennan 3d Is Christened," May 23, 1933.

"I don't want": *Newark Sunday Call,* "Chips of the Old Blocks," Oct. 22, 1939.

was the son of: *NYT,* "Shelton Pitney, 53, A Leading Lawyer," Jan. 14, 1946.

required guests: Kipp, *Personal History of the Firm,* p. 17.

30 tidy profit: David S. Jobrack, *Mr. Justice Brennan . . . the Man and the Judge,* N.J.B.J. 241 (spring 1959).

senior partner aghast: WJB interview, July 16, 1986 (1-9).

Allegaert assumed: John Allegaert interview, Aug. 7, 1989.

31 shortly after he arrived: In a 1956 interview, Brennan recalled he had only been at the firm two months when he was given this assignment. Charles L. Whipple, "Justice Ace Trouble-Shooter; Labor Leaders Trust Him," *BG,* Oct. 8, 1956.

Pulaski Skyway: Steven Hart, *The Last Three Miles* (New York: New Press, 2007).

mistook Brennan: Charles L. Whipple, "The Brennan Family Story," *BG,* Oct. 7, 1956.

32 Brennan quickly impressed: Allegaert interview, Aug. 7, 1989.

initially ruled against: NLRB press release, April 13, 1935 (on file with authors); this was a successor to the National Labor Board created by President Roosevelt under the NIRA rather than the modern National Labor Relations Board established by the National Labor Relations Act. Brennan mistakenly recalled that the case was heard by the NLB.

displayed everywhere: Lewis Lord, "An Eagle That Didn't Take Off," *U.S. News & World Report,* Aug. 10, 2003.

obtaining an injunction: *NYT,* "Court Stays Blue Eagle Bans," Apr. 25, 1935.

NIRA unconstitutional: *Schechter Poultry Corp. v. United States,* 295 U.S. 495 (1935).

upheld the law's constitutionality: *Nat'l Labor Relations Bd. v. Jones & Laughlin Steel Corp.,* 301 U.S. 1 (1937).

resisted organizing drives: *In re Elk Tanning Co.,* 1940 WL 11427 (NLRB) (Dec. 1940).

33 "The labor leaders": Whipple, "Justice Ace Trouble-Shooter."

"So far he": *Newark Sunday Call,* "Chips of the Old Blocks."

"Bill 'Unity and Unionism'": Hunter R. Clark, *Justice Brennan: The Great Conciliator* (Secaucus, NJ: Carol Publishing Group, 1995), 41.

"That was one": Thomas L. Morrissey interview with Wermiel, undated.

"I never lost": WJB interview, Feb. 5, 1987 (10-3).

courteous manner: Abraham Weiner interview, Aug. 4, 1990.

World Series game: Kipp, *Personal History of the Firm,* pp. 38–39.

34 eleventh partner: *Newark Sunday Call,* "Chips of the Old Blocks."

western slope: Ibid.

He could now afford: WJB interview, June 10, 1987 (18-8 to 18-9).

sponsored Brennan's membership: Allegaert interview, Aug. 7, 1989.

could often be found: *Newark Sunday Call,* "Chips of the Old Blocks."

card table: WJB III interview, Sept. 6, 1988.

"He was the policy maker": Hugh Brennan interview, Mar. 18, 1987.

incensed driver: WJB III interview, Sept. 6, 1988.

35 trusts and estate work: See *Chandler v. Hardgrove,* 2 A.2d 661 (1938); *Blanchard v. Blanchard,* 174 A. 431 (1934).

$14 million tax assessment: *NYT,* "Doris Duke Gets $13,834,924 Tax Bill," July 2, 1941; Brennan joined: *NYT* "Jersey Tax Fought by Mrs. Cromwell," July 15, 1941.

a client quite like: Stephanie Mansfield, *The Richest Girl in the World: The Extravagant Life and Fast Times of Doris Duke* (New York: Putnam, 1992).

36 Her abrupt request: WJB to Donald Kipp, May 8, 1980.

He was meeting: Ibid. Brennan recalled he was originally scheduled to travel to Hawaii the following week to conduct the deposition.

swimming pool: Mansfield, *Richest Girl in the World,* p. 166.

"Are you in the habit": *NYT,* "Mrs. Cromwell Fights Huge Tax," Jan. 21, 1942; Corinne Hardesty, "Amount of Her Wealth Just Deep Mystery to Doris Duke," *WP,* Jan. 31, 1942.

37 looks out of place: family photo provided to authors.

He was called out: Morris Schnitzer, a New Jersey attorney who knew Brennan, suggested that Robert Wood Johnson might have been responsible for recruiting WJB or at least bringing him to the attention of Campbell. *Conversations with Morris M. Schnitzer,* 47 RUTGERS L. REV. 1391 (1995). Johnson, the president and chairman of his family's New Jersey–based business, Johnson & Johnson, was a top officer in the

Army Ordnance Department at the time Brennan entered the service. In his biography of Brennan, Eisler credited Johnson with helping enlist Brennan for military service and also suggested he had retained Brennan as a labor lawyer for his company. Kim Isaac Eisler, *A Justice for All: William J. Brennan, Jr., and the Decision That Transformed America* (New York: Simon & Schuster, 1993), 38, 43. Brennan never mentioned Johnson, either in the context of his law firm work or Army service.

"He was so happy": Allegaert interview, Aug. 7, 1989.

cut in salary: Waldron Ward to ATV, Jan. 31, 1952, ATV papers.

could not supplement: Kipp interview, June 11, 1987.

Army grew from: Alan L. Gropman, *Mobilizing US Industry in World War II: Myth and Reality* (Washington, DC: Institute for National Strategic Defense Studies, National Defense University, 1996), 93.

three thousand labor strikes: Gropman, *Mobilizing US Industry*, pp. 127, 130; two-week period: Keith Eiler, *Mobilizing America: Robert P. Patterson and the War Effort, 1940–1945* (Ithaca, NY: Cornell University Press, 1998), 291.

38 similar program employed: Byron Fairchild and Jonathan Grossman, *The Army and Industrial Manpower* (Washington, DC: Office of the Chief of Military History, 1959), 29–36.

To reduce absenteeism: Elizabeth McFadden, "Brennan's Rise Included War Service," *NEN*, Feb. 10, 1952.

greater sacrifice: *LAT*, "West Coast's War Task Outlined to Ad Club," Jan. 12, 1944.

giant military pageant: *LAT*, "'Los Angeles Attacks' Will Feature Show," Dec. 30, 1943; *LAT*, "More Troops Swell Camp for Coliseum Show," Jan. 3, 1944; *LAT*, "Mighty 'Battle' Thrills 100,000 at Coliseum," Jan. 9, 1944.

Brennan was promoted: War Department press release, July 11, 1944 (on file with authors).

vital war materials: Fairchild and Grossman, *Army and Industrial Manpower*, p. 152.

39 had been shot down: *NEN*, "Capt. F. W. Brennan Reported Missing," Dec. 26, 1944.

filled the letter: Charlie Brennan to WJB, Dec. 31, 1944, WJB personal files.

Army notified: *NEN*, "S/Sgt. C. F. Brennan Reported Killed," Feb. 27, 1945.

40 getting in the way: WJB interview, Nov. 23, 1987 (25-3 to 25-4).

inform Frank about: Frank Brennan interview, Dec. 29, 1986.

"a tower of strength": President Truman considered nominating Patterson to the Supreme Court in 1945 but opted to nominate him for secretary of war instead. Patterson died in a January 1952 plane crash. Eiler, *Mobilizing America*, p. 443.

"Newark's most aristocratic": "Bill Brennan Jr. Has Gone Far after Ably Abetting Himself," Nov. 11, 1945, NPL collection.

41 "You deserve the job": Joseph Nolan interview, July 17, 1990.

he attracted: Brennan's list of corporate clients included Western Electric, Jersey Bell Telephone, Phelps-Dodge, and American Hair and Felt. Charles L. Whipple, "Justice Never Tough, Yet Never Hedges," *BG*, Nov. 11, 1956.

daily scorecard: *NEN*, "Strike Summary," Jan. 4, 1946.

phone service: *NEN*, "Long Line Phones Crippled; Most Local Service Good," Jan. 9, 1946.

strike turned violent: *NEN*, "WE Workers Injured in Picket Line Fights," Jan. 4, 1946; *W. Elec. Co. v. W. Elec. Emp. Ass'n*, 45 A.2d 695 (1946).

42 temporary injunction: *NEN*, "Wekearny Pickets Limited by Court," Jan. 16, 1946.

Even as Brennan stood: *NEN*, "Picketing Ban Is Permanent," Feb. 11, 1946; *NEN*, "Kearny Strikers Defy Court's Picket Order," Feb. 14, 1946; *NEN*, "Chancery Is Still Defied," Feb. 15, 1946.

Brennan then sought: *NEN*, "Court Cites WE Pickets," Feb. 28, 1946.

"approaching anarchy": Ibid.

posse deputized: *NEN*, "Pickets March Off after Sheriff Reads Riot Act," Mar. 1, 1946.

reach an agreement: *NEN*, "Wekearny Strike Settled; Telephone Tieup Averted," Mar. 7, 1946; *NEN*, "Back to Work after Long WE Strike," Mar. 11, 1946.

43 "vital public importance": reprinted in 69 N.J.L.J. 145 (May 9, 1956).

"when we must": *NEN*, "Calls for Limits on Labor Power," Sept. 25, 1946.

defended the measure: *NEN*, Oct. 22, 1947, NPL collection.

defended labor against: *NEN*, "Unions Are Seen As Communist Foes," June 5, 1946.

colleagues marveled: Robert Levitt interview, Aug. 3, 1990.

carve out time: Hugh Brennan interview, Mar. 19, 1987.

set up lamps: Peter Allegaert to Wermiel, Aug. 5, 1989.

"If Father ever said": WJB III interview, Sept. 6, 1988.

44 Shelton Pitney died: *NYT*, "Shelton Pitney, 53, A Leading Lawyer," Jan. 14, 1946.

"a little larger": WJB interview, July 16, 1986 (1-14).

pressed the governor: "Meet Bill Brennan Junior."

"I know this": *NYT*, "Moore Says Dad Will Be Pleased," Feb. 21, 1939.

started his own: Arthur T. Vanderbilt II, *Changing Law: A Biography of Arthur T. Vanderbilt* (New Brunswick, NJ: Rutgers University Press, 1976).

45 finally paid off: Vanderbilt himself played a minimal role at the constitutional convention. He was angered over Governor Driscoll's handling of it, and after suffering a stroke in May 1947 he spent the summer at his vacation home in Maine.

46 "I began to believe": Charles L. Whipple, "Why Top Lawyer Sacrificed Big Income for Judgeship," *BG*, Oct. 8, 1956.

did not envy: Barbara Allegaert interview, Aug. 7, 1989.

"It's going to cost": Gotthelf, *Brennan's Career in N.J.*

"We saw one another": WJB interview, Aug. 25, 1989 (54-8); According to Eisler, Vanderbilt intervened using Kipp as an intermediary when Jacobs's entreaties failed to convince Brennan to accept. Eisler, *Justice for All*, pp. 65–66. But in 1976 Kipp recalled, when he spoke at an unveiling of Brennan's portrait at the New Jersey Supreme Court, being surprised when Brennan told him he intended to leave the firm to become a judge. Kipp repeated that account in a June 11, 1987, interview.

Kipp was happy: Kipp interview, June 11, 1987.

soon concluded: Frank went to work for a subsidiary of Standard Oil and in 1954 moved to Ballantine, the brewery where their father had worked. After seventeen years at Ballantine, he ultimately attained the title of vice president and secretary. He later worked for the Rheingold Brewery in Brooklyn and ended his career as vice president and general counsel of Gallo Winery in Modesto, California.

Lincoln Continental: Gotthelf, *Brennan's Career in N.J.*

47 "The Senate should": Editorial, "An Excellent Choice," *Newark Star-Ledger*, Jan. 5, 1949.

3. ASCENDING THE BENCH

48 greatest test yet: *NYT*, "Local Campaigns Near End in Jersey," May 8, 1949.

tomatoes and boos: *Chicago Daily Tribune*, "Boos Instead of 'Boss' Greet Today's Hague," May 5, 1949.

49 voting machines: *NYT,* "Jersey City Ruled 32 Years by Hague," May 11, 1949.
count on votes: Dayton David McKean, *The Boss: The Hague Machine in Action* (Boston: Houghton Mifflin, 1940), 64, 139.
"the magic ballot box": *NYT,* "Ballot Inquiry Ordered," April 9, 1949.
Brennan issued: *Witkowski v. Burke,* 65 A.2d 781 (N.J. Super. Ct. Law Div. 1949); *NYT,* "Ballot Upset Rejected," Apr. 15, 1949.
would be impractical: Leo Egan, "Hague Pins Hopes on a Divided Vote; Sees 50,000 Margin," *NYT,* May 10, 1949.
spotted burning: Leo Egan, "Kenny to Ask Court for Order to Seize Jersey City Books," *NYT,* May 12, 1949. Hague's fall did not mean a happy ending for Jersey City. Kenny ran as a reformer but became just as corrupt a boss as Hague, earning him the nickname the Pope of Jersey City and a 1970 indictment for extortion and tax invasion.
municipal zoning decisions: *Protomastro et al. v. Board of Adjustment of City of Hoboken et al.,* 3 N.J. Super. 539 (1949); contract disputes: *Condenser Service & Engineering Co, Inc. v. Mycalex Corporation of America,* 7 N.J. Super. 427 (1950); garbage-removal contract: *Albanese et al. v. Machetto et al.,* 5 N.J. Super. 605 (1949).
50 rejected a labor injunction: *NYT,* "Injunction Denied in Jersey Pier Row," July 31, 1949; upheld a wage increase: *Int'l Ass'n of Machinists, Lodge 1292 v. Bergen Ave. Bus. Owners' Ass'n,* 67 A.2d 362 (N.J. Super. Ct. Law Div. 1949).
weekly reports detailing: WJB, *After Eight Years: New Jersey Judicial Reform,* 43 ABA J. 499 (1957).
"If any of the": ATV to WJB, July 7, 1952, ATV papers.
First introduced: For more detail about New Jersey's pretrial practice at the time, see Harry D. Nims, *Pre-trial* (New York: Baker, Voorhis & Co., 1950). One of Brennan's pretrial orders was included as a model in this guide to pretrial procedure (pp. 305–7.)
Vanderbilt had championed: Harry D. Nims and the American Bar Association, *Report of Committee on Pre-trial Procedure* (New York: Baker-Voorhis & Co., 1950), 1.
silently rebelled: ATV, *Our New Judicial Establishment: The Record of the First Year,* 4 RUTGERS L. REV. 353, 367 (1950); overcome that resistance: ATV to WJB, July 7, 1952, ATV papers.
clubby band: Mark Sullivan interview, July 27, 1989.
"intelligent application": Francis P. McQuade and Alexander T. Kardos, *Mr. Justice Brennan and His Legal Philosophy,* 33 NOTRE DAME L. REV. 321, 342 (1958), citing William J. Brennan Jr., *Does Business Have a Role in Improving Judicial Administration?* 28 PENN B.A.Q. 238 (1957).
Brennan conceived: WJB, *After Eight Years,* p. 564.
51 thus taken aback: Haydn Proctor interview, July 25, 1989.
"a charmer": Mark Sullivan interview, July 27, 1989.
98 percent: ATV, *Our New Judicial Establishment,* p. 363.
"I must learn": WJB to ATV, Dec. 5, 1949, ATV papers.
sensitive task: *In re: Wittreich,* 74 A.2d 258 (N.J. 1950). In a June 19, 1950, decision, the New Jersey Supreme Court recommended a two-year suspension of the attorney's license, though Vanderbilt argued for disbarment in his dissenting opinion. Wittreich was subsequently indicted for embezzlement and three counts of false swearing for statements he made at the hearing where Brennan presided. *NYT,* "Wittreich Is Indicted," June 28, 1950.
"Dear Chief": WJB to ATV, Aug. 5, 1949, ATV papers.
52 "The only thing": ATV to WJB, Aug. 6, 1949, ATV papers.

looked back fondly: Daniel J. O'Hern, *Brennan and Weintraub: Two Stars to Guide Us,* 46 RUTGERS L. REV. 1049 (1994).

"He made friends": "Hear Ye!" Jon Byrne, WJB personal files.

"I'm prone to": WJB to ATV, July 17, 1950, ATV papers.

53   bristling mustache: *NYT,* "Wilfred H. Jayne, Ex-Judge, 73, Dies," Aug. 13, 1961.

apply to the states: The Court accomplished this through the due process clause of the Fourteenth Amendment, finding that provisions of the Bill of Rights were part of the guaranteed "liberty" with which states could not interfere without providing due process. This constitutional approach was called incorporation, because, one by one, the Court incorporated most provisions of the Bill of Rights into the Fourteenth Amendment.

defendant was absent: *Cohen v. Scola,* 80 A.2d 643 (N.J. Super. Ct. App. Div. 1951).

"The citizen holds": *Cortese v. Cortese,* 76 A.2d 717, 720–21 (N.J. Super. Ct. App. Div. 1950), quoting *State v. Damm,* 266 N.W. 667 (S.D. 1936).

rare bursts: He scolded an attorney for failing to include the lower-court judgment in the filing to the appellate court. *In re Gotchel's Estate,* 76 A.2d 901, 903 (N.J. Super. Ct. App. Div. 1950). Similarly, he scolded a lower-court judge who supplied jurors with a dictionary at their request while they were deliberating, without first notifying the defendant or her attorney. *Palestroni v. Jacobs,* 77 A.2d 183, 184 (N.J. 1950).

54   attend a matinee: Elizabeth McFadden, "Brennan's Rise Included War Service," *NEN,* Feb. 10, 1952.

"the ideal selection": Ward to ATV, Jan. 31, 1952, ATV papers.

overrepresented: Brennan would be the fourth from Essex: Chief Justice Vanderbilt lived in Short Hills, Justice William A. Wachenfeld lived in Orange, and Jacobs lived in Livingston.

over dinner: *NEN,* "O'Mara Says No to Bench," Feb. 6, 1952; William F. O'Connor, "Jacobs and O'Mara to Supreme Court," *NEN,* Feb. 5, 1952.

A few minutes later: Franklin Gregory, "Driscoll to Name Judge Brennan of Newark as Fourth Essex Justice for Supreme Court," *Newark Star-Ledger,* Feb. 8, 1952.

"rich experience": Ibid.; *NEN,* "Court Post to Brennan," Feb. 7, 1952.

"It may be said": *NEN,* "Good Appointment," Jan. 5, 1949.

55   "I had no intention": WJB interview, June 10, 1987 (18-8).

sworn in together: *NEN,* "Supreme Court Bench Is Filled," Mar. 24, 1952. The *New Jersey Reports,* the official court records of the state, incorrectly lists the date Jacobs was sworn in as March 17, 1952, and Brennan as having been sworn in separately on March 19, 1952. March 17 was the date that Jacobs was approved by the state senate. *NEN,* "Court OKs Jacobs, Holds on Brennan," Mar. 17, 1952.

fifty onlookers: "Supreme Court Bench Is Filled."

"Harvard ends": WJB recalled at 1976 unveiling of his portrait at New Jersey Supreme Court, 69 NJ XLIV. Brennan and Jacobs had heard a couple cases together on the Appellate Division.

"My aversion": Nathan Jacobs diary, June 1952, WJB personal files.

own misgivings: Voorhees Dunn, "Chief Justice Arthur T. Vanderbilt and the Judicial Revolution in New Jersey" (Ph.D. thesis, Rutgers University, 1987), 153.

56   traveled by train: Morris M. Schnitzer interview, June 28, 1994.

same chambers: James C. Pitney interview, Mar. 6, 1991.

divorce decree: *Shammas v. Shammas,* 88 A.2d 204 (N.J. 1952); personal-injury case: *Stacy v. Greenberg,* 88 A.2d 619 (1952).

"Discipline must be": *In re Howell,* 89 A.2d 652, 654 (N.J. 1952). Brennan favored similarly harsh punishments in two other attorney-discipline cases when he was on the

New Jersey Supreme Court. See *In re Backes,* 109 A.2d 273 (N.J. 1954), where he urged disbarment. And in a third case he again argued for disbarment, where the majority favored a two-year suspension. *In re Frankel,* 120 A.2d 603, 609, (N.J. 1956) (Brennan, J., dissenting).

57 original sod: *Time,* "Sport: Too Much Fuss," Aug. 14, 1950.

adjacent estate: The estate had been owned by a member of the McCarter family. Another member of the family was president of the Public Service Corporation, the company that Brennan's father had faced off against during Newark's 1916 trolley workers' strike.

additional $18,000: 1040 Tax Records (1952), WJB personal files; WJB described renovations in a January 5, 1981, letter to the subsequent owner of the house, Raymond Cleary.

"Everything is right": Isabelle Shelton, "Mrs. Brennan Looks Forward to Capital," *Washington Evening Star,* Oct. 10, 1956.

despite allergies: Nancy Brennan interview, July 20, 2009.

small burial plot: This was the burial plot for the McCarter family.

58 later discovered: David Harrison interview, Aug. 4, 1990.

preferred to write: John C. Giordano Jr. (WJB clerk 1955–56) interview, June 12, 1996.

most significant case: *State v. Tune,* 98 A.2d 881 (N.J. 1953).

59 sparkling prose: J. L. Bernstein, "The Philosophy of Mr. Justice Brennan," *Reporter,* Nov. 1956.

willingness to disagree: Brennan's son Bill later suggested that his dissent in the case "ought to be regarded as my father's declaration of independence" from Vanderbilt. Barbara Gotthelf, *Brennan's Career in N.J. Showed Little Liberalism,* 149 N.J.L.J. (1997).

ruthless enforcer: Brennan recalled Vanderbilt telling him, "One man in this set up has to be the son of a bitch and I'm it." Arthur T. Vanderbilt II, *Changing Law: A Biography of Arthur T. Vanderbilt* (New Brunswick, NJ: Rutgers University Press, 1976), 218.

coauthored the manual: The *Manual of Pretrial Practice* by the Supreme Court of New Jersey does not list any authors. But as ATV wrote at the time WJB was selected for the U.S. Supreme Court, "The successive editions of the New Jersey *Manual of Pretrial Practice* is more largely his work than that of any other man." ATV, *New Members of the Supreme Court of the United States: Mr. Justice Brennan,* 43 A.B.A. J. 526 (1957); ATV's papers include a July 7, 1952, letter to WJB in which he provides feedback on WJB's draft manual.

"Brennan was the workhorse": Ed McConnell interview, Feb. 3, 1989.

no particular ideological bent: Pitney interview, Mar. 6, 1991, and Giordano interview, June 12, 1996.

key piece of evidence: In a 1959 article for the journal of the New Jersey State Bar Association, David Jobrack characterized Brennan as a "realistic liberal or liberal realist." David S. Jobrack, *Mr. Justice Brennan . . . the Man and the Judge,* 2 N.J. St. B.J. 270 (1959). In a 1978 doctoral thesis, Edward V. Heck characterized Brennan as a "pragmatic liberal" during his tenure on the New Jersey Supreme Court. Edward V. Heck, "Justice Brennan and the Changing Supreme Court" (Ph.D. thesis, Johns Hopkins University, 1978).

60 King James Bibles: *Tudor v. Bd. of Educ.,* 100 A.2d 857 (N.J. 1953).

denying an operating license: *Adams Theatre Co. v. Keenan,* 96 A.2d 519 (N.J. 1953).

Brennan emphasized: For an early analysis of Brennan's jurisprudence as a state judge, see McQuade and Kardos, *Mr. Justice Brennan,* p. 321.

"precious to free men": *State v. Fary,* 117 A.2d 499, 501 (N.J. 1955).
could be compelled: *In re Pillo,* 93 A.2d 176 (N.J. 1952).
"The law values": *Davis v. Hellwig,* 122 A.2d 497, 499 (N.J. 1956).
"The plea of": *State v. Midgeley,* 105 A.2d 844, 847 (N.J. 1954), quoting *State v. DiGiosia,* 70 A.2d 756 (N.J. 1950).
featured speaker: *RBR,* "300 Men Expected to Hear Justice Brennan," Sept. 10, 1953; *RBR,* "Holy Name Men to Hear Brennan," Mar. 8, 1956.
Marjorie volunteered: *RBR,* "Rumson Appeal Officers Map October Drive," July 1, 1954; treasurer: *RBR,* Sept. 1, 1955.
61 He was elected: *RBR,* "Hospital Board Elects Two Rumson Residents," Oct. 20, 1955; Monmouth County organization for Social Service: *RBR,* "Bad Welfare Services Cost More State Heads Tells MCOSS," Apr. 26, 1956.
He delivered speeches: *RBR,* "Justice Brennan Hails Legal Aid," Feb. 3, 1955; *RBR,* Feb. 24, 1955; *RBR,* "Vespucci Society Honors Giordano," Apr. 28, 1955; *RBR,* "Friends to Fete John Pillsbury," June 2, 1955.
Marjorie regularly cooking: Hugh Brennan interview, Mar. 19, 1987.
"If the matter": Griswold to WJB, May 24, 1955, WJB personal files.
"a better job": WJB to Griswold, May 27, 1955, WJB personal files.
he was engaged: *RBR,* "Roxey Atwood Engaged to W. J. Brennan, 3d," Aug. 25, 1955; *NYT,* "Roxey L. Atwood Will Be Married," Aug. 21, 1955; *NEN,* "Roxey Atwood Is Fiancée of William Brennan III," Sept. 21, 1955.
62 "was a dreadful kid": Hugh Brennan interview, Mar. 19, 1987.
stole the mayor's car: Ibid.
"A lot of them": Ibid.
socialized regularly: David Freeman (Rumson friend) interview, July 27, 1989.
Arthur Murray instructor: Mrs. John Ballentine interview, July 1989.
Marjorie seemed content: June Young interview, July 24, 1989.
63 shielded his children: William J. Brennan III interview, Sept. 6, 1988.
keynote address: *NEN,* "Brennan Says U.S. Courage Unweakened by Witch Hunts," Mar. 18, 1954; *Boston Herald,* "Charitable Irish Society Eyes Menace of Soviet Communism," Mar. 18, 1954; *BG,* "Witch Hunts Passing Aberration, Charitable Irish Society Told," Mar. 18, 1954.
"This is the day": WJB (keynote address, Charitable Irish Society, Boston, MA, Mar. 17, 1954).
65 "driving the snakes": Thomas C. Reeves, *The Life and Times of Joe McCarthy: A Biography* (New York: Stein and Day, 1982), 581.
generally less popular: William V. Shannon, *The American Irish* (New York: Macmillan, 1963), 383.
"a game to be played": Reeves, *Life and Times,* p. 59.
"hapless and helpless": WJB (keynote address, Charitable Irish Society).
"The thing was": WJB interview, Jan. 28, 1987 (9-3).
66 indirectly criticized: *NEN,* "Favors Rein on M'Carthy," Nov. 11, 1954; WJB (speech, Monmouth Rotary Club, Feb. 23, 1955).
public relations man: Haydon Proctor interview, July 25, 1989.
favorable write-up: *NYT,* "Jersey Judges Go on a Penal Tour," Apr. 9, 1954.
led demonstrations: Thomas J. Hooper, "N.J. Shows Court Plan," *NEN,* Aug. 23, 1955.
"I acquired my": WJB (speech, North Carolina Bar Association, June 25, 1954).
come to share: WJB interview, Aug. 15, 1986 (2-16).
equally assertive: For discussions of Vanderbilt court activism, see Dunn, "Chief Justice Arthur T. Vanderbilt," pp. 240–42. Edward V. Heck, who conducted the most

thorough review of Brennan's jurisprudence in New Jersey, saw hints of Vanderbilt's "activist" orientation in some of Brennan's decisions, particularly workers' compensation cases where he interpreted statutory language broadly. Heck, "Justice Brennan and the Changing Supreme Court," p. 82.

business partnership: Ed McConnell interview, Feb. 3, 1989; Friendly Sons: picture of them attending event in Dermot Quinn, *The Irish in New Jersey* (New Brunswick, NJ: Rutgers University Press, 2004), 179.

Vanderbilt was grooming: David Harrison interview, Aug. 4, 1990; Bernstein, "The Philosophy of Mr. Justice Brennan," p. 1.

shared his convictions: WJB interview April 4, 1989 (48-5).

67 "This is the most": Anthony Lewis, "Bar Chiefs Study Delays in Trials," *NYT*, May 22, 1956.

writers later claimed: For one version of this story, see Stanley H. Friedelbaum, "Justice William J. Brennan Jr.: Policy-Making in the Judicial Thicket," in *The Burger Court: Political and Judicial Profiles*, ed. Charles M. Lamb and Stephen C. Halpern (Chicago: University of Illinois Press, 1991), 100, 102.

continue to do so: Two weeks after the DOJ conference, Brennan delivered a speech titled "Jersey Justice Refurbished" to the Kansas City Bar Association on June 7, 1956.

68 never been on the schedule: Robert Seaver interview, July 13, 1990.

"It is very": Proceedings of Attorney General's Conference on Court Congestion and Delay in Litigation (1956).

particularly good impression: Brennan recalled that they had previously met when he testified before the congressional commission to which Rogers served as counsel during World War II.

"Unlike other judges": Charles L. Whipple, "Why Top Lawyer Sacrificed Big Income for Judgeship," *BG*, Oct. 8, 1956.

4. IKE'S MISTAKE

71 he picked up: For an earlier account of Brennan's nomination, see Stephen Wermiel, *The Nomination of Justice Brennan: Eisenhower's Mistake? A Look at the Historical Record*, 11 CONST. COMMENT. 515 (1995).

"Uh-oh, here it is": WJB interview, Oct. 28, 1986 (5-22). On September 20, Brownell had announced that Arthur T. Vanderbilt was among the eleven members of a new Justice Department committee on court congestion and delay. *WP*, "Rogers to Head Study of Courts," Sept. 20, 1956.

were busy stacking: Clyde Szuch interview, June 11, 1987.

preoccupied with a case: WJB interview, Oct. 28, 1986 (5-22); *In re Herr*, 125 A.2d 706 (N.J. 1956).

Brownell persisted: WJB interview, Oct. 28, 1986 (5-23). Brownell offered a similar account in a Feb. 10, 1988, interview.

72 arrive in Washington: *NEN*, "Brennan Home, Happy Over Post and Dodgers," Sept. 29, 1956.

"Come on": WJB interview, Oct. 28, 1986 (5-24).

"slipping fast": Minton to Truman, Dec. 27, 1955, cited in David J. Garrow, *Mental Decrepitude on the U.S. Supreme Court: The Historical Case for a 28th Amendment*, 67 U. CHI. L. REV. 995, 1043-45 (2000). In addition to his seven years as justice, Minton had served eight years on the U.S. Court of Appeals for the Seventh Circuit.

72 "appreciation": Allen Drury, "Minton Retiring from High Court; Cites Ill Health," *NYT*, Sept. 8, 1956.

73 masked his annoyance: Ann Whitman, diary entry, Sept. 7, 1956, DDE papers.
"terribly handicapped": *U.S. News & World Report*, "Change in the Court," Sept. 14, 1956, 8.
Eisenhower had privately confided: David A. Nichols, *A Matter of Justice: Eisenhower and the Beginning of the Civil Rights Revolution* (New York: Simon & Schuster, 2007), 106.
emergency surgery: Edwin L. Dale Jr., "Block 'Bypassed,'" *NYT*, June 10, 1956.
August Gallup Poll: *Newsweek*, "Ike's Health and Politics," Aug. 20, 1956.

74 denied strenuously: Bernard Shanley interview, June 11, 1987.
votes of Jews: Stephen Ambrose, *Eisenhower: The President* (New York: Simon & Schuster, 1984), 353.
stag dinners: DDE presidential schedule, accessed at http://millercenter.org/scripps/archive/documents/dde/diary.

75 frequent guest: John Cooney, *The American Pope: The Life and Times of Francis Cardinal Spellman* (New York: Crown, 1991), 111.
His conduit: Shanley would later suggest in a June 11, 1987, interview that this initial meeting occurred in 1956. But Shanley wrote in a diary entry that he reminded Eisenhower about Spellman's suggestion when the president was in Denver. The president was in Denver, where he often vacationed, in September 1953 at the time Chief Justice Fred Vinson died and again in October 1954 at the time of Justice Robert Jackson's death, but not during the period following Minton's announcement in 1956.
No Catholic had served: Barbara Perry, *The Life and Death of the "Catholic Seat" on the United States Supreme Court*, 6 J.L. & Pol. 55, 74, 83 (1989). In all, five Irish Catholics had previously served on the Court, starting with Roger Brooke Taney, who became chief justice in 1836.
Spellman argued: Bernard Shanley, undated diary entry (p. 1687), DDE papers.
"The president is under": Daniel F. Cleary, "Catholics and Politics," in *Catholicism in America: A Series of Articles from the Commonweal* (New York: Harcourt, Brace, 1956), 101–102.
Earl Warren's surrogates: Jim Newton, *Justice for All: Earl Warren and the Nation He Made* (New York: Riverhead Books, 2007), 8.
Shanley reminded: Bernard Shanley, undated diary entry (p. 1687), DDE papers.

76 "does show the acute": DDE, diary entry, Nov. 16, 1954, in *The Papers of Dwight David Eisenhower*, ed. L. Galambos and D. van Ee, doc. 1157. World Wide Web facsimile by the Dwight D. Eisenhower Memorial Commission of the print edition; Baltimore, MD: Johns Hopkins University Press, 1996, www.eisenhowermemorial.org/presidential-papers/first-term/documents/1157.cfm.
draw up a list: DDE to Brownell, Mar. 8, 1955, in *Papers of Dwight David Eisenhower*, ed. Galambos and van Ee, doc. 1334, www.eisenhowermemorial.org/presidential-papers/first-term/documents/1334.cfm.
paper stealthily prepared: Michael O'Brien, *John F. Kennedy: A Biography* (New York: Thomas Dunne Books/St. Martin's Press, 2005), 313–14.
"start thinking again": Ann Whitman, telephone call summaries, Sept. 7, 1955, DDE papers.

77 repeated the message: Ibid.
"reasonable age": *NYT*, "President Keeps Court Post Open," Sept. 12, 1956.
Thomas E. Dewey: *NYT*, "Dewey Mentioned for Supreme Court," Sept. 9, 1956.
William Henry Hastie: Doris Fleeson, "The New Justice," *New York Post*, Oct. 1, 1956.

fifth on his agenda: "Pre-press conference notes," Sept. 11, 1956, DDE papers.

helped lead the push: Herbert Brownell and John P. Burke, *Advising Ike: The Memoirs of Attorney General Herbert Brownell* (Lawrence: University Press of Kansas, 1993), 100.

"How about being": Ibid., p. xiii. There was precedent in Brownell's family: his great-uncle William H. H. Miller held the same job for President Benjamin Harrison.

Eisenhower entrusted: David Alistair Yalof, *Pursuit of Justices: Presidential Politics and the Selection of Supreme Court Nominees* (Chicago: University of Chicago Press, 1999), 42.

78 only Catholic appellate judge: Ibid., p. 59.

Brownell asked Rogers: William Rogers interview, Sept. 1, 1987.

Brownell quizzed: George Williams interview, Feb. 4, 1989.

79 handled almost entirely: John V. Lindsay interview, July 16, 1990. Lindsay was later elected mayor of New York City.

"well reasoned": Brownell interview, Feb. 10, 1988.

Shanley had known: Brennan's father laid tracks for the trolley-car company owned by Shanley's grandfather when he first moved to Newark.

80 "was the first": Shanley interview, June 11, 1987.

earned Hickey's gratitude: WJB interview, Oct. 28, 1987 (23-2).

"Our files reflect": FBI memo Sept. 25, 1956, Subject: "Judge William Joseph Brennan Jr.," obtained under Freedom of Information Act.

"was like manna": Brownell interview, Feb. 10, 1988.

met in the Oval Office: Sherman Adams appointment books, Sept. 28, 1956, Adams papers.

"But it seemed so": *Life*, "A Fine Judge Ready for His Biggest Job," Oct. 29, 1956, 116.

only promotion: WJB interview, July 12, 1988 (41-13).

81 Eisenhower expressed regret: WJB interview, Oct. 28, 1986 (5-25).

"apparently didn't hurt": WJB, oral history interview by Anthony Lewis, May 13, 1992, Federal Judicial Center.

"My father": William J. Brennan III, "First Words to the Nation," in *The Common Man as Uncommon Man: Remembering Justice William J. Brennan, Jr.*, ed. E. Joshua Rosenkranz and Thomas M. Jorde (New York: Brennan Center for Justice, 2006), 6-7.

82 "God bless you": *Washington Evening Star*, Oct. 16, 1956.

"Oh Jesus!": WJB interview, Oct. 28, 1986 (5-26).

initial positive review: *Philadelphia Inquirer*, "Choice of Brennan Hinged on Investigation by Segal," Sept. 30, 1956.

would have disrupted: Allen Drury, "President Adds West Coast Trip to His Campaign," *NYT*, Oct. 1, 1956.

sixty-mile barnstorm: James Reston, "Stevenson in Jersey," *NYT*, Oct. 3, 1956.

had few details: *NEN*, "Decision to Name Brennan to Top Court Was Sudden," Oct. 1, 1956.

"I never saw": Charles L. Whipple, "Why Top Lawyer Sacrificed Big Income for Judgeship," *BG*, Oct. 8, 1956.

sitting smiling: George Beveridge, "New Jersey Democrat Named to High Court," *Washington Sunday Star*, Sept. 30, 1956.

recess appointment: There have been a total of twelve recess appointments to the Supreme Court. Nine of these occurred earlier in the nation's history, between 1791 and

1862. From 1862 to 1953 there were no recess appointments to the Court, and then President Eisenhower used the power three times, with Warren in 1953, Brennan in 1956, and Potter Stewart in 1958; see Note, *Recess Appointments to the Supreme Court — Constitutional but Unwise?* 10 Stan. L. Rev. 124 (1957).

83 "I really don't understand": Beveridge, "New Jersey Democrat Named to High Court."

first visit there: Brennan said he had appeared before the Court as attorney during the appeal of Doris Duke's tax case, *Township of Hillsborough v. Cromwell*, 326 U.S. 620 (1946). He is not listed as arguing the case, but Brennan remembered accompanying Shelton Pitney and another son of a former justice, Charles Evan Hughes Jr., who acted as cocounsel, to the oral argument in December 1945. WJB interview, Feb. 5, 1987 (10-5). William Douglas, who wrote the opinion in the case, also recalled Brennan's appearance. William O. Douglas, *Justice Brennan as a Jurist,* 4 Rutgers-Cam. L.J. 5 (1972).

"almost bombastically pretentious": Fred J. Maroon and Suzy Maroon, *The Supreme Court of the United States* (New York: Thomasson-Grant & Lickle, 1996), 39.

"This building just awes": Phyllis Turner, "Justice for All," *Crystal City Magazine,* winter 1990, 28.

84 quietly rejoiced: WJB interview, Oct. 21, 1988 (45-5).

made himself at home: Chriss Winston, *The University Club of Washington DC: One Hundred Years of Fellowship* (Washington, DC: Regnery Publishing Inc., 2004), 70.

leisurely lunches: Interviews with Jesse Choper (Warren OT '60 clerk) and Michael E. Smith (Warren OT '65 clerk), January 2008.

exchanged pleasantries: WJB interview, April 11, 1988 (32-4).

saw a picture: WJB interview, Oct. 28, 1986 (5-30).

horde of photographers: Ibid.

85 Marjorie had barely had time: *NEN,* "Brennan Dinner Party Becomes Celebration," Sept. 30, 1956.

Szuch heard the news: Szuch interview, June 11, 1987.

rags-to-riches tale: AP, "Justice Brennan, Son of Irish Immigrants, Came Up the Hard Way to Highest Tribunal," WJB scrapbook.

"I'm no Horatio Alger": *Life,* "A Fine Judge Ready for His Biggest Job," Oct. 10, 1956.

carried his own bag: Charles L. Whipple, "The Brennan Family Story," *BG,* Oct. 7, 1956.

handy in the kitchen: *Allentown Evening Chronicle,* "New Supreme Court Justice Handy Man in Kitchen with Skillet, Pot," Oct. 6, 1956.

began a pattern: In a tribute after his retirement, Nina Totenberg described Brennan's "mischievous Irish grin" and called him "the leprechaun of the Supreme Court." Nina Totenberg, et al., *A Tribute to Justice William J. Brennan, Jr.,* 104 Harv. L. Rev. 33, 34, 39 (1990).

"a jaunty judge": *NYT,* "A Jaunty Judge," Sept. 30, 1956.

"storytelling Irishman": *Time,* "The Ninth Justice: A Happy Irishman," Oct. 8, 1956, 25.

"moderate liberal": *WP,* "Brennan for the Court," Oct. 1, 1956.

"comparative obscurity": *NYT,* Editorial, "The Supreme Court," Oct. 1, 1956.

86 administration official: *U.S. News & World Report,* "An Experienced Judge for Supreme Court," Oct. 12, 1956, 70.

"Prediction in print": J. L. Bernstein, "The Philosophy of Mr. Justice Brennan," *Reporter* (Nov. 1956), 1, 4.

"for bestowing": Bowler to DDE, Oct. 22, 1956. All letters to White House officials were contained in Justice Department file on Brennan's nomination obtained on August 10, 1989, under Freedom of Information Act.

would not vote: WJB interview, Oct. 21, 1988 (45-4).

"Being a Roman Catholic": Paula Jackson to DDE, Jan. 17, 1957. President Harding received nearly identical letters thirty-four years earlier when he nominated another Catholic, Pierce Butler. One alarmed citizen warned that Butler's nomination would tighten "the papal noose around the neck of America almost to the strangulation point." Sanford Levison, *Confrontation of Religious Faith and Civil Religion: Catholics Becoming Justices*, 39 DEPAUL L. REV. 1047, 1067 (1990), quoting David Danelski, *A Supreme Court Justice Is Appointed* (New York: Random House, 1964), 92.

"Just about ten minutes": Alice Gothard to Sherman Adams, Sept. 28, 1956.

87 Shanley called: Shanley interview, June 11, 1987.

Spellman did not believe: Cooney, *American Pope*, p. 237.

during a ceremony: Shanley interview, June 11, 1987.

Sunday in church: Tom Barrett, "Brennan Neighbors Join Ovation to New Justice," publication unknown, Oct. 1, 1956, WJB scrapbook.

almost embarrassed: WJB interview, June 17, 1987 (19-6).

made coffee: Barrett, "Brennan Neighbors Join Ovation."

88 mistakenly referred: *RBR*, Dec. 23, 1958.

Brennan borrowed: WJB to Frank Ritchie, Jan. 20, 1964, WJB personal files.

"Washington's gain": "Brennan Credits Job to Vanderbilt Regime," publication unknown, Oct. 1, 1956, WJB scrapbook.

Vanderbilt was surprised: A decade later, Warren biographer Leo Katcher quoted an anonymous former American Bar Association official as saying that Vanderbilt "blew up" upon hearing about Brennan's nomination. Leo Katcher, *Earl Warren: A Political Biography* (New York: McGraw-Hill, 1967), 355. But Katcher's version of events was later contradicted by all the key decision makers—as well as Vanderbilt himself. For further discussion of Vanderbilt's reaction, see Wermiel, *Nomination of Justice Brennan*.

Vanderbilt's son: Brownell interview, Feb. 10, 1988.

89 highest regard: Williams interview, Feb. 4, 1989.

"could not have been": Bernard Segal interview, Aug. 23, 1989.

"wonderful appointment": Miriam Ottenberg, "Middle of the Road Independent Thinker," *Washington Sunday Star*, Sept. 30, 1956.

Vanderbilt wrote letters: ATV to Robert S. Snively, Oct. 3, 1956, ATV papers.

"truly magnificent": ATV to WJB, Oct. 5, 1956.

Ill health: WJB to ATV, Oct. 17, 1956.

"your personal recommendation": WJB to ATV, Feb. 4, 1957.

"receiving it from": WJB (speech, New Jersey State Bar Association, Atlantic City, NJ, May 18, 1957).

fedora in one hand: photograph by Alfred Eisenstaedt, *Justice William J. Brennan Walking Out of Empty Office, w. Robe Over His Arm* © 1956 by Time, Inc., from Life Magazine Photo Archive, http://images.google.com/hosted/life (under "Search Life Images" type "William Brennan").

90 Three admitted: Doris Fleeson, "A Pitch for Votes in the Big States," *Washington Star*, Oct. 1, 1956.

often exaggerated: Bruce Allen Murphy, *Wild Bill: The Legend and Life of William O. Douglas* (New York: Random House, 2003).

clerk dutifully did: William Cohen (WOD OT '56 clerk) interview, June 13, 1993.

"about my brother-designate": FF to Jacobs, Oct. 4, 1956, FF papers, LOC.

91 "I am chagrined": Freund to FF, Oct. 9, 1956, FF papers, LOC.

"With this commendable": Robert H. Newman, "The Brennan Appointment," *Harvard Crimson*, Oct. 13, 1956.

"I confidently expect": FF to C. C. Burlingham, Oct. 3, 1956, FF papers, LOC.

"I look forward": FF to WJB, Oct. 1, 1956.

"I cannot hope": WJB to FF, Oct. 3, 1956, FF papers, LOC.

typical photograph depicted: Josephine Bonomo, "Mrs. Brennan Up in Clouds," *NEN*, Oct. 7, 1956.

92 "Sometimes he tells me": Ibid.

"be sorry to give": Ibid.

photo shoot: photograph by Alfred Eisenstaedt © 1956 by Time, Inc., in Life Magazine Photo Archive, http://images.google.com/hosted/life (under "Search Life Images" type "William Brennan").

93 insisted on driving: Roger K. Newman, *Hugo Black: A Biography* (New York: Pantheon Books, 1994), 426.

World Series: Brennan later suggested in interviews that it was the first game of the World Series. WJB, interview by Nina Totenberg, *All Things Considered,* National Public Radio, Jan. 29, 1987. But he was still in New Jersey attending to business on the state Supreme Court rather than in Washington, D.C., for Game 1 on October 3, 1956. WJB arrived in Washington on October 9 and did not actually visit the Court until October 10, 1956, which was the date of Game 7. In a Dec. 23, 1974, note to Milton M. Abramoff, WJB wrote, "I came here on October 9."

94 "Do you smoke?": WJB interview, Jan. 7, 1987 (8-5).

gathered for a picture: *Washington Evening Star,* "Nine Justices and Brennan Call at White House," Oct. 12, 1956.

no intention of: *Washington Evening Star,* "Grateful Mother Sees Brennan Take Oath," Oct. 16, 1956.

"If Eisenhower had lost": WJB interview, Sept. 13, 1986 (42-8).

found a furnished apartment: WJB to Everett Goulard, Dec. 5, 1956.

Marjorie would need: *WP,* "No School for Nancy as Dad Takes Oath," Oct. 16, 1956.

95 a school bell: Ibid.

5. JOINING THE COURT

96 black judicial robe: Max Wiener, "Ceremonies Over, Brennan Starts Job," *NEN,* Oct. 17, 1956.

97 twenty-six family members: *Washington Evening Star,* "Grateful Mother Sees Brennan Take Oath," Oct. 16, 1956.

first full oral argument: Brennan first sat in on the conclusion of a hearing in a condemnation case from Kansas. *Butler v. Michigan* was the first in which he participated fully.

family lunched: Marie McNair, "A Great Day for the Brennans," *WP,* Oct. 17, 1956.

second argument: *Brownell v. Chase National Bank,* 352 U.S. 36 (1956).

tour of the White House: Frank Brennan interview, Dec. 29, 1986.

did not realize: WJB interview, Apr. 11, 1988 (32-6); jointly celebrating: WOD, *Justice Brennan as a Jurist,* 4 RUTGERS-CAM. L.J. 5, 7 (1972).

Bazelon was the ninth: Marilyn Berger, "David Bazelon Dies at 83; Jurist Had Wide Influence," *NYT,* Feb. 21, 1993.

groundbreaking opinion: *Durham v. United States,* 214 F.2d 862 (D.C. Cir. 1954).

98 came away impressed: WJB (remarks, dinner in honor of Judge David Bazelon, Cosmos Club, Washington, DC, Nov. 9, 1974).

"had a good": David L. Bazelon, *A Tribute to Justice William J. Brennan, Jr.,* 15 HARV. C.R.-C.L. L. REV. 282, (1980). Brennan later remembered meeting Bazelon for the first time at a Sunday brunch, but Bazelon recounted earlier that it was at the Douglas party, and Bazelon's son later recalled him coming home from the party at Douglas's house that night and describing the meeting.

first opinion: *Putnam v. Comm'r,* 352 U.S. 82 (1956); first dissent: *La Buy v. Howes Leather Co.,* 352 U.S. 249 (1957); most controversial: *Jencks v. United States,* 353 U.S. 657 (1957).

had already worked: Edward V. Heck, *The Socialization of a Freshman Justice: The Early Years of Justice Brennan,* 10 PAC. L. J. 707 (1979).

"direct from a circus": Fred J. Maroon and Suzy Maroon, *The Supreme Court of the United States* (New York: Thomasson-Grant & Lickle, 1996), 33.

99 not necessarily prepare: WJB, "State Court Decisions and the Supreme Court" (speech, Pennsylvania Bar Association, Pittsburgh, PA, Feb. 3, 1960).

"considerable astonishment": WJB, "The United States Supreme Court: Reflections Past and Present" (speech, Marquette University, Milwaukee, WI, Feb. 25, 1965), published as WJB, *The United States Supreme Court: Reflections Past and Present,* 48 MARQ. L. REV. 437 (1965).

"an adventure into": WJB, "State Court Decisions and the Supreme Court."

any misgivings: WJB (speech, Harvard Law Review Banquet, Boston, MA, Apr. 11, 1959).

observed no signs: Edward Keane (WJB OT '57 clerk) interview, June 1, 1989; Richard Rhodes (WJB OT '56 clerk) interview, Mar. 15, 1989.

"He is never plagued": Jack Alexander, "Mr. Justice from New Jersey," *Saturday Evening Post,* Sept. 28, 1957.

a little overwhelmed: Si Liberman, "Supreme Court a 7-Day a Week Job for Justice Brennan," *Asbury Park Press,* Jan. 20, 1957.

100 first writing assignment: *Putnam v. Comm'r,* 352 U.S. 82 (1956).

"Your opinion however": HLB to WJB, Nov. 15, 1956.

"I am sorry": JMH to WJB, Nov. 13, 1956.

Brennan had sought: WJB to Freund, Oct. 19, 1956.

"If you want": FF, *Felix Frankfurter Reminisces* (New York: Reynal, 1960), 249.

enlisting the assistance: WJB to Freund, Oct. 19, 1956.

101 "he will, I am": FF to WJB, Oct. 25, 1956, FF papers, HLS.

"It will give me": FF handwrote his reply on WJB's invitation.

"Frankfurter took over": Frank Brennan interview, Dec. 29, 1986.

hand them cocktails: Keane interview, June 1, 1989.

Frankfurter believed firmly: Philip B. Kurland, *Mr. Justice Frankfurter and the Constitution* (Chicago: University of Chicago Press, 1971), 5.

due process clause: Section 1 of the Fourteenth Amendment, ratified in 1868, states, "No State shall make or enforce any law which shall abridge the privileges or immunities of citizens of the United States; nor shall any State deprive any person of life, liberty, or property, without due process of law; nor deny to any person within its jurisdiction the equal protection of the laws." U.S. CONST. amend. 14, § 1.

102 incremental application: Melvin I. Urofsky, *Felix Frankfurter: Judicial Restraint and Individual Liberties* (Boston: Twayne, 1991), 97. See, for example, *Wolf v. Colorado*, 338 U.S. 25 (1949).

"their prejudices": Melvin I. Urofsky, *Conflict Among the Brethren: Felix Frankfurter, William O. Douglas and the Clash of Personalities and Philosophies on the United States Supreme Court*, 1988 DUKE L. J. 71, 105.

"On more than one": FF to Hand, Oct. 25, 1956, FF papers, LOC.

103 "And Felix really": WJB interview, Apr. 4, 1988 (31-8).

Frankfurter lined up: FF to Hand, Oct. 25, 1956, FF papers, LOC.

"Felix wanted me": Jeffrey T. Leeds, "A Life on the Court," *NYT Magazine*, Oct. 5, 1986, 24.

first dissent Brennan joined: *Mass. Bonding Co. v. United States*, 352 U.S. 128 (1956).

104 possible death sentence: *Fikes v. Alabama*, 352 U.S. 191 (1957).

"fundamental fairness": In *Fikes v. Alabama*, Frankfurter referred to this as "what may fairly be deemed the civilized standards of the Anglo-American world." *Fikes v. Alabama*, 352 U.S. 191, 199 (1956).

first dissent Brennan wrote: *La Buy v. Howes Leather Co.*, 352 U.S. 249 (1957).

"I am glad": FF wrote this on WJB's Dec. 12, 1956, draft.

pop in unannounced: Clyde Szuch interview, June 11, 1987.

"he'd go into": WJB interview, Jan. 7, 1987 (8-10).

"I'm serious": FF to WJB, undated.

"We are all": EW to WJB, Nov. 28, 1956.

trip to Philadelphia: Liberman, "Supreme Court a 7-Day a Week Job."

a private car: WJB interview, Jan. 7, 1987 (8-3).

They ate breakfast: Jim Newton, *Justice for All: Earl Warren and the Nation He Made* (New York: Riverhead Books, 2006), 350.

105 would soon graduate: *Quantico Sentry*, Feb. 22, 1957; *NYT*, "Marines Hear Brennan," Feb. 17, 1957.

owner's box: Evan Thomas, *The Man to See* (New York: Simon & Schuster, 1991), 177.

Warren preferred: WJB interview, May 30, 1990 (63-7).

"we just got along": WJB interview, Apr. 11, 1988 (32-4).

"naturally gregarious": WJB, "Chief Justice Warren," 88 HARV. L. REV. 1, 1 (1974).

106 angrily reject: WJB interview, June 21, 1994.

Just as Warren: G. Edward White, *Earl Warren: A Public Life* (New York: Oxford University Press, 1982), 185.

Warren asked Black: Roger K. Newman, *Hugo Black: A Biography* (New York: Fordham University Press, 1997), 427.

met with Black: Ibid., p. 471.

"I suppose we": Leeds, "A Life on the Court," p. 24.

107 antitrust lawsuit: *United States v. E. I. du Pont de Nemours & Co.*, 353 U.S. 586 (1957).

shown a willingness: *United States v. E. I. du Pont de Nemours & Co.*, 351 U.S. 377 (1956).

all made clear: WOD conference notes, WOD papers.

recused himself: Clark also recused himself, as did Charles E. Whittaker, since the case was argued prior to his appointment, leaving just six justices to hear the case.

Brennan argued: WOD conference notes, WOD papers.

108 "He'd be frankly": Szuch interview, June 11, 1987.

got noticed by clerks: William H. Allen interview, May 23, 1989.

"When I think back": WJB to Ginger Atwood, Apr. 19, 1957.

109 crated all the bulbs: WJB interview, Apr. 4, 1988 (31-1).

"find self-fulfillment": Dorothy K. Goldberg, *A Private View of a Public Life* (New York: Charterhouse, 1975), 152.

No one still expected: Miriam Kellner Bazelon Knox, *A Salute to Life: Mickey's Memoir* (Washington, DC: K2 Pub., 2002), 66.

might show up: Nancy Brennan interview, Sept. 1, 1988.

talk about dogs: Tim Phelps interview, May 29, 2007.

110 only two invitations: Liberman, "Supreme Court a 7-Day a Week Job."

first state dinner: Marie McNair, "Justice Was Served — Formally," *WP,* Jan. 30, 1957.

"She was a very": Alice Knight interview, Aug. 13, 1990.

"Both Mrs. Brennan": Jean Campbell, "Irish Roots in Jersey Soil," *Suburban Life,* Oct. 1959, 46.

"She loved it": WJB interview, June 10, 1987 (18-13).

particularly enjoyed: WJB to James Auchincloss, Mar. 27, 1957.

Brennan recoiled: James E. Clayton, *The Making of Justice: The Supreme Court in Action* (New York: E. P. Dutton, 1964), 158.

111 "was much too busy": Liberman, "Supreme Court a 7-Day a Week Job."

injured railroad workers: *Rogers v. Mo. Pac. R.R. Co.,* 352 U.S. 500 (1957).

in most cases: At the time, there was a category of cases known as mandatory appeals that the Supreme Court had less discretion to turn down. Congress repealed most of the Court's mandatory jurisdiction in 1988. *Certiorari* is Latin for "to be informed," and litigants asking the Supreme Court to review their case are literally petitioning the Court to become informed about their case by requesting that the lower courts send up the record. Lee Epstein and Jack Knight, *The Choices Justices Make* (Washington, DC: CQ Press, 1998), 26.

two hundred claims: Newman, *Hugo Black,* p. 473.

"I do not conceive": FF to WJB, Apr. 10, 1957, FF papers, HLS.

112 first time he encountered: WJB (speech, Harvard Law Review Banquet, 1959). In this speech, Brennan said he did not write an opinion in the case, nor is there record of the Appellate Division's per curiam reversal.

"When the state": WJB (speech, Harvard Law Review Banquet, 1959).

In re Groban: 352 U.S. 330 (1957).

Brennan switched sides: WJB to HLB, Feb. 25, 1957, HLB papers.

113 "into the hands": Reed to WJB, Feb. 25, 1957.

retired that day: *Time,* "Supreme Court: Reed Steps Down," Feb. 11, 1957.

"hard core liberal wing": Melvin I. Urofsky, *Felix Frankfurter,* p. 143, citing FF to Hand, June 30, 1957.

noticeably centrist: Edward V. Heck, *The Socialization of a Freshman Justice: The Early Years of Justice Brennan,* 10 PAC. L. J. 707, 711 (1979).

"with a fine-tooth comb": Jay Lewis, "Johnston Plans Inquiry Into Brennan's Record," *WP,* Nov. 19, 1956.

requiring segregation on buses: *Gayle v. Browder,* 352 U.S. 903 (1956). The per curiam opinion in its entirety read, "The motion to affirm is granted and the judgment is affirmed." *Brown v. Board of Education,* 347 U.S. 483 (1954); *Mayor and City Council of Baltimore v. Dawson,* 350 U.S. 877 (1955); *Holmes v. Atlanta,* 350 U.S. 879 (1955).

114 victoriously declared: Taylor Branch, *Parting the Waters: America in the King Years, 1954–63* (New York: Simon & Schuster, 1989), 193, 196.

"did not anticipate": Lewis, "Johnston Plans Inquiry."

"supremely unfit": AP, Feb. 22, 1957, WJB scrapbook.

"waging a guerilla war": *Washington News*, "Brennan Will Be Opposed by McCarthy," Jan. 15, 1957.

"It is safe": *Washington Star*, "McCarthyism Wanes," Feb. 28, 1957.

severe drinking: Thomas C. Reeves, *The Life and Times of Joe McCarthy: A Biography* (New York: Stein & Day, 1982), 669.

115 "None of the praise": *Asbury Park Press*, "McCarthy Honors Brennan," Jan. 8, 1957.

viewed as inappropriate: WJB interview, Oct. 21, 1987 (22-8).

"demonstrated an underlying": Senate Committee on the Judiciary, *Nomination of William Joseph Brennan Jr.: Hearings Before the Committee on the Judiciary*, 85th Cong., 1st sess., 1957. All quotes from the hearing come from this transcript.

117 "For a few hours": *Washington Star*, "McCarthyism Wanes."

"At this late date": *NY Post*, "Judgment Day for a Judge," Feb. 28, 1957.

"going to the mat": Daniel M. Berman, *Mr. Justice Brennan: A Preliminary Appraisal*, 7 CATH. U. L. REV. 1, 7 (1958), citing an Apr. 17, 1957, conversation with WJB.

"He'd rather walk": Szuch interview, Dec. 21, 2007.

"If there's a kid": WJB (lecture, Salzburg Seminar, Salzburg, Austria, July 1987).

118 "Roman Catholicism is engaged": *Catholicism in America: A Series of Articles from the Commonweal* (New York: Harcourt, Brace, 1954), 75.

objected to the question: Richard L. Lyons, "Senate Committee Ends Hearings on Brennan; Approval Is Expected," *WP*, Feb. 28, 1957.

119 gone too far: Berman, *Mr. Justice Brennan*.

"confused and negative": Ibid., citing *Commonweal*, Apr. 5, 1957, 5.

"Whatever one's religion": Michael O'Brien, *John F. Kennedy: A Biography* (New York: Thomas Dunne Books/St. Martin's Press, 2005), 418.

"Why in God's name": WJB interview, Jan. 28, 1987 (9-7).

Stone accurately predicted: I. F. Stone, "The Last Stand of Low Blow Joe," *I. F. Stone's Weekly*, Mar. 4, 1957.

120 obscure statute: 28 U.S.C. 4 states, "Associate justices shall have precedence according to the seniority of their commissions. Justices whose commissions bear the same date shall have precedence according to seniority in age."

signed the commission: *NYT*, "Justice Commissioned," Mar. 22, 1957.

Whittaker's commission: WJB (speech, Yale Law Journal, New Haven, CT, Apr. 13, 1957). WJB also describes the chronology of events in a Mar. 21, 1957, letter to ATV.

"Warren was a": Edward de Grazia, *Girls Lean Back Everywhere* (New York: Random House, 1992), 274.

Was it enough: Anthony Lewis, "Sex and the Supreme Court," *Esquire*, June 1963, 83.

121 several states: Frederick F. Schauer, *The Law of Obscenity* (Washington, DC: Bureau of National Affairs, 1976), 10.

increasingly alarmed: Ibid., pp. 12–13.

"Does your argument": Lewis, "Sex and the Supreme Court," p. 82.

justices tied: *Doubleday & Co. v. New York*, 335 U.S. 848 (1948).

122 losing battle: David Halberstam, *The Fifties* (New York: Ballantine Books, 1994), 570–71.

Butler v. Michigan: 352 U.S. 380 (1957).

"I confess": WJB to FF, Feb. 19, 1957, FF papers, LOC.

with titles such as: Schauer, *Law of Obscenity*, p. 33.

123 Fisher sent: Roger Fisher interview, Feb. 12, 2008.

The justices passed: Grazia, *Girls Lean Back Everywhere*, pp. 302–3.

"Everybody knew": WJB interview, Apr. 13, 1989 (49-4).

encountered obscenity before: *Adams Theatre Co. v. Keenan,* 96 A.2d 519 (N.J. 1953).
Szuch hid: Szuch interview, Dec. 21, 2007.

124 "well-defined and narrowly": *Chaplinsky v. New Hampshire,* 315 U.S. 568 (1942).
so impressed: WJB interview, June 17, 1987 (19-16). No such memo survives in Brennan's papers, but Jerome Cohen, Frankfurter's clerk that term, vividly recalled writing one with the details Brennan remembered.
"In light of this": *Roth v. United States,* 354 U.S. 476, 483 (1957).
smiled mischievously: Richard Rhodes interview, Mar. 15, 1989.

125 companion case: *Alberts v. California,* 354 U.S. 476 (1957).
"when legislators and judges": *WP,* "Obscenity in Court," June 30, 1957.
looked fixedly: Alexander, "Mr. Justice from Jersey."

126 first decision: *United States v. E. I. du Pont de Nemours & Co.,* 353 U.S. 586 (1957).
twenty minutes: Alexander, "Mr. Justice from Jersey."
8,283-page transcript: Tinsley E. Yarbrough, *John Marshall Harlan* (New York: Oxford University Press, 1992), 67-69.
"Now that my lips": JMH to FF, June 3, 1957, FF papers, LOC.
Frankfurter was so worried: FF to Warren, June 3, 1957, FF papers, LOC.
"Justice Brennan's opinion introduced": *Fortune,* "Brennan on Bigness," July 15, 1957.

127 case reminded Brennan: *State v. Tune,* 98 A.2d 881 (N.J. 1953).
"big mistake to open": WOD, Oct. 19, 1956, conference notes, WOD papers.
only where the defense: TC to conference, Nov. 27, 1956, WOD papers.

128 typical cartoon: Arthur E. Sutherland Jr., *Foreword: The Citizen's Immunities and Public Opinion,* 71 HARV. L. REV. 85, 86 (1957).
"Liberal leanings": *WSJ,* Washington Wire, June 7, 1957.
"B.B.D. & W.": *Time,* "The Temple Builder," July 1, 1957.
a play on the name: Roger K. Newman, *The Warren Court and American Politics: An Impressionistic Appreciation,* 18 CONST. COMMENT. 661, 689 (2001).
"as much as any": *Life,* "The Warren Court," July 1, 1957, 33.
"the framers": Newman, *Warren Court,* p. 690.
the "Jesus Quartet": Yarbrough, *John Marshall Harlan,* p. 144.
"I have been depressed": WEB to HAB, July 11, 1957, HAB papers.
four additional subversion decisions: *Service v. Dulles,* 354 U.S. 363 (1957), *Watkins v. United States,* 354 U.S. 178 (1957), *Sweezy v. New Hampshire,* 354 U.S. 234 (1957), *Yates v. United States,* 354 U.S. 298 (1957).

129 American serviceman: *Wilson v. Girard,* 354 U.S. 524 (1957).
justices had sided: Barry Friedman, *The Will of the People: How Public Opinion Has Influenced the Supreme Court and Shaped the Meaning of the Constitution* (New York: Farrar, Strauss, and Giroux, 2009), 250.
Georgia legislature overwhelmingly: Bernard Schwartz, *Super Chief: Earl Warren and His Supreme Court; A Judicial Biography* (New York: New York University Press, 1983), 250.
common enemy: Walter F. Murphy, *Congress and the Court* (Chicago: University of Chicago Press, 1962), 86.
"Vesuvian eruption": Fulton Lewis Jr., *Washington Report,* June 16, 1957.
had not helped: Murphy, *Congress and the Court,* p. 86.

130 one-man protest: *RBR,* "Brennan Is Cited for Way of Life," July 25, 1957.
"I don't understand": WJB interview, Mar. 13, 1987 (11-3).
"How do you like": WJB to Agnes Brennan, Oct. 25, 1956, WJB personal files.
"confess to considerable": WJB to FF, Aug. 31, 1957, FF papers, LOC.

"The past is": FF to WJB, Sept. 4, 1957.
Rhodes concluded: Rhodes interview, Mar. 15, 1989.
gun-shy: Lucas A. Powe, Jr., *The Warren Court and American Politics* (Cambridge, MA: Belknap Press, 2000), 140–41.
"yellow press": WJB interview, Mar. 13, 1987 (11-2).
131 "Believe me, there's": WJB, "The United States Supreme Court: Reflections Past and Present" (speech, Marquette University, 1965).

6. COLD WAR

132 "columnists' row": Drew Pearson, "Columnist Beset by Animal Rites," *WP,* Oct. 18, 1958.
133 officers stopped Brennan: William J. Brennan III, "Breakfast with the Police," in *The Common Man as Uncommon Man: Remembering Justice William J. Brennan, Jr.,* ed. E. Joshua Rosenkranz and Thomas M. Jorde (New York: Brennan Center for Justice, 2006), 11–12.
"Don't worry about": Jack Alexander, "Mr. Justice from New Jersey," *Saturday Evening Post,* Sept. 28, 1957.
134 out of gas: Daniel O'Hern interview, Mar. 28, 2007.
"I sincerely appreciate": WJB to FF, undated (summer 1957), FF papers, LOC.
Perez v. Brownell: 356 U.S. 44 (1958).
Trop v. Dulles: 356 U.S. 86 (1958).
135 later credited Frankfurter: WJB interview, May 19, 1987 (15-1).
"is reasonably calculated": WJB to FF, Mar. 21, 1958.
"The more you": Bernard Schwartz, *Supreme Court—October 1957 Term,* 57 MICH. L. REV. 315, 326 (1959).
"just dead wrong": WJB interview, May 19, 1987 (15-1).
"Congress is constitutionally": *Kennedy v. Mendoza-Martinez,* 372 U.S. 144 (1963).
Speiser v. Randall: 357 U.S. 513 (1958).
badly divided: Harold Burton to WJB, June 23, 1958.
136 Brennan focused: George Anastoplo, *Justice Brennan, Due Process and the Freedom of Speech: A Celebration of* Speiser v. Randall, 20 J. MARSHALL L. REV. 7, 10 (1986).
be central: Ibid., citing Leonard W. Levy et al., eds., *Encyclopedia of the American Constitution* (New York: Macmillan, 1986).
"He made me": Norman Dorsen, "Brennan's Magic: Always Time to Talk," *LAT,* July 27, 1997.
Harlan did ultimately: JMH to WJB, June 25, 1958.
137 Brennan would use: For a full discussion of Brennan's use of *Speiser,* see Laurence H. Tribe, *In Memoriam: William J. Brennan Jr.,* 111 HARV. L. REV. 41 (1997).
"a passionate concern": Daniel M. Berman, *Mr. Justice Brennan: A Preliminary Appraisal,* 7 CATH. U. L. REV. 1, 14–15 (1958).
"courage and independence": WOD to Fred Rodell, Mar. 2, 1957.
"fringes of the bloc": Edward V. Heck, *The Socialization of a Freshman Justice: The Early Years of Justice Brennan,* 10 PAC. L. J. 707, 716 (1979).
more apt to write: Ibid., p. 718. Heck also cites *Beilan v. Board of Education,* 357 U.S. 399 (1958), and *Gore v. United States,* 357 U.S. 386 (1958), as two other examples of 1957 term cases where Brennan "generally reached a libertarian result on narrow grounds."

"Justice Brennan has seemed": *Life*, "One Supreme Court," June 16, 1958.

"I wish he were": FF to JMH, undated, JMH papers.

Frankfurter even joked: FF to WJB, Jan. 2, 1958. In *Brown v. United States*, 356 U.S. 148 (1958), Frankfurter wrote for the 5–4 majority that a defendant could not invoke the Fifth Amendment privilege against self-incrimination after testifying voluntarily about related matters in a denaturalization proceeding. Rather than join Black's dissent, which included Warren and Douglas, Brennan wrote his own.

138 offered a gushing: Drew Pearson, "Justice Copies Queen's Dinner," *WP,* Nov. 20, 1957.

"I get more confused": DDE to Rogers, May 12, 1958, DDE papers.

"This capital": Daniel M. Berman, "The Supreme Court's New Liberal Swing," *Washington Sunday Star*, June 23, 1957.

held out: Preble Stolz (Burton OT '57 clerk) interview, Feb. 5, 1990.

"expressed disappointment": Harold H. Burton diary entry, July 17, 1958, HHB papers.

139 Abraham included it: Henry J. Abraham, *Justices and Presidents: A Political History of Appointments to the Supreme Court,* 3rd ed. (New York: Oxford University Press, 1992), 266.

Richardson's 1979 biography: Elmo R. Richardson, *The Presidency of Dwight D. Eisenhower* (Lawrence: Regents Press of Kansas, 1979), 108; Tony Mauro, "Intern Spikes Ike's," *Legal Times,* Aug. 20, 1990.

did not use: Decades later, Brennan's clerks referenced the line at a party in his chambers celebrating his twenty-eighth anniversary on the Court, where they hung a handmade sign that read, "I like Ike's Mistake" behind his desk; U.S. Supreme Court Office of the Curator's photo collection.

only account: Fred Friendly interview, May 4, 1990.

140 angrily canceled his membership: Jim Newton, *Justice for All: Earl Warren and the Nation He Made* (New York: Riverhead Books, 2007), 356.

dangers of: *WP & Times-Herald,* "Warren Denounces Court Delays," Aug. 26, 1958.

warned the crowd: Tom Cameron, "Brennan Says Courts Need Modern Methods," *LAT,* Aug. 26, 1958.

"There has to be": Jeffrey T. Leeds, "A Life on the Court," *NYT Magazine,* Oct. 5, 1986, 24.

141 finagled a tour: WJB to Stanley Weigel, Sept. 2, 1958.

planned to continue: Brennan's speech files contain remarks prepared for delivery at Stanford University on August 26 and the Ninth Circuit Judicial Conference in Los Angeles on August 29.

Southern defiance: Numan V. Bartley, *The Rise of Massive Resistance: Race and Politics in the South During the 1950s* (Baton Rouge: Louisiana State University Press, 1969), 64.

"full compliance": *Brown v. Bd. of Educ. (II),* 349 U.S. 294 (1955).

142 surprising symbol: J. Harvie Wilkinson III, *From Brown to Bakke: The Supreme Court and School Integration* (New York: Oxford University Press, 1979), 88–89.

143 boarded a plane: photograph by Ed Clark, *Justice Earl Warren and His Family Arriving with William J. Brennan Jr. for a Special Session of the US Supreme Court* © 1956 by Time Inc., from Life Magazine Photo Archive, http://images.google.com/hosted/life (under "Search Life Images" type "William Brennan").

"Well, Chief": WJB interview, Apr. 13, 1989 (49-5).

Cooper v. Aaron: 358 U.S. 1 (1958).

chief justice met privately: Newton, *Justice for All,* p. 360.

last-minute maneuvering: Ibid., p. 366.

rushed through: Russell Baker, "Eisenhower Hints Desire for 'Slower' Integration," *NYT,* Aug. 28, 1958.

"slower movement": Ibid.

"Faubus's resistance": Dennis Lyons interview, Apr. 6, 1989.

144 tan business suit: Russell Baker, "Courtroom Hushed as Drama Unfolds," *NYT,* Aug. 29, 1958.

did not bother applying: Juan Williams, *Thurgood Marshall: American Revolutionary* (New York: Times Books, 1998), 52.

"surrender to obstructionists": Ibid., p. 270, citing *NY Post,* Aug. 28, 1958.

145 retorted acidly: Baker, "Courtroom Hushed."

Brennan asked: Anthony Lewis, "High Court Hears Little Rock Plea," *NYT,* Sept. 12, 1958.

146 "didn't bother": WJB interview, Feb. 5, 1987 (10-6).

called upon: Brennan recalled it was a St. Louis munitions factory. WJB interview, Aug. 25, 1989 (54-1). But Arthur Krim, his wartime colleague who accompanied Brennan on the trip, recollected that the plant was in Georgia. Arthur Krim interview, Aug. 22, 1989.

"You know": Hunter R. Clark, *Justice Brennan: The Great Conciliator* (Secaucus, NJ: Carol Pub. Group, 1995), 150.

breakaway parish: Unpublished history of Epiphany Church provided by church staff in December 2007.

147 first black Catholic pastor: *WP,* "Negro Priest Assigned to DC Parish," Sept. 1, 1952.

agonizing work: WJB interview, Jan. 7, 1987 (8-1).

"nearly colorless compromises": Lyle Denniston, "Angry Justice Brennan," *Trenton Times,* Apr. 2, 1971.

Plessy v. Ferguson: 163 U.S. 537 (1896).

148 Black suggested: WJB to conference, Sept. 17, 1958.

more dramatic: Ibid.

"Under our constitution": TC draft dissent, undated, TC papers.

frequent visits: WJB interview, Sept. 13, 1988 (42-4).

149 "So that's": WJB interview, Apr. 4, 1988 (31-2).

Harlan suggested that: JMH to conference, Sept. 23, 1958, HLB papers.

"grave mistake": WJB to conference, Sept. 24, 1958.

either Harlan or Frankfurter: There is some disagreement over who originated the idea of having all nine justices sign the opinion. In his memoirs, Warren recounts that it was Frankfurter who made the suggestion. Earl Warren, *The Memoirs of Chief Justice Earl Warren* (Garden City, NY: Doubleday, 1977), 299. But in *Super Chief,* Schwartz cites a Harlan draft that suggests it was actually Harlan. Schwartz, *Super Chief: Earl Warren and His Supreme Court; A Judicial Biography* (New York: New York University Press, 1983), 299. Douglas wrote a memo to his files on Oct. 8, 1958, in which he indicates it was first suggested by Harlan.

Marbury v. Madison: 5 U.S. 137 (1803).

attacked by conservative critics: See Edwin Meese III, *The Law of the Constitution,* 61 Tul. L. Rev. 979 (1987); Michael Stokes Paulsen, *The Most Dangerous Branch: Executive Power to Say What the Law Is,* 83 Geo. L.J. 217, 223–25 (1994).

Brennan rejected: WJB to JMH, Sept. 24, 1958.

later insisted: WJB interview, Apr. 13, 1989 (49-7).

150 "It became apparent": Anthony Lewis, "Supreme Court Forbids Evasion or Force to Balk Integration," *NYT,* Sept. 30, 1958.

each of the justices: Douglas, who had already left on a canoe trip to Minnesota, missed the historic occasion.

until two decades later: Daniel J. Hutchinson, *Unanimity and Desegregation: Decision-making in the Supreme Court, 1948–1958,* 68 GEO. L. J. 1 (1979). Brennan provided access to his files on the case to New York University law professor Bernard Schwartz, who was working on the biography of Warren published as *Super Chief.*

could not be persuaded: Burton diary, Sept. 29, 1958, HHB papers.

"After sleeping on it": FF to JMH, Sept. 12, 1958, JMH papers.

151 "These are not": FF to JMH, Sept. 25, 1958, JMH papers.

"peculiarly qualified": FF to C. C. Burlingham, Nov. 12, 1958, FF papers, LOC.

"vindication of Brown": FF to JMH, Oct. 11, 1958, JMH papers.

"Some of my brethren": Ibid.

Frankfurter angrily rebuffed: Schwartz, *Super Chief,* p. 302.

"Isn't this bound to": James F. Simon, *The Antagonists: Hugo Black, Felix Frankfurter, and Civil Liberties in Modern America* (New York: Simon & Schuster 1989), 232.

152 "his words today seemed": *NYT,* "Justice Deplores Arkansas Tactics," Oct. 7, 1958.

Warren did repeatedly: *Time,* "Warren v. Frankfurter," May 5, 1961.

153 "little bastard": Melvin I. Urofsky, *Felix Frankfurter, William O. Douglas, and the Clash of Personalities and Philosophies on the United States Supreme Court,* 1988 DUKE L. J. 71, 106.

as both Vinson: Bruce Alan Murphy, *Wild Bill: The Life and Legend of William O. Douglas* (New York: Random House, 2003), 301; and Black: Roger K. Newman, *Hugo Black: A Biography* (New York: Pantheon Books, 1994), 485.

"If he was unhappy": Jeffrey Nagin interview, Mar. 23, 2007.

subversion and criminal-procedure cases: See *Uphaus v. Wyman,* 360 U.S. 72 (1959); *Barenblatt v. United States,* 360 U.S. 109 (1959); *Bartkus v. United States,* 359 U.S. 121 (1959).

"were consistently with": Anthony Lewis, "Conflict Growing in Supreme Court," *NYT,* July 5, 1959.

"We would be inclined": Dennis Hutchinson, *Felix Frankfurter and the Business of the Supreme Court, OT 1946 to OT 1961,* 1980 SUP. CT. REV. 143, 205.

"He tried very hard": WJB interview, Apr. 4, 1988 (31-8).

154 "the Admiral from Newark": Peter Fishbein interview, June 1, 1989, re: *Romero v. International Terminal Operating Co.,* 358 U.S. 354 (1959).

"Brother Frankfurter": WJB to conference, Feb. 6, 1959, re: *Bartkus v. Illinois,* 359 U.S. 121 (1959).

"A young fellow": FF to WJB, undated, re: *Abbate v. United States,* 359 U.S. 187 (1959).

"I was a student of": WJB (speech to Harvard Law Review Banquet, Boston, MA, Apr. 11, 1959).

Irvin v. Dowd: 359 U.S. 394 (1959).

155 "clear, deep rooted understanding": FF to conference, Mar. 23, 1959.

forwarding to Stewart: WJB to PS, Oct. 22, 1958.

"They will make": PS to WJB, Oct. 22, 1958.

"the Stewarts will make": WJB to Board of Governors of the Chevy Chase Club, Oct. 7, 1959.

Brennan's initial sense: Lyons interview, Apr. 6, 1989.

156 One litigator joked: James E. Clayton, *The Making of Justice: The Supreme Court in Action* (New York: E. P. Dutton, 1964), 216.

"Your opinion in the above": WJB to PS, June 4, 1962.

"You had to work with Potter": WJB interview, Mar. 16, 1988 (30-7).

"very carefully reasoned": Fishbein interview, June 1, 1989.

an article appeared: Henry M. Hart Jr., Note, *Foreword: The Time Chart of the Justices*, 73 HARV. L. REV. 84 (1959).

Hart regularly denigrated: Daniel Rezneck interview, Aug. 24, 2007.

157   brushed off Hart's complaints: Fishbein interview, Mar. 27, 2007.

"I have always envied": WJB to Rodell, Dec. 16, 1957.

"Why don't you just ask us?": Kenneth Mott e-mail to Stern, Mar. 25, 2008.

write a rebuttal: Thurman Arnold, *Professor Hart's Theology*, 73 HARV. L. REV. 1298 (1960). According to Eisler, Douglas and Brennan's friend Judge Bazelon enlisted Arnold as a proxy. Kim Isaac Eisler, *A Justice for All: William J. Brennan, Jr., and The Decision That Transformed America* (New York: Simon & Schuster, 1993), 163. But Dennis Lyons, Brennan's former clerk who at the time was working at the law firm, recalled it was Arnold's idea. Lyons helped edit the article but said he never discussed it in advance with Brennan. Dennis Lyons interview, June 29, 2007.

briefly served: Arnold was a judge on the U.S. Court of Appeals for the D.C. Circuit between 1943 and 1945.

"It's both brilliant and devastating": WJB to AF, Dec. 28, 1959.

158   "for your eyes only": WOD to WJB, May 1960, re: *United Steelworkers of America v. Warrior and Gulf Navigation*, 363 U.S. 574 (1960).

Memos Brennan circulated: WJB to EW, HLB, WOD, re: *Campbell v. United States*, 365 U.S. 85 (1961).

"Lyons served Brennan's purpose": Paul Bender interview, Dec. 18, 2007.

"This is just a": EW to WJB, Aug. 19, 1960.

The conversation turned: WJB interview, Apr. 4, 1988 (31-8).

159   psychological problems: H. N. Hirsch, *The Enigma of Felix Frankfurter* (New York: Basic Books, 1981), 81–82.

One Halloween: Alice Knight interview, Aug. 13, 1990.

would drop everything: Andrew Kaufman (FF OT '56 and OT '57 clerk) to Richard Cooper (WJB OT '69 clerk), Nov. 20, 1969.

"Don't tell the secrets": FF to Nancy Brennan, undated.

"He was absolutely": WJB interview, Jan. 7, 1987 (8-5).

tutor Nancy: Nancy Brennan interview, Sept. 1, 1988.

160   returning there in 1959: WJB to Donald Kipp, Feb. 18, 1959.

Nancy once sent Warren: Nancy Brennan to EW, Mar. 19, 1961, EW papers.

Warren's daughter: Brennan's son Bill later recalled a movie date with Warren's beautiful and much-courted daughter Virginia after he got out of the Marines as "one of the nicest days of my life." Newton, *Justice for All*, p. 350.

"a knitting of compromised work": Donna Haupt, "Justice William J. Brennan Jr.," *Constitution*, winter 1989, 54.

161   "Papa could be": Georgie Brennan interview, Dec. 1, 2007.

Roxey was already engaged: *NYT*, "Brennan-Fox," June 25, 1959.

"He was just an alcoholic": WJB interview, July 28, 1989 (52-9).

He was enrolled: Jean Campbell, "Irish Roots in Jersey Soil," *Suburban Life*, Oct. 1959, 45.

7. IRISH OR HARVARD

162   made a friendly wager: John J. Cain to WJB, Dec. 19, 1963.

"the Republicans did better": WJB to Mr. and Mrs. Albert Buerck, Dec. 5, 1960.

remained in bed: WJB interview, July 28, 1989 (52-8).

Seated two rows in front: *CT,* "Seating Arrangement for Inauguration," Jan. 19, 1961.

163 "Be more Irish than Harvard": Thomas Maier, *The Kennedys: America's Emerald Kings* (New York: Basic Books, 2004), 363.

Conspicuously absent: Thurston Clarke, *Ask Not: The Inauguration of John F. Kennedy and the Speech that Changed America* (New York: Henry Holt & Co., 2004), 188.

made known: John Cooney, *The American Pope: The Life and Times of Francis Cardinal Spellman* (New York: Times Books, 1984), 268.

new president greeted: Clarke, *Ask Not,* p. 202.

arrived for a nightcap: Robert W. Merry, *Taking on the World: Joseph and Stewart Alsop, Guardians of the American Century* (New York: Penguin, 1997), 358.

Kennedy had suggested Brennan: Edward M. Kennedy interview, Feb. 18, 2008.

wrote to congratulate Ted: WJB to Edward M. Kennedy, Apr. 24, 1959.

much closer: Kennedy interview, Feb. 18, 2008.

164 more of Kennedy: WJB interview, June 3, 1988 (38-23).

"You can't tell me": Robert O'Neil interview, June 9, 1989.

165 continued attending Sunday Mass: Maier, *Kennedys,* p. 306.

two out of every: Nancy Brennan interview, Aug. 22, 2007.

appeared at a Mass: *Catholic University of America Bulletin,* Apr. 1957; marking his death: Kenneth Dole, "Eisenhower Heads U.S. Notables at Cathedral Mass for Pope Pius," *WP,* Oct. 15, 1958; dedication of the National Shrine: John D. Morris, "Catholics Dedicate National Shrine in Washington," *NYT,* Nov. 21, 1959; student orators' competition: *WP,* "5 Catholic Orators Vie in Contest," Mar. 31, 1958.

every January: The date of the Red Mass later shifted from January to prior to the start of the Court's term in October.

"He was happy": Paula Smith interview, Mar. 7, 2009. Paula Smith and the Crawleys were related to Brennan's mother. Brennan was unable to locate any members of his father's family in Ireland.

166 "taking care of the poor": WJB, oral history interview by Anthony Lewis, May 28, 1992, Federal Judicial Center.

Saint Thomas Aquinas: In a 1964 speech, Brennan said, "Perhaps some of you may detect, as I think I do, a return to the philosophy of Saint Thomas Aquinas in the new jurisprudence. Call it a resurgence if you will of concepts of natural law. . . ." WJB, "Religion, Education and the Law" (speech, Jewish Theological Seminary, New York, Nov. 15, 1964).

"espoused an enlightened liberality": Philip Gleason, "American Catholics and Liberalism, 1789–1960," in *Catholicism and Liberalism: Contributions to American Public Policy,* ed. R. Bruce Douglass and David Hollenbach (Cambridge: Cambridge University Press, 2002), 65.

disliked eating cabbage: Connie Phelps interview, July 1, 2007.

did not pressure: Georgie Brennan interview, Oct. 30, 2007.

Bill drifted away: WJB III interview, Sept. 6, 1988.

started talking about: Nancy Brennan interview, Aug. 22, 2007.

informing Stone Ridge's headmaster: WJB to Mother M. O. Mouton, Mar. 8, 1961.

Elsewhere, he said: WJB interview, Nov. 22, 1988 (47-7).

167 Georgie suspected: Georgie Brennan interview, Dec. 1, 2007.

no Masses celebrated: Maier, *Kennedys,* pp. 362–63.

Papal Nuncio's Office called: Peter Fishbein (WJB OT '58 clerk) interview, June 1, 1989.

joined reading and writing: John T. McGreevy, *Catholicism and American Freedom: A History* (New York: W. W. Norton & Company, 2003).

168 The First Amendment: "Congress shall make no law respecting an establishment of religion, or prohibiting the free exercise thereof. . . ." U.S. Const. amend. I.
1930 case challenging: *Cochran v. Louisiana State Bd. of Educ.,* 281 U.S. 370 (1930).
Everson v. Board of Education: 330 U.S. 1 (1947).
an Illinois law: *McCollum v. Bd. of Education,* 333 U.S. 203 (1948).
upholding New York City's: *Zorach v. Clauson,* 343 U.S. 306 (1952).
ducking the question: Court denied cert. in *Tudor v. Bd. of Educ.,* 100 A.2d. 857 (1953), the New Jersey Supreme Court holding against distribution of Gideon Bibles by volunteers, 348 U.S. 816 (1954).
changed his position: Robert Dallek, *An Unfinished Life: John F. Kennedy, 1917–1963* (Boston: Little, Brown and Co., 2003), 146–47.
sole presidential hopeful: Michael O'Brien, *John F. Kennedy: A Biography* (New York: Thomas Dunne Books, 2005), 417.

169 "unthinkable that any": Maier, *Kennedys,* p. 399.
"I asked": Ibid., p. 400.
Engel v. Vitale: 370 U.S. 421 (1962).
Sunday- closing laws: *Braunfeld v. Brown,* 366 U.S. 599 (1961); *Gallagher v. Crown Kosher Super Market,* 366 U.S. 617 (1961); *McGowan v. Maryland,* 366 U.S. 420 (1961); *Two Guys v. McGinley,* 366 U.S. 582 (1961).
Orthodox Jewish merchants: *Braunfeld v. Brown,* 366 U.S. 611 (1961).

170 faced the same case: *Tudor v. Bd. of Educ. of Borough of Rutherford,* 100 A.2d 857 (1953).
nothing voluntary: Harry N. Rosenfeld, *Separation of Church and State in the Public Schools,* 22 U. Pitt. L. Rev. 561, 581–582 (1961), citing P. Baum, Summary of Argument Before Supreme Court of New Jersey in Gideon Bible Case, CLSA Reports 4 (Commission on Law & Social Action, Am. Jewish Congr., mimeo, Oct. 12, 1953).
Fears of growing secularism: Richard P. McBrien, *Caesar's Coin: Religion and Politics in America* (New York: Macmillan, 1987), 171.
Only Stewart expressed: WOD conference notes, Apr. 3, 1962, WOD papers.
honored Black: Anthony Lewis, "Supreme Court Outlaws Official School Prayer in Regents Case Decision," *NYT,* June 26, 1962.
"The clear implication": Ibid.

171 largest volume of mail: Lucas A. Powe, Jr., *The Warren Court and American Politics* (Cambridge, MA: Belknap Press, 2000), 187.
all other business: Anthony Lewis, "Court Again Under Fire," *NYT,* July 1, 1962.
"They put": Lewis, "Supreme Court Outlaws Official School Prayer."
fuel for Communist propaganda: Anthony Lewis, "Both Houses Get Bills to Lift Ban on School Prayer," *NYT,* June 27, 1962.
"tragic misreading": *NYT,* "Spellman Renews Attack on Court's Decision," June 28, 1962.
Kennedy came to: *NYT,* "Transcript of President's News Conference," June 28, 1962.
"one of the most": Wallace Terry, "Area Religious Leaders Split in Views on Court Decision," *WP,* June 30, 1962.
caught off-guard: Frank Michelman interview, Apr. 25, 2007.
Clark broke with: James E. Clayton, *The Making of Justice: The Supreme Court in Action* (New York: E. P. Dutton, 1964), 21–22.
"The tradition that judges": *Look,* "A Visit with Justice Brennan," Dec. 18, 1962.

172 "I was afraid": WJB interview, May 13, 1987 (14-6).
looking pale: O'Neil interview, Apr. 11, 2007.
had been sloppy: Ibid.

clerks' urging: Ibid.

exhaustively researching: AP, "Long Hours, Much Research Go Into Brennan's Opinions," *Washington Star,* July 5, 1963.

173 accept no offers: OT '62 Term History, p. 2.

"This takes an awful": AP "Long Hours, Much Research."

174 *Sherbert v. Verner:* 374 U.S. 398 (1963).

The practical effect: *Sherbert* and the principle of accommodation remained the dominant approach and was even expanded beyond the employment context until Brennan's last weeks on the Court. In *Employment Division v. Smith,* 494 U.S. 872 (1990), Justice Scalia's majority opinion did not overrule *Sherbert* but did change the premise so that government is not required to accommodate religious beliefs if a law's requirements are applicable to everyone in a neutral, evenhanded way.

"specific and outspoken": Clayton, *Making of Justice,* p. 284.

"There were four majority": AP, "High Court Found Imperiled by Foes," *NYT,* Aug. 30, 1963.

"Indeed, our mail": WJB to Charles Alan Wright, Aug. 7, 1963.

real-world impact: Bruce J. Dierenfield, *The Battle over School Prayer: How Engel v. Vitale Changed America* (Lawrence: University Press of Kansas, 2007), 183.

Marjorie silently fumed: Nancy Brennan interview, Aug. 22, 2007.

"Thank God, our Constitution": Kenneth Dole, "Bishop Raps Neutral Stand on Religion," *WP,* Jan. 27, 1964.

175 remained stone-faced: Taylor Branch, *At Canaan's Edge: America in the King Years 1965–68* (New York: Simon & Schuster, 2006), 651.

Marjorie had already: Nancy Brennan interview, Aug. 22, 2007.

performed the novena: Ibid.

176 "It wasn't safe": Ibid.

He had remarried: *NYT,* "Father Escorts Mary F. Crown at Her Wedding," Aug. 27, 1961.

"It was as if": Hugh Brennan Jr. interview, July 10, 2008.

177 the comfort food: WJB interview, May 7, 1987 (13-3).

earned the appreciation: Richard M. Cohen, "The Unquenchable Spirits of Milton Kronheim," *WP Magazine,* April 27, 1975.

178 status symbol: Bart Barnes, "Friend of Presidents Milton Kronheim Dies," *WP,* Sept. 5, 1986.

Kronheim insisted: Milton Kronheim, oral history interview by Ellen Epstein, Center for Oral History, Feb. 6, 1977, p. 82; used with permission of Jacob Stein.

have a hand: Cohen, "The Unquenchable Spirits."

"If you had friends": Ibid.

pleaded no contest: Barnes, "Friend of Presidents."

179 surrogate father: Mickey Bazelon Knox interview, July 25, 2007.

"They can relax": Philip Taubman, "Milton Kronheim's, Where the Justices Adjourn for Lunch," *NYT,* July 15, 1979.

Brennan invested: David Bazelon to WJB, May 25, 1960.

180 closest friends: Richard Bazelon interview, June 22, 2007.

"They were cut": Abe Krash interview, Aug. 15, 2007.

"most students of the Court": AP, "New Jersey Jurist Makes Strong Imprint on US Supreme Court," *Daily Home News,* Aug. 9, 1962.

"Courts have a creative job": WJB, "Law and Social Sciences Today" (Gaston Lecture, Georgetown University, Washington, DC, Nov. 25, 1957).

"some brooding omnipresence": WJB, "Fiftieth Anniversary Celebration" (speech, St. Alban's, Washington, DC, May 25, 1959).

"have survived the tests": WJB, "Law and Social Sciences Today."

Adhering to precedent: WJB (speech, Duquesne Law School, Pittsburgh, PA, Feb. 3, 1960).

181 "Of course I would": Jon Newman (Warren OT '57 clerk) interview, May 15, 1990.

"There are 'absolutes'": Hugo Black, *The Bill of Rights*, 35 N.Y.U. L. REV. 865 (1960).

closeted himself: Daniel Rezneck interview, Aug. 24, 2007.

police in 1960 could: David G. Savage, *Turning Right* (New York: John Wiley & Sons, 1992), 44.

"Crises at hand": WJB, *The Bill of Rights and the States*, 36 N.Y.U. L. REV. 761 (1961).

182 *Mapp v. Ohio:* 367 U.S. 643 (1961).

allegedly obscene materials: Carolyn N. Long, *Mapp v. Ohio* (Lawrence: University Press of Kansas, 2006), 9.

Since 1914: *Weeks v. United States,* 232 U.S. 383 (1914).

Wolf v. Colorado: 338 U.S. 25 (1949).

"Wouldn't this be": Bernard Schwartz, *Super Chief: Earl Warren and His Supreme Court; A Judicial Biography* (New York: New York University Press, 1983), 393.

"Of course you know": WJB to TC, May 1, 1961.

"If you don't mind": Schwartz, *Super Chief,* p. 396, citing JMH to TC, May 1, 1961, TC papers.

183 "an ideal opportunity": WJB to WOD, HAB, and EW, Mar. 2, 1961, EW papers.

hour or two: Mary Fowler interview, Aug. 30, 1988.

most important of his tenure: Earl Warren, *The Memoirs of Chief Justice Earl Warren* (Garden City, NY: Doubleday & Company, 1977), 306.

184 "Courts ought not": *Colegrove v. Green,* 328 U.S. 549 (1946).

Baker v. Carr: 369 U.S. 186 (1962).

gave little weight: WJB interview, Nov. 16, 1987 (24-11).

rejecting the way: *Gomillion v. Lightfoot,* 364 U.S. 339 (1960).

Stewart would be the key: Gene S. Graham, *One Man, One Vote: Baker v. Carr and the American Levelers* (Boston: Little, Brown, 1972), 220–21.

gesticulating: Tony Lewis, *In Memoriam: William J. Brennan Jr.,* 111 HARV. L. REV. 30, citing Richard Arnold diary.

an error akin: Lewis, *In Memoriam,* p. 30, citing Richard Arnold diary.

"the purpose of": WOD conference notes, WOD papers.

185 "I find it necessary": FF to conference, Oct. 10, 1961, TC papers.

"At the very least": WJB to conference, Oct. 12, 1961.

Harlan quietly penned: Harlan to PS and Whittaker, Oct. 11, 1961; FF papers, LOC.

"You have rendered": FF to JMH, Oct. 11, 1961, JMH papers.

"taking his blinders": FF to Hand, July 4, 1961; letter provided by Stanford Law School professor Gerald Gunther with permission from Hand family. Hand died six weeks later at the age of eighty-nine.

"Why do I bother": FF to JMH, Mar. 5, 1962, JMH papers.

lost cause: Roy Schotland interview, Apr. 6, 2007.

186 "Frankfurter without mustard": Tinsley E.Yarbrough, *John Marshall Harlan* (New York: Oxford University Press, 1992), xii.

talked so late: WJB interview, Sept. 13, 1988 (42-4); Nancy Brennan interview, Sept. 1, 1988.

"Hiya, Johnny Boy": Schotland interview, Apr. 7, 2007.

"I strongly believe": FF to JMH, undated, "Re: South Carolina," JMH papers.

"against getting": WOD conference notes, WOD papers.

"a capricious and arbitrary": Ibid.

bear a heavy burden: OT '61 Term History, p. 3.

Black and Douglas favored: Ibid., pp. 3–4.

187 "a judicial sleight": Richard Hasen, *The Benefits of "Judicially Unmanageable" Standards in Election Cases Under the Equal Protection Clause,* 80 N.C. L. REV. 1469 at 1476 (2002).

"It is hard to avoid": Michael McConnell, *The Redistricting Cases: Original Mistakes and Current Consequences,* 24 HARV. J. L. & PUB. POL'Y 103, 107 (2000).

"There was a broad": WOD, *The Autobiography of William O. Douglas: The Court Years 1939–1975* (New York: Random House, 1980), 136.

188 Harlan pleaded: JMH to PS, Feb. 8, 1962, JMH papers.

"try to bring": PS to JMH, Feb. 8, 1962, JMH papers.

Douglas circulated: WOD to conference, Feb. 13, 1962.

in a funk: Schotland interview, Feb. 2, 1989.

received a telephone phone call: Ibid.

stayed in the car: Schotland interview, Apr. 6, 2007.

189 had not even talked with Clark: OT '61 Term History, p. 5.

"I am sorry to say": TC to JMH, Mar. 7, 1962, JMH papers.

"That's the way": WJB interview, Sept. 13, 1988 (42-2).

"The changes represent": WJB to HLB, WOD, and EW, Mar. 10, 1962.

190 "it is a great": EW to WJB, undated.

"pallid and technical": *WP,* "What the Court Decided," Mar. 28, 1962.

"There's nothing that": WJB interview, Nov. 16, 1987 (24-15).

"a perfect illustration": Powe, *Warren Court and American Politics,* p. 202.

"The Justices did not": Anthony Lewis, "Decision on Reapportionment Points Up Urban-Rural Struggle," *NYT,* April 1, 1962.

Time magazine observed: *Time,* "The Supreme Court: Fragmented Bench," Apr. 6, 1962,

191 "What is the timetable": *Newsweek,* Apr. 9, 1962, 32.

only seventy-seven minutes: Ibid.

"is burning like a prairie fire": Layhmond Robinson, "22 States Battle on Redistricting," *NYT,* Aug. 6, 1962.

"Where did all these": Daniel Rezneck to WJB, Mar. 27, 1962.

192 "In some important way": Steven Goldberg (WJB OT '74 clerk) interview, Aug. 15, 2007.

the dangers of: Geoffrey Stone (WJB OT '72 clerk) interview, July 26, 2007.

8. TRIUMPHANT

196 left Bazelon crestfallen: WJB interview, Sept. 13, 1988 (42-6).

almost certainly knew: Richard Bazelon interview, June 22, 2007.

published shortlists: Anthony Lewis, "Ailing Justice Whittaker Leaving Supreme Court," *NYT,* March 30, 1962.

disappointed Frankfurter: FF interview with A. McLaughlin, John F. Kennedy Library Oral History Program, 54, JFK Library.

mobilize the union vote: Liva Baker, *Miranda: Crime, Law, and Politics* (New York: Atheneum, 1983), 33.

Times-Dispatch lamented: *NYT,* "Opinion of the Week: At Home and Abroad," Sept. 2, 1962.

197 "The Secretary's phone": James E. Clayton, *The Making of Justice: The Supreme Court in Action* (New York: E. P. Dutton, 1964), 158.

walked down the hall: Robert O'Neil interview, Apr. 11, 2007.

Christmas decorations: Ibid.

"And where, Arthur": Robert O'Neil, *Clerking for Justice Brennan,* SUP. CT. HIST. J. (1991).

could not recall: Arthur Goldberg interview, June 10, 1987.

crossed paths: Dennis J. Hutchinson, *The Man Who Once Was Whizzer White* (New York: Free Press, 1998), 179.

198 only person Kennedy: Ibid., p. 311.

"The same issues": Ibid., p. 339.

Throughout his first term: Ibid., p. 338.

Brennan came back: O'Neil, *Clerking for Justice Brennan.*

"Perhaps on no other": Clayton, *Making of Justice,* p. 233.

Gideon v. Wainwright: 372 U.S. 335 (1963).

199 *Fay v. Noia:* 372 U.S. 391 (1963).

had expanded: Lucas A. Powe, Jr., *The Warren Court and American Politics* (Cambridge, MA: Belknap Press, 2000), 420–21.

200 "Far too many": WJB, *The Bill of Rights and the States,* 36 N.Y.U. L. REV. 761 (1961).

"As the Supreme Court": WJB, *Federal Habeas Corpus and State Prisoners: An Exercise in Federalism,* 7 UTAH L. REV. 423 (1961).

"will have far-reaching": JMH to conference, Dec. 3, 1962.

"I submit with all": WJB to conference, Dec. 10, 1962.

Brennan devoted more: WJB interview, Jan. 28, 1987 (9-2).

201 Warren said he agreed: WOD conference notes, Jan. 11, 1963, WOD papers.

"deliberately bypassed": Brennan advocated the same approach in a 1961 speech at the University of Utah. See WJB, *Federal Habeas Corpus and State Prisoners.*

"Your opinion in Fay v. Noia": AG to WJB, Feb. 6, 1963.

"a magnificent opinion": *WP,* "The Great Writ," Mar. 20, 1963.

"I hope the": Lee to WJB, Apr. 30, 1963.

"This decision": *Fay v. Noia,* 372 U.S. 448 (1963); "The history of federal": *Fay v. Noia,* 372 U.S. 448, 449 (1963).

202 "*Fay v. Noia* did": WJB interview, Oct. 19, 1989 (55-6).

Townsend v. Sain: 372 U.S. 293 (1963).

held up four fingers: O'Neil, *Clerking for Justice Brennan.*

"The Court is creating": James E. Clayton, "Court Showing Other Two Branches How to Innovate," *WP,* June 23, 1963.

203 "the emergence of": UPI, "Top Court Guards Individual," Apr. 7, 1963.

"At 56": *Look,* "A Visit with Justice Brennan," Dec. 18, 1962.

"the atmosphere of disregard": FF to JMH, May 28, 1963, FF papers, LOC.

"Some well-meaning people": *NYT,* "Harlan Cautions on Role of Court," Aug. 14, 1963.

passed over: Harlan served on the Visiting Committee between 1963 and 1969.

204 conflicts of interest: Brennan recused himself from a number of cases due to his son's ties to law firms or parties in the case. An early example was *Schneider v. Rusk,* 377 U.S. 163 (1964), when Bill was a summer associate at Arnold, Fortas & Porter.

"varied backgrounds": Erwin Griswold interview, June 13, 1989.

"Harvard in those days": Stephen Friedman interview, April 27, 2007.

not connected to his decision: Brennan made this contention in his interviews with Wermiel, letters to Freund, and in an interview with Nat Hentoff: "The Constitutionalist," *New Yorker*, Mar. 12 1990.

"I now feel": WJB to Freund, April 26, 1965.

"I can understand": Freund to WJB, April 30, 1965.

205 felt guilty about: O'Neil interview, Mar. 19, 2008.

never entirely believed: Friedman interview, April 27, 2007.

Freund's idea: Hentoff, "The Constitutionalist," p. 60.

bridge foursome: Marian Burros, "Grand Slam Bridge Lunches," *Washington Star*, Jan. 22, 1969.

everyone gathered around: Luther Youngdahl to WJB, Jan. 10, 1978.

usually off-key: Dorothy K. Goldberg, *A Private View of a Public Life* (New York: Charterhouse, 1975), 150.

embassy tours: *WP*, "A Star Line-Up on Goodwill Embassy Tour Today," May 5, 1962; fashion shows: *WP*, "Clothes Case for Court Wives," Oct. 23, 1964.

orthopedist diagnosed: WJB interview, July 28, 1989 (52-8).

probably begun drinking: Nancy Brennan interview, Mar. 11, 2008.

206 maintained no contact: Hugh Brennan Jr. interview, July 10, 2008.

fill the silence: Nancy Brennan interview, Sept. 1, 1988.

"You bothered me": Fred Rodell to WJB, April 28, 1961; Brennan ignored: WJB to Rodell, May 3, 1961.

"He had the ability": Richard Cotton (WJB OT '70 clerk), interview by Charlie Rose, "A Remembrance of Justice William J. Brennan," *Charlie Rose Show*, July 24, 1997, www.charlierose.com/view/interview/5437.

Nancy, later wondered: Nancy Brennan interview, Mar. 11, 2008.

207 had not increased: The salary for an associate justice increased to $39,500 in 1964.

he had suffered: Frank Ritchie to WJB, Jan. 30, 1962, WJB personal files.

"I've been at my wits end": WJB to Ritchie, Feb. 1, 1962, WJB personal files.

"I had the sense": Nancy Brennan interview, Mar. 11, 2008.

"She said that home": Nancy Brennan to WJB, Sept. 1963, WJB personal files.

208 "heartfelt gratitude": WJB, "Holton-Arms School Dedication" (speech, Bethesda, MD, Oct. 27, 1963).

"She made it": Nancy Brennan interview, Aug. 22, 2007.

9. DISARMING THE SOUTH

209 powerful enough to: Taylor Branch, *Parting the Waters: America in the King Years 1954–63* (New York: Simon & Schuster Inc., 1988), 759.

junior high school students: *Washington Star*, "Justice Brennan Tells Students About Court," Apr. 25, 1963.

210 "tragic deaths": WJB, "Law as an Instrument of Social Justice" (speech, University of Pennsylvania, Philadelphia, Sept. 29, 1964.)

"Real tolerance means": WJB, "What Does 'Ordered Liberty' Mean to the Youth of America?" (speech, Detroit, MI, Jan. 22, 1963.)

black-tie gala: Noel J. Lipson, "Justice Brennan Hails City Library," *NEN*, May 2, 1963.

"It was quite a lesson": WJB interview, July 12, 1988 (41-10).

211 "It was half": Dennis Lyons (WJB OT '58 clerk) interview, June 29, 2007.

rushing into: Robert O'Neil (WJB OT '62 clerk) interview, June 9, 1989.

treated Hood: Stephen Goodman (WJB OT '66 clerk) interview, Aug. 23, 1989.

"the last plantation": Nina Totenberg, "The Last Plantation," *New Times*, July 1974.

employed as a bludgeon: Robert Jerome Glennon, *The Jurisdictional Legacy of the Civil Rights Movement*, 61 Tenn. L. Rev. 869 (1994).

212 Court prohibited segregation: *Boynton v. Virginia*, 364 U.S. 454 (1960).

rare in-chambers oral argument: Frank I. Michelman, *Brennan and Democracy* (Princeton, NJ: Princeton University Press, 1999), 139–44.

213 "Well, we lost": WJB interview, Jan. 7, 1987 (8-8).

"I knew that old adage": WJB to TM, Sept. 12, 1962.

kept the races apart: Branch, *Parting the Waters*, 126.

first citizen: Ibid., p. 277.

214 Alabama refused: Glennon, *Jurisdictional Legacy*, p. 894.

circulated an exhaustive: WJB to AG, BRW, Oct. 5, 1962. He sent a separate cover memo to each.

Black objected: WJB to HLB, Nov. 23, 1962.

215 "a means for achieving": *NAACP v. Button*, 371 U.S. 415 (1963).

justices and clerks gathered: Peter Low (Warren OT '63 clerk) interview, June 9, 1989.

216 turn his head away: Stephen Barnett interview, Apr. 11, 2007.

White drove out: Dennis J. Hutchinson, *The Man Who Once Was Whizzer White* (New York: Free Press, 1998), 354.

called Goldberg: Taylor Branch, *Pillar of Fire: America in the King Years 1963–65* (New York: Simon & Schuster, 1998), 174.

mourned at home: Nancy Brennan interview, Mar. 11, 2008.

"I can't say": WJB to John Cain, Dec. 23, 1963.

emissaries arrived: Bernard Schwartz, *Super Chief: Earl Warren and His Supreme Court; A Judicial Biography* (New York: New York University Press, 1983), 495.

sat in the front row: Walter Trohan, "Aims Outlined by Johnson," *CT*, Nov. 28, 1963.

first sit-in case: *Garner v. Louisiana*, 368 U.S. 157 (1961).

217 attacked as "extreme": FF to JMH, Dec. 1, 1961, JMH papers.

Five more sit-in cases: For a full discussion of the sit-in cases, see Brad Ervin, *Result or Reason: The Supreme Court and the Sit-In Cases*, 93 Va. L. Rev. 181 (2007).

218 "pappy": OT '61 Term History, p. 14.

broadly as possible: Schwartz, *Super Chief*, p. 511.

heated argument ensued: OT '63 Term History, p. 13.

angered other justices: Ibid., p. 14.

Bell v. Maryland: 378 U.S. 226 (1964).

219 "The case does not": HLB to conference, May 15, 1964.

"abdication of judicial authority": WOD to conference, June 18, 1964.

"His great mistake": Jeffrey T. Leeds, "A Life on the Court," *NYT Magazine*, Oct. 5, 1986, 24.

220 claiming the ad's: Anthony Lewis, *Make No Law: The Sullivan Case and the First Amendment* (New York: Random House, 1991), 11.

the *Times* faced: Ibid., p. 35.

221 millions of dollars: Ibid., p. 36.

glancing reference: Brief for the Petitioner at 68, *New York Times v. Sullivan*, 376 U.S. 254 (1965).

beyond the protection: *Beauharnais v. Illinois,* 343 U.S. 250 (1952).

222 "Taken together": Harry Kalven, *A Worthy Tradition: Freedom of Speech in America* (New York: Harper & Row, 1988), 61.

slipped the civil rights leader a copy: Branch, *Pillar of Fire,* p. 204.

223 Brennan suggested: WOD conference notes, Jan. 10, 1964, WOD papers.

"As money is": WJB, "Dedication of the Samuel I. Newhouse Law Center" (speech, Rutgers University, Newark, NJ, Oct. 17, 1979), reprinted as WJB, *Address,* 32 RUT-GERS L. REV. 173 (1979).

marry newspaper reporters: Nancy's first husband, Tim Phelps, would have a distinguished career at the *St. Petersburg Times, Newsday,* and the *Los Angeles Times.* Bill's wife, Georgie, was a reporter at the *Newark Star Ledger.*

"I did put my foot": WJB to Luis Blanco Lugo, Feb. 21, 1962.

"There is just": WJB to Marietta College, Oct. 1966.

224 relied heavily: Lewis, *Make No Law,* p. 166.

Kansas Supreme Court: *Coleman v. MacLennan,* 98 P. 281 (1908).

where they found it: Barnett interview, Apr. 11, 2007.

not gone far enough: Concurring opinions circulated by Goldberg (Feb. 25, 1964) and Black joined by Douglas (Feb. 26, 1964).

"In order to get": WJB interview, July 12, 1988 (41-14).

225 eschewed absolutes: Edward V. Heck, "Justice Brennan and the Changing Supreme Court" (Ph.D. thesis, Johns Hopkins University, 1978.)

"there are circumstances": WJB interview, Dec. 17, 1986 (7-19).

"At the time": William J. Brennan Jr., *The Supreme Court and the Meiklejohn Interpretation of the First Amendment,* 79 HARV. L. REV. 1 (1965), citing David Reisman, *Democracy and Defamation: Fair Game and Fair Comment,* 42 COL. L. REV. 1085 (1942).

worried here: WJB interview, Apr. 4, 1988 (31-3).

Harlan circulated: JMH to conference, Mar. 3, 1964.

Black insisted: HLB to WJB, undated.

226 Clark told Brennan: WJB to clerks, Mar. 5, 1964.

Harlan, too, backed down: JMH to conference, Mar. 9, 1964.

viewed as a great occasion: Lewis, *Make No Law,* p. 181.

"You know of course": HLB to WJB, undated.

"a victory of first importance": *NYT,* "Free Press and Free People," Mar. 10, 1964.

227 "may prove to be": Harry Kalven Jr., *The New York Times Case: A Note on 'The Central Meaning of the First Amendment,'* 194 SUP. CT. REV. 1 (1964).

proved crucial: Lewis, *Make No Law,* p. 158.

"The case could have": Anthony Lewis, "High Court Curbs Public Officials in Libel Actions," *NYT,* Mar. 10, 1964.

standard was criticized: Richard A. Epstein, *Was New York Times v. Sullivan Wrong?,* 53 U. CHI. L. REV. 782 (1986); David A. Barrett, *Declaratory Judgments for Libel: A Better Alternative,* 74 CAL. L. REV. 847 (1986).

"Oh well": WJB interview, June 3, 1987 (17-8). In an opinion issued the term following Brennan's retirement, the Court suggested judges use a less confusing phrase in jury instructions such as "with knowledge of falsity or reckless disregard as to truth or falsity," rather than "actual malice." See *Masson v. New Yorker Magazine, Inc.,* 501 U.S. 496 (1991).

Dombrowski v. Pfister: 380 U.S. 479 (1965).

228 sharply circumscribed: *Younger v. Harris,* 401 U.S. 37 (1971).

most acute need: Glennon, *Jurisdictional Legacy,* p. 869.

Stanley Weigel: Brennan first met and befriended Weigel in the late 1950s before he became a federal District Court judge in San Francisco. In 1959 Brennan recommended Weigel, a Republican, as a potential judicial nominee to Attorney General William Rogers (WJB to Rogers, Sept. 4, 1959). By that point Brennan's suggestions were not necessarily welcome in the Eisenhower administration, and as with Brennan, it would be a president of the opposite party — John F. Kennedy — who ultimately nominated Weigel, in 1962.

"Both we": WJB to Weigel, June 20, 1964.

229   "To walk": WJB (eulogy for Baron Robert Silvercruys, National Cathedral, Washington, DC, Apr. 8, 1975.)

"The party of our fathers": Branch, *Pillar of Fire,* p. 493.

"It is hardly": WJB, "Law as an Instrument of Social Justice."

10. CRIME & CRITICISM

230   top priority: Rick Perlstein, *Before the Storm: Earl Warren and the Nation He Made* (New York: Hill and Wang, 2001), 110.

Indianapolis Motor Speedway: Jim Newton, *Justice for All: Earl Warren and the Nation He Made* (New York: Riverhead Books, 2007), 386.

Dallas suggested hanging: Perlstein, *Before the Storm,* p. 151.

"Thanks for letting me": PS to WJB, Feb. 1961.

invariably elicited: WJB interview, May 30, 1990 (63-1).

231   "there was plenty of time": WJB to Stanley Weigel, Aug. 20, 1962.

"have greatly conflicted": Delta Tau Delta, Auburn Chapter, to WJB, May 22, 1963.

"segregationists and security mongers": Alexander M. Bickel, "Mr. Justice Black: The Unobvious Meaning of Plain Words," *New Republic,* Mar. 14, 1960, 13.

thwarted the will: Alexander Bickel, *The Least Dangerous Branch: The Supreme Court at the Bar of Politics* (Indianapolis: Bobbs-Merrill, 1962).

"is taking too much": Anthony Lewis, "Supreme Court Moves Again to Exert Its Powerful Influence," *NYT,* June 21, 1964.; see also *U.S. News & World Report,* "How Supreme Court Is Reshaping the Country," July 6, 1964; and *Time,* "The Limits That Create Liberty & the Liberty That Creates Limits," Oct. 9, 1964.

"A vote for Barry Goldwater": Perlstein, *Before the Storm,* p. 465.

232   "Almost every decision": WJB (lecture, Seventh Circuit Judicial Conference, Chicago, IL, May 11, 1965).

favoring Communists: William Moore, "Rips Warren 'Pro' Votes in Red Rulings," *CT,* May 3, 1962.

It was not personal: Nancy Brennan interview, Aug. 22, 2007.

first coined: Keenan D. Kmiec, *The Origin and Current Meanings of "Judicial Activism,"* 92 CAL. L. REV. 1442 (2004).

many different complaints: Ibid.

233   "has with more or less": *U.S. News & World Report,* "In the 13th Year of the 'Warren Revolution,'" June 20, 1966, 48.

"The Court is not": WJB, "The U.S. Constitution" (speech, Maxwell Air Force Base, Montgomery, AL, Sept. 9, 1963), reprinted as "The U.S. Constitution: An Address by Justice William J. Brennan Jr.," 2 *Air War College Supplement* 3, 43.

"our government": *Look,* "A Visit with Justice Brennan," Dec. 18, 1962.

"Law is again": WJB (lecture, American Jewish Theological Seminary, New York, NY, Nov. 11, 1964).

"no one doing": WJB, Bouton Lecture (Princeton University, Princeton, NJ, Feb. 4, 1969).

234 "roving commission": Alexander M. Bickel, *The Supreme Court and the Idea of Progress* (New York: Harper & Row, 1970), 134. The venue at which Bickel spoke was the same one where Hand criticized the "bevy of platonic guardians": the Oliver Wendell Holmes Jr. lecture.

set out to reform: Lincoln Caplan, *The Tenth Justice: The Solicitor General and the Rule of Law* (New York: Vintage Books, 1988), 66.

235 "To impose upon": "Proceedings of the Twenty-Eighth Annual Judicial Conference, Third Judicial Circuit of the United States," 39 F. R. D. 495 (Sept. 10, 1965).

audience dismayed: Yale Kamisar interview, May 1, 2007.

coughed or squirmed: Ibid.

sat stone-faced: Sidney E. Zion, "Attack on Warren Court Heard by Warren," *NYT*, Sept. 10, 1965.

"As the Chief Justice": Fred Graham, "Law: Fresh Attack on the Court," *NYT*, Sept. 12, 1965.

as powerful: Michael W. Flamm, *Law and Order* (New York: Columbia University Press, 2005), 6.

Uniform Crime Reports: Liva Baker, *Miranda: Crime, Law, and Politics* (New York: Atheneum, 1983), 39.

1964 Harris Poll: Flamm, *Law and Order*, p. 51.

236 "Let us not be": DDE (speech, Republican National Convention, San Francisco, CA, July 14, 1964), available on Eisenhower Memorial Commission website at: www .eisenhowermemorial.org/speeches/19640714%20Republican%20National %20Convention%20Speech.htm.

"Crime grows faster": Baker, *Miranda*, p. 40.

"Is Crime": *U.S. News & World Report*, "Is Crime in US Out of Hand?" Mar. 22, 1965, 38.

237 "I am aware": WJB, "The Role of the Court — the Challenge of the Future" (lecture, Georgetown University Law Center, Washington, DC, March 16, 1965).

"a private citizen": WJB interview, Oct. 21, 1988 (45-3).

felony rap sheet: Baker, *Miranda*, p. 10.

proposed it: EW to WJB, May 9, 1966.

238 Brennan was uneasy: OT '65 Term History, p. 41.

"These suggestions are": WJB to EW, undated.

"I feel guilty": WJB to EW, May 11, 1966.

talked more: WJB interview, Jan. 28, 1987 (9-2).

239 "Obviously, it would": Ibid.

police chief predicted: Baker, *Miranda*, p. 176.

"Some people think": Milton Lewis, "McClellan Set to Attack Rule Freeing Killer," *World Journal Tribune*, Feb. 23, 1967.

three other landmark decisions: *Mapp v. Ohio*, 367 U.S. 643 (1961); *Gideon v. Wainwright*, 372 U.S. 335 (1963); *Escobedo v. Illinois*, 378 U.S. 478 (1964).

Malloy v. Hogan: 378 U.S. 1 (1964).

gained widespread acceptance: Arthur Sutherland Jr., *Crime and Confession*, 79 HARV. L. REV. 21, 35 (1965).

240 "We were plowing": WJB interview, Jan. 28, 1987 (9-2).

trial by jury: The Seventh Amendment provides, "In suits at common law, where the

value in controversy shall exceed twenty dollars, the right of trial by jury shall be preserved, and no fact tried by a jury, shall be otherwise reexamined in any court of the
United States, than according to the rules of the common law."
very different view: *Schmerber v. California,* 384 U.S. 757 (1966).
reverse his conviction: The four dissenters differed in their disagreement with
Brennan. Justices Hugo Black and William Douglas rejected as too narrow Brennan's view that the Fifth Amendment privilege did not apply because the self-
incrimination was neither personal testimony nor a means of communication. They
argued that the Fifth Amendment should be given a more generous reading.
Chief Justice Earl Warren and Justice Abe Fortas relied on Warren's earlier dissent in *Breithaupt v. Abram,* 352 U.S. 432 (1957), in which a blood sample was
taken without consent from an unconscious car accident victim and tested for alcohol.

241 legitimate law enforcement needs: In 1990, Brennan wrote an 8–1 decision for the
Court extending the nontestimonial rationale to uphold police authority to videotape
drunk-driving suspects and use footage of their slurred speech as nontestimonial evidence at trial without first advising the defendant of their constitutional rights. *Pennsylvania v. Muniz,* 496 U.S. 582 (1990).
"People are not neutral": WJB (speech to Washington, DC, Bar Association, Washington, DC, June 14, 1978).
"In some circles": David Bazelon, "The Education of an Activist," (lecture, Albert Ein-
stein College of Medicine, Nov. 12, 1972), Bazelon papers.
holding chronic alcoholism: *Easter v. District of Columbia,* 361 F.2d 50 (1966).
"Giving them": David Bazelon, "Law and Order without Justice" (speech to New York
Civil Liberties Union, New York, NY, Feb. 22, 1966), Bazelon papers.
"welfare criminology": Roger Wilkins, "A Federal Judge Who Questions the Status
Quo," *NYT,* Mar. 21, 1979, quoting Stephen J. Morse, who was then a law professor at
the University of Southern California.
load up their briefs: Fred Barbash, "Judge Bazelon's 'Network': The Salon of the Ultimate Liberal," *WP,* Mar. 1, 1981.

242 "The issue": *WP,* "Brennan Urges Greater Rights for Defendants," May 10, 1963.
"These provisions would": David Bazelon, *Questioning Authority* (New York: Knopf,
1988), 158–68; reprints full text of letter exchange.

243 "one of the worst": Sanford J. Ungar, "The Bazelon Opinions: No One Is Ever Neutral," *WP,* Oct. 17, 1971.
some accused: Ibid.
one uncommitted jurist: Joseph C. Goulden, *The Benchwarmers: The Private World of
the Powerful Federal Judges* (New York: Random House, 1976), 253.
"the avant-garde": WEB to HAB, Oct. 31, 1960; HAB papers.
privately mocked: Goulden, *Benchwarmers,* p. 253.
"It was a blood feud": WJB interview, Mar. 6, 1988 (30-1).
more in common: Jeffrey Branden Morris, *Calmly to Poise the Scales of Justice* (Durham, NC: Carolina Academic Press, 2001), 202–3.

244 "You can be thankful": WEB to HAB, Feb. 3, 1960, HAB papers.
"Things will need": WEB to HAB, Apr. 29, 1961, HAB papers.
"The horrible thing": WEB to HAB, June 20, 1961, HAB papers.
"Brennan was his usual": WEB to HAB, Aug. 6, 1962, HAB papers.

245 "In the present": WEB to HAB, Sept. 4, 1967, HAB papers.
a transplant: Jack Bass, *Unlikely Heroes* (Tuscaloosa: University of Alabama Press,
1990), 113.

"They couldn't even": Ronald Goldfarb, "We Are, All of Us, Free-Born Americans," *WP,* Aug. 8, 1988.

246 most hated man: Bass, *Unlikely Heroes,* p. 115.

Wright joked: J. Skelly Wright, *A Colleague's Tribute to Judge David L. Bazelon, On the Twenty-Fifth Anniversary of His Appointment,* 123 U. PA. L. REV. 250 (1974–75).

single entity: Arthur S. Miller, *A Capacity for Outrage: The Judicial Odyssey of J. Skelly Wright* (Westport, CT: Greenwood Press, 1984), 195.

"When I get": Bass, *Unlikely Heroes,* p. 116.

"Here is a man": WJB, *Tribute to Judge J. Skelly Wright,* 1985 ANN. SURV. AM. L., ix.

"Your work on": Wright to WJB, Oct. 24, 1967.

glowing terms: Joseph Onek interview, Mar. 19, 2008. Onek clerked for both Bazelon and Brennan.

bruising rebuke: *Vermont Yankee Nuclear Power Corp. v. NRDC,* 435 U.S. 519 (1978).

the last thing: WJB interview, Apr. 13, 1989 (49-10).

247 "demanding taskmaster": Timothy S. Robinson, "Bazelon Relinquishes Title of Chief Appeals Judge Here," *WP,* Mar. 29, 1978.

"He was a private person": E. Joshua Rosenkranz, *Remembering a Constitutional Hero,* 43 N.Y. L. SCH. L. REV. 13, 18 (1999).

248 "So much of who": Geoffrey Stone (WJB OT '72 clerk) interview, Mar. 16, 1989.

11. ANGERING THE LEFT

249 would affirm: *Ginzburg v. United States,* 383 U.S. 463 (1966).

250 mental note: Frank Gregory (WJB OT '67 clerk) interview, Mar. 30, 1990.

even handing clerks: Richard Arnold, *A Remembrance: Mr. Justice Brennan — October Term 1960,* SUP. CT. HIST. J. (1991).

"mock conference": WOD, *The Autobiography of William O. Douglas: The Court Years 1939–1975* (New York: Random House, 1980), 229.

something of a sham: Bob Woodward and Scott Armstrong, *The Brethren: Inside the Supreme Court* (New York: Simon & Schuster, 1979), 61.

251 "People jumped to": WJB interview, June 17, 1987 (19-11).

"He'd come in": WJB interview, April 11, 1988 (32-3).

Brennan took pains: Ibid.

Perhaps the only parallel: Robert Henry, "The Players and the Play," in *The Burger Court: Counter-Revolution or Confirmation?* ed. Bernard Schwartz (New York: Oxford University Press, 1998), 20.

252 "Who am I": Stephen Barnett (WJB OT '63 clerk) interview, Oct. 30, 1989.

"liberating this country": Anthony Lewis, "Sex . . . and the Supreme Court," *Esquire,* June 1963, 82.

"hopelessly divided": WJB to JMH, June 9, 1962.

Manual Enterprises v. Day: 370 U.S. 478 (1962).

253 American critics': Lucas A. Powe, Jr., *The Warren Court and American Politics* (Cambridge, MA: Belknap Press, 2000), 339.

254 "an ultimate censor": *Jacobellis v. Ohio,* 378 U.S. 184 (1964).

"the Court spokesman": AP, "New Jersey Jurist Making Strong Impression on US Supreme Court," *Daily Home News,* Aug. 9, 1962.

"has emerged as": AP, "Chief Arbiter on Obscenity," *NEN,* Aug. 13, 1964. The press focused on Brennan's opinion at the time but it would be Potter Stewart's declaration

about obscenity in his concurrence, "I know it when I see it," that became the most enduring line from this case — and the most oft-quoted of Stewart's entire career.
"a flood of": Rick Perlstein, *Before the Storm: Earl Warren and the Nation He Made* (New York: Hill and Wang, 2001), 483.
several horror stories: O. K. Armstrong, "The Damning Case against Pornography," *Reader's Digest*, Dec. 1965.

255 "Many Catholics": William H. Mooring, "Supreme Court Does It Again on Movie Ruling," *Catholic Standard and Times*, July 3, 1964.
"an acceptance of degeneracy": *The Tablet*, "Cardinal Charges Supreme Court Accepts 'Beatnik Mentality' as the American Way," Aug. 13, 1964.
"Like other": O'Meara to Haverty, Feb. 1, 1965.

256 "He flays me": WJB to EW, Nov. 3, 1964; EW papers.
"reflects the misreading": WJB to O'Meara, Nov. 11, 1964.
"The sheer weight": Joseph O'Meara and Thomas L. Shaffer, *Obscenity and the Supreme Court: A Note on* Jacobellis v. Ohio, NOTRE DAME LAWYER (Dec. 1964,) 1, 5.
"dirty books day": Andrew Kopkind, "May It Please the Court," *New Republic*, Dec. 9, 1965, 9.

257 "most of the lawyers": Ibid.
could not hide: Charles Rembar, *The End of Obscenity: The Trials of Lady Chatterley, Tropic of Cancer, and Fanny Hill* (New York: Random House, 1968), 443.
"I'm sure this": Fred P. Graham, "How to Avoid Reading Spicy Books," *NYT*, Dec. 8, 1965.
"The Court may": Edward de Grazia, *Girls Lean Back Everywhere* (New York: Random House, 1992), 503.

258 convinced him: Bob Reitman, *Freedom on Trial: The Incredible Ordeal of Ralph Ginzburg* (San Diego, CA: Publishers Export Co., 1966), 33.
"Love and sex are beautiful": *Playboy*, "Playboy Interview: Ralph Ginzburg," July 1966.
The 9 million: Ralph Ginzburg, *Eros on Trial* (New York: Book Division of Fact Magazine, 1966), 4.
relied on mailing lists: Reitman, *Freedom on Trial*, 47.
"the presses of this": Grazia, *Girls Lean Back Everywhere*, p. 509.

259 "dirt for dirt's sake": *United States of America v. Ginzburg*, 338 F.2d 12 (1964) (citing trial findings).
cause célèbre: Reitman, *Freedom on Trial*, p. 143.
invited the Court: Rembar, *End of Obscenity*, p. 420.
Bender sensed: Paul Bender interview, Dec. 18, 2007.
"The publication of this magazine": Robert Christgau, "Portrait of a Man in Trouble," *NYHT Magazine*, Apr. 17, 1966.
just happened: *Playboy*, "Playboy Interview."
was not thinking: Bender interview, Dec. 18, 2007.

260 tersely indicated: WOD conference notes, Dec. 10, 1965, WOD papers.
"Contrary to my principles": AF to WOD, Apr. 15, 1966, WOD papers.
Warren persuaded Fortas: OT '65 Term History, pp. 19–20.
Fortas would recall: AF to WOD, Apr. 15, 1966, WOD papers.

261 Fortas also suggested: OT '65 Term History, p. 20.
"the quizzical expression": EW to WJB, undated.
"You have made": Ibid.
"terrible decision": Bender interview, Dec. 18, 2007.
"Just send Bender": Powe, *Warren Court*, p. 346.

262 later joke with Bender: Bender interview, Dec. 18, 2007.
prepared two statements: Christgau, "Portrait of a Man in Trouble."
"Today's decision was": *NYT,* "Publisher of Erotica, Ralph Ginzburg," Mar. 22, 1966.
supported not only: Christgau, "Portrait of a Man in Trouble."
"It is obvious": Russell Baker, "Observer: Some Advice to the Supreme Court," *NYT,* Mar. 24, 1966.
"These are dark": Peter Bart, "As the Censors Move In . . ." *NYT,* Apr. 10, 1966.
"the majority found": Robert J. Donovan, "Effects of Obscenity Ruling Yet to Be Felt," *LAT,* Mar. 23, 1966.
"massive prosecutions": Sidney E. Zion, "The Ginzburg Decision," *NYT,* Mar. 24, 1966.
scrambled to replace: Paul L. Montgomery, "Booksellers Here Staging a Cleanup," *NYT,* Mar. 23, 1966.
Outraged liberals: The reflexive rush by liberals to defend Ginzburg may seem anachronistic in light of the critique of pornography during the 1980s by feminist legal scholars who asserted it was a form of sex discrimination and violated women's civil liberties. See Catharine A. Mackinnon, *Pornography, Civil Rights, and Speech,* 20 HARV. C. R.-C. L. L. REV. 1 (1985).
"It was a grim": *New Republic,* "Obscenity and the Law," Apr. 3, 1966, 5.
263 "the silliness to which": *Nation,* "Demeaning the Court," Apr. 4, 1966.
"drawing a line": E. Earle Ellis to WJB, May 10, 1966; "The Ginzburg case": anonymous to WJB.
view shared: Bender interview, Dec. 18, 2007.
"not the world's": Ibid.
"If the Supreme Court": Arnold to AF, Mar. 29, 1966, AF papers.
"It certainly reflects": WJB to AF, undated. Brennan's reply is written on Fortas's Apr. 8, 1966, note forwarding Arnold letter; AF papers.
"I think": AF to WOD, Apr. 15, 1966, AF papers.
264 the obvious choice: Robert O'Neil interview, May 7, 2007.
father gave him: Stephen Labaton, "For Defense Lawyer in Bomb Case, Latest in a Line of Unpopular Clients," *NYT,* June 9, 1995.
wrote an article: Michael Tigar, "Freedom of Debate Marks Youth Festival," *People's World,* Aug. 18, 1962, 2; spearheaded an effort: Michael E. Tigar, *Fighting Injustice* (Chicago: American Bar Association, 2002), 43.
"This wasn't 1955": O'Neil interview, May 7, 2007.
"I don't want": Ibid.
accepted immediately: Tigar to WJB, June 17, 1965.
265 listened over and over: Tigar, *Fighting Injustice,* p. 52.
"Frankly, there may": Tigar to WJB, July 13, 1965.
"The summer of": Tigar, *Fighting Injustice,* p. 53.
first hint: Ibid.
issued a report: Lawrence E. Davies, "Berkeley Called Red Infiltrated," *NYT,* May 7, 1966.
"charges of communism": *LAT,* "Reagan Demands Legislative Quiz on UC Charges," May 13, 1966.
"A remarkable thing": James J. Kilpatrick, "The Lady and the Tigar," *Richmond Virginia News Leader,* June 8, 1966.
266 "horrible and shocking": John P. MacKenzie, "High Court Law Clerk Appointee Is Victim of Right Wing Barrage," *WP,* July 17, 1966.
"deeply grieved": Bennett to WJB, June 21, 1966.

"a fiery young": Bill Schulz, "Radical Leftist Named Law Clerk for Supreme Court Justice Brennan," June 22, 1966.

red-eye flight: Tigar, *Fighting Injustice*, p. 54.

"I am ready": Tigar to WJB, June 26, 1966.

267 would refuse: Tigar, *Fighting Injustice*, p. 57.

began packing: Ibid., p. 58.

come to his chambers: WJB interview, Oct. 21, 1988 (45-14).

private line: Laura Kalman, *Abe Fortas: A Biography* (New Haven: Yale University Press, 1990), 312.

"How do you": WJB interview, Jan. 30, 1990 (57-6).

suspect Fortas: WJB interview, Oct. 21, 1988 (45-14).

"I never bothered them": WJB interview, Nov. 16, 1987 (24-5).

"a matter personal": EW to Murphy, June 22, 1966, EW papers.

268 Warren insisted: Jim Newton, *Justice for All: Earl Warren and the Nation He Made* (New York: Riverhead Books, 2007), 228. Warren is not completely innocent when it comes to controversial hiring decisions affected by charges of Communist ties. He came under criticism while serving on the California Commission on Judicial Qualifications in his capacity as state attorney general. Warren cast the deciding vote in 1940 against Max Radin to be a member of the state Supreme Court. Radin, a noted Berkeley law professor, had been frequently targeted as a Communist during the 1930s and came to the defense of a group of city employees in Stockton, California, who refused to answer questions from a state legislative committee investigating Communist infiltration. See Ed Cray, *Chief Justice: A Biography of Earl Warren* (New York: Simon & Schuster, 1997), 108–11.

former clerk joked: Andrew Kopkind, "Brennan v. Tigar," *New Republic*, Aug. 27, 1966, 21.

made clear: : Newton, *Justice for All*, p. 396.

Warren thought Reagan: Roger K. Newman, *The Warren Court and American Politics: An Impressionistic Appreciation*, 18 CONST. COMMENT. 661, 678 (2001).

"a small minority": Rick Perlstein, *Nixonland: The Rise of a President and the Fracturing of America* (New York: Scribner, 2008), 83.

"Brown as head": *Human Events*, "Brown, Berkeley, Brennan," June 25, 1966.

269 Tigar later recalled: Tigar interview, Oct. 20, 1988.

Fiss said he: Owen Fiss, e-mail message to Stern, Apr. 14, 2008.

stopped to visit friends: Tigar, *Fighting Injustice*, p. 58.

tone was grave: Ibid.

Tigar asked for: Tigar to Wermiel, Apr. 5, 1994.

no matter what: Tigar, *Fighting Injustice*, p. 59.

"had a very long": WJB to Weigel, July 12, 1966.

successfully defended: Wolfgang Saxon, "Judge Stanley Weigel, 93, Dies; Acted to Improve Prisons," *NYT*, Sept. 4, 1999.

"Overnight I": WJB to Weigel, July 14, 1966.

270 came to believe: Goodman interview, May 25, 2007; Mary Fowler interview, Aug. 30, 1988.

admit to doing such: Goodman interview, May 25, 2007.

"The notion that": WJB interview, Oct. 21, 1988 (45-14).

271 100,000 protestors: Perlstein, *Nixonland*, p. 80.

"I felt we": WJB interview, Aug. 25, 1989 (54-7).

three Army soldiers: *Washington Evening Star*, "Brennan Rejects Plea by 3 GIs in Viet Case," Oct. 12, 1966.

angry letters: Brennan saved three folders of letters he received in opposition.

requiring public teachers: *Keyishian v. Board of Regents* 385 U.S. 589 (1967).

272 "How can I": Frederick S. Benson to WJB, Jan. 25, 1967.

letter alarmed Brennan: WJB to J. Edgar Hoover, Jan. 26, 1967.

"His appointment meant": James Marquis to WJB, July 18, 1966.

"The pressures you": Marshall Krause to WJB, Aug. 8, 1966.

"Go tell them": WJB interview, Nov. 16, 1987 (24-6).

"egregiously mistaken": Tigar to friends, July 28, 1966; enclosed in July 28, 1966, letter to WJB.

273 "Though both": Ibid.

"I see nothing": WJB to Tigar, Aug. 2, 1966.

"strongly recommended": Robert J. Pack, *Edward Bennett Williams for the Defense* (New York: Harper & Row, Publishers, 1983), 351.

Tigar, who declined: Tigar, *Fighting Injustice*, p. 61.

figures far more controversial: Stephen Labaton, "For Defense Lawyer in Bomb Case," *NYT*, June 9, 1995.

decided to write: Tigar, *Fighting Injustice*, p. 61.

He was surprised: Ibid.

"I'm deeply touched": Brennan to Tigar, July 14, 1977.

closest they came: Tigar interview, Oct. 20, 1988.

274 "To Mike Tigar": Tigar, *Fighting Injustice*, p. 63.

"I wish to hell": WJB interview, Nov. 16, 1987 (24-5).

"I behaved": Tigar to WJB, Nov. 13, 1990.

"That morning": WJB to Tigar, Nov. 19, 1990.

thirty-five-page book: Ralph Ginzburg, *Castrated: My Eight Months in Prison* (New York: Avante Garde Books, 1973).

275 of "high crimes": Ibid., p. 33.

cheeky consumer newsletter: Adam Bernstein, "Ralph Ginzburg; Pushed Envelope as a Publisher," *WP*, July 7, 2006.

"My regret": Ralph Ginzburg, "Injustice in an 'Obscenity' Case," *NYT*, Feb. 18, 1988.

"I thought you": Ginzburg to Wermiel, Feb. 2, 1988.

Hentoff recalled: Nat Hentoff, "Supreme Court Obscenity," *Village Voice*, July 18, 2006.

"Had he made": Shoshana Ginzburg interview, May 3, 2007.

12. PASSAGES

276 speaking in Gaelic: Judi Brennan (WJB's niece) interview, Mar. 1, 2009.

277 "Your counsel": Paul Reardon to WJB, Apr. 1, 1966.

Griswold decided: Erwin Griswold interview, June 13, 1989.

"It is the best": Griswold to WJB, July 1, 1966.

"I am greatly": WJB to Griswold, July 13, 1966.

"Brennan has more": Erwin N. Griswold, *William J. Brennan, Jr. — Legal Humanist*, 80 HARV. L. REV. 4 (1966).

"In the entire": Earl Warren, *Mr. Justice Brennan*, 80 HARV. L. REV. 1 (1966).

278 a compilation: WJB, *An Affair with Freedom: A Collection of His Opinions and Speeches Drawn from His First Decade as a United States Supreme Court Justice*, ed. Stephen J. Friedman (New York: Atheneum, 1967).

comfortable rhythm: One measure of Brennan's job satisfaction was his answers to a

Harvard Law School survey mailed to alumni in November 1966. For the question, "Are you satisfied with your present work?" Brennan checked "Very satisfied" — the highest rating. When asked what satisfied him in his work, Brennan marked off "subject matter," "intellectual stimulation," "independence," "people with whom I work," "variety of work," "organization for which I work," and "importance of problems." He did not check "high prestige of profession," "helping people," "high income" — or, least surprisingly, "opportunity for advancement."

read all: Clerks still read cert. petitions when they arrived in the summer, which Brennan considered good training.

prepare a history: Brennan had his clerks in the 1959–60 and 1960–61 terms write short memos on unpublished opinions and the first fuller narrative was produced by his clerks in the 1961–62 term.

Brennan came up: WJB interview, Oct. 24, 1986 (4-37).

279   "Hugo Black may be": Sidney Zion, "The Supreme Court," *New York Post*, Feb. 4, 1965.

themes were echoed: George Carmack, "Brennan: Core of Liberals," *New York World Telegram*, Feb. 16, 1965.

"Mr. Zion is very": WJB to William H. Borden, Feb. 12, 1965.

"the center of gravity": Edward V. Heck, *Justice Brennan and the Heyday of Warren Court Liberalism*, 20 SANTA CLARA L. REV. 841, 846 (1980).

had dissented only: Ibid.

280   Pope Pius XI came out: John T. McGreevy, *Catholicism and American Freedom: A History* (New York: W. W. Norton & Company, 2003), 221.

"mutual masturbation": David J. Garrow, *Liberty & Sexuality: The Right to Privacy and the Making of Roe v. Wade* (New York: Macmillan Publishing Company, 1994), 118.

"When the long arm": Fowler W. Harper's Jurisdictional Statement in Brief for the Appellants, 1960 WL 98679 *2, *Poe v. Ullman*, 376 U.S. 497 (1961) (No. 60–61).

281   At best: John W. Johnson, *Griswold v. Connecticut: Birth Control and the Constitutional Right of Privacy* (Lawrence: University Press of Kansas, 2005).

technological advances: Ibid., pp. 57–58.

1890 article: Louis Brandeis & Samuel Warren, *The Right to Privacy*, 4 HARV. L. REV. 193 (1890).

"The makers": *Olmstead v. United States*, 277 U.S. 438 (1928).

Poe v. Ullman: 367 U.S. 497 (1961).

282   Douglas's urging: Garrow, *Liberty & Sexuality*, pp. 191–92, citing interviews with Brennan's OT '60 clerks, Richard Arnold and Daniel Rezneck.

"We must indeed": Ibid., p. 199.

Brennan made clear: Ibid., p. 193.

283   approved the sale: David Halberstam, *The Fifties* (New York: Ballantine Books, 1994), 605.

Warren expressed reservations: WOD conference notes, Apr. 2, 1965, WOD papers.

"realm of privacy": Ibid.

Douglas declined: Bruce Allen Murphy, *Wild Bill: The Legend and Life of William O. Douglas* (New York: Random House, 2003).

"He didn't really": WJB interview, Apr. 4, 1989 (48-5).

284   "While I agree": WJB to WOD, Apr. 24, 1965.

Douglas quickly recast: WOD to WJB, Apr. 27 1965.

285   well received: Posner to WJB, Apr. 27, 1965.

evoked a mixture: Garrow, *Liberty & Sexuality*, p. 249.

"many good and able": *Griswold v. Connecticut*, 381 U.S. 479, 522 (1965).

claim more credit: WJB interview, Mar. 12, 1990 (58-12). Brennan said, "I gave him the idea."

286 openly questioned: Leslie Woodcock Tentler, *Catholics and Contraception: An American History* (Ithaca, NY: Cornell University Press, 2004).

"long overdue": Garrow, *Liberty & Sexuality*, p. 257.

no reference to Brennan: Fred Rodell, "It Is the Earl Warren Court," *NYT Magazine*, Mar. 13, 1966.

"was never free": Herbert Stein, "Perry Wins the Case of the Dazzled Lawyers," *Pittsburgh Post-Gazette*, Feb. 1960, WJB scrapbook.

"Honey — sitting behind": WJB to Marjorie Brennan, undated.

happily obliged: WJB to Raymond Burr, Mar. 3, 1966.

287 Marjorie enjoyed teasing: Frank Brennan interview, Dec. 29, 1986.

puckish delight: Robert O'Neil, *Clerking for Justice Brennan*, Sup. Ct. Hist. J. (1991), 11, 12.

subordinates wrote back: Harry Walker agency to WJB, July 9, 1968.

out of step: Roger K. Newman, *Hugo Black: A Biography* (New York: Pantheon Books, 1994), 542.

increasingly broke: Heck, *Justice Brennan*, pp. 859–60.

resented that Warren: Bernard Schwartz, *Super Chief: Earl Warren and His Supreme Court; A Judicial Biography* (New York: NYU Press, 1983), 630; Newman, *Hugo Black*, pp. 565–66.

"[Warren] didn't": Newman, *Hugo Black*, p. 565.

288 went too far: Ibid., p. 564.

"dear and sincere": Hugo L. Black and Elizabeth Black, *Mr. Justice and Mrs. Black* (New York: Random House, 1986), 176.

walking together: Newman, *Hugo Black*, p. 588.

deciding vote: 23 Cong. Q. Almanac 1154 (1967).

Black's "defection": Fred P. Graham, "Shift in Court's Trend," *NYT*, June 14, 1967.

significant losses: Michael W. Flamm, *Law and Order* (New York: Columbia University Press, 2005), 81.

testily complained: HLB to conference, Dec. 7, 1966, re: *Fortson v. Morris*, 385 U.S. 231 (1966).

"chilling effect": WJB to WOD, Nov. 8, 1966, re: *Adderley v. Florida*, 385 U.S. 39 (1966).

289 "Hugo of today": Newman, *Hugo Black*, p. 570, citing 1968 Drew Pearson interview with WJB.

eleven decisions: Schwartz, *Super Chief*, p. 676.

Walker v. Birmingham: 388 U.S. 307 (1967).

"I expect that": WJB to conference, June 6, 1967.

290 "before 'Black Power'": Ibid.

too much for Warren: OT '66 Term History, p. 32.

panicked white residents: Richard Reeves, "Hatred and Pity Mix in Views of Whites on Newark Negroes," *NYT*, July 22, 1967.

291 Occidental Restaurant: Dennis Lyons to WJB, Apr. 8, 1964.

spoke so candidly: Peter Fishbein (WJB OT '58 clerk) interview, Mar. 27, 2007.

mixing bloody marys: Frank Michelman interview, Apr. 25, 2007; Daniel O'Hern, interview by James M. McGovern Jr. and Robert Honecker, Aug. 4, 2000, *Remembering the 20th Century: An Oral History of Monmouth County*, Monmouth County

Library Headquarters, Manalapan, NJ, www.visitmonmouth.com/oralhistory/bios/ OHernDaniel.htm.

commissioning a portrait: Michelman interview, Apr. 25, 2007.

surprising Brennan's clerks: Roy Schotland interview, Apr. 6, 2007.

292 "I hope the artist": WJB (remarks at portrait unveiling, Harkness Commons, Harvard Law School, Cambridge, MA, Apr. 29, 1967).

all gathered: Michelman interview, Apr. 25, 2007.

"The school has": WJB, "The Responsibilities of the Legal Profession" (speech, Harvard Law School, Cambridge, MA, Sept. 23, 1967), reprinted as WJB, *The Responsibilities of the Legal Profession*, 54 A.B.A. J. 121 (1968).

"Fear of": *Time*, "Violence in America," July 28, 1967.

Brennan's schedule: New York University, press release, July 21, 1967.

Hesburgh had written: WJB to Hesburgh, Oct. 15, 1960, Hesburgh papers.

293 leading champion: Michael O'Brien, *Hesburgh: A Biography* (Washington, DC: Catholic University of America Press, 1998), 71.

had chosen this: Theodore Hesburgh interview, Mar. 17, 2008.

Grace treated Brennan: WJB to Grace, Sept. 11, 1967.

"a number of": Hesburgh interview, Mar. 17, 2008.

wanted to meet: Alice Knight interview, Aug. 13, 1990.

full of gratitude: WJB to Hesburgh, Sept. 28, 1967, Hesburgh papers.

persuaded the State Department: Nancy Brennan interview, Aug. 22, 2007.

294 told the alumni magazine: *Pennsylvania Gazette*, "Nancy Brennan '71 CW 'Vibrant Intellectual Community,'" Jan.–Feb. 1968, 11.

"Before I finished": WJB to Hesburgh, Sept. 28, 1967, Hesburgh papers.

convinced her mother: Nancy Brennan interview, Aug. 22, 2007.

295 first person ever: *NYT*, "Tom C. Clark, Former Justice, Dies; On the Supreme Court for 18 Years," June 14, 1977.

traded gossip: Juan Williams, *Thurgood Marshall: American Revolutionary* (New York: Times Books, 1998), 321.

privately administered: *Thurgood Marshall Becomes First Negro Justice*, 23 CONG. Q. ALMANAC 1164 (1967).

ease his transition: Frank Gregory (WJB OT '67 clerk) interview, Mar. 30, 1990.

invited Brennan: WJB interview, Jan. 7, 1987 (8-8); WJB interview, Mar. 8, 1988 (28-8).

13. TUMULT

296 Transistor radios: Ben W. Gilbert and the Staff of the Washington Post, *Ten Blocks from the White House: Anatomy of the Washington Riots of 1968* (New York: F. A. Praeger 1968), 19–29.

school-desegregation case: *Green v. County School Board*, 391 U.S. 430 (1968).

"I don't like": Bernadette Carey, "4000 Hear Dr. King at Cathedral," *WP*, Apr. 1, 1968.

297 clergy of all denominations: Louis Dombrowksi, "Capital Bows in Cathedral to Honor King," *CT*, Apr. 6, 1968.

"Hugo Black more": Nicholas von Hoffman, "President Leads Mourners," *WP*, Apr. 6, 1968.

tolled mournfully: Isabel McCraig, UPI, "'God, Forgive Us,' Leader Prays in Memorial Rite," *Chicago Daily Defender*, Apr. 8, 1968.

rearview mirror: Raymond Fisher interview, June 13, 2007.

five hundred fires: Gilbert, *Ten Blocks*, p. 85

"soul brother": Ward Just, "City's Mood: Resignation, Bitterness," *WP*, Apr. 7, 1968.

Nancy had gone: Nancy Brennan interview, Aug. 22, 2007.

298   steps of the Capitol: Gilbert, *Ten Blocks*, p. 88.

total of 13,600 federal troops: Ibid., p. 89.

biggest military occupation: Ibid., p. 89.

"excesses of protest": WJB (Law Day Dinner speech, Federal Bar Association of New York, New Jersey and Connecticut, New York, NY, May 1, 1968).

"However just": WJB (speech, Talmudic Academy of Baltimore, Baltimore, MD, May 19, 1968).

299   only standing ovation: *Time*, "The Crucible," Jan. 26, 1968.

"Some of our courts": Christopher P. Banks, *Judicial Politics in the D.C. Circuit Court* (Baltimore, MD: Johns Hopkins University Press, 1999), 26.

equally alarmist: Lucas A. Powe, Jr., *The Warren Court and American Politics* (Cambridge, MA: Belknap Press, 2000), 410.

displayed a chart: Ibid., p. 409.

300   "I hope you": WJB to EW, Mar. 14, 1968, EW papers.

"written in a rhetoric": OT '67 Term History, p. 33.

"crime in the streets": WJB to EW, Mar. 14, 1968, EW papers.

301   *United States v. O'Brien:* 391 U.S. 367 (1968).

302   Protestors let out: *Time*, "Turmoil in Shantytown," June 7, 1968.

Fisher emerged: Fisher interview, June 13, 2007.

"raided" the building: WJB interview, May 7, 1990 (61-19).

opened the case: C. D. DeLoach to Clyde Tolson, FBI Memorandum, June 4, 1968; accessed at http://foia.fbi.gov/wbrennan/brennan_pto8.pdf.

He pleaded: Ibid.

303   "In light of": WJB to Harvard, June 7, 1968.

"unjust and immoral": *Harvard Crimson*, "Commencement 1968," June 13, 1968, www .thecrimson.com/article.aspx?ref=128639.

King's widow: *Harvard Crimson*, "Today's Events," June 12, 1968, www.thecrimson .com/article.aspx?ref=127653.

"Unhappily, the joy": WJB (address, Harvard Law School, Cambridge, MA, June 12, 1968), reprinted as WJB, "A Judge Looks at Student Dissent," 19 *Harvard Law Bulletin* 9 (1968).

304   all the more likely: Ed Cray, *Chief Justice: A Biography of Earl Warren* (New York: Simon & Schuster, 1997), 494.

sensitive request: Jim Newton, *Justice for All: Earl Warren and the Nation He Made* (New York: Riverhead Books, 2007), 489.

"Hugo told me": Hugo L. Black and Elizabeth Black, *Mr. Justice and Mrs. Black* (New York: Random House, 1986), 195.

"absolutely stunned": WJB interview, April 13, 1989 (49-7).

Warren confided: WJB interview, July 5, 1989 (51-4).

Brennan was mentioned: *Time*, "Warren: Out of the Storm Center," June 28, 1968.

305   shared widely: Black and Black, *Mr. Justice and Mrs. Black*, p. 195.

"thought fate might": Ibid., p. 196.

"an utterly delightful": *Time*, "Chief Confidant to Chief Justice," July 5, 1968.

harbored deep reservations: WJB interview, Jan. 30, 1990 (57-4).

306   "I must say": WJB to WOD, Aug. 5, 1968, WOD papers.

substantial payment: Laura Kalman, *Abe Fortas: A Biography* (New Haven, CT: Yale University Press, 1990), 351.

lengthy, searing attacks: 24 CONG. Q. ALMANAC 531 (1968).

307 "who do not partake": WJB, "Landmarks of Legal Liberty" (speech, New York University School of Law, Oct. 1, 1968).

"walk of a queen": Brennan was quoting the last lines of Yeats's 1902 play *Cathleen ní Houlihan*. The old lady is widely interpreted to symbolize a free Ireland. See Alexander Norman Jeffares, *A New Commentary on the Poems of W. B. Yeats* (London: Macmillan, 1984), 79–80.

pick Spiro Agnew: Joseph Onek interview, Apr. 5, 1989.

"He thought he": Abner Mikva interview, Oct. 22, 2007.

308 "a jackass Catholic": Michael Beschloss, "A Question of Anti-Semitism," *Newsweek*, Oct. 18, 1999.

"I needn't tell you": WJB to AG, June 26, 1988.

"He was so": WJB interview, Jan. 30, 1990 (57-4).

still regret: Henry J. Reske, UPI, "Justice Goldberg Reflects on Remarkable Career," *LAT*, Dec. 7, 1986.

Brennan's clerks recounted: OT '68 Term History discussion of *Younger v. Harris*, 401 U.S. 37 (1971); the case was first argued in April 1969 but was not ultimately decided until February 1971.

309 "There just wasn't": WJB interview, Oct. 28, 1986 (5-9).

starting a fire: James C. Young, "Probe Starts a Fire Fatal to 3 at Penn Yule Party," *Philadelphia Inquirer*, Dec. 11, 1967; AP, "Penn Campus Fire Kills 3 at Party," *NYT*, Dec. 11, 1967; *NYT*, "Penn Student Says He Accidentally Set Fire that Killed 3," Dec. 15, 1967.

worried about her testifying: Nancy Brennan interview, Aug. 22, 2007.

only reference: *Philadelphia Inquirer*, "Roommate Tells How He Helped Noble to Flee," Nov. 15, 1968; UPI, "Drunkeness Cited in Fraternity Fire," *NEN*, Oct. 17, 1968.

310 political firestorm: AP, "Organized Crime Said to Infiltrate Jersey Legislature," *NYT*, Dec. 12, 1968; AP, "Jersey Disclosure on Crime Links Due," *NYT*, Dec. 16, 1968.

mob retribution: Georgie Brennan interview, Dec. 1, 2007.

scheduled to testify: Ronald Sullivan, "Jersey Legislature Names Panel for Inquiry on Links to Mafia," *NYT*, Dec. 28, 1968.

"He's new at this": Sidney E. Zion, "Brennan Recital Is Called Flimsy," *NYT*, Dec. 31, 1968.

relieved of his job: Ronald Sullivan, "Brennan Relieved in Crime Inquiry," *NYT*, Jan. 7, 1969.

special legislative committee: Ronald Sullivan, "Sills Applauds Report in New Jersey," *NYT*, Jan. 16, 1969.

311 soured Bill: *NYT*, "Brennan Reflects on '68 Accusation," Dec. 10, 1972.

"passionate protests": WJB, "Bouton Lecture" (speech, Princeton University, Princeton, NJ, Feb. 4, 1969).

"Are we willing": WJB (speech, Notre Dame University, South Bend, IN, Feb. 8, 1969). In between his appearances at Princeton and Notre Dame, Brennan spoke at New York University on Feb. 6, 1969.

"defended the 'social activism'": AP, "Brennan Defends High Court," Feb. 15, 1969, WJB scrapbook.

Brennan's secretary answered: Unless otherwise noted, this account of Landau's visit comes from a March 17, 1969, memo Brennan wrote about the incident.

press secretary: Landau would go on to lead the Reporters Committee for Freedom of the Press, an organization dedicated to protecting reporters' access to public information. In that role, he would lead a campaign to prevent Nixon from removing 40 million White House documents from the public domain. Douglas Martin, "Jack C. Landau, Who Fought for Right of News Reporters, Is Dead at 74," *NYT,* Aug. 20, 2008.

trio of cases: *Alderman v. United States, Butenko v. United States,* and *Ivanov v. United States,* 394 U.S. 165 (1969).

312 Justice Department nervous: Earl Warren, *The Memoirs of Chief Justice Earl Warren* (Garden City, NY: Doubleday & Company, 1977), 341.

313 "this outrageous attempt": Ibid., p. 340.

released its opinions: *Giordano v. United States,* 394 U.S. 310 (1969); *Taglianetti v. United States,* 394 U.S. 316 (1969); denial of rehearing in *Ivanov v. United States,* 394 U.S. 939.

"It seems pretty": WOD to file, Mar. 17, 1969; WOD papers.

rehear a case: *Utah Pub. Serv. Comm'n v. El Paso Natural Gas,* 395 U.S. 464 (1969).

Catholic layperson: The award is so named because it is announced on Laetare Sunday, the fourth Sunday of Lent. Eligibility for the medal was later extended to include Catholic clergy.

"We take great pride": Hesburgh to WJB, Mar. 14, 1969.

314 "I am just": WJB to Hesburgh, Mar. 14, 1969, Hesburgh papers.

"Nothing has given": WJB to Hesburgh, June 11, 1969, Hesburgh papers.

grew suspicious: Tim Phelps interview with Wermiel, undated.

"This will not only": WJB to W. H. Lawrence, Mar. 3, 1969.

also made inquiries: WJB to Nancy Brennan, Apr. 16, 1969, WJB personal files.

315 They expected Nancy: Nancy Brennan interview, Aug. 22, 2007.

"marriage was": WJB, "Holton Arms School Dedication" (speech, Dedication of Holton Arms School, Bethesda, MD, Oct. 27, 1963).

Nancy attended: Toni House, "25 Happy Debutantes Make Bow," *Washington Star,* Dec. 23, 1967.

wanted to pursue: Nancy Brennan interview, Aug. 22, 2007.

"Vacuuming the living room": Betty Friedan, *The Feminine Mystique* (1963; repr., New York: Norton, 2001), 121.

Gender consciousness: Ruth Rosen, *The World Split Open* (New York: Viking, 2000), 67–78.

further raised: The ban on sex discrimination had been intended by sponsors to sink the measure.

316 more assertive wave: Martha Weinman Lear, "The Second Feminist Wave," *NYT Magazine,* Mar. 10, 1968, 24.

"He was making": Nancy Brennan interview, Aug. 22, 2007.

"He can't stay": Kalman, *Abe Fortas,* p. 368.

not take him back: Ibid., p. 380.

"There is no profession": *NEN,* "Brennan Opinion Cites Bar's Duty," Oct. 4, 1956; *In re Herr,* 125 A.2d 706 (1956).

317 refused to invite: Tim Phelps interview, May 29, 2007.

"Fortas's departure, coupled": John P. MacKenzie, "Denies Doing Wrong," *WP,* June 16, 1969.

"The whole face": WJB interview, Oct. 28, 1986 (5-6).

decisions alone did not: Michael W. Flamm, *Law and Order: Street Crime, Civil Unrest, and the Crisis of Liberalism in the 1960s* (New York: Columbia University Press, 2005), 126.

"I'm sick of": Ibid., p. 1.
318 *Brandenburg v. Ohio:* 395 U.S. 44 (1969).
Fortas had circulated: AF to conference, Apr. 11, 1969.
Brennan took over: WJB to conference, Apr. 11, 1969.
"clear and present danger": *Schenck v. United States,* 249 U.S. 47 (1919).
were together: Richard Bazelon interview, Oct. 26, 1989.
319 "There are reasons": Lyle Denniston, "Jerseyan May Shape Burger Court," *Trenton Times,* June 27, 1969.
"What can one man": WEB to HAB, Mar. 31, 1969, HAB papers.
"Douglas is next": Fred Graham, "The Delicate Issue of Judging the Judges," *NYT,* June 1, 1969.
"We have the responsibility": 115 CONG. REC. 12687–88 (1969).
sought to disqualify: Philip Warden, "Dealings of 2 Court Members Keep Ethics Issue Boiling," *CT,* May 17, 1969.
published stories: *NYT,* "Court to Let Brennan Hear Case Despite Real Estate Partnership," May 27, 1969.
he resigned: Lyle Denniston, "Apartment Investment Links Severed by Justice Brennan," *Washington Evening Star,* June 12, 1969.
320 He sold off: AP, "All Activities Outside Court Given Up by Justice Brennan," *Bridgeport Telegram,* June 12, 1969.
"Have you written": Onek interview, Apr. 5, 1989.
Three other justices: *Washington Star,* "Four Justices to Restrict Outside Role," June 23, 1969.
"It's a decision": WJB to Hesburgh, June 11, 1969, Hesburgh papers.
321 "I seem fated": WJB to Frank Ritchie, Jan. 20, 1964, WJB personal files.
"We're getting on": WJB interview, June 10, 1987 (18-12).
modest ceremony: WJB to Hesburgh, Mar. 27, 1969, Hesburgh papers.
322 master of ceremonies: Black and Black, *Mr. Justice and Mrs. Black,* p. 223.
more public tribute: John P. MacKenzie, "Warren Termed 'Emancipator,'" *WP,* June 30, 1969.
"Your wonderful remarks": Hesburgh to WJB, June 16, 1969, Hesburgh papers.
"pantheon": WJB, *Chief Justice Warren,* 88 HARV. L. REV. 1, 4–5 (1974); Brennan's efforts to burnish Warren's reputation would continue the rest of his life. In an effort to make sure Warren got his proper due, Brennan provided copies of his term histories to Warren biographer Bernard Schwartz. At the behest of Warren's son-in-law, Brennan also sought to get the postal service to issue a stamp in his honor in 1988. In what may well have been his last public speech, Brennan delivered taped remarks for a 1994 symposium on Warren in Oklahoma.
"Every day": Wermiel attended this event on May 7, 1990.
That morning: Fred Graham, "Justices Curbing Off-Bench Roles," *NYT,* June 9, 1969.
323 Brennan's smile disappeared: Barry Schweid, e-mail message to Stern, May 1, 2007.
misremembered the details: WJB interview, Dec. 14, 1987 (26-15).
so "livid": Fred Graham, *Happy Talk: Confessions of a TV Newsman* (New York: W. W. Norton & Company, 1990), 140; Graham also wrote that he believed Brennan was angry with him for not covering an earlier case, *United States v. Wade,* an account both Brennan and his clerk that term, Stephen Goodman, disputed at the time Graham's book was published. Goodman interview, May 10, 1990.
He blamed Graham: WJB interview, Dec. 14, 1987 (26-15).
"It's a camp": WJB to Stanley Weigel, Aug. 26, 1969.

324 Marjorie's doctor called: W. Taylor Reveley III (WJB OT '69 clerk) interview, Apr. 29, 1992.

14. NEW CHALLENGES

327 none seemed angrier: Hugo L. Black and Elizabeth Black, *Mr. Justice and Mrs. Black* (New York: Random House, 1986), 226.

Brennan appreciated: WJB, *Chief Justice Warren*, 88 HARV. L. REV. 1, 1–2 (1974).

328 still moved: Bob Woodward and Scott Armstrong, *The Brethren: Inside the Supreme Court* (New York: Simon & Schuster, 1979), 30.

Brennan reverted: WJB to WEB, Sept. 29, 1969.

chatting cordially: Robert Weinberg interview, July 9, 2007.

329 "They were reasonably": Black and Black, *Mr. Justice and Mrs. Black,* p. 232.

emergency appeal: *Alexander v. Holmes County Bd. of Educ.*, 396 U.S. 19 (1969).

most flagrantly obstructionist: J. Harvie Wilkinson III, *From Brown to Bakke: The Supreme Court and School Integration: 1945–1978* (New York: Oxford University Press, 1979), 79.

330 The reality was: J. Anthony Lukas, *Common Ground: A Turbulent Decade in the Lives of Three American Families* (New York: Vintage Books, 1986), 232.

growing exasperated: WJB interview, Nov. 16, 1987 (24-17).

Green v. County School Board of New Kent County: 391 U.S. 430 (1968).

not a single: Wilkinson, *From Brown to Bakke,* p. 115.

chose to italicize: Raymond Fisher (WJB OT '67 clerk) interview, June 13, 2007.

331 "When this opinion": EW to WJB, May 22, 1968.

lowered state flags: Bernard Schwartz, *Super Chief: Earl Warren and His Supreme Court; A Judicial Biography* (New York: New York University Press, 1983), 706.

liberal college towns: James T. Wooten, "Rocky Road for Busing," *NYT,* Nov. 3, 1969.

bomb was thrown: Donald Janson, "Bomb Mars Start of Chicago Busing," *NYT,* Mar. 12, 1968, 27.

"the school bus": Wooten, "Rocky Road for Busing." *Keyes v. Sch. Dist. No. 1,* 396 U.S. 1215, 1217 (1969) (mem.) (citing *Green v. County Sch. Bd.,* 391 U.S. 430, 439 (1969)), *vacating* 303 F. Supp. 279 (1969).

332 "chaos and confusion": Lucius Jefferson Barker and Twiley W. Barker, Jr., *Freedom, Courts, Politics: Studies in Civil Liberties* (Englewood Cliffs, NJ: Prentice-Hall, 1972), 193.

"There is no longer": *Alexander v. Holmes County Bd. of Educ.*, 396 U.S. 1218, 1220 (1969) (mem.), *aff'g suspension of United States v. Hinds County Sch. Bd.*, 417 F.2d 852 (1969).

333 Burger said he would: OT '69 Term History, p. 63.

privately consulted: WEB to conference, Oct. 25, 1969, WOD papers.

"at the earliest possible time": WEB to conference, Oct. 28, 1969.

drafting a revision: WJB handwritten draft, Oct. 26, 1969.

read the resulting draft: There is a notation on the handwritten copy of Brennan's notes dated Sunday, Oct. 26, 1969, indicating he read it over the phone to Justice Black's secretary at "about 12:00 Sunday."

Black soon circulated: HLB to conference, Oct. 26, 1969.

"forthwith": WEB to conference, Oct. 28, 1969.

"remove the impression": WJB to WEB, Oct. 28, 1969.

334 Other justices would: JMH to conference, Oct. 28, 1969; PS to conference, Oct. 28, 1969; WOD papers.
Burger visited: OT '69 Term History, p. 71.
"In some respects": WEB to conference, Oct. 29, 1969.
"It was an ugly business": WJB to Stanley Weigel, Nov. 17, 1969.
"He did not": Weinberg interview, July 9, 2007.
335 burden of planning: Nancy Brennan interview, Aug. 22, 2007.
Brennan was responsible: Ibid.
"This was not": W. Taylor Reveley interview, Apr. 29, 1992.
336 she was shocked: Alice Knight interview, Aug. 13, 1990.
Goldberg v. Kelly: 397 U.S. 254 (1970).
began funding: Robert W. Bennett, "The Burger Court and the Poor," in *The Burger Court,* ed. Vincent Blasi (New Haven, CT; Yale University Press, 1983), 46–47.
337 "right to live": Israel Shenker, "Guarantee of 'Right to Live' Is Urged," *NYT,* Sept. 28, 1969.
barring the presence: *King v. Smith,* 392 U.S. 309 (1968).
Shapiro v. Thompson: 394 U.S. 618 (1969).
insisting on keeping: Joseph Onek (WJB OT '68 clerk) interview, April 5, 1989.
338 Critics suggested: See, for example, Todd Zubler, *The Right to Migrate and Welfare Reform: Time for* Shapiro v. Thompson *to Take a Hike,* 31 VAL. U. L. REV. 893 (1997).
attorneys balked: Martha F. Davis, *Brutal Need: Lawyers and the Welfare Rights Movement, 1960–1973* (New Haven, CT: Yale University Press, 1993), 81.
widely read article: Charles A. Reich, "The New Property," 73 YALE L. J. 733 (1964).
339 Brennan cited Reich: WJB, "Centennial Address" (speech, Centennial Convocation of the George Washington University Law School, Washington, DC, Oct. 12, 1965), reprinted as WJB, *Centennial Address,* 34 GEO. WASH. UNIV. L. REV. 189 (1965).
"Once they lost": WJB interview, July 16, 1986 (1-4).
targeted New York: Davis, *Brutal Need,* p. 87.
Kelly was the victim: Factual account of the case from the original complaint filed in U.S. District Court in New York on Jan. 29, 1968, and Davis, *Brutal Need.*
340 Diamond, quickly realized: David Diamond interview, Nov. 1, 1995.
eating spoiled food: Tony Mauro, "Fair Hearing: Legacy to the Poor," in *Reason and Passion: Justice Brennan's Enduring Influence,* eds. E. Joshua Rosenkranz and Bernard Schwartz (New York: W. W. Norton & Company, 1997), 237.
three-judge: Three-judge district courts, consisting of one circuit judge and two district judges, were convened by federal law to hear constitutional challenges to enjoin the operation of state laws and federal laws. The requirement was first created by Congress in 1911, modified several times, and repealed in 1976, except for narrow classes of cases. The law also provided for direct appeal to the Supreme Court from the decision of a three-judge district court.
341 flagged the case: WJB interview, Apr. 15, 1987 (12-14).
vote to hear: John M. Harlan, Potter Stewart, Byron R. White, and Abe Fortas voted to hear the case.
related case from California: *Wheeler v. Montgomery,* 397 U.S. 280 (1970).
White and Marshall seemed inclined: WOD conference notes, Oct. 17, 1969, WOD papers.
342 "I'd have to write": WOD to WJB, Oct. 17, 1969, WOD papers.
labeled it "offensive": Davis, *Brutal Need,* p. 113.

343 laid out: JMH to WJB, Dec. 11, 1969.
344 underlined much: HLB markup of WJB to conference, Dec. 12, 1969, HLB papers.
so riled up: Black and Black, *Mr. Justice and Mrs. Black*, p. 234.
declare extemporaneously: Fred P. Graham, "High Court Upsets City Welfare Rule,"
NYT, Mar. 24, 1970.
praised Black's dissent: James J. Kilpatrick, "Burger for the Dissent," *LAT,* Apr. 3,
1970.
less favorable: *New York Daily News,* "More Judge-Made Law," Mar. 30, 1970.
"I pick up": Pete Hamill, "The Revolt of the White Lower-Middle Class," in *The White
Majority: Between Poverty and Affluence,* ed. Louise Kapp Howe (New York: Random
House, 1971), 11.
345 setting a ceiling: *Dandridge v. Williams,* 397 U.S. 471 (1970); unannounced inspections: *Wyman v. James,* 400 U.S. 309 (1971); pay different benefits: *Jefferson v. Hackney,*
406 U.S. 535 (1972); driver's license: *Bell v. Burson,* 402 U.S. 535 (1971); terminating parole: *Morrissey v. Brewer,* 408 U.S. 471 (1972); disability payments: *Matthews v. El-
dridge,* 424 U.S. 319 (1976); civil service workers: *Arnett v. Kennedy,* 416 U.S. 134 (1974);
untenured assistant professor: *Board of Regents v. Roth,* 408 U.S. 564 (1972).
"This deceptively simple": Stephen G. Breyer, "Goldberg v. Kelly: Administrative Law
and the New Property," in Rosenkranz and Schwartz, *Reason and Passion,* p. 246.
"twenty years later": Charles A. Reich, *Beyond the New Property: An Ecological View
of Due Process,* 56 BROOKLYN L. REV. 731 (1990).
"due process explosion": Henry J. Friendly, *Some Kind of Hearing,* 123 U. PA. L. REV.
1267, 1268 (1975).
came out of funds: Richard A. Epstein, *No New Property,* 56 BROOKLYN L. REV. 747,
767–81 (1990).
346 "I had no idea": WJB interview, May 16, 1988 (34-6).
touch off: WJB, "Reason, Passion, and 'The Progress of the Law'" (Forty-Second Annual Benjamin N. Cardozo Lecture, Bar Association of the City of New York, New
York City, Sept. 17, 1987), reprinted as WJB, *Reason, Passion and "The Progress of the
Law,* 10 CARDOZO L. REV. 3 (1988).
"I wonder if": WEB to conference, Feb. 7, 1970.
direct-mail marketers: *Rowan v. Post Office Dept.,* 397 U.S. 728 (1970).
"distaste for absolutes": JMH to conference, Apr. 23, 1970.
"It may be that": WJB to WEB, Apr. 28, 1970.
Burger instead grew: WEB to WJB, Apr. 28, 1970.
347 parents ought to have: OT '69 Term History, p. 11.
Growing up blocks: HAB to E. Barrett Prettyman, Apr. 10, 1964, HAB papers.
Blackmon had wired: Ibid.
348 "appears strikingly like": Fred P. Graham, "Burger and Blackmun Opinions Similar,"
NYT, Apr. 15, 1970.
"no hesitation whatsoever": *Harry A. Blackmun: Hearing Before the S. Judiciary
Comm.,* 91st Cong. 39 (1970).
"very pleasant, outgoing": HAB, oral history interview by Harold H. Koh, Apr. 24,
1995, Federal Judicial Center.
"Please bear with": HAB to WJB, May 21, 1970.
touching toast: Black and Black, *Mr. Justice and Mrs. Black,* p. 242.
349 long enough: Their third grandchild, Hugh's daughter, Marianne, was born in 1967.
so exhausted: WJB to Mr. and Mrs. Harry Crawley, Sept. 11, 1970.
"I love her more": Black and Black, *Mr. Justice and Mrs. Black,* p. 245.

15. FRUSTRATION RISING

350 "It is monstrous": *Harris v. NY,* 401 U.S. 222 (1971).
Louisiana state law: *Labine v. Vincent,* 401 U.S. 532 (1971).
"Let's blow them": Richard Cotton interview, Mar. 13, 1990.

351 children of American citizens: *Rogers v. Bellei,* 401 U.S. 815 (1971).
left the mock dissent: Loftus Becker interview, July 3, 1990.
"Justice Brennan now appears": Lyle Denniston, "Angry Justice Brennan," *Trenton Times,* Apr. 2, 1971. The article was originally written for the *Washington Star.*
"the increasingly vinegary": Fred P. Graham, "Justices Are Losing Their Cool," *NYT,* Apr. 11, 1971.
"have an angry": Glen Elsasser, "Sees Angry Bite in High Court Rifts," *CT,* May 31, 1971.

352 returned to his chambers: Thomas Jorde (WJB OT '73 clerk) interview, Mar. 12, 1990.
no ambition: Gerald Rosberg (WJB OT '72 clerk) interview, Mar. 6, 1990.
was hospitalized: WJB to Dr. H. A. Grennan, Apr. 26, 1971, and T. Crandall Alford, M.D., to WJB, Apr. 17, 1981; both WJB personal files.

353 "It's a trend": WJB to Mr. and Mrs. Harry Crawley, Jan. 14, 1971. The Brennans had two more grandchildren, Hugh's sons Michael and James, born in 1974 and 1976, respectively.
stripped the D.C. Circuit: Christopher P. Banks, *Judicial Politics in the D.C. Circuit Court* (Baltimore, MD: Johns Hopkins University Press, 1999), xii, 27–29.
Black was fading: Roger K. Newman, *Hugo Black: A Biography* (New York: Fordham University Press, 1997), 619. At the time, the longevity record was held by Justice Stephen Field, who served for thirty-four years and eight months from 1863 to 1897. Douglas subsequently surpassed that record.
"three musketeers": Newman, *Hugo Black,* p. 604.
voted the same way: Stephen L. Wasby, *Justice Harry A. Blackmun in the Burger Court,* 11 HAMLINE L. REV. 183, 191 (1988).
"President Nixon has already": Nathan Lewin, "There Is No Mistaking the Swing of the Pendulum," *NYT,* June 27, 1971.

354 visiting Black: Hugo L. Black and Elizabeth Black, *Mr. Justice and Mrs. Black* (New York: Random House, 1986), 268.
plan the funeral: Brennan saved several pages of handwritten notes regarding funeral plans and a note from Hugo Black Jr. thanking him for his help.
could not understand: Tim Phelps interview, May 29, 2007.
paralyzed: Tinsley E. Yarbrough, *John Marshall Harlan* (New York: Oxford University Press, 1992), 334.
shocked to see: WJB interview, Jan. 30, 1990 (57-2).
"will turn more": *Time,* "Now the Nixon Court and What It Means," Oct. 4, 1971.
counterrevolution: Vincent Blasi, ed., *The Burger Court: The Counter-Revolution That Wasn't* (New Haven, CT: Yale University Press, 1983); Bernard Schwartz, ed., *The Burger Court: Counter-Revolution or Confirmation?* (New York: Oxford University Press, 1998).

355 telegram arrived: WEB to WJB, Aug. 26, 1970.
Swann v. Charlotte-Mecklenburg Bd. of Educ.: 402 U.S. 1 (1971).
Only 2 percent: Bernard Schwartz, *Swann's Way* (New York: Oxford University Press, 1986), 8, 14.

The home of: Frye Gaillard, *The Dream Long Deferred* (Chapel Hill: University of North Carolina Press, 1988), 35.

hung in effigy: Schwartz, *Swann's Way*, p. 21.

went into effect: Gaillard, *Dream Long Deferred*, p. 79.

more than doubled: *NYT*, "Year of Desegregation a Trying One in South," Apr. 18, 1971.

356 rambling pronouncements: WJB interview, May 7, 1987 (13-10).

crisp presentations: WJB, *Chief Justice Warren*, 88 Harv. L. Rev. 1–2 (1974). Brennan noted how "lucidly and concisely" Warren presented cases at conference.

sloppy with assignments: PS to WEB, Dec. 29, 1970.

purpose of keeping: WJB interview, Oct. 21, 1987 (22-11).

complaining about: Richard Cotton (WJB OT '70 clerk) interview, Mar. 13, 1990.

more thoughtful: Douglas received similar treatment when he later got sick.

freewheeling discussion: HAB conference notes, Oct. 17, 1970, HAB papers.

spoke against it: WOD memo to file, Apr. 20, 1971, WOD papers.

offering to draft: Ibid.

357 "the only way": WJB to WEB, Dec. 30, 1970.

undoing the effects: *United States v. Jefferson County Bd. of Educ.*, 372 F.2d 836 (5th Cir. 1966).

Brennan believed: WJB to WEB, Dec. 30, 1970.

"deep-seated judicial philosophy": Bernard Schwartz, *The Ascent of Pragmatism: The Burger Court in Action* (Reading, MA: Addison-Wesley Publishing Co., 1990), 22.

narrow opinions: Vincent L. Broderick, *Justice Potter Stewart*, 12 N.C. Cent. L.J. 297 (1981).

appalled Blackmun: *Time*, "Agreeing to Disagree," July 10, 1972. That young veteran, John Kerry, was later elected a Democratic senator from Massachusetts and was the Democratic nominee for president in 2004.

reflexively liberal: Laurence Tribe (PS OT '67 clerk) interview, Nov. 18, 2008.

Stewart took issue: PS to WEB, Dec. 29, 1970.

358 privately circulated: PS to WJB, Feb. 19, 1971; PS to WOD, Feb. 10, 1971; both WOD papers.

urged: WOD to PS, Feb. 16, 1971, WOD papers.

better position: OT '70 Term History, p. 35.

extremely unpopular: *Time*, "The Busing Issue Boils Over," Feb. 28, 1972.

359 *Keyes v. School District No. 1*: 413 U.S. 189 (1973).

almost every major city: Christopher Jencks, "Busing—The Supreme Court Goes North," *NYT Magazine*, Nov. 19, 1972.

360 "extreme solicitude": WHR, "Who Writes Decisions of the Supreme Court?," *U.S. News & World Report*, Dec. 13, 1957, 74.

Rehnquist had opposed: Leroy F. Aarons and Ken W. Clawson, "Rehnquist: Admired Yet Decried," *WP*, Nov. 3, 1971.

government surveillance: David E. Rosenbaum, "William Hubbs Rehnquist," *NYT*, Oct. 22, 1971.

"So when he": WJB interview, Mar. 14, 1988 (29-13).

"with an eye": Dan Levine, "Opening the Rehnquist Files," *Recorder (CA)*, Nov. 18, 2008.

could claim roots: John C. Jeffries, Jr., *Justice Lewis F. Powell, Jr.: A Biography* (New York: Charles Scribner's Sons, 1994). Like Brennan and Blackmun, Powell had Frankfurter as a professor at Harvard Law School, meaning a third of the Court were now his former pupils.

361 mostly silent: Jeffries, *Justice Lewis F. Powell, Jr.,* p. 178.
saw no point: LFP internal memo to clerks, July 31, 1972, LFP papers.
"In my view": LFP internal memo to clerks, Jan. 6, 1973, LFP papers.

362 "permeates the entire system": HAB memo to file, Sept. 28, 1972, HAB papers.
initially drafted: OT '72 Term History, p. 11.
delay making a decision: HAB to WJB, Jan. 9, 1973.
frustrated Brennan: OT '72 Term History, p. 42.
he would drop: WJB to conference, April 3, 1973.
Burger suggested holding: WEB to conference, May 30, 1973.

363 proposal infuriated Brennan: OT '72 Term History, p. 45.
"I most strenuously": WJB to WEB, May 30, 1973, WOD papers.
"fundamentally unnecessary": John P. MacKenzie, "Brennan Opposes 'Mini-Court,'" *WP,* May 24, 1973; full speech reprinted as WJB, *The National Court of Appeals: Another Dissent,* 40 U. CHI. L. REV. 473 (1973).
made it moot: HAB to WJB, May 30, 1973.
picked up: *NYT,* "Denver Districting Is Unconstitutional," June 22, 1973.
Milliken v. Bradley: 418 U.S. 717 (1974).

364 intermittent victories: Blackmun provided the fifth vote in *Dayton Bd. of Educ. v. Brinkman,* 443 U.S. 526 (1979).
Protestors bombarded: J. Anthony Lukas, *Common Ground: A Turbulent Decade in the Lives of Three American Families* (New York: Vintage Books, 1986), 244–45.
"good jobs": Ronald P. Formisano, *Boston Against Busing: Race, Class, and Ethnicity in the 1960s and 1970s* (Chapel Hill: University of North Carolina Press, 1991), 179.
argument echoed: Nathan Glazer, *Affirmative Discrimination: Ethnic Inequality and Public Policy* (New York: Basic Books, 1975).

365 "I feel indebted": Garrity to WJB, Jan. 11, 1978.
banning only: Frederick F. Schauer, *The Law of Obscenity* (Washington, DC: Bureau of National Affairs, 1976), 44.
Brennan instead joined: *Stanley v. Georgia,* 394 U.S. 557 (1969).
as late as 1971: *United States v. Thirty-Seven Photographs,* 402 U.S. 363 (1971).
unsuccessfully urging him: Becker interview, Dec. 10, 2008.

366 Brennan concluded that: WJB interview, Dec. 17, 1986 (7-20).
Miller v. California: 413 U.S. 15 (1973).
"worsen an already": WJB to conference, May 22, 1972.
"I think that": WJB to conference, June 13, 1972.

367 famously declared: *Jacobellis v. Ohio,* 378 U.S. 184 (1964).
Paris Adult Theatre v. Slaton: 413 U.S. 49 (1973).
set the tone: OT '72 Term History, p. 16.
"has a distinct appeal": HAB to conference, Nov. 20, 1972.
"exceedingly well done": HAB to WJB, Jan. 9, 1972. The memo was misdated as 1972 though circulated in 1973.

368 only learn later: OT '72 Term History, p. 24. There is evidence of this correspondence in HAB's papers.
reconfigured test: WEB memorandum to conference, Jan. 4, 1973, TM papers.
"Dear Harry": OT '72 Term History, p. 25.
brought back word: Ibid., p. 26.
Burger had managed: HAB to WEB, May 9, 1973, HAB papers.
planned to join: HAB to conference, May 15, 1973.

369 more of them directed: OT '72 Term History, p. 69.
Roe v. Wade: 410 U.S. 113 (1973).

370 late-December memo: WJB to WOD, Dec. 30, 1971.

Eisenstadt v. Baird: 405 U.S. 438 (1972).

even some liberals: Ruth Bader Ginsburg, *Some Thoughts on Autonomy and Equality in Relation to* Roe v. Wade, 63 N.C. L. REV. 375 (1985).

371 "Bill Douglas never": WJB interview, May 19, 1987 (15-6).

"the core constitutional question": WJB to HAB, May 18, 1972.

"He didn't want": William J. Maledon interview, May 1, 1990.

"particular attention": HAB to WJB, Nov. 21, 1972.

vented his irritation: OT '71 Term History, p. 11.

372 first-of-its-kind: David Garrow, *Liberty & Sexuality: The Right to Privacy and the Making of Roe v. Wade* (New York: Macmillan, 1994), 311.

voiced anguish: Ibid., p. 414.

"I wouldn't under": WJB interview, Jan. 28, 1987 (9-8).

"It never crossed": Ibid.

"He was obviously": Maledon interview, May 1, 1990.

arguing that unborn children: William J. Maledon, *The Law and the Unborn Child: The Legacy and Logical Inconsistencies,* 46 NOTRE DAME LAW. 349 (1970). Maledon listed the article on the resumé he sent to Brennan in Sept. 1971 after being recommended for the clerkship.

"arbitrary": HAB to conference, Nov. 21, 1972, HAB papers.

Powell indicated: LFP to HAB, Nov. 29, 1972, LFP papers.

373 "no particular commitment": HAB to LFP, Dec. 4, 1972, HAB papers.

soon followed up: HAB to conference, Dec. 11, 1972, HAB papers.

Douglas indicated: WOD to HAB, Dec. 11, 1972; "the opinion's present": TM to HAB, Dec. 12, 1972.

"technically inconsistent": WJB to HAB, Dec. 13, 1972.

"I have in mind": HAB to conference, Dec. 15, 1972, HAB papers.

"I have tried": HAB to conference, Dec. 21, 1972.

374 "was involved": WJB interview, May 23, 1988 (36-4).

"made no suggestions": HAB interview, Aug. 10, 1988.

1993 article: Kim Eisler, "The Real Story of Roe v. Wade," *Washingtonian,* October 1993; "This is hogwash": Linda Greenhouse, *Becoming Justice Blackmun: Harry Blackmun's Supreme Court Journey* (New York: Times Books, 2005), 138.

drafted an announcement: HAB to conference, Jan. 16, 1973, TM papers.

"Our practice": WJB to conference, Jan. 17, 1973, TM papers.

375 "an unspeakable tragedy": *NYT,* "Statement by 2 Cardinals," Jan. 23, 1973.

O'Boyle accused: Marjorie Hyer, "Cardinal O'Boyle Asks Pastors to Preach Against Abortion Rule," *WP,* Jan. 25, 1973.

"Notably, one": Lester Kinsolving, "He's Embroiled Over O'Boyle," *Washington Evening Star,* Feb. 17, 1973.

sitting justices: Retired chief justice Earl Warren attended.

asked priests: Hyer, "Cardinal O'Boyle Asks Pastors to Preach Against Abortion Rule."

half-dozen picketers: Marjorie Hyer and William A. Elsen, "Ruling on Abortions Criticized in Sermons," *WP,* Jan. 29, 1973; soon echoed: Marion K. Sanders, "Enemies of Abortion," *Harper's Magazine,* March 1974, 26; Sanders identified the publications as the *Wanderer* and *Triumph.*

Maledon sensed: Maledon interview, May 1, 1990.

noticed a pattern: Geoffrey Stone (WJBOT '72 clerk) interview, July 26, 2007; Randall Bezanson (HAB OT '72 clerk) interview, Aug. 21, 2007.

"to congratulate you": OT '72 Term History, pp. 69–70.

376 often hateful: Blackmun received letters in the week after the decision was announced comparing him to Adolf Hitler, Joseph Stalin, and Genghis Khan; HAB papers.

offer Blackmun: Maledon interview, Sept. 6, 2007.

shared the news: HAB to WJB, Dec. 22, 1982, HAB papers.

"anguish": HAB to WJB, May 16, 1983, HAB papers.

punishment later proposed: After the Vatican issued a "doctrinal note" in 2003 affirming the obligation of Catholic politicians to oppose abortion, those asked not to receive Communion included California governor Gray Davis, Massachusetts senator John Kerry, and New Jersey governor Jim McGreevey. Ramesh Ponnuru, "Rites and Wrongs," *National Review*, May 31, 2004.

most taken aback: WJB interview, May 13, 1987. In 1990 Brennan told the *Los Angeles Times* that he left his parish church because of criticism of the *Roe* decision. Jim Mann, "Justice William J. Brennan Jr.: A Lifetime of Ensuring That Law Embraces Justice," *LAT*, Apr. 22, 1990. In fact, Brennan did not switch parishes until he moved out of Georgetown later in the 1970s. He appears to have been mixing up *Roe* with what happened after criticism of the Court's school-prayer decisions, which prompted Marjorie to stop attending church regularly a decade earlier.

never made him regret: WJB interview, May 27, 1987 (16-3).

377 knew where to find: In a June 7, 1982, memo to the justices regarding a case under consideration, Burger joked, "to avoid canceling Bill Brennan's ferry reservation, I enclose a typescript draft of dissent in this case." Two weeks later, Powell wrote in a cover note to Brennan, "We will get you to Woods Hole in time for the ferry" to Nantucket; LFP to WJB, June 22, 1982, re: *Board of Education v. Pico* 457 U.S. 853 (1982), LFP papers.

Marjorie had rebounded: WJB to Leon Jaworski, Apr. 14, 1972.

"to spend another": WJB to Shimon Agranat, Oct. 27, 1972.

clerk lore: Peter Busch, "Jet Fuel," in *The Common Man as Uncommon Man: Remembering Justice William J. Brennan, Jr.*, ed. E. Joshua Rosenkranz and Thomas M. Jorde (New York: Brennan Center for Justice, 2006), 16–17. Busch was an OT '79 clerk.

daily routine: William Dougherty (Nantucket friend) interview with Wermiel, undated; WJB interview, Sept. 22, 1988 (43-4).

wooden sign: Robert F. Cross, "No Reserved Seats for the Mighty," *Historic Nantucket* summer 1993, 24–26.

plead ignorance: Nancy Brennan interview, Mar. 11, 2008.

378 "We've developed": WJB to HAB, July 24, 1976, HAB papers.

379 senior Nixon aides: Those indicted included former attorney general John Mitchell, who had come to the Court to tell Warren that Fortas had to go because of his own scandal.

followed news accounts: Lawrence Pedowitz (WJB OT '73 clerk) interview, Nov. 24, 2008.

take the steam out: Linda Mathews, "Nixon Lawyers Warn High Court It Could Upset Balance of Powers," *LAT*, July 2, 1974.

evidence most likely: WJB to Ball, Jan. 4, 1988, cited in Howard Ball, *We Have a Duty: the Supreme Court and the Watergate Tapes Litigation* (New York: Greenwood Press, 1990), 88.

Brennan persuaded: Ball, *We Have a Duty*, p. 88.

380 visited each of his colleagues' chambers: OT '73 Term History, p. 52.

Reporters speculated: Linda Mathews, "Shun Impeachment Role, Court Warned," *LAT*, July 9, 1974.

renewed his argument: OT '73 Term History, p. 58.

Brennan suggested: OT '73 Term History, p. 58.

381 "Thank God": WJB interview, May 20, 1988 (35-7).

"appeared particularly moved": Lesley Oelsner, "Earl Warren Is Buried in Army Rites at Arlington; References to Opposition," *NYT,* July 13, 1974.

"the Super-Chief": WJB, *Chief Justice Warren,* 88 HARV. L. REV. 1–5 (1974).

382 *United States v. Nixon:* 418 U.S. 683 (1974).

"my effort": WEB to conference, July 15, 1974.

Burger's delivery: OT '73 Term History, p. 82.

"All of us know": WEB to conference, Aug. 26, 1974, HAB papers.

turning point: HAB, oral history interview by Harold H. Koh, June 27, 1995, Federal Judicial Center.

383 Burger had unleashed: WJB interview, Oct. 21, 1987 (22-11). Brennan said the case was *Sea-Land Servs., Inc. v. Gaudet,* 414 U.S. 573 (1974).

Leahy peeked in: Edward Leahy interview, May 2, 1990.

"I had no feeling": HAB, oral history interview by Harold H. Koh, Apr. 24, 1995, Federal Judicial Center.

horribly gaunt: Bruce Allen Murphy, *Wild Bill: The Legend and Life of William O. Douglas* (New York: Random House, 2003), 486.

384 not always make sense: OT '74 Term History, pp. 25–27. The case was *Antoine v. Washington,* 420 U.S. 194 (1975).

justices conspired: Seven of the justices agreed to this highly unusual decision, with only White objecting. BRW to conference, Oct. 20, 1975.

agonized: Stanley Fickle (WJB OT '75 clerk) interview, Mar. 9, 1990.

"horribly difficult": WJB interview, Apr. 11, 1988 (32-10). Brennan denied ever encouraging Douglas to retire.

"One frequently reads": Cathy Douglas to WJB, Nov. 21, 1975.

16. PEDESTALS & CAGES

385 seeking a way: *Goosby v. Osser,* 409 U.S. 512 (1973).

became so nervous: Ann Torregrossa interview, May 25, 2007.

worried she might: WJB to HAB, Feb. 6, 1973, HAB papers.

helpfully leading questions: John C. Jeffries, Jr., *Justice Lewis F. Powell, Jr.: A Biography* (New York: Charles Scribner's Sons, 1994), 479.

"He was so": Torregrossa interview, May 25, 2007. Brennan did not find out Torregrossa had named her son after him until Blackmun ran into her relative in a Rochester, Minnesota, restaurant in 1977.

386 Torregrossa's favor: In the case, *Goosby v. Oser,* 409 U.S. 512 (1973), the Court directed the District Court to hear the claims asserted by Torregrossa on behalf of her clients.

"the Court's clearest": Ruth Bader Ginsburg and Wendy Webster Williams, "Court Architect of Gender Equality," in *Reason and Passion: Justice Brennan's Enduring Influence,* E. Joshua Rosenkranz and Bernard Schwartz, eds. (New York: W. W. Norton & Company, 1997), 186.

"When it comes": Nina Totenberg, *A Tribute to William J. Brennan Jr.,* 104 HARV. L. REV. 1, 36 (1990).

opportunity excited: Alison Grey Anderson interview, May 11, 2007.

"Send me someone else": In 2007, O'Neil and Barnett both recalled in separate interviews having been the one to call Grey. She recalled it was Barnett in a May 11, 2007, interview.

Douglas had hired: Artemus Ward and David L. Weiden, *Sorcerers' Apprentices: 100 Years of Law Clerks at the United States Supreme Court* (New York : New York University Press, 2006), 90.

"the appropriate young man": Pollak to WJB, Sept. 16, 1966, and WJB to Pollak, Sept. 22, 1966.

387 women accounted: Ruth Rosen, *The World Split Open* (New York: Viking, 2000), 79.

10 percent: Ruth B. Cowan, *Women's Rights through Litigation: An Examination of the American Civil Liberties Union Women's Rights Project,* 8 COLUM. HUM. RTS. L. REV. 373, 377 (1976)

Even Warren: Jim Newton, *Justice For All: Earl Warren and the Nation He Made* (New York: Riverhead Books, 2007), 56–57.

thirty cases: Fred Strebeigh, *Equal: Women Reshape American Law* (New York: W. W. Norton & Company, 2009), 122.

388 tease him: WJB interview, Apr. 4, 1988 (31-3).

having to watch: Joseph Onek (WJB OT '68 clerk) interview, 2007.

"It's a strange": Abner Mikva interview, Oct. 22, 2007.

Burger warned: Strebeigh, *Equal*, p. 375.

not even occurred: Robert O'Neil interview, May 7, 2007.

agreed instead: Barnett to WJB, Dec. 15, 1970.

389 "So I just wrote": Grey Anderson interview, May 11, 2007.

Ginsburg mumbled: David Margolick, "Trial by Adversity Shapes Jurist's Outlook," *NYT*, June 25, 1993.

made the *Harvard Law Review:* Elinor Porter Swiger, *Women Lawyers at Work* (New York: Messner, 1978), 55.

at first balked: Gerald Gunther, *Ruth Bader Ginsburg: A Personal, Very Fond Tribute,* 20 U. HAW. L. REV. 583, 584 (1998).

"Young lady": *NYT*, "Confronting Limits on a Woman's Role," June 25, 1993.

390 so insecure: David Von Drehle, "Conventional Roles Hid a Revolutionary Intellect; Discrimination Helped Spawn a Crusade," *WP*, July 18, 1993.

inquire whether: Deborah L. Markowitz, *In Pursuit of Equality: One Woman's Work to Change the Law,* 14 WOMEN'S RTS. L. REP. 335(1992); citing RBG to Wulf, Apr. 6, 1971.

Reed v. Reed: 404 U.S. 71 (1971).

391 poll taxes: *Breedlove v. Suttles,* 302 U.S. 277 (1937).

bartending except: *Goesaert v. Cleary,* 335 U.S. 464 (1948).

jury lists: *Hoyt v. Florida,* 368 U.S. 57 (1961).

incensed Harlan's secretary: John Rhinelander (JMH OT '61 clerk), e-mail to Stern, Oct. 3, 2008.

expanded the roster: *Shapiro v. Thompson,* 394 U.S. 618 (1969).

California Supreme Court: *Sail'er Inn, Inc. v. Kirby,* 485 P.2d 529 (Cal. 1971).

obscure 1920 decision: *F. S. Royster Guano v. Virginia,* 253 U.S. 412 (1920).

best of both worlds: RBG, "Advocating the Elimination of Gender-Based Discrimination: The 1970s New Look at the Equality Principle" (speech, University of Cape Town, Cape Town, Western Cape, South Africa, Feb. 10, 2006). remaining shielded: Mark V. Tushnet, *A Court Divided: The Rehnquist Court and the Future of Constitutional Law* (New York: W. W. Norton, 2006), 107.

harmful stereotypes: Neil A. Lewis, "Rejected as a Clerk, Chosen as a Justice," *NYT*, June 15, 1993.

392 "once thought": Brief for Appellant at 17, *Reed v. Reed*, No. 70–4, 404 U.S. 71 (1971).

"The pedestal upon": *Sail'er Inn, Inc. v. Kirby*, 485 P.2d 529, 541 (Cal. 1971).

watched silently: Reed's attorney accepted assistance on the brief but would not let ACLU lawyers argue the case.

men were better: Tushnet, *Court Divided*, p. 109.

quiet and reserved: David Margolick, "Trial by Adversity Shapes Jurist's Outlook," *NYT*, June 25, 1993.

embodied the stereotype: Cowan, *Women's Rights through Litigation*, p. 394.

helped in part: Ginsburg described "Appendix E" in her 2006 speech at the University of Cape Town, "Advocating the Elimination of Gender-Based Discrimination."

393 "with a strong": RBG interview, Feb. 13, 2008.

Air Force lifted: *Struck v. Sec'y of Def.*, 460 F.2d 1372 (9th Cir. 1972).

quarreled with Levin: RBG to Joseph J. Levin Jr., Oct. 24, 1972, and Levin to RBG, Oct. 27, 1972; both RBG papers.

fallback position: Brief of ACLU as Amicus Curiae at 8, 23, *Frontiero v. Laird*, 409 U.S. 1123 (1972).

1972 article: Gerald Gunther, *Foreword: In Search of Evolving Doctrine on a Changing Court: A Model for a Newer Equal Protection*, 86 HARV. L REV. 1 (1972).

394 seemingly "benign": Brief of ACLU as Amicus Curiae at 34, *Frontiero v. Laird*, 409 U.S. 1123 (1972).

"It had to be": RBG interview, Feb. 13, 2008.

her students' suggestion: Ibid.

"No, your honor": *NYT*, "Confronting Limits on a Woman's Role," June 25, 1993. The case was *Duren v. Missouri*, 439 U.S. 357 (1979).

"They are just": RBG et al., *In Memoriam: William J. Brennan, Jr.*, 111 HARV. L. REV. 1, 3 (1997).

395 left her wondering: RBG interview, Feb. 13, 2008.

"We need not": OT '72 Term History, p. 81.

intellectually dishonest: Geoffrey Stone interview, Mar. 16, 1989.

remembered leaving: Ibid.

had already circulated: WJB to conference, Feb. 14, 1973.

additional impetus: PS to conference, re: *San Antonio School Dist. V. Rodriguez*, Feb. 8, 1973.

"In light of": WJB to conference, Feb. 14, 1973.

White almost immediately: BRW to WJB, Feb. 15, 1973.

Douglas said: WOD to WJB, Feb. 14, 1973.

396 Powell indicated: LFP to WJB, Feb. 15, 1973.

"until we know": Ibid.

"All in all": HAB memo, Oct. 18, 1971, HAB papers.

"clearly justified": draft circulated, Feb. 28, 1973.

397 questioned "the desirability": LFP to WJB, Mar. 2. 1973.

entering "the arena": HAB to WJB, Mar. 5, 1973.

"Since rejection": WJB to conference, Mar. 6, 1973.

"it now seems": *Time*, "Trouble for ERA," Feb. 19, 1973.

"The 'suspect' approach": WJB to conference, Mar. 6, 1973.

398 concur in the result: PS to WJB, Mar. 7, 1973.

"It is unnecessary": LFP to conference, Mar. 14, 1973.

Brennan rejected: OT '72 Term History, p. 86.

"The decision fell": Warren Weaver Jr., "Air Force Woman Wins Benefit Suit," *NYT*, May 15, 1973.

jubilantly predicted: *NYT*, "A 'Flaming Feminist' Lauds Court," May 22, 1973.

"Brennan's opinion": RBG to Jane Lifset, May 15, 1973, RBG papers.

"far more spectacular": RBG (speech, New York County Lawyers' Association, Nov. 14, 1973), RBG papers.

Ginsburg was disappointed: RBG interview, Feb. 13, 2008.

399 prepared to recommend: Barnett's fellow Berkeley faculty member and Brennan clerk, Robert O'Neil, who had helped recommend Alison Grey in 1970, had left the school to become provost of the University of Cincinnati in 1971.

once again requested: Stephen Barnett interview, Aug. 13, 2007.

1971 lawsuit: Fred Strebeigh, *Equal*, p. 166.

400 Barnett told Berzon: Marsha Berzon interview, Aug. 22, 2007.

"Mr. Justice": Barnett to WJB, Jan. 12, 1974. This letter is not in Brennan's papers.

admitted he was wrong: Barnett interview, Aug. 14, 2007.

401 Brennan wrote Berzon: WJB to Berzon, Jan. 17, 1974.

careful about how: Berzon interview, Oct. 27, 1988.

went to work: Ward and Weiden, *Sorcerers' Apprentices*, p. 90.

felt uneasy: Thomas Jorde interview, Mar. 12, 1990.

"generational chivalry": Berzon interview, Aug. 22, 2007.

402 wound up leaving: Berzon interview, Oct. 27, 1988.

encouraging reply: WJB to Hugh Brennan Jr., Sept. 28, 1970.

became roommates: Connie Phelps interview, July 1, 2007.

Minnie Mouse ears: Steven Goldberg interview, Aug. 15, 2007.

conspiratorial sweet tooth: Connie Phelps interview, July 1, 2007.

"You're not supposed": Marsha S. Berzon, "Justice Brennan's Childcare Issues," in *The Common Man as Uncommon Man: Remembering Justice William J. Brennan Jr.*, ed. E. Joshua Rosenkranz and Thomas M. Jorde (New York: Brennan Center for Justice, 2006), 77–78.

403 "That is not": Connie Phelps interview, July 1, 2007.

after he agreed: RBG to Stephen Wiesenfeld, Dec. 27, 1972, RBG papers.

404 required male officers: *Schlesinger v. Ballard*, 419 U.S. 498 (1975); disability insurance: *Geduldig v. Aiello*, 417 U.S. 484 (1974); property-tax exemption: *Kahn v. Shevin*, 416 U.S. 351 (1974).

Weinberger v. Wiesenfeld: 420 U.S. 636 (1975).

In hindsight: Berzon interview, Aug. 22, 2007; Berzon argued a major sex-discrimination case before the Court, *United Auto Workers v. Johnson Controls, Inc.*, 499 U.S. 187 (1991), and was later appointed to the U.S. Court of Appeals for the Ninth Circuit by President Clinton.

405 "major victory": Warren Weaver Jr., "Justices Back Widowers' Equal Rights," *NYT*, Mar. 20, 1975.

"the route to": *NYT*, "Toward Equal Rights," Mar. 24, 1975.

"Wiesenfeld gets us": RBG to Philip Kurland, Apr. 4, 1975, RBG papers.

"I cried too!": Milicent Tryon to RBG, Mar. 21, 1975, and RBG to Tryon, Mar. 24, 1975; both RBG papers.

victory party: Strebeigh, *Equal*, p. 380.

recounted a rumor: Schafran to RBG, Apr. 4, 1975, RBG papers.

mentioned it too: Cowan, *Women's Rights through Litigation*, p. 381.

did not surprise: RBG interview, Feb. 13, 2008.

406 thirty-four women: RBG, "The First Female Law Clerks," in *Supreme Court Decisions and Women's Rights*, ed. Clare Cushman (Washington, DC: CQ Press), 236–37.

"Believe me": WJB interview, Oct. 19, 1988 (44-6).

the plot focused: *The Paper Chase,* "The Sorcerer's Apprentice," season 1, episode 11 (1978); episode information available on the Internet Movie Database at www.imdb .com/title/tt1420908/.

No one uttered: Frederic Woocher interview, Feb. 9, 1990.

Craig v. Boren: 429 U.S. 190 (1976).

"non-weighty interest": Cushman, ed., *Supreme Court Decisions,* p. 64.

407 "We don't have": RBG to Fred P. Gilbert, Jan. 26, 1976, RBG papers. She also advised, "Don't remind Brennan that in Frontiero he copied from Sail'er Inn without acknowledging the source."

local lawyers resisted: RBG to Fred P. Gilbert, Jan. 15, 1976, RBG papers.

what she considered: *Califano v. Goldfarb,* 430 U.S. 199 (1977).

"go along": HAB to WJB, Nov. 11, 1976.

Califano v. Goldfarb: 430 U.S. 199 (1977).

408 come to fruition: Markowitz, *In Pursuit of Equality,* p. 95.

"an embarrassment": RBG to Esther Raditti Schacter, Feb. 26, 1976, RBG papers.

opinions in three: *Califano v. Goldfarb,* 430 U.S. 199 (1977); *Weinberger v. Wiesenfeld,* 420 U.S. 636 (1975); *Frontiero v. Richardson,* 411 U.S. 677 (1973).

"First he was": Patricia Brennan, "Seven Justices, One Camera," *WP,* Oct. 6, 1996.

decision of her own: *U.S. v. Virginia,* 518 U.S. 515 (1996).

"Without you": Steven Chanenson (WJB OT '95 clerk) interview, June 26, 1996.

17. DEATH & DIGNITY

409 "I'm absolutely convinced": WJB interview, May 8, 1989 (50-10).

410 later traced: Brennan talked about this experience in three separate interviews on Nov. 21, 1986 (6-11), May 8, 1989 (50-7), and July 5, 1989 (51-7).

meant electrocution: Hugo A. Bedau, *Death Sentences in New Jersey 1907–1960,* 19 RUTGERS L. REV. 1 (1964).

fall and rise: Stuart Banner, *The Death Penalty* (Cambridge, MA: Harvard University Press, 2002).

New Jersey judges: Bedau, *Death Sentences in New Jersey,* p. 10.

411 drop reflected: Banner, *Death Penalty,* p. 227.

involving death sentences: See *State v. Tune,* 110 A.2d 99 (N.J. Sup. Ct. 1954). In an earlier version of this case, 98 A.2d 881 (N.J. Sup. Ct. 1953), Brennan wrote a revealing dissenting opinion that tracked what he would later argue in *Jencks v. U.S.,* 353 U.S. 657 (1957). But in a subsequent appeal, Tune had been sentenced to death, and the New Jersey Supreme Court, with Brennan joining the majority, found no reversible error in the conduct of the trial, which led to the murder conviction. John Henry Tune was executed on August 21, 1956.

first such case: *State v. Peterson,* 89 A.2d 680 (N.J. Sup. Ct. 1952). Irving Peterson was executed by electrocution on August 26, 1952.

rejected defendants' appeals: See, e.g., *State v. Vaszorich,* 98 A.2d 299 (N.J. Sup. Ct. 1953), *State v. Walker,* 105 A.2d 531 (N.J. Sup. Ct. 1954), affirming murder conviction, Brennan in majority; *State v. Beard,* 106 A.2d 265 (N.J. Sup. Ct. 1954), affirming murder conviction, Brennan in majority; *State v. Roscus,* 109 A.2d 1 (N.J. Sup. Ct. 1955), affirming murder conviction, Brennan in majority; *State v. Rios,* 112 A.2d 247 (N.J. Sup. Ct. 1955), affirming murder conviction, Brennan in majority; *State v. Wise,* 115 A.2d 62 (N.J. Sup. Ct. 1955), affirming murder conviction, Brennan in majority.

"I was always": WJB interview, May 8, 1989 (50-6).

as a given: The Fifth Amendment, for example, barred depriving anyone "of life, liberty or property without due process of law," and says that no person shall "be twice put in jeopardy of life or limb" for the same offense or be compelled "to answer for a capital, or otherwise infamous crime."

firing squads: *Wilkerson v. Utah*, 99 U.S. 130 (1878); electrocution: *In re Kemmler*, 136 U.S. 436.

fell into disfavor: Banner, *Death Penalty*, p. 146.

412 no trouble voting: Daniel Rezneck (WJB OT '60 clerk) interview, Aug. 24, 2007.

expressed personal misgivings: Banner, *Death Penalty*, pp. 238–39.

"are gratefully encouraging": WJB to Norman Redlich, Mar. 3, 1965.

Duncan's lawyer gave up: WJB interview, Apr. 4, 1989 (48-10).

Frank arrived: Frank Brennan interview, Dec. 29, 1986.

413 Duncan was executed: *NYT*, "Mrs. Duncan Loses 2 Pleas for a Stay," Aug. 8, 1962.

clerks to research: That clerk, Alan Dershowitz, went on to a famous legal career of his own as a professor, criminal defense lawyer, and author.

Goldberg condemned: The full text of Goldberg's memo is reprinted in Arthur J. Goldberg, *Memorandum to the Conference RE: Capital Punishment*, 27 S. TEX. L. REV. 493 (1986).

Filipino penal code: The Philippines had become a U.S. colony following the 1898 Spanish-American War.

Weems v. United States: 217 U.S. 349 (1910).

"evolving standards of decency": *Trop v. Dulles*, 356 U.S. 86 (1958).

414 "sleep for a while": WOD memo to files, Oct. 17, 1963, reprinted in Melvin Urofsky, *The Douglas Letters* (Bethesda, MD: Adler & Adler, 1987), 189.

convinced Brennan: Brennan also later recalled being influenced by the anti–death penalty writings of French philosopher Albert Camus; WJB interview, Nov. 21, 1987 (6-9). It is not clear whether Brennan was referring to Camus' 1947 essay "Neither Victims Nor Executioners" or his 1957 book *Reflections on the Guillotine*.

Brennan suggested framing: Alan Dershowitz interview, Apr. 19, 1989.

followed that approach: *Rudolph v. Alabama*, 375 U.S. 889 (1963).

most apparent: Banner points out that the number of executions in the South also decreased from 105 in 1947 to 48 in 1957 and 13 in 1963. Banner, *Death Penalty*, p. 230.

58 percent: Michael Meltsner, *Cruel and Unusual: The Supreme Court and Capital Punishment* (New York: Random House, 1973), 75.

rising proportion: Brief for Petitioner at 38, *Aikens v. California*, No. 68-5027, 406 U.S. 813 (1971); Jack Greenberg et al. attorneys note that sixteen southern states and the District of Columbia accounted for 2,306, or 60 percent, of the 3,859 persons executed between 1930 and 1967.

415 Incremental victories: Meltsner, *Cruel and Unusual*, pp. 66–69.

"Last Aid Kits": Ibid., p. 112.

fell from forty-two: United States National Criminal Justice Information and Statistics Service, *Capital Punishment, 1978* (Rockville, MD: National Institute of Justice, 1979).

Federal Kidnapping Act: *United States v. Jackson*, 390 U.S. 570 (1968).

"death qualified" juries: *Witherspoon v. Illinois*, 391 U.S. 510 (1968). This case was not brought by the LDF, though it did file an amicus brief.

directly challenged: *Boykin v. Alabama*, 395 U.S. 238 (1969).

416 presented statistical evidence: *Maxwell v. Bishop*, 398 U.S. 262 (1970).

came up again: *McGautha v. California*, 402 U.S. 183 (1971).

417 recalled talking about: WJB interview, Nov. 21, 1986 (6-15). That former judge, Bartholomo Bartholomew, said in a July 1989 letter to Wermiel that he had "no clear recollection" of discussing the death penalty with Brennan.

"Justice Brennan's position": OT '69 Term History, p. 14.

"repulsive": Banner, *Death Penalty*, p. 239.

seemed dead set: Loftus Becker interview, Dec. 10, 2008.

"Maybe they might": WJB interview, Nov. 21, 1986 (6-26).

finally ready: OT '71 Term History, p. 135.

Brennan suggested: Ibid.

Black argued: Ibid.

They ultimately agreed: WJB and BRW to conference, June 14, 1971. The California case, *Aikens v. California*, 406 U.S. 813 (1972), was dismissed after California's Supreme Court struck down the state's death penalty statute on state constitutional grounds.

418 Becker included: Becker to WJB, July 26, 1971.

"the basic premise": WJB interview, June 6, 1988 (39-17).

Brennan placed: Peter Irons noted the "striking parallel" between Brennan's rhetoric in the speech and Catholic social thinkers. Peter Irons, *Brennan v. Rehnquist: The Battle for the Constitution* (New York: Knopf, 1994), 34–35. In the first invocation of the term in a speech after joining the Court, Brennan cited a fourteen-year-old *Yale Law Journal* article (Harold D. Lasswell and Myres S. McDougal, *Legal Education and Public Policy*, 52 YALE L.J. 203, 212 (1943)) for the proposition that "the supreme value of democracy is the dignity and worth of the individual." WJB, "Law and Social Sciences Today" (lecture, Georgetown University Law Center, Washington, DC, Nov. 25, 1957).

1961 Newark speech: WJB, "The Essential Dignity of Man" (speech before the Morrow Citizens Association on Correction, Newark, NJ, Nov. 21, 1961).

Rerum Novarum: Marvin L. Krier, *Catholic Social Teaching and Movements* (Mystic, CT: Twenty-Third Publications, 1998), 27.

419 1906 book: John A. Ryan, *A Living Wage* (New York: Macmillan, 1906), vii.

German constitution: See Alan Gewirth, "Human Dignity as the Basis of Rights," in *The Constitution of Rights*, ed. Michael J. Meyer and William A. Parent (Ithaca, NY: Cornell University Press, 1992), 10. For a critical discussion of the applicability of European notions of human dignity to the U.S. legal system, see Neomi Rao, *On the Use and Abuse of Dignity in Constitutional Law*, 14 COL. J. EUR. L. 201 (2008).

upholding the internment: *Korematsu v. United States*, 323 U.S. 214, 241 (1944).

Black and Douglas: See *Abbate v. United States*, 359 U.S. 187 (1959), and *Ullman v. United States*, 350 U.S. 422, 449 (1956).

seven different constitutional amendments: For full discussion of prior Court usage, see Stephen Wermiel, *Law and Human Dignity: The Judicial Soul of Justice Brennan*, 7 WM. & MARY BILL RTS. J. 223 (1998).

forty states: The Death Penalty Information Center says forty state statute were struck down by *Furman*. In their January 18, 1972, stories, the *WP* said forty-one states, while the *NYT* said thirty-seven.

420 not tolerate executions: John P. MacKenzie, "Justices Hear Death Penalty Called Cruel, Aimed at Poor," *WP*, Jan. 18, 1972.

cited Goldberg's: WOD conference notes, WOD papers.

421 "a basic lack": LFP to conference, May 12, 1972.

"serves no useful purpose": HAB to conference, June 8, 1972, HAB papers.

Stewart's clerk delivered: OT '71 Term History, pp. 147–48.

422 "consistent ethic": James J. Megivern, *The Death Penalty: An Historical and Theological Survey* (New York: Paulist Press, 1997).

earlier than any: It was not until 1980 that the U.S. Council of Bishops issued a statement arguing for the abolition of the death penalty because of the "unique worth and dignity of each person."

other contexts: Where human dignity had first been invoked a century earlier by the Church in the context of economic rights, it would in the years to come be used by Pope John Paul II and his successor, Benedict XVI, to argue against everything from poverty and war to artificial insemination, human cloning, abortion, and divorce.

have to apply: Jeffrey J. Pokorak, *Death Stands Condemned: Justice Brennan and the Death Penalty*, 27 CAL. W. L. REV. 239, 259 (1991).

423 no more difficult: Martha Minow, "Equality and the Bill of Rights," in *The Constitution of Rights*, ed. Michael J. Meyer and William A. Parent (Ithaca, NY: Cornell University Press, 1992), 118.

single out his use: See Robert H. Bork, *The Tempting of America: The Political Seduction of the Law* (New York: Free Press, 1990), 219–21. It was not just conservative lawyers who would criticize human dignity as a slippery concept. In response to the Bush administration's release of a 2008 report titled "Human Dignity and Bioethics," noted Harvard psychology professor Steven Pinker dismissed human dignity as "a squishy, subjective notion, hardly up to the heavyweight moral demands assigned to it." Steven Pinker, "The Stupidity of Dignity," *New Republic*, May 28, 2008.

"Respect for": Raoul Berger, "Brennan, 'Dignity,' and Constitutional Interpretation," in Meyer and Parent, *Constitution of Rights*, p. 134.

"Brennan's humanistic": Leonard W. Levy, *Original Intent and the Framers' Constitution* (New York: Macmillan Publishing Co., 1988), 372.

"utterly groundless": WJB interview, June 6, 1988 (39-15).

"If the interaction": WJB, "Text and Teaching Seminar" (speech, Georgetown University, Washington, DC, Oct. 12, 1985).

gender bias: *Roberts v. United States Jaycees*, 468 U.S. 609 (1984); refusing to offer: *Paul v. Davis*, 424 U.S. 693 (1976).

424 watching the movie: *Newsweek*, "The Court on the Death Penalty," July 10, 1972, 20.

viewers jeered: Howard Hughes, *Crime Wave: The Filmgoers' Guide to the Great Crime Movies* (New York: I. B. Tauris, 2006), 120.

inmates learned: *Newsweek*, "The Court on the Death Penalty."

Jubilant convicts: Morton Mintz, "Joy on Death Row: Praise, Scorn on the Hill," *WP*, June 30, 1972.

lying on his bunk: *Time*, "Closing Death Row," July 10, 1972.

425 only half the public: Corinna Barrett Lain, *Furman Fundamentals*, 82 WASH. L. REV. 1 (2007), citing David W. Moore, "Americans Firmly Support Death Penalty," *Gallup Poll Monthly*, June 1995.

Violent crime rose: Brad R. Tuttle, *How Newark Became Newark* (New Brunswick, NJ: Rivergate Books, 2009), 9. Violent crime rose 91 percent in Newark.

evolving in favor: Banner, *Death Penalty*, p. 268.

"lost contact": Barrett Lain, *Furman Fundamentals*, p. 1, citing Meltsner, *Cruel and Unusual*, p. 290.

just as liberal: Brennan hired a handful of conservative clerks, most notably Michael Chertoff, who went on to be a Republican-appointed judge on the U.S. Court of Appeals for the Third Circuit and was secretary of homeland security during the Bush administration, and Michael McConnell, who became a judge on the U.S. Court of

Appeals for the Tenth Circuit. Richard Posner, who later became a judge on the U.S. Court of Appeals for the Seventh Circuit, did not consider himself conservative at the time of his clerkship.

426 ultimately stayed home: Michael Davis and Hunter Clark, *Thurgood Marshall: Warrior at the Bar, Rebel on the Bench* (New York: Carol Pub. Group, 1992), 320.

427 White House dinner: *NYT*, "Among Ford's Guests Are Potential Nominees," Nov. 25, 1975.

mild-mannered moderate: Lesley Oelsner, "Ford Chooses a Chicagoan for Supreme Court Seat; Nominee is Appeals Judge," *NYT*, Nov. 29, 1975.

highest grade point average: Jeffrey Rosen, "The Dissenter," *NYT Magazine*, Sept. 23, 2007.

excessive praise: WJB to JPS, Dec. 29, 1976.

428 opted to write: Bob Woodward and Scott Armstrong maintain in *The Brethren* that Brennan was "so discouraged that he virtually turned the cases over to one of his clerks." Brennan disputed that account. *The Brethren: Inside the Supreme Court* (New York: Simon & Schuster, 1979), 517.

perfunctory: Robert A. Burt, *Disorder in the Court: The Death Penalty and the Constitution*, 85 Mich. L. Rev. 1741, 1767 (1987).

level of support: Banner, *Death Penalty*, p. 275.

just two majority opinions: Pokorak, *Death Stands Condemned*, p. 309 n. 192 (1991). The two cases were *Frances v. Franklin*, 471 U.S. 307 (1985), and *South Carolina v. Gathers*, 490 U.S. 805 (1989). Gathers was overturned by *Payne v. Tennessee*, 501 U.S. 808 (1991).

five other appeals: *Pulliam v. Georgia; Hallman v. Florida; Sullivan v. Florida; Sawyer v. Florida;* and *Spenkelink v. Florida*, 428 U.S. 911 (1976).

429 three more times: *Collins v. Arkansas* and *Neal v. Arkansas*, 429 U.S. 808 (1976), *Douglas v. Florida*, 429 U.S. 871 (1976).

single joint dissent: The first joint dissent using Brennan's boilerplate language appeared May 31, 1977, in *Floyd v. Georgia*, 431 U.S. 949 (1977).

similar stock dissents: On double jeopardy, Brennan filed a stock dissent from denials of cert. based on his belief that the Fifth Amendment required that all charges from a single criminal act must be brought in one trial. See, for example, *Rivera v. Ohio*, 459 U.S. 957 (1982); on the Eleventh Amendment, he dissented over the granting of immunity to states from lawsuits by their own citizens. See, for example, *Schuster v. New York*, 434 U.S. 910 (1977); on obscenity, Brennan, sometimes joined by Stewart and Marshall, dissented from appeals of convictions where prosecutions did not involve exposure to minors or to unwilling adults. See, for example, *Int'l Amusements v. Utah*, 434 U.S. 1023 (1978).

"a kind of": Burt, *Disorder in the Court*, pp. 176–79. See also Michael Mello, *Adhering to Our Views: Justice Brennan and Marshall and the Relentless Dissent to Death as a Punishment*, 22 Fla. St. U. L. Rev. 591 (1995).

"In my book": Weigel to WJB, July 7, 1976.

430 detailed defense: WJB, *In Defense of Dissents*, 37 Hastings L. J. 427 (1985).

"Their names": Fred Barbash, "Two Old Men v. Executioners," *WP*, Dec. 19, 1983.

"battle to keep": James S. Kunen, "Justices Marshall and Brennan Battle to Keep Liberalism Alive at the U.S. Supreme Court," *People*, July 7, 1986.

431 "More than my father's": *Legal Times*, "Free Spirits," March 1, 1993.

"soul brothers": During a speech at a ceremony unveiling Brennan's portrait at the New Jersey Supreme Court in 1976, Joseph Nolan recounted Marshall using the term

(69 NJ Reports XXXI); Mary McGrory, "He Opened the Door to Freedom," *WP*, Jan. 28, 1993.

did not like: Brennan asked his biographer to use "great discretion" when addressing his disappointment about Marshall. "It could be horribly misunderstood," Brennan said in a Mar. 8, 1988, interview (28-11).

reputation for laziness: Juan Williams, *Thurgood Marshall: American Revolutionary* (New York: Times Books, 1998), 13.

"What the hell happened": WJB interview, Mar. 8, 1988 (28-8). The only public hint of his disappointment came in an interview with *Playboy*, in which Brennan said, "When he does put himself to it, the resultant product is just as good as it used to be in his trial days, when he was regarded — and with justification — as one of the ablest trial lawyers in the country." Nat Hentoff, "The Playboy Interview," *Playboy*, July 1991.

432 "massa" in a deep slave dialect: Williams, *Thurgood Marshall*, p. 376.

body began failing him: Ibid., pp. 348, 359.

"I'm afraid it's": WJB to Vartan Gregorian, Mar. 25, 1980.

"resented Thurgood's 'deification'": Hunter R. Clark, *Justice Brennan: The Great Conciliator* (Secaucus, NJ: Carol Publishing Group, 1995), 276.

433 "salve its conscience": TM to conference, July 31, 1980.

"Perhaps no advocate": WJB (speech, University of Maryland, Baltimore, MD, Oct. 9, 1980).

came to believe: There were at least four dozen cert. denials during the 1980s in which Brennan wrote just a one-paragraph boilerplate dissent while Marshall wrote a lengthier dissent.

"My way of approaching": WJB interview, Nov. 21, 1986 (6-15).

"I don't like": WJB interview, Apr. 5, 1990 (59-4).

18. UNEXPECTED ALLY

434 "We wonder why": WJB to Peter Artaserse, Oct. 28, 1976.

435 refashioned the hotel's image: *NYT*, "Children Now Welcomed Where 'Bunnies' Romped," Sept. 16, 1975.

still patterned: Lee Dembart, "A Skiing Novice on a Skiing Weekend," *NYT*, Jan. 25, 1976.

evening featured: Herb Jaffe, "State Bar Honors 'Our Very Own' Justice Brennan," *Newark Star Ledger*, May 24, 1976.

The portrait was: Robert Cohen, "Brennan Is Put in Perspective . . . ," *Newark Star Ledger*, May 25, 1976.

worn wooden: Picture of event provided to authors by the New Jersey State Bar Foundation.

436 "I said the hell": WJB interview, Jan. 27, 1988 (27-5). The Associated Press and *Washington Post* both published stories about Brennan's speech based on texts provided in advance, so their stories do not reflect what he actually said that night. See John P. MacKenzie, "Brennan Praises State Court Rulings," *WP*, May 23, 1976, and *Newark Star Ledger*, June 20, 1976.

widely quoted: The article was ranked nineteenth in a 1985 ranking of the most cited law review articles since 1947, having been cited in 176 law review articles; Fred Shapiro, *The Most Cited Law Review Articles*, 73 CAL. L. REV. 1540, 1550 (1985). Shapiro's subsequent study of the most cited articles of all time ranked Brennan's article twenty-sixth, with 346 citations. Fred Shapiro, *The Most-Cited Law Review Articles Revisited*, 71 CHI-KENT. L. REV. 751, 768 (1996).

Harvard Law Review: WJB, "State Constitutions and the Protection of Individual Rights," 90 HARV. L. REV. 489 (1977). Some of the punchiest — and often quoted language — was added postdelivery. That includes the charge that "under the banner of the vague, undefined notions of equity, comity and federalism the Court has condoned both isolated and systematic violations of civil liberties."

a renaissance: Ann Lousin, *Justice Brennan: A Tribute to a Federal Judge Who Believes in State's Rights*, 20 J. MARSHALL L. REV. 1, 5 (1986); see also Robert F. Williams, *Justice Brennan, the New Jersey Supreme Court, and State Constitutions: The Evolution of a State Constitutional Consciousness*, 29 RUTGERS L. J. 763, 764 (1998). Williams, who became a leading scholar of the use of state constitutions, says Brennan is "credited with stimulating the reemergence of state constitutional law."

already begun: See Robert Force, *State 'Bill of Rights': A Case of Neglect and the Need for a Renaissance*, 3 VAL. U. L. REV. 125 (1969); Vern Countryman, *Why a State Bill of Rights?* 45 WASH. L. REV. 454 (1970); *Project Report: Towards an Activist Role for State Bill of Rights*, 8 HARV. C.R.-C.L. L. REV. 271 (1973).

"phoenix-like resurrection": Stanley Mosk, *The New States' Rights*, 10 CALIF. L. ENF. 81 (1976), cited in Dick Howard, *State Courts and Constitutional Rights in the Day of the Burger Court*, 62 VA. L. REV. 873 (1976).

"reform-minded lawyers": Linda Mathews, "Law Strategy: Don't Take It to High Court," *LAT*, May 10, 1976.

What triggered: *State v. Johnson*, 346 A.2d 66 (N.J. 1975); U.S. Supreme Court had earlier: *Schneckloth v. Bustamonte*, 412 U.S. 218 (1973).

437 case of a photographer: *Paul v. Davis*, 424 U.S. 693 (1976).

"Today's distortion": *Michigan v. Moseley*, 423 U.S. 96 (1975).

picked up the same: See also *Baxter v. Palmigiano*, 425 U.S. 308 (1976), and *United States v. Miller*, 425 U.S. 435 (1976).

"What a frustrated": *Billings (MT) Gazette*, "Liberal Justice Urges Courts to Go Own Way," Apr. 28, 1975.

had not been thinking: Stewart Pollock interview, Mar. 10, 2009.

Pollock cited Brennan's: See *Right to Choose v. Byrne*, 450 A.2d 925 (N.J. 1982) (holding that a New Jersey statute prohibiting Medicaid funding for abortions except where medically indicated to be necessary to preserve the mother's life violated the state constitution's equal protection provision).

438 "the Magna Carta": Stewart Pollock, *State Constitutions as Separate Sources of Fundamental Rights*, 35 RUTGERS L. REV. 707 (1983).

"Like the fox": Mary Ann Glendon, *A Nation Under Lawyers* (New York: Farrar, Straus and Giroux, 1994), 158.

"Brennan may have lost": Mark S. Pulliam, "State Courts Take Brennan's Revenge," *WSJ*, Jan. 4, 1999.

"false prophet": Earl M. Maltz, *False Prophet — Justice Brennan and the Theory of State Constitutional Law*, 15 HASTINGS CONST. L.Q. 429 (1988).

439 warfare: Jeffrey Toobin, *Opening Arguments: A Young Lawyer's First Case* (New York: Penguin Press, 1992), 149–50.

"The impression that comes through": UPI, "Supreme Court Shifts Away from Brennan," *Jacksonville Times-Union and Journal*, June 6, 1976.

"beleaguered": Lyle Denniston, "Supreme Court Is a Different Place Without Douglas," *Washington Star*, June 20, 1976.

upheld that limited extension: *Maryland v. Wirtz*, 392 U.S. 183 (1968).

National League of Cities v. Usery: 426 U.S. 833 (1976).

Stewart switched: Bob Woodward and Scott Armstrong, *The Brethren: Inside the Supreme Court* (New York: Simon & Schuster, 1979), 483. According to *The Brethren,* Stewart initially said he would be the sixth vote but not the fifth for overruling the precedent but changed his vote after White accused him of adopting a "chicken shit position."

440 "one-man strong": Warren Weaver Jr., "Mr. Justice, Dissenting," *NYT Magazine,* Oct. 13, 1974. In the 1977–78 term, Brennan and Rehnquist aligned in just 17.9 percent of cases, the least Brennan agreed with any justice in any term of his entire tenure.

Lone Ranger: Evan Thomas, "Reagan's Mr. Right," *Time,* June 30, 1986.

monastery: John A. Jenkins, "The Partisan," *NYT Magazine,* Mar. 3, 1985.

Burger rejected: Burger did organize a coffee break during the justices' conference meetings where he would bring refreshments. WJB interview, May 7, 1987 (13-9).

gently spoofing: WHR to conference, Nov. 29, 1974; WJB to WHR, Dec. 2, 1974.

invariably ruled: David L. Shapiro, *Mr. Justice Rehnquist: A Preliminary View,* 90 HARV. L. REV. 293 (1976).

"a roving commission": WHR, *The Notion of a Living Constitution,* 54 TEX. L. REV. 693, 698 (1976).

started off: The limerick in the 1974 case, *Corp. Comm'n of Oklahoma v. Fed. Power Comm'n,* 415 U.S. 961 (1974), read:

> There was a young lady from Niger
> Who smiled as she rode on a tiger.
> They returned from the ride
> With the lady inside,
> And the smile on the face of the tiger.

"I shall soon": WHR memo to conference, Mar. 3, 1977.

"Wasn't Rehnquist": Milton Katz, *Tribute to Mr. Justice Brennan,* 15 HARV. C.R.-C.L. L. REV. 292 (1980).

441 first time since: "National League of Cities v. Usery," in *Oxford Companion to the Supreme Court,* ed. Kermit L. Hall (New York: Oxford University Press, 2005), 573.

apocalyptic tone: Earl Maltz, *The Chief Justiceship of Warren Burger 1969–1986* (Columbia: University of South Carolina Press, 2000), 65.

"as caustic": *WP,* "The Revival of States Rights," July 2, 1976.

Blackmun scribbled: HAB papers, *National League of Cities v. Usery* case file.

"Although I": JPS to WJB, June 9, 1976.

442 "did get some": OT '75 Term History, p. 88.

Buckley v. Valeo: 424 U.S. 1 (1976).

rejected the idea: OT '75 Term History, p. 64.

443 "much too sharp": WJB interview, July 1, 1987 (21). Brennan was not entirely chastened. Michael Rubin, one of his 1980–81 clerks, recalled Brennan would make dissents "shriller and less temperate," Rubin interview, Oct. 28, 1988. Michael Chertoff, an OT '79 clerk, similarly recalled Brennan "punching up" their language. Chertoff interview, Sept. 1, 1990.

They talked over: Whit Peters interview, Apr. 15, 2009.

"Telling the lower courts": Gerard Lynch, e-mail message to Stern, Oct. 18, 2007. Lynch was nominated to be a U.S. district court judge in the Southern District of New York by President Clinton and promoted to the U.S. Court of Appeals for the Second Circuit by President Obama in 2009.

"These were not": Whit Peters interview, May 3, 1990.

"This is garbage!": WJB draft, June 24, 1978, in *FCC v. Pacifica Found.*, 438 U.S. 726 (1978), LFP papers.

"No doubt you": LFP to HAB, June 26, 1978, LFP papers.

444 "I am convinced": HAB to LFP, June 27, 1978, LFP papers.

"No one is kinder": LFP note atop copy of WJB draft dissent in *Engle v. Isaac*, 465 U.S. 107 (1982), LFP papers.

"I know from experience": LFP memo to clerks, Apr. 21, 1978, re: *Monell v. New York City Dept. of Soc. Serv.*, 436 U.S. 658 (1978), LFP papers.

Monroe v. Pape: 365 U.S. 167 (1961).

445 had dodged: *DeFunis v. Odegaard:* 416 U.S. 312 (1974).

feared that a majority: OT '77 Term History, p. 10.

the Court voted: Powell, Rehnquist, Stevens, Stewart, and White voted to hear the case.

446 "You do not take": Lyndon B. Johnson, "To Fulfill These Rights" (commencement address, Howard University, Washington, DC, June 4, 1965), accessed at www.lbjlib .utexas.edu/johnson/archives.hom/speeches.hom/650604.asp.

black college enrollment: Joel Dreyfuss and Charles Lawrence III, *The Bakke Case: The Politics of Inequality* (New York: Harcourt Brace Jovanovich, 1979), 145.

white ethnics: Dreyfuss and Lawrence, *Bakke Case*, p. 107.

447 dating back to: *United States v. Carolene Prods. Co.*, 304 U.S. 144, 152 n. 4 (1938).

Powell laid out: LFP to conference, Nov. 22, 1977; TM papers.

448 "Short-term race consciousness": WJB to conference, Nov. 23, 1977.

"reasonableness" test: Bernard Schwartz, *Behind Bakke: Affirmative Action and the Supreme Court* (New York: New York University Press, 1988).

less enthusiastic: Whit Peters interview, Apr. 10, 2009.

urged his colleagues: HAB to conference, Dec. 5, 1977.

449 "If the case": OT '77 Term History, p. 23.

sore throat: WJB to Anthony Lewis, May 12, 1977.

recommended by Powell: LFP to WJB, Feb. 26, 1977.

"I am advised": WJB to conference, Dec. 16, 1977, HAB papers.

450 "You are in": HAB to WJB, Dec. 17, 1977, HAB papers.

"We find it": LFP to WJB, Dec. 14, 1977, LFP papers.

talked about their treatment: David Carpenter interview, Oct. 5, 2007.

despondent: Carmen Legato interview, Mar. 15, 1990.

Brennan feared: David Carpenter interview, Mar. 16, 1989.

Court released: Lyle Denniston, "Throat Cancer Is Unlikely to Disable Justice Brennan," *Washington Star,* Jan. 11, 1978.

Doctors discovered: WJB to Mr. and Mrs. Crawley, Feb. 1978.

faced the strain: WJB interview, May 20, 1988 (35-6). In this interview, Brennan accurately related details of Marjorie's condition though scrambled the dates, which he often did when discussing her health.

451 not be necessary: WJB to conference, Jan. 17, 1978, HAB papers.

"It's a tremendous relief": WJB to Frank Brennan, Feb. 23, 1978.

had not wanted: HAB memo to self, Aug. 24, 1977, HAB papers.

handwritten outline: Linda Greenhouse, *Becoming Justice Blackmun* (New York: Times Books, 2005), 130–31.

"I could not join this": Ibid., p. 131.

452 He was torn: OT '77 Term History, p. 31, re: *Franks v. Delaware*, 438 U.S. 154 (1978).

"the Davis program": HAB to conference, May 1, 1978.

was pessimistic: Robert Comfort to LFP, Feb. 8, 1978, LFP papers.

"differ so substantially": WJB to LFP, May 10, 1978.

earlier mulled: OT '77 Term History, p. 37.

453 complained to their colleagues: HAB to WHR, Feb. 27, 1980, HAB papers.

"deputy prime minister": OT '75 Term History, re: *Nebraska Press v. Stuart,* 427 U.S. 539 (1976).

"Damn right": OT '77 Term History, p. 44.

"We are not": TM to conference, Apr. 13, 1978, HAB papers.

Blackmun credited: HAB to conference, May 1, 1978.

454 left Powell speechless: John C. Jeffries, Jr., *Justice Lewis F. Powell, Jr.: A Biography* (New York: Charles Scribner's Sons, 1994), 487.

"In terms of 'judgment'": LFP to WJB, June 23, 1978. Brennan did add a modifier to his language that limited it "at least when appropriate findings have been made by judicial, legislative, or administrative bodies with competence to act in this area."

455 headline on the cover: *Newsweek,* "No Quotas — But Race Can Count," July 10, 1978.

upholding an agreement: *United Steelworkers of America v. Weber,* 443 U.S. 193 (1979).

19. DARKEST YEARS

456 as usual: Dennis Lyons to WJB, Sept. 10, 1979.

457 on the ferry: WJB to Worrall F. Mountain, Sept. 26, 1979.

returned to work: WJB interview, June 3, 1988 (38); *WP,* "Justice Brennan Suffers Stroke," Sept. 18, 1979; Lyle Denniston, "Justice Brennan Has 'Small Stroke,' Is Back at Work," *Washington Star,* Sept. 19, 1979; WJB letter to conference, Sept. 10, 1979.

"several close associates": *WP,* "Justice Brennan Said to Consider Stepping Down," Oct. 23, 1979.

458 "I've never": WJB interview, June 3, 1988 (38-6).

"most unwelcome news": LFP to WJB, Oct. 23, 1979, LFP papers.

"It is to be": WJB to David S. Fine, Oct. 30, 1979.

459 "I was really": Nancy Brennan interview, Mar. 11, 2008. Nancy recalled that, without any prompting, Brennan acknowledged Marjorie's problem to her years later over another lunch in his chambers. By then, Nancy had developed her own drinking problem.

"He's so active": William Dougherty interview with Wermiel, undated.

"Pop without": Hugh Brennan interview, Mar. 19, 1987.

"She thought it": WJB interview, July 28, 1989 (52-4).

had hired: *NYT,* "Brennan Hires Clerks, Indicating He'll Stay," Nov. 27, 1979.

460 "I finally decided": WJB to Daniel Rezneck, Dec. 6, 1979.

The spark: Bob Woodward and Scott Armstrong, *The Brethren: Inside the Supreme Court* (New York: Simon & Schuster, 1979).

pending cases: Steven Reiss (WJB OT '77 clerk) interview, June 1, 1989.

"Rumor has it": WJB to Alfred Knopf, Apr. 27, 1979.

had introduced Brennan: Alfred Knopf to WJB, May 10, 1963.

"accumulated a staggering": David Beckwith, "Coming: Woodward's Book — The Biggest Leak of All," *Legal Times,* June 19, 1979.

The first excerpt: Bob Woodward and Scott Armstrong, "Inside the Supreme Court: Burger's First Test," *WP,* Dec. 2, 1979.

accompanying news story: Fred Barbash, "Author's View: No True Leader," *WP,* Dec. 2, 1979.

was shocked: Brennan actually had an inkling a few weeks earlier that copies of his term histories had gotten out, when syndicated columnist Jack Anderson wrote a column revealing the existence of what he described as Brennan's "secret memoirs." Jack Anderson, "A Look Inside the Supreme Court," *WP*, Nov. 20, 1979.

461 Armstrong later explained: *Oakland Tribune*, "Woodward, Armstrong and the Court," Jan. 24, 1980.

Woodward later revealed: *Playboy*, "Interview with Bob Woodward," Feb. 1989.

still refused: Graham wrote Brennan a lengthy letter on June 19, 1978, requesting an interview, and Brennan replied with a curt rejection two days later.

thought it best: WJB interview, Dec. 14, 1987 (26-15).

462 replied tartly: Nina Totenberg interview, Aug. 21, 2007.

photographer on assignment: Donald M. Morrison, "Apostle of Justice," *Pennsylvanian Gazette*, Oct. 1977.

"Here is": Peter Harkness interview, Nov. 9, 2007.

"in the heat": WJB (address to S. I. Newhouse Center for Law and Justice, Newark, NJ), reprinted as WJB, *Address*, 32 Rutgers L. Rev. 173 (1979).

What prompted: *Gannett Co. v. DePasquale*, 443 U.S. 368 (1979). A trial judge had granted a request by two criminal defendants' lawyers to exclude reporters from a pretrial hearing on the admissibility of evidence out of concern adverse publicity would impair their ability to receive a fair trial.

"down the ominous": *LAT*, "A Disastrous Assault," July 4, 1979; "a free hand": Austin C. Wehrwein, "An Eloquent Dissent in the Closed-trial Case," *Minneapolis Star*, July 11, 1979.

unusual public rebuttals: Burger, Powell, Blackmun, and Stevens all talked about the ruling that summer. Curt Matthews, "Justices Break with Tradition in Comments on Trial Press-ban Ruling," *Baltimore Sun*, Sept. 14, 1979.

463 "hard words": *WP*, "Justice Brennan Tells Off the Press," Oct. 22, 1979. In the case of *Richmond Newspapers v. Virginia*, 448 U.S. 555 (1980), the Court found a right of public and media access to criminal trials in the First Amendment without overruling the earlier ruling in *Gannett*. The *Richmond* ruling was by a 7–1 vote, but the majority was composed of four separate opinions and, thus, did not really turn on a single theory like the ideas put forth by Brennan in the Rutgers speech.

ambiguous enough: A *University of Pennsylvania Law Review* article concluded that "the portrait offered of Justice Brennan seems to be the most favorable," shown to be "on the correct side of the substantive issues, as conscientious, effective, friendly, and humane, but somewhat prone to political manipulation within the Court." Paul Bender, *Book Review*, 128 U. Pa. L. Rev. 716 (1980). In contrast, a *University of Chicago Law Review* article stated that "Brennan appears to be a whimpering, petty, hate-filled, disappointed Don Quixote, frustrated by the failure of the new Chief to follow where his predecessor had led." Philip Kurland, *Book Review*, 47 U. Chi. L. Rev. 176, 185 (1979).

"most energetic advocate": Woodward and Armstrong, *Brethren*, p. 48.

464 "He cajoled": Ibid., pp. 48–49.

"kill off": WJB interview, Aug. 15, 1986 (2-22).

"Like all good": Mark Tushnet, *Themes in Warren Court Biographies*, 70 N.Y.U. L. Rev. 748, 764 (1995).

out of his way: Fred Barbash, "Justices Meet Book Queries with a Studied Nonreaction," *WP*, Dec. 4, 1979. On Dec. 11, 1979, Brennan wrote Burger a note assuring him that Woodward and Armstrong "obtained them without my knowledge or consent." Burger replied the next day that "I totally reject the suggestion that you 'leaked' any of your 'history' to the 'gentlemen,'" and added, "The silly intimation that you should resign was unmitigated nonsense not worthy of comment." WEB to WJB, Dec. 12 1979.

new smattering of condemnation: Virgil C. Blum, "Brennan and Abortion," *Catholic Standard*, Jan. 24, 1980.

"no independent recollection": WJB to D.C. Bar Counsel, Jan. 30, 1980, reprinted in Robert S. Barnett, *In the Ring: The Trials of a Washington Lawyer* (New York: Crown Publishers, 2008), 104. Brennan later explained, "I certainly didn't want to get into it." WJB interview, May 8, 1989 (50-3). The D.C. Bar subsequently dropped the investigation.

"damnable lie": WJB to John P. Frank, Jan. 7, 1980, WJB personal files. In referring to thirty-one years on the bench, Brennan included his tenure as a state judge in New Jersey. Brennan's own notes show that while at conference he voted to overturn Moore's conviction, he later switched his vote to uphold it. Such a switch is not unusual and explains nothing about his motives. Brennan had always been sensitive to any suggestion that justices might trade votes. After reading Anthony Lewis's *Gideon's Trumpet*, he wrote Professor Charles Alan Wright on Aug. 18, 1964, taking exception to "a sentence at page 41 suggesting that we engage in judicial logrolling in the matter of granting certs. He says something to the effect that each of us gets votes for a favorite case of his by promising to vote to take a case some colleague would like to have reviewed. He's dead wrong about it. We don't treat cases as fungible goods. If we did, we would justify the severest condemnation."

465 not provided: Mary Ann Hogan, "Woodward, Armstrong and the Court," *Oakland Tribune*, Jan. 24, 1980.

"I only wish": WJB to Paul Hoeber, Mar. 7, 1980.

Brennan also resented: Michael Chertoff (WJB OT '79 clerk) interview, Sept. 1, 1990.

troubled by their suspicions: Peter Busch (WJB OT '79 clerk) interview, Oct. 27, 1988.

"to edify or enrich": William Safire, "Our Brethren's Keepers," *NYT*, Dec. 10, 1979.

"So gross": James J. Kilpatrick, "Lowdown on the High Court," *LAT*, Dec. 13, 1979.

"Brennan appears": George V. Higgins, "The Court's Curveball," *BG Magazine*, Dec. 30, 1979.

"My daughter and granddaughter": WJB to Walter Murphy, Jan. 7, 1980, WJB personal files.

466 first person: A handwritten draft of a portion of the history of the *Regents of the University of California v. Bakke* case written by his clerks was inadvertently included in the case files open to the public at the Library of Congress. Because clerks wrote the term histories in the first person at the time, scholars who subsequently found it there incorrectly concluded it was written by Brennan. See Lee Epstein and Jack Knight, *Piercing the Veil: William J. Brennan's Account of Regents of the University of California v. Bakke*, 19 YALE L. & POL'Y REV. 341 (2001). Howard Ball utilized this term history, which he referred to as a "diary" in his account of the *Bakke* case. See Howard Ball, *The Bakke Case: Race, Education, and Affirmative Action* (Lawrence: University of Kansas Press, 2000). After a decade of writing them in the first person, his clerks went back to writing them in the third person in the 1983–84 term.

vary greatly: The history covering the 1977–78 term, for example is 140 pages long while the one the next year is only 13 pages. The longest in length appears to be the 179-page single-spaced edition in the 1984–85 term.

"wetbacks": OT '81 Term History, p. 9.

unmemorable 1970 case: OT '69 Term History, p. 11.

"an embarrassment": OT '83 Term History, p. 51, re: *Lynch v. Donnelly*, 465 U.S. 668

(1984); "an unqualified disaster": OT '84 Term History, p. 40, re: *U.S. v. Young*, 470 U.S. 1 (1985); "a long and incoherent": OT '85 Term History, p. 40, re: *Pembauer v. City of Cincinnati*, 475 U.S. 469 (1986).

Understanding these limitations: Brennan granted his biographer full access to his term histories and provided a portion to law professor Bernard Schwartz, for his work on a biography of Earl Warren. Schwartz used nearly verbatim portions of the histories without attribution in his Warren biography *Super Chief*, as well as other books he subsequently wrote such as *Behind Bakke*. Brennan made a set available to Anthony Lewis, who used them as sources in his book about the *NYT. v. Sullivan* case, *Make No Law: The Sullivan Case and the First Amendment* (New York: Random House, 1991), and a law review article about *Baker v. Carr, In Memoriam: William J. Brennan, Jr.*, 111 HARV. L. REV. 29 (1997). After Brennan's death, his son William J. Brennan III provided a set to another Warren biographer, Jim Newton, who subsequently wrote about them in a series of articles published in the online magazine *Slate*, at www.slate.com/id/2156940/entry/2157320/. The original copies reside in the Library of Congress, separated from Justice Brennan's other papers in an even more secure storage area.

considered destroying: WJB to WJB III, Nov. 20, 1980, WJB personal files.

467 "I have never": WJB to Murphy, Jan. 7, 1980, WJB personal files.

"reference materials": WJB to Alfred Knopf, Dec. 26, 1979, WJB personal files.

"had raided": Stephen Goodman (WJB OT '66 clerk) interview, May 25, 2007.

468 "The authors": William A. Fletcher, *The Brethren*, 68 CALIF. L. REV. 168, 169 (1980).

"I did so": Geoffrey Stone to WJB, Oct. 10, 1979.

"I've always worked": WJB to Erwin Griswold, Dec. 6, 1979. Griswold had joined the law firm Jones & Day after leaving his post as solicitor general in 1973.

"I've personally come": WJB to Geoffrey Stone, William Maledon, and Gerald Rosberg, Dec. 14, 1979.

most damning charge: Woodward and Armstrong, *Brethren*, p. 266.

wrote a letter: unpublished letter, Dec. 11, 1979.

"hit-and-run journalism": Anthony Lewis, "Supreme Court Confidential," *New York Review of Books*, Feb. 7, 1980.

lengthy rebuttal: Bob Woodward and Scott Armstrong, "The Evidence of 'The Brethren': An Exchange," *New York Review of Books*, June 12, 1980. It is not possible to add much to that debate. Brennan, Hoeber, and Woodward all adhered to their respective positions about the case in subsequent years.

469 "I can't adequately": WJB to Anthony Lewis, May 19, 1980, WJB personal files.

becoming less forthcoming: White responded to the book by speaking less candidly with his own clerks and stopped having lunch with clerks from other chambers. Dennis J. Hutchinson, *The Man Who Once Was Whizzer White* (New York: Free Press, 1998), 385.

eventually reveal: Goodman interview, May 25, 2007.

Woodward later approached: Miriam Kellner Bazelon Knox, *A Salute to Life: Mickey's Memoir* (Washington, DC: K2 Pub., 2002), 128.

"I don't want": WJB interview, May 8, 1989 (50-1). Brennan again had reason to be angry at the press in 1981 when the *Wall Street Journal* published a front-page story that mischaracterized his role in the Court's consideration of a lawsuit regarding a New Jersey real estate sale in which his son Bill was involved as an attorney. *WSJ*, "How a New Jerseyite Stands to Lose Fortune Over His Sale of Land," Feb. 27, 1981. Brennan was furious that the newspaper did not run a letter to the editor he wrote correcting the error and that the editor did not respond to his letter. A correction ran two months later. *WSJ*, "Corrections & Amplifications," Apr. 27, 1981.

unsolicited career advice: Curtis Gans, "Marshall, Brennan Must Quit," *CT*, Aug. 18, 1980.

quietly laid: Sean Wilentz, *The Age of Reagan: A History, 1974–2008* (New York: HarperCollins, 2009), 85

470 GOP platform: Linda Greenhouse, "Bar Panel Opposes GOP's Plank for Judges Who Support Abortion," *NYT*, Aug. 8, 1980.

"We can only": Letter to the Editor, "Reagan's View of the Supreme Court," *NYT*, Oct. 10, 1980.

Reagan swept: The popular vote tallies were closer: Reagan received 43,201,220 or 51 percent of the vote compared to Carter's 34,913,332 (42 percent). John Anderson, the independent candidate, received 5,581,379 or 7 percent of the vote.

471 managed to win: Carter also carried the District of Columbia as well as Georgia, Hawaii, Minnesota, and West Virginia.

first time: Brennan later recalled having first met Reagan and his then-wife Jane Wyman in January 1944 during the "mock battle" at the Los Angeles Coliseum he helped plan. WJB interview, Feb. 5, 1987 (10-7). Press coverage of the event, which details participation by several Hollywood personalities, does not reference Reagan, who was serving as an Army captain in California at the time. But Reagan often attended fundraising events and war bond drives during his military service, so it is still possible that he did attend.

eight justices present: Rehnquist had a previously scheduled speaking engagement.

cherubic smile: Adam Clymer, "Manager of Only Show in Town," *NYT*, Nov. 7, 1980.

"he didn't have horns": Lou Cannon, *President Reagan: The Role of a Lifetime* (New York: Public Affairs, 2000), 79.

472 "The two of them": *Bergen (NJ) Record*, "Supreme Court's Guardian of Civil Rights," Apr. 6, 1984.

made a point: WJB to Mark O. Hatfield, Dec. 18, 1980.

how upset: Elliot Polebaum (WJB OT '80) interview, May 2, 1990.

did not see much: Brennan was invited to a White House state dinner in February 1982 held in honor of Egyptian president Hosni Mubarak. *WP*, "Guest List," Feb. 4, 1982.

Smith signaled: Fred Barbash, "U.S. Changes School, Job Bias Policy," *WP*, May 23, 1981.

473 "The groundswell": *NYT*, "Excerpts from Attorney General's Remarks on Plans of Justice Department," Oct. 30, 1981.

quietly passed word: William French Smith, *Law and Justice in the Reagan Administration: The Memoirs of an Attorney General* (Stanford, CA: Hoover Institution Press, 1991), 63.

how enthusiastic: Polebaum interview, May 2, 1990.

particularly hard: LFP to PS, June 18, 1981, LFP papers.

took issue: Lou Cannon, "Reagan Names Woman to Supreme Court," *WP*, July 8, 1981.

nontraditional: Joan Biskupic, *Sandra Day O'Connor* (New York: EcCO, 2005), 76.

474 knew nothing: WJB interview, Mar. 8, 1988 (28-4).

"Legal scholars doubt": Ed Magnuson, "The Brethren's First Sister," *Time*, July 20, 1981.

"positively cooing": WSJ, Aug. 27, 1981.

"She ceased immediately": Jeffrey T. Leeds, "A Life on the Court," *NYT Magazine*, Oct. 5, 1986; Brennan was even more effusive when he spoke at a conference of women judges in 1989. "If only every other woman who follows here is like Sandra Day O'Connor, we're all going to be very, very fortunate."

475 "She has certainly": WJB to C. A. Crawley, Sept. 28, 1981.

He arrived: Brennan found some relief from the increasing isolation at home thanks to a new VCR he received for Christmas. His clerks laughed when he told them he had rented an off-color comedy by the Cheech & Chong duo. Still, Brennan later recalled being far more excited to meet Benny Goodman, the famous jazz clarinetist and bandleader, than Steven Spielberg, who had directed the enormously popular movies *E.T.* and *Indiana Jones*, when the three received honorary degrees from Brandeis University in May 1986.

Plyler v. Doe: 457 U.S. 202 (1982).

thousands of children: The brief for the schoolchildren said that estimates went as high as twenty thousand kids throughout the state of Texas and that twelve thousand had enrolled in schools after a federal district court blocked Texas from enforcing its law. Brief of Appellees at 3, n.2, *Texas v. Certain Named & Unnamed Undocumented Alien Children, decided sub. nom. Plyler v. Doe*, No. 80-1934, 457 U.S. 202 (1982).

"wetbacks": OT '81 Term History, p. 9.

"the unusual step": WJB to LFP, Jan. 25, 1982.

months of negotiations: For evolution of the decision, see Linda Greenhouse, *What Would Justice Powell Do: The "Alien Children" Case and the Meaning of Equal Protection*, 25 Const. Comment. 29 (2008).

476 ruled nine years earlier: *San Antonio Independent School District v. Rodriquez*, 411 U.S. 1 (1973).

"profoundly troubled": WEB to LFP, Apr. 9, 1982, LFP papers.

"painstaking and generous": LFP to WJB, June 16, 1982.

felt completely overwhelmed: SOC interview, Mar. 14, 2008.

out of his way: SOC interview, Mar. 14, 2008.

477 daughter of his friend: In 2007 Abner Mikva said it was Bazelon who had advocated on her behalf, though he acknowledged that Brennan would have certainly recognized her name. Mikva had previously clerked for Prentiss Marshall, a district court judge Brennan respected.

awkward interactions: Mark Campisano interview, Sept. 6, 1990.

"You could sense": Mary Mikva interview, Mar. 15, 1989.

"He couldn't even": Abner Mikva interview, Oct. 22, 2007.

"you may be": WJB to conference, Dec. 9, 1981.

"I feel so strongly": Biskupic, *Sandra Day O'Connor*, p. 121, citing WJB to WEB, Dec. 16, 1981, LFP papers.

478 increasingly frustrated: OT '81 Term History, p. 7.

state judges' frustration: SOC, *Trends in the Relationship between the Federal and State Courts from the Perspective of a State Court Judge*, 22 Wm. & Mary L. Rev. 801 (1981).

479 *Rose v. Lundy:* 455 U.S. 509 (1982).

"In scarcely": Campisano recalled that reference was suggested by a Blackmun clerk.

question whether: Stephen Wermiel, "Low-Roading on the High Court," *WSJ*, Sept. 13, 1982. The *Washington Post* also noted the sharp language of opinions; see Fred Barbash, "Justices Are Exchanging Fighting Words," *WP*, April 22, 1982.

Rehnquist accused Brennan: *Larson v. Valente*, 456 U.S. 228 (1982).

"No one is kinder": *Engle v. Isaac* file, LFP papers.
480 "I wonder if we": LFP to conference, Sept. 17, 1982.
incident reinforced: SOC interview, Mar. 14, 2008.
nevertheless offended: Ibid.
"I've got to": Campisano interview, Sept. 6, 1990.
"to express": SOC to WJB, June 28, 1982.
rental agent assured: Old North Wharf Company to WJB, Dec. 30, 1981.
"We do thank you": WJB to Old North Wharf Company, Jan. 5, 1982.
481 Lyme disease: Rehnquist forwarded an article he found on Lyme disease in *Yankee Magazine.* WHR to WJB, Sept. 21, 1982.
looked terribly thin: Edward Kelly interview, Mar. 21, 1990.
considered retiring: Mildred "Vergie" Ching interview, July 19, 1990.
482 "I will offer": Hesburgh to WJB, Dec. 9, 1982, Hesburgh papers.
"Marjorie often reminisced": WJB to Hesburgh, undated, Hesburgh papers.
"How can I live": Hugh Brennan interview, Mar. 19, 1987.
"I'll be joining": Connie Phelps interview, July 1, 2007.

20. REBIRTH

485 Schapiro was surprised: John Schapiro interview, July 21, 1988.
486 "It's no fun": Marsha Berzon interview, Aug. 22, 2007.
"We could see": Hugh Brennan interview, Mar. 19, 1987.
he started asking: Mickey Bazelon Knox interview, July 25, 2007.
initially puzzled: Mary Fowler interview, Aug. 30, 1988.
"You're out of": Bazelon Knox interview, July 25, 2007.
487 harbored romantic feelings: WJB interview, Nov. 17, 1988 (46-6).
did not want to wait: Ibid., p. 5.
peeked in: Schapiro interview, July 21, 1988.
"For Christ sakes": Fowler interview, Aug. 30, 1988.
newlyweds dined: Arnie Shaw interview, May 19, 1987.
488 somewhat awkwardly: WEB to conference, Mar. 30, 1983, HAB papers.
wrote back: WEB to conference, Apr. 4, 1983, HAB papers.
"I knew you were": Mildred "Vergie" Ching interview, July 19, 1990.
"When they came": Perry Dane interview, Aug. 12, 1990.
mark the dedication: Chapin Wright, "Brennan Hails NJ Courts," *Trenton Times,* Mar. 16, 1983.
"Brennan is his ebullient": Al Kamen, "Justice's Renaissance," *WP,* Oct. 28, 1985.
489 "His entire existence": Dane interview, Aug. 12, 1990.
made plans to jet: WJB to HAB, July 14, 1983, HAB papers.
her wedding ring: Nancy Brennan interview, July 20, 2009.
buying a condominium: Shaw interview, May 19, 1987.
490 clerks for lunch: Bruce Lerner (WJB OT '83 clerk) interview, May 4, 1990.
over for dinner: WJB to HAB, Dec. 1983, HAB papers.
"You made history here": Ruggero J. Aldisert to WJB, Feb. 10, 1986.
rethinking was prompted: Bernard Schwartz, *Super Chief: Earl Warren and His Supreme Court; A Judicial Biography* (New York: New York University Press, 1983).
491 "I must say": WJB to Aldisert, June 11, 1984.
"It is increasingly": Stephen Gillers, "The Warren Court — It Still Lives," *Nation,* Sept. 17, 1983.

"Schwartz's argument belies": Dennis J. Hutchinson, *Hail to the Chief: Earl Warren and the Supreme Court*, 81 Mich. L. Rev. 922, 923 (1983).

"If any single": Ibid., 930.

"He was extremely generous": WJB to Norman Dorsen, Sept. 20, 1983.

492 reliability of police informants: In *Illinois v. Gates*, 462 U.S. 213 (1983), the majority overruled the Aguilar-Spinelli test from *Aguilar v. Texas*, 378 U.S. 108 (1964), and *Spinelli v. United States*, 393 U.S. 410 (1969).

U.S. v. Leon: 468 U.S. 897 (1984).

merited coverage: Francis X. Clines and Warren Weaver Jr., "Briefing," *NYT*, May 18, 1982.

no interest in returning: SOC interview, Mar. 14, 2008.

more success relating: John J. O'Connor III to WJB, May 7, 1985, and WJB to John J. O'Connor III, May 9, 1985.

493 "Thank you for": WJB to SOC, Mar. 21, 1983.

Brennan replied praising: WJB to SOC, Apr. 12, 1983.

he expected her: OT '82 Term History, p. 49.

Minnesota civil rights law: *Roberts v. U.S. Jaycees*, 468 U.S. 609 (1984).

"I continue to have": SOC to WJB, June 19, 1984.

494 asserted in separate books: Jan Crawford Greenburg, *Supreme Conflict: The Inside Story of the Struggle for Control of the United States Supreme Court* (New York: Penguin Press, 2007), 124; Joan Biskupic, *Sandra Day O'Connor* (New York: Ecco, 2005), 247.

O'Connor rejected: SOC interview, Mar. 14, 2008.

"He was fired up": John Savarese interview, Mar. 13, 1990.

"Under the banner": WJB, "Some Judicial Aspects of Federalism" (speech, San Juan, Puerto Rico, Dec. 15, 1983), reprinted in 3 Rev. Jur. U.P.R. 1 (1983).

"crippling" federal judges: Carol Cioe, "Justice Brennan Criticizes Court Colleagues," *Palm Beach Post*, Feb. 11, 1984.

495 "just to make": TM interview, July 13, 1988.

"It has to be": WJB interview, Mar. 14, 1988 (29-12).

"once considered part": Al Kamen, "Supreme Court's Moderate Bloc Is Shrinking," *WP*, July 14, 1986.

provided the key vote: *Garcia v. San Antonio Metro. Transit Auth.*, 469 U.S. 528 (1985).

National League of Cities v. Usery: 426 U.S. 833 (1976).

496 found it difficult to apply: *Transp. Union v. Long Island R. Co.*, 455 U.S. 678 (1982); *FERC v. Mississippi*, 456 U.S. 742 (1982); *EEOC v. Wyoming*, 460 U.S. 226 (1983).

"Nevertheless, after much": *Marsh v. Chambers*, 463 U.S. 783 (1983).

nativity display: *Lynch v. Donnelly*, 465 U.S. 668 (1984).

Lemon test: *Lemon v. Kurtzman*, 403 U.S. 602 (1971).

497 paying public school teachers: *Aguilar v. Felton*, 473 U.S. 402 (1985).

Michigan, program: *School Dis. of Grand Rapids v. Ball*, 473 U.S. 373 (1985).

"splendid birthday present": OT '84 Term History, p. 19.

Alabama law: *Wallace v. Jaffree*, 472 U.S. 38 (1985).

came to regret: John C. Jeffries, Jr., *Justice Lewis F. Powell, Jr.* (New York: Charles Scribner's Sons, 1994), 530.

Bowers v. Hardwick: 478 U.S. 186 (1986).

vehicle to recognize: The previous term, Brennan had dissented from the Court's denial of certiorari in the case of a public high school guidance counselor who alleged she was fired because she told coworkers she was bisexual. In a dissent joined by Marshall, Brennan wrote that the petitioner had legitimate First Amendment and equal protection claims the Court should have considered, and noted that homosexuals "have historically been the object of pernicious and sustained hostility." *Rowland v. Mad River Local Sch. Dist.*, 470 U.S. 1009 (1985).

assuming incorrectly: Larry Kramer interview, Mar. 16, 1989.

498 six major: Jeffries, *Justice Lewis F. Powell, Jr.*, p. 500, citing *Fullilove v. Klutznick*, 448 U.S. 448 (1980); *Firefighters Local Union No. 1784 v. Stotts*, 467 U.S. 561 (1984); *Wygant v. Jackson Bd. of Educ.*, 476 U.S. 267 (1986); *Local 28, Sheet Metal Workers Int'l Ass'n v. EEOC*, 478 U.S. 421 (1986); *Local No. 93, Int'l Ass'n of Firefighters v. Cleveland*, 478 U.S. 501 (1986); and *United States v. Paradise*, 480 U.S. 149 (1987).

Jackson, Michigan, school board: *Wygant v. Jackson Bd. of Educ.*, 476 U.S. 267 (1986).

minority firefighters: *Local No. 93, Int'l Ass'n of Firefighters v. Cleveland*, 478 U.S. 501 (1986).

Powell joined much: *Local 28, Sheet Metal Workers Int'l Ass'n v. EEOC*, 478 U.S. 421 (1986).

"outrageously long": LFP copy of May 25, 1986, WJB draft; "too many statements": LFP internal memo, May 30, 1986, LFP papers.

499 "gerontocracy": Raymond Coffey, "Who's Got a Gerontocracy Now?" *CT*, Mar. 17, 1985.

"three old goats": David G. Savage, *Turning Right: The Making of the Rehnquist Supreme Court* (New York: Wiley, 1992), 211.

dangerously heavy bleeding: Jeffries, *Justice Lewis F. Powell, Jr.*, p. 539.

500 intelligence-gathering mission: Charles Curtis (WJB OT '84 clerk) interview, Apr. 7, 1989.

Gregg decision: *Gregg v. Georgia*, 428 U.S. 153 (1976).

"You could tell": Donald Verrilli interview with Wermiel, undated.

501 "A pattern seems": *Woodward v. Hutchins*, 464 U.S. 377, 380 (1984) (Powell, J., concurring).

502 "is at best": *Stephens v. Kemp*, 469 U.S. 1043 (1984) (Brennan, J., dissenting from denial of cert).

"reckless pursuit of efficiency": David Kaplan, "The Court and the Switch," *NYT*, Dec. 7, 1984.

"a person should not": *Stephens v. Kemp*, 469 U.S. 1098 (1984) (stay denied).

first volts: AP, "Murderer Electrocuted in Georgia after Appeals Fail," *NYT*, Dec. 13, 1984.

503 "These old fools": Sheldon M. Novick, *Honorable Justice: The Life of Oliver Wendell Holmes* (Boston: Little, Brown, 1989), 292.

underestimated Brennan: William Bradford Reynolds interview, Oct. 23, 2007.

Reagan appointed: Reagan announced Meese's nomination in January 1984 but he was not confirmed until February 1985, due to an ethics investigation.

very archetype: Bradford Reynolds interview, Oct. 23, 2007; Stephen J. Markman interview, Sept. 20, 2007.

"Brennan was the most articulate": Gary McDowell interview, Nov. 17, 2007.

"There is no individual": Stephen J. Markman and Alfred S. Regnery, "The Mind of Justice Brennan: A 25-Year Tribute," *National Review*, May 18, 1984, 30.

enjoyed the attention: Saverese interview, Mar. 13, 1990.

war of ideas: Steven M. Teles, *Transformative Bureaucracy: Reagan's Lawyers and the Dynamics of Political Investment*, 23 STUDIES AM. POL. DEV. 61 (2009).

504 "The Constitution is not": *Marsh v. Chambers,* 463 U.S. 783, 816 (1983).
into the open: Bradford Reynolds interview, Oct. 23, 2007; McDowell interview, Nov. 17, 2007.
At the urging: Verrilli interview with Wermiel, undated.
Brennan's clerks waded: Rory Little interview, Oct. 26, 1988.

506 front-page news: Stuart Taylor, Jr., "Brennan Opposes Legal View Urged by Administration," *NYT,* Oct. 13, 1985.
"impressive survey": Editorial, "The 20th-Century Justice," *NYT,* Oct. 15, 1985.
"It is highly unusual": *LAT,* "Justice, Brennan Style," Oct. 16, 1985.
"For all his fumbling": Stuart Taylor Jr., "Meese v. Brennan," *New Republic,* Jan. 6 & 13, 1986, 17.
criticized Brennan: AP, "Reynolds Attacks Brennan for Views, 'Egalitarianism,'" *WP,* Sept. 13, 1986. Reynolds's tenure in charge of the Civil Rights Division was a controversial one and the Senate Judiciary Committee had refused to advance his nomination to be associate attorney general, the Justice Department's third-highest post, in 1985.

507 "Justice Brennan thus prefers": William Bradford Reynolds, "Securing Equal Liberty in an Egalitarian Age" (speech, University of Missouri Law School, Columbia, MO, Sept. 12, 1986), 5.
"The whole approach": WJB interview, Nov. 23, 1987 (25-11).

21. TWILIGHT

508 mysterious trail: E. Joshua Rosenkranz, "A Lot to Answer For," in *The Common Man as Uncommon Man: Remembering Justice William J. Brennan Jr.,* ed. E. Joshua Rosenkranz and Thomas M. Jorde (New York: Brennan Center for Justice, 2006), 45.
"My Lord, Bill": Ibid., p. 46.

509 O'Connor sent a reply: Larry Kramer (WJB OT '85 clerk) interview, Mar. 16, 1989.
"health and life to you": Edward M. Kennedy to WJB, Apr. 25, 1986.
While in Alabama: Black had sat for a television interview in 1968 after completing thirty years on the Court.
sake of fairness: WJB to UPI, Feb. 4, 1986.
emphasizing how much: Stuart Taylor Jr., "Brennan: 30 Years and the Thrill Is Not Gone," *NYT,* Apr. 16, 1986. Other interviews included Philip Hager, "Brennan, Near 80, Holds Firm to Court Post," *LAT,* Apr. 19, 1986; Kathryn Kahler, "Brennan Speaks Out as Liberal Voices Fade," *Newark Star Ledger,* July 20, 1986.
"How's my movie star": WJB interview, Oct. 24, 1986 (4-21).

510 become overexposed: WJB interview, May 27, 1988 (37-2).
lengthy layover: Floyd Abrams, the noted First Amendment lawyer who was traveling with Brennan, recounted this anecdote in *In Memoriam: William J. Brennan Jr.,* 111 HARV. L. REV. 21 (1997).
"Insofar as": Philip Hager, "Brennan Now a Dissenter as High Court Edges Right," *LAT,* July 5, 1985. Brennan used the same line in a May 2, 1985, address to the American Jewish Committee.
"You've done enough": WJB interview, June 3, 1988 (38-15).
"He had that irrepressible": Mark Haddad interview, Dec. 18, 2007.

511 "Bill is usually thorough": WHR to LFP, Jan. 18, 1985, LFP papers.
often recycled: Brennan delivered almost the exact same speech at Brandeis University's commencement in 1986 as he had at Trinity College in 1960.

again denounced: The lecture was later published as WJB, *Constitutional Adjudication and the Death Penalty: A View from the Court,* 100 HARV. L. REV. 313 (1986).

renewed his call: The lecture was later published as WJB, *The Bill of Rights and the States: The Revival of State Constitutions as Guardians of Individual Rights,* 61 N.Y.U. L. REV. 535 (1986).

stood out as fresh: WJB, "Space Settlements and the Law" (speech, American Law Institute Annual Dinner, Mayflower Hotel, Washington DC, May 21, 1987). He delivered the same speech to the Bicentennial Conference of Judges of the U.S. Court of Appeals on Oct. 26, 1988.

"get some younger": Hesburgh to WJB, June 20, 1986, Hesburgh papers.

exhibited symptoms: Mickey Bazelon Knox interview, July 25, 2007.

medical degrees: Dean Hashimoto clerked for Brennan the following term.

poignantly renewed: Abner Mikva interview, Oct. 22, 2007.

512 greatly appreciated: Richard Bazelon to WJB, June 15, 1987.

grew closer: WJB III interview, Sept. 6, 1988.

turned down offers: WJB interview, Dec. 17, 1986 (7-5).

began stopping by: WJB IV interview, Aug. 7, 2007.

thought it was endearing: WJB interview, July 12, 1988 (41-11). Like his father, William J. Brennan IV pursued a career as a corporate lawyer, eventually becoming a partner at Pepper Hamilton LLP in Philadelphia.

new but familiar: Jack O'Hara interview, Feb. 27, 2008.

513 holding placards: Bruce Rosen, "Supreme Court's Guardian of Civil Rights," *Bergen (NJ) Record,* Apr. 6, 1984.

"a devout Roman Catholic": WJB, interview by Nina Totenberg, *All Things Considered,* National Public Radio, Jan. 30, 1987.

"Much less disconcerting": HAB to WJB, Oct. 2, 1989, HAB papers.

514 deeply religious professor: Ruth Marcus and Susan Schmidt, "Scalia Tenacious after Staking Out a Position," *WP,* June 22, 1986.

unusually affable: Ronald J. Ostrow, "Scalia Described as Persuasive, Affable," *LAT,* June 18, 1986.

skilled as a writer: Ruth Marcus, "Judge a Favorite with Conservative Lawyers, Activists," *WP,* June 18, 1986.

going too far: Marcus and Schmidt, "Scalia Tenacious after Staking Out a Position."

press focused: Stuart Taylor Jr., "More Vigor for the Right," *NYT,* June 18, 1986; Philip Hager, "Move to Provide New Conservative Strength," *LAT,* June 18, 1986.

cocaine-filled balloons: *United States v. Montoya De Hernandez,* 473 U.S. 531 (1985).

"Bill, I'm on": OT '84 Term History, p. 148.

515 singing "Happy Birthday": Charles Curtis (WJB OT '84 clerk) interview, Apr. 7, 1989.

"We're not great buddies": WHR interview, Nov. 19, 1990.

wearing a skullcap: *Goldman v. Weinberger,* 475 U.S. 503 (1986).

readily agreed: WJB to WHR, Feb. 14, 1986; WHR to WJB, Feb. 18, 1986.

He genuinely wanted: WJB interview, Mar. 14, 1988 (29-13).

laughed the first: WJB interview, June 17, 1987 (19-11).

Rehnquist consulted with him: WJB interview, Mar. 14, 1988 (29-13).

"The present chief": Q&A with National Association of Women Judges, Nov. 1989.

thirteen of his first forty-two: Al Kamen, "Scalia Making Conservatives Nervous," *WP,* Mar. 8, 1987.

"I'm afraid his place": WJB interview, May 13, 1987 (14-4).

Louisiana's law: *Edwards v. Aguillard,* 482 U.S. 578 (1987).

handicapped persons: *School Bd. of Nassau County v. Arline,* 480 U.S. 273 (1987).

516 election campaign law: *FEC v. Mass. Citizens for Life,* 479 U.S. 238 (1986).

publicly expressing concern: Kamen, "Scalia Making Conservatives Nervous."

"I think we will": AS to WJB, Nov. 3, 1986.

form of intermarriage: David G. Savage, *Turning Right: The Making of the Rehnquist Supreme Court* (New York: Wiley, 1992), 23.

"He is an uncle": AS interview, July 3, 1990.

"I'm bold enough": WJB interview, Mar. 13, 1987 (11-13).

tough questions: Stuart Taylor Jr., "Vigor in the Court, Laughter in the Court," *NYT,* Oct. 14, 1986.

"adroit grilling": Al Kamen, "Rehnquist Court Veers Away from Dullness," *WP,* Dec. 18, 1986.

"There's no sense": WJB interview, Mar. 13, 1987 (11-13).

Johnson v. Santa Clara Transportation Agency: 480 U.S. 616 (1987).

517 1979 ruling: *United Steelworkers v. Weber,* 443 U.S. 193 (1979).

United States. v. Paradise: 480 U.S. 149 (1987).

"It is Justice": Stuart Taylor Jr., "To Reagan's Consternation, Brennan Leads Court in Big Cases," *NYT,* Mar. 30, 1987.

"the 81-year-old": James J. Kilpatrick, "It Was Bill Brennan's Term," *WP,* July 23, 1987.

McCleskey v. Kemp: 481 U.S. 279 (1987).

518 failed to prove: McCleskey was executed in Georgia's electric chair in 1991.

particularly devastated: SOC to LFP; LFP papers.

"Was it springtime": Aric Press and Ann McDaniel, "Renaissance of an Octogenarian Liberal," *Newsweek,* July 6, 1987.

519 "I'd just have": WJB interview, Oct. 28, 1987 (23-3).

"I think they rather": Ibid., p. 2.

Senate rejected: The closest Bork and Brennan came to facing off was on the nearby campus of Georgetown's law school, where Bork's daughter and Brennan's grandson both enrolled a year after Bork's failed confirmation. Brennan's grandson remembers they took positions opposite of their famous relations for the sake of argument during one classroom civil procedure debate.

520 disappointed conservatives: Linda Greenhouse, "Reagan Nominates Anthony Kennedy to Supreme Court," *NYT,* Nov. 12, 1987.

Griswold v. Connecticut: 381 U.S. 479 (1965).

"increasingly independent": WJB interview, Mar. 8, 1988 (28-4).

Patterson v. McLean Credit Union: 491 U.S. 164 (1989).

Runyon v. McCrary: 427 U.S. 160 (1976).

521 favor overruling *Runyon:* HAB conference notes, HAB papers.

"crestfallen and virtually speechless": OT '87 Term History, p. 51.

highly unusual dissents: *Patterson v. McLean Credit Union,* 485 U.S. 617 (1988) (ordering reargument).

"Is this an omen": HAB draft, undated, HAB papers.

"What do you think?": HAB to WJB, Mar. 7, 1988, HAB papers.

surprising fifth vote: OT '88 Term History, p. 32.

draft privately: AMK to WJB, Nov. 15, 1988.

522 Kennedy advised: AMK to WJB, Dec. 2, 1988.

did not hear: AMK to WJB, Apr. 27, 1989.

"What the Court declines": WJB to conference, June 12, 1989. Brennan did not open with that line in an earlier draft circulated on June 8, 1989.

complained privately: AMK to WJB, undated.

"barbs about": AMK to conference, June 13, 1989.

Hustler Magazine v. Falwell: 485 U.S. 46 (1988).

same high standard: Plaintiffs had to prove that the statements were made with actual malice, meaning knowing falsehood or reckless disregard of the truth or falsity.

school officials could censor: *Hazelwood School Dist. v. Kuhlmeier,* 484 U.S. 260 (1988).

523 "It would have been": WJB interview, July 5, 1989 (51-9).

"The big strength": WJB interview, May 2, 1988 (33-8).

"You had your day": Lynn Rosellini, "The Most Powerful Liberal in America," *U.S. News & World Report,* Jan. 8, 1990, 27.

"I'm probably thinking": WJB interview, Oct. 19, 1989 (55-3).

"the cabal": Edward Lazarus, *Closed Chambers: The First Eyewitness Account of the Epic Struggles Inside the Supreme Court* (New York: Times Books, 1998), 251.

"Now I know": OT '88 clerks, joint interview, May 24, 1989.

the mentally retarded: *Penry v. Lynaugh,* 492 U.S. 302 (1989); nor teenagers: *Stanford v. Kentucky,* 492 U.S. 361 (1989).

Mayo Clinic: AP, "Justice Brennan Undergoing Prostate Tests at Mayo Clinic," *WP,* Aug. 11, 1987.

524 laying out every detail: HAB to WJB, Aug 2, 1987.

"had more stamina": Rosenkranz, "A Lot to Answer For," p. 45.

shingles: WJB to Guido Calabresi, Jan. 19, 1988.

living will: LFP to WJB, Aug. 17, 1988.

"He was a man": WJB, "Eulogy of the Honorable J. Skelly Wright" (Washington Cathedral, Washington DC, Aug. 17, 1988).

diagnosed pneumonia: Al Kamen, "Justice Brennan Hospitalized for Pneumonia," *WP,* Dec. 9, 1988.

removing his gallbladder: Al Kamen and Susan Okie, "Brennan Has Gallbladder Removed," *WP,* Dec. 13, 1988.

surgery was a success: A few days later, Brennan heard that Burger had been admitted to a hospital, suffering from pneumonia. He called Burger and jokingly warned, 'Warren, you better get out of there quickly. If they think you have pneumonia they'll take your gallbladder out." *NYT,* "Brennan's Advice on Illness," Apr. 2, 1989.

525 "It was a marvelous": Hugh Brennan Jr. interview, July 10, 2008.

Blackmun noticed: HAB interview, Aug. 10, 1988.

remained the commander: Einer Elhauge (WJB OT '87 clerk) interview, Mar. 11, 2008.

decisively determined: Timothy Bishop (WJB OT '88 clerk) interview, Dec. 7, 2007.

526 *Texas v. Johnson:* 491 U.S. 397 (1989).

"followed the party": WJB interview, Mar. 8, 1988 (28-5).

"Bill and I": AS (speech, The Judiciary Act of 1789: A Bicentennial Conference, Washington, DC, Sept. 22, 1989).

"In my experience": AS interview, July 3, 1990.

527 listeners inundated: Evan Caminker (WJB OT '89 clerk) interview, Jan. 8, 2008.

passed a resolution: Senate Resolution 151, 101st Cong., 1st. sess. (1989), passed the Senate on June 22, 1989, by a vote of 97-3, declaring that the Senate "expresses its profound disappointment that the Texas statute prohibiting the desecration of the flag was found to be unconstitutional."

Congress quickly enacted: Flag Protection Act of 1989, Pub. L. No. 101–131, 103 Stat. 777 (1989) (amending 18 U.S.C.A. § 700).

warnings from legal experts: Among those who testified that legislation would not suffice and that the Constitution would have to be amended to protect the flag was

Robert Bork, the defeated Supreme Court nominee. Robin Toner, "Amendment Needed to Protect the Flag, Bork Tells Senators," *NYT*, Aug. 2, 1989.

Bush called for: Robin Toner, "President to Seek Amendment to Bar Burning the Flag," *NYT*, June 28, 1989.

attended a ceremony: Patricia Cappon, "Justice Served," *Newark Star Ledger*, Sept. 17, 1988.

"I really don't think": *WSJ*, "Effort to Revoke Honor to Justice Brennan Ended," Aug. 11, 1989.

draped an American flag: Mary Fowler interview, June 23, 1989.

striking down: *United States v. Eichman*, 496 U.S. 310 (1990).

528 *Webster v. Reproductive Health Services.*: 492 U.S. 490 (1989).

activists announced plans: Bill Wolfe, "Archbishop Won't Attend Spalding Commencement Slated to Include Brennan," *Louisville Courier-Journal*, May 10, 1989.

"bitterly disappointed": Ibid.

"Pray for death": John Billotta, UPI, "Anti-Brennan Prayer Asked," *WP*, June 2, 1986.

"I know you can": Frank Brennan to WJB, June 3, 1986.

replied reassuringly: WJB to Frank Brennan, June 6, 1986. Television evangelist Pat Robertson did not confine his death wish to Brennan when he addressed the North Carolina state legislature in May 1987. Robertson suggested that many of the nation's social problems would be solved if Brennan, Marshall, and Stevens "were to be either retired or to be promoted to that great courtroom in the sky." *Legal Times*, "Heaven Help Us," May 25, 1987.

decided to cancel: Robin Garr and Bill Wolfe, "Brennan, Amid Controversy, to Skip Spalding Ceremony," *Louisville Courier-Journal*, May 12, 1989.

"It offends my sense": Robin Garr, "Brennan Presence Felt at Graduation as Spalding Honor Draws Abortion Foes," *Lousville Courier-Journal*, May 15, 1989.

529 "I am proud": John E. Selent to WJB, May 16, 1989, and WJB to Selent, May 19, 1989.

death threats: *LAT*, "Justice Blackmun Shot At Through Window of Home," Mar. 4, 1985.

bullet crashed through: Ibid.

FBI concluded: Savage, *Turning Right*, p. 237.

"a kind of heroic": Michael Kimmelman, "Richard Serra in Shows of Drawing and Sculpture," *NYT*, Nov. 22, 1989.

"It is a good": HAB to WJB, Nov. 20, 1989, HAB papers.

530 Ohio law requiring notification: *Ohio v. Akron Ctr. for Reprod. Health*, 497 U.S. 502 (1990).

Minnesota law: *Hodgson v. Minnesota*, 497 U.S. 117 (1990).

Brennan believed that Blackmun: OT '89 Term History, p. 26.

Brennan made a point: *Clemons v. Mississippi*, 494 U.S. 738, 756 (1990) (Blackmun, J., concurring in part and dissenting in part); *Lewis v. Jeffers*, 497 U.S. 764, 794 (1990) (Blackmun, J., dissenting); *Walton v. Arizona*, 497 U.S. 639, 677 (1990) (Blackmun, J., dissenting).

"Hit them harder": OT '89 Term History, p. 27.

"I so love": Sean O. Murchu, "Lone Justice: An Interview with Justice William Brennan Jr.," *Irish America*, June 1990.

His resolve had: Eric Rakowski (WJB OT '88 clerk) interview, Dec. 14, 2007.

"It's always stuck": WJB interview, May 2, 1988 (33-10).

grown more insistent: WJB interview, May 2, 1990 (60-14).

531 "I'd go crazy": WJB interview, July 12, 1988 (41-7).

"The appointment": Timothy Healy to WJB, Apr. 16, 1990.

old fool portrayed: Undated cartoon in the collection of the U.S. Supreme Court Office of the Curator.

badly overweight: Savage, *Turning Right*, p. 78.

appeared hopelessly lost: David J. Garrow, *Mental Decrepitude on the U.S. Supreme Court: The Historical Case for a 28th Amendment*, 67 U. CHI. L. REV. 99, 10735 (2000).

Rehnquist noticed: Savage, *Turning Right*, p. 345.

Kennedy wondered: AMK interview, Apr. 9, 1991.

forgot details: Rosellini, "The Most Powerful Liberal in America."

532 recycled whole passages: WJB (Memorial in Remembrance of the Honorable Arthur J. Goldberg, Department of Labor, Washington, DC, Apr. 6, 1990). Brennan crossed out "Robert" and wrote in "Arthur" as well as other identifying information but kept a reference to a *New York Times* editorial that praised Silvercruys.

Metro Broadcasting Inc. v. FCC: 497 U.S. 547 (1990).

policy of giving preference: *Winter Park Commc'ns v. FCC*, 873 F.2d 347 (D.C. Cir. 1989).

distress sale: *Shurberg Broad. of Hartford, Inc. v. FCC*, 876 F.2d 902 (D.C. Cir. 1989).

City of Richmond v. J. A. Croson Co.: 488 U.S. 469 (1989).

533 Brennan believed: WJB typed statement for the Court's conference.

he remained optimistic: WJB OT '89 clerks, joint interview with Evan Caminker, Regina Maloney, Jonathan Massey, and Nory Miller.

"tough" case: HAB conference notes, Mar. 30, 1990, HAB papers.

534 clerk reported back: OT '89 Term History, p. 36.

private memo: WJB to BRW, July 13, 1990.

Red Lion Broadcasting Company v. FCC: 395 U.S. 367 (1969).

new draft: WJB to conference, June 15, 1990.

535 also weighed: JPS to WJB, June 18, 1990.

22. "SO LONG, BILL"

536 "Bill is going": John McInespie interview, Mar. 11, 1992.

remained undecided: WJB III interview, Feb. 28, 1991.

537 first African American: Marcella David, a graduate of the University of Michigan Law School, had previously clerked for Brennan's friend Judge Louis Pollak on the U.S. District Court in Philadelphia.

last vote: AP, "Virginia Executes Man for Murder," *NYT*, July 21, 1990, re: *Boggs v. Muncy*, 497 U.S. 1043 (1990).

Cosmos Club: WJB to Admissions Committee, June 29, 1988. After his retirement, Brennan wrote letters of recommendation for Totenberg's sister, Amy, to become a state or federal judge in Georgia.

"We all have": Nina Totenberg to WJB, Dec. 16, 1988.

"It's not an easy": Nina Totenberg, *A Tribute to Justice William J. Brennan Jr.*, 104 HARV. L. REV. 1, 34 (1990).

538 was upset: Mary Fowler interview, July 23, 1990.

Blackmun heard: HAB, interview by Harold H. Koh, Dec. 1, 1995, Federal Judicial Center.

"earned an": Ethan Bronner, "Ailing Brennan, Key Liberal, Resigns from Supreme Court," *BG*, July 21, 1990.

"one of the greatest": Editorial, "A Day for the Law," *San Francisco Examiner*, July 22, 1990.

"The damage that": *National Review*, "The Oligarch," Aug. 20, 1990.

"Brennan cannot": James H. Rubin, "Marshall Critical of Bush's Choice," *Spokesman-Review*, July 27, 1990.

539 heartbreaking: Phyllis Turner, "Justice for All," *Crystal City*, winter 1990, 26, 29.

second floor: The Court's second floor is actually its third floor, as the floors are referred to as ground, 1, and 2.

soon to meet: John A. Farrell, *Tip O'Neill and the Democratic Century* (Boston: Little, Brown, 2001), 688.

whose ranks: The list of Brennan clerks who became federal judges includes Marsha Berzon, Raymond Fisher, William Fletcher, Frank Gregory, Merrick Garland, Gerard Lynch, Richard Posner, and Richard Arnold, whose health problems precluded President Clinton from nominating him to the Supreme Court as planned; law school deans: Geoffrey Stone of the University of Chicago, Evan Caminker of the University of Michigan, Larry Kramer of Stanford, and Robert Post of Yale; corporate CEO: Jeff Kindler; Republican cabinet member: Michael Chertoff served as President George W. Bush's second secretary of homeland security.

red carpet: Mary Doyle interview, Sept. 8, 2007, and Patrick Gudridge (University of Miami law professor who cotaught class) interview, Sept. 11, 2007.

540 helped further secure: Smith had also given Brennan $20,000 in cash gifts. On a financial disclosure form released in May 1991, Brennan revealed that $80,000 of the gifts and forgiven loans came prior to his retirement. *WSJ*, "Ex-Justice Brennan Discloses Developer's $20,000 in Cash Gifts," May 20, 1991.

just a single time: There was an opinion issued under his name in one of the cases argued on Nov. 22: *Tenngasco Exch. Corp. v. FERC*, 952 F.2d 535 (1992) (Brennan, Assoc. J., Retired).

Brennan would not recall: Nat Hentoff, "The Justice Breaks His Silence," *Playboy*, July 1991, 120.

treatment for cancer: Richard Arnold to WJB, Aug. 24, 1993.

"try to act": DHS to WJB, Aug. 16, 1990.

"I do hope": WJB to DHS, Aug. 22, 1990.

541 "one of the most": Senate Committee on the Judiciary, *Hearings on the Nomination of David H. Souter to Be Associate Justice of the Supreme Court of the United States*, 101st Cong., 2nd sess. (1990).

expected a warm handshake: DHS, Remarks (Salute to WJB, Harvard Club, Washington, DC, Sept. 30, 1992), 4. Copy in authors' possession.

"As fond as": David H. Souter interview, Oct. 23, 2007.

his inspiration: Ibid.

"Their collective influence": DHS, Remarks.

"The President could": WJB to RBG, June 15, 1993.

"Dear Bill": RBG to WJB, June 16, 1993.

When Ginsburg wrote: *United States v. Virginia*, 518 U.S. 515 (1996).

542 So too did Blackmun: *Callins v. Collins*, 510 U.S. 1141 (1994) (Blackmun, J., dissenting from denial of certiorari).

one last poignant visit: Brennan categorically denied an account that he searched Marshall's desk looking for a bottle so he could drink a toast. WJB to Wermiel, Apr. 18, 1995. The account is in Hunter R. Clark, *Justice Brennan: The Great Conciliator* (Secaucus, NJ: Carol Publishing Group, 1995), 278.

"If I have drawn": WJB, "What the Constitution Requires," *NYT*, Apr. 28, 1996.

regular visitors: RBG interview, Feb. 13, 2008.

543 "I am a woman": Gabriel Escobar, "Brennan Remembered As an 'American Hero,'" *WP,* July 29, 1997.

"So long, Bill": Mary McGrory, "So Long, Pal," *WP,* July 31, 1997.

"Let him speak": RBG, *In Memoriam: William J. Brennan Jr.,* 111 HARV. L. REV. 1, 3 (1997).

next to Marjorie: Mary Brennan was buried on the other side of Brennan, and the date of her death was added to the headstone after she died of cancer on March 28, 2000.

"There is no": The speech was reprinted the next day, Apr. 28, 1996, in condensed form as an op-ed in the *New York Times.* WJB, "What the Constitution Requires."

544 "They're not": WJB interview, May 2, 1988 (33-8).

"I think it'll be": Ibid.

"quite remarkable": Linda Greenhouse, "A Court Liberal's Legacy," *NYT,* July 27, 1997.

made the "we": Patricia Brennan, "Seven Justices, On Camera," *WP,* Oct. 6, 1996.

545 "probably the most": Ibid.

lasted longer: Stevens surpassed Brennan's tenure in 2009. At the time of his retirement, Brennan was the seventh-longest-serving justice in American history.

Liberals pined: Dahlia Lithwick, "I Need a Hero," *Slate,* Feb. 3. 2009. After Sonia Sotomayor's nomination, Marjorie Cohn, president of the National Lawyers Guild, released a statement saying, "Obama has missed an opportunity to tap a liberal intellectual giant like William Brennan who will have a major impact on the Court for years to come." Institute for Public Accuracy, "Sotomayor Nomination," press release, May 26, 2009.

546 openly questioned: Jeffrey Toobin, "Bench Press," *New Yorker,* Sept. 21, 2009, 42; Jeffrey Rosen, "What's a Liberal Justice Now?" *NYT Magazine,* May 31, 2009.

"heroes of mine": Barack Obama, interview with *Detroit Free Press* editorial board, Oct. 3, 2008, accessed at: www.freep.com/article/20081003/OPINION01/810030434/ Obama — Aim-for-fundamental-change.

547 "So it is": WJB (keynote address, Charitable Irish Society, Boston, MA, Mar. 17, 1954).

Index

Mishkin, Edward, 256, 257, 261, 262
Mitchell, James, 79–80
Mitchell, John, 312, 313, 316
Mobilization for Youth (MFY), 336, 339, 340
Monell v. New York City Department of Social Services, 444–45
Moneysworth (newsletter), 275
Monroe v. Pape, 444
Montgomery bus boycott, 113–14, 144
Moore, Harry, 44
Moore, "Slick," 461, 468
Moral Majority, 470, 473
Morrissey, Thomas, 33
Mosk, Stanley, 436
Mudd, Roger, 218
Murphy, Frank, 75, 102, 232, 419
Murphy, George, 267
Murphy, Michael, 234–35
Murphy, Walter, 465
Murray, John Courtney, 176, 286
Murrow, Edward R., 64
Muskie, Edmund, 179–80

NAACP (National Association for the Advancement of Colored People), 211, 213–14
NAACP v. Button, 214–15
NAACP Legal Defense and Educational Fund (LDF), 142, 144, 212, 332, 336, 392, 414–16, 421
Nabokov, Vladimir, 122
Nagin, Jeffrey, 153
Naked and the Dead, The (Mailer), 122
Naked Truth, The (film), 11, 21, 60
Nantucket, WJB family vacation on, 195, 228–29, 323, 377–78, 380, 381, 388, 459, 474, 480–81, 489
National Coalition to Abolish the Death Penalty, WJB honored by, 539
Nationality Act (1940), 134
National Industrial Recovery Act (NIRA), 31–32
National Labor Relations Act, 32, 43
National League of Cities v. Usery, 439, 441–42, 495–96
National Organization for Women, 316, 387
National Shrine, dedication of, 165
Neoconservatives, 470
Newark, New Jersey, 24
  and Brennan family, 5–6, 7, 9, 12, 14, 15 (*see also* Brennan, William Joseph, Sr.)
  and WJB, 17, 28, 210
  Depression in, 27
  riots in (1967), 290

New Deal coalition, 317, 446, 470
New Jersey court system, WJB in overhaul of, 44–45, 50, 66, 67
New Jersey Law Journal, WJB on, 45
"New judicial federalism," 438
New Rochelle, school desegregation case in, 212–13
New York Times v. Sullivan, 220, 221, 222–27, 228, 238, 288, 461, 466, 522
Nichols, Terry, 273
Nixon, Richard, 73, 162, 163, 268, 304, 307–8, 318, 319, 353, 354, 360, 361, 427
  and crime/race issue, 299, 317
  inauguration of, 311
  and obscenity commission recommendations, 366
  vs. school busing, 332, 359
  and Watergate, 227, 378–80, 381–82
  resignation of, 382
Noble, Richard, 309
Noia, Charles, 199
Nolan, Joe, 435

Obama, Barack, xiv, 546
O'Boyle, Patrick Cardinal, 313–14, 375
O'Boyle, Rose, 17
O'Brian, John Lord, 103
O'Brien, David Paul, 301
Obscenity law, 97, 120–22, 256–57, 261–64, 365–68
  and WJB, 97, 122–25, 223, 252–56, 352, 366
  and "community standards," 125, 254
  difficulty in defining obscenity, 252–53, 366
  and *Fanny Hill*, 256, 258, 260, 261, 262
  and Ginzburg, 249–50, 256, 257–62, 263, 274–75
  and *Jacobellis v. Ohio*, 253–55, 257
  and *Miller v. California*, 366–67, 368
  and Mishkin, 256, 257, 261, 262
  pandering theory in, 260
  and *Paris Adult Theatre v. Slaton*, 367, 368
  and "prurient interest," 124–25
  and *Roth* decision, 122–23, 252, 253, 254, 257, 258, 261, 366
  and social-value standards, 257, 261, 368
  and *Tropic of Cancer*, 253
  See also Censorship
O'Connor, John, III, 473, 492–93
O'Connor, Sandra Day, xii, 473–74, 476, 477–80, 492–94, 497, 498, 509, 517, 518, 520, 526, 529, 534–35, 543, 545
O'Hara, Jack, 512–13, 543
O'Hern, Daniel, 134, 247–48
Oliphant, Dayton, 55